ALMOST A Dynasty

ALMOST A
Dynasty

THE RISE AND FALL OF THE
1980 PHILLIES

WILLIAM C. KASHATUS

PENN

UNIVERSITY OF PENNSYLVANIA PRESS

PHILADELPHIA

Published by
University of Pennsylvania Press
Philadelphia, Pennsylvania 19104-4112

Printed in the United States of America on acid-free paper
10 9 8 7 6 5 4 3 2 1

A Cataloging-in-Publication Record is available from the
Library of Congress
ISBN-13: 978-0-8122-8
ISBN-10: 0-8122-4036-7

for

MICHAEL JACK,
my boyhood hero,

and to the memory of
TUG,
a sorely missed friend.

Contents

INTRODUCTION

THOSE WHO LIVED AND DIED with the Philadelphia Phillies during their glory years of 1976 to 1983 will never forget the evening of Tuesday, October 21, 1980. Game Six of the World Series was being played at Veterans Stadium in South Philadelphia. The Phillies held a three-games-to-two lead over the American League champion Kansas City Royals. Perennial losers who had reached the Fall Classic just twice before in their ninety-seven-year history, the Phils had pinned their hopes for their first world championship on the left arm of their pitching ace, Steve Carlton.

Through seven innings on that cool, crisp autumn evening, Carlton was unhittable. He alternated between a 90-mph fastball, a wicked curve, and a devastating slider, limiting the Royals to a single run on 4 hits while striking out 7 before he was pulled from the game in the eighth inning. Mike Schmidt, who would later be named the Most Valuable Player of the Series and one of the most feared power hitters in the game, gave Carlton all the support he needed in the third inning when he singled to left to drive in two runs. The Phils added another two runs in the sixth for a 4-0 lead.

Tug McGraw, the Phillies' colorful reliever, entered the game in the eighth with two runners on base and no outs. After walking the bases loaded, he managed to retire the side allowing just one run. Ever the showman, Tugger provided more drama in the top of the ninth when, with one out and the Fightin' Phils clinging to a 4-1 lead, he loaded the bases again.[1]

Curiously, Philadelphia's infamous fans, the so-called Boo Birds, held their tongues. They had grown accustomed to disappointment after the Phillies won three straight division titles in 1976, '77, and '78, only to lose in the playoffs each year. Somehow they *knew* tonight would be different.

1

Kansas City's second baseman Frank White came to bat and swung at McGraw's first delivery, popping a high foul ball near the Phillies' dugout. Catcher Bob Boone leaped from behind home plate in pursuit of the ball as Pete Rose, the team's spark plug, converged from first base. Boone expected "Charlie Hustle" to call him off, but he heard nothing.

"Where is he?! Where the hell is he?!" Boone panicked, as he neared the edge of the dugout. Normally, the Phillies catcher would simply let the ball fall to him, but now, not knowing where Rose was, he felt he would have to fight his teammate for the ball. Rose stopped short as Boone reached out to make the catch, but the ball glanced off the heel of his mitt. Ever alert, Rose snatched the ball for the second out of the inning.[2]

"We can't lose now," thought Larry Bowa, the Phillies' fiery shortstop who had been with the team since the hard luck days of the early 1970s. "Not even if fuckin' Babe Ruth himself comes up."[3]

Fortunately for Phillies fans, Ruth's playing days were long over. But Kansas City did have one more threat, Willie Wilson, a dangerous leadoff man, who had a reputation for hitting in the clutch. When Wilson stepped to the plate, the "Vet," the Phils' sterile concrete stadium, rocked with anticipation as more than 65,000 screaming fans took to their feet.

City policemen on horseback lined the warning tracks down the left and right field foul lines. Attack dogs had also been brought onto the field to discourage fans from rushing the players.

McGraw, so exhausted that he considered asking manager Dallas Green to lift him if he couldn't get Wilson, eyed his surroundings, desperately searching for inspiration to face one more hitter. "Anything," he thought. "Let me find anything to get through this last hitter." Just then, the comic reliever noticed a horse over by the warning track in foul territory. The steed was in the process of dropping a big, brown mud pie right there on the Astroturf. "Hmm, if I don't get out of this inning," McGraw mused, "that's what I'm going to be in this city. Nothing but a pile of horse shit."[4] In Philadelphia, such negative motivation often produces the desired result.

McGraw worked a 1-2 count on the Royals left fielder and looked for another sign; not from the catcher, but from his surroundings. Staring at a German shepherd seated next to the Phillies' dugout, the reliever thought, "K-9." "This is the ninth inning and I need a K—the baseball score sheet mark for strikeout," he later explained.[5]

Confident that supernatural forces were behind him, McGraw, at 11:29 P.M., toed the rubber and drew a deep breath, preparing to deliver the pitch that would unlock nearly a century's worth of pent-up frustration for the City of Brotherly Love. He fired the ball toward home plate. It was, as he would say later, "the slowest fastball I ever threw" because "it took ninety-seven hard years to get there."[6]

Wilson swung and missed.

For a solitary moment, time seemed to stop. All the years of losing, the decades of last-place finishes, the eternal frustration that had been passed down from one generation of fans to the next now belonged to the history books. Amid all the tears, laughter, and sheer jubilation was the realization that a miracle had happened—the Phillies had finally won their very first world championship. McGraw raised his arms and jumped skyward.

Schmidt dashed in from third base as Phillies converged on the mound from every conceivable direction. Just before the players could close ranks to embrace each other, Michael Jack, in a rare display of emotion, dove onto his teammates. Photographers freeze-framed the scene for posterity, indisputable proof that the Phillies *really did* capture a world championship. The celebration had begun.

More than a million turned out for the parade down Broad Street the following day and to hear McGraw deliver one of the city's most memorable quips. "All through baseball history, Philadelphia has taken a backseat to New York City," said the comic reliever, whipping the crowd into a wild frenzy. "Well, New York City can take this world championship and stick it!" he roared, thrusting a copy of the "We Win!" *Philadelphia Daily News* skyward.[7]

Sound unprofessional? Perhaps. But the remark also resonated deeply with Phillies' fans, who had always taken a backseat to the Big Apple and that city's historically successful sports teams. Philadelphians, having long suffered the reputation of perennial losers, had finally been given reason to believe in something bigger than a baseball game. They could now bask in the national spotlight that had eluded them for nearly a century.

"The world is different today," wrote Gil Spencer of the *Philadelphia Daily News*, "because a Philadelphia baseball team is on top of it."[8]

Between 1980 and 1983 the Philadelphia Phillies captured two pennants (1980 and '83) and a world championship. The team was even stronger in 1981. The experience of a pennant race and winning both the National League Championship Series and World Series prepared the club for a return to the Fall Classic. The previous year's rookies had a season of major league experience to their credit. All of the veterans returned with the exception of Greg Luzinski, who was sold to the Chicago White Sox. There was also an important addition. Gary Matthews, a dependable .300 hitter, was acquired from the Atlanta Braves to replace Luzinski in left field. Accordingly, the Phils, barring injuries, were odds-on favorites to repeat as world champions in '81.[9]

If they had accomplished that feat, the Phillies would have established a dynasty, a team that captures two or more world championships and three or more pennants in five years or less. They would have joined the illustrious ranks of the Philadelphia Athletics clubs of 1910–14 and 1929–31, the 1926–28 New York Yankees, the 1969–71 Baltimore Orioles, and the 1972–74 Oakland Athletics—

baseball teams among the greatest in history because of their ability to win consistently over a prolonged period of time.[10] But a Phillies dynasty never occurred because of a players' strike that resulted in a sixty-day work stoppage. The Phils, who had been in first place before the strike, were unable to regain their winning ways after play resumed in the split season. They lost a best-of-five-game playoff against the Montreal Expos, who became division champions.[11]

The 1981 season was a watershed not only for the Phillies, but for the national pastime itself. Afterward, labor relations between an increasingly powerful Players Association and owners who were equally inflexible became more acrimonious than ever before. While labor conflict had resulted in a series of work stoppages during the previous decade, never had there been a split season with a mini-playoff to determine divisional championships. Although free agency, established in 1975, spelled the end of the reserve clause binding a player to one team unless he was traded, sold, or released, it affected only an elite group of performers. After 1981 player salaries skyrocketed and many others followed the money trail, leaving the club that originally signed them. Old loyalties were forgotten and the notion of a homegrown team, like the 1980 Phillies, was a thing of the past. Family-operated teams, like the Carpenters who had owned the Phillies since 1943, became frustrated with the ongoing labor conflict and sold to new, corporate owners who were more concerned about profits than winning.

Fan interest in the game also waned after 1981. Cable television increased the number of viewer outlets, bringing the game into people's homes and delivering a sharp blow to attendance. More fans chose to stay at home or watch professional football, a more action-packed alternative to baseball. Further eroding the fan base was the growing publication of kiss-and-tell books, which revealed the seedier side of the ballplayers' lives, their infidelity and alcohol and drug abuse.[12] Together with the exorbitant salaries players were demanding and the constant threat of a strike, the sordid revelations destroyed player reputations among fans who turned elsewhere for role models. Only by examining the 1980 Phillies in the context of these dramatic changes can we understand why the team failed to repeat as world champions in 1981 and why they would become one of the last homegrown teams in baseball history.

Caught in the growing chasm that divided a more stable era of the past from the uncertainties of the future were four Phillies who distinguished themselves as the talented cornerstone of the 1980 world champions: Tug McGraw, Steve Carlton, Mike Schmidt, and Pete Rose. McGraw, the Phils' comical relief pitcher, was the emotional soul of the team. Passionate, funny, and quintessentially Philadelphia, Tug entertained the fans with his humorous quips, irreverent personality, and heart-stopping performances in the late innings. Acquired from the New York Mets in 1975, the left-handed screwball specialist proved to be an immediate success, saving 14 games and winning 9 while posting a 2.97 earned run average that year. He also brought a much-needed presence to the clubhouse, keeping the Phillies loose when they almost lost the National League's Eastern Division championship after building a huge lead in 1976.

In 1980, McGraw compiled a 5-4 record, 1.47 earned run average, and 20 saves in 57 appearances. He was even more impressive during the pennant race. After coming off the disabled list on July 17, the screwball specialist posted five victories and five saves in a three-week period. McGraw pitched in all five playoff games against the Houston Astros, saving the first and fourth contests. In the World Series, he pitched in four of the six games against Kansas City, winning Game Five and saving the opener and the final contest. During the strike-abbreviated season of 1981, McGraw saved 10 games for the Phillies and continued to be among the league leaders in appearances with 34 for each of the next two seasons. But when the Phillies reached the post-season in 1983, the Tugger was relegated to the bench, having relinquished his role as closer to Al Holland. He retired after the 1984 season.[13]

While McGraw may have forged his impressive career with the Miracle Mets of '69 and their pennant-winning successors of '73, he will always be remembered by Phillies fans as the "Tugger," the colorful pitcher who sealed the team's one and only world championship. Both a "showhorse" and "workhorse," he gave creative names to all the pitches in his repertoire. The "John Jameson," for example, was a fastball that was "straight"—the way McGraw "liked his whiskey." Other pitches were named for Peggy Lee ("Is that all there is?"), Bo Derek ("It has a nice little tail on it"), and Frank Sinatra ("Fly me to the moon").[14]

McGraw was different from the vast majority of Philadelphia's professional athletes because he genuinely cared about the fans. Once, when asked by baseball writer Roger Angell how he managed to survive such a tough crowd pitching in Philly, Tug replied: "I love them. Whenever I need something extra, I look up in the stands and there it is."[15] His trademark "Ya gotta believe!" was more than a late season rally cry; it was a citywide inspiration for the little guy who was down on his luck, the senior citizen who was struggling with the infirmities of old age, the impressionable adolescent who had given up hope, and those who were fighting for their lives against a terminal illness. McGraw encouraged Phillies fans to believe in the community and in the missions of its many charitable organizations. Most important, he inspired fans to believe that if they chased after their dreams—no matter what they might be—those dreams would come true.

If McGraw was the emotional soul of the team, Steve Carlton gave the Phillies an air of quiet professionalism. He was the team's ace, a power pitcher for most of his 14-year career in the City of Brotherly Love. Acquired from the St. Louis Cardinals in 1972, Carlton quickly won over the fans going 27-10 for a Phillies club that won only 59 games that season. "Lefty," as he was dubbed by teammates and fans alike, won 20 or more games in 1976 and '77, but emerged as one of the National League's most dominant pitchers in 1980 when he posted a 24-9 record with 286 strikeouts and a 2.34 ERA. His brilliant performance earned him the third of four Cy Young Awards he garnered over the course of a twenty-three-year career in the majors. During the post-season, Carlton defeated Houston 3-1 in the opener and, in the World Series against Kansas City, emerged as the winning pitcher in the second and sixth games.

During the strike-shortened season of '81, Carlton still managed to win 13 games in 24 starts and notched his 3,000th strikeout as well as his first Gold Glove. In '82, the tall left-hander was even better. Not only was he the National League's only 20-game winner, but led the league in strikeouts (286), complete games (19), and shutouts (6) earning him his fourth Cy Young Award. Although a nagging back injury limited Carlton to just 15 victories in 1983, when the Phils captured another pennant, he still led the league in strikeouts (275) and innings pitched (284). Carlton also defeated the Dodgers twice to clinch the pennant in post-season play.

Lefty posted a 13-7 record in 1984, his last effective year for the Phillies. Plagued by injuries over the next two years, the Phillies released the forty-one-year-old hurler in June 24, 1986. Convinced he could still pitch in the majors, Carlton attempted comebacks with the San Francisco Giants, Chicago White Sox, Cleveland Indians, and Minnesota Twins before retiring in 1989.

Carlton possessed a special blend of power and finesse that allowed him to win a total of 329 games during his major league career as well as a place in the National Baseball Hall of Fame. He was fanatical about conditioning, working out nearly two hours a day with a personal fitness coach. But his was not an easygoing personality.

Believing that the mental aspect of the game was every bit as important as the physical, Carlton eliminated all outside influences. On game days he rarely talked with teammates and stuffed cotton in his ears when he pitched. He consistently avoided the press and by 1978 refused to give interviews altogether. Throughout his career, Carlton remained an intense competitor and a seemingly unemotional person, though teammates knew a more supportive and humorous side.[16]

Mike Schmidt, one of baseball's premier power hitters during the 1970s and '80s, anchored the Phillies lineup for a remarkable seventeen-year career. Signed by Phillies in June 1971, Schmidt's greatest achievement was his ability to survive in the major leagues on two bad knees. He was the most talented member of a group of highly rated prospects that came up through the Phillies farm system and played together for eight years in the majors. Although the 18 home runs and 52 RBI Schmidt compiled in his rookie year of 1973 were overshadowed by his .196 batting average and 136 strikeouts, he would rebound to lead the National League in home runs for the next three seasons.

For the power-hitting third baseman, 1980 was a career year. He was singularly responsible for the Phillies' good fortune at various times throughout the season, including 4 game-winning RBI in the Phillies last five regular season victories. Schmitty's dramatic home run against the Expos at Montreal on the final day of the season clinched the division title for the Phillies and propelled them into the playoffs against Houston. Schmidt was not only named the National League's Most Valuable Player for the .286 batting average, 48 home runs, and 121 RBI he compiled that year, but his remarkable performance during the World Series (.381, 2 HR, 7 RBI) earned for him the MVP of the Fall Classic.

The following year Schmidt was even better with a .316 average, 31 homers, and 91 RBI in a strike-shortened season. He repeated as the National League's MVP and nearly captured the coveted Triple Crown, for leading the league in all three hitting categories. Schmitty's 40 home runs and 109 RBI vaulted the Phillies into post-season play, once again, in 1983. He continued to average 35 homers and 92 RBI for each of the next four seasons, his finest coming in 1986 when he captured a third National League MVP award for a .290 batting average, 37 home runs, and 119 RBI. Schmidt retired from the game in May 1989 and was enshrined at Cooperstown five years later.

Unfortunately, Michael Jack's introspective personality and graceful, seemingly effortless play was mistaken for a "cool" approach to the game during most of his seventeen-year career in Philadelphia. He was one of the most severely criticized athletes in the city's history for not showing more emotion on the playing field, a discreet but strong commitment to his Christian faith, and failing to meet the unreasonable expectations of the fans and the media. In fact, Schmidt put more pressure on himself than either group imagined. He took failure very personally and worked harder than anyone else on the team, with the possible exception of Carlton. Sometimes Schmitty could be his own worst enemy, especially when he spoke candidly to the press about his frustrations. At the same time he took his responsibilities as a role model seriously and was widely admired among youngsters and parents alike. An active fundraiser for many local and national charities, Schmidt set a refreshing example for other professional athletes in an era when the cult of the antihero was popular.[17]

Finally, there was the legendary Pete Rose, who played first base for the Phillies from 1979 to 1983. One of the greatest performers in the history of baseball, Rose, who began his career with Cincinnati's "Big Red Machine," is often credited as the catalyst for '80 Phils. He was the experienced veteran whose unrelenting desire to win inspired his younger teammates.

Signed by the Phillies as a free agent in 1979, Rose, at age thirty-eight, went on to hit .331, score 90 runs, and steal 20 bases that year. In 1980, his average slipped to .282, but he emerged as the key figure in the Phillies' quest for a world championship. He ignited three different rallies in the division-clinching 6-4 victory over the Montreal Expos. In the League Championship Series against

Houston, Rose hit .400 and scored the winning run in the Phillies 5-3 victory in Game Four when he bowled over Astro catcher Bruce Bochy. Though he hit just .261 in the World Series, Rose's never-say-die attitude inspired his teammates time and again. His penultimate contribution came in the ninth inning of Game Six when he snatched victory from defeat with a split-second catch of a pop foul that glanced off Bob Boone's mitt.

Rose had another banner year in 1981 when he hit .325 and broke the National League's all-time record for most hits. Age began to catch up with Charlie Hustle in 1982 when his average dipped to .271. Another subpar season followed in '83 when he slipped to .245 and rode the bench for the first time in his career. But Rose bounced back in the post-season to hit .375 in the League Championship Series against the Los Angeles Dodgers and .313 in the World Series against the Baltimore Orioles. Shortly after the Series he was released by the Phillies and played briefly with the Montreal Expos before returning to the Cincinnati Reds as a player-manager. Suspended by Commissioner A. Bartlett Giamatti for betting on baseball in 1989, Rose's career came to a tragic end.[18] Despite his life-long ban from the game, there are still many baseball writers, former players and fans who believe that he deserves a place in Cooperstown.

Rose was a seasoned veteran whose leadership was the intangible that vaulted the Phillies to their only world championship. Interestingly, he didn't have much natural ability. He was not fast by big league standards, but he demonstrated superb instincts as a base runner. He didn't have great range in the field or a strong throwing arm, but he rarely made a defensive mistake. Nor was Rose a great natural hitter. Instead, he disciplined himself to become a contact hitter in order to advance the runner or simply to get on base. Yet he took the Phillies to a higher level of competition by sacrificing himself for the team, taking media pressure off of Schmidt and Carlton, and bringing a fire that burned white-hot to a club that had failed to clinch a pennant on three previous occasions in the mid- to late 1970s.

McGraw, Carlton, Schmidt, and Rose were the nucleus of the team. As they went, so went the Phillies. The supporting cast was solid but not nearly as talented as the core. They were a collection of homegrown veterans, castoffs from other clubs, and fair-haired rookies. Veterans like Bob Boone, Larry Bowa, and Greg Luzinski had, along with Schmidt, come up through the Phillies farm system and had been expected to clinch a pennant for Philadelphia. Since all of them were in their mid- to late twenties when they were promoted to the majors, there was an intense rivalry among them. No one was able to emerge as the genuine leader of the team. While they managed to reach the playoffs each year from 1976 through 1978, these talented ballplayers could not clinch the National League championship and, by 1980, they realized they were running out of time.

Owner Ruly Carpenter and general manager Paul Owens brought in other veteran players to get to the World Series. Between 1974 and 1980, McGraw came from the New York Mets, Garry Maddox came from the San Francisco Giants, Bake McBride and Ron Reed from the St. Louis Cardinals, Dick Ruthven from the Atlanta Braves, Greg Gross and Manny Trillo from the Chicago Cubs, and, of course, Pete Rose from the Cincinnati Reds. Farm director Dallas Green added rookies Lonnie Smith, Marty Bystrom, Bob Walk, Dickie Noles, George Vukovich, and Keith Moreland to the mix. This was the team that would make baseball history in Philadelphia. They were also a very special part of my life.

Those Phillies were the only professional sports team I ever lived and died with. Veterans Stadium was hallowed ground for me. From the first time I set foot in it in April 1971 to the last game on September 28, 2003, the "Vet" and the red-pinstriped teams who played there served as treasured benchmarks in my own life. My father and I sat in the nosebleeds and shared a host of memorable moments: Carlton's 20th victory in 1972; Schmidt's game-winning homer off Tug McGraw to defeat the New York Mets, 5-4, in the 1974 season opener; Dick Allen's return in 1975; Larry Bowa's grand slam against the Reds in 1977; and even the painful playoff losses of '76, '77, and '78. Those shared experiences allowed us to bond, even during my adolescence, when it seemed we didn't have much to discuss.

Back then, what made baseball so special for me was the continuity of the game. There were only two divisions in the National League and you could count on seeing the Cubs, Reds, and Dodgers more than once a season. Aside from the organ music, an animated scoreboard, and some of the wackiest promotions—"Kiteman," cash scrambles, the "Human Cannonball," and the Great Wallenda's tightrope walk—the game was still pretty pure. Many fans came to watch a promising young team play, rather than for the carnival-like atmosphere that surrounded them. The platoon system and free agency had not yet become commonplace and fans could follow the same lineup just about every night each season.

Like every other baseball-playing adolescent reared in Philadelphia, I idolized Mike Schmidt, going so far as to switch my uniform number to 20, change positions from catcher to third base, and grow a mustache. His chiseled physique and seemingly laid-back approach to the game made him "cool." But his prowess as a home run hitter who had the moral courage to live by a strong set of values made him my hero. Along with Steve Carlton, Schmitty carried the Phillies to post-season berths for three straight years between 1976 and '78.

By 1980, the Vet had become a dating ground. Like my unconditional loyalty to the Phillies, I gave my heart to just one girl. Initially she tolerated baseball, but eventually looked forward to going to games with me. She admired center fielder Garry Maddox, reveled in Pete Rose's gutsy headfirst slides, and went crazy during McGraw's nerve-racking performances. She quickly learned not to disturb me when Michael Jack was at the plate vying for yet another of the 548 home runs he would hit during his career. I threatened to propose to her over "Phan-o-vision," but she swore that if I did, she'd not only turn me down but never go to another game. We've been married now for twenty years. In the blink of an eye, the promising young team of my boyhood became the "Wheeze Kids" of my adulthood, seasoned veterans who managed to eke out another pennant in 1983 before they went into a free fall and faded away.

Writing this book was a labor of love. While the research allowed me to connect with my own past, the final product offers a more objective treatment than earlier works on the 1980 Phillies.[19] Hopefully, readers of my generation will discover that the story resonates with their own experience and younger readers will understand what it means to have patience with and faith in the hometown team.

Rarely do the Phillies make the post-season; rarer still do they make it to the World Series. That's why 1980 will forever remain a special season. A talented team of homegrown players, intensely competitive veterans from other clubs, and enthusiastic rookies finally achieved the goal that had eluded the fans for nearly a century—winning a world championship. In the process, the Phillies were embraced by an entire city that learned to believe in itself and its heroes.

CHAPTER 1

LEGACY OF LOSING

WHEN THE PHILLIES BLEW THEIR THIRD straight bid to capture the National League pennant in October 1978, Pulitzer Prize-winning author James A. Michener admitted to his long-standing disappointment with the club. "Since 1915 I have been cheering for the Philadelphia Phillies, and if that doesn't take character, what does?" he said. "In such circumstances it is traditional to say, 'I supported them in good years and bad.'" "There were no good years," he concluded. "I cheered in bad and worse."[1]

Michener was a passionate baseball buff whose greatest misfortune was to be born a Phillies fan. Growing up in Doylestown, Bucks County, he was just a trolley ride away from the old Baker Bowl where he spent many summer afternoons sympathizing with the futility of his hometown team. Michener accepted his fate admitting that he "favored local partisanship." If it came down to a World Series between his beloved Phils and the regal New York Yankees, whom he deplored, the novelist "felt sure that even a moron would be able to detect where [his] enthusiasm lay."[2]

Fortunately, Michener developed over the years a sharp wit and special appreciation for tragic comedy, which enabled him to survive all the seasons of losing and still remain loyal.

To be sure, the silent majority of Phillies fans are similar to James Michener. They possess a fairly good understanding of the game, act respectfully at the ballpark, tend to suffer in private, and in spite of all the losing, still give their unconditional loyalty to the team. They are genuine fans who view their allegiance as a special legacy handed down through the generations. There are, however, an unattractive vocal minority called the "Boo Birds," whose loyalty extends only as far as the win column. They revel in their notorious reputation and function in

11

a black-and-white world of heroes and bums. The Boo Birds thrive on the negativity of sports talk shows and embrace only those athletes who aren't afraid to
get their uniforms dirty, who show their emotions as well as their humanness,
warts and all. They are reactionaries who demand immediate gratification and,
failing to get it, express their displeasure by throwing beer cups, insults, or other
profanity-laced accusations at the players. Regardless of the profile, it is difficult
to deny the Phillies fan sympathy. No other major league franchise can claim as
woeful a history or fans who've suffered more.

Chicago Cubs fans believe that their team is cursed because they haven't won
a World Series since 1908. But the Cubs have two world championships and sixteen pennants to their credit.[3] The Phillies, on the other hand, possess just one
world championship and five pennants. There are also the Boston Red Sox. Until
Boston won the 2004 World Series, Red Sox fans pitied themselves for the "Curse
of the Bambino."[4] Dan Shaughnessy, a sportswriter for the *Boston Globe* who
popularized the theory that Babe Ruth cursed the Sox when he was sold to the
New York Yankees in 1920, rejects the notion that any other club can be as disappointing as the Red Sox and still retain the love of its fans. He acknowledges
Philadelphia's historic frustration with its team, but insists that the 1980 world
championship put an end to the "love/hate relationship between the Phillies
and their fans." "The Phils aren't special anymore," he concludes. "They are just
another ball team."[5]

In fact, the Phillies *are* pathetically unique, especially when compared to Boston. The Red Sox had already won 6 world championships before Ruth was sold
to the Yankees. The tragedy of the Red Sox was that they were often in contention
but somehow managed to blow the pennant or the championship. The Phillies,
on the other hand, have elevated losing to an art form.

No other major league team has suffered more losses in its history (10,000+),
including a record 23-game losing streak in 1961. No other team has had as many
last-place finishes (26).[6] No other team has blown a pennant with a 6½-game
lead and just twelve games left to play in the regular season. But the '64 Phillies
somehow managed to do that by dropping 10 straight and finishing in a tie for
second place.[7] Even when the Phillies reached the World Series they found a way
to go down in flames. After winning the first game of the 1915 Fall Classic against
the Red Sox, the hapless Phils dropped the next four contests, all by one-run margins.[8] In 1950 the Fightins were swept in four straight games by the New York
Yankees.[9] In 1983, it took the Baltimore Orioles just five games to dispatch the
hapless Phils.[10] And in 1993, Mitch Williams, Philadelphia's closer, served up a
walk-off home run to Toronto's Joe Carter in Game Six to end a championship
series that had been Philadelphia's for the taking.[11] If the Phillies aren't cursed,
no team is.

The foiled heroism, generations-long mismanagement, and just plain bad luck began in 1876 when the National League of Professional Baseball Players was organized. Two Philadelphia baseball clubs existed at the time, the Athletics and the Quakers. But the new league awarded the city's franchise to the Athletics, who joined seven other charter members: Boston, Chicago, Cincinnati, St. Louis, Hartford, New York, and Louisville. The Athletics lost the very first game they played, 6-5. It was a relatively low-scoring contest played against the Boston club before 3,000 spectators at Twenty-Fifth and Jefferson Streets. The A's went on to win just 14 of their 59 games that season and, along with the New York Mutuals, were expelled from the league for refusing to make the final scheduled road trip to the west.[12] The die had been cast—Philadelphia was not only a loser but a poor one at that.

The Quaker City was without a professional baseball team until 1883 when the Worcester (Massachusetts) Brown Stockings were transferred to the City of Brotherly Love and renamed the "Phillies." Financed by Alfred J. Reach, a sporting goods magnate, and Colonel John I. Rogers, a Pennsylvania state politician, the team played at Recreation Park located on a misshapen plot of land bordered by Columbia and Ridge Avenues and Twenty-Fourth and Twenty-Fifth Streets. Accordingly, the ballpark had some of the most idiosyncratic dimensions of any field in baseball history: 300 feet down the left field line; 331 feet to straightaway center; 369 feet in right center; and a remarkably short 247 feet down the right field line. Odder than those dimensions, however, were the curious collection of players who called the ballpark "home."

The Phillies were a team of fringe major leaguers managed by their ill-tempered second baseman, Bob Ferguson. Nicknamed "Death to Flying Things," Ferguson was a supreme contortionist able to catch anything hit his way. Sid Farrar was the team's first baseman who hit ninth. Had he not fathered famed opera star Geraldine Farrar, he would have been completely forgotten by history. John Coleman was considered the "ace" of the pitching staff, though he lost 48 of the 65 games he pitched that season. The first loss came on opening day, May 1, 1883, against the Providence Grays. The Phils spotted Coleman a 3-0 lead after seven innings, but Providence rallied with four runs in the eighth to win, 4-3. Thus, the Phillies picked up where the Athletics had left off, losing all but four of their first seventeen games. Frustrated, Ferguson resigned and was made business manager. It would prove to be the first of many moves within the organization where a bungling manager was rewarded for his incompetence by being promoted to the front office.

Outfielder Blondie Purcell became the new skipper by default and the Phillies went on to the first of their many last-place finishes with a miserable record of 17 wins and 81 losses. In addition to pitcher John Coleman's 48 defeats, the Phillies set another inglorious record that season: a 28-0 whitewashing by Providence, which still stands as the most lopsided defeat in major league history.[13]

After that first wretched season, Harry Wright, a former manager of the famed
Cincinnati Red Stockings, was hired as the Phillies' skipper and the team's fortunes improved dramatically. Led by Charlie Ferguson, a rookie pitcher and 20-
game winner, the Phils more than doubled their victory total of the previous year
and finished sixth in the eight-team league. The club advanced to third place in
1885 behind the pitching of Ferguson and rookie Ed Daily, both of whom won
26 games. The Phillies remained contenders until 1896 when the club dropped
to eighth place in what was then a twelve-team league. The closest the Phils came
to clinching a pennant, however, was in 1887 when they finished just 3½ games
behind league-leading Detroit.[14]

It was a banner year for the team, who moved into a new ballpark at Fifteenth
and Huntington Streets in the northern section of the city. Built on a city dump
that was lower than street level, the lot took some 100,000 wagonloads of dirt to
fill the gullies on the field and another 20,000 loads to make the site even with
the adjacent streets and railroad tracks. But by the time the ballpark was completed, it was the most modern and advanced of the time period. Unlike the
other wooden bandbox parks of the day, Philadelphia Ball Park incorporated brick
seating pavilions, topped by 75-foot-high turrets, and ornamental moldings, giving the appearance of a castle from the outside. Seating was spacious with a
capacity of 12,500. Like Recreation Park, the new ballpark also had lopsided
dimensions: 400 feet from home plate to the left field wall; 408 feet to straightaway center; and a short 300 feet down the right field line.[15] Considered a showplace at the time, Philadelphia Ball Park would, over the next half century,
become the scene of high humor and awful tragedy.

The inaugural game was played on April 30 when the Phillies defeated the
New York Giants, 19-10. The team boasted three 20-game winners in Ferguson,
Dan Casey, and Charlie Buffinton. Bolstered by this impressive trio, the Phillies
were poised to win their first pennant in 1888 until tragedy struck. Ferguson contracted typhoid fever in spring training and died at the end of April. Without his
pitching prowess, the Phils finished in third place.[16]

The 1888 campaign witnessed the signing of the Phillies' first true power hitter, Ed Delahanty, a twenty-year-old outfielder who would go on to forge a Hall
of Fame career in the Quaker city. The Phillies purchased his contract from the
Wheeling, West Virginia, club for $1,900 in July. Although he only hit .228 that
year, Delahanty would become the first member of an all-star outfield to arrive.[17]
The other members of that outfield were Sam Thompson, who came in 1889
and led the league with 20 home runs, and Billy Hamilton, who joined the Phils
in 1890 and became one of the best hitters and base-stealers in the game. The
trio played together from 1891 to 1895 and all three outfielders hit over .400 during the '94 season.[18] With such outstanding players, Philadelphia, by the mid-
1890s, was known as "the best baseball city in the world."[19] At the same time,

most reputable Philadelphians—like most respectable Americans—were appalled by the notion of "professional" baseball. Being paid to play a child's game was considered even less reputable than vaudeville.

The sport's poor reputation was reinforced by the constant competition for players between the National League and the American Association, established in 1882, as well as the wrangling of team owners, who controlled everything from ticket prices to player salaries. The cornerstone of their authority was the "reserve clause," which required the five best players of each team to reserve their services in perpetuity to the club for which they played. In these early years, baseball was dominated by the same kind of economic structure and labor relations that existed in the nation's industrial sector. In both cases, owners were entrepreneurs seeking upward mobility at the expense of the workers, who were deprived of control over their wages, working conditions, and terms of employment.[20] The annual salary for most players was less than $2,000.[21] Disgruntled with their low wages, the players organized a union and, in 1890, established their own league.

The Players League marked a significant departure from the earlier circuits in that players and owners shared power and profits equally. The new circuit consisted of eight teams, including one in Philadelphia. Some of the Phillies who jumped were lured back by raises. But the Phils lost their two best pitchers, Charlie Buffinton and Ben Sanders, along with second baseman Bill Hallman, first baseman Sid Farrar, and outfielders George Wood, Jim Fogarty, and Ed Delahanty.[22]

Suddenly in need of talent to replace the jumpers, Reach and Rogers purchased outfielder Billy Hamilton from the Kansas City club of the American Association. With Hamilton's hitting prowess (.325, 49 RBI) and speed on the base paths (102 stolen bases), the Phillies added to an already potent offense powered by Sam Thompson (.313, 102 RBI) and catcher Jack Clements (.315, 74 RBI). Together with the pitching of Kid Gleason, who won 38 games, the Phillies' impressive hitting allowed the team to finish third in 1890.[23] But internal problems continued to plague the game.

Three major leagues and twenty-four teams proved to be too many for fans, who had become disgusted with all the infighting and stayed away from the ballpark. The National League responded by declaring a baseball war. When the Players League folded in 1891 and the American Association died a year later, the National League and its owners had prevailed.[24] For the first time since 1883, the Phillies had the city to themselves and made a strong effort to revive fan interest in the game. Although team president John Rogers refused to allow the defecting players back on to his club, he made an important exception in re-signing Ed Delahanty. Rogers was no fool. Delahanty was a valued prospect before he jumped. The fans adored "Big Ed" and would keep the turnstiles moving to see him play. Unfortunately, they had to be content with the exploits of individual stars during the 1890s because the team never finished higher than third place.[25] To be sure, there *were* some remarkable individual performances during the decade.

Delahanty developed into the team's biggest star and future Hall of Famer, hitting over .300 for 10 straight seasons between 1892 and 1901. He was the league's best hitter in 1899 with a .410 average and was the league leader twice in slugging with a .495 average in 1892 and a .583 average in 1893.[26] Between 1897 and 1900, Napoleon Lajoie, another future Hall of Famer, became an all-star second baseman and consistently hit .324 or higher. In 1897, he led the National League in slugging average (.569) and total bases (310) and finished third in home runs with 9. The following year Lajoie topped the league in doubles (43) and RBI (127).[27]

By 1900, there was room for competition in major league baseball. A pressing need to address the decline in the quality of play and umpiring coupled with gambling and the rowdy behavior of the players, led to the creation, in 1901, of a rival "American League." National League teams were losing money at the gate and their owners were divided into two warring camps over players' salaries and other administrative expenses. To survive economically, the National League was forced to drop four teams from its organization, teams that were quickly assumed by the new American League. Once again, the Phillies were forced to share the city with another team—the Philadelphia Athletics, managed and partly owned by Connie Mack.[28]

Almost from the moment that he set foot in the City of Brotherly Love, Mack created controversy. He persuaded Benjamin F. Shibe, a business partner of sporting goods dealer Al Reach, to invest in his club. The offer wouldn't have seemed so conspiratorial if Reach hadn't been a part owner of the Phillies, but Mack persisted. He even sweetened the deal by arranging to have the Reach company's baseballs selected as the official ball of the new American League. After clearing the offer with Reach, Shibe purchased 50 percent of the A's stock and became president of the club.[29] But Mack didn't stop there.

Stating that the purpose of the new American League was "to protect the players," unlike the National League, which sought "to protect the magnates," the brash baseball entrepreneur proceeded to raid the roster of the rival Phillies by offering sizable pay increases to their stars.[30] Not only did Mack land a pitching staff for his team by signing Chick Fraser, Bill Bernhard, and Wiley Piatt, he captured a real prize when Lajoie defected to the A's for $5,500.[31] Roster raiding was made easier by the National League's refusal to pay any individual player more than $2,400 a season. American League clubs promised no salary cap and made more lucrative offers, and a total of 74 National Leaguers jumped to the new circuit.[32] When Rogers discovered Mack's scheme, the Phillies president took him to court, arguing that the reserve clause prevented players from jumping to another team or league unless they were first released by their original club. The case was thrown out in common pleas court on the grounds that National League contracts "lacked sufficient mutuality." But the Phillies appealed the decision to the Supreme Court of Pennsylvania, which ruled in their favor. The Phils obtained court injunctions against Lajoie, Fraser, and Bernhard, preventing them from playing for any club except theirs.[33]

John McGraw, the feisty manager of the National League champion New York Giants, was so enraged by Mack's efforts that he spited the A's by predicting they would turn out to be a money loser, the "White Elephants" of the new league. Mack, who could be spiteful as well as humorous, countered by adopting the animal as his team's mascot, attaching a small white elephant on the left breast pocket of each player's dark blue warm-up sweater.[34] Nor did he have any intention of giving in to the National League on the Lajoie ruling.

Since the Pennsylvania Supreme Court's decision could only be enforced within the state, American League president Ban Johnson, with Mack's blessing, transferred the contracts of Lajoie and Bernhard to the Cleveland Americans so the National League would be deprived of their services. Whenever Cleveland played against the A's in Philadelphia, neither player was permitted to take the field in accordance with the injunction. Instead they spent a paid vacation in Atlantic City.[35] Shortly after the arrangement had been sealed, Mack boasted of his vindication to the press: "The American League and the Athletics are here to stay, whether Lajoie is with us or not."[36] It was a prophetic statement. Mack's A's not only survived, but went on to capture six American League pennants and three World Series titles between 1902 and 1914.[37] The Phillies' fortunes, on the other hand, were not as bright.

Before the 1902 season began, the Phils lost almost every star player they had to the American League and dropped to seventh place. Attendance fell to just over 100,000—a decrease of more than 50 percent—and the owners were forced to take a sizable loan to remain afloat. Disgusted by their financial misfortune and drop in the standings, Rogers and Reach sold the Phillies in 1903 to a syndicate headed by James Potter, a Philadelphia stockbroker.[38]

Peace talks between the rival leagues began just before the 1903 season. According to a "National Agreement," the two circuits agreed to coexist, abstaining from raiding each other's rosters. The reserve clause would be observed and territories clearly defined. New York, Boston, Chicago, Philadelphia, and St. Louis would be shared by both circuits. While the National League held special rights to teams in Cincinnati and Pittsburgh, the American League would establish exclusivity in Washington, Detroit, and Cleveland. Finally, a National Commission was established to govern baseball and clean up its scandalous image. Composed of the president of each league and a third member chosen by the other two, the commission cracked down on umpire baiting but was less successful in addressing the chronic problems of gambling and alcoholism. On the field, base-ball was a low-scoring game. Home runs were rare. The ball remained largely inside the park, and teams manufactured runs inning by inning. The hit-and-run, stolen base, squeeze play, and bunt were common. The ball was also heavier because of a rubber core, giving this period of baseball history the name "Dead-Ball Era."[39]

Between 1904 and 1913, the Phillies continued to forge a well-deserved repu-tation as perennial losers. The 1904 club was the first of fourteen in the club's history to drop at least 100 games. A parade of forgettable players, managers, and owners followed until 1913, when William F. Baker, a former New York City police commissioner, assumed ownership of the team.[40] Under the leadership of manager Charlie Dooin, the Phils finished second to the New York Giants that season after leading the league throughout the first half. The pitching staff was outstanding. Tom Seaton posted a 27-12 record in 322 innings of work to lead the league in both categories. Grover Alexander, who had won 28 games as a rookie two years earlier, compiled a 22-8 record and a 2.79 ERA. Ad Brennan won another 14 games and Eppa Rixey and Erskine Mayer nine each. The offense was powered by right fielder Gavvy Cravath, who led the league in home runs (19), RBI (128) and hits (179) and finished second in batting average (.341). Left fielder Sherry Magee (.306, 11 HR, 70 RBI) and first baseman Fred Luderus (.262, 18 HR, 86 RBI) were among the club's other top hitters. Fans returned in droves to watch the team at Philadelphia Ball Park, renamed "Baker Bowl" for the new owner. More than 470,000 fans came out to the rickety old bandbox during the season. Some of the incorrigibles sat in the sun-drenched bleachers and flashed mirrors in the faces of the opposing team when they came to bat, resulting in at least one forfeited game.[41]

The highlight of Baker's tenure came in 1915, when the Phillies won their first pennant (Figure 1). Throughout the season the Phils were never lower than second place. Alexander was brilliant. During the month of June the future Hall of Famer pitched three one-hitters en route to the first of three straight 30-win seasons. He finished the season with a 31-10 record and led the National League with a 1.22 ERA and 12 shutouts. Offensively, Cravath (.285, 24 HR, 115 RBI) and Luderus (.315, 7 HR, 62 RBI) were among the league leaders in hitting. On September 29, Alexander clinched the pennant by defeating the Boston Braves, 5-0, at Braves Field.

The Phillies faced the American League champion Boston Red Sox in the World Series. Game One was played at Philadelphia's Baker Bowl on a soggy, rain-soaked field. The Phillies scored the first run of the game in the fourth inning. Center fielder Dode Paskert reached base on a bloop single to center field. Gavvy Cra-vath bunted him to second. Paskert advanced to third on a fielder's choice and scored when Possum Whitted beat out a grounder to second. Alexander held the

Red Sox hitless through seven innings before surrendering Boston's lone run of the game in the eighth. The Phils won the game with a two-run rally in the bottom of the inning and Philadelphia had its first World Series victory ever, 3-1.

The Red Sox evened the Series the following day with a 2-1 victory. The highlight of the game took place off the field as Woodrow Wilson traveled to Philadelphia, becoming the first United States president to witness a World Series contest. The Series moved to Boston for Game Three on Monday, October 11. Alexander returned to the mound pitching on just two days' rest. He pitched well, surrendering two runs on six hits. But Boston's Dutch Leonard was better, giving up just one run on three hits. The deciding run was a heartbreaker coming in the bottom of the ninth. The Phils also dropped the next two games by one run margins. Spitballer George Chalmers lost to Boston's Ernie Shore in Game Four, 2-1. Eppa Rixey, taking over for Erskine Mayer, lost the final game back at Baker Bowl, 5-4, as the Phils lost their first bid for a world championship. But the Phillies certainly didn't go quietly.

Several beer kegs awaited the losers in the clubhouse. Whether or not they cried in the beer is uncertain. What is known is that the party ran well into the evening. Many players were so drunk they passed out, including catcher Bill Killefer who had to be carried to a nearby station and loaded onto a train that would take him home to Michigan.[43]

The Phillies finished in second place for the next three seasons. With World War I raging in Europe, Baker, fearing he would lose Alexander to military

FIGURE 1. The 1915 Phillies won the first National League pennant in the club's inglorious history. They were led by the pitching of future Hall of Famer Grover Alexander, pictured in the center row, fifth from left. Courtesy of the *Philadelphia Daily News*.

service, sold his star pitcher to the Chicago Cubs in 1918. Selling marquee players for desperately needed cash would become common among future owners,
who never seemed to have enough operating capital to survive, let alone field a
contender. As a result, the team finished as high as fifth place just once during
the next two decades.[44]

Anyone who was traded during those miserable years must have felt as if he
had escaped from purgatory. One of the lucky players was Casey Stengel, who
would go on to become a Hall of Fame manager with the New York Yankees.
Stengel got the news that he was dealt in mid-1921 to the New York Giants during a rain-delayed game. Half-dressed, he raced from the clubhouse outside into
the pouring rain. Although the field was nothing but mud, he circled the bases,
sliding into each bag. Later, when asked why he put on such a display, the mud-
caked right fielder replied, "I was celebrating my liberation from the cellar."[45]

While the Phillies struggled during the Roaring Twenties, baseball was in the
throes of its golden age. Nationwide there was a new popularity to the game. To
prevent the possibility of another game-fixing scheme on the level of the infamous 1919 "Black Sox Scandal," the owners abolished the three-man National
Commission and hired Judge Kenesaw Mountain Landis as commissioner with
full powers to act as he saw fit in the interests of baseball. Soon after, Landis ban-
ished from the game the eight Chicago White Sox implicated in the 1919 scandal with the decree that "regardless of the verdict of juries, no player that throws
a game" or "sits in a conference with crooked players or gamblers" intending to
throw a game and doesn't tell his club "will ever play professional baseball again."
Landis's pronouncement and the powers vested in the new office served to reinforce how critical baseball was to American life at the time.[46]

On the field, the ball was livelier than ever before. Home runs were flying out
of ballparks at a record pace, especially in the American League. Babe Ruth of
the New York Yankees revolutionized the game by hitting 54 home runs in 1920
alone. Fans turned out in droves to see the home run. Attendance figures rose
to a record 9.3 million during the decade. National League teams stocked their
rosters with sluggers like Rogers Hornsby of the St. Louis Cardinals and Hack
Wilson of the Chicago Cubs. Not to be outdone, William Baker, in 1928, signed
outfielder Chuck Klein, who immediately became one of baseball's great sluggers. Klein led the National League in home runs for four years between 1929
and 1933, setting a personal high of 43 in 1929. He was voted the league's Most
Valuable Player in 1931 by the *Sporting News* and again, in 1932, by the Baseball
Writers. Klein's greatest season, however, came in 1933 when he won the coveted
Triple Crown for leading the National League in three hitting categories with a
.368 batting average, 28 home runs, and 120 RBI.[47]

Meanwhile, the allegiance of Philadelphia's baseball fans turned to the Athletics who were in the process of building another championship dynasty (Figure 2).

Connie Mack boasted an impressive cast of characters, including seven future Hall of Famers: Ty Cobb, Eddie Collins, Mickey Cochrane, Jimmie Foxx, Lefty Grove, Al Simmons, and Zack Wheat. The A's were sharp-witted and strong, reckless and carefree, brutally candid and shamelessly self-indulgent—much like the Roaring Twenties in which they played. They also captured two World Series titles and three pennants between 1929 and 1931.[48]

Cobb almost brought his winning ways to the Phillies in 1929. Having ended his playing career the year before, he was anxious to get back into baseball and partnered with real estate agent Raymond H. Greenberg to negotiate a deal with Phils owner William Baker. Greenberg planned to buy the team and Baker Bowl for about $900,000. He would then turn the Phillies over to Cobb who would serve as manager and put up some of his own money toward the purchase price of the team. Meanwhile, Greenberg arranged with Connie Mack to move the Phillies to Shibe Park, home of the Athletics. He would then demolish Baker Bowl and use the space to erect an office building. But when the Phillies won eight games in a row, jumping from eighth to sixth place in the standings, Baker

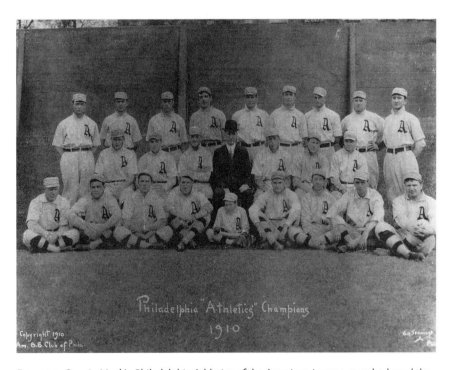

FIGURE 2. Connie Mack's Philadelphia Athletics of the American League overshadowed the Phillies, capturing nine pennants and five world championships during their half century in the City of Brotherly Love. Courtesy of the National Baseball Hall of Fame Library, Cooperstown, New York.

became convinced that his asking price was too low. Naturally, he increased the price by another $100,000. Cobb became infuriated and killed the deal, leaving another generation of Phillies fans to wonder "what might have been."[49]

The Phillies continued to be tail-enders during the early 1930s with a pitching staff that was the worst in the National League. Attendance plummeted and those fans who did go to Baker Bowl went to mock the team. One wag went so far as to vandalize a huge soap advertisement posted on the right field wall that read: "The Phillies use Lifebuoy." Taking a white paintbrush to the billboard, he added the words: "and they still stink."[50] Only the condition of the team's decrepit ballpark was worse than their play.

Coal dust billowed into the ballpark from the nearby train yards. The seats were grimy, the field was shoddy, and the press box, enclosed with chicken wire, was a popular target of jokes among scribes from other cities. When the Phillies were on the road, the ballpark was used for fire department parades, midget auto races, and donkey baseball. Only the truly discerning fan could tell the difference between the latter and the team's comedic play. One Chicago beat writer called the park the "Toilet Bowl." By 1938, ownership agreed and approached Connie Mack with the request to share Shibe Park with the Athletics. Fortunately, Mack had gotten over his early bitterness and welcomed the Phils.[51]

The final game at Baker Bowl was played on June 30 against the New York Giants. Appropriately, the Phillies lost the contest, 14-1. "Baker Bowl passed out of existence as the home of the Phillies," wrote Bill Dooly of the *Philadelphia Record*. "Equal to the occasion, the Phillies almost passed out with it by providing one of their inimitable travesties, a delineation in which they drolly absorbed a 14-1 pasting."[52]

The Phillies constantly struggled to meet their financial obligations as the Great Depression lingered on. In 1932, Gerald Nugent, the team's business manager, became president. To balance the books he traded away the Phillies' best players for lesser ones, making sure that a sizable amount of cash accompanied every deal. Among the stars auctioned off were catcher Spud Davis, shortstop Dick Bartell, third baseman Pinky Whitney, first baseman Dolph Camilli, pitchers Curt Davis, Claude Passeau, and Kirby Higbe, and, worst of all, Klein himself. The club's financial problems became so severe that after the 1942 season the National League assumed control of the franchise and sold it to a group headed by Bill Cox, a New York lumber broker. Cox lasted one year before being banned from baseball by Commissioner Landis for betting on games.[53]

Landis's action was a blessing in disguise for the beleaguered franchise. The Phillies were sold to Robert R. M. Carpenter, a wealthy DuPont Corporation executive and prominent sportsman from Wilmington, Delaware, who gave the club to his son, Robert Jr., as a birthday present. The $400,000 transaction was made on November 23, 1943, and the younger Carpenter was immediately installed as

president. His first act was to hire as general manager Herb Pennock, a personal
friend and former Yankee great. Unlike previous owners, Bob Carpenter was a
full-time club president who invested his energies and fortune into the franchise
for the next three decades. While he never took a salary or expected to make a
profit from the team, Carpenter wasn't willing to lose money. A self-described
skinflint, he once admitted that he "always wanted to make money because
there's no satisfaction in doing something if you don't make a success of it."[54]

Carpenter brought a certain dignity to what had been a mediocre, poorly run
franchise. He was a player's owner who lavished huge bonuses on talented young
prospects, loaned money to veterans who wanted to purchase businesses or
homes, and often assumed responsibility for their expenses when they had financial problems. While Carpenter endeared himself to many of his players because
of his generosity, he could be a strict disciplinarian when he needed to be. He
opposed too much late-night carousing and was known to sermonize in clubhouse meetings. Once the DuPont heir went so far as to hire detectives to follow
some of his more incorrigible ballplayers.[55] Unfortunately, Carpenter's tenure is
also remembered for his club's poor treatment of Jackie Robinson in his 1947
quest to break the color barrier.

The Phils' infamous reputation as a racially segregated team in a racially segregated city was born that year as the Phillies treated the Dodgers rookie worse
than any other National League team did. Encouraged by manager Ben Chapman,
Phillies pitchers threw at Robinson's head, infielders purposely spiked him on
the base paths, and—in one of the lowest moments in baseball history—the Phils
humiliated the Dodger first baseman by standing on the steps of their dugout,
pointing their bats at him, and making gunshot sounds.[56] The Phillies were also
the last team in the National League to integrate. They did not field an African
American player until 1957 when infielder John Kennedy appeared in five games
for the Phils—a full decade after Robinson broke the color line. Even then, the
Phillies maintained segregated spring-training facilities, a practice that was finally
abandoned in 1962.[57]

At the same time, Carpenter was able to bring the Phillies their first pennant
since 1915. Together with Pennock, he signed and cultivated a group of young players known as the "Whiz Kids," including first baseman Eddie Waitkus, second
baseman Mike Goliat, shortstop Granny Hamner, third baseman Willie "Puddin'
Head" Jones, left fielder Dick Sisler, right fielder Del Ennis, catcher Andy Seminick, and pitchers Curt Simmons, Bob Miller, and Jim Konstanty. The most talented players of the group, however, were center fielder Richie Ashburn and
pitcher Robin Roberts, both of whom would go on to forge Hall of Fame careers
in Philadelphia. Fans adored the young team, treating them like movie stars.

Scratching their way to the top of the National League pennant race largely on
cunning and daring, the Whiz Kids clinched the flag on the final day of the 1950

season, beating out the Dodgers at Brooklyn's Ebbets Field. The Phillies scored first when Jones singled to left in the sixth inning to score Sisler. The Dodgers tied the score in the bottom of the inning when Brooklyn shortstop Pee Wee Reese hit a controversial home run that lodged at the base of a wire screen in right center field.

The score was still tied at 1-1 when the Dodger came to bat in the bottom of the ninth. Cal Abrams led off with a walk and Reese singled him to second. Duke Snider followed with a line drive to center field. Richie Ashburn fielded the ball on one hop and, with Abrams streaking toward home, fired to the plate. Catcher Stan Lopata gloved the throw and put the tag on Abrams for the first out of the inning. The Phillies center fielder had saved the season. Roberts retired the side and the Phillies sent the game into extra innings.

In the top of the tenth, Dodgers starter Don Newcombe began to show signs of fatigue. He surrendered base hits to Roberts and Waitkus before notching the first out on a sacrifice by Ashburn. With two runners on base, Dick Sisler came to the plate. After getting ahead in the count one ball and two strikes, Newcombe threw the Phillies first baseman a fastball on the outside corner of the plate and Sisler belted it into the left field stands for a three-run homer. Roberts, with a 4-1 lead, retired the Dodgers in order in the bottom of the tenth and the Phillies had clinched the second pennant in the club's history.

It was a short-lived celebration, though. Three days later, the New York Yankees arrived in Philadelphia to play the World Series. Manager Eddie Sawyer, in a surprise move, started reliever Jim Konstanty, who would later be named the Most Valuable Player of the National League. Opposing him was Vic Raschi, who had compiled a 21-8 record for the Yankees during the regular season. Both pitchers were brilliant. The only run of the game came in the fourth inning when the Yankees' Bobby Brown stroked a leadoff double down the left field line. He was advanced to third by Hank Bauer's 400-foot fly to deep center field, and scored on Jerry Coleman's sacrifice fly to left.

Robin Roberts faced the Yanks' Allie Reynolds in Game Two. Again, the Phils lost by a single run when, with the score deadlocked at 1-1 in the top of the tenth, Yankee Clipper Joe DiMaggio belted a 400-foot home run into the left field bleachers to give New York a 2-1 victory.

The Series shifted to New York for Game Three. With his pitching staff badly depleted, Phillies skipper Eddie Sawyer chose veteran southpaw Ken Heintzelman against the Yankees' Ed Lopat. Although the Phils outhit New York 10-7, they failed to capitalize on several scoring opportunities and dropped the game, 3-2. A Yankee victory was a foregone conclusion going into the fourth and final game of the Series. Sawyer was forced to start rookie Bob Miller, still ailing from a sore arm, against Whitey Ford, New York's twenty-one-year-old left-hander who had won nine straight decisions for the Yankees during the regular season. The

Fightins went down to a 5-2 defeat, becoming the first team since the 1939 Cincinnati Reds to be swept in the World Series. It was the Yankees' 13th world championship in 17 Series.[58]

Because the 1950 Whiz Kids sported an average age of twenty-six, Phillies fans believed that better years were ahead for the team. They had also won over the loyalty of the city's fans. The Athletics were in decline. Unable to draw at the gate or attract star players, the Mack family sold the franchise to Chicago businessman Arnold Johnson. When the A's relocated to Kansas City after the 1954 season, the Phillies were, once again, the only baseball team in town.[59] In honor of Mack's legendary career, Carpenter renamed Shibe Park, "Connie Mack Stadium." Mack, who died shortly after, predicted that better days were ahead for his former archrivals. He was wrong. In the seasons that followed the Phils were unable to replicate their pennant-winning success.

By 1960 Carpenter had had his fill of losing seasons. Unrealized expectations in an aging group of Whiz Kids convinced him it was time to rebuild. Sawyer confirmed that belief when, after losing the first game of the season, he resigned as manager. Frustrated at the prospect of another tail-ender, Sawyer explained his decision to general manager John Quinn, saying: "I'm forty-nine years old, and I'd love to live to be fifty."[60] Quinn seized the opportunity to overhaul the club. He started at the top, immediately hiring Gene Mauch, manager of the American Association's Minneapolis Millers, as skipper.

At thirty-four years of age, Mauch was a young disciplinarian who had come through the Brooklyn Dodgers organization in the late 1940s. His career batting average of .239 underscored that the game had not come easy to him.[61] He was a better tactician than player, and one who studied the game with an exceptional attention to detail. A trait that would later earn him the moniker "Little General." On good days, Mauch was able to "steal a victory by manipulating his roster one step a head of the opposing manager." On bad days, he would overmanage, costing his team a victory that had been in reach. No one could deny, however, that Mauch had the temperament to manage. He was surly, sharp-witted, and refused to back down from anyone, regardless of size or authority. The sportswriters loved him for the ease with which he conducted a postgame interview, serving up some of the most colorful—if not printable—quotes imaginable.[62]

Mauch inherited a bad ball club that would only get worse before it got better. The 1960 Phillies finished in last place, 36 games behind first-place Pittsburgh. The following season the Phils hit rock bottom. The team not only finished in last place for the fourth straight season, but the Phillies suffered a twenty-three-game losing streak, a major league record that still stands today. It began on July 29 with a 4-3 loss to the San Francisco Giants at home, and continued well into the dog days of August. Even the newspapers in other cities followed the losing streak with a macabre fascination. "To lose 20 straight ball games takes quite a bit of doing," reported the *New York Herald Tribune.* "And if the Phillies have not yet exhausted the possibilities of losing ball games, they certainly have explored them thoroughly. They have lost games in the first inning and in the ninth, on the mound, at the plate and in the field. They have employed all the old methods and developed a few new ones. We make these observations with sympathy and even respect. There has been suspense in watching the Phillies lose. How long can they keep it up? When will their luck change? Can they go on like this forever? These are the questions being asked today—and probably tomorrow. And we hate to think of the answers."[63] Finally, the losing streak ended on August 20, when the Phils won the second game of a doubleheader, 7-4, against the Braves at Milwaukee.[64]

The only thing that prevented the Phillies from finishing last in 1962 was the addition of two expansion clubs, the New York Mets and the Houston Colt .45s. The club's 34-win improvement from the previous season was largely due to beating up on these two clubs. The Phillies stumbled out of the gate again in 1963 and found themselves mired in last place until mid-July. But they rebounded to win 56 of their last 91 games to finish fourth.[65]

The following season was one of the most memorable—and tragic—in Phillies history. For 150 games it seemed the Phillies couldn't lose. Jim Bunning (19-8, 219 K, 2.63 ERA) and Chris Short (17-9, 181 K, 2.20 ERA) were the workhorses of the pitching staff. Rookie third baseman Richie Allen (.318, 29 HR, 91 RBI) and right fielder Johnny Callison (.274, 31 HR, 104 RBI) were the only two regulars and carried the offense. Mauch established an extremely effective platoon system. Bobby Wine and Ruben Amaro shared playing time at shortstop. Tony Taylor and Cookie Rojas split second base. Clay Dalrymple and Gus Triandos shared catching duties. Frank Thomas, John Herrnstein, Roy Sievers, Vic Power, and Danny Cater all saw playing time at first base. Tony Gonzalez and Johnny Briggs split time in center field and Wes Covington and Adolfo Phillips and Alex Johnson did the same in left. What's more, the team enjoyed a special chemistry (Figure 3). It was the first truly integrated squad in the organization's history with Latinos, whites, and African Americans. Most of the players were in their mid-twenties and reveled in the clubhouse camaraderie.

The 1964 season was an almost magical one that catcher Gus Triandos dubbed the "Year of the Blue Snow." Jim Bunning pitched a perfect game to defeat the New York Mets, 6-0, at Shea Stadium on Father's Day. Johnny Callison hit the winning home run at the All-Star Game. The Phillies had a stranglehold on first place for most of the season. Up 6½ games with just 12 left to play, the pennant was within reach. Fans were so confident that the elusive flag was theirs for the taking that they snatched up as many World Series tickets as possible. Even the programs had been printed by the front office, inflating their hopes. Only then did the cruelest thing happen.

On September 21, the Phils spiraled into a horrific losing streak. Mauch panicked. Desperate to clinch, the Little General, on three separate occasions during the stretch, gave Bunning or Short the ball with only two days' rest. Never did they refuse. Nor could they win, being exhausted by that point. By the final weekend of the regular season, the Phils had dropped ten straight and finished a game behind the pennant-winning St. Louis Cardinals. It was the greatest collapse in the history of major league baseball. Just as tragic, not until 1976 would the team again come as close to capturing the flag.

From 1965 to 1969, injuries, poor trades, and personal conflict among the players prevented the Phillies from finishing any higher than fourth place. Thus, a team that had the potential to contend for the next five seasons became tail-enders for the balance of the decade.[66] Fan disappointment continued to grow. Failing to appreciate the depth of the historic frustration, the players, most of whom were in Philadelphia as a way station to greater fortunes with other clubs, maligned the fans. "Phillies fans are so rough," quipped Bob Uecker, a journeyman catcher,

FIGURE 3. The infamous 1964 Phillies included (from left to right) Cookie Rojas, Johnny Callison, Richie Allen, and Manager Gene Mauch. Courtesy of the *Philadelphia Daily News*.

"they'd boo unwed mothers on Mother's Day. I've even seen people standing on street corners booing each other."[67]

More than any other team in Philadelphia's sports history, the 1964 Phillies saddled the city with a reputation for being a "loser." Even when victory seemed certain, Philadelphia always found a way to lose. Predictably, Phillies fans came to demand so much from the team, but deep down expected so little. Call it "chronic bad luck" if you will, but the Phillies' infamous reputation became so ingrained in the fabric of the city's sports culture that the ghosts of that tragic season were exorcised time and again whenever any of the city's sports teams contended for a championship.

"Rooting for the Phillies," wrote Joe Queenan, author of *True Believers: The Tragic Inner Life of Sports Fans*, "was the Vale of Tears, the Stations of the Cross, the Crown of Thorns, the Bataan Death March, and the Babylonian Captivity all rolled into one."[68] As a result, there were only two reasons for being a Phillies fan during the first century of the team's existence: either you were geographically predisposed to that fate having been born and raised in Philadelphia, or you adopted your father's childhood team. Most of us really had no choice. All we could do is learn to find the humor in a painful situation, season after forgettable season.

Vindication would not come until 1980.

CHAPTER 2

DOWN ON THE FARM

ROBERT RULIPH MORGAN CARPENTER, III, may have been born with a silver spoon in his mouth, but it didn't prevent him from embracing the family business with an exceptional work ethic and special passion. Nicknamed "Ruly," the twenty-three-year-old DuPont heir had been an outstanding three-sport athlete at Tower Hill, a prestigious prep school in Wilmington, Delaware. He spent his summers at Connie Mack Stadium as a gofer, entering the organization at the ground floor. When the team was on the road, his father sent him to his grandparents' dairy farm in rural Delaware. If nothing else, milking cows at five o'clock in the morning and baling hay sometimes as late as nine-thirty at night cultivated character as well as an impressive work ethic in the youngster.[1]

Matriculating at Yale University in 1958, Ruly majored in American studies and lettered in both football and baseball. Although he intended to pursue a career in law, the dismal fortunes of his father's baseball team changed his mind. "The teasing and criticism from my classmates convinced me that I wanted to help my father build a winning ball club," he later admitted. "It was a personal challenge."[2] After graduating from Yale in 1962, Carpenter enrolled at the University of Delaware, where he took courses in accounting to prepare for the financial challenges of running a baseball franchise. The following year he spent six months working for Phillies treasurer George Harrison in the club's accounting department. Shortly after, Bob Carpenter dispatched his son to the minor leagues to continue the apprenticeship.[3] It was a humbling experience.

Eight-hour bus rides, hand-me-down uniforms from the parent club, rickety, old bandbox parks, flea-bitten hotels and boardinghouses were the hard realities of life in the minors during the 1960s. Only the pay was worse. Those who played in the rookie or "high A" leagues earned $600 per month, plus meal money, which amounted to another $10 per day. If the player was lucky, he received a signing bonus that would help him survive the early years in pro ball. If he made it to Triple-A ball, the prospect's salary increased to $750 per month, and the meal money to $15 per day. Unless the minor leaguer enjoyed a split contract, which guaranteed a certain pay and benefits if he made the majors, he had no agent, no protection, and no leverage.[4] In short, minor leaguers, during the 1960s, played for nothing more than a genuine love of the game.

Carpenter's first exposure to the minors came at Leesburg, Florida, the lowest level of the Phillies farm system. Assigned camp administrator, he worked under Paul Owens, a California scout who coordinated minor league spring training for the organization. "Ruly was in charge of all the business operations and I took care of all on-the-field matters," Owens remembered. "It didn't take him long to get involved with everything we were doing."[5] That included the evaluation of player talent.

"Night after night we would talk baseball," said Carpenter. "Paul believed that everything revolved around scouting, player development, and the minor leagues. It was obvious to me during those six weeks at Leesburg what our problem was. We just didn't have enough players who could basically run, hit, and throw. Of the more than 100 kids we had in that camp, 25 percent of them weren't as good as my teammates at Yale. It was a real eye-opener."[6] While Carpenter understood that the Phillies lacked talent at the minor league level, he was still young enough to empathize with players who were around the same age.

One evening, when a young pitcher from Panama complained that he hadn't been given a "fair shake," Ruly went to Owens's hotel room, got him out of the shower, and asked him to reconsider. Owens agreed to return to the ballpark to watch the young pitcher throw. "I had hardly dried off," recalled Owens, chuckling at the memory. "I got Dick Teed, one of our young managers, and we went to the park. We get the kid cranked up and he throws to Teed. Ruly's watching from behind home plate. Finally, he says, 'Aw, you guys are right.'"

When Owens and Carpenter told the pitcher that they couldn't use him, he became so irate he threatened to burn down the decrepit old hotel where the team was staying. Realizing that the place was a fire hazard, Ruly was so worried that he stayed up all night ready to catch the potential arsonist. The next morning, he accompanied the young pitcher to the local airport in a police car and put him on a plane to Panama.[7] It was a telling experience. Carpenter would learn not only to make the hard decisions necessary to build a winning baseball organization, but to walk a fine line between trusting the judgment of the baseball men in the organization and listening to the concerns of the players. Even Owens had to admit that Carpenter's "dedication and intensity were so great" that, "once he got experience, Ruly would make a fine baseball executive."[8]

To be sure, Owens and Carpenter were very much alike (Figures 4 and 5). Grassroots baseball men, they thrived on long hours and outworked anyone to make the Phillies a winning organization. But life had not come as easily for Owens as it had for his young protégé.

Born February 7, 1924, at Salamanca, New York, Owens was the son of a rail-road worker who had quit school at age thirteen. His mother emphasized the importance of education and strictly supervised his study habits in the hope that her son would go on to college. Owens, who played football, basketball, and base-ball in high school, grew to 6' 3" and earned a full scholarship to Rider College as a basketball player. In 1943, he left Rider to join the military. Over the next two years he would serve as a combat engineer in Belgium, France, and Germany and see action during D-Day and the Battle of the Bulge. He also met and married a beautiful French nurse, Marcelle.[9]

After the war, Owens transferred to St. Bonaventure, where he prepared for a teaching career and continued to play basketball and baseball. During his senior year of 1951, the tall power hitter captured the attention of the Olean, New York, club, which signed him to a professional contract at $175 per month. That season Owens hit .407 in 111 games and collected 17 home runs and 101 RBI. He spent the next three years teaching school and playing ball for Olean. Baseball was additional income that he could earn during the summer months. That changed in 1955 when the Phillies purchased the Olean club.[10]

"The Phillies offered me $4,500 to become a player-manager," Owens recalled. "That was $1,500 more than I could make teaching. I figured I didn't have any-thing to lose and if baseball didn't work out, I'd still get a chance to teach again."[11] The twenty-five-year-old schoolteacher accepted the offer and, after the 1957 sea-son, he was transferred to California to manage the Phillies' Bakersfield club. In 1959 he served as the Phillies' West Coast scout and ran their minor league spring training.

When Bob Carpenter, Jr., fired farm director Clay Dennis in 1965, he acted on his son's suggestion to name Owens the new director of Minor Leagues. "The only way I would take the job was if I had complete control of player devel-opment and scouting," insisted Owens, who had seen enough of the organiza-tion to know that the scouting ranks had to be overhauled. "Bob Carpenter was always dedicated to his people and a lot of them took advantage of him. I was never going to be a 'yes' man and Bob knew it. If I failed, I could always go back to California and scout."[12] Owens took the job with the understanding that he was to mentor Ruly Carpenter and prepare him to assume the presidency of the club sometime in the future.

Together, Owens and his protégé began to overhaul the farm system. They persuaded Bob Carpenter to invest $250,000 for an expanded training complex in Clearwater, Florida, so the minor leaguers could train together instead of at various sites across Florida. They also convinced the owner to spend another $30,000 to enter a team in the winter Instructional League. Those two investments resulted in a dramatic improvement in the uniformity and quality of instruction and player development.[13] Nor did the changes stop there.

Shortly after he was named farm director, Owens began a critical evaluation of the twenty scouts employed by the Phillies to find out how productive each one had been. "Some of those scouts had been with the club for twenty years or more," said Ruly Carpenter in a recent interview. "We evaluated each one based on who they had signed, the level those players had reached at that point in time, and what kind of bonus money they had offered a prospect. We made quite a few changes based on the outcome of that evaluation."[14] Carpenter understated the case. Owens fired half of the team's scouting staff. When some of the disgruntled scouts took their complaints to the owner, he supported Owens's decision. "Some of those guys were my friends," explained the Phillies farm director. "But they were too worried about protecting their jobs and they weren't producing. I had to change that. This was a business and to be frank, the Phillies were doing terribly for too long because they weren't signing big league players."[15]

Owens and Carpenter understood that good scouting was a key to success in any highly competitive organization. The Phillies, like every major league organization, employed between twenty and thirty full-time scouts, most of whom

FIGURE 4. Ruly Carpenter was an heir to the DuPont fortune and worked as an assistant to Paul Owens before assuming the presidency of the club for his father, Robert R. M. Carpenter, Jr., in 1972. Courtesy of the National Baseball Hall of Fame Library, Cooperstown, New York.

were former pro ballplayers themselves. Each one of the scouts was assigned a specific geographical territory and rated prospects in terms of five fundamental abilities, or "five tools": running, throwing, fielding, hitting, and hitting with power. "You really had to know your scouts," said Carpenter. "What, for example, did they mean by a grading system? We used the lettering system. Other clubs used a numerical system. Paul and I believed that the grading system gave us a better frame of reference, but we had to know what the scout meant by his grade and the only way to do that was to review the kids he signed. What we discovered was that some of our scouts were overgrading in order to sell their prospects to management."[16]

Just as important as good scouting was the ability to differentiate those who were best at amateur free agent scouting from those who were better at scouting the minor leagues. Amateur scouts identified the best prospects from high schools, colleges, and summer leagues. They had the difficult task of projecting the development of a youngster. In addition to assessing a player's current skills accurately, the amateur scout had to be able to project what kind of a hitter the prospect would be in five or six years against a pitcher who could throw 90 miles per hour and could hit the corners of the plate. The amateur scout usually had several associate scouts, or "bird dogs," working for him. These were often umpires, high school coaches, or others who were involved in amateur baseball. When they

FIGURE 5. Paul Owens was Phillies farm director. Courtesy of the National Baseball Hall of Fame Library, Cooperstown, New York.

identified a prospect, they reported him to the amateur scout. The bird dog usually got paid expenses plus a commission when one of the prospects he recommended got drafted.[17]

Tony Lucadello was among the Phillies' best amateur scouts. A short, unassuming man who favored snap-brim hats, Lucadello began working for the Phillies in 1957. His territory included the Midwest states of Ohio, Illinois, and Indiana. Logging thousands of miles in a rented Chevy each season, he employed some of the most unusual scouting methods. When Lucadello discovered a raw talent, he became almost paranoid in his behavior. Not wanting to tip his hand to any of the other scouts, he hid behind bushes or watched the player from the backseat of his station wagon, going to great lengths to keep his secret.[18] Other tactics were more amusing. "One of the stories I used to hear about Tony was that he worked on the mother when he wanted to sign a prospect," said Ruly Carpenter. "He knew that mothers were always concerned about how the club was going to take care of their son now that he was leaving home. Tony had an old trick. He'd put a little onion juice near his tear ducts so his eyes would be watering when he went in to talk to the mother. That sealed the deal because she knew he cared."[19]

Lucadello's paranoia over hiding his prospects from other scouts was understandable because of the introduction of the amateur draft in 1965. The draft created fierce competition for the most highly rated prospects. If another scout knew Lucadello's feelings about a certain prospect, he could lose the player to another organization. As a result, Lucadello had to rely on his bird dogs even more than he had in the past. "Tony was incredibly well organized," recalled Carpenter. "He created one of the best bird dog systems of any scout I ever saw. Not only did he have these guys on his part-time payroll, he had every high school and college coach in his area in his back pocket. His bird dogs were extremely loyal to him and wouldn't tip his hand to any other organization's scout. Once these guys got Tony 'in the door' to sign a player, the kid was ours."[20]

If Lucadello was among the Phillies' top amateur scouts, Hugh Alexander was among the organization's best professional scouts, those who evaluated talent at both the minor and major league levels. Sitting in the stands behind home plate, Alexander not only possessed an exceptional ability to evaluate a player's physical tools, but also his work ethic, coachability, and self-confidence. A gruff Oklahoman who'd lost his left hand in an oil-rig accident, "Uncle Hughie," as he was called within the Phillies organization, quickly became Owens's confidant. "The relationship that Hughie and I had was amazing," recalled Owens. "We were always on the same page. When I became general manager I traveled with the club most of the time so I'd get to see the National League. I'd focus on two or three guys every game and by season's end I had pretty much seen them all. I trusted Hughie with the American League. If we were getting to the point where we needed a player, I'd call Hughie and tell him to get me a left-handed-hitting outfielder or whatever the need was. He always seemed to know what we needed and he always had a few names ready for me."[21]

Like Owens, Alexander was part of the "old school," former pro players who didn't use stopwatches or radar guns because they didn't need them to time a runner's speed to first base or a pitcher's fastball. They knew those things intuitively as well as a player's psychological makeup. "Any scout can recognize a five-tool player," insists Ruly Carpenter, "but Paul had a unique ability to analyze what was inside a player. He could predict how the guy was going to react in pressure situations, if he could handle adversity, if he was mentally tough. When you get to the highest level in any sport, all players have physical ability or they wouldn't be there. That's when the 'little things' really start to make a difference."[22]

Just five years after Owens was named farm director, the Phillies won the Topps award for best minor league program in baseball.[23] The organization enjoyed the best spring training facilities in the majors, had their best young players competing in the Florida Instructional League, and the scouts were signing much better prospects than they had in the past. Among them was a temperamental shortstop from Sacramento, California, named Larry Bowa (Figure 6).

Signed by the Phillies in 1965, Bowa was a fine example of the kind of scrappy player that fit into the Phillies' future plans. Having been cut by his high school

FIGURE 6. Larry Bowa was cut from his high school baseball team, but caught the attention of the Phillies playing shortstop at Sacramento City College. Courtesy of the *Philadelphia Daily News.*

baseball team, he played American Legion ball and eventually made the team at Sacramento City College. Eddie Bockman, who scouted northern California for the Phillies, discovered the fiery shortstop there. After being ejected in the first inning of both games of a doubleheader, Bowa, still fuming, was boarding the team bus when Bockman caught up with him. "He was throwing helmets and trashing bats," recalled the Phillies scout. "I told him, 'I'll be back to see you. You'll be a pretty good player if you can keep your head in the game.' He asked me who I was and when I told him, that pretty much quieted him down."[24]

Although Bowa was bypassed in the June 1965 amateur draft, the Phillies still showed an interest in him. Impressed by the scrawny shortstop's scrappy defense and intensity, Bockman invited him to play for a Phillies rookie league team he managed on the San Francisco Bay Peninsula. The invitation was contingent on Bowa behaving himself. "If you start throwing any helmets and bats or abusing any umpires," the Phillies scout told him, "you're through."[25] Early that autumn Bockman began to promote the young shortstop within the organization. According to an October 2, 1965, scouting report, Bockman admitted that while Bowa's "attitude would make you throw up at times," he possessed the "accuracy of a major league shortstop's arm," "can hit the fast ball," and "has some strength in the hands." "If he can keep the bugs out of his head," Bockman concluded, "he is a definite major league prospect."[26]

Later that month, Bockman met with Owens in Los Angeles where the Dodgers were playing the Minnesota Twins in the World Series. The two men went up to Owens's hotel room, tore the sheet off the bed and tacked it to the wall for a movie screen. Bockman showed his boss an eight-millimeter film of Bowa hitting, playing shortstop, and running the bases. "Slow down the film," ordered Owens, who thought something was wrong with the projector. "I can't see the kid run, there's nothing but a blur." Assuring him that the projector was in perfect working condition, Bockman insisted that Bowa's speed made up for his weak hitting.

"Does he want a lot to sign?" asked Owens, always careful to manage limited bonus money.

"He'll take anything we give him," replied Bockman.

"Then sign him for $2,000."[27]

While Bockman may have been eager to secure the services of the fiery young shortstop, there were others who were more reluctant. "I didn't want him to sign," recalled Paul Bowa, the shortstop's father, a career minor leaguer in the St. Louis Cardinals organization. "I thought he could have gotten more money. But if he didn't, I didn't want to be the one to kill Larry's chances of playing in the major leagues."[28] Paul Bowa actually discouraged his son from pursuing a baseball career because he didn't want him to face the same disappointment he had experienced. The game had not been very good to him. After bouncing around the minors for the better part of the 1940s, Paul's last stop was at Duluth, Minnesota, where he was the player-manager of a Class A team. The constant travel had taken a tremendous toll on his family and at the end of the season he retired. He spent the remainder of his working years driving a beer truck and tending bar. But the elder Bowa also taught his son two important lessons that would ensure his success: (1) "Never quit, no matter what happens"; and (2) "Don't take any crap from anybody. If they don't like it, fuck 'em."[29] Larry Bowa learned those lessons well.

Bowa scratched and clawed his way up the professional ladder: Class A ball at Spartanburg, South Carolina; Double-A ball at Reading, Pennsylvania; and Triple-A at Eugene, Oregon. While his fielding and speed impressed various coaches and managers, Bowa's weak hitting raised serious questions about his ability to make it to the big leagues. When the young shortstop stepped into the batter's cage at Clearwater, Florida, during spring training in 1967, one Philadelphia sportswriter observed that Bowa's swing "looked like he was flailing at baseballs with a rolled up newspaper."[30] Phillies manager Gene Mauch was even more critical. Noting that Bowa's performance was "one of the worst at bats that he'd ever seen," Mauch walked away from the cage mumbling that he "couldn't even HEAR him swing."[31] Bowa was dismissed from camp the very next day.

Although he continued to work extremely hard during the next few years, Bowa was never projected as anything more than a utility infielder, and he knew it. Fortunately, the shortstop was paired from the very beginning of his pro career with second baseman Denny Doyle. They not only made a great double play combination, but Doyle served as an important stabilizing influence for him. "Denny was very mature," recalled Bowa, years after he made it to the majors. "He'd been to college. He had a family. When I lost my temper or if I got down on myself, he'd sit me down and say, 'Man, you can't do that.' I was lucky to play with someone that mature. If I was playing with someone as high strung as me, we'd have been tearing down walls."[32] Unbeknownst to Bowa, Doyle suggested the idea of fining his double play partner if he was thrown out of a game. Spartanburg manager Bob Wellman liked the idea so much he implemented it and, as a result, drastically reduced Bowa's unattractive behavior.[33]

Wellman knew how to get the most out of his young shortstop, who worried constantly about his performance. While he could be tough-minded, he also knew when to encourage him. For example, Bowa's very first game at Spartanburg was played against the New York Mets' Greenville farm club, which sent a young pitcher by the name of Nolan Ryan to the mound. When the game was over, Spartanburg had lost 1-0, and the young shortstop had collected four strikeouts. Disgusted with his performance, Bowa, in a rare admission of defeat, approached his manager and said, "Skip, if this is what it's like, I'd better pack up and go home now."

"Let me tell you something," Wellman replied, "this kid Ryan is going to be unbelievable. You're not going to face many pitchers like that." He was correct. That season Ryan compiled a 17-2 record and 272 strikeouts. More important for the Phillies, Bowa's performance helped Spartanburg win 26 games in a row during that season. The 1-0 loss against Ryan was the only defeat the team suffered in a month's time, making Spartanburg one of the best teams in the low minors in 1966.[34]

By 1969 the Phillies were prepared to promote Bowa to the majors as a utility player. On the final day of spring training, the shortstop approached manager Bob Skinner and said, " I don't want to be in the big leagues yet."

Surprised by the remark, Skinner asked why.

"I want to play every day when I get there," insisted Bowa. "I want to be a regular, not a sub."

"Okay," replied the Phillies manager. "If you feel that way, I want you to go to Eugene and learn how to switch-hit. That's the only way you're going to make the big leagues as a regular."[35]

To his credit, Bowa, a natural left-handed hitter, went down to Eugene and not only made himself a switch-hitter, but inadvertently learned to hit with some power from the opposite side of the plate. One night Frank Lucchesi, the Emeralds manager, decided to get a few laughs and entered his light-hitting shortstop

FIGURE 7. Greg Luzinski turned down a Notre Dame football scholarship to sign with the Phillies. Courtesy of the National Baseball Hall of Fame Library, Cooperstown, New York.

in a pregame home run hitting contest with some of the team's bona fide sluggers. The shortstop went along with the gag and smacked the only home run of the contest, hitting right-handed![36] Of course, Bowa, who somehow managed to collect 15 home runs over the course of a sixteen-year major league career, was *not* a power hitter. Fortunately, the Phillies had more able sluggers in the farm system. Among them was a 6′ 1″, 200-pound prospect by the name of Greg Luzinski.

Signed as the Phillies' first pick in the 1968 draft, Luzinski was a catcher–first baseman at Notre Dame High School in Niles, Illinois, where he lettered in both football and baseball. Luzinski (Figure 7), a scholastic linebacker, was offered more than forty football scholarships, including two from Kansas and Notre Dame. But he wanted to play baseball. Frank Piet, who scouted the youngster, was immediately impressed by his hitting skills. "Basic fundamentals on hitting actions are great," he wrote in his scouting report. "Keeps head and bat steady swinging from shoulder. Can hit to all fields with power. You can fool him with a pitch, but throw it again and he'll hit it out of the park."[37] Although Piet projected Luzinski as a first baseman, the nineteen-year-old prospect would be converted to the outfield in the minors.

During his first season of pro ball at Huron, New York, in 1968, Luzinski led the Northern League with 13 home runs in 57 games. Paul Owens was so

FIGURE 8. Bob Boone, a Stanford graduate, considered giving up minor league baseball for medical school. Courtesy of the National Baseball Hall of Fame Library, Cooperstown, New York.

impressed by the young slugger that he nicknamed him the "Baby Bull."[38] Dallas Green, Luzinski's first manager, would have a profound impact on his career. Green, once a Phillies prospect himself, had had an unremarkable career as a journeyman pitcher after injuring his arm in the low minors. But he was ambitious and after his playing days ended in 1967, Owens persuaded him to join the Phillies as a minor league manager.[39] Green had a strong intuition for a player's potential. He could project what players would be able to do in the future and never hesitated to convert them from one position to another if he felt it would improve their chances to make the majors. Luzinski was a prime example. One of several catchers at Huron, Bull would compete for the position with a slightly built Latino named Manny Trillo. Green didn't see either player making it to the majors at that position, though, so he converted Trillo to the infield and Luzinski to the outfield.[40] "Dallas did me a favor," said Luzinski in a recent interview. "The Phillies already had Deron Johnson at first base then and Deron averaged 30 home runs a season. So playing the outfield gave me the opportunity to get to the big leagues quicker."[41] Those were the kinds of decisions that made Green an important member of the organization and one who would eventually replace Owens as farm director when he was promoted to general manager in 1972.

The following season Luzinski was sent to Raleigh-Durham in the Carolina League where he experienced his first hitting slump. Walter Brock, the general manager, wanted to send him back to Huron and probably would have if manager Nolan Campbell didn't insist on keeping him. But Brock persisted. The tightfisted general manager infuriated Luzinski by selling his bats.[42] Shortly thereafter, the young power hitter got even.

Frank Dolson, a sportswriter for the *Philadelphia Inquirer*, came down to Durham to write a story on Luzinski. When Brock, eager to impress the big-city sportswriter, invited him to dinner, Dolson innocently asked if Luzinski could come along. Brock bit his tongue. He realized that Dolson knew nothing of his ongoing feud with the young power hitter and agreed to take Luzinski along. Bull, who had an impressively big appetite, took advantage of the situation. "Greg hit all the high spots on the menu," recalled Dolson. "Maybe it was my imagination, but you could see Walter Brock flinch every time Luzinski signaled for a waiter. Greg was in rare form that night. I'll say this for Brock—he never uttered a word of protest. He was either playing the role of a perfect host or struck speechless by the size and quantity of Luzinski's order. And I lean toward the latter theory."[43]

Luzinski continued to struggle at the plate. He began to press harder and when his hitting still didn't improve he became lethargic. "I kept watching his average drop," recalled Owens. "No home runs, no RBI, nothing. So I phoned him and really let him have it. I told him I'd be down there in two weeks and he'd better have his average back up where it belonged, or I'd get rid of him."[44] Owens was a master at hard love, a skill he would employ countless times over the next two decades. He took his players' successes and failures personally, as if he was a surrogate father. He was as proud as a braggart when they succeeded and as furious as a tsunami when they didn't. Together with his facial resemblance to Pope Paul VI, Owens's authority was so commanding that he was nicknamed "Pope." "Boy, that phone call really woke me up," Luzinski admitted, cringing at the memory more than three decades later. "I had been feeling sorry for myself but he scared the hell out of me. He saw me play three games and I think I hit five home runs. That conversation really turned it around for me. No question, I owe Pope a lot."[45]

Luzinski went on to hit a series of tape-measure home runs that season. One, in Red Springs, North Carolina, cleared a light tower over the left field fence and landed some 500 feet from the plate.[46] But his appetite was just as prodigious as his power hitting. Bob Boone (Figure 8), who played with Luzinski at Raleigh-Durham, recalled that the two players and their families shared a little house for $500 a month on Clearwater Beach during spring training in 1970. Both Boone and Luzinski were married and both had a baby, so they were on tight budgets. "We look back on it and just laugh," said Boone. "We started out splitting the groceries. You know who took the short end of the stick on that. Greg would come in, make a sandwich and take a whole package of bologna."[47]

One evening, Boone, his wife, Sue, and Jean Luzinski were sitting in the living room watching television. Greg was in the kitchen making popcorn. A few minutes later, he walked into the living room with two huge bowls full of the snack, sat down and, without offering any to the others, began eating from both bowls. His wife and the Boones just sat there staring at him, without saying a word. Finally, Bull looked up and, noticing their disbelief, asked, "Oh, would you like some?"[48]

Luzinski would struggle with significant weight gain throughout his professional career. At times, the Phillies' treatment of him was humiliating. Howie Bedell, a coach in the Phillies farm system, remembers watching Luzinski work off the excess weight at the Carpenter Complex during spring training in 1970. "Greg was jogging around a track wearing a rubber suit," said Bedell. "Tied to his waist was a sled used to drag the infield and he was pulling it along as he ran. It was really very archaic. I never felt so sorry for a guy in my whole life. This was nonsense for a twenty-year-old kid who was considered a prospect. I wouldn't have done that to any kid, even if he wasn't a prospect. But that was the way things were done back then and not just with Greg, but with any player who reported to camp overweight."[49]

The ghastly sight of Luzinski pulling that sled motivated Bedell to create a more humane—and more effective—conditioning program. Known as the "continuous motion program," the regimen was ninety minutes in length and consisted of stretching and a series of running events that combined fielding and aerobic conditioning. The program drastically improved a player's recovery time, resulted in better conditioning than the traditional method, and was eventually adopted by several other major league clubs.[50] Owens quickly recognized Bedell's value to the ball club and convinced him to abandon his plans to teach high school. Bedell gradually worked his way up the ranks from Class A manager to director of the minor leagues in 1980. Each step of the way, his contributions to player development helped to transform the farm system into the crown jewel of the Phillies organization. Along with Dallas Green and Hughie Alexander, Bedell became part of the remarkable brain trust that Owens would rely on to make the most critical decisions regarding player development, contract negotiations, and staff evaluations over the next decade.

Another prospect who played a significant role in the fortunes of the Phillies during the 1970s and early '80s was Bob Boone. Boone's father, Ray, played infield for the Cleveland Indians and Detroit Tigers in the late 1940s and '50s. As a result, Bob learned at an early age not only how to play the game the "right way," but also to "respect it." "I had a fantastic childhood," Boone said. "Every day after school I'd be at the ballpark trailing my Dad around. While he taught me that baseball was a lot of fun, he also made me tough. He was 'Old School.' There weren't any excuses for not playing hard. You learned to run out ground balls. You learned to be part of a team, to help make your teammates better. In my family, you learned to respect the game and your teammates. That's how I was raised."[51]

Selected by the Phillies in the sixth round of the 1969 amateur draft, Boone was a product of Stanford University, where he majored in psychology, pitched, and played third base. Eddie Bockman, who scouted Boone, called him a "high class boy with all the ability to play in the majors." Bockman's only concern was that Boone was "confused" by being shuttled between the pitcher's mound and third base and suggested that he "stay at one position."[52] It was an easy decision for Boone to make. "When it finally came time to sign," recalled the Stanford product, "I asked Eddie if he was going to take me as a pitcher or a third baseman. When he told me third base, I agreed. I really didn't like pitching. I didn't like the soreness that came with it. I didn't like the fact that I'd get fewer at bats because I wasn't in the lineup every day. So third base was just fine with me."[53] But Boone quickly discovered that the Phillies had other plans for him.

Despite the fact that he hit .300 during his first season in the minors, Boone was not the most favored third base prospect when he arrived in the Instructional League. The Phillies already had Don Money, who was a year away from the majors, and John Vukovich, who wasn't far behind. In 1970, all three players were invited to the big league spring training camp, where they were told by manager Frank Lucchesi that there were "no set positions on the field" and that "everyone had a chance." "I actually believed him," Boone said. "With a season already under my belt, I expected to go the majors. That spring I played a lot of third base and hit over .400. So you can imagine how crushed I was when I didn't make the first cut." Shortly after he arrived at Double-A Reading, Boone received a notice to report for reserve duty at Fort Campbell, Kentucky, where he spent most of his summer.[54]

When Boone returned to the Instructional League at the end of the season, he was asked to change positions. The Phillies were in need of a catcher. Since he realized that there wasn't much of a future for him at third base, Boone decided to give catching a try. He headed for spring training in 1971 as a backstop, but spent most of his time in the bullpen before being cut. Reassigned to Reading, he found himself competing for the position with three other players. "Instead of catching me, they played me at third base," Boone recalled. "But whenever a Phillies' scout showed up they'd move me behind the plate. When he left, I was back at third base. It was getting real frustrating for me. By the time spring training rolled around in 1972, I decided that if I wasn't sent to Triple-A to catch every day I was going to quit and go to medical school."[55]

As things turned out, Boone was sent to Triple-A at Eugene, Oregon, in 1972, where he played for the former Whiz Kids' catcher Andy Seminick. "Andy took me under his wing," said Boone. "He gave me two seasons' worth of experience at catcher in one year. I caught 138 of Eugene's 142 games that season and by the end I was ready for the call-up to Philadelphia."[56] Although Boone had a strong throwing arm and would eventually develop an exceptional talent for pitch calling, he was not a prototypical catcher of the 1970s. Those were players like Johnny Bench, power-hitting backstops with take-charge attitudes. Boone was more laidback in his approach to the game and his bat didn't compare to Luzinski's or any of the other power hitters in the farm system. What the young catcher did possess, however, was an innate intelligence for the game, a remarkable psychology for handling pitchers, and a physical toughness that belied his calm exterior. Those intangible qualities would allow him to become the anchor of the Phillies pitching staff during the team's glory years as well as a voice of reason as the National League's player representative during the acrimonious strike negotiations of 1981.[57]

Mike Schmidt was the last of the four players who would become the homegrown nucleus of the 1980 Phillies. He soon became the team's franchise player, but one who almost went unnoticed had it not been for Tony Lucadello. Schmidt was one of those rare prospects Lucadello coveted. In the spring of 1965, when Mike was still a sophomore at Fairview High School in Dayton, Ohio, the Phillies scout received a phone call from one of his bird dogs, Ed French, who was quite impressed with the youngster. French insisted that Lucadello see him play. When Lucadello followed up on the tip, he saw that Schmidt was an "excellent athlete" and "an above average prospect." But he was still a raw talent. "Sometimes he would do things that would amaze me," recalled the idiosyncratic scout. "Other times he would make errors or just look terrible at the plate. This gave me an edge right away because other scouts would see him play and pick at all those flaws. But I sensed that Mike Schmidt was a late bloomer."[58]

Over the next two years, while Schmidt was still in high school, Lucadello watched him play a dozen times but he never contacted the young prospect, his family, or his coach for fear that another scout would find out about his interest. Instead, he watched Schmidt perform from a distance. He befriended the school's janitor who allowed him on the roof of a building that overlooked the ball diamond. At other times, he settled in behind a tree or the opposing team's dugout.[59] While Lucadello continued to be impressed by Schmidt, other scouts dismissed him as "damaged goods." Football injuries to both knees prevented him from attracting much interest either from the minor leagues or colleges. Only small, Division III schools such as DePauw, Defiance, and Marietta expressed interest in him.[60] But few realized the hard work Schmidt invested in the game.

"Mike was a power hitter, who struck out a lot," said Dave Palsgrove, one of Schmidt"s high school baseball coaches. "He'd hit it a mile or strike out. He had a good, strong arm and he could field. The thing you worried about was, could he hit the ball enough? There's no question though, Mike was determined. He had operations on both knees, and that held him back for a while. But he made up his mind that he wanted to excel at the game and he did." Bob Galvin, who coached Schmidt in his senior year at Fairview, agreed: "Schmidt advanced a heckuva long way because he loved the game and worked hard. When I said practice was over, Mike didn't want to go home. He'd say, 'Coach, it's still too early,' and it would be dark. Or he'd say, 'Loan me some equipment and I'll get somebody to stay around and hit me pop-ups.'"[61]

Since no scout expressed an interest in signing him and no college offered him an athletic scholarship, Schmidt decided to attend Ohio University and pursue a career in architecture. He was interested in architectural engineering and knew that the school had an excellent department in architecture. Although he still intended to pursue his interest in baseball, Schmidt realized that there were more attractive players who were drawing attention from both professional ball clubs as well as Division I programs. What's more, he understood that his injured knees made him a risk for any college to recruit. "I was about the fourth or fifth best baseball player in high school—a .250 hitter," Schmidt recalled, "and if you don't hit .400 in high school, nobody knows you're alive. I was always the kid with potential, but even that potential was jeopardized by a couple of major injuries in high school."[62]

Bob Wren, the coach at Ohio University, learned of Schmidt while recruiting his teammate Ron Neff at Fairview. Although Wren didn't have any scholarship money to offer the young shortstop, he did invite him to try out for the squad.

Schmidt made the team in his freshman year as a backup to shortstop Rich McKinney. Bobcat trainer Al Hart also put him on a carefully supervised conditioning program to strengthen his knees. Schmidt was conscientious, pushing himself to redevelop his leg strength. He also abandoned an experiment with switch-hitting, discovering that he could only hit a low and inside pitch when he hit left-handed. Returning to his natural, right-handed approach, Schmidt began to crush the ball, hitting more consistently and with power.[63]

When McKinney was drafted by the Chicago White Sox in 1968, Schmidt took his place, helping Ohio University to the first of three straight Mid-American Conference championships. The next year Ohio qualified for the College World Series, defeating Southern Cal, the nation's top-ranked team, in the first round. The Bobcats eventually lost to Texas and Florida State to finish fourth in the tournament, but Schmidt had captured national attention with his stellar defense and .313 average. He also earned first team NCAA All-American honors that year.

Schmidt's success came largely as the result of growing self-confidence. "It was in college that I started to gain the maturity and insight into life generally, that I needed to make it to the majors," he admitted. "I realized that teammates appreciated my ability and looked up to me, and that I had the qualities necessary to become one of the respected players of whatever team I was on—to become a leader. It looked like I might have a shot at the dream I'd once had."[64]

In his senior year, Schmidt compiled a .330 average with 10 home runs and 45 RBIs, earning him All-American honors once again. He was also named the shortstop on the *Sporting News* 1971 All-America squad and set a school record with 27 career home runs. Success didn't come without a lot of hard work, though.

"Mike was one of the most dedicated players I've ever had," said Wren. He worked hard to strengthen those knees and developed great upper body strength in the process. Scouts kept coming to me and asking about him, always mentioning the knees, and I pointed out that he never missed a game with us and could do anything physically required of him."[65] Two of those scouts paid close attention to Wren—Lucadello and Carl Ackerman of the California Angels. Lucadello was so impressed with Schmidt that he insisted that Paul Owens fly out to Ohio to see Schmidt play a Saturday doubleheader against Bowling Green State University. The Bobcat shortstop impressed Owens, hitting a home run, going from first to third on a routine single, and going deep in the hole at short to throw out a runner at first. Not only could Schmidt hit, run, and throw with some of the best prospects Owens had seen in years, but he was the kind of aggressive player the Phillies sought. Owens immediately projected him as a third baseman.[66]

During the last few months of the 1971 college season, before the June draft, Lucadello protected his own interest in Schmidt by reminding other scouts of his bad knees. "Mike's name would come up," admitted the Phillies scout, "and I'd say, 'Well, there's his knees, you know.' The others would nod in agreement and

I could see them moving him down a notch on their lists. What they didn't know was that Mike had been on a strict weight program until his knees were as good as new."[67] At the same time, Lucadello tried to convince Owens to make Schmidt the Phillies' first pick in the draft. Unfortunately, his history of knee problems dropped Schmidt into the second round and the Phillies selected Roy Thomas, a pitcher from California, instead. "My heart just sank," Lucadello confessed. He knew that Ackerman had Schmidt high on his list as well and thought the Phillies had lost him to the Angels. But when the Angels made their first round selection they also chose a pitcher—Frank Tanana—and the Phillies took Schmidt in the second round (Figure 9).[68]

On June 11, Lucadello met with Mike and his parents at a Holiday Inn in North Dayton and signed him for $32,500 with a series of additional $2,500 bonuses for each time he advanced through the farm system from Single-A to Triple-A.[69] The next day, Schmidt and his father flew to Philadelphia. There he worked out with the Phillies at Veterans Stadium, taking ground balls alongside the organization's budding young shortstop Larry Bowa and hitting in a group that included Ron Stone, Byron Browne, and Oscar Gamble—fringe players on a team that was going nowhere. Twenty-four hours later, Schmidt made his professional debut at Reading's Municipal Stadium against the Phillies' Class AA Eastern League farm team.

"It just so happened that Bowa was unable to play and the Phillies asked me

FIGURE 9. Mike Schmidt, a two-time All-American shortstop at Ohio University, was the Phillies second round pick in the June 1971 amateur draft. Courtesy of the *Philadelphia Daily News*.

if I would want to take his place with the big league club," Schmidt recalled. "John Vukovich played third. Denny Doyle played second. Deron Johnson was playing first and there I was, playing shortstop." His first hit was a home run to left field off a Mike Fremuth fastball. It proved the margin of victory for the Phils, 4-3.[70] When Schmidt crossed the plate, Bob Boone, who was catching for Reading, said, "Nice hitting, Mike." He would never forget the compliment, or Boone's friendship as they climbed through the Phillies farm system together.[71]

Although Schmidt's contract called for him to be sent to Peninsula, Virginia, the Phillies' Class A affiliate at the time, he remained in Reading as a shortstop and third baseman. He hit mostly out of the eighth slot that first season in the minors, and earned $500 a month.[72] When he finished with a .211 average and only 8 homers and 31 RBIs in 74 games, Lucadello "caught a little heat." But the scout stood by Schmidt telling the Phillies' braintrust: "This kid's a late bloomer, I've seen it before. He'll develop."[73] Some of Schmidt's difficulty was his inability to hit breaking pitches. He admitted that "from the time I got out of college until almost half way through my Triple-A year, I couldn't hit breaking balls at all. They'd just freeze me at the plate."[74] The other part of his dilemma was adjusting to life in the minor leagues.

Minor league ball is baseball in its purest form. The players haven't become cynical, rich, or lazy yet. Their dreams allow them to tolerate the long bus rides, bland food, and cheap motels. All seem to arrive with raw talent and the potential for stardom. But only a few come to realize their dream of playing in the majors. Some minor leaguers become bitter, envious of another player's talent or perhaps luck. Others form a special bond, having gone through the hard times together. They come to know each other's likes and dislikes and they learn to support each other. Schmidt was fortunate to have the support of Bob Boone during those early years of his professional career. Schmidt appreciated Boone "taking [him] under his wing." He was a "guy who could relate to my position, being drafted out of college. He knew I had already experienced better conditions playing college ball. He knew I was one of the 'big-deal' guys on my college team and now I was in an environment where I was starting all over, and I was away from home."[75]

Schmidt and Boone would be promoted to Triple A-Eugene in '72. When Schmidt struggled at the plate during the early part of the season, Owens suggested that it might be in his best interests to send him back to Reading. Manager Andy Seminick disagreed. When his average dropped to .201, Seminick decided to switch Schmidt with second baseman John Vukovich who was also mired in a slump. It worked. Schmidt had been worrying about his hitting so much that he had jinxed himself at the plate. Having to learn a new position would take some of the pressure off. "I started playing second and it seemed like I totally concerned myself with my defense, forgetting about the pressure that was on me to hit," he said.[76]

Seminick was just the kind of manager Schmidt needed. The former Phillies catcher was an integral part of the 1950 Whiz Kids, the organization's last pennant winners. At 6' and 230 pounds of muscle, Seminick was an imposing figure who could be intimidating when he needed to be. But he also had a special intuition for reading his players. Above all, he taught his players to respect the game. "Andy was all about attitude," recalled John Vukovich in a recent interview. "He was 'old school,' a carryover from his playing days in the 1950s. There was no such thing as being tired or hurt. And you had to play the 'right way,' to respect the game. If you didn't, he had the muscle to back it up. Andy was a demanding guy but you knew he had your best interests at heart."[77]

By the end of August, Schmidt's average climbed to .291 and he had recorded 26 homers and 91 RBIs. Although he registered an eye-catching 145 strikeouts, his mental approach changed at the plate. He was more relaxed. No longer did he try to power the ball out of the park. Additionally, Schmidt's fine play at second base also bolstered the Emeralds' defense in the middle infield. A very respectable .976 fielding average with only 8 errors, showed the Phillies that they had a fine-fielding second baseman who could fill in at shortstop or switch to third base.[78] Then things unraveled. In a game in Hawaii Vukovich fielded a ground ball at third and flipped to Schmidt who was covering second. When he spun around to complete the double play, his left knee locked. When the Emeralds returned to Oregon, Schmidt saw a doctor who determined that he had torn the cartilage on the outside of the knee and that he would need surgery. While the Emeralds were competing in the Pacific Coast League playoffs, Schmidt was rehabbing the leg, preparing to go to Philadelphia for the mid-September call-up.[79]

Shortly after the minor league playoffs, Schmidt was scheduled for surgery at Philadelphia's Temple University Hospital. At 6:00 A.M. the day of the surgery, Dr. John R. Moore, chairman of orthopedic surgery, entered the room and looked at the knee.

"Son," he said, "I want you to follow me."

Leading the Phillies prospect out into the hallway, Moore told him to "get in a three-point stance like a wide receiver."

Schmidt dutifully obliged.

"Now," continued Moore, "I want you to fire out and go as hard as you can down the hallway."

Groggy from medication and half-clad in a hospital gown, Schmidt got down in the three-point stance and took off, limping down the hall. The knee was so badly swollen that he could only go a few yards.

When he stopped, Moore rendered his decision: "I'm scrapping the surgery. I want you to go back and see the trainer. Rehab the knee and let me know what happens."[80]

Schmidt started on a rehab program and within a week's time was back in uniform, this time with the Philadelphia Phillies. He made his major league debut on September 12 in a game against the New York Mets at Veterans Stadium. He was inserted into the lineup in the third inning to replace third baseman Don Money. In the fifth he got his first major league hit—a single off right-hander Jim McAndrew. The following week Schmidt belted his first homer in the majors, a three-run shot off Montreal's Balor Moore that gave the Phils a 3-1 victory over the Expos. It was the only home run he hit for the Phillies in the 13 games in which he appeared for the big league club that season. His totals for the brief stint were: 7 hits and 15 strikeouts in 34 plate appearances for a .206 average.[81]

Schmidt considers that season with Eugene a pivotal one in his career. "Being on that team with players like John Vukovich, Andy Thornton, Bill Robinson, and Bob Boone—all of whom made it to the majors—made me realize how close I was to being in the big leagues," he said. "It was one of the most fun years in my entire baseball career. You're experiencing hard times with a lot of guys that you've really become close to and care about. You spend time with them. You get to know their families. They're pivotal years, and you experience it all together."[82]

To be sure, the minor leagues were a humbling experience for Schmidt, Boone, Luzinski, and Bowa. Little came easy for them. Injuries, hitting slumps, and self-doubt were unavoidable parts of the apprenticeship. But along the way, each of them learned to respect the game. Farm director Paul Owens taught them that there was a significant difference between playing "good" and playing "right." The former approach was based on statistical success, hitting home runs, collecting RBI, pitching complete games, striking out the side. The latter approach was more subtle and based on the manner in which a player conducted himself on and off the field. Playing the game "right" meant doing the little but important things like hustling on the field, wearing the uniform properly, respecting teammates, listening to coaches, and playing the game the way it is supposed to be played. Owens referred to these intangibles as the "Phillies' Way," the unique method of instruction emphasized by coaches throughout his farm system.[83] In so doing, they cultivated a sense of pride that was informed by both an innate respect for the game as well as the expectation of winning every time a player took the field against an opponent. It was also the foundation on which Owens intended to build a championship team. Those minor leaguers who refused to adopt the approach didn't have any future in the organization. Those who did had a shot at the majors.

Schmidt, Boone, Luzinski and Bowa bought in to the program, realizing that to be released would not only mean the end of a career but the end of a boyhood dream. They earned their shot at the majors. Only time would tell if they deserved to stay there.

CHAPTER 3

THE VET

THE PHILLIES' EFFORT TO REBUILD their organization in the late 1960s included plans to construct a brand new multipurpose stadium in South Philadelphia. The team's old ballpark, Connie Mack Stadium, located at Twenty-First Street and Lehigh Avenue in North Philadelphia, had become obsolete by 1970. Originally called Shibe Park after Benjamin F. Shibe, the sporting goods magnate who built it, the stadium was opened in 1909 as the home of the American League Philadelphia Athletics. The Phillies moved to the park in 1938 and shared it with the A's until they relocated to Kansas City after the 1954 season. Once compared to a French Renaissance castle in its appearance, the ballpark's name was changed to Connie Mack Stadium and looked more like a run-down warehouse. Over the years several patchwork additions were made. Except for the grandstand walls meeting at Twenty-First and Lehigh where the domed tower of the entrance stood, it would be difficult to see any resemblance to the original ballpark.[1]

Inside, space was limited. The dugouts were smaller than those of many of the existing parks around the National League and the clubhouse was just as crowded. The main locker area had a cold concrete floor and was bounded by a small manager's office at one end and an equipment room at the other. There were only five showers, so players were forced to take turns. The trainer worked in a small loft jammed with a whirlpool, a diathermy machine, two rubbing tables, and a supply cabinet. Above the clubhouse were the offices of owner Bob Carpenter, general manager John Quinn, and farm director Paul Owens. Larry Shenk, the public relations director, had his office above the employee entrance at Twenty-First and Lehigh. The traveling secretary and the sales and promotion staff also had their offices in this area. The Phillies' finance department worked in a third set of offices in the domed tower at the corner of Twenty-First and Lehigh.[2] "None of the offices were connected," recalled Shenk. "If I wanted to see the general manager, I had to go down one flight of stairs, across the third base side of the concourse, and up another flight of stairs. We had one small elevator that took you up to the press box, but it only fit three people. It was a tough place to communicate. You had to do it mostly by phone because we were so spread out."[3] The press box, located at the top of the second level, seated about 40 writers and presented a similar challenge. "You'd get there by taking an elevator to the press box level and then navigating a little catwalk from the landing," recalled Allen Lewis, who covered the Phillies for the *Inquirer.* "It wasn't the easiest place to get to. The press box was also pretty high so you didn't see ground balls too well, though you did have a nice view of the entire playing field."[4]

At the same time, Connie Mack Stadium was fan-friendly. Admission prices hadn't increased much since the 1930s. A bleacher seat cost only 75 cents, general admission $1.50, a reserved seat $2.25 and a box seat just a dollar more at $3.25. Fans could purchase a scorecard for 15 cents, and that included a pencil. A Coke cost the same amount. Ortlieb's beer was only 40 cents a can, a hot dog 50 cents, and Cracker Jack 25 cents.[5] There was also a special intimacy to the old ballpark. The grandstands, which had a seating capacity of 33,000, hugged the infield, allowing the fans to see the expressions of the players and feel as if they were part of the unfolding drama of the game. Players seemed to respond to their approval and rejection. Adding to the excitement were the idiosyncratic dimensions of the ballpark: 334 feet from home plate down the left field line, 447 feet to center field, and 329 feet down the right field line. A 60-foot-long scoreboard in right center field towered above the 34-foot fence on either side. Batted balls hitting the scoreboard were still in play, as were balls hitting a 10-foot-high "Ballantine Beer" sign on top of it. If, however, a ball hit the Longines clock above the beer sign—75 feet above the playing field—it was ruled a home run.[6] Bobby Wine, who played shortstop for the Phillies in the 1960s and later became a bench coach for the team, considered Connie Mack a "romantic ballpark." "It looked like a fortress on the outside, but inside it was a great place to play," he said. "It always gave me a warm feeling. The stands were close along the sidelines, though there was plenty of foul territory. Each spectator's wooden seat made them seem like they were sitting right across from you at the Thanksgiving table."[7]

For all its intimacy, however, Connie Mack Stadium was situated, by 1970, in a dangerous neighborhood. Once a white, working-class enclave, the North Penn district was now predominantly 97 percent minority. Lower-middle-class and poor blacks and Hispanics inhabited the row houses vacated by the Irish, Polish, and Germans.[8] Exide Battery, Baldwin Locomotive, Budd Manufacturing, and Philco, the factories that once were the lifeblood of the community, had left the area. Small but vital businesses like Acme supermarkets, theaters, banks, bakeries, pharmacies, and small convenience stores were also closing down.[9] "Car fleec-ing" by the neighborhood kids—the practice of directing drivers to empty spots and offering to "watch" their car for a fee—was the smallest of concerns. Black frustration with unemployment and poor housing turned to anger and resent-ment toward the white baseball fans who came into the neighborhood from the suburbs to see a game. Vandalism, drugs, assaults, and muggings by black gangs who laid claim to the neighborhood as their turf kept white fans away from the ballpark. In August of 1964 the neighborhood exploded into a bloody race riot that lasted for nearly three days. Predictably, the police referred to the area as "the Black Belt" or, worse, "the Jungle."[10] The growing crime rate drove down not only property values but also attendance at Phillies games.

In 1964, when the Phillies contested for the pennant most of the season, the team attracted 1.4 million fans. But after an August riot that year there was a steady decline in ballpark attendance. In 1965, the Phillies drew 1.2 million; 1966, 1.1 million; 1967, 800,000; 1968, 660,000; and 1969, just 500,000. "Connie Mack Stadium represented white baseball, white Philadelphia," according to Bruce Kuklick, author of *To Every Thing a Season: Shibe Park and Urban Philadel-phia, 1909–1976*. "Black residents saw white people coming into their neighbor-hood to do their 'white thing' and resented it."[11]

Phillies owner Bob Carpenter had been pleading with the city for a new sta-dium as early as 1954. Despite the support of Mayor Joseph Clark, the City Plan-ning Commission vetoed the idea. Two years later, the new mayor, Richardson Dilworth, appointed a stadium commission and appropriated $35,000 for a study to recommend a host of possible sites. It proved to be inconclusive. Other study commissions followed with similar results, though a site located at Thirtieth and Arch Streets along the Pennsylvania Railroad appeared to be the most favored possibility. By the early 1960s, more than twenty other sites emerged, including one at the corner of Broad Street and Pattison Avenue in South Philadelphia. Mayor James H. J. Tate recommended to City Council that a $22.7 million bond issue, the cost of the new stadium, be placed before the city's voters. But City Council rejected the loan question, and vehement opposition by South Philadel-phia's residents defeated the idea.[12]

With no action in sight, Carpenter became determined to pursue his own plans for a new stadium. Purchasing nearly one hundred acres of land in Cherry Hill, New Jersey, the Phillies president threatened to build the ballpark there and relocate his team. "It was just a ploy to put pressure on the city to get its act together," Ruly Carpenter, the owner's son, admitted years later. "I don't think he would've moved the team to New Jersey."[13] The ploy worked. Stunned by Car-penter's action, City Council began discussions for a new stadium. The two par-ties agreed to a multipurpose facility that would accommodate both baseball and football. They also agreed that the best site for the new stadium would be South

Philadelphia since the location would be accessible to a large portion of Philadelphia's fan base, which came from New Jersey, Delaware, and Delaware County. Despite continued opposition from a small but vocal civic group, City Council approved the South Philadelphia location and voted to place a bond issue on the November 3, 1964, ballot. On that day, Philadelphians approved the loan by a margin of 40,823 votes and Mayor Tate confidently proclaimed that the new stadium would open in 1967.[14] His prediction proved to be too optimistic.

The final year that the Phillies played at Connie Mack Stadium was 1970, and like most of the previous ones, the season was a forgettable one. The team was in a rebuilding process. Dick Allen, who had been the franchise player on a team that had come close but never captured a pennant during the 1960s, was traded to the St. Louis Cardinals shortly after the '69 season ended. Allen, the Phillies' first African American superstar, had worn out his welcome by that time. A fiercely independent individual, Allen's prodigious power hitting was only exceeded by his unruly behavior. Pregame beer-drinking, chronic lateness, unexcused absences from games, and candid opinions had made him unpopular among the fans and the press, who made Allen the scapegoat for the Phillies' perennial failure to win the National League pennant. While the fans jeered the enigmatic star, or worse, threw pennies, beer bottles, and bolts at him whenever he played in the outfield, the sportswriters accused him of manipulating racism to force a trade. In fact, Allen was a victim of racism and the Phillies' shameful history of race relations that dated to its humiliating treatment of Jackie Robinson during his quest to break baseball's color barrier in 1947.[15] Carpenter finally yielded to Allen's constant pleas for a trade on October 7, 1969, when the Phillies packaged Allen along with infielder Cookie Rojas and pitcher Jerry Johnson to the Cardinals for catcher Tim McCarver, outfielders Curt Flood and Byron Browne, and reliever Joe Hoerner.[16] Flood, a black, thirty-one-year-old veteran, refused to report to his new team, telling baseball commissioner Bowie Kuhn that he did not feel that he was "a piece of property to be bought and sold irrespective of [his] wishes."[17] Instead, he challenged the reserve clause, filing a $4.1 million antitrust suit against Major League Baseball and took his case all the way to the Supreme Court. Although he eventually lost the battle, Flood's action set in motion a chain of events that led to the 1975 arbitration ruling that granted players the right to free agency.[18]

While Allen's turbulent career in Philadelphia had come to an end with a legal explosion that would rock the baseball world for years to come, it also left the Phillies with a team that was closer in talent to a Triple-A club than a major league one. Allen's departure wasn't the only reason for the poor team the Phillies fielded in 1970. "We had mortgaged our future by trading young talent to get a pennant after the near-miss in '64," said Rick Wise, who had become the pitching ace of the team. "We lost a lot of talent, including [pitcher] Ferguson Jenkins who went on to become a Hall of Famer with the Chicago Cubs. So, by 1970, we were losing two out of every three ball games we played. It was very tough to compete."[19]

Frank Lucchesi presided over the rebuilding process. Having spent nineteen years as a manager in the minor leagues, the personable skipper had paid his dues. Climbing the ladder from the low minors at such places as Medford, Thomasville, Pine Bluff, and Pocatello to Triple-A ball at Little Rock and Eugene, Lucchesi was a natural teacher, a man with an abundance of patience and an impressive reputation for getting the most out of his players. His teams won a total of seven championships, and he was voted "Manager of the Year" five times over the course of two decades.[20] Lucchesi was also an emotional individual who was extremely dedicated to the Phillies organization. When he was hired to manage the Phillies on September 26, 1969, Lucchesi, unable to control his feelings, wept at the press conference, admitting: "I don't bleed blood. I bleed Phillies red."[21] He wept again during the pregame introductions on opening day of the 1970 season when the fans gave him a standing ovation. To be sure, Philadelphia's fans genuinely loved Lucchesi and wanted desperately for him to succeed. Unfortunately, he inherited a pathetic team.

Few teams open a season with rookies at shortstop and second base because the game demands a strong middle infield. But Lucchesi had to play Larry Bowa at short and Denny Doyle at second, players recently promoted from Triple-A. At least he knew their potential from having managed them in the minors, but Bowa was still too temperamental to handle the daily pressures of the game. By the end of April he was hitting just .130 and the Philadelphia sportswriters began to pass judgment on his hitting, comparing him to a "little leaguer." General manager John Quinn was ready to send him back to the minors. Summoning Lucchesi to his office, Quinn asked, "How long are you going to go with this kid, Bowa?"

"Mr. Quinn," replied the Phillies skipper, "the way I feel, Larry Bowa is my shortstop tonight, tomorrow, next week, next month and all year."

Shocked at the response, Quinn, who was known to overrule his manager without a second thought, deferred to Lucchesi's judgment. "Look, Frank, you're the manager. If you want to keep Bowa, we'll keep him up here, but he better start hitting more."[22] That afternoon Lucchesi called Bowa into his office. He could see how dejected the young shortstop was and realized that he fully expected to be sent down to Triple-A. Putting his arm around Bowa's shoulder, Lucchesi said, "Larry, listen to me. You're my shortstop today, tomorrow, next week, all year. One day you're going to prove me right and be one of the best fielding shortstops around."

Stunned by the confidence of his manager, Bowa had to regroup. "You mean, you're not going to send me down?"

"No!" replied Lucchesi. "That's it. That's all I have to say. Now get the hell out of here!"[23]

Shortly after, Billy DeMars, the Phillies hitting coach, joined forces with Lucchesi to refine Bowa's approach to the game, both mentally and physically. "If it wasn't for Frank I don't know what would have happened to Bowa," said DeMars recently. "He let him play everyday. At the beginning of the season, Bowa's name was penciled into the line-up even though he was only hitting .130. If it was some other manager, he might not have given him the chance. I also worked with Larry on his hitting. We'd go out there on the field before home games and work on hitting down into the ball. He had a terrible habit of pulling away and swinging up. That's what we did every day while we were at home and at the end of the season Larry was hitting .250."[24]

Lucchesi's patience and encouragement paid off. Bowa respected him and listened to his advice. He began to check his temper on the field and show more confidence in his ability to hit. "The reason I stuck with Larry Bowa," said Lucchesi years later, "was that I knew what was inside of him. I knew a lot of people considered him a 'red-ass,' but that was his emotional makeup. He wanted to win so bad that if he didn't do things perfectly, he'd show his anger or frustration. We came to have a lot of respect for each other. I think my patience paid off because Larry Bowa went on to become one of the best shortstops in the game."[25]

While Lucchesi could be sympathetic with younger players, he didn't have much patience with some of the veterans. When catcher Tim McCarver broke his hand in early May and backup Mike Ryan suffered a similar injury on the same day, the Phillies were forced to platoon four catchers for most of the season. McCarver returned in September, but since he hadn't faced major league pitching for nearly four months, his timing and swing were off. When he asked Lucchesi for extra batting practice, the Phils' manager refused stating that if a "guy couldn't hit by September, he wasn't going to learn how to do it at that point." While McCarver could understand the anxiety his manager felt presiding over a last-place team, the Phillies were only seven games out of first. It didn't make sense not to capitalize on every opportunity to make the lineup stronger. McCarver wasn't asking for Lucchesi's sympathy, he wanted his empathy for a common cause—to help the team win. After going hitless in the game, the Phillies catcher stormed around the clubhouse criticizing his manager's policy. Lucchesi responded the following day by calling a team meeting in which he accused McCarver of being a "clubhouse lawyer" and adding that no one was "going to tell [him] how to run the team."[26] Relations between the two men never improved. McCarver was used as trade bait for the next year until he was finally sent to Montreal in mid-season of 1972 for a less talented catcher named John Bateman.

The Phillies finished the 1970 campaign with a 73-88 record, 15½ games behind the Pittsburgh Pirates, who clinched the Eastern Division title. It was a remarkable achievement, considering the team's lack of talent. Jim Bunning, who had once been the Phillies' ace, was in decline as was the number two pitcher, Chris Short. The two hurlers could only muster nineteen victories between them. Rick Wise possessed the best arm on the staff with a 13-14 record. With the exception of first baseman Deron Johnson (.256, 27 HR, 93 RBI), the infield was young and inexperienced. The outfield was more seasoned but struggled at the plate. Center fielder Larry Hisle, who had been a Rookie of the Year candidate the season before, slumped, finishing the season with a .205 batting average and just 10 home runs. Ron Stone, the right fielder, was a .262 hitter who drove in just 39 runs, and had just 3 homers. The left fielder, Johnny Briggs (.270, 9 HR, 47 RBI), wasn't much better. As a team, the Phillies' .238 batting average was just a tenth of a percentage point better than the last-place Montreal Expos, and one of the worst in the major leagues.[27] The 1970 Phillies would be remembered not for their on-field performance but for sporting new polyester home uniforms with a stylized burgundy "P" logo and pinstriping and bird's-egg-blue road uniforms as well as being the last team to play at Connie Mack Stadium.

The final game at the old ballpark was played on October 1, 1970, with a near-capacity crowd of 31,822 on hand to watch the Phillies play their archrivals, the Montreal Expos, in a game that would determine last place in the division. A gala celebration had been planned for the closing. Bill Giles, recently hired as the club's vice president, was in charge of the event. "We planned to give away replacement slats from the wooden seats as souvenirs," he recalled in a recent interview. "I thought it was a pretty neat idea to give the first 5,000 paying customers something to remember the old stadium by. Each one of the slats was stamped with the date 'October 1, 1970' and the words. 'I was there.'"[28] But Giles's good intentions turned into a nightmare.

By the fourth inning, the wooden slats were being used as hammers to dislodge seats from the dilapidated ballpark. Some fans even used the slats as projectiles to throw onto the field when they disagreed with an umpire's call. Others brought toolboxes to remove signs, turnstiles, concession stands, and even a urinal from one of the restrooms.[29] Still others, with no tools, sat in the long rows of wooden-and-metal seats and rocked on them until they could pry the rows out of the concrete in which they were anchored.[30] As the game wore on, distinguished-looking men and women joined youngsters in running onto the field to scoop up dirt or grass, or into the dugout to pilfer hats, bats, balls, or gloves. "I made repeated requests for order," recalled Art Wolfe, the public address announcer. "But they kept running out. Finally, I announced that if they wouldn't stay off the field, the Phillies would have to forfeit the game."[31] It didn't matter. The contest had become incidental to the destructive rampage that was now taking place around it.

With the game tied, 1-1, at the end of the ninth inning, Lucchesi and Expos manager Gene Mauch huddled with the umpires behind home plate and agreed that if a run wasn't scored in the tenth inning, the game would be stopped. Fortunately for the Phils, Tim McCarver singled, stole second, and scored on a single by Oscar Gamble to give the Phillies a 2-1 victory. As Lucchesi ran onto the field to give Gamble a congratulatory hug, he was followed by dozens of unruly fans. Gamble, fearing for his life, brushed aside his manager, yelling, "Run, man, run like hell! We'll be happy later!"[32]

A helicopter hovered over the rampage waiting to land and dislodge home plate. The closing ceremony called for the immediate transport of the plate to the Phillies new multipurpose stadium in South Philadelphia. But after an hour, the pilot gave up and left.[33] "Instead of dying like the graceful, grand place it was," editorialized the *Philadelphia Daily News* the following day, "Connie Mack Stadium ended its life literally shrieking in pain from the torments of being torn apart as the fans raped the old park."[34] It was a sad but appropriate epitaph to an old ballpark that had seen better days, at least when the Philadelphia Athletics played there. The Phillies would have to write a new, hopefully better history at their new home, Veterans Stadium.

Built on a 67-acre tract that was once marshland, Veterans Stadium (Figure 10) cost $52 million and was constructed by McCloskey and Company. The massive structure was made of 87,000 cubic yards of concrete and 9,000 tons of steel. It measured 840 feet in diameter and rose 135 feet above street level. Designed in the shape of an octorad, the stadium's exterior was punctuated by a series of concrete ramps supported by 1 7/8-inch cables with 40,000 pounds of stress on each point. As many as four of these walkways were supported by a single cable.[35] Outside, the stadium looked much like the other multipurpose facilities of the era, including Houston's Astrodome, Busch Stadium in St. Louis, Fulton County Stadium in Atlanta, Riverfront Stadium in Cincinnati, and Three Rivers Stadium in Pittsburgh.[36] "It's hard to believe that this elegant stadium

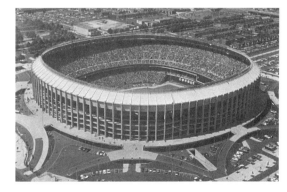

FIGURE 10. Multi-purpose Veterans Stadium, completed in 1971, had a seating capacity of 56,371, making it the largest stadium in the National League. Courtesy of the National Baseball Hall of Fame Library, Cooperstown, New York.

now stands on what was a dump," said Lonny Sciambi, project manager for the construction firm. "I know—I played on it. I grew up less than a mile from home plate."[37]

Inside, the "Vet," as it quickly came to be known, was state-of-the-art. Twin 100- by 25-foot animated scoreboards that cost $4 million were situated above the green wall in the outfield. An $800,000 "home run spectacular," especially designed for the youngest fans, was located in center field. Whenever a Phillie would hit a home run, an animated character dressed in colonial garb and called "Philadelphia Phil" would swing his bat against a replica of the Liberty Bell. The loud sound of a clapper could be heard as a light flashed from the bell to another animated character named "Philadelphia Phillis," who pulled a rope setting off a cannon. Green-colored "dancing waters" would then spurt up from behind the outfield fence as a Betsy Ross flag unfurled across the center field wall. Together with the animated scoreboards and the "home run spectacular," the orange, red, brown, and yellow theater-type plastic seats gave the Vet a circuslike atmosphere.[38]

With a seating capacity of 56,371, the Vet was the largest of any stadium in the National League. Fans could sit in a field box seat for a reasonable $4.25, or climb to the 700-level "nosebleeds" for just fifty cents. There were 60 concession stands with a picnic area for groups and private, air-conditioned luxury boxes on the press level leased for five-year terms at an annual rental fee of $12,000 to $15,400. For those fans who wanted to dine before or during the game, the Vet offered a stadium club with a 200-foot-long bar and seats for 400 diners. The field surface was 146,000 square feet covered with green Astroturf, with the exception of the base cutouts and the brown, rubberized warning track. The Vet's dimensions were much more symmetrical than those of Connie Mack, being 330 feet from home plate to both the left and right field fences and 408 to straightaway center field. Just as outstanding was the brand-new squad of miniskirted usherettes called "Fillies." Directed by Rosemary Sudders, the usherettes were shapely young women dressed in white sleeveless blouses, high white go-go boots, and fire-engine red miniskirts. They would chase down foul balls along the warning tracks, direct fans to their seats, and, at the lower levels, serve food and beverages.[39]

"The new stadium is a symbol of Philadelphia's modern-day accomplishment," boasted Bill Giles, the team vice president who had previously worked in public relations for the Houston Astros. "This is something we all can rally around. From personal experience I know what the Astrodome did for Houston and I feel our new stadium also can do more than just provide a place for the Phillies to play. It can be something that will make Philadelphia a better place to live."[40] The remark was prophetic. Within the next decade, Giles would transform Philadelphia baseball from a tired old game to cutting-edge entertainment.

Bill Giles was the son of Warren Giles, former National League president. Born in 1934 in Rochester, New York, where his father was a minor league executive, Giles grew up around the game.[41] His earliest memory of baseball came at age six after his father had joined the Cincinnati Reds' front office as general manager. It occurred at the seventh game of the 1940 World Series, which pitted the Reds against the Detroit Tigers. "I was sitting with my mother and father," he recalled, "and after the Reds had clinched the title, I tugged on my mother's dress and asked, 'Mom, we did win, didn't we?'

"'Yes, we did,' she replied.

"'Then why is Daddy crying?'"[42]

It was a very poignant scene that forged a deep impression with the youngster. Two years later, his mother passed away, and Bill's life revolved around his father and Cincinnati's Crosley Field. While the elder Giles took a very active role in his only child's upbringing, he refused to be a doting father or a disciplinarian. Nor did he force baseball on his son. What was important to Warren Giles was that his son knew the value of hard work, how to make his own decisions in life, and to "be the best at whatever [career he] decided on." Naturally, Bill decided to follow his father's example.[43]

"To meet and talk with the players in the dugout, watch them practice, shag fly balls in the outfield—all of it got into my blood at a very young age," said Giles. "By the age of fifteen, I knew two things about baseball: first, that I wasn't good enough to play past high school, and second, that I wanted to be the general manager of a major league baseball team before I was forty years old." Giles pursued his dream to run a baseball team with an exceptional passion. At nineteen, he volunteered to become general manager of a financially troubled independent league team in Morristown, Tennessee. Although the league folded soon after, Giles's efforts were recognized by Gabe Paul, president of the Reds. After three years in the Air Force, Giles returned to baseball as general manager of the Reds farm club in Nashville. Once again, Paul was impressed by the young man's work ethic and asked Giles to go with him when major league baseball expanded to Houston in 1962. Giles jumped at the offer. Shortly after Paul was installed as president of the Houston Colt .45s, he appointed Giles as the team's traveling secretary and publicity director.[44]

Within five years, Giles earned an exceptional reputation for promotions and was promoted to vice president.[45] After the Astrodome opened in 1965, Houston built an amusement park called Astroworld, and Giles was appointed marketing director for the entire complex. "We used to have the rodeo in the Astrodome," he recalled. "We had motorcycle races, polo matches, and bloodless bull fights. I even promoted three of Muhammad Ali's fights. But I found myself spending more time on all these other events and less and less on baseball. I wanted to be a baseball executive; not a promoter." Phillies president Bob Carpenter was familiar with Giles's exceptional reputation and realized that with the move to a new stadium, the organization would have to be much more aggressive in marketing if the Phillies wanted to expand their fan base.[46] In September 1969, Carpenter offered Giles (Figure 11) the newly created position of vice president of marketing operations with the understanding that, in time, his responsibilities would include running the team itself. Giles jumped at the opportunity. "When Mr. Carpenter interviewed me, he explained that he was going to retire in a few years and that he wanted me and his son, Ruly, to run the team," Giles recalled in a recent interview. "That's what really energized me. I thought that Ruly would become president and I would become general manager. Mr. Carpenter did not use those exact words, but that's how I interpreted it."[47]

Publicity director Larry Shenk was initially skeptical about Giles's hiring. "Bill had been a PR man with Houston," Shenk explained, "and when he was hired I thought that was the end for me. But Bill actually opened the door for us. We started the winter caravan, taking a group of players to meet fans and the local press in various towns and cities in the tristate area. That was extremely important in developing a larger fan base. We also took writers to the Instructional League so they could begin following our prospects; something you can't do these days for ethical reasons. I learned a lot from Bill. He was a very progressive and image-conscious person and he took this organization to a much higher level as far as marketing and promotions were concerned."[48]

FIGURE 11. Bill Giles was hired by the Phillies in 1969 as vice-president of marketing operations. Twelve years later he was a principal owner and president of the team. Courtesy of the National Baseball Hall of Fame Library, Cooperstown, New York.

Giles would make the Vet one of the most entertaining venues in the city with some of the most fascinating pregame performers and memorable giveaways for fans of all ages. "My basic philosophy was that Philadelphians had gotten out of the habit of caring about baseball and going to the game," Giles explained recently. "The year before I came, the Phillies only drew 425,000 at Connie Mack Stadium. They had very limited promotions and did very little marketing of any kind. I implemented a staircase concept of marketing. That is, I did anything that made sense to try and get a person to the game one time, things like a Dionne Warwick concert. There might have been some of her fans who didn't really care about baseball, but they came to see her. This is where the staircase came in. If we got a person to come to one game and they liked it, we believed that they'd return for two or three more games. Then, the next season, we'd try to upgrade them to a small ticket plan of fifteen games. If that worked, we had them hooked on baseball and they'd eventually sign up for a full season ticket plan."[49]

Giles also believed that children made a lot of decisions for their parents. As a result, he targeted families by "creating an atmosphere where the parents and kids could go to the game and enjoy themselves." More important, the family's enjoyment "wouldn't depend on whether the Phillies won or not," because the team "wasn't very good in those early years." Giles began advertising giveaway games on the Saturday morning television shows, which were targeted to a child audience. Bats, balls, caps, plastic batting helmets were all part of the early give-aways. "The most popular item by far, though, was the Phillies warm-up jacket," he recalled. "It was a pretty darn good-looking jacket. I think each one only cost us $1.25, but it looked like a $15 warm-up jacket. We must have had 100,000 people trying to get into the Vet on jacket day, especially since we only had a $1.00 general admission fee for kids then. It was quite a bargain."[50]

Giles lured fans to the game by hiring Harry Kalas, the play-by-play radio announcer for the Houston Astros. Kalas teamed up with Richie Ashburn, the former Phillies center fielder, and long-time Philadelphia baseball broadcaster By Saam to bring the game into the living rooms, backyards, and summer homes of fans throughout the Delaware Valley. Over the next three decades, his silky-smooth voice would generate a large listening audience as he popularized such catch phrases as "Outta here" and "Watch that baby."[51]

Giles's trial run came on April 10, 1971, when the Vet opened its gates for the first time. It was a cold, cloudy, blustery afternoon with some 55,352 fans in attendance to see the Phillies take on the Montreal Expos. It was the largest crowd to that date to see a baseball game in the Commonwealth of Pennsylvania. Organist Paul Richardson kept the fans entertained with his lively keyboard, playing everything from pop music to polkas. About 1:45 P.M., the Hegeman String Band played some of the tunes made popular by city's annual Mummers' Day Parade. Shortly after, four F-106 Air Force jets staged a flyover. Mayor Tate unveiled a plaque dedicating the stadium to the city's veterans, and Expos general manager Jim Fanning entered the park riding a dogsled, adding a Canadian twist to the opening day ceremonies. After the singing of the Canadian and American national anthems, Phillies catcher Mike Ryan caught a baseball dropped from a helicopter hovering some 150 feet above the stadium and presented it to Frank Mastrogiovanni, a twenty-year-old marine corporal who had lost his legs in Vietnam. Mastrogiovanni, a South Philadelphia resident, then threw the ball out to the Phils' regular catcher, Tim McCarver, who returned it to him as a souvenir.[52]

Montreal manager Gene Mauch, not one to give compliments easily, was clearly impressed by his surroundings. "It's got to be the best new park in baseball," he said before the game as he scoped the colorful seats, plush green Astroturf, and animated twin scoreboards. "Looks like they've taken the good things from all the other new parks, added some things of their own, and whipped them into a pretty good plan."[53] Baseball commissioner Bowie Kuhn, who sat in Bob Carpenter's luxury box, was more effusive: "It certainly ranks with the finest new stadiums. The scoreboard is just spectacular as it was forecast to be and I'm certainly impressed with the overall attractiveness inside the stadium."[54]

By 2:20 P.M. the ball game was underway and Phillies right-hander Jim Bunning delivered the very first pitch to Montreal's Boots Day, who hit a ground ball back to the pitcher's mound for the first out. The first hit came off the bat of Phillies shortstop Larry Bowa, who singled to right field off Montreal's Bill Stoneman in the bottom of the first inning. The Expos scored the first run in the top of the sixth when Ron Hunt stroked a line drive that bounced into the right field stands for a ground rule double. He scored on Bob Bailey's hit to center. But the Phillies prevailed in the bottom of the sixth when Don Money hit the first home run in the Vet's history. The Phils added three additional runs that same inning on two key hits by Deron Johnson and Roger Freed and a sacrifice fly by McCarver. The Phillies went on to win the game, 4-1. Bunning, who allowed six hits, struck out four, and walked three, got the decision for his 220th career win. Joe Hoerner earned the save.[55]

Aside from the opening of the Vet, 1971 was another forgettable season. The Phillies acquired Roger Freed from the Baltimore Orioles before the season began in hopes of adding some power to their feeble offense. But Freed, the regular right fielder, disappointed, hitting just .221 with 6 home runs and 37 RBI. Left fielder Oscar Gamble (.221, 6 HR, 23 RBI) was just as bad. Don Money (.223, 7 HR, 38 RBI) and rookie John Vukovich (.166, 0 HR, 14 RBI) split time at third base. Although they were strong defensively, both struggled to hit big league pitching, which was unacceptable at a position reserved for power hitters. The pitching was terrible. Bunning (5-12, 58 K, 5.48 ERA) and Short (7-14, 95 K, 3.85 ERA) continued their slide. It would be Bunning's last season in the majors, and Short's second to last with the Phillies. Management had high expectations for two other starting pitchers, Barry Lersch and Ken Reynolds. But they, too, failed to deliver, gaining just 10 victories between them. Naturally, the Phillies completed the season in last place with a record of 67-95, 30 games behind the Pittsburgh Pirates, who went on the capture the World Series.[56] There were bright spots, though.

Rick Wise, who had become the pitching ace of the team, compiled a 17-14 record including a no-hitter against the Reds on June 23 at Cincinnati's Riverfront Stadium. Wise was impressive, using an assortment of pitches to keep the Big Red Machine's powerful hitters off-kilter. "Rick threw 56 fast balls and 39 breaking balls," according to pitching coach Ray Ripplemeyer, who kept track of the deliveries. "He made 19 pitches in the ninth inning, and 17 were fast balls, which shows you how he was mixing them up until the final frame."[57] Wise had a perfect game until he walked Reds shortstop Dave Concepcion in the sixth inning with one out. "Right there, I think I was starting to tire briefly," he admitted after the game. Phillies catcher "Tim [McCarver] came out and told me to take a few deep breaths and relax. I took my inside shirt off between innings and I was a lot cooler after that."[58] After the brief letdown, Wise was perfect, not allowing a single base runner.[59]

The final out came off the bat of the Reds' scrappy right fielder, Pete Rose, who hit a screeching line drive toward third base. "Rose was the last guy in the world I wanted up there hitting with two outs in the ninth," McCarver admitted later in the clubhouse. "Nobody can say that Rick didn't earn that last out. Pete was really grinding. When the ball left his bat, my heart jumped into my throat, but it went right at [third baseman John] Vukovich."[60] Wise was just as impressive at the plate, where he hit two home runs and collected three RBI to seal the 4-0, shutout for himself.[61]

The Phillies were also blessed with some young talent, including Willie Montanez, a colorful center fielder who proved to be among the leading candidates for the Rookie of the Year Award. Promoted from Triple-A before the season, Montanez had been sent by the St. Louis Cardinals to the Phillies as compensation for Curt Flood when the disgruntled outfielder refused to report after being traded to Philadelphia. A first baseman by trade, Montanez was converted to center field since the Phils already had a bona fide slugger in Deron Johnson at first base. The young Puerto Rican exceeded the club's wildest expectations, hitting 30 home runs and driving in 99 runs while playing brilliantly in the outfield. Flipping his bat defiantly as he strutted from the on-deck circle to home plate, Montanez basked in the spotlight and quickly won over the hearts of the fans, who dubbed him "Willie the Phillie."[62]

Larry Bowa also proved for the second straight year that he was a major league caliber shortstop. What he lacked in gracefulness, Bowa made up for with his scrappy defense. His .987 fielding percentage was among the highest for major league shortstops and he was among the league leaders in turning double plays (97) and stealing bases (28).[63] Bowa's defense was especially remarkable against the Montreal Expos, whose manager Gene Mauch became so infuriated that he referred to him as a "fucking gnat."[64] On one occasion, Mauch, realizing how much Bowa struggled as a hitter, tried to intimidate him by positioning all three of his outfielders just off the infield cutout. It appeared as if the Expos were playing seven infielders. Motivated by the insult, Bowa hit a game-winning triple over the right fielder's head.

"You fucking gnat," screamed Mauch, fuming at the sight of the Phillies shortstop on third base. "You'll never hit a ball like that again in your life!"

Bowa, standing on third, dusted himself off, turned in the direction of the Expos dugout, and, in one swift motion, pounded his left hand onto his right bicep. The shortstop's forearm shot up in the air with the middle finger of his hand protruding unmistakably for all to see—a gesture more commonly known as "flipping the bird." Then he pointed to Mauch, saying, "That one's for you!"[65]

Greg Luzinski was also promoted to the majors in September 1971. When he stepped into the batting cage at Veterans Stadium to take his cuts, the hulking outfielder blasted pitch after pitch into the left field stands, some into the upper deck. Lucchesi, desperate for offense, inserted him into the lineup. The Bull's first big league home run came on September 7, a fast ball delivered by the Cardinals' Reggie Cleveland that landed in the 500 level seats.[66] In 28 games, Luzinski compiled a .300 average, collecting 30 hits, including 8 doubles, 3 home runs, and 15 RBI.[67] The Bull was in the big leagues to stay.

Finally, Bill Giles and his attractive new showplace appeared to have won back the fans with pre-game ceremonies, special events and promotional giveaways. Lured by the new stadium, Philadelphians turned out in droves to watch baseball allowing the team to set a record attendance mark with 1,511,223 patrons in 1971.[68] In the years ahead, the Vet would give a new, more exciting meaning to baseball in the City of Brotherly Love.

CHAPTER 4

LEFTY

T HE PHILLIES BECAME ONE OF the most fan-friendly organizations in baseball during the early 1970s. Veterans Stadium, with its circuslike atmosphere and giveaway days, appealed to young and old alike. Talented young players like Larry Bowa and Greg Luzinski were exciting to watch and represented a promising future. But the club still lacked a marquee player, a veteran star who could fill the seats and raise the team's performance to a more competitive level. In 1972, Steve Carlton became that player.

Carlton was not the most likable individual. He was born with a magnificent left arm and a streak of independence that were only exceeded by his impetuousness. In March 1965, the St. Louis Cardinals auditioned the 6' 4" rookie in an exhibition game. In four innings of work, Carlton surrendered 2 runs on 5 hits, hardly an impressive performance. But the lanky southpaw refused to accept the blame for his poor showing. Afterward, in the Cardinal locker room, he approached catcher Tim McCarver while he was shaving.

"Hey," began the twenty-year-old hurler. "You've gotta call for more breaking pitches when we're behind in the count."

McCarver couldn't believe that a rookie had the gall to tell him how to call a game. He was, after all, a veteran and the club's regular catcher. Just five months earlier, he hit .478 in the World Series and smacked a three-run homer in Game Five to help the Cards clinch the championship against the storied New York Yankees. He was a bona fide major leaguer, and yet here was a rookie questioning his judgment.

"You son of a bitch!" McCarver exploded, appalled at Carlton's brashness. "Who the hell do you think you are telling me that? You've got a lot of guts. What credentials do you have?"

Unimpressed by the tirade, Carlton simply shrugged his shoulders and walked away. The next day, McCarver apologized, but the Cardinal rookie brushed him off again. Looking him straight in the eye, Carlton said, "I wasn't listening anyway."[1] It was an inauspicious beginning for a young pitcher who years later would credit the veteran catcher as being a large part of his success. The two men would become inseparable when they played for the Phillies, leading the affable catcher to predict: "When Steve and I die, we're going to be buried sixty feet six inches apart."[2]

Born on December 22, 1944, in Miami, Florida, Steven Norman Carlton shied away from organized sports as a youngster. He was twelve years old when his father signed him up for Little League, but he quit after one practice, saying that the game was "no fun." When Carlton finally did start playing baseball at North Miami High School, he excelled at pitching and attracted the interest of the St. Louis Cardinals, who signed him in 1963. Promoted to the majors in mid-September 1964 to watch the Cards clinch their first pennant in eighteen years, the tall, lanky, 185-pound Carlton was nicknamed "Ichabod" after Washington Irving's schoolteacher Ichabod Crane.[3] The following year he was back at Tulsa in the Pacific Coast League where he was putting together an impressive, nine-win season when his manager, Charlie Metro, told him, "Get packed, you're going to Cooperstown."

Carlton, always quick with a quip, replied: "Me? The Hall of Fame already?"

The promotion, to pitch at the annual "Hall of Fame [exhibition] Game," was actually a desperate move by the Cards to save a heavily depleted pitching staff. Mired in the bottom of the standings, the team was out of contention and seeking help from the farm system to replace some of the injured arms. With a 9-5 record, Carlton became a logical choice. Facing the Minnesota Twins at Cooperstown, the young hurler struck out 10 hitters en route to a 7-5 victory. "I'm sure that game changed the club's mind about bringing me up," he said afterward. "The Twins had some pretty good hitters—Harmon Killebrew, Tony Oliva, Don Mincher—and all those big guns were swinging away in that small park at Cooperstown."[4]

Over the next six years, Carlton won 77 games for the Red birds, helping them to two National League pennants and a world championship. He also developed a slider to go with his lively fastball and devastating curve. "I figured I obviously needed another pitch," he admitted after slipping to 13-11 during the 1968 season. "I needed something to keep the right handed batters away from the plate. I wasn't throwing the fastball inside on right-handers enough, and sometimes when I got it inside, it would sail right over the plate—and that's a bad pitch. Now a batter can't come up to the plate knowing he has to guess only curve or fastball. He has to think about the slider. I've been throwing the slider about 25% of the time. It's easier to control than a big, sweeping curve."[5] Carlton's slider was so effective that he was able to win 17 games in 1969. His earned run average dropped from 3.00 to 2.17 and he posted 210 strikeouts, including a brilliant performance against the New York Mets in which he set a modern major league record for a nine-inning game by striking out 19 batters.[6] Success spawned controversy, though.

Carlton believed that his performance deserved a sizable pay increase and he wanted his salary doubled from $25,000 to $50,000 for the 1970 campaign. When Cardinals owner Augustus "Gussie" Busch, Jr., offered to raise the pitcher's salary to $32,000, Carlton countered with a $40,000 figure. Busch held firm and Carlton refused to report to spring training. "I don't give a damn if Steve Carlton never pitches another ball for us," fumed Busch to the press on March 9 at the Cards' St. Petersburg training complex. "He got a 25% increase with a club that finished way down in the standings. I only hope that some of the other owners have the guts to take the stand I have, and return things to normal."[7] To counter Carlton's hold out, the Cardinals, on March 11, enacted a unique provision of the controversial reserve clause allowing the club to renew his contract under the same terms of the previous one for a period of one year. The renewal clause protected ownership from free agency and allowed the team to supervise the rebellious player as he got into shape for the upcoming season. Carlton was now "legally obligated" to report to spring training or face a considerable fine.[8] The impetuous hurler also realized that unless he signed a contract, he wouldn't be eligible for additional pension plan benefits, nor would he be covered by the players' insurance plan if injured. "With the generous pension fund the players have," said Busch, driving the point home, "I don't see how Carlton can say we're tightfisted. We've been so fair with these players. You have no idea. I'm no attorney, but if you ask me, this is another challenge to the reserve clause."[9] Despite the tough talk, Busch relented and Carlton signed a two-year contract worth $40,000 a year.[10]

But Carlton's performance hardly merited the raise. In 1970, he posted a 10-19 record and an inflated earned run average of 3.72. The strain on his arm from throwing the slider forced him to abandon the pitch and he found himself relying too much on his fastball. Determined to improve his performance in 1971, Carlton lifted weights and did stretching exercises during the off-season. He bulked up to 225 pounds, but retained the flexibility and strength to become an effective power pitcher. The work paid off as the Cardinal southpaw compiled a 20-9 record for a team that contended most of the season, finishing in second place, seven games behind the division-leading Pittsburgh Pirates.[11] Once again, Carlton believed that his performance earned him a significant increase in salary and he asked for $65,000. And again Gussie Busch refused, but this time he was determined to hold the line.[12] He would use Carlton as an example in an effort to intimidate the Major League Baseball Players Association.

Labor relations between the owners and the players had become increasingly antagonistic as the March 31, 1972, expiration of the 1969 Basic Agreement neared. Initially, Marvin Miller, the players' negotiator, had taken a cautious approach. Hired by the players' union in the mid-1960s. Miller, once a negotiator for the United Steelworkers of America, was a patient man. Instead of immediately challenging the reserve system, he secured limited but winnable objectives in order to earn the players' confidence. Over the course of five years, Miller improved both the players' salary scale and working conditions. The minimum salary was raised from $6,000 to $10,000 and the maximum pay cut reduced to 20 percent. Spring training expense money was raised from $25 to $40 a week and players now enjoyed first-class travel and hotel accommodations. These achievements might sound "modest" by today's standards, but players' salaries and working conditions hadn't improved since 1947.[13]

By 1970, however, Miller had become much more aggressive. He pressed for a structural change in the Basic Agreement called "grievance arbitration" whereby a player, if he believed his contractual rights were being violated and the union supported him, could take the matter to an independent arbitrator who would serve as a mediator between labor and management. Under the existing system, the baseball commissioner remained the absolute authority in disputes between players and teams, as well as between leagues and between teams.[14] Miller also wanted a 17 percent increase in the owners' annual contribution to the pension plan to match the previous three years' inflation, what amounted to an annual payment of $6.5 million. Naturally, the owners rejected both proposals, publicly portraying Miller as "a labor boss who dictated terms to the players." In private, they referred to the player negotiator as a "Jew bastard."[15] Still, Miller persisted. To ease their out-of-pocket costs, he proposed that the $800,000 surplus accrued from the pension plan be applied to the benefits increase, drastically reducing the cost to the clubs. Surprisingly, the owners, led by Gussie Busch, rejected the proposal and decided to take the union on.[16]

Busch and the other owners believed that the Players Association was still weak and could be broken. They belonged to an era when players and owners were bound to each other by a mutual love of the game. While the players weren't paid well, the owners showed their appreciation by giving them job security and perks that would reinforce a personal commitment to them. In 1972, while the players and their agents were trying to drive salaries up to the $125,000 range, only six players were earning that kind of annual salary: Frank Robinson, Carl Yastrzemski, Frank Howard, Willie Mays, Hank Aaron, and Bob Gibson. These were an elite group of players who compiled league-leading statistics year after year. Now there was emerging a new breed of ballplayer who demanded to be paid for his services, whether or not he turned in a consistent performance. Busch saw players like Steve Carlton as the crux of the problem. When Carlton, who had never won twenty games before 1971, asked for $65,000, Busch told his general manager, Bing Devine, "Give him fifty and if he won't play for that, get rid of him!"[17]

Bob Carpenter of the Phillies was locked in a similar stalemate with pitcher Rick Wise. Wise had posted 17 wins, including a no-hitter, in 1971 and was asking that his $32,500 salary be doubled. Carpenter refused the demand, telling his general manager John Quinn to offer Wise an additional $10,000 and no more. When Wise held out, he became expendable. On February 25, 1972, Carpenter and Busch decided to show the Players Association that the owners still ruled the game by trading the two, rebellious frontline pitchers for each other. It was a new tactic in labor-management relations that had little to do with salary demands or improving the quality of their teams. Carlton and Wise were almost mirror reflections of each other. Carlton, age twenty-seven, had compiled 77 victories in 7 seasons with the Cardinals. He was asking for $65,000, but St. Louis refused to give him more than $60,000. Wise, age twenty-six, had posted 75 wins in 7 seasons with the Phillies. He was asking for $65,000, but Philadelphia refused to pay him more than $45,000. Yet after they were traded each pitcher was paid essentially the same salary he had asked his former club to pay him.[18]

When Wise learned of the trade from Phillies general manager John Quinn, he was elated. "It's a great opportunity," he told the press. "You get tired of being a .500 pitcher, when you've been with a second division club. The Cardinals just gave me a raise bigger than all the combined raises I ever got from Philadelphia."[19] Years later, however, Wise admitted that he was "stunned" by the deal since he had "grown up in the Phillies organization" and that "it hurt to be traded." "In retrospect," he said, "I learned that the trade was all about money and the power management exercised to control the lives of the players. What it came down to was, 'if you're not going to sign the contract we offer, you're gone.' Then Steve and I signed basically for what we had asked for to begin with."[20] Carlton, on the other hand, was in shock after learning of the trade. He considered the Phillies "an awful team" and didn't want to pitch for them. "I was panic-stricken," Carlton admitted years later. "The Phillies were a last-place club at that time and the Cardinals were always competing for first place. I thought, 'Oh my God, there goes my career.' I called [Cards general manager] Bing Devine and said, 'I'll take the money you offered me. I'll take anything.' But it didn't matter because it was a done deal by then."[21] Devine admitted that the trade had been provoked by Carlton's stubborn negotiating tactics two years earlier and that the Cardinals could "sense a similar situation developing."[22] Shock soon turned into anger for Carlton who expressed his displeasure to the *New York Daily News*. "I'm mad," he admitted. "I came up through the Cardinals' organization and I didn't have anything to say about it. I thought we were working things out. Then, all of a sudden I'm traded cold turkey. If you ask me, the reserve clause is unconstitutional."[23]

After Phillies general manager John Quinn agreed to Carlton's salary demand of a one-year contract at $65,000, the former Cardinal hurler accepted the situation. He adopted a "wait-and-see" attitude, much like the Phillies. Only Quinn and Lucchesi seemed to be convinced that Carlton had "what it takes to become a great one." Others in the Phillies brain trust as well as the fans were less optimistic. Wise had been the club's ace pitcher. Perhaps he had caused headaches with his recent contract demand, but he still managed to win with a second division team. Carlton, on the other hand, had posed chronic problems in contract negotiations and if he allowed as many runs in Philadelphia as he did with the Cardinals, there were doubts that he would win as many games for the Phillies.[24] Nor would Quinn be around to see if his prediction came true. He was relieved of his responsibilities as general manager that June and replaced by farm director Paul Owens.

Near the end of spring training, the Players' Association, seeking a cost-of-living increase in pension benefits, voted to go on strike unless the owners agreed to submit the dispute to arbitration. Determined to fight the demand, the owners refused. "We voted unanimously to take a stand," declared Gussie Busch, who emerged as the leading spokesman for the owners. "We're not going to give the players another god-damned cent! If they want to strike, let 'em!"[25] On April 1 the players walked out of their spring training camps marking what the *Sporting News* called "the darkest day in sports history."[26] Days later, as Busch and most of the other owners settled in for the long haul, Phillies owner Bob Carpenter softened his position and allowed his striking players to work out at the team's spring training fields in Clearwater, Florida. The White Sox and Pirates did the same for their striking players. Having broken with each other, the owners, after thirteen days, finally agreed to the players' cost-of-living increase. They also sustained the financial losses of the 86 games that had been canceled, while the players agreed to forfeit their pay for their time away. The strike was over, but the owners' hold on the game was beginning to weaken.[27]

Two months later, on June 19, the United States Supreme Court rejected Curt Flood's challenge to baseball's reserve clause. The court, by a vote of five to three, ruled in favor of baseball and its exemption from antitrust laws, keeping the reserve clause intact. But the decision was hardly an unconditional endorsement of the reserve system. The court, in handing down the ruling, admitted that baseball's exemption was "an aberration" and insisted that it was "time for Congress—not the Court—to remedy the problem."[28] Although Flood lost his bid to eliminate the reserve clause, his challenge turned public opinion to the players' side. Shortly after the Supreme Court rendered its decision, a national poll revealed that fans opposed the reserve clause by an eight to one margin.[29] Congress also began to pay closer attention. "Even if I believed the solemn predictions of the pro sports industry spokesmen, and I don't," said Senator Sam Ervin of North Carolina, who would become famous two years later for his role in chairing the Watergate hearings, "I would still oppose a system that demands lordlike control over serflike hired hands."[30] Fearing that the reserve clause might be taken from them, the owners announced that any player with ten major league seasons to his credit, including five seasons with his current team, could veto any trade he didn't approve.[31] It was a last-ditch effort to avoid the inevitable dissolution of the reserve system.

In Philadelphia, Steve Carlton won over the hearts of the fans when he put together one of the greatest seasons in baseball history. On opening day at Chicago's Wrigley Field, Carlton pitched eight strong innings to lead the Phils to a 4-2 victory over the Cubs. A few days later, he blanked his old Cardinal teammates, hurling a 3-hitter for a 1-0 win. His performance was even better in his next starting assignment against the San Francisco Giants, the defending National League Western Division champions. Alternating his fastball, curve, and slider, Carlton struck out 14 hitters, tying a club record, and surrendered just one hit in the 3-0 victory. More impressive, the Phillies southpaw threw just 103 pitches in the one hour and forty-seven minutes it took him to dispatch the Giants for his second consecutive shutout.[32] Both of those statistics were exceptional considering the average pitch count was 120 deliveries and most games were completed in two hours or more. "My slider's a great pitch," Carlton mused after the game. "In 1970, when I held out and got a late start, I had problems throwing it. I was getting underneath the slider and releasing it improperly. It gave me a sore arm before the season was over so I decided to scrap it."[33] But Phillies pitching coach Ray Ripplemeyer convinced the hurler to return to the slider during spring training. Carlton agreed to the experiment and was able to throw the pitch pain-free through the early spring. "His slider is as good as any I've seen," boasted Ripplemeyer after the 3-0 shutout of San Francisco. "I couldn't understand why he didn't want to use it last year. All I told him was that if he started using the slider again, not to let it change him into a breaking ball pitcher. He can get any hitter in the world out with his fastball and, at his age, he's still got to think of himself as primarily a fastball pitcher. Besides, his fastball, curve and slider are all A+. It's the first time I've ever rated a pitcher excellent on all three."[34] In fact, of the 20 times Carlton used his slider in the game, he threw 17 for strikes.[35] The slider, when thrown properly, can fool even the best hitters because it looks like a fastball when it is released but breaks sharply when it crosses the plate. Carlton used the slider whenever he got behind in the count or when he needed a strikeout, though he didn't throw the pitch nearly as much as he would in later years.

Carlton lost his fourth start, 4-0, against the San Diego Padres, though he pitched shutout ball for six innings. Undaunted by the loss, he returned to his winning ways on May 3, when he struck out 9 hitters to beat the Los Angeles Dodgers, 5-1, on a six-hitter. Four days later, he returned to the mound and defeated the

Giants again, 8-3. He also struck out 13 batters to bring his career total to 1,007. Tim McCarver, who had also caught Carlton in St. Louis, was impressed by how much more effectively the southpaw was throwing. "Steve has great control on the inside edge of the plate on right-handed hitters," he observed. "As a rule, we don't pitch in there that much to right-handed hitters, but his location is so exceptional we decide to go there a lot. His slider is great, too. Sometimes it will come in and down, and when it does that pitch is unhittable. But the key to his success is his concentration. He's in a trance when he's on the mound as he works rapidly in a cadence that's the mark of a truly outstanding pitcher. Steve learned that from [St. Louis pitcher] Bob Gibson."[36] Carlton was now sporting a 5-1 record. Not once in those six starting assignments did he need help from the bullpen—all were complete game performances. "I can't remember if I've ever had this good a start before," said the Phillies ace. "I know I've always had a good record going into the All-Star Game, but this might be my best start for putting everything together."[37]

Carlton's brilliant pitching was one of the few bright spots for the Phillies, who continued to lose when he wasn't on the mound. As the losses mounted, Lucchesi became more frustrated with his players and began to reevaluate his off-field policies. After the Phils manager banned the customary two cases of beer on an off-day charter flight, McCarver approached him and demanded to know why he was treating the players "like children." Ignoring the challenge, the Phillies skipper turned and walked away. A few days later, Lucchesi called the catcher into his office and informed him that new general manager Paul Owens had traded him to the Montreal Expos for catcher John Bateman. McCarver was stunned. Although he was only hitting .237 at the time, he was a .260 hitter lifetime and an excellent defensive catcher who had played on three pennant winners and two world championship teams in St. Louis. Bateman, on the other hand, had a lifetime batting average of .245 while playing nine seasons for last-place teams in Houston and Montreal. After collecting himself, McCarver asked who else was involved in the trade.

"Well, there'll probably be a minor leaguer involved," replied Lucchesi, too embarrassed to admit that the deal was a one-for-one acquisition.

"If you didn't get any more for me than Bateman, you got fucked!" snapped McCarver as he stormed out of the manager's office.[38]

Lucchesi would make his own exit on July 10, with the Phillies firmly entrenched in last place. On that day, Paul Owens announced that his longtime friend would be relieved of his responsibilities as Phillies manager and that he would takeover the team, serving the dual roles of general manager and field manager.[39] "It's the same old story," said a teary-eyed Lucchesi at the press conference announcing his dismissal. "You can't fire the troops, so you have to fire the general." Nevertheless, he accepted his fate, realizing that "there's only 18 inches between a pat on the back and a kick in the butt."[40] Years later, Lucchesi admitted that he "still really doesn't know why they made the change." He had always been under the impression that the team was in a rebuilding process and that he knew his young players—both in the farm system at on the parent club— well enough to supervise the process. "I wasn't mad, just hurt because I loved the Phillies," he said. "I thought I was going to be there quite a few years." While other managers might become vindictive after being dismissed, Lucchesi was loyal and remains so to this day. "I still believe that Bob Carpenter was the most wonderful owner of any major league club I managed. He rewarded loyalty. I had been with the Phillies organization for almost seventeen years when I applied for the manager's job. It came down to three finalists and I got the job because Mr. Carpenter respected my commitment to the organization."[41]

Regardless of the team's lackluster performance on the field, Lucchesi had made an important contribution. His patience with and commitment to the young players at the earliest stage of the Phillies' rebuilding process allowed individuals like Montanez, Luzinski, and especially Bowa to gain the confidence necessary to succeed at the major league level. "If it wasn't for Frank Lucchesi, I probably wouldn't have stayed in the majors," said Bowa in a recent interview. "His patience with me and his confidence in my ability to play shortstop made my career possible. If it was any other manager, I might not have been given the chance of a big league career."[42] Lucchesi had also been popular with the Philadelphia press, who roundly criticized his firing and questioned Owens's motives for naming himself as the replacement.

Few baseball executives have the confidence to assume the responsibilities of field manager. The day-to-day demands of the position are daunting and can easily detract from the broader administrative duties that must be addressed in the front office. But if members of the press believed that Owens's decision was based purely on ego, they were wrong. There was no one else in the Phillies organization at that time who commanded as much respect among the players as he did. Owens had signed and developed most if not all of the young talent and would not hesitate to make them accountable. "Not everyone can make the transition from the front office to field manager," admitted Ruly Carpenter, who would soon take over as the team president. "But Paul was able to do that because the players had a tremendous amount of respect for him. They knew he played professionally and, of course, he had signed many of them. Nor did we expect that things would go smoothly. Paul didn't have a problem chewing their assess out when they didn't perform. He wasn't afraid of anybody. We also knew that as field manager, he would find out which guys really wanted to play and which ones didn't. You can only do that by being with the team on a daily basis."[43] Owens said as much on the day he announced his dual responsibilities. "I took over with the idea of learning our personnel and the personnel around the league," he explained, "and I thought I could do that better as manager than I could from the general manager's office."[44]

The forty-eight-year-old Owens also cited the need for the club to "develop the everyday players, the young guys who'll be playing together for eight or nine years."[45] Having spent the last decade as farm director, he realized that the Phillies had the talent to build a contender in their organization. Triple-A Eugene, managed by Andy Seminick, was en route to the Pacific Coast League's Western Division title with such All-Stars as Bob Boone, Mike Schmidt, and Craig Robinson. Single-A Spartanburg, piloted by Bob Wellman, would clinch the Western Carolinas League championship that season thanks, in large part, to the hitting of All-Star outfielder Jerry Martin, a .316 hitter who led the league in hits (162), doubles (30), RBI (112) and total bases (240). Even double-A Reading, which was not a championship caliber team, enjoyed an outstanding manager in former Phillies ace Jim Bunning, who was being groomed to become the future manager of the parent club.[46] If those minor leaguers continued to develop, Owens knew he could trade for whatever missing players he needed to build a winner. After all, he was an old school negotiator, the kind of general manager who closed the hotel bar night after night in his quest to make the "right" deal. Holding court amidst the haze of cigarette smoke and stiff scent of whiskey and gin, Owens, in the early hours of the morning, would consummate most of his deals. Never did he question his own judgment because he had the intuition of a hardened baseball man and he knew, deep down, that he "was right, that [he] was going to win [his] way."[47]

Meanwhile, Carlton continued his masterful season. For three-day stretches, the Phillies were an awful team. But on the fourth day when their ace left-hander took the mound, they became almost unbeatable. After dropping five straight games in May, Carlton rallied to win 15 consecutive contests. During that remarkable streak, he hurled 5 shutouts and 5 games in which he allowed just one run. Beginning on June 25, when he defeated Montreal, 1-0, Carlton completed 12 of his 13 starts. His fourteenth victory came in Philadelphia on Sunday afternoon, August 13, against the Expos, but was overshadowed by one of Bill Giles's most fascinating promotions.

Karl Wallenda, the patriarch of world-famous family of high-wire performers, walked a two-inch wide steel cable close to 900 feet from foul pole to foul pole across the top of the Vet between games of a double-header. He performed the stunt at a height of nearly 200 feet and without a net. Midway across the stadium, the sixty-seven-year-old Wallenda stopped and did a headstand while hovering over second base. The feat, accomplished in just seventeen minutes, was greeted with a standing ovation by the more than 32,000 fans on hand. It had never been done before in a major league stadium.

The Phillies paid Wallenda $3,000 for the performance, but had to take an insurance policy out from Lloyd's of London. "It was a little nerve-wracking for me," admitted Giles. "I was worried that he might fall. As I watched him walk across the high-wire, I became more confident, figuring he had done this plenty of times before. But when he came down from the roof and asked for six martinis, I knew he was scared."[48] Not even Carlton's fourteenth straight win could top Wallenda's act.

Four days later, on August 17, the tall left-hander notched his twentieth win, a 9-4 victory over the powerful Cincinnati Reds. "The thing Steve Carlton does to his team is incredible," observed Bill Conlin, a beat writer for the *Philadelphia Daily News.* "He walks to the mound and the Phillies become a snarling wolf pack of opportunists who score enough runs to win, to make the right plays, and hustle. They display the machismo of a rising star in the National League firmament."[49] Whenever Carlton took the mound he infused so much confidence in his teammates that the opponent didn't matter, even if it was a perennial winner like the Cincinnati Reds or Los Angeles Dodgers. First baseman Tommy Hutton compared the situation to "David fighting Goliath." "When Carlton pitched, we had an 'All-Midget Infield' with myself, Bowa, and Doyle," he explained. "None of us were close to six feet and we weren't the most powerful hitters either. But with Carlton on the mound we knew we had a good chance to win. He was a fierce competitor, so you knew you had better be at the top of your game."[50] Larry Bowa echoed that sentiment. "Steve had a way about him that elevated everybody's play," said the Phillies shortstop recently. "As bad as we were, as young as we were, we knew that if we made one or two runs we had a chance to win."[51] Not since the glory days of the Athletics of 1929-31, led by Lefty Grove, had Philadelphians seen such a dominating southpaw. While the fans and the sportswriters dubbed him "Super Steve," Carlton's teammates honored him by giving him the nickname "Lefty" (Figure 12).

When asked to explain his success, Carlton cited the four-man rotation and his ability to concentrate as the keys. "Defeat? I never consider it," he insisted after notching his twenty-second victory in early September. "Pressure? It doesn't exist. I just lock into this inner strength, this concentration that allows me to make the key pitches under pressure," he said. "Once I hit that stride, it seems like I never throw a pitch down the heart of the plate. I just constantly work the corners. It's so easy pitching every fourth day to have that kind of rhythm and pace. I didn't have that advantage in St. Louis where we used a five-man rotation."[52]

Carlton finished the '72 season with a 27-10 record. He was responsible for 45.8 percent of the Phillies' 59 victories that year, the highest ratio in baseball history. Carlton also topped the majors with 15 consecutive victories and 30 complete games. Together with his 1.97 ERA and 310 strikeouts in a staggering $346\frac{1}{3}$ innings, those impressive statistics earned him the first of four Cy Young Awards. Aside from Carlton's brilliance, Greg Luzinski proved to be a reliable outfielder hitting .281 with 18 homers and 68 RBI that season. Bill Robinson, a veteran once hailed by the Yankee organization as the "next Mickey Mantle," also provided the Phillies with some consistent play in the outfield. The strength of the organization, however, could be found in the minor leagues where such prospects as Mike Schmidt and Bob Boone were refining their raw talent.[53]

In November, Bob Carpenter called a press conference to announce that he was resigning as president of the team and that his son would assume that responsibility. "Ruly is ready," he insisted. "He knows all phases of the operation. I just feel that the time has come for him to take over."[54] While the elder Carpenter was content with his decision to step down, his son expressed his regrets. "I begged my father not to retire," he admitted. "I knew we were on the way to something special and I wanted him to be part of it. Sure, we had a mediocre club with the exception of the days when Carlton pitched. We were 30 games out of first place by mid-August, but when he took the mound there were still 35,000 fans in the seats and it doesn't take a Harvard Business School graduate to figure out that if we could get the pitching, the fans were behind us."[55] Giles agreed that there was a promising future on the horizon, but that it wasn't based solely on good pitching. "I look at whether a player is interesting or not," he explained

FIGURE 12. In 1974, Steve Carlton won 27 games for the last-place Phillies, being responsible for nearly half of the team's 59 victories that season. He also captured the first of four Cy Young Awards. Courtesy of the *Philadelphia Daily News*.

to Bill Conlin of the *Philadelphia Daily News*. "We have athletes who are colorful as well as interesting to watch—Carlton, Bowa, Montanez, Luzinski to name a few. If we can play .500 baseball, we're going to be the kind of club where a fan is willing to pay $4.25, and even bring the wife and kids to a game. There's no question that 1973 is a key year for the Phillies. When you finish last, its very important to start fast in order to get the fans interested and then play at least .500 ball. If we do that, I think we can draw 1.8 million. If we hang in for the pennant race, we could do as well as 2 million."[56] How to attract and retain a sizable fan base was only one of the Phillies' concerns that off-season. The other, more pressing issue was to find a manager.

Owens had achieved his purpose by taking the reins of the team for the final three months of the '72 campaign. He was now able to identify a nucleus of players around which he could build a contender. At the same time, that nucleus was very young and he needed a manager who was not only patient, but also knowledgeable. Three candidates, in particular, immediately surfaced: Jim Bunning, Dave Bristol, and Richie Ashburn. Bunning, who had just completed his first year of managing at Double-A Reading, was interviewed after the season by Bob and Ruly Carpenter, Paul Owens, and new farm director Dallas Green. Green later confirmed that Owens, in particular, was impressed, giving Bunning the impression that he was going to be offered the job. A week later, however, Bunning learned from Ray Kelly, a beat writer from the *Philadelphia Bulletin*, that he wasn't a serious candidate. Kelly, who was covering the World Series in Oakland, was sitting at a hotel bar with Owens, who admitted that "there was no way Jim Bunning was ever going to manage the Phillies."[57] Interestingly, Bristol, a former manager with the Reds and Brewers, and Ashburn also left their interviews with the impression that the Phillies were going to offer them the job.[58] Ashburn, the sparkplug of the 1950 pennant-winning Whiz Kids, returned to the organization as a broadcaster in the early 1960s and was beloved by the fans. After his interview, he confided to Bill Giles that Bob Carpenter told him he "should be the new manager."[59] In the end, the Phillies executives fooled everybody. As it turned out, Giles had already recommended the successful candidate, Danny Ozark, a forty-eight-year-old third base coach for the Los Angeles Dodgers.[60]

When the Phillies hired Ozark, both the press and the fans were shocked. Few people knew him and those who did didn't consider him a likely candidate. Ozark had been in the Dodger organization for more than two decades as a player, minor league manager, and major league coach. Within the Dodger organization, it was assumed that Ozark would succeed longtime manager Walter Alston when he decided to retire. But Alston had no plans to quit in the near future. Therefore, Ozark, with Alston's blessing, applied for the Phillies job. "I knew the Phillies farm system pretty well," he said in a recent interview. I had managed in the Pacific Coast League and saw a lot of their players at Eugene, Oregon. I liked what

I saw in guys like Luzinski, Boone and Schmidt and I thought it would be a good fit for me."[61] Despite his fierce loyalty to Ashburn, Bob Carpenter left the final decision to his son, respecting his authority as the new president of the team. Ruly didn't need much convincing to hire Ozark. He was impressed with individuals who had a long-term commitment to an organization, especially when they came from as successful a franchise as the Dodgers. The younger Carpenter also felt that Bunning and Bristol would create controversy because of their reputations as disciplinarians. "With all due respect to the other candidates," said Ruly, "Danny had a lot more experience with the younger kids as a minor league manager. Since we had a lot of kids at that time, I felt he would complement the team much better."[62]

When he arrived at the Phillies' spring training complex in Clearwater, Florida, Ozark made it clear that he would emphasize the fundamentals. He intended to bring the "Dodger style" to the Phillies, explaining the concept as an "expectation of winning, pride in the organization and proper instruction." "You're going to see a club that is going to show a lot of pride in winning," he told the press. "We'll hit, run, steal and take advantage of a club's weaknesses. They won't know what hit 'em." "It'll be beyond their apprehension," Ozark added, foreshadowing the malapropisms that would become a trademark of his press conferences.[63] The decision to focus on the fundamentals would prove to be beneficial to a very young team, sorely lacking in the basics.

At the same time, Owens, who returned full-time to the front office, began making trades to secure the necessary veteran leadership. Realizing that the Phillies needed starting pitching and believing that Mike Schmidt had the potential to be the club's third baseman of the future, the general manager traded Don Money to the Milwaukee Brewers for Jim Lonborg and Ken Brett. Money, who had been acquired from Pittsburgh in 1968, had been the Phillies third baseman since 1970. Although he hit .295 with 14 homers and 66 RBIs that year, he never managed to hit higher than .223 during the next two seasons and became expendable.[64] Lonborg, on the other hand, had won the Cy Young Award with Boston in 1967, helping the Red Sox to an American League pennant. Although his career had been sidetracked by injuries, Owens believed that the tall right-hander still had the potential to be a consistent winner.[65]

Brett, the older brother of George Brett of the Kansas City Royals, was a solid young hurler who was worth a risk. Owens believed that he was an "outstanding pitcher" who had "not yet matured" and predicted that '73 would be the "turnover year for him." As a result of the trade, Ozark had three solid starters on his pitching staff. Since Carlton wanted to pitch every fourth day, he planned to use Lonborg as his number two starter and Brett and Wayne Twitchell (5-9, 112 K, 4.05 ERA) would round out the four-man rotation. If Lonborg needed an extra day's rest, he could go with Barry Lersch (4-6, 3.03 ERA). Ozark was more guarded about the bullpen. Dick Selma (2-9, 5.55 ERA) and Billy Wilson (1-1, 3.30 ERA) who had been the club's long relievers were both trying to come back after arm injuries. He realized that he might have to rely more on rookies Larry Christenson and Ron Diorio. Ozark was also prepared to turn over the catching duties to another rookie, Bob Boone. "We're confident that Boone has progressed enough to be an outstanding major league catcher," he told the press. "He has a live bat, a strong, accurate throwing arm, and has improved greatly behind the plate in terms of calling a game. [Veteran] Mike Ryan gives us an excellent defensive backup."[66]

The infield also needed to be reconstructed at the corner positions. With Deron Johnson gone, Owens needed a regular first baseman so he moved center fielder Willie Montanez there and traded outfielders Oscar Gamble and Roger Freed to the Cleveland Indians for Del Unser, a fine defensive center fielder who had displayed promise as a line-drive hitter earlier in his career. At third base, Schmidt would split time with a journeyman veteran infielder, Cesar Tovar.[67]

The '73 campaign was a much better one than Philadelphia baseball fans had seen in years. The Phillies played competitive baseball throughout the summer and headed into the Labor Day weekend only five games out of first place, though the season proved to be an emotional roller coaster for Mike Schmidt. There were occasions when Schmidt displayed remarkable power, but at other times he looked lost at the plate. Frustrated, he tried swinging for the fences every time up to bat. As the strikeouts mounted, Ozark began meeting regularly with Owens and new farm director Dallas Green to discuss the twenty-three-year-old rookie. Owens and Green wanted to send him back to the minors, believing that he was overmatched at the plate. Ozark convinced them to keep Schmidt put. He realized that the future rested with a young power-hitter like Schmidt. Why not let him play and learn? "Mike had proven he could hit Triple A pitching, what was he going to prove down there?" reasoned Ozark. "I said to Owens, we might as well let him play. He had great hands, quick reactions, and his swing was like a Ben Hogan golf swing. The ball came off the bat like a rocket. He didn't muscle the ball. It was all timing and bat speed. He had so much talent, it was only a matter of time before he put it all together."[68]

At the same time, Ozark displayed a paternalistic attitude toward Schmidt. He began calling his rookie third baseman "Dutch," a term of endearment for players of German ancestry. He summoned Schmidt to his office on almost a daily basis to give him advice. Against some of the tougher right-handers, Ozark would bench him, particularly when Schmidt was in a slump.[69] While Ozark's intentions were good, his approach was clumsy at best. Schmidt resented being called "Dutch," as if he was a "big, dumb kid." He interpreted Ozark's treatment of him as critical, almost as if he were acting like a father. "Danny never taught me much as a player," Schmidt said years later reflecting on his rookie season. "He thought I was a stubborn kid. He treated me more like my father, disciplining me, yelling at me, using me as an example."[70]

Schmidt was also going through the hazing process all rookies experienced in those days. Montanez, who had suffered the same ridicule two seasons earlier, was merciless in his treatment of the rookie third baseman. Whenever Schmidt walked past him in the batting cage, he would pretend to sneeze as though he had caught a cold from Schmidt's swings and the draft they created—an unpleasant reminder of his high strikeout ratio.[71] Bowa, who had a chip on his shoulder from the first day he heard that the Phillies signed Schmidt, a college All-American shortstop, also rode him endlessly. Bowa felt that he had already paid his dues, scratching and clawing his way up through the Phillies farm system. A fiery, intense competitor who had to work hard at the game, Bowa felt threatened by Schmidt and his more natural abilities. The more threatened he felt, the more he antagonized his younger teammate.[72]

Between Ozark's paternalism, his teammates' hazing, and the incessant booing of the hometown fans, Schmidt became depressed. The more he struggled at the plate, the more frustrated and bewildered he became. "All I wanted to do my first season," he said, "was hit the ball out of sight. I got into trouble by pulling away from the plate instead of simply swinging the bat to make contact."[73] Schmidt tried to forget about his problems by partying every night. He'd get lost in the nightlife of Philadelphia's dance clubs. "If I do good, I celebrate by partying," he admitted. "If I do badly, I forget it by partying. I'm young, I can handle it."[74]

Carlton saw that Schmidt was struggling and took him under his wing. The two teammates began going out to dinner and playing golf together as Lefty encouraged his young teammate to take a more positive approach to the game. He was a good mentor. On days when he pitched, Carlton prepared with a quiet professionalism that was only exceeded by the fierce competitiveness he displayed on the mound. But off the field he enjoyed life and taught his younger teammates to enjoy it as well. A connoisseur of fine wines, Carlton hosted his own entourage of young players at some of the best restaurants on the road. He taught them how to take pleasure in the life of a professional athlete.[75] But he could also be critical, especially when it affected his game.

Catcher Bob Boone was the target of Carlton's wrath his rookie year. The tall southpaw criticized the way Boone located his glove in the middle of the plate and then moved it to receive pitches. Nor did he like the rookie catcher's tendency to waste pitches when he was ahead in the count. Carlton wanted to go right after the hitter, to strike him out with the fewest number of pitches possible.[76] "I don't like to keep shaking a catcher off," he complained to Ozark. "It bothers my concentration. I like to get it over with. I only have three pitches and [Boone and I] are always four pitches apart."[77] Ozark found himself in a bind. He had made a commitment to Boone as his regular catcher and realized that the young backstop was just as stubborn as his left-handed ace. There was no way Boone was going to change his style to accommodate Carlton. Ozark also believed that the southpaw was looking for a scapegoat for his own inability to win games that season. "I knew Steve had problems with Bobby," he admitted in a recent interview. "He didn't pitch nearly as well in '73 as he had the year before and I think he blamed Bobby for his poor performance when it had nothing to do with the catcher."[78] Ozark also realized that Boone had a wonderful working relationship with the other pitchers. "I thought Bob was developing into a fine catcher during his rookie season," said Jim Lonborg, the Phillies' number two pitcher and a former Cy Young Award winner himself. "We had a great relationship in terms of communicating with each other. Before games we'd talk about hitters and review scouting reports and were able to incorporate those preliminary discussions into a game plan that worked very smoothly for us."[79]

To be sure, Carlton was in the midst of a nightmarish season in which he would eventually lose 20 games. Bill Conlin, the beat writer for the *Philadelphia Daily News*, exacerbated the pitcher's miseries by lambasting him on the sports pages. "I got into trouble with Carlton because I reported that he wasn't taking care of himself," admitted Conlin, known for his provocative and acerbic prose. "That wasn't done to titillate, or to blow the whistle on him. It was an attempt to explain how a guy who was one of the most dominant pitchers in the majors one year—a guy who compiled a 27-10 record for an absolutely wretched team— could come back the next year and lose 20 games with a better club." Conlin insisted that he "owed [his] readers that much" and that Carlton only had himself to blame for the dismal performance. "It was well known that he spent the winter after the 1972 season on the banquet circuit accepting every major sportswriters' award in the nation," remarked the *Daily News* scribe. "If he resented any implication that he was boozing it out, I can't do anything about that."[80]

Although Carlton rarely read the newspapers, well-meaning teammates fed him stories or quotations, often out of context. When he learned of Conlin's criticism, Lefty snubbed him in postgame interviews. Although he continued to cooperate with the rest of the media for the balance of the season, Carlton kept his remarks brief and delivered them in an almost trancelike state, staring off into the distance, an idiosyncrasy that earned him the nickname "Sphinx of the Schuylkill."[81]

To be sure, Lefty was confused and desperate for help. After being knocked out of a game against St. Louis in late July, he approached his old batterymate Tim McCarver, who had returned to the Cardinals as a backup catcher, and asked him for help. McCarver immediately identified one of the problems. "You're not getting any pop on your fastball," he told Lefty. "It's flat and gliding in because you're dropping your hand and pushing the ball instead of throwing it."[82] Having caught him for so many years, McCarver knew that Carlton's success depended on perfect arm position and delivery. He was surprised, however, that the impetuous rookie who had questioned his judgment nearly a decade earlier was now coming to him for his advice. Carlton had apparently found a catcher he could trust, though they no longer played on the same team. McCarver's advice helped solve the mechanical problem with Lefty's fastball, but the tall the left-hander continued to lose.

Ozark tried to accommodate Carlton by making Mike Ryan his personal catcher. When that didn't seem to work, the Phillies skipper went to a five-man rotation to give him an additional day of rest. If the tall left-hander got into trouble in the late innings of a game, Ozark would lift him for a reliever, even if the Phillies had a lead. But the manager's actions only seemed to make the situation worse. Carlton was convinced that his earlier success was due to pitching every fourth day. Nor did he appreciate being lifted from a game with a lead. He had grown accustomed to completing his own games and working out of late-inning jams. Infuriated by Ozark, Carlton, in September, went to Owens and complained about the manager's treatment of him. Coupled with the fact that the Phillies had fallen into last place —16 games below the .500 mark—and that the fans and press were also carping at Ozark, Carlton's criticism placed the first-year manager's job in jeopardy. Determined to assuage his ace pitcher, Owens went to the press and admitted that Ozark had "failed to develop a line of communication with the players" and that if he did not "establish a better rapport with them" he would "consider making a change."[83] After hearing the ultimatum, Ozark, ever the malapropist, promised Owens that "my repertoire will be better."[84]

Whether or not Carlton was the only player to complain is debatable. That he was unquestionably the franchise player on the team during the early 1970s is not. That fact alone forced Owens to act. Shortly after the season ended, the Phillies general manager, in another move to mollify Carlton, traded Boone, along with rookie pitcher Larry Christenson, to the Detroit Tigers for veteran catcher Bill Freehan and outfielder Jim Northrup. Freehan's best days were already behind him, but he was a veteran catcher whose game-calling was well respected among the pitchers he caught. Owens had already sealed the deal with a handshake, but when Ruly Carpenter learned of the trade the following day, he forced his general manager to cancel the deal.[85] Ruly wasn't about to part with two prized rookies when he had already committed to building on the strength of a very talented farm system. Owens—and Carlton, for that matter—would have to live with that commitment. As for Ozark, Ruly was just as loyal to him. He strongly believed that Ozark was the right manager for his young team. The former Dodgers coach had the background, knowledge, and temperament to cultivate a budding contender. Nor did Ruly appreciate his general manager's disparaging comments about Ozark in the press and told him so.[86]

"We were lucky to have a manager like Danny Ozark," said Larry Christenson, echoing Carpenter's sentiments. "He let us play the game without constantly interfering, and he took a lot of heat for it, too. But you'd never hear him blast a player in the press. Sure, he'd take the ball from a pitcher who was getting hit hard and none of us liked it. That's the emotional make-up of a starting pitcher. But Carlton took it to extremes. He didn't listen to anybody at that time. Lefty was his own man. He didn't realize how fortunate he was to have Danny and not some other manager telling him what he needed to do."[87]

Despite problems with Carlton, Ozark did a commendable job in his first year. Under his leadership, the Phillies showed clear signs of improvement in 1973. With a record of 71-91 the team improved by 12 victories over the previous year and were in a tight pennant race until early September when they faded to last place. The pitching was solid. Lonborg, Brett, and rookie Wayne Twitchell each won 13 games. Dick Ruthven, a spot starter signed in the January 1973 amateur draft, went 6-9 with 98 strikeouts, demonstrating that he could compete at the big league level. Had Carlton not slipped to 13-20, the Phils might have been in contention for a division title.

Most of the offensive power was supplied by Greg Luzinski (.285, 29 HR, 97 RBI) and Bill Robinson (.288, 25 HR, 65 RBI). Montanez's production dropped off (11 HR, 65 RBI), but he still hit a respectable .263 and played well defensively at first base. Schmidt contributed 18 home runs and 52 RBIs in his rookie season, though he also struck out an alarming 136 times in 367 at bats. Del Unser, the new center fielder, hit .289 and played solid defense, and Boone performed admirably behind the plate for a rookie, while also hitting .261 and contributing 61 RBI. By all indications, the Phillies were headed in the right direction. The fans recognized that fact, too, as the Vet set a new attendance record of 1,475,934, 132,000 more than the previous season when Carlton was the main attraction.[88] Lefty, once the franchise player, would have to share the spotlight with his younger teammates in the future.

CHAPTER 5

"YES WE CAN"

W HILE MANAGER DANNY OZARK guided the young Phillies on the playing field, Paul Owens worked behind the scenes to secure the talent
necessary to contend. Owens's vision, more than any other single factor, paved the way for the organization's success during the mid to late 1970s.
Fiercely independent, the Phils general manager never paid much attention to
the naysayers. They told him that no bona fide star would agree to play for the
Phillies because of the inglorious history of the club, the city's mean-spirited
press, and the impossible expectations of the fans. Even if the Phils general manager was able to persuade an impact player like Tug McGraw or Pete Rose to come
to Philadelphia, he would be, according to the argument, unable to do it without
dismantling the young nucleus of his club.[1] To his credit, Owens never listened.

Before free agency was established in 1975, there were only two ways to build
a contender: a club either developed the talent within its own farm system or
traded for it. Both methods involved natural risks. To rely strictly on the farm
system could be a painfully slow process. It took patience to make a long-range
commitment, a quality that is usually not shared by the fans. Trading for talent,
on the other hand, was difficult because no organization is willing to give up a
quality player without receiving one in return. Gambling with another club's castoffs—injured or aging players—is even more dangerous because there are no
guarantees of success. But Owens succeeded by blending both methods more
effectively than any other general manager in major league baseball during the
1970s. Among the first steps he took was to hire Dallas Green and Howie Bedell
to develop the organization's farm system.

Owens first met Green in 1956 when he was a twenty-one-year-old pitching
prospect out of the University of Delaware. "I liked his make-up right away," said

84

Owens. "He was a very personable guy. Tough. No-nonsense. He was a competitor, and he was the same all the time. He didn't change his personality when he had to talk to the manager or a coach." What's more, Owens recognized that Green shared his own unwavering loyalty to the organization. "If you didn't love the Phillies 110 percent, Dallas didn't want to have anything to do with you," he explained. "And that was a lot like me."[2] Three years later, in April 1959, while pitching for Buffalo, Green's arm gave out, but he refused to quit. He made it on to the Phillies roster in 1960, only to be used sparingly by manager Gene Mauch. Then, in July 1964, when Mauch was struggling to keep his young team in first place, Green was knocked out of a game against the St. Louis Cardinals. Afterward, the Little General, infamous for making snap judgments, told the tall right-hander that he was being sent down to Triple-A Little Rock. "It was really a blow," Green admitted years later. "My dad was dying of cancer at the time. When he heard that I was being sent down, he just gave up. He died two weeks later. I still think that's what killed him."[3] Released by the Phillies at the end of the '64 campaign, Green pitched three more years with the Senators and Mets and, again, with the Phillies, before retiring. He rejoined the Phillies as a minor league manager, first at Huron, New York, in 1968 and then at Pulaski, Virginia, the following year. But Green was ambitious and set his sights on a front office job and Owens cultivated him.

In 1970, the Pope, then the Phillies farm director, made Green his assistant. Two years later, when Owens was hired as the Phillies general manager, he immediately promoted Green to director of the minor leagues and scouting.[4] "Pope was my mentor," Green admitted. "He played a very special role in my life. There is no question about that. Among the many things he taught me was that the best hire you make is the guy who can take your job because you know you're getting a quality guy. And I don't know of many farm directors or general managers who'd tell you that because they'd be worried about their own job. Not Paul. He was more concerned about building a winner and he knew that it would take quality people to do it."[5]

Green was a taskmaster. He could drink and curse with the best in the front office and wasn't afraid to speak his mind or make the scouts accountable to the organization. Once, in his early years as farm director, Green, angered by the poor quality of recently signed players, weeded out his scouts by having them attend a workout. Each of the players was wearing a jersey with the last name of the scout who signed him on his back. Whenever that player made a mental or physical mistake on the field, Green confronted the scout who signed him. By the end of the workout, most of the players were released and the scouts who signed them, fired.[6] After that, Green himself scrutinized the signing of prospective talent, by employing a "free-for-all" approach. He would gather all of the organization's scouts into a large room, shut the door, and referee the fisticuffs that would invariably result when the competition for bonus dollars became heated.[7] Outside the organization there were rumors that the Carpenter family could afford to sign the best prospects because they spent lavishly on bonuses and created top-of-the-line facilities to develop the organization's talent. It wasn't true. Bob and Ruly Carpenter spent their money carefully, relying more on the personnel they hired to identify and develop the organization's young talent.[8] Green's efforts were instrumental in that success. He had a special knack for identifying and securing exceptional talent in the June amateur draft. Among those he drafted were ten prospects who would later make significant contributions to the 1980 world championship team: pitchers Warren Brusstar, Larry Christenson, Randy Lerch, Dickie Noles, Dick Ruthven, Kevin Saucier, and Bob Walk; catcher Keith Moreland; and outfielders Lonnie Smith and George Vukovich. In addition, Green drafted infielder Ryne Sandberg, who would go on to forge a Hall of Fame career with the Chicago Cubs.

FIGURE 13. Dallas Green and Howie Bedell ran the Phillies minor league system in the mid-1970s. Green was chiefly responsible for scouting. Courtesy of the *Philadelphia Daily News*.

When Howie Bedell became Green's assistant in 1974, the Phillies farm system boasted some of the finest young talent in the major leagues (see Figures 13 and 14). But no two personalities could have been more different. Bedell, who played in the Milwaukee Braves organization in the 1960s, was more reserved than Green and preferred to work behind the scenes. He also had the reputation of a "straight arrow," actively avoiding the hard lifestyle of the others in the front office. Like Green, however, he quickly attracted the attention of Paul Owens who convinced him to abandon his plans to become a high school teacher for a career in the Phillies farm system. Bedell's first managerial assignment was at Walla Walla, Washington, in the Northern League in 1970. From there, he moved rapidly through the farm system managing at Spartanburg, Peninsula, and then Double-A Reading, where he coached for Jim Bunning.[9]

While Bedell was a "no-nonsense" manager when he needed to be, he was also a "teacher-coach," who tended to be more diplomatic with his players than

FIGURE 14. Howie Bedell focused on player development. Courtesy of the *Philadelphia Daily News*.

other managers.[10] Once, while managing at Spartanburg, he became so disgusted with the slovenliness of his players that he kept them for two hours after a game to show them how to shower and wear the uniform properly. To register the point, Bedell walked out of his office completely naked and proceeded to take each piece of the uniform and dress himself, from jock strap to cap. "Imagine a naked guy in his late thirties, giving a lesson on how to wear the uniform," he recalled years later, referring to the stunt. "After I finished, I had all the players dress and undress and then I marched them all into the shower and showed them how to bathe. Freddie McNeal, the clubhouse attendant, thought I had lost my mind. But from that time on, they wore the uniform properly and there were never any dirty sanitary socks or uniforms lying around on the floor. And the team used more soap than we had for an entire month before my demonstration."[11]

Despite their differences in personality—or maybe because of them—Bedell and Green formed an effective partnership. From 1974 until he was dismissed by the Phillies in 1980, Bedell was responsible for player contracts, development, and personnel issues, including the assignment of players, managers, and coaches to the various farm clubs in the organization as well as the hiring and firing of managers and coaches. Green, on the other hand, was primarily responsible for the scouting of players and the amateur draft. Both men subscribed to Owens's philosophy of "working together as a single unit to achieve the same goal."[12] As a result, Bedell and Green collaborated on some important innovations that later became commonplace throughout minor league baseball.

"We were the first organization to add a pitching coach to each farm club," said Bedell. "We also added a third coach to compliment the manager's weakness at a given level. If the manager wasn't good at teaching hitting, for example, the third coach would focus on that aspect. Roving instructors for catching and in-fielding were added as well. And we also eliminated the practice of written reports by giving each manager a recording device to report on the progress of each player on a regular basis. All of those innovations were popular inside the organization and quickly caught on elsewhere."[13] Other ideas were more controversial, like limiting the number of innings a starting pitcher would throw at the beginning of the season.

While it was standard procedure to identify the starters, middle relievers, and closers on a pitching staff during the first month of the season, Bedell believed that the Phillies farm clubs weren't able to do justice to all the young hurlers because they weren't given enough opportunity to pitch in different parts of a game. As a result, he directed his managers to create a five-man rotation, but only allow the starters to throw three or four innings, which was never enough to get the win. At first, the managers cringed at the notion of limiting a potential starter's innings. They believed that the more experience a starter gained in the early part of the season, the longer—and more effectively—he would pitch later in the season. Bedell, however, felt that the middle relievers in particular were getting cheated of innings and that their role would become increasingly important as the game evolved. "If you limited the starter to three or four innings in the first thirty days of a season," he reasoned, "you would soon find out which of the eleven or twelve pitchers on your staff were best suited to the role of a middle reliever. It wasn't a very popular idea, but in 1977 the pitching staff and Peninsula won some 100 games and took the Class A pennant because they were able to make effective use of their middle relief corps. That's how we identified Kevin Saucier and Dickie Noles as middle relievers, the very same role they would later assume on the 1980 Phillies team that won the World Series."[14]

Owens gave Green and Bedell a tremendous amount of responsibility, but he also made sure they were accountable to the organization. Accordingly, he employed some of his veteran scouts, former career minor leaguers and longtime advisers, to serve as his "eyes and ears." Hughie Alexander and Lou Kahn fulfilled these roles for the Pope. "These guys were throwbacks from the 1930s," recalled Bedell. "We called Alexander 'Uncle Hughie' because he was a colorful character who was always around watching the players and the coaches. Lou was more gruff. He'd sit around in his lounge chair, heavily hung over, chewing tobacco and spitting all over himself. But he knew his baseball. If there was a negative, he'd find it. If there was a positive, he wouldn't talk about it. I just had to assume that things were going well. Both of these scouts were mouthpieces for Paul when he couldn't be around. They'd report back to him at night and I knew that. I was called on the carpet a few times because of it, but as long as they reported honestly, I had no problem with it."[15]

While Green and Bedell identified and developed prospective major leaguers, they relied on Ruben Amaro to scout and provide them with Latin American talent. Amaro was a teammate of Green's on the Phillies in the early 1960s. Although he did not have a strong bat, he was outstanding defensively at shortstop. He also had a knack for teaching the game. After his eleven-year career in the majors ended in 1969, Owens enlisted the personable Mexican to scout the winter leagues in Latin America, where he had played and managed. "Paul Owens wanted to create a new position," Amaro recalled in a recent interview. "He wanted to make me the coordinator of the Phillies' Latin American program. The idea interested me, so I took a swing at it. I went down to Puerto Rico and Venezuela with Hughie Alexander, the Phillies advance scout, and examined the possibility."[16] Amaro was displeased by what he saw. The Phillies were paying their Latin American scouts a fraction of what their scouts in the United States were making. Nor did the Latin American scouts enjoy the same bonus money to sign players, or reimbursement for their traveling expenses. "Look," Amaro told Dallas Green when he returned to Philadelphia. "If you're only going to pay the Latino scouts $250, you're only going to get players that are worth $250. If I'm going to be in charge of the Latin American situation, my budget must be much greater than what it is now and my scouts have to be treated better than they are now."[17] Owens and Green agreed, realizing that the Latin American market was rich with prospects and held possibly the largest pool of future major leaguers.

The Dodgers, Giants, Reds, and Cardinals had already committed significant financial resources to Latin American programs and were beginning to reap the rewards. But the Pittsburgh Pirates surpassed all major league clubs with the success of its Latin American players. Featuring such stellar performers as Roberto Clemente, Manny Sanguillen, and Jose Pagan in the 1950s and '60s, the Pirates went on to become a perennial contender in the early 1970s, defeating a heavily favored Baltimore Orioles club for the 1971 world championship.[18]

Having secured a firm commitment from Owens and Green, Amaro began to plot his strategy. He targeted players in the largest Latin American markets— Puerto Rican, Venezuela, and the Dominican Republic—but also sent his scouts to Panama and Colombia. Mexican players would be the easiest for him to sign because of his family's connections there. Both he and his father had competed in the Mexican leagues and were well respected in their native land. Although he only had four scouts for all those areas, he gave them all cars, raised their salaries to $10,000 each, and paid their traveling expenses. Amaro also established a working relationship with ball clubs in Puerto Rico and Venezuela to field young Phillies players in the winter league. As a result, the organization's best prospects played winter ball there from 1972 on, including Mike Schmidt, Bob Boone, Dick Ruthven, Larry Christenson, Bobby Dernier, and Ryne Sandberg.[19]

"Ruben was the Phillies connection to the Lain American market," said Bedell. "Without his efforts we wouldn't have been able to sign any quality player from those countries. He had a great rapport with them and we benefited from it. We were able to sign future big league stars like Julio Franco, George Bell, and Juan Samuel, thanks to Ruben."[20] Amaro was more humble in discussing his success. "It really was a learning experience," he admitted. "Sure, we signed some good players, but we also had some disappointments, like Jorge Lebron, a thirteen-year-old infielder who had fantastic skills but wasn't mature enough to play away from home. He was washed up by the age of sixteen. The reason we were successful was because of Francisco 'Quique' Acevedo, a scout and part owner of a Dominican ball club. He scouted from his heart and he really knew about the players. Whenever I went down there he took me all over and introduced me to some unbelievable players. At the same time, I told him, 'I'm here to protect the interests and financial resources of the Carpenter family. If you steal so much as five cents of that money, you're stealing from me.' He understood that and we got along quite well."[21]

Like Owens, Amaro, Green, and Bedell were critical to Ruly Carpenter's vision of the "Phillies family," an organization based on unconditional loyalty to all its members regardless of their place in the club hierarchy. "It didn't matter if you were in the front office, on the playing field, or the grounds crew, everyone mattered," said Mark Carfagno, who worked on the team's grounds crew from 1971 to 2002. "That was Ruly's goal and he set the example for everyone else. This was a rich guy with a degree from Yale, but it didn't stop him from sitting down with us and watching games from the tunnel in back of home plate. We were the 'little guys' in the organization, but he would sit and joke with us like he was one of the gang. Paul Owens was the same way. He made it a point to know us. Every day he'd come into the Mud Room where we kept the equipment and ask about our day, tell a joke, or just sit down and talk with us. It made you feel like a million bucks."[22]

Owens made sure to remember everyone who worked for the Phillies. He lived at the ballpark when the team was playing at home and in the off-season. He seemed to genuinely care about the concession workers, electricians, clubhouse attendants, security guards, and mechanics as much as the players. The Pope realized that "everyone in the organization had to take pride in it if the team was ever to become successful" and that an "occasional pat on the back" or a "simple gesture of appreciation" went a long way.[23] Unlike other general managers who preferred to stay in the office and work the telephones, the Pope spent most of his time with the team. When the Phillies were on the road, so was he. "I can learn more about a player during one road trip than I can watching him play an entire home schedule," he explained. "I can find out about his eating habits, what he does in his spare time, how he handles himself with the fans in a hotel lobby, things that might seem inconsequential when it comes to getting a clutch base hit or striking out a batter with the game on the line. But they all mean something to me because I'm able to spot something about him that might otherwise go undetected."[24] Owens paid just as much attention to the players on opposing teams, hoping to fill the voids in the lineup. Talent was not the only consideration either. Those players had to be quality human beings able to fit into the "Phillies family."

After the '73 season, Owens saw that the Phils needed a veteran presence in the lineup to give his young club the leadership it lacked. Carlton provided that leadership every fourth day when he took the mound, but he couldn't do it on a daily basis. Owens solved the problem by acquiring Dave Cash from the Pittsburgh Pirates for pitcher Ken Brett. Brett, who was coming off a 13-win season, was a fan favorite. But the Phils general manager was willing to part with him to secure Cash, a bona fide leadoff hitter.[25] A scrappy veteran second baseman with Pittsburgh, Cash, at the young age of twenty-five, knew what it was like to win. Signed by the Pirates in 1969, he took over second base from Bill Mazeroski two years later and became an instrumental player on a team that captured three division titles and a world championship. His experience, enthusiasm, and aggressive play were just what the young Phillies needed. "I like Cash because he's a team leader," admitted Owens. "I know he'll pass some of that along to our guys. I also feel that with Larry Bowa, who we think is one of the finest fielding shortstops in baseball, Willie Montanez at first and Mike Schmidt at third, our infield will be one of the best in baseball for years to come."[26]

Cash made an immediate impact, providing a steadying influence in the infield and giving the team the confidence they needed to win (Figure 15). During spring training the veteran second baseman quickly bonded with his new teammates on and off the field. A regular at the dog track, Cash told Bowa that he had a tip on a dog named "Jiff Jones," and the shortstop wanted in on the bet. So did pitchers Steve Carlton and Jim Lonborg. When Cash returned from the races, they asked him if they'd won anything and the Phillies second baseman exclaimed: "Yes we did!" Afterwards, other teammates picked up the catchy slogan. If someone was asked, "Can you hit this pitcher?" or "Can you beat this team?" The answer was always, "Yes we can!" Shortly after the season opened, Cash made a brilliant defensive play against the St. Louis Cardinals and screamed, "Yes we can!" Bowa, bewildered by the remark, asked, "Who you talkin' to, man?" Without missing a beat, Cash replied: "Anyone who'll listen."[27] Apparently, Mike Schmidt was listening.

On opening day at Veterans Stadium against the New York Mets, the Phillies found themselves trailing 4-3 in the ninth with one out and a runner on first

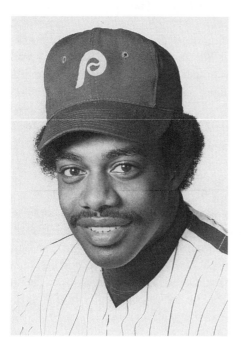

FIGURE 15. Veteran second baseman Dave Cash provided a young Phillies team with inspirational leadership and the rally cry, "Yes We Can." Courtesy of the National Baseball Hall of Fame Library, Cooperstown, New York.

base. Schmidt came to bat facing reliever Tug McGraw and homered to left field to win the game, 5-4.[28] That at bat seemed to set the tone for Schmidt's entire season. His most impressive display of power came in a June 10th at bat in Houston's Astrodome. In the first inning, Cash, the leadoff hitter, walked and Bowa followed with a single. Schmidt, hitting out of the third slot, jumped on a Claude Osteen fastball, hitting it so high and so hard that the Astros center fielder, César Cedeño, retreated to the wall just to see how far it would sail. But after soaring 340 feet in the air, the ball crashed into a public-address speaker 110 feet above straightaway center field. It dropped straight down, landing about 325 feet from the plate. Had the speaker not been there, the Astrodome's engineers estimated that Schmidt would have had himself a home run measuring anywhere from 500 to 600 feet. Instead, he had a ground rule single, since the speaker, as a fixed object, is in fair territory. Just to prevent a repeat occurrence, the Astros raised the speaker to 173 feet after the game, a 12-0 Phillies victory.[29]

"I knew the ball was going out," admitted Cedeño after the game, "but I continued running because I wanted to see how far it would go. I know one thing—it was over everything. I never saw a ball hit so hard in my life. I've seen some real line shots by Richie Allen and guys like that, but nothing like this."[30] Schmidt was just as amazed. "I knew it was a good hit," he said, "but the ball doesn't carry well in the Astrodome so I didn't know how far it was going. Running to first base, I realized it hit something up there. I didn't know what, but something. It all happened so fast, I really wasn't sure of the ground rule. What can pop into your mind at a time like that? But after the umpire held me at first base, I realized the ball had hit the speaker and that it cost me a home run. I'd like to have seen it go all the way, just to see how far it would've gone."[31]

By mid-June the Phils found themselves in unfamiliar territory being alone in first place. The pitching staff was the most dominant in the National League's Eastern division. Carlton had already collected 69 strikeouts and was sporting a 3.00 ERA. Ruthven (44 K, 3.10 ERA) and Ron Schueler (39 K, 3.22 ERA) weren't far behind, and Lonborg posted his 100th major league victory. Schmidt was hitting at a .310 clip and crushing the ball with 14 homers and 46 RBIs. Cash seemed to be at the center of the success, inspiring his teammates in the clubhouse and on the playing field. Offensively, he exceeded all expectations, hitting safely in 40 of 49 games, collecting 61 hits from the leadoff slot for a .302 average while striking out just 11 times in 202 at bats.[32]

"I've always thought of myself as a guy who starts something," he said of his quick start. "You have to be that way to be a leadoff hitter." But there was more to his example than his offensive exploits or defensive play. Cash had played with future Hall of Famers in Pittsburgh, individuals like Roberto Clemente, Willie Stargell and Bill Mazeroski. He recognized genuine talent when he saw it. "When I got here, I watched everyone for a while and then said, 'You guys don't know how damn good you are,'" he explained. "There are players on this team as good as any in the league, but they're never recognized. No one pays attention when you finish in last place. In spring training they started making comparisons with other players on other clubs and they started to realize, 'Hey, I'm better than he is.' They started believing in themselves."[33]

Shortstop Larry Bowa benefited most by Cash's inspirational example. "Dave has been a big influence on me," he admitted. "Last year, I'd go 0 for 4 and that would be on my mind the next day, worrying me that I'd go 0 for 8, then 0 for 12. Dave pointed out that if you give 100 percent you have to be satisfied and forget it. Just start from scratch again the next day. That's how I've tried to keep my attitude this year. My mind is more at ease." Cash also reminded Bowa constantly of just how talented he was. It meant a lot to the fiery shortstop who felt that he had been overlooked by fans and opposing managers for All-Star honors. "But I don't feel that way now," he admitted. "Dave tells me that I'm the best he's ever seen. I don't know if he's blowing smoke or not, but I'm starting to believe it myself."[34]

Bowa, in many respects, had been his own worst enemy. Until Cash arrived, his success was based on negative motivation. Tell him that he "can't do something" and he'd give his all to prove that he can. He worked three to four times harder than anyone else, because he harbored his own self-doubt that he didn't measure up. Accordingly, if an umpire made a call against him, Bowa would allow his nasty temper to take over, erupting into a fusillade of profanity or throwing a childish tantrum in front of the crowd. It was as if the umpire had robbed him of all the hard work he had invested in making the play and he certainly wouldn't stand for that. "I tried to convince Larry that he could help the team more on the field than in the clubhouse after getting tossed out," Cash said of his influence on the twenty-eight-year-old shortstop. "I'd tell him, 'You have to calm down. Just because an umpire makes a bad call doesn't mean he's going to change it. That call stands no matter how much ranting and raving you do. The only thing that's going to happen is that you're going to hurt the club if you get tossed out of the game.' I think it registered with Larry because in 1975 he was thrown out of only three or four games, a big difference from '74.[35]

Cash and Bowa were inseparable on and off the field. They even made a record together titled, "Ting-a-ling, Double Play." Released by Molly Records of Philadelphia, the 45 rpm record was a corny little song with a catchy chorus that went: "Ting-a-ling is what the people say when everybody wants to see that double play; Tingle-a-ling will be the only way that Larry and Dave can put the side away." A tone-deaf Bowa would then "sing": "Here comes that grounder I can get it to Dave." Cash, who wasn't much better, followed: "I tag the bag, throw to first, the game has been saved!" Then, together: "Let's hear a ting-a-ling and you can do your thing so we can put the side away."[36] Played on radio stations throughout the Delaware Valley, the record stirred up greater interest in a team that Philadelphians had largely ignored in the previous decade.

Cash also had a strong impact on Mike Schmidt, the Phillies' second-year third baseman. "When I came to the Phillies in 1974, Mike had all the tools but he didn't have the confidence," recalled Cash. "He was a real sensitive guy who constantly doubted himself. There were some guys on the team that directed a lot of negative stuff towards him and the fans rode him pretty hard, too. I just tried to be as positive as I could with him. I told him, 'You got a chance to be one of the best players in the game. You got all the talent. You're a good hitter. You got power. You got an above average throwing arm, and you run pretty well. You got five tools that other guys dream about having.' I guess I said it enough times that it finally sunk in."[37]

Cash's encouragement let Schmidt ease up on himself, allowing his natural abilities to take over. Together with the "homer that wasn't" in Houston's Astrodome, Schmidt's remarkable power-hitting captured national attention, provoking a write-in campaign to get the twenty-four-year-old third baseman elected to the National League's All-Star squad. Because he had such a dismal rookie season, Schmidt's name didn't appear on the ballot. But with the aid of a write-in campaign conducted by Howard Eskin, a young intern at a Philadelphia radio station, and the Phillies who hired a helicopter to airlift 100,000 votes to All-Star headquarters to beat the election deadline, Schmidt finished second to the Dodgers' Ron Cey. National League manager Yogi Berra of the Mets eventually picked the power-hitting third baseman for the squad, adding: "The guy is having a fantastic year. And besides, I don't want to get shot next time I go to Philly."[38]

Schmidt joined Carlton, Bowa, and Cash as the Phillies' representatives to the All-Star game, which was played in Pittsburgh that year. More important, his election to the team gave him confidence that he could compete with the very best in the major leagues. Schmidt finished the '74 campaign with a league-leading 36 homers, 116 RBI and a .282 average, 86 points higher than in his rookie season. Other Phillies demonstrated significant improvement as well.

Cash led the National League in at bats with 687 and hitting .300. Inspired by the second baseman's example, Bowa raised his batting average to .275—64 points higher than his average of the previous season. Montanez returned to the .300 mark. Boone proved to be more than adequate behind the plate and handled a respectable pitching staff with the savvy of a seasoned veteran. The pitching improved as well. Lonborg led the staff in victories with 17, Carlton chalked up 16 wins, Ron Schueler who joined the Phils from Atlanta, added another 11 victories, and Dick Ruthven contributed an additional 9. With those kinds of numbers, the Phillies led their division through most of the summer only to fall behind Pittsburgh in late August. Still, they finished the season in third place, only 8 games out. It was the first time the team finished out of the cellar since

1971, and the first time they finished higher than fifth place since 1969 when the National League was reorganized into eastern and western divisions.[39]

When asked to explain his change in fortune from a dismal rookie year, Schmidt replied: "I guess I just learned to relax. Last year I was in and out of the lineup and when I was in I probably tried too hard to do well because I was wondering if I'd be in the next day. I wanted to relax last season, but I couldn't. I was as tight as a drum. This year, when I go to the plate, I'd say 70 to 80 percent of the time, I'm at ease just looking to hit the ball hard somewhere. When you come up to the plate that way, your natural instincts take over."[40]

Schmidt also acknowledged the tremendous impact that Cash and outfielder Bill Robinson had on his own attitude. "Before those guys came to the Phillies it wasn't too much fun to come to the ballpark," he admitted. "Robbie had a lot to do with the early success in my career. He was one of the first guys who gave me a lot of confidence by telling me that I was a good player and that I was going to be successful some day. Dave Cash also helped me in terms of having a good, positive attitude around the clubhouse. He always seemed to say the right things to me. That was a big difference from guys like Bowa, Luzinski, and Montanez who were ragging on me all the time, kidding me about striking out. There was a bit of jealousy there and I saw it as mean-spirited, no question. I found a solace from the black players who, for some reason, took a liking to me. There was just a sensitivity there that I felt very comfortable with."[41]

Philadelphia's sportswriters and even members of the Phillies front office have, over the years, emphasized the jealousy that existed among the homegrown nucleus of Schmidt, Bowa, Luzinski, and Boone. According to the argument, none of these players would allow each other to assume a leadership role on the club because they were all about the same age and constantly competed with each other for the limelight. They point to the ongoing competition to explain why Pete Rose's signing in 1978 was essential to the team's ultimate success of winning a world championship. While there is much merit to that argument, Owens's earlier efforts to secure the veteran leadership necessary to win a world championship are often overlooked. Dave Cash was the first of many veteran players who filled that need and were successful enough to get the Phillies to the National League playoffs for three straight years between 1976 and 1978. There is also some question as to how much resentment actually existed between Schmidt, Bowa, Luzinski, and Boone.

Luzinski and Boone, for example, were close friends and roommates who came up together through the Phillies farm system. Bowa also counted the Bull among his closest friends on the Phillies. And Luzinski insists that there was nothing more than a "friendly competition between all of us."[42] Boone agreed, calling the "personal jealousy" and "lack of leadership" among the members of the homegrown nucleus "a lot of folklore." He dismisses the notion that the Phillies teams of the 1970s lacked leadership. "Good teams, like ours, weren't looking for a leader, it just happened," insists Boone. "There wasn't one guy. In our case everybody led. Everyone thought Bowa led in those early years because he was so fiery. We all just laughed at Bowa. We were pros. We knew what we had to do to win. Early on we got our butts beat, but Pope kept on adding the players we needed to win a championship and by 1980 those pieces were all in place."[43]

Perhaps Boone didn't see any competition or jealousy, but there certainly was some understandable resentment toward the enormously talented Schmidt, especially among the young power hitters on the team. Montanez was twenty-six years old, Luzinski was only twenty-three, and Schmidt was twenty-four. All were about the same age. All of them had tremendous offensive potential but had only begun to tap into it. Montanez enjoyed an outstanding '71 season, hitting 30 home runs and driving in 99 runs, a performance that earned him a second-place finish in the balloting for Rookie of the Year that season. His flamboyant play in the field and the almost casual manner in which he walked up to the plate, flipping the bat in one hand from handle to barrel, made him popular with the fans who dubbed him, "Willie the Phillie." By '74, however, Montanez's home run production had slipped to 7 and Schmidt's success only added to the pressure he was already feeling to produce.[44]

Luzinski, the Phillies' No. 1 pick in the 1968 June free agent draft, also enjoyed an impressive rookie season in 1972, collecting 18 home runs, 68 RBIs, and a .281 average. The following season he established himself as one of the top power hitters in the game by clouting 29 homers, driving in 97 runs, and compiling a .285 average. Big things were predicted for the "Bull" in 1974. He was being compared to some of the premier power hitters in the game like Dick Allen, Willie Stargell, and Johnny Bench. At 6' 1" and 225 pounds, he was built like a defensive lineman, leading the prognosticators to believe that a 50-homer season was well within his reach. But Luzinski battled a weight problem and in 1974 that problem landed him on the disabled list for most of the season when he tore a ligament in his right knee.[45] Schmidt's bat filled the offensive void left by Luzinski in the lineup that season and his 36 homers, 116 RBI and a .282 average were better than the numbers the Bull had produced in the past and Luzinski knew it. When asked recently about his relationship with Schmidt, the Bull admitted that the two power hitters "weren't the best of friends," but that they "got along fine." "I think the press tried to make more out of Mike hitting third and me hitting fourth than there was," he added. "If my hitting behind him helped him see some better pitches, that's great. That's what I was there for. But Schmitty still had to hit the ball and he helped us win a lot of games."[46]

Bowa's relationship with Schmidt was more complicated. The fiery little shortstop worked hard, toiling in the Phillies farm system for four years before making it to the majors in 1970. When the Phillies made Schmidt their number two selection in the June 1971 draft, they had planned to make him their future short-stop. Word got back to Bowa. "Right away, I've got a chip on my shoulder," he admitted years later. When they flew Schmidt to Philadelphia to work out with the big league club, Bowa was seething with anger. "I said, 'Screw this guy, Mike Schmidt.' Who does he think he is, some big deal? He's a college kid. Everything's cool with him. He takes ground balls with me at the Vet and after he worked out they sent him to Reading—double A—and he tore it up. I remember a comment he made, something like, 'I plan on playing shortstop in Philadelphia.' And my reply was, 'Not as long as I'm here!' So I kept working and the more I read about Mike Schmidt, the harder I worked. You know the rest of it . . . he ended up play-ing third base!"[47]

Predictably, Schmidt viewed Bowa as a hard-nosed competitor who tended to place individual success above team success in their early years together. "Larry was always quick to criticize other peoples' work habits," he recalled. "[When] he first came into the [Phillies] organization it was really hurting. He was forced into the big leagues and had to learn to play at that level. Whatever he lacked in ability he made up for in desire and hard work." According to Schmidt, Bowa was consumed by the game and always seemed to feel that he should get more out of it because he put more into it than many other players. "I probably put a hell of a lot more work into playing the game later in my career than I did in my first four or five years because I started setting standards as a player that couldn't be kept up without that kind of work ethic. Still, I don't think I've ever had the kind of work habits that Bowa had. He got the most of the talent he had and, to his credit, he became a .300 hitter."[48]

To be sure, Schmidt and Bowa were two very different personalities who, ini-tially, were competing for the same position. Bowa was scrappy, aggressive, and competitive to the point of being ruthless at times. He was not naturally gifted, having to work for everything he got in terms of his fielding and hitting. Even then, his style wasn't too pretty. He simply got the job done, both offensively and defensively. Schmidt, on the other hand, was a naturally gifted athlete who made the hard plays look easy, almost graceful in his execution. He spent only two years in the minor leagues and though he struggled with his hitting, his bat was always very capable of spelling the margin of victory in a game. Although Schmidt was every bit as intense as Bowa, he tended to internalize those feelings. That's what irked Bowa the most about him. "I knew that it was killing him inside when he was in a slump," said the fiery, little infielder. "I'd ask him, 'Why don't you show some emotion? Hit something. Go mad. Go berserk!'"[49] Schmidt didn't appre-ciate it either.

"Larry was a great clubhouse needler, but he didn't have great timing," said Schmidt. "There were times when he didn't needle people and I think he should have. There were times when he needled me that I thought it would be best to lay off. One time, I got so angry in a clubhouse in Houston that I almost wanted to kill him. I probably would have if there weren't four other players there to separate us."[50]

Bowa admits that he probably set new standards when it came to riding teammates: "Oh yeah, I did a good job. I'd get on players. But I'd know who to get on. I got on Luzinski a lot more than I ever got on Schmidt. But Greg knew me. We were close friends. He also took a lot of crap from the fans and, in my opinion, not deservedly so. I thought that he was a much better clutch hitter than Schmidt in those early years. Back then, Bull would come up when we were behind and hit one out. Schmitty would always hit his homers when the score was 7-1, 7-2."[51]

Schmidt and Bowa gave each other respect only begrudgingly during their early years together. It was inevitable. Over the next six years both players matured, proving worthy of the other's respect. Winning had a way of mending their personal conflict, and the Phillies would become perennial winners. Paul Owens made sure of that by acquiring the veteran talent to fill the club's needs. After the '74 campaign, Pope was convinced that the team needed a quality closer to contend.

On December 3, 1974, Owens acquired relief pitcher Tug McGraw and outfielders Don Hahn and Dave Schneck from the New York Mets for center fielder Del Unser, reliever Mac Scarce, and John Stearns, a promising young catcher. McGraw, age thirty, was the key to the deal for the Phillies.[52] The comic left hander had been one of the game's premier relievers until arm troubles limited his pitching to a 6-11 record and just 3 saves in '74. McGraw was largely credited for the Mets' pennant the previous year when his 25 saves allowed the team to rebound from last place in July to capture the Eastern Division in the final week of the season.[53] But New York thought that McGraw's best days were behind him.[54] Only Baltimore and Boston of the American League and Philadelphia expressed any interest in him.[55] When he learned that he was going to the Phillies, McGraw called it a "Jack Daniels' trade," assuming that Owens and Mets general manager Joe McDonald made the deal over a bottle of whiskey at the winter meetings in New Orleans. "How else do you explain the Mets trading me to a division rival?" he quipped. "No one in their right mind does that!"[56]

Not everyone was happy with the deal, though. "I was pissed off," admitted Dallas Green, who projected John Stearns to be the Phillies' future catcher. "Pope had to fight like hell to sell me on that one. I didn't want to see him part with our top catching prospect for a guy who battled arm troubles all last season."[57] Owens realized that he was taking a chance, but he also knew that the Phillies wouldn't finish any higher in the standings "until we straightened out the bullpen."[58] Nor was McGraw very happy with the trade. "It really hurt me at the time," he admitted. "I'd been with the Mets from the start and thought I'd always be a

Met. They were my baseball family. I'd had a taste of the spotlight in New York, and I loved it. I didn't want to leave."[59]

To be sure, McGraw had flourished in New York, where he was regarded by many fans as "the heart and soul of the Mets," if not a folk hero.[60] A self-proclaimed "flake," the comic reliever had come to the Big Apple from Vallejo, California. Born August 30, 1944, Frank Edwin McGraw, Jr., came from a dysfunctional family. His mother gave him the name "Tugger" because of his aggressive teething while she was nursing him. After his parents divorced, he and his two brothers were raised by their father, a janitor and later a water department plant manager. Their household was more of a fraternity than a home. Tug idolized his older brother, Hank, who signed with the Mets as a catcher immediately after high school. Though his professional baseball career never amounted to much—in part because of his rebellious nature—Hank helped his younger brother get his first contract by threatening to quit the Mets organization if they didn't sign him.

Tug was only 5' 9" and 160 pounds when he signed with New York in the summer of 1964. He threw a fastball, curve, and a mediocre changeup and split his initial season between Cocoa Beach, Florida, and Auburn, New York. The following spring he was promoted to the Mets where he posted a 2-7 record in 97 innings of work. After the season, McGraw spent six months in the Marine Corps training as a guerrilla fighter in the event that he was called to serve in Vietnam. Returning to baseball in April 1966, the Mets shipped McGraw to Jacksonville, Florida, where he completed the season. Later that year, in the Florida Instructional League, McGraw learned the pitch that would make him a successful reliever—the screwball. Thrown like a reverse curveball, the "scroogie" sailed inside and dropped on a right-handed batter. It was an extremely difficult pitch to hit because it looked like a curveball as it approached home plate. But just before crossing the plate the screwball dropped sharply, fooling the hitter who had already chased after it. McGraw threw the screwball so effectively that he used it as his "out pitch," the pitch he used when he needed a strikeout.

His breakout season came in 1969 when the "Miracle Mets" overcame a wretched start to upset the Chicago Cubs and clinch the National League pennant as well as the World Series. McGraw was used primarily as a relief pitcher that season, posting a 9-3 record with 12 saves and a 2.24 ERA. Manager Gil Hodges credited him as an "instrumental factor" during the stretch drive. To his dismay, McGraw did not pitch in the '69 World Series. That opportunity would come four years later when the Mets, in another miracle finish, came from last place to win the Eastern Division title and the pennant. Coining the famous phrase "Ya gotta believe!" Tug proved to be indispensable in the Mets' assault on the National League. Though he made five appearances in the World Series, posting a win and a save, the Mets lost to the Oakland A's in 7 games.[61] With that kind of personal history, Mets fans of all ages adored the Tugger and were extremely upset when they learned of his trade to the Phillies.

"Tug McGraw was the heart and soul of the Mets," wrote Philip Zalon of Brooklyn in a letter to the editor of the *New York Times*. "Without him, we have no one left to root for, no one left to love." Sixteen-year-old Liz Jennings of Glen Cove, Long Island, was devastated. "Trading Tug McGraw is like New York without the Empire State Building, or like Christmas without Santa Claus," she lamented. "It's hard to believe that they traded 'You Gotta Believe' and it will be harder to believe without Tug." Stan Glitelman of Plainview, Long Island, cut to the core of fan disappointment when he wrote that McGraw was the "spirit of the Mets" because he "generated excitement" by "leaping off the mound" and "slapping his glove against his thigh" after a big out. He made us "all believe."[62] New York's loss was Philadelphia's gain, though it didn't appear that way when McGraw arrived at Clearwater, Florida, for spring training in February.

Astonished to learn that the Mets said nothing to Owens about his shoulder problems, McGraw explained that he had been experiencing some "sporadic pain in [his] scapula" during the '74 season and that he started taking painkillers to deal with the problem. When he asked the Mets to "find out what was wrong with [him]," they "didn't take a strong interest in it." Instead, they pulled him from the bullpen and made him a starter. It was then that Tug realized he was "trade bait," being "put on display for other teams."[63] When the Phillies sent McGraw to Jefferson Hospital to identify the problem, a mass of tissue was discovered below his left shoulder blade.[64] Although the Phillies might have made a case that the Mets had sent them "damaged goods," Owens insisted that there would be "no effort to negate the deal" since the Phils had been sent McGraw's X-rays and medical reports before the trade and were "satisfied that the reliever was in good health."[65] On March 19, McGraw was operated on by Dr. John Templeton, a thoracic surgeon. A benign mass of tissue, the size of a small walnut, was removed from a back rib.[66] The comic reliever requested that he be allowed have it and placed the fleshy lump into a small jar to show his new teammates.[67] After five weeks of rehab, McGraw was "able to throw freely" and vowed that he would "give the Phillies the closer they're looking for." "Besides," he chuckled, "baseball is mostly between the ears, why should I worry about my arm?"[68]

After watching his teammates in spring training, McGraw became excited about the team's prospects. Tug pointed out that the Phillies were a "young team" with players "who are just reaching their full potential, like the "Miracle Mets of 1969." But he also noted that they were "too serious" and that they "needed a shot of adrenaline." "I figured that my screwball personality was just as much a reason for the trade as my relief pitching," he added. "So I'll provide a little comic relief."[69]

With the addition of McGraw and Gene Garber, promoted from Triple-A

Toledo, the Phillies had a closer and setup man who were among the best in the National League. The rest of the pitching staff was solid. Carlton had signed a new, three-year deal for nearly $500,000, ensuring his role as the team's ace in the future. Lonborg, Ruthven, and Twitchell had already proven their mettle and, if they failed, youngsters Larry Christenson and Tommy Underwood would be given the opportunity to start. Cash, Bowa, Schmidt, and Montanez were finally being recognized around the league as a formidable infield, both offensively and defensively. The outfield was less predictable. Luzinski, in left field, was the only constant as long as he remained free of injuries. Alan Bannister, Mike Anderson, and Bill Robinson would compete for center field. Bannister, a rookie, was an unknown at the major league level. Anderson had had three straight disappointing seasons. His statistical totals for the three-year period averaged .233, 5 home runs, and 22 RBI. The year 1975 would be Anderson's "make-or-break" year. Robinson had performed well in '73 when he hit .288 with 25 home runs, but his production dropped sharply in '74 when he became a utility player. Right field would also be open to competition between Jay Johnstone, who signed as a free agent after his release by the Cardinals and Mike Rogodzinski, a Phillie farm hand with less than 100 at bats at the major league level during the previous two seasons.[70]

Owens still believed he needed another power hitter to take some of the pressure off of Luzinski and Schmidt. Throughout the winter he had explored the possibility of acquiring veteran slugger Rusty Staub of the New York Mets. When Carlton began complaining about Boone's pitch calling two years earlier, the Phillies general manager considered the young backstop expendable. The back troubles Boone experienced during the previous season seemed to reinforce Owens's feeling that the Phillies needed another catcher. He was prepared to deal Boone until manager Danny Ozark insisted on keeping the struggling catcher. "I'm a hard-headed S.O.B.," said Ozark, explaining his decision to retain Boone. "Sometimes I just have these gut feelings. But I've gone with Bobby for two years, and my gut feeling is that I want him as my catcher."[71]

Owens then turned his attentions to Dick Allen, who had informed the Chicago White Sox that he was "retiring" the previous September, but never submitted a written statement. At the baseball winter meetings in New Orleans, the Atlanta Braves gave the White Sox $5,000 for the negotiating rights to Allen, but the enigmatic slugger informed the Braves that he "would never agree to play in the South again after the horrific experience [he] had had in Arkansas as a minor leaguer in the Phillies organization." At the same time, Allen did suggest that he "might be interested in returning to Philadelphia," a remark that shocked the baseball world.[72]

Allen had a controversial career since leaving the Phillies in 1969. He spent single seasons with the St. Louis Cardinals and Los Angeles Dodgers, teams that believed he could make the difference in their lineup. But his enigmatic personality divided the clubhouse. Both organizations gave up on him and traded him off for considerably less talent than he was worth. He landed with the Chicago White Sox in 1972 and put up numbers that earned him the American League MVP that year. Perhaps the change to a new league was the answer. Allen enjoyed three very productive seasons in Chicago before retiring in September of 1974. He returned to his farm in Perkasie, Pennsylvania, intending to pursue his "other passion"—raising thoroughbred horses. But the Phillies believed that Allen still had a lot of baseball left in him. The .302 average and 32 homers he compiled in '74 certainly seemed to reinforce that feeling.

In April, a small contingent of Phillies—Schmidt, Cash, and broadcaster Rich Ashburn—paid the recently retired slugger a visit. "It was a conversation I wouldn't forget," said Allen. "Schmidt was talking about the Phils needing some additional clout, a big stick in the lineup to go with his and Luzinski's. He said something about 'Schmidt-Luzinski-Allen firepower.' Cash was rapping about the brothers on the Phils' team and how they could use a veteran to inspire them. And ol' Richie Ashburn was telling tales about how much the city of Philadelphia had changed for the better. That was as specific as it got, but I got the message: 'Come home, Dick. We love you. They're gonna love you!'

"At first I figured it had to be a joke. It's not my style to return to the scene of the crime. But I had to admit the idea of coming home did fire me up a bit. I always did like surprises—even when the surprises were on me. When they left the farm that day, I hugged them all. I was touched to feel wanted by guys who played for the Phillies."[73]

That visit was followed by another from Ashburn and Hall of Famer Robin Roberts. Again, the Phillies attempted to reconcile with their one-time Rookie of the Year. "No specific requests were made and no promises given," insists Allen.[74] A few days later, the *Philadelphia Inquirer* reported that Commissioner Bowie Kuhn was investigating the Phillies for tampering with the retired slugger. In the meantime, Ozark, who was the Dodgers' third base coach when Allen played for Los Angeles, openly expressed his reservations about managing the controversial slugger. "I want to win badly," he told the *Philadelphia Inquirer*. "But there would have to be a lot of sacrifices made by me and the players on this club if we got Richie Allen. We'd have to shut our eyes to a lot of things."[75] The Allen drama would play out over the course of the spring.

The Phillies opened the '75 season against the Mets at New York's Shea Stadium. It was a pitcher's dual that pitted Steve Carlton against Tom Seaver, two of the best hurlers in the game. Despite an impressive performance in spring training, Lefty struggled with his control during the early innings of the game. In the fourth, he worked a 0-2 count on slugger Dave Kingman and then tried to get him to chase a slider outside. But the pitch didn't break, sailing over the middle of the plate, and Kingman smashed a 400-foot home run to dead center. For the next four innings both pitchers were unhittable, the score deadlocked at 1-1. Carlton lost the game in the ninth inning, though, when second baseman Felix Millán singled to right, advanced to second on a walk, and scored on Joe Torre's base hit to left.[76]

Carlton continued to struggle through the spring and early summer, in part, due to recurring pain in his left elbow. Instead of relying on his fastball and slider—like the power pitcher he was—Lefty tried to work the corners of the strike zone with off-speed deliveries. As the season progressed, he only became more frustrated, again blaming his difficulties on catcher Bob Boone. Nor was the center field platoon of Bannister-Robinson-Anderson very successful. None of the three outfielders could provide the speedy defense or offense the Phillies needed at that position. Fortunately, Christenson and Underwood stepped into the starting rotation and pitched masterfully. Together with the power-hitting of Schmidt and Luzinski, the two young starters and the bullpen allowed the team to remain in the first division during the early months of the season.

Owens solved the center field problem on May 4 when he traded first baseman Willie Montanez to the San Francisco Giants for Garry Maddox.[77] The trade was not popular with either the fans or the players at first. Maddox, a Vietnam veteran, began his major league career with the Giants in 1972. He hit .319 the following year, but slumped to .284 in '74. At the time of his trade to the Phillies, the tall, lanky center fielder was in a hitting slump. Nor did he have a very colorful personality, like Montanez. A soft-spoken, religious individual, Maddox preferred to keep to himself and was known sit quietly by his locker reading the Bible before games.[78]

News of the deal reached the Phillies clubhouse as the players packed their bags for a flight to St. Louis for a series against the Cardinals. Montanez, a fan favorite, was told to report to Owens's office on the third floor of the Vet. When he got there, Pope informed the first baseman that he had been traded to San Francisco. "We both had a good cry for ourselves," Owens later admitted. "He's done a helluva job for us and we'll miss him." Caught off guard by the deal, the usually upbeat Montanez returned to the clubhouse in a daze to say good-bye to his friends. Bowa was incredulous. "Are you kidding me!" he chirped. "We traded Montanez for Garry Maddox? What's he hitting a buck twenty-five? Is that all we got for Willie?" In fact, Maddox was hitting .135 at the time, but he was one of the best defensive center fielders in baseball. So good that Owens called him "the best center fielder since Willie Mays." "Maddox plays shallower than anybody," he insisted, "and nobody shuts down the alleys like him." As the Phillies boarded the buses for the airport, "Willie the Phillie" wished them well and admitted to Bill Conlin of the *Philadelphia Daily News* that he "hated to leave such a good bunch of guys," but he understood that "that's how the game is."[79]

With Montanez's departure, the Phillies needed a first baseman and the negotiations for Dick Allen heated back up. When Allen made clear that there was "no way [he'd] play for Atlanta," the Braves, on May 7, dealt him to Philadelphia along with catcher Johnny Oates for Jim Essian, a young backstop and outfielder Barry Bonnell . . . both of whom had seen limited time in the majors.[80] Fans, sportswriters, and even the Phillies themselves began talking about winning the pennant. But Allen downplayed the popular expectation at a press conference the following day, insisting that he was "no messiah" and that his primary goal was to "entertain the fans." Referring to his troubled early career with the Phillies, the veteran slugger said: "I'm not anticipating any trouble. I've learned a lot through my journeys. There's a lot of difference between the man I am now and the boy I was back then."[81]

Allen's decision to return to the Phillies took the city by surprise. It was as unpredictable as the black superstar's personality. But two things were certain: Allen was blessed with exceptional talent and, at the age of thirty-three, he still had not realized his full potential. He knew it, too. Allen understood that he had not fulfilled anybody's expectations—the fans, the baseball world's, or, sadly, his own. In 11 previous seasons, he hit 40 home runs once, drove in 100 runs three times, and never had the experience of being on a pennant winner. Only twice did he match the offensive productivity of his 1964 Rookie of the Year season— in 1966 when he belted 40 homers and in '72 when he hit .308, with 37 homers and drove in 113 RBI to win the American League's MVP Award. Instead, his career was troubled by an odd assortment of injuries and an inability to cope with people who had difficulty understanding him.[82] Perhaps a second chance in Philadelphia was what he needed.

Ashburn was correct in his belief that Phillies baseball had changed in the six years since Allen had last played for the team. There was no more Connie Mack Stadium. Instead, the Phillies played in a brand new Veterans Stadium. The crowds were suburban and white. There was a new owner in Ruly Carpenter who seemed more compassionate, more approachable than the sterile, ultra-conservative style exhibited by his father in the 1960s. Conditions seemed right for a reconciliation and, with a little luck, that pennant that Allen desired. He was excited to return to his old team, which, as he put it, "finally entered the twentieth century in terms of race." In the 1960s, Allen believed that he represented "a threat to white people in Philadelphia." "I wore my hair in an Afro," he recalled. "I said what was on my mind. I did my own thing. And I'll admit that I was something of a jerk. But it seemed like Philadelphia and its fans had changed. I saw players like Dave Cash, who represented a new generation of talented black ballplayers. They were proud of their playing abilities and sure weren't going to take a back seat to anybody. So the race thing wasn't an issue anymore. In terms of pure baseball, those Phillies had one of the best infields in the game with Mike Schmidt at third base, Cash at second, Bowa at short, Bob Boone behind the plate. I thought I could make a pretty solid contribution at first. We also had the starting pitching to contend, with guys like Carlton and Lonborg, and McGraw in the bullpen. Sure, I was pretty excited about coming back to Philly."[83] Not everyone was excited about Allen's return, though.

Ozark had serious reservations about the kind of influence Allen would bring to his young team. Shortly after the deal was made, the Phils manager, usually known for his relaxed approach, instituted five team rules that he swore to enforce and distributed them in the clubhouse:

1. Players are to be in their rooms two hours after the team bus leaves the ballpark during road trips after a night game and midnight after a day game.
2. I control alcoholic beverages on team flights and no beverage of any type will be taken out of the clubhouse.
3. All players must be on the bench five minutes before the game starts.
4. All players—except the starting pitcher—must be on the field for infield practice.
5. All players must report to the ballpark by the time the team bus arrives on the road and at posted times when the team is at home.[84]

It was no coincidence that the rules targeted areas of personal behavior that Allen broke repeatedly throughout his career: beer-drinking during games; arriving late to the ballpark, or not at all; and routinely breaking curfew. When one sportswriter pointed out that the rules seemed to contradict his usually "laid back" style of managing, Ozark replied: "If my head's going to roll, I want to be the one who rolls it!"[85]

Allen returned to the Phillies lineup against the Cincinnati Reds on May 14. It was a hero's homecoming. Before the game, Allen was reunited with his close friend, Pete Cera, the assistant clubhouse manager. The slugger had developed a close friendship with Cera in the minor leagues when he was experiencing the turmoil of racial discrimination. Allen nicknamed him "Mother Cera" because he was always checking up on him, taking care of his needs, and lending a sympathetic ear whenever he needed it. As the two men embraced, the Phillies' prodigal son promised the clubhouse attendant that it was "My turn to take care of you."[86] Out on the playing field Allen was greeted just as warmly.

As the Phillies were taking the field, a few members of the grounds crew, finishing up their work on the base paths, yelled out, "Hey 15! Welcome back!" "We didn't expect any response," said Mark Carfagno, a member of the crew, "but he turned our way and said, 'Thanks.' After that, he referred to us as his 'Gang.'"[87] Allen's new teammates also embraced him. The energy level on the club seemed to soar. The fans were even more receptive, even patronizing. Allen received a tremendous ovation after he singled to center in his first at bat. But even if Allen made a miscue during those first few games back—as he did several times, having missed all of spring training—it was excused. He was cheered constantly for regular defensive plays and routine fly-ball outs, even though he was in the middle of a career-low .233 slump. Perhaps the most exaggerated expression of fan appreciation came in a game against San Francisco. After struggling all evening against Giant pitching, Allen, in the eleventh inning, hit a sharp liner down the left field line that dribbled through the third baseman's legs. When the winning run scored on the error, Phillies fans erupted with applause and demanded a curtain call from their new hero.[88]

Even the Philadelphia press was friendly. Allen found himself glibly answering the questions of sportswriters he had refused to talk to six years earlier. Now they followed the fans' lead, a band of admirers toting pads and pens, hanging on to his every word. Six years before, the press had run Allen out of town, steadfastly continuing to call him "Richie," knowing fully that he thought it was denigrating because it sounded like a boy's name and whites tended to think of blacks as "boys." He had requested time and again, that he be referred to as "Dick Allen." Now, they graciously deferred to his request.[89] While all the media hype unfolded, Ruly Carpenter, who understood the fickle nature of the local press, stood by watching, concerned that they would run his new slugger out of town again. "I hope to hell they leave him alone," he said quietly. "I could never understand why they got on him so when he was here before. He's a serious dedicated athlete, he's a great team player, and really, he never did anything you could consider bad for the game of baseball. Hell, Babe Ruth was drunk all the time, whored around like mad, set a lousy example for kids, and there was never a bad word written about him. Allen would show up late for a practice once and they'd crucify him. How do you explain it?"[90]

More explicable were the dismal fortunes of Dick Ruthven, the hard-throwing right-hander drafted by the Phillies out of Fresno State two years earlier. Believing that "Rufus" had the talent, ability, and poise to compete at the major league level, the Phils immediately made him part of the pitching staff. He responded with a 6-9 record and improved his performance by three more victories the following season. Ruthven was a brash, aggressive competitor with a devastating curveball. But in '75 he was hit hard and began to experience pain in his right elbow. After compiling a 2-2 record and an inflated 4.17 ERA, he had surgery on his elbow and was sent down to Triple-A Toledo.[91] "I would never have gone down to the minors if I hadn't had surgery on my elbow," Ruthven insisted in a recent interview. "It kept on swelling up on me because I had never pitched 200 innings in a season before, like I did in '74. After the surgery I couldn't throw anywhere near as hard as I once did. Besides that, to come straight out of college and expect someone to know how to pitch, how to change speeds effectively, would be like expecting a six-year-old to paint like Picasso. It's physically and mentally impossible to do."[92]

The Phillies had done Ruthven a disservice by rushing him to the majors before he learned how to pitch properly. Jim Bunning, the Toledo manager, would help him regain that confidence. Rufus reminded Bunning of himself at the same stage in his own pitching career and immediately took a liking to him. "I loved pitching for Jim," said Ruthven. "I had more fun pitching for him in Toledo than I had the previous three seasons in the majors. I actually felt cheated not going to the minors before."[93] Another individual who was instrumental in helping the young hurler to get his career back on track was Wayne Simpson, a right-handed pitcher who briefly enjoyed stardom with the Cincinnati Reds. By 1975, Simpson, once a power pitcher, was struggling to make it back to the majors with the Toledo Mud Hens.

Shortly after being sent down, Ruthven was knocked out of a game against the Richmond, Virginia, Braves. He didn't even get through the first inning. "Wayne came up to me in the clubhouse and told me, 'Don't you ever quit,'" he recalled. "'I went through the same thing you're going through. Don't give up. If you do, it's going to be you and me, one on one.'"

Later that season Simpson found himself pitching a seven-inning no-hitter in the first game of a doubleheader against Syracuse. Rufus was charting pitches in the dugout and cheering on his teammate. After the game he approached Simpson to congratulate him, saying: "As badly as I want to go back up, they should take you."

"Don't ever say you'd rather have someone else go up," Simpson shot back. "You can get buried down here."[94]

Ruthven listened and learned. At the end of the season, he was dealt to the Chicago White Sox, who traded him to the Braves. Rufus would return to the Phillies in 1978 a different athlete. His two and a half seasons with Atlanta allowed him to make the transition from a "hard thrower" to a "control pitcher," thanks in large part to the tutelage of the club's ace, Andy Messersmith. But in 1975, mired in the Phillies farm system, Ruthven feared that his career was over. He wasn't the only one who was struggling that year, either. Bob Boone and Mike Schmidt were also riding an emotional roller coaster.

After the Phillies acquired Johnny Oates from Atlanta in the Allen deal, Ozark benched Boone. Demoted to backup catcher, Boone began to feel sorry for himself. He believed that he had earned the starting role and that he should be playing rather than Oates.[95] Then, in early July, when the Boston Red Sox released Tim McCarver, Owens jumped at the opportunity to reunite Carlton with his former catcher. When Lefty made his next start against the Houston Astros, McCarver was behind the plate. With the exception of a two-run homer he surrendered to Bob Watson in the first inning, Carlton blanked the Astros for the rest of the game, limiting them to two singles.[96] He would go on to win 3 of his next 4 starts. Boone was made a third-string catcher, but, to his credit, he put team success before his own. At the same time the Stanford graduate was determined to show Ozark and Carlton just how good he was behind the plate when the opportunity presented itself.[97]

Schmidt was also disillusioned with his situation, though he enjoyed regular playing time. Like all prodigious hitters, he continued to battle the strikeout. In 1973, his rookie year, Michael Jack hit 18 home runs, batted a career-low .196 and struck out 136 times in 367 plate appearances. The following year he led the league with 36 homers, improved his average by nearly 100 points, batting .282, but also continued to lead the league in strikeouts with 138. In '75, Schmidt's home run production increased to 38 and so did his strikeout total with 180, while his average dropped to .249.[98] Near the end of the season, Ozark dropped him from third to sixth in the batting order and began to question his intensity. "He started off bad and instead of getting mad, gritting his teeth and working harder, he began fighting himself . . . and thinking," he said of the young slugger. "He's thinking all the time. Now he's so confused he doesn't know what to do. And to top it off, I think he's scared of the ball. In this business, if you're scared of the ball, you've had it. I'm really afraid for him."[99] The Philadelphia press chimed in, nicknaming him "Captain Cool." And the fans booed him mercilessly.[100] Dick Allen, who had been treated similarly by the fans and the media, took the beleaguered third baseman under his wing.

Like Allen, Schmidt had superstar potential and an extremely sensitive ego. Both men were natural athletes in the truest sense of the term. Both were blessed with muscular, athletic builds. Both were power hitters with high strikeout ratios. And both had to labor under the unrealistic expectations of the Philadelphia fans and the local media. The same was said about Allen as was said about Schmidt in 1975: "The only thing that can keep Mike Schmidt from being a superstar is Mike Schmidt. He has all the tools and it is only a matter of applying himself and not getting fatheaded."[101] It was almost as if Schmidt inherited Allen's legacy. In that sense, it was Schmidt's good fortune that the Phillies acquired the enigmatic slugger when his own career was at a critical juncture.

"Growing up," said Schmidt, "I admired Dick Allen. I pretended I was like him when I was up at bat playing Legion ball in Ohio. I was fortunate that we became good friends on the Phillies and that I learned a lot from him."[102] Allen would help Schmidt learn to cope with the press, the Boo Birds, the fickleness of Philadelphia baseball itself. He was really the only person who could, having experienced it himself six years earlier. "Schmidt had as much talent as anybody I've ever seen play the game," said Allen of his younger teammate. "Quick wrists. Strong. Perfect baseball body. But he was trying to hit every pitch out of the park, and when he didn't, he'd sulk about it. When I got to Philly in '75 he didn't seem to be having fun playing the game. I talked to him about swinging down on the ball. The downswing is the ticket. Schmidt picked up on it pretty quick. The other thing about him was his attitude. He was moody and if he had a bad game, he'd take it home with him. I used to take him out after a game for a couple of beers and we'd talk about things, have a few laughs, put the ballyard behind us. I used to tell Schmitty to pretend he was back in the sandlots of Ohio where he grew up. Get out there and bang that ball like you did in high school. He began to get the message in '75 but he still had some work to do."[103]

With little more than a week remaining in the season, the Phillies were 6 games behind the Pittsburgh Pirates in the National League East, heading for a second place finish. On September 22, Pittsburgh's Bruce Kison beat Tommy Underwood, dropping the Phils seven games behind with six left to play. Afterward, D. Byron Yake, the Pittsburgh Associated Press chief, asked Ozark how he felt about his team's season. "We aren't out of it if we win every game and they lose every game," the Phillies manager said incredulously. When informed that his team had been mathematically eliminated, Ozark, bewildered, said: "That's disheartening."[104] Ozark later insisted that he was "only kidding" with Yake, thinking that the AP chief was "some country bumpkin." [105] But the damage had been done. The Phils manager had lost his credibility with the fans and the press. It would be difficult for either group to take him seriously in the future. To be sure, Ozark's forgetfulness was due to the pressure he was feeling over the front office's expectations. Their patience was wearing thin after three years. Owens had given Ozark an awesome team that featured both 1974 home run champions (Schmidt and Allen), two former Cy Young Award winners (Carlton and Lonborg), the best second base-shortstop combination in the game (Cash and Bowa), a top-notch bullpen led by Tug McGraw, and a quality bench. Of the twenty-four major league teams, only Cincinnati and Oakland could match the Phillies in terms of all-around talent. Yet Ozark couldn't lead the team to a division championship. Now the front office would have to concoct the excuses to explain the team's failure. Among them were: Carlton's sore elbow, Lonborg's two months on the disabled list due to a groin injury, and Allen's anemic hitting (.233, 12 HR, 62 RBI).[106]

While the Phillies' second-place finish was a tremendous disappointment, there were some bright spots. Cash, Bowa, and Maddox gave the team an excellent defense up the middle of the playing field. Cash also contributed mightily to the offense, topping the National League in hits with 213, scoring 111 runs, and batting .305.[107] In addition to Schmidt's 38 homers and 95 RBI, Luzinski, who was rebounding from his injury of the previous season, contributed some formidable power with 34 homers and a league-leading 120 RBI. McGraw went (9-6) with 14 saves out of the bullpen, establishing his role as closer. Journeyman Jay Johnstone, found a home in Philadelphia's outfield as a platoon player with a reputation as a solid contact hitter who rarely struck out.[108] What's more, the Phillies had a good mix of young ballplayers and seasoned veterans, all of whom were returning the following season. In 1976 pitchers Tom Underwood and Larry Christenson were, at twenty-two years old, the youngest players on the team. Cash (28), Bowa (30), Luzinski (25), Schmidt (26), Maddox (26) and Boone (28), had not yet reached their prime. Allen (34), Lonborg (34), Carlton (31) and McGraw (31) had had enough experience with winning to provide the kind of leadership necessary for a contender.[109]

An organization that as recently as three years before was a perennial loser had come to believe in itself. The success was evident throughout the franchise, as each part performed its particular set of responsibilities. The Carpenter family provided the money; Paul Owens, the vision; Dallas Green, Howie Bedell, the coaches, managers, and scouts of the farm system, the sweat equity. In many respects, Danny Ozark and his team were simply the beneficiaries of all that hard work, the public face of the Phillies. In the process, "Yes We Can!" had become not only the rallying cry for a talented club of youngsters and veterans, but for an entire organization committed to winning a world championship for the city of Philadelphia.

CHAPTER 6

CONTENDERS

T HE PHILLIES' HOPES FOR A PENNANT almost came true in 1976. After dropping three of their first four games, the Phillies, it seemed, couldn't lose.[1]
The springboard to the winning season came seven days later at Chicago's
Wrigley Field, when Mike Schmidt hit four consecutive home runs to lead the
Phils to an 18-16 victory over the Cubs in a ten-inning marathon. Schmidt, who
had struggled at the plate earlier that spring, was pressing. Ozark tried to break
the slump by hitting him out of the leadoff spot, believing that the free-swinging
third baseman would be forced to take more pitches. It didn't work.

To make matters worse, Rich Ashburn, a former Phillie, broadcaster, and writer
for the *Bulletin*, was highly critical of the manager's strategy in his column. Ashburn, who had tired of Schmidt's lack of discipline at the plate suggested that he
be dropped to the sixth slot. "You can take pitches there just as easily," he reasoned. "And if Schmidt happens to drive the ball, at least he has the chance to
knock in some runs."[2] When Schmidt read the column on the flight to Chicago,
a shouting match erupted between the two men. As it turned out, the altercation
did more to break the young slugger's slump than anything else.

Ozark took Ashburn's advice and dropped Schmidt to the sixth slot in the
opening game against the Cubs. It was a beautiful but windy spring day—a hitter's day at Wrigley. Before the game, Dick Allen pulled Schmidt aside and offered
some helpful advice: "Mike, you've got to relax. You've got to have some fun.
Remember when you were a kid and you'd skip supper to play ball? You were
having fun. Hey, with all the talent you've got, baseball ought to be fun. Enjoy
it. Be a kid again."[3] Schmidt took the words to heart. He also made some other
changes. Instead of using his own bat, he borrowed veteran Tony Taylor's, which
was an inch shorter and an ounce lighter than his own. Terry Harmon, a utility

infielder and fellow Ohio University alum, lent Schmidt his tattered blue T-shirt for good luck with the tip that "it's got a lot of hits stored up in it."[4]

Carlton started the game but was knocked out in the second inning. Seven more pitchers followed in a slugfest that saw the Phillies trail 12-1 at one point. Schmidt put on an impressive display of firepower. After a fourth-inning single, he homered in each of his next four at bats. Two of his home runs came off Cub starter Rick Reuschel, a two-run shot in the fifth and a solo homer in the seventh. His third home run came in the eighth inning, a 3-run shot off right-handed reliever Mike Garman. With the game tied 16-16 in the tenth, Schmidt came to bat again and nailed a Paul Reuschel fastball into the left field bleachers for his fourth home run. In so doing, he became the tenth player in major league history to collect four homers in a single game.[5] The Phillies' 18-16 victory went to Tug McGraw, who pitched the eighth inning and surrendered two runs in the ninth to send the game into extra innings. Afterward, the comic reliever boasted: "Schmitty never would have done it without me!"[6]

Any other player might have taken advantage of the opportunity to criticize the manager for dropping him in the batting order, but Schmidt respected Ozark's decision. After the game he admitted that his manager "has a job to do and he can put people wherever he wants to." "If he wants to hit me third, I'll bat third," he added. "If he wants me sixth, I'll hit sixth. And if he wants me to bat ninth, then I'll bat ninth."[7] Schmidt, who was locked in an early season competition for home runs with Dave Kingman of the Mets, went on a tear after that game. While Kingman hit 6 round trippers in a five-game stretch that April, Schmidt blasted 7 in a four-game period and finished the month with a National League record-tying 11 home runs.[8]

On May 9, Jim Lonborg defeated the Dodgers, 10-3, and the Phillies took over first place in the Eastern Division for good. Everyone was contributing. Boone, who resumed the role of regular catcher after Johnny Oates suffered a shoulder injury on opening day, regained Ozark's confidence with his handling of the pitching staff. Luzinski sported a .300 average and was on pace to hit 20 or more home runs. The right field platoon of Jay Johnstone, Ollie Brown, and Bobby Tolan was proving to be successful, both offensively and defensively. Jim Kaat and Ron Reed, two off-season acquisitions, bolstered an already strong pitching staff. Kaat, previously a starting pitcher with the Minnesota Twins and Chicago White Sox, was an effective "spot starter," who provided insurance in the event that Lonborg or Carlton ended up on the disabled list. Reed pitched magnificently out of the bullpen as a middle reliever.[9]

On May 20, Lonborg defeated Tom Seaver and the New York Mets, 5-3, at Shea Stadium for the Phils' twelfth straight road victory, setting a new club record. He beat Seaver again five days later on May 25. Inspired by the impressive achievement, Carlton took the mound the following day and three-hit the Mets. Homers by Luzinski and Brown propelled Lefty to the 5-0 victory. The Phillies ended the month with a 30-11 record, the second best start in the National League's history. The team was now firmly entrenched in first place, 6½ games ahead of the second-place Pittsburgh Pirates. They continued their domination of the National League the following month, launching a 20-hit assault on Tommy John and the Los Angeles Dodgers for an easy 14-2 win on June 8. After the game, John, a respected veteran hurler, was asked to compare the Phils with the world champion Cincinnati Reds. "That's like trying to compare the hydrogen bomb and the atom bomb," he replied. "They both kill."[10]

Boone, with restored confidence behind the plate, began to assert himself at bat as well. His grand slam on June 27 against the St. Louis Cardinals keyed the Phils' 6-2 win. "My dad [former major leaguer Ray Boone] hit eight [career grand slams], so I guess it proves that it's not heredity!" he deadpanned after the game. Two days later, on June 29, Boone won another game with a suicide squeeze, as the Phils closed out the month with a 50-20 record.[11]

Carlton was pitching like the Cy Young Award winner of four years earlier. Considered by many sportswriters as "washed up" after a 44-47 three-year slump, Lefty improved his record to 9-3. Carlton's turnaround can be attributed to several factors. First, he felt more comfortable pitching to his close friend and personal catcher Tim McCarver. "When I came back to Philadelphia in '75 Lefty needed some help," said McCarver. "He was confused by his three subpar years and his relationship with the press was starting to wear on him. He'd been trying too hard for his own good. I might have helped him relax a little bit by talking with him about his mechanics, but I certainly didn't structure him for victory. Steve did that himself. He did it with his physical conditioning and his mental approach to the game."[12] Second, Carlton abandoned the traditional training routine of running and calisthenics and became a disciple of Gus Hoefling, a martial arts instructor who taught him how to keep his mind and pitching sharp through a Zen-like personal conditioning program. Third, Carlton made a slight mechanical change by pitching to right-handed hitters from the right side of the rubber instead of from the left. The change allowed him to throw his fastball inside on a right-handed batter instead of hanging it over the heart of the plate. It also gave him the ability to push off the mound with greater force and to better locate his pitches.[13] Finally, Carlton isolated himself even further from the press, agreeing occasionally to go on record with selected writers. Instead, McCarver became his media relations person, entertaining the media with his colorful assessment of Lefty's performance in postgame interviews.[14]

At the All-Star break the Phillies held a commanding 10-game lead over the second-place Pirates. They had been playing .650 baseball since the beginning of June. Eleven of the Phils were hitting .300 or better. Lonborg was 11-5 at midseason, which included a near perfect game against the Dodgers. Together with

Carlton, he combined to win 12 consecutive decisions. The team was having so much fun, Cash and Bowa convinced Schmidt, Luzinski, and Maddox to cut another 45 rpm record with them. Produced by Walt Kahn of Grand Prix Records, "Phillies Fever" had a disco beat and, to the relief of professional vocalists, a lot of talking. Some of the dialogue was quite amusing. In one segment, Cash, Luzinski, and Maddox, using the citizens band radio jargon that was popular in the mid-'70s, promote the team:

> CASH: "Breaker 19 for some local info."
> LUZINSKI: "Go ahead local info."
> CASH: "Hey, good buddy, can you tell me what the hottest thing in Philadelphia is?
> MADDOX: "Got to be the Phillies, good buddy.
> CASH: "That's a big 10-4. Say, Greg, you goin' out for batting practice?"
> LUZINSKI: "Yeah, Dave, soon as I finish these three cheeseburgers!"

Needless to say, the five athletes were much better at playing baseball than singing, which was limited to the chorus:

> We'll all go dancin', dancin' in the streets,
> 'Cause we're the Phillies, we know we can't be beat;
>
> So c'mon, baby, won't you get on down?
> Veterans Stadium is the hippest place in town.[15]

While the Phils were padding their lead in the National League's Eastern Division, vice president Bill Giles came up with a host of promotions to keep the turnstiles spinning during the Bicentennial year. On opening day, he arranged to have a horseback rider dressed as Paul Revere, deliver the game ball to Veterans Stadium. The reenactor, lantern in hand, had already spent a week riding from Boston to Philadelphia on horse by the time he entered the Vet to turn the baseball over to "Rocketman," who jetted around the stadium before throwing out the first pitch to catcher Johnny Oates. The Phillies wore red-and-white pinstriped, pillbox caps like the nineteenth-century players, a practice they continued for Sunday afternoon games that season.

On May 31, the Great Wallenda returned to the Vet for an encore performance. To commemorate the nation's Bicentennial, the seventy-one-year-old high-wire artist placed American flags on each end of his balancing pole. Once again, Wallenda did a headstand at the halfway point and, again, he was greeted with a standing ovation by the 52,211 fans on hand to observe the 21-minute act. Two years later, Wallenda fell to his death while performing on a high wire in Puerto Rico.[16]

But the highlight of the Phillies Bicentennial celebration was the All-Star Game that was played at the Vet that year. The night before the midsummer classic, Giles rented an area of Independence Mall, with the Liberty Bell and Independence

Hall serving as a backdrop. It was a festive and uniquely "Philadelphia" occasion that featured a Mummers band, soft pretzels, and cheesesteaks.[17] The following day 63,974 baseball fans—the third largest in the history of the event—packed the Vet to watch the All-Star Game. Greg Luzinski started in left field for the National League, though Bowa, Boone, Cash, and Schmidt were also named to the squad. President Gerald Ford was on hand to throw out the celebratory first pitch. The National League continued its dominance by defeating their American League rivals, 7-1. It was the fifth straight victory for the National League, the thirteenth of the last fourteen contests.[18]

The Phillies increased their lead to 15½ games by August 1. Thomas Boswell of the *Washington Post*, one of the more astute baseball writers, stated that the Phils were "on the sort of natural, unrealistic high that blesses a team perhaps once every 20 years. They can beat you every way: power, average hitting, speed, defense, and brains."[19] The Phillies' play during the so-called dog days of August, when a team can either stay in the pennant race or fold, reinforced Boswell's observation. On August 11, Tommy Underwood, on his way to a 10-win season, defeated the Braves. Three days later, the heroes were Tolan, Maddox, and Bowa, each of whom collected three hits in a 13-2 romp of the San Francisco Giants. Johnstone was the hot hitter for the next six games and boosted his average to a league-leading .344. On August 24, Carlton, en route to his second 20-win season with the Phillies, defeated the Atlanta Braves for his sixth straight victory. Tolan, Carlton, and Bowa powered the offense in the 14-3 rout.[20]

Then, beginning August 27, the team went into a two-week tailspin, losing 13 of their next 15 games, while the second-place Pirates won 12 of their next 14. The Phillies were overdue for a letdown. They had been playing .600 baseball for most of the season, and it's difficult for any team, regardless of how talented they are, to keep up that kind of pace. Baseball is a 162-game grind. In addition to pitching, hitting, and defense, those teams who contend must also enjoy a certain degree of luck. In late August, the Phillies' luck had changed. On days they had good pitching, nobody hit. On days when the team hit, they didn't get the pitching. As a result, the Phils' lead dwindled to just three games.[21] All the regulars were mired in terrible hitting slumps. Cash, in the two-week skid, had just 13 hits in 45 at-bats. Schmidt was 9 for 55, Bowa, 8 for 52, Luzinski, 7 for 32, Boone, 9 for 33, and Allen, 1 for 25, before being benched. The team was hitting an anemic .128.[22]

Predictably, the Philadelphia media began blaming Ozark for not resting his regulars when the team enjoyed such a huge lead in August. To his credit, the Phils manager didn't panic, but conducted himself as if he expected to win the division. "What else was I going to do?" Ozark said, in a recent interview. "Once you get into a situation like that when you're losing game after game, it's natural to try to overmanage. What got us out of it was just letting the players play, letting them do what came naturally to them."[23] Instead of second-guessing himself, the Phils skipper simply continued to fill out the lineup and let his players assume responsibility for the game. He also offered the press some interesting postgame insights. When asked if his team was suffering from a morale problem, for example, Ozark, master of the malaprop, insisted that "morality is not a factor on this team." Similarly, after losing a Labor Day doubleheader against Pittsburgh, he reminded the sportswriters that "even Napoleon had his Watergate."[24]

Nevertheless, fans and the press began to envision the ghosts of 1964 when the Phillies, with a 6½ game lead and 12 left to play, lost ten straight to blow the pennant.[25] "It was a nightmare," said Schmidt. "The hate mail, the letters saying we were choking, the abuse. I'd be out there trying to catch a tough grounder, thinking that what I did would decide whether we'd be 2½ in front the next day or 4½. Blow this one, I'd think, and I'll need cops to guard my house."[26] Bowa received a letter on one road trip that threatened him with being "tarred and feathered" when the team "gets back home."[27] Even Tug McGraw, who rarely criticized the fans, admitted that when he pitched for the Miracle Mets, who weren't expected to win, he had "everything to gain and nothing to lose." But in Philadelphia, "for the first time in [his] career," he felt as if he had "everything to gain and everything to lose." "People in Philly expect us to win," he told Red Foley of the *New York Daily News*. "We're expected to win the division and the playoffs. People have been putting pressure on this club from the beginning of the season. With the talent we have, if we don't win, there will be no excuse."[28]

Finally, on September 26, the Phillies clinched the division title. Jim Lonborg pitched the Phils past the Montreal Expos in the first game of a doubleheader at Jarry Park. Luzinski sealed the 4-1 victory in the sixth inning with a tremendous three-run homer. [29] It was the first time the Phils would go to post-season play in twenty-six years. "I was pretty calm all day," said Lonborg after the game. Then it was the ninth inning and I was as pumped up as I've ever been in my life. Winning this game will remain the highlight of my career. Nothing will ever top it."[30]

But even in victory the Phillies were unable to escape controversy. As the team celebrated the pennant-clinching win in the visitors' clubhouse, Schmidt, Allen, Cash, and Maddox gathered in a nearby equipment room where Allen offered a prayer of thanks. Tug McGraw, who was frolicking around the clubhouse dousing his teammates with champagne, noticed that the four players were missing from the celebration and made a flippant remark about the "Brothers meeting" elsewhere.[31] Some of the other players noticed the absence as well and complained about the "attitude" of their four missing teammates.[32] Afterward, the Phillies headed to St. Louis for their final regular season series and Allen returned to Philadelphia. He was mired in a slump and Ozark agreed to let him have the time off. When Bill Conlin of the *Philadelphia Daily News* learned of the events, he began to raise questions about racial dissension in the clubhouse, focusing his attention on Dick Allen.[33]

Dave Cash insists that "there was nothing racial about the [separate] meeting" and that it "should have never been reported that way by the press." "To set the record straight," he said in a recent interview, "yes, we did have a meeting in the back of the clubhouse after the first game of the doubleheader. It was 9:30 at night and it was about 35 degrees outside, too cold to hang out in the dugout. All the starting players were in that room, not just Dick, Garry, Mike, and myself. That small group just wanted to get together to thank the good Lord that he had taken us that far. But the press purposefully misinterpreted the remarks of one teammate, which was meant to be taken humorously, and made a racial thing out of it."[34] Maddox echoed Cash's feelings, stating that "race never entered [his] mind when the four players isolated themselves for the prayer meeting.[35]

To be sure, Cash, Allen, Schmidt, and Maddox were the core of a small but growing group of Christian Athletes on the team. Because of the negative stereotype associated with fundamentalist Christianity among most ballplayers, it would have been logical for them to separate themselves in order to worship God. While McGraw, who gave new meaning to the term "free spirit," would never be mistaken for a "born again Christian," he certainly was not racist either. The relief pitcher respected and was genuinely interested in the religious, ethnic, and racial backgrounds of others. What did disturb McGraw, a consummate "team player," was the double standard that he felt was being created for Allen, specifically allowing the veteran slugger to be excused from traveling with the rest of the club.

At the same time, tension *did* exist in the Phillies clubhouse and it *did* revolve around Allen and the playing time of the black players. When the team arrived in St. Louis for a three-game series against the Cardinals on September 27, Ozark called a clubhouse meeting to clear the air. At that meeting, McGraw criticized Allen for distancing himself from the team. "He makes $250,000 a year," said the reliever. "Doesn't that mean he has a responsibility to be with the team on the road? [Management] says he's been hitting an hour and a half every day at home. What the hell does he think we're doing here?"[36]

Maddox took exception to McGraw's remarks. "Why should anybody be upset over Dick's going home?" asked the black center fielder. "He got permission from Danny and he told him he could [go home]." Maddox, angered by the notion of a double standard, also made reference to the reliever's earlier comment about the post-pennant-clinching "Brothers meeting" in Montreal. Pointing out that it was McGraw who "brought up all this race stuff," Maddox added: "Somebody's been fooling me this season. I never saw a sign of race problems all year."[37]

"I don't see this as a strictly race thing," McGraw shot back. "I see it as a thing where some guys, black and white, who really admire Dick and his independent ways are letting him influence their attitude toward the club."[38] But the effort to temper the discussion failed and the meeting became more heated.

One of the black players raised the issue of Ozark's inconsistency in regard to playing time. He pointed out that Bobby Tolan, a black utility player who had been crushing the ball, was not being given sufficient time at first base when Allen was removed from the game in late innings. Instead the weaker-hitting Tommy Hutton served as Allen's replacement. Nor had Ollie Brown, a black reserve, been in the pennant-clinching lineup in Montreal when he had played right field against left-handed pitchers all season. Instead, Ozark went with the right-handed-hitting Jerry Martin, who was white. Maddox agreed, admitting that he was "mad about [the situation]."[39]

"Ollie knows why he wasn't in the lineup," Ozark replied. "That's between him and me. As far as putting Bobby [Tolan] at first base when Allen comes out, hey, his regular position is the outfield. Why should I put him at first when I have a great defensive first baseman like Tommy Hutton?" The Phils skipper was becoming noticeably irritated as the meeting continued. Believing that he didn't need to defend his decisions any longer, Ozark posed the rhetorical question: "Who's the manager here anyway?" No one said a word. "All playing decisions will be made by me," he added, putting an abrupt end to the discussion.[40] But the issue wasn't over.

Allen, before flying home from Montreal, apparently gave Ozark an ultimatum: unless Tony Taylor was made eligible for the playoffs, he would refuse to play in the postseason. It was a difficult decision for Ozark, who had to cut the postseason roster to twenty-five players, which meant that Taylor, a veteran reserve infielder, would probably not be eligible. The Cuban-born second baseman was a fan favorite, who had played with the Phillies for 15 seasons and had never made it to the playoffs. Allen was a close friend of Taylor's, going back to the mid-1960s when they came up together in the Phillies organization. "To my way of thinking, nothing could be more unfair than for the Phillies to take Tony Taylor's uniform," he fumed. "He played 19 seasons in the big leagues, but never in a World Series. He was a model player in the Phillies' organization, mostly through the club's worst times. He was the one guy that would walk to the box seats and sign autographs before every game. He was the one guy who would volunteer to do a post-game interview when the rest of us were turning our backs on the press. In all his years, he never complained. Tony Taylor was Philadelphia Phillies baseball."[41]

Allen took the snub personally. "With God as my witness," he told the front office, "if you take Tony Taylor's uniform off his back, you'll have to take mine too."[42] It was no idle threat. Allen desperately wanted a World Series ring, but it wasn't going to be without his close friend and teammate.

"Much as I love Tony Taylor and as much as I'd like to see him play in a World

Series," said Ozark, when presented with the ultimatum, "I'm not going to go to one of my pitchers and ask him to sit out."[43] The Phils manager eventually agreed to keep Taylor in uniform for the playoffs, but placed him on the roster as a coach. "I certainly didn't see race as being part of that decision," Ozark explained. "We had to make some tough choices and I thought we could do justice to Tony by making him a coach. If there was any racism in that, I can't see it."[44]

"It really was a dirty deal," said Taylor, years later. "I was forty-two years old at the time, but the club could have made room for me. I was happy that they included me as a coach, but it's not the same as being a player. I told Dick, 'Look, there's nothing we can do about it. Just go play ball. The team needs you.' Then the press made the whole thing into a race issue. I don't think it was. I just think the Phillies wanted to go with younger players, that's all."[45]

Having resolved the issue, the Phillies prepared to take on the defending world champion Cincinnati Reds in the best-of-three-game National League playoffs. Cincinnati dominated baseball in the decade of the 1970s. Known as the "Big Red Machine" for its offensive prowess, the team carried itself with a controlled arrogance, realizing just how good it was. Led by catcher Johnny Bench (.234, 16 HR, 74 RBI) and third baseman Pete Rose (.323, 10 HR, 63 RBI), the Reds featured such other superstars as first baseman Tony Perez (.260, 19 HR, 91 RBI), right fielder Ken Griffey (.336, 6 HR, 74 RBI), shortstop Davey Concepcion (.281, 9 HR, 69 RBI), center fielder Cesar Geronimo (.307, 2 HR, 49 RBI), left fielder George Foster (.306, 29 HR, 121 RBI), and second baseman Joe Morgan (.320, 27 HR, 111 RBI), who won consecutive National League Most Valuable Player awards in 1975 and 1976. The pitching staff was not as impressive, but didn't need to be with all the support it received from the offensive juggernaut. Gary Nolan (15-9, 3.46 ERA) was the ace of the staff. Pat Zachry (14-7, 2.74 ERA), Fred Norman (12-7, 3.10 ERA), Jack Billingham (12-10, 4.32 ERA), and Don Gullett (11-3, 3.00 ERA) rounded out the starting rotation. Rawly Eastwick (11-5, 26 SV, 2.08 ERA) and Will McEnaney (2-6, 7 SV, 4.85 ERA) headed a strong bullpen.[46]

During the 1970s, the Reds averaged 95 wins a season and were perennial contenders, having captured four pennants and a world championship. Their experience in post-season play gave the Reds a significant advantage over the Phillies. On the other hand, the Phils had won 7 of the 12 regular season contests against Cincinnati and featured the kind of team that could dominate a short, three-game series. They had stronger pitching with a rotation that included Carlton (20-7, 3.13 ERA), Lonborg (18-10, 3.08 ERA), Christenson (13-8, 3.67 ERA), and Underwood (10-5, 3.52 ERA). They also had comparable power in Schmidt (.262, 38 HR, 107 RBI), Luzinski (.304, 21 HR, 95 RBI), Allen (.268, 15 HR, 49 RBI), and Maddox (.330, 6 HR, 68 RBI).[47]

"I thought we had a team that matched up pretty well with the Reds," said Jim Lonborg. "We had finished up the season on a strong note and that's the kind of thing that enables a team to go into a tough, three-out-of-five-game series with a positive attitude. Statistically, our pitching was better, and, offensively, we had power hitters like Schmidt and Luzinski who were just as good as Perez, Foster, and Bench."[48] But the Reds' depth and post-season experience proved to be too much for the Phils.

The National League Championship Series opened in Philadelphia on Saturday, October 9, with Steve Carlton facing Don Gullett. More than 62,000 fans turned out to watch the Phils take a 1-0 lead in the first inning when Dave Cash scored on a sacrifice fly by Mike Schmidt. But the Reds tied the game in the third on a sacrifice fly by Tony Perez. Carlton surrendered two more runs before McGraw entered the game in the eighth. Gullett pitched flawless baseball after the first and helped his own cause by collecting two hits and driving in three runs. Although the Phils added two more runs in the ninth off reliever Rawly Eastwick, the Reds won the game, 6-3.[49]

Lonborg faced Pat Zachry in Game Two and held the Reds hitless through the first five innings. With a 2-0 lead heading into the sixth, the Phillies saw their lead evaporate. An error by Dick Allen and two questionable hits opened the floodgates, and Cincinnati scored four runs, "I had had great control until the sixth," said Lonborg. "I always enjoyed pitching against the Reds because they were an aggressive hitting team. They didn't stand at the plate and wait for pitches. Anything that was close, they'd swing at. That approach was beneficial to my style of pitching because when I was on I could work the corners pretty well."[50] The Reds added another two runs in the seventh inning, one against McGraw, and the other against Ron Reed, winning the game by a 6-2 margin.[51] The Phillies had their backs to the wall. They would have to sweep the Reds in Cincinnati now to make it to the World Series.

"You could cut the tension in the clubhouse with a knife," recalled Dave Cash. "It was do or die for us after that second game. Everybody—the fans, the press, the front office—expected us to win. But those two games just showed that we weren't prepared to face Cincinnati. They had all that postseason experience going back to 1970. They knew what to expect in a playoff atmosphere. We were a young team with no playoff experience and it caught up with us as the series went on. When we couldn't hold a lead in our own ballpark during the first two games, that more than anything else, destroyed our confidence."[52]

The series moved to Riverfront Stadium for Game Three on Tuesday, October 12. Ozark gambled by starting veteran Jim Kaat, who had only won two of his last 12 decisions during the regular season. But he opted for Kaat believing a veteran with World Series experience would handle the pressure better than either Larry Christenson or Tommy Underwood, the youngest pitchers in the rotation. Ozark's hunch proved to be correct. Kaat pitched brilliantly, taking a 3-0 shutout into the seventh inning. Back-to-back doubles by Luzinski and Schmidt gave the

Phils a 1-0 lead in the fourth off Reds starter Gary Nolan. Philadelphia increased its lead by two runs in the seventh on a walk and doubles by Schmidt and Maddox. But the Reds came back in the seventh. After allowing the first two runners to reach base, Kaat was replaced by Ron Reed, who promptly surrendered four earned runs on three hits. Down 4-3, the Phils battled back, scoring twice in the eighth and once in the ninth for a 6-4 lead. Unfortunately, Reed surrendered back-to-back home runs by George Foster and Johnny Bench and the Reds tied the game. Ozark brought in Gene Garber, who surrendered a single to Dave Concepcion. Garber was then lifted for Tommy Underwood who proceeded to load the bases. Ken Griffey knocked in the winning run, and Cincinnati clinched its second straight pennant with a 7-6 victory.[53]

Shortly after the playoffs, Allen was released. In the two seasons since his return to Philadelphia, the veteran first baseman hit just .250, averaging 13 home runs and 55 RBI each season. Allen had hoped to contribute much more than he did, but he was hampered by a weak Achilles tendon in his right leg. He had been spiked there during his final season in Chicago and, though he had the tendon surgically repaired, it was still painful for him to play with. He couldn't drive the ball as far as he had in the past because of the inability to plant this back foot in the batter's box, though he never used it as an excuse and never informed the Phillies of the ongoing problem.[54] Still, Allen's decline in production was sorely disappointing for a team that needed positive veteran leadership. He would play one more, unproductive season for the Oakland Athletics before retiring for good in 1977. The loss of Dave Cash to free agency was more painful.

Cash had asked the Phillies for a long-term contract. "I really wanted to stay in Philly because I thought we had the chance to win for a number of years," he admitted in a recent interview. "But in 1975, I led the National League in hits, fielding percentage, and all the offensive and defensive categories at second base and I didn't get a raise."

After that season, Cash met with Phils owner Ruly Carpenter to discuss a long-term contract. But Carpenter balked at the idea.

"If we sign you to a huge contract, how much are we going to have to pay Schmidt when its time for him to re-sign?" asked Carpenter.

"I'm not concerned about that," Cash retorted. "I'm concerned about myself. This is a business, and I'm not going to be playing this game that long. I can only make as much as I can right now."

The negotiations continued into the summer of the '76 season. Cash told his agent, Jerry Kapstein, that if the Phillies didn't "get something done by the All-Star break, [he] didn't want to talk anymore."[55]

Failing to receive the long-term contract he sought from the Phils, Cash, at the end of the season, signed with the Montreal Expos for $1.5 million over a five-year period.[56] "I had to look out for myself and my family's interests," insisted the All-Star second baseman. "I looked at Montreal and they had a very talented, young team. Gary Carter was their catcher, Tony Perez played first, Larry Parrish played third, and Chris Speier was at short. In the outfield they had Warren Cromartie in left, Andre Dawson in center, and Ellis Valentine in right. It was the same kind of talent we had in Philly when I arrived in '73. So I could easily see myself fitting into Montreal's lineup. In fact, we were in the pennant race every year between 1977 and 1979. Had the Expos' front office kept the team together, we could have won it all."[57]

Despite the loss of two key players and their quick elimination by the Reds in the playoffs, the '76 Phillies did demonstrate significant improvement. The team compiled a club-record 101 victories and 2,480,150 fans (another franchise record) showed their appreciation by turning out to watch the team play. Steve Carlton returned to form as one of the most dominant pitchers in the majors with a 20-7 record. Talented players like Schmidt, Luzinski, Bowa, and Boone were finally recognized outside of Philadelphia, being selected to the National League All-Star squad. Maddox finished third in the league's batting race with a .339 average. He was also hailed as the "Secretary of Defense" because of his ability to consistently cut off sinking line drives as well as to spear deep fly balls with over-the-shoulder catches. Finally, Ozark was named Manager of the Year by the *Sporting News* and the National League Manager of the Year by United Press International and the Associated Press[58] (Figure 16).

FIGURE 16. Danny Ozark managed the Phillies from 1973 to 1979. Three times he led the team to the playoffs and three times he failed to clinch a pennant. Courtesy of the National Baseball Hall of Fame Library, Cooperstown, New York.

124   CHAPTER 6

The Associated Press's award was especially gratifying for Ozark, whose decision-making as well as rapport with the media had been questioned repeatedly by Ralph Bernstein, who covered the Phillies for the syndicate and was also the chairman of the local Baseball Writers' Association. Earlier in the season, Bernstein got into a shouting match with the Phillies skipper over his handling of the press. The particular incident involved Ozark's last-minute decision to remove Dick Allen from the starting lineup of a mid-April game. The truth of the matter was that Allen had arrived late and in no condition to play, but admitting to that would only fuel the sportswriters' intrusive curiosity about clubhouse chemistry. When Bob Fachet of the *Washington Post* asked Ozark, at the postgame press conference, why he made the decision, the Phillies manager snapped. "He didn't play because I didn't think he was right to play!" he shot back. "What a stupid question."

Fachet realized he had struck a nerve. An uneasy silence followed. Then, unexpectedly, Ozark lost his temper. "Out!" he shouted, storming into his office. "The whole fucking bunch of you!" While the writers began packing up to leave, Bernstein went after the Phils' pilot.

"You can't do that," screamed the AP writer.

Infuriated, Ozark threatened to punch Bernstein if he didn't leave him alone.

"Go ahead, hit me," challenged the sportswriter.

Ozark charged him, but was restrained by clubhouse manager Kenny Bush.

After the ugly episode, Bernstein and several angry writers marched up to the Phillies executive offices, demanding to see Ruly Carpenter. They met him in the lobby as he was about to catch the elevator. Initially, the team president was cordial and listened patiently to Bernstein describe the details of the confrontation. But when charges of "unprofessionalism" and "double standards" began to fly, Carpenter also became angry.

"Look Ralph, Danny is sick and tired of this bullshit," he snapped. "Every game he loses, you go down and second-guess him. I'm getting sick and tired of it, too." As he entered the elevator, Ruly muttered an insulting reference to the press corps as the "sons of bitches of the Fourth Estate." If there had been any questions about his attitude toward the local media, they disappeared after that incident. When asked about his relationship with the Philadelphia press in the future, Carpenter would respond defensively with the phrase: "When you allow the press to control your team, you know you're in trouble."[59]

In the end, Ozark prevailed. Forced to present the AP's Manager of the Year Award at the Philadelphia Sportswriters' Banquet, Bernstein handed the Phils' skipper the award and whispered to him, "I didn't vote for you." At that point, Ozark revealed a big red boxing glove he had tied onto his left hand and had kept hidden behind his back. "I've got something for you, too, Ralph," he quipped, holding the glove in front of the writer's nose.[60] Both men began to laugh, breaking the unmistakable tension in the room. But the repartee still didn't do much to improve the antagonistic relationship that existed between the club and the local media.

For better or worse, there were three daily newspapers in Philadelphia that covered the Phillies: the *Evening Bulletin*, the *Inquirer*, and the *Daily News*. The *Bulletin*, published by Robert Taylor, enjoyed the highest circulation. It was the most staid newspaper of the three dailies because it refrained from taking controversial editorial positions. Instead, the *Bulletin* concentrated on an impartial printing of the news gathered by a highly competent staff of reporters, including Ray Kelly, the beat writer for the Phillies whose columns were also reprinted by the *Sporting News*. He was regarded as a ballplayer's writer, fair, concise, and reflecting a good, sound knowledge of the game. Rich Ashburn, former Phillie turned broadcaster, also wrote a weekly column offering personal insights into the team and its players.[61]

The *Philadelphia Inquirer*, published by Knight Ridder, competed for the *Bulletin's* readers by printing the news in the morning and in a more colorful fashion. Allen Lewis was the primary baseball writer, but Frank Dolson, Bruce Keidan, and Larry Eichel also covered the game and its personalities.[62] Like Kelly, Lewis was a ballplayer's writer whose columns often alternated with Kelly's on the pages of the *Sporting News*. Because he grew up in nearby Havertown and attended Haverford College, Lewis was often accused of being partial to the Phillies in his writing. But he believes that he was able to empathize more with the circumstances of the ballplayers. This stemmed from the fact that he played baseball through his college years at Haverford. "I honestly believe that if you didn't play the sport you were covering, it's very difficult to write about it," said Lewis. "I was passionate about baseball long before I was a writer. I played the game in grade school, prep school, and college. That experience taught me that baseball looks a lot easier than it really is."

One of the ways Lewis ensured his objectivity was to attend a dozen high school and college games each season. The experience reinforced his belief that the "routine play" in the majors is often extremely difficult for players at the lower levels of the game to execute. "Watching those games," he said, "reminded me that baseball is one of the most difficult sports to play, and you had better be careful before criticizing a professional ballplayer. I never believed in writing negatively if I didn't have to. Sure, if a guy wasn't hustling, I'd write about it. But I'm not going to rip a guy if he's not hitting well. I'd give him the benefit of the doubt that he's trying."[63]

For the sportswriters at the *Philadelphia Daily News*, however, Lewis's attitude was "old school." The *Daily News*, a satellite of the *Inquirer*, was a tabloid that made very little effort to cover national or international news other than what was made available by the wire service. Instead, the newspaper promoted itself as the "people paper" and concentrated on stories of local human interest with a high emphasis on sports. Often accused of sensationalizing the news, the paper's sportswriters tended to make ballplayers flashier—and sometimes, more controversial—personalities than they really wore. Stan Hochman started the trend.

Hochman represented a new breed of aggressive young sportswriters known as the "chipmunks" when he served as the Phillies beat writer in the 1960s. The chipmunk writers sought to go beyond the statistics and narrative description of the game to focus on the players' personalities and clubhouse controversy. Forced to adjust their writing styles by the increasing popularity of television—which already brought to fans the events of the game—the chipmunks resorted to intrusive questioning in their postgame interviews and to scrutinizing the performances as well as lifestyles of the players.[64] Bill Conlin, who began his career with the *Bulletin* in 1964, switched to the *Daily News* the following year and quickly adopted the controversial style. By the 1970s, he was covering the Phillies as the paper's beat writer and Hochman became a columnist.

Hochman and Conlin set a precedent for Philadelphia's sportswriters. No longer could the beat writer afford to sit in the press box and wax eloquent about the game. The "scoop" was in the postgame interview, and the writer had to get it, no matter how intrusive he became. Fans were more interested in the players' personalities and their off-field behavior. The *Daily News's* afternoon deadline made the paper ideal for running those kinds of stories. "What was the point of getting to the ballpark at 3:30 in the afternoon when, with a 6:00 A.M. deadline, I had full run of the clubhouse?" asked Conlin. "I could walk right into the manager's office, sit down, and shoot the shit with him after the *Inquirer* and *Bulletin* beat writers went up to meet their deadlines. That's when I did my best interviewing and got the 'inside' stuff that always gave the *Daily News* an edge on the morning newspapers. While they were reporting what kind of pitch was hit for a home run, I was reporting whether the guy was sober or hung over when he hit it."[65] Nor did Conlin entertain any reservations about reporting controversial stories.

"I'm one of those old-fashioned, loyal guys," said the *Daily News* scribe. "I've always felt that my first responsibility was to my readers and to the newspaper I work for. Everything else should follow that. As a beat writer, you need to tell the story of the baseball season—warts and all—without permanently hurting too many people. I can tell you stuff that happened on the road involving writers and players. Incidents of adultery, players getting high on LSD, or dropping something in someone's drink at a party, players going AWOL on the club. None of that stuff was ever written about because there is a certain trust that exists between the press and the players. At the same time, if it's necessary to offend some people, or to step on some toes, well, that goes with the territory. The fact is, a beat writer travels with the club. There's no place to hide. You have to go into the clubhouse after the game. You have to pull your neck in, grin and bear it while a manager is calling you a cocksucker. That goes with the territory."[66]

Conlin's philosophy grated on Ruly Carpenter and Danny Ozark. They felt that the *Daily News* writers, in particular, broke the trust that once existed between the ballplayers and the sportswriters. "You could be straight with writers like Ray Kelly, Allen Lewis, and Frank Dolson because they traveled and drank with the players," said Carpenter in a recent interview. "There was a certain level of trust that developed between the two. You didn't have to worry about what they'd write because they focused on the game. But there were others I had trouble with, like Stan Hochman and Bill Conlin, who wrote for the *Daily News*. I wasn't naive. I realized that being in professional sports you and your team are going to be crit- icized. I also realized the writers had a job to do. But when there were *factual* inaccuracies and clear distortions, that's when I'd call them in and we'd talk it out."[67] Ozark echoed his former employer's feelings. "The Philadelphia press was very critical about the things I did," he recalled. "They inflated many of my quotes and, I think, egged on the fans when we weren't winning."[68] Many of the play- ers agreed with Ozark's assessment.

"There was an undercurrent of suspicion surrounding our team among the Philadelphia sportswriters," Tug McGraw explained. "We were labeled spoiled, overpaid underachievers. We didn't have the guts to win. So whenever we'd win a big game, you'd hear the guys in the clubhouse say, 'Take that overpaid crap and shove it up your ass.'"[69] Mike Schmidt was a bit more tactful, if not humor- ous. Schmidt, after reading an especially galling story by Bill Conlin, quipped: "Philadelphia is the only city where you can experience the thrill of victory and the agony of reading about it the next day."[70]

While Carpenter, Ozark, and the players may have had their problems with the media, Paul Owens never did. "Pope understood the press," said Conlin. "He was a 'no-bullshit' person and I was the same way. That's why we respected each other. But that never deterred me from criticizing him in print when I felt it was necessary. He understood that I had a job to do and never stopped talking to me after something I wrote."[71]

To be sure, the local press *did* fuel the negativity of the fans by scrutinizing the players on and off the field. The newspapers were the fans' most direct con- nection to the team at a time when the players and management were isolating themselves from the public. With the escalation of salaries, free agency, and de- clining loyalties between employer and employee, athletes no longer lived in the city where they played. Those who did lived in the wealthier suburbs and jeal- ously guarded their privacy. Fewer and fewer agreed to make public appearances, even if they were paid to do so. As a result, the fans relied increasingly on the newspapers to learn about their hometown heroes, their personalities, and their shortcomings. If the team didn't win, the newspapers would be the first to point out that the players didn't deserve the high salaries they were making. If the ball-player didn't get his uniform dirty and show his emotions on the playing field, the sportswriters would call him a "prima donna," someone who felt as if he was better than his teammates. Phillies fans, already disappointed with years of los-ing, were influenced by those judgments and registered their disapproval at the ballpark. The problem was exacerbated by the nature of the game itself.

One of the reasons baseball, more than any other sport, is considered the national pastime is due to the common man's ability to relate with it. He may not know a "hit-and-run" from a "suicide squeeze," but he's still convinced that he can play the game at least as well as the athletes who are paid extravagant sums of money to do it. Oftentimes, the players themselves try to appease the fans by saying that "they know the game," in the hope that such a sign of "respect" will keep the jeers at bay. Tony Taylor, for example, was a fan favorite in Philadelphia for many years not only because he hustled, but because he swore by Phillies fans as "very knowledgeable, the best in the game." He claimed that the faithful "get a bad rap" because, "knowing the game so well, they will make you accountable."[72]

Mike Schmidt, who spent all seventeen years of a Hall of Fame career in Phil-adelphia, had a different perspective. "Our fans overreact both ways," he observed, in the mid-1970s. "When you're in a slump, they're brutal and when you're going good they make you come out of the dugout and tip your cap for every little thing. They're so passionate it scares the hell out of me. You're trying your damnedest. You strike out and they boo you. I act like it doesn't bother me, like I don't hear anything. But the truth is I hear every word and it kills me."[73] Of course, Phillies fans begrudged Schmidt because he refused to get visibly angry, kick a water cooler, or pick a fight with an opposing player when things didn't go his way. When asked why he didn't show more emotion on the diamond, Schmidt simply replied: "What good would it do? The pitcher doesn't get me out. I get myself out."[74]

Perhaps Jim Lonborg, who enjoyed the advantage of playing in several differ-ent cities, provided the most diplomatic assessment of Phillies fans when he said that they gave him "quite an education." "It was one thing coming from Boston where the fans were tremendously nice and very knowledgeable," observed the gentleman right-hander who won a Cy Young Award with the Red Sox. "In Mil-waukee, the fans were dealing with a rebuilding situation so they had more of a 'let's-go-to-the-game-and-have-fun' mentality as opposed to getting on the play-ers. Then I came to Philadelphia, and it was pretty different. I got booed a lot. But that got to my wife more than it got to me. I tried to tell her that they weren't booing me, personally, that I just happened to be the guy who wasn't pitching very well. I think, eventually, I won over the hearts of the fans. I left Philadel-phia [in 1979] feeling very good about them. I think they felt the same way about me, realizing that I had contributed to the team's success."[75]

To be sure, Phillies fans, more than most, believe themselves entitled to a winner, especially the so-called Boo Birds. That small but vocal minority will provoke, jeer, and cajole the ballplayers when they fail to meet their expectations, which are impossibly high. As a result, the City of Brotherly Love has earned the reputation as the cradle of the "boo," it's very own Cooperstown. Sportswriter Frank Dolson, who covered the team for the *Philadelphia Inquirer*, understands that mentality, though. Phillies fans, he explains, have "learned to live with adversity, but never to accept it." "In the late 1960s and early 1970s, the fans waited for next year, and the year after that, and the year after *that*, swearing at their frequently flawed heroes." But Dolson also insisted that the fans, deep down, "realize that as bad as the bad years were, they served a useful purpose—making the good years, and the world championship when it finally arrived in 1980, seem even better."[76] By 1977, that championship was just around the corner.

The '77 Phillies were a more versatile club than the '80 world champions. They had tremendous depth, a tight defense, a powerful offense that chalked up enough runs to end a game in the early innings, an effective bullpen, and a strong starting rotation. To replace Dave Cash, who left for Montreal, the Phillies acquired Ted Sizemore from the Los Angeles Dodgers in exchange for catcher Johnny Oates. Sizemore had been the Rookie of the Year in 1969 and, in the eight years he played for L.A. and St. Louis, had forged a reputation as a "team player" who provided a steady defense at second base and hit for a .260 average.[77] The Phillies dipped into the free agent market and gave a three-year, $600,000 contract to Richie Hebner to fill their need at first base. Hebner, an off-season gravedigger, had been a third baseman for the Pittsburgh Pirates and an integral part of the teams that captured five division championships and a world championship in 1971. A steady .275 hitter, he was the Phils' very first free agent signing and became a major contributor to the team's offense. "I loved Philadelphia," Hebner said in a recent interview. "It was a blue collar town and I'm a blue collar guy. I fit in well there. I knew I was going to have to move over from third base to play first, but I didn't care. The Phillies had a great team, and however I could help them out, I'd do it." [78] Together with Bowa and Schmidt, Sizemore and Hebner gave the Phils a better infield, offensively and defensively, than they had enjoyed the previous season.

The outfield was solid. Luzinski provided an adequate defense in left and power at the plate. If he needed a rest, Jerry Martin, a better defensive outfielder and .250 hitter, could provide some relief. Maddox, widely acknowledged as the best defensive center fielder in baseball, had also rediscovered his batting stroke and could hit for both power and average. Right field was platooned by three players. Jay Johnstone, a .300 hitter, played against right handers. Ollie Brown and Jerry Martin split time against left handers.

Carlton was the ace of the pitching staff, with Christenson, Lonborg, and

Lerch rounding out the starting rotation. Kaat and Underwood were spot starters.
McGraw, Garber, Reed, and Warren Brusstar were in the bullpen. The bench
was anchored by seasoned veterans: Ollie Brown, Terry Harmon, Tommy Hutton, Davey Johnson, Jay Johnstone, Tim McCarver, and Bobby Tolan. Brown,
Johnstone, and Tolan gave Ozark flexibility in the outfield, while Hutton, Harmon, and Johnson provided versatility and experience in the infield. McCarver
continued to be Carlton's personal catcher and spelled Boone when necessary.[79]

The Phillies also had a special chemistry that was kept intact by pranksters
like Tug McGraw and Jay Johnstone, self-confessed flakes. Johnstone, who had
developed a lighthearted relationship with Danny Ozark during their years together in Los Angeles, kept his teammates entertained with his uninhibited clubhouse antics. He was infamous for playing Oscar Madison to Ozark's Felix Unger
in baseball's version of the "Odd Couple." Johnstone especially liked to break in
the rookies by giving hotfoots in the dugout, nailing their spikes to the floor, and
charging room service to their hotel bills on the first road trip. The fans loved
him as well. The flaky outfielder entertained them during rain delays with headfirst belly slides across the wet infield tarp, placing towels under his uniform
shirt to make it bulge so he could imitate Babe Ruth's "called shot," and sneak-
ing in from right field to pick off a runner who was taking a big lead off first
base. "That was a great trick play," recalled first baseman Richie Hebner. "I set
up about ten feet behind the runner and you'd get some guys who weren't paying attention. They thought I wasn't holding 'em on and Johnstone would quietly cheat his way up the first base line. Boone, who had a real accurate arm,
would make a snap throw on the inside of the bag. If Jay got the tag down quickly
the runner was out. It was an absolute joke, but that play got us out of a couple
serious jams."[80] Hardly a game went by that some fan didn't hang a bed sheet
in the upper deck with the rhythmic plea to "Play Jay Every Day."[81] McGraw,
whom Johnstone called a "pre-meditated joker," was even more beloved.[82]

No matter how poorly the Phillies played in the post-season, or how badly he
might have pitched on occasion, the Tugger refused to allow disappointment to
spoil his fun. During spring training in 1976, he asked pitching coach Ray Ripplemeyer to add him to the rotation on his favorite holiday, St. Patrick's Day,
even though he had just hurled the previous day. Ripplemeyer agreed and when
he called him in to pitch, McGraw entered the game with a green uniform in
honor of St. Paddy. "Tug had gotten together with the clubhouse guy and comes
in to the game in a white and red pinstriped Phillies' uniform, dyed completely
green," recalled Ripplemeyer. "The fans went crazy," he added.[83] So did the
umpire, who threw McGraw out of the game for wearing an "illegal" uniform,
one that did not match those of his teammates. But that didn't stop Tug. Once
again, on St. Patrick's Day in 1977, McGraw asked to pitch. Again he was called
on to relieve. "What, no green uniform this year?" asked the home plate umpire,

referring to the earlier prank. The irreverent Irishman responded by turning his behind to home plate and dropping his drawers to reveal green underwear. Once again, he was thrown out of the game.[84]

McGraw could be just as fun loving with his teammates. Since he and Mike Schmidt lived in suburban Media, they would often drive to the Vet together during home stands. When he wasn't driving, Tug made a habit of reading aloud the *Daily News* sports pages. "Did ya read this, Mike?" he would ask, spotting a headline about his successful outing in the previous night's game. "MCGRAW SHUTS DOWN THE METS TO SEAL PHILS' WIN," blared the comic reliever in full voice. Naturally, Tug would then recap his performance in full detail, just to rub it in. "Oh yeah," he would add, "there's a small line about you, too, Schmitty." Then, in a quiet, squeaky voice—"Schmidt hit 2 homers and drove in 5 runs." McGraw would then volunteer the editorial comment "Big deal" and return to the account of his own pitching exploits.[85] Larry Christenson was another favorite target. On days when Christenson started, Tug would prance up to his locker and say: "Hey, Larry, you pitchin' today?" When L.C. answered in the affirmative, McGraw would quip "Me, too!"—the suggestion being that Christenson couldn't complete his own games.[86]

Because of his buoyant personality and his genuine interest in the fans, Tug quickly became the Phillies' greatest ambassador. He was visible to the public, making himself accessible to the fans, and he rarely charged for autographs. McGraw performed with the Philadelphia Orchestra, sketched a weekly newspaper comic called "Scroogie," based on a pitching leprechaun with eternal optimism, and was the first to volunteer his services to community organizations during the off-season.[87] Once, Tug, who served as sports chairman for Philadelphia's Muscular Dystrophy Foundation, made a 16-day, 900-mile bicycle journey to spring training to promote that cause. Accompanied by Larry Christenson, Steve Carlton, Jerry Martin, and Eagles quarterback Roman Gabriel, the Tugger and his entourage stopped to visit with muscular dystrophy patients along the way.[88] Predictably, Tug was in constant demand as a speaker, though his humor was not always appreciated.

When the Westtown School, where he sent his children, for example, asked if he would be the parent chairman for the Quaker boarding school's capital campaign, McGraw eagerly agreed. During the kickoff event, he ended his speech with a prediction about just how successful the campaign would be. Evoking the image of the first humans standing naked in the Garden of Eden, the Tugger told his audience that his excitement rivaled Adam's when he said to Eve, "Better back off, baby, there's no telling how big this thing will get!"[89] According to John Nicholson, who served on the Westtown Board of Trustees, "it was a hilarious line, but not for a straitlaced Quaker audience." Moments earlier, people had been laughing at McGraw's one-liners, quips, and humorous anecdotes. It seemed as if the campaign was off to a great start. But after Tug made the phallic reference, "you could actually hear the wallets of the large donors snapping shut," recalled Nicholson.[90] Afterward, McGraw was more careful to do his homework before speaking to an audience. But even Tug's humor couldn't erase the sting of poor play.

The Phillies got off to a slow start in 1977, losing four straight games. The Chicago Cubs dominated the early going. By late April, the team found itself mired in last place. Schmidt was hitting an anemic .182 and 3 of his 7 hits were home runs. Once again, Ozark grew tired of all the third baseman's strikeouts. In one particularly dismal performance against the Pittsburgh Pirates, Schmidt whiffed in three straight plate appearances. There would be no fourth at bat. Ozark lifted Michael Jack in the eighth inning for pinch hitter Jay Johnstone. "He was struggling and I thought I would put a better hitter up there with two men on in the eighth," Ozark said, explaining the move. "Johnstone gave me a lot of clutch hits in the past as a pinch hitter."

When Ray Kelly of the *Bulletin* asked what the move would do to Schmidt's confidence, Ozark replied: "It might ease things for him. He might come back tomorrow with a different attitude. This could make him a bigger man than he is."[91] Once again, Ozark was delivering his point through the press. While he might have been trying to motivate Schmidt, the Phils manager only distanced himself more from the sensitive third baseman, who tended to be his own worst critic. To Schmidt's credit, he responded diplomatically when Kelly asked for his side of the story. "Hey, it's early in the season," he told them. "I haven't batted 50 times yet. Besides, my teammates have confidence in me. I know that much. They've seen me strike out three times in a row and then hit a home run. That could have happened tonight, if I had that fourth at-bat. But I can't second-guess the manager. Maybe if I was in his position, I would have done the same thing."[92]

The team's fortunes began to turn on May 7 when Kaat, Garber, Reed, and Underwood pitched shutout relief against the Dodgers for a 7-4 victory at Los Angeles. Carlton went on a streak that stretched to 16 straight home victories. Luzinski went on an offensive tear, hitting at a .360 clip, which allowed the Phillies to win 8 of 10 games during the last two weeks of the month. On May 31, the Phils found themselves in fourth place, just 3 games behind the division-leading Cubs, when they suffered another tailspin. Although Luzinski continued his hot hitting into June, the Phils had difficulty winning. After their fourth straight loss, on June 15, Paul Owens traded pitcher Tommy Underwood and outfielders Dane Iorg and Rick Bosetti to the St. Louis Cardinals for Bake McBride, a speedy right fielder who had been Rookie of the Year in 1974. The Cards believed that his career was over because of chronic knee problems. Instead, McBride became a dependable leadoff hitter and a serious threat on the base paths. He also proved to be tremendously popular with the fans, who nicknamed him,

"Shake-and-Bake."[93] McBride joined Luzinski and Maddox to give the Phillies one of the best outfields in baseball with a potent combination of speed, defense, and power at the plate. The acquisition saved the season for the Phillies, who rediscovered their winning ways.

On June 19, Carlton defeated the Atlanta Braves, 4-2, for his 100th career victory as a Phillie putting the Phils in second place, 5½ games behind Chicago. During the Sunday afternoon game a top-heavy, exotic dancer by the name of Morganna Roberts, bounced out of a third base field box, wrapped her arms around Mike Schmidt's neck, and planted a kiss on his lips. Michael Jack was speechless, taken completely by surprise. But after the game he admitted that the fans could "boo all they want if they keep sending them out like that!"[94] If nothing else, the incident seemed to motivate the slumping third baseman.

Three days later, Schmidt led the Phillies in a 15-9 assault against the Cincinnati Reds, hitting his 17th and 18th home runs of the seasons and driving in four runs. Bowa, hit a grand slam in the seventh inning and, as he circled the bases, told Pete Rose to "take a ride on that one."[95] Schmidt continued his hot streak over the next two weeks, hitting three more home runs and driving in 16 more runs. Luzinski was also hot, on pace to hit 40 home runs. McBride was the sparkplug, starting the offensive rallies and hitting in the clutch.

Fans were visiting the Vet in droves, inspired not only by the team's winning performance, but also some of the greatest promotions in major league baseball, including trapeze acts, a motorcycle ridden on a high wire, parachute jumpers, cow-milking contests, and a "cash scramble," where fans raced around the field scooping up as much money as they could find. An old-timers game, which pitted former Phillies against a collection of former major league All-Stars, was also popular with the fans. Even the Playboy Bunnies participated in a softball game.[96] Attendance was at record levels. On July 2, the Phils topped the one million mark, the earliest date in club history. Two days later, on July 4, 63,283 spectators packed the Vet to see Ollie Brown's two-run triple beat the New York Mets, 3-1. It was the largest regular season crowd in the history of Philadelphia baseball.[97]

The Phillies finally took over first place on August 5 with an 8-3 win over the Dodgers and never looked back. During the next two weeks they went on a 13-game tear, sweeping the Dodgers at Veterans Stadium, winning three more against the Expos at home, and then traveling to Chicago where they won another four-game series. Carlton's performance was especially impressive. On August 21, he struck out 14 Houston Astros en route to a 7-3 victory. Ten days later, Lefty won his 15th straight game at the Vet. On September 5, he improved his season record to 20-8 in an 11-1 rout of the Pittsburgh Pirates. After the game, an exasperated Willie Stargell said, "Hitting Carlton was like trying to drink coffee with a fork."[98] Lefty's 16th consecutive victory at the Vet came on September 9 against the St. Louis Cardinals, a performance in which he struck out 14 hitters. Carlton would go on to win two more starting assignments to complete the regular season with a 23-10 record. Together with the 198 strikeouts and 2.64 ERA he compiled, Lefty's 23 victories earned him a second Cy Young Award.[99]

Carlton's success can be attributed to his almost singular preoccupation with the mental aspect of the game. "My job was my performance on the field," he insisted. "So I found ways to eliminate any outside influence in order to give the best of my mental and physical capabilities. Then I go out there and I know I'm going to win. Every game. I don't lose. I never mention that word."[100] On days he was scheduled to pitch, the tall left-hander avoided teammates, cloistering himself inside a small room adjoining the clubhouse. Known as the "mood room," Carlton, eyes closed and in a meditative state, would visualize the lanes of home plate: inside, outside, and center. "Steve would tell himself, 'The plate is 17 inches wide. The center lane, which is 12 inches, belongs to the hitter, explained his catcher Tim McCarver. The inside and outside—which are 2½ each— are mine. If I pitch to spots properly, there's no way the batter can hit the ball hard on a consistent basis.'"[101]

Carlton was also a devotee of the martial arts, which emphasized the need to integrate the physical being with the mind and soul for a productive life. He became well read in Eastern philosophies like Taoism and Buddhism, and abandoned the traditional pitcher's workout of running and calisthenics for strength and flexibility training. Lefty followed a program that was designed on a 360-degree range of motion, giving him much greater flexibility than he possessed at the beginning of his career. One of the most unusual practices was plunging his pitching arm into a huge barrel of white rice and slowly pushing it to the bottom. He also walked around the clubhouse squeezing two steel balls to strengthen his wrist and forearm. Tim McCarver, his personal catcher, claimed that those activities gave Lefty such strong forearms that he was able to "get a tight spin on his slider, making him such an effective pitcher." In fact, Carlton was so devoted to his conditioning that he sometimes carried the steel balls with him wherever he went. Once, the two teammates were eating at the Maisonette, a French restaurant in Cincinnati. Lefty, who had been squeezing the balls during the meal, forgot them. As the two players walked out to their car, the maître d' came running out of the restaurant, shouting: "Monsieur Carlton, you left your balls on ze table!"[102]

Carlton's desire to "eliminate any outside influence" also included the press. The decision to stop all interviews was a gradual one that began in 1973 when *Daily News* sportswriter Bill Conlin attributed his poor pitching to the "off-season banquet circuit." Carlton, an intensely private individual, took exception to the remark and shunned Conlin for quite some time, though he continued to speak with other members of the press. The two men reconciled during spring training in 1976, but it was short-lived. That spring, the owners, in a last-ditch effort to protect the reserve system, locked the players out of camp. To register his frustration with baseball's ongoing labor conflict, Conlin wrote a sarcastic piece about the hypocrisy of the players who were complaining about "poor working conditions" when they enjoyed such a luxurious lifestyle. As an example, he pointed to a "Bloody Mary drinking contest" Carlton had organized the year before during a delayed flight from Atlanta to San Diego. Lefty, allegedly, collected $20 from each of his teammates and instructed the bartender to keep the vodka and tomato juice on hand until the money ran out or the flight was called. After Carlton heard about the article, he stopped talking to all the writers, though he did agree to go on record occasionally with a select few when he was in an especially generous mood.[103] The final break came in 1978, according to Tim McCarver, when after winning his 200th career victory, Lefty agreed to a mass interview. *Daily News* columnist Stan Hochman was the first to ask a question.

"Danny [Ozark] has a theory . . . ," he began.

Before Hochman could complete his question, Carlton, whose disdain for Ozark was well known, chuckled and remarked: "This oughtta be good."

The following day, Hochman made reference to the quip in his column. Infuriated, Carlton refused to speak to the press again until he was released by the Phillies in June 1986.[104]

When asked, years later, why he refused to cooperate with the media, Carlton insisted that "it was just something I had to do." "I found that talking to the press took my focus away," he explained. "I thought about it for more than a year and finally decided I was cheating the fans and myself by allowing myself to be diverted mentally. It was one less obstacle for me, like the hitter."[105] Ultimately, members of the press didn't care if Carlton spoke with them or not as long as he won whenever he pitched. Instead, they dismissed him as an "eccentric" and simply continued to report his Hall of Fame achievements, relying on McCarver for color commentary, which he readily gave.

The Phillies finally clinched the National League's Eastern Division on September 27 when Larry Christenson won his own game, 15-9, with a grand slam home run against the Cubs at Wrigley Field. Five days later, they ended the regular season 5 games ahead of the second-place Pirates, equaling the club's record for victories with 101. Privately, the front office claimed that this was the best team in the organization's nearly century-old history. It featured one of the best pitching staffs in the National League, led by Cy Young Award-winner Steve Carlton (23-10, 198K, 2.64 ERA). Larry Christenson enjoyed the finest season of his career with a 19-6 record. Jim Lonborg contributed 11 wins, and Randy Lerch another 10. The bullpen was just as strong with McGraw, Gene Garber, Ron Reed, and Warren Brusstar combining for 29 victories and 46 of the team's 47 league-leading saves. Offensively, the Phils were even better. They had the National

League's most potent one-two punch in Schmidt (.274, 38 HR, 101 RBI) and Luzinski (.309, 39 HR, 130 RBI), who finished second in the voting for the league's Most Valuable Player. McBride (.339, 11 HR, 41 RBI) exceeded all expectations, providing the team with a reliable leadoff hitter. Similarly, Hebner (.285, 18 HR, 62 RBI) and Sizemore (.281, 4 HR, 47 RBI) improved significantly the right side of the infield. As a team, the Phils led the National League with a .279 average and 847 runs. Their 186 homers set a new all-time mark in franchise history.[106]

The Phillies faced the Los Angeles Dodgers in the playoffs. The Dodgers finished 10 games ahead of the defending world champions Cincinnati Reds in the National League's Western Division. The key to their success was their starting pitching. Burt Hooton (12-7, 2.62 ERA) was their ace, though he had an off-season. Don Sutton (14-8, 3.19 ERA), Tommy John (20-7, 2.78 ERA), Rick Rhoden (16-10, 3.75 ERA), and Doug Rau (14-8, 3.44 ERA) rounded out the rotation. The Dodger bullpen was less reliable. With the exceptions of closer Charlie Hough (22 SV, 3.33 ERA) and set-up man Mike Garman (12 SV, 2.71 ERA), the relief corps had neither the depth nor the experience of the Phillies bullpen.

The Dodgers infield was not as good defensively as the Phils, but they did pose a mighty offensive threat. Catcher Steve Yeager (.256, 16 HR, 55 RBI) was a solid defensive catcher who was capable of hitting the ball out of the park. Shortstop Bill Russell (.278, 4 HR, 51 RBI) and second baseman Davey Lopes (.283, 11 HR, 53 RBI) were good, steady ballplayers capable of stealing a base as well as hitting home runs. First baseman Steve Garvey (.297, 33 HR, 115 RBI) and third baseman Ron Cey (.241, 30 HR, 110 RBI) were more dangerous. The outfield also produced runs. Right fielder Reggie Smith (.307, 32 HR, 87 RBI) and left fielder Dusty Baker (.291, 30 HR, 86 RBI) were young power hitters who could deliver in the clutch. Rick Monday (.230, 15 HR 48 RBI), the center fielder, wasn't much of an offensive threat, but he covered a lot of ground in the outfield.[107]

The experts believed that if the Phillies could earn a split in Los Angeles, where the series opened, they would be a cinch to win the pennant, having posted a 60-21 regular season record at the Vet. Carlton faced Tommy John in the opener and enjoyed a 5-1 lead going into the seventh when he surrendered a grand slam home run to Ron Cey. But Schmidt broke the deadlock in the ninth on a one-run single, and the Phillies added another run and managed to hang on for the 7-5 victory, their first postseason win in twenty-seven years.[108] "Momentum's a big thing in a short series like this," said the slugging third baseman after the game. "The momentum took a drastic turn on Cey's home run. For us to rise to the occasion and turn the momentum around—that's a tough thing to do."[109] Luzinski was even more confident. "I've got a feeling this thing could be three in a row," predicted the Bull, who hit a two-run homer to dead center in the first inning. "We're practically unbeatable at home. I can't see any way we'll lose two out of three at the Vet."[110] Luzinski had spoken too soon.

Lonborg faced Don Sutton in Game Two. It looked as if the Phils might get more than a split in Los Angeles when Bake McBride hit a solo home run in the third to give Lonnie a 1-0 lead. But the Dodgers tied the game in the bottom of that inning. Los Angeles went ahead for good in the fourth when Lonborg hung a slider to Dusty Baker, who crushed the ball for a grand slam home run. The Dodgers had evened the series with a 7-1 victory.[111]

The Phillies were still confident as the series moved to the Vet. Larry Christenson faced Burt Hooton in Game Three before a sellout crowd of 63,719. L.C. surrendered two runs in the top of the second inning, but the Phils rallied in the bottom half. Hooton became wild, to the delight of the Boo Birds. The more they jeered the Dodger pitcher, the more unnerved he became. When the inning had finally ended, Hooton had issued four straight walks to force three runs across the plate, and the Phillies held a 3-2 lead. "I don't think I've ever heard noise like that," remarked Bowa. "They hooted the guy right off the mound."[112] Stan Hochman of the *Daily News* would later applaud the fans' boorish behavior, calling it a "clutch performance" worthy of an "MVP—'Most Valuable Patrons'—Award."[113]

The Phillies added another two runs and enjoyed a 5-3 lead going into the ninth. Gene Garber retired the first two batters and then the floodgates opened. Garber surrendered an infield single to pinch hitter Vic Davalillo. Manny Mota, another pinch hitter, followed. He hit a catchable line drive toward the warning track in the left field corner. Luzinski got his glove on the ball but couldn't hold on to it. When he retrieved it, the Bull threw home in an attempt to peg Davalillo at the plate. But second baseman Ted Sizemore botched the relay throw, allowing Mota to advance to third. Now the Dodgers had the tying run in scoring position.[114]

"I can't understand why Danny left Bull in the game," Bowa said later. "All year long, he'd take him out for a defensive replacement late in the game. Sure as hell, a fly ball goes out there to Jerry Martin, he'd just suck it up. If he's out there, we'd win the game."[115]

With the Phillies clinging to a one-run lead, Dodger second baseman, Davey Lopes, smashed a hard liner to third. The ball hit off Schmidt's left leg and deflected to an alert Bowa who threw to first in a last-ditch effort to get the final out. It was a bang-bang play, but umpire Bruce Froemming ruled Lopes safe as the tying run crossed the plate. Bowa, incredulous, went after Froemming, screaming that he had blown the call. First baseman Richie Hebner beat him to it and Ozark was forced to restrain both of them.[116] "Lopes was out," Hebner insisted in a recent interview, still reeling at the memory. "That was a big ass play in the game, and it really broke our backs. But what are you going to do? It didn't go our way. We just couldn't beat 'em."[117]

More chaos followed. An errant pick off attempt by Garber and a single by Dodger shortstop Bill Russell scored Lopes, giving Los Angeles a 6-5 lead, which they preserved in the bottom of the inning for the victory.

During the postgame interview, Ozark was asked to explain why he didn't replace Luzinski with Jerry Martin in the ninth inning, an obvious defensive move he had made throughout the season when the Phillies had a lead. "In this kind of a series, you don't know what's going to happen," insisted the Phils manager. "If the Dodgers tie it or go ahead in the ninth, I still have Bull coming to bat in the bottom of the inning."[118]

The press honed in for the kill. Bruce Keidan of the *Inquirer* referred to the 6-5 loss as "giveaway day at the Vet."[119] His colleague, Frank Dolson, called Ozark's reasoning "astounding." "Instead of managing to protect a two-run lead in the top of the ninth," he wrote, "Ozark was concerned with having his top RBI man available to bat in the bottom of the ninth in the event that the Dodgers scored two or three runs. It was negative thinking carried to the extreme."[120] Dolson had a valid criticism.

Ozark should have quit while he was ahead. Instead, he made the situation worse by trying to defend Luzinski's miscue. "Bull broke in on the ball a little bit," he explained. "If he got back right away, he'd have caught it very easily. If I knew the same ball was going to be hit, I'd have put Martin in there. But Mota's a guy that doesn't pull the ball."[121] Realizing that he was getting nowhere, Ozark changed the subject. He diverted blame for the loss to Froemming's controversial call at first base. "He was stunned by Bowa's throw," insisted Ozark. "He just anticipated that Bowa couldn't make the throw. He didn't know what the fuck to call it, so he called it safe."[122] The writers didn't care about Froemming's call, though. The following day Ozark was excoriated in the newspapers for blowing the game by leaving Luzinski in left field.

"The Philadelphia sportswriters were always trying to get Danny fired," said Richie Hebner. "I could never understand it. Here's a guy who won 100 games two years in a row and took us to the playoffs, but it still wasn't good enough for them. Some of the players even complained about his moves. I'd just tell 'em, 'Look, if you can't play for this guy, who can you play for?' I played for a lot of managers and, to me, Danny Ozark was one of the best because he made out the lineup and he let you play."[123]

Regardless of who was to blame, the game was the most heartbreaking loss for a team that was perhaps the best ever in the history of the organization. In a strange way, the defeat embodied all the hard luck that seemed to follow the Phillies, generation after generation, validating the pessimism of the city's fans, who learned to live by Murphy's Law.

Game Four was a rain-soaked rematch between Steve Carlton and Tommy John, whose sinker was unhittable. Baker smacked a two-run homer in the second inning, which provided all the runs the Dodgers needed in their 4-1, pennant-clinching victory.[124] "They said we didn't belong on the same field with the Phillies," boasted Dodger manager Tommy Lasorda, a Norristown native, after the game. "They said we couldn't win at the Vet. But we believed from the first day of spring training that we could beat anybody."[125]

Perhaps the most fitting epitaph to the Phillies' tragic postseason came from Bill Conlin of the *Daily News,* who compared the final two playoff games to forensic medicine. "Does death occur when the heart stops, or when the brain ceases to function?" he asked his readers. "The Phillies heart stopped when [Bake] McBride became [Tommy] John's eighth strikeout victim [to end Game Four]," he replied. "But the Phillies' brain ceased to function the day before in the ninth inning when they let victory slip away. Death had come to the executioners. The Phillies had met the enemy and it was them."[126]

If there was a silver lining to the season, it had to be credited to Paul Owens, who made sure that 95 percent of the players were signed through the next season, and many for two-to-four-year commitments. "I'll guarantee that, barring injuries, we'll be in contention for the next four years," predicted the Phils general manager. "We've got players in their prime and the sort of program that's ideal for continuity."

Owens had masterfully blended the nucleus of homegrown players with veterans acquired through trades. Of the 1978 twenty-five-man roster, nine were products of the farm system (Boone, Bowa, Brusstar, Christenson, Harmon, Lerch, Luzinski, Martin, and Schmidt) and another nine (Carlton, Hutton, Kaat, Lonborg, Maddox, McGraw, Reed, Sizemore, and McBride) were acquired through trades in which the Phillies benefited. Owens also strengthened the Phillies by signing other teams' castoffs, including Ollie Brown, Davey Johnson, Jay Johnstone, and Tim McCarver, all of whom he picked up on waivers.[127] The disadvantage to the organization, however, was a $3,474,325 payroll, second only to the Yankees' at $3,497,900 in 1978. Even then, the average salary on the Phillies was $140,000, about $1,000 more than the average Yankee salary, while the average major league salary was considerably lower at $76,349.[128] With that kind of payroll, the press and the fans expected nothing less than a trip to the World Series, and the players knew it.

"The guys know they should have won it all last year," said Ozark in spring training. "I think they'll be kicking themselves in the butt this season and go to it from the start."[129] The Phillies manager was prophetic. His team got off to a great start, winning a club record 10 games in April. That same month, the Phillie Phanatic made his debut. Named after the fanatical Phillies fans, the 7-foot, 300-pound furry green creature had a huge, round belly and a large circular beak. Inside the beak was a curled, red tongue that shot out whenever he disagreed with an umpire's call or wanted to capture the attention of a fan. The Phanatic was the brainchild of the Phillies marketing department, which sought to create a "mascot that would rival the San Diego Padres' chicken." Dave Raymond, a former University of Delaware football player who was interning with the Phillies, jumped at the opportunity to wear the costume. Over the next few years, Raymond would give the Phanatic a mischievous, but fun-loving personality and win rave reviews from fans and players across the nation. The Phanatic entertained crowds during all eighty-one of the Phillies' home games. He began with a twenty-minute pregame performance, cajoling opposing players and dancing with fans atop the Phils' dugout. A similar display would follow the bottom of the fifth inning, and, after the seventh inning, he would lead the crowd in singing, "Take Me Out to the Ball Game." During the contest itself, the Phanatic roamed the stands, visiting fans, giving "Happy Birthday" wishes, and stealing a kiss from attractive young women.[130] It was yet another masterstroke by Bill Giles and his public relations staff.

As the June 15 trade deadline neared, Owens reacquired Dick Ruthven from the Atlanta Braves for reliever Gene Garber. Ruthven had been unhappy in Atlanta. But he benefited from the mentoring of the Braves' ace Andy Messersmith, and returned to Philadelphia as a very effective control pitcher. Happy to be out of Atlanta, Rufus went on to win 13 of his next 18 decisions. Carlton (16-13), Christenson (13-14), and Lerch (11-8) pitched much better than their records indicated, and the Phillies found themselves in first place for most of the season. Their biggest lead was 11½ games on August 12, but the Pirates went on a tear, winning 20 of 22 games. The Bucs cut the Phillies' lead to 3½ games with 4 left to play on September 30, and the division title came down to a season-ending series in Pittsburgh.

The Pirates swept the Phillies in a Friday night doubleheader, beating Carlton and Reed. With just a 1½ game lead, Ozark sent Randy Lerch to the mound the next day. Willie Stargell hit a mammoth grand slam home run in the first inning to give the Bucs a 4-1 lead. But Lerch calmed down and led the comeback with two homers of his own. Luzinski's three-run homer and a three-run double by Hebner put the Phils on top, 10-4. Although the Pirates rallied for 4 runs in the ninth, Ron Reed struck out Stargell and forced Phil Garner to ground out, sealing the division-clinching victory.[131]

Once again, the Phillies faced the Los Angeles Dodgers in the playoffs. This time, the series opened in Philadelphia and the Phils were out for revenge. Ozark predicted that his team would beat the Dodgers in "three straight." Larry Christenson faced Burt Hooton in the opener and was knocked out of the game early, surrendering 7 runs, six of them earned, on 7 hits in just 4⅓ innings. To make matters worse, it started raining and a puddle formed near the third base cutout. Schmidt, charging a slow roller that landed in the puddle, committed an error that led to one of the seven runs. The 63,460 fans who turned out for the game seemed shell-shocked, recovering enough to voice their displeasure at the end of the game. Los Angeles first baseman Steve Garvey hit a three-run homer, which proved to be the decisive blow in the Dodgers' 9-5 victory.[132]

Having witnessed postseason disappointment the previous two years, Stan Hochman of the *Daily News* adopted a whimsical attitude over the Phils' chances of capturing a pennant. "Swing those bats, mop those puddles," he wrote, in mock derision of the team's performance, "and all together now, follow the bouncing ball as everyone sings, 'Raindrops Keep Falling on My Head.'"[133] Frank Dolson of the *Inquirer* adopted more of a "wait-and-see" position. He approached Ozark after the game and asked about his earlier prediction. "I predicted three in a row," deadpanned the Phils' skipper. "But I didn't predict what order."[134]

Ozark sent Dick Ruthven to the mound for Game Two against Tommy John. Rufus pitched perfect ball through the first three innings before surrendering a solo home run in the fourth to Davey Lopes. It was all the support John needed. Capitalizing on his sinker, the Dodger veteran threw 18 ground ball outs and Los Angeles won 4-0. Banners demanding the firing of Danny Ozark could be seen in the outfield. Fan disappointment gave way to infuriation as the 60,643-strong crowd showered the Phillies with boos starting in the sixth inning. Many, having seen enough, left the game after the seventh.[135]

Jim Murray, a columnist for the *Los Angeles Times*, provided some negative motivation for the Phillies when the series moved to southern California. Murray, a humorist, wrote a story about Philadelphia, attacking the city, the Phillies, and their fans. "They used to have great baseball teams in Philadelphia," began the column. "But nobody cared. Connie Mack had to sell them off. Philadelphia preferred teams like the rest of the town—second rate." The Phillies are "a perfect team" for the "city's fans," claimed Murray, because "excellence annoys them" and "competence even bores them." The fans want "somebody to blame, not praise."

Turning his attention to the Phillies, Murray insisted that they "couldn't win in the old Pacific Coast league" because they "have no pitching," "no .300 hitter," and a manager who "forgot to put a left fielder in with a two-run lead in the top of the ninth last year." Ozark, "for reasons best known to himself, started a pitcher named Larry Christenson" in the first game of this year's playoffs. "Larry proved to be a true Phillie," wrote Murray, "giving up three home runs, two triples and a double." "The Phils, as usual, sank to the occasion," he concluded. "A pity because the World Series could use a laugh this year."[136]

The Phillies responded to the humiliating column by beating the Dodgers, 9-4, in Game Three. Carlton pitched a complete game for his first postseason win as a Phillie. He also hit a home run and drove in four runs to help his cause.[137] "Carlton did a great job, offensively and defensively," said Dodger first baseman Steve Garvey. "We just didn't capitalize on the breaks. But I'm sure you'll see a different team tomorrow."[138]

Game Four went into extra innings deadlocked at 3-3. The Phillies failed to score in the top of the tenth, and McGraw retired the first two Dodger hitters in the bottom of the inning. Then Dusty Baker hit a soft line drive to center field. Garry Maddox got his glove on the rapidly sinking ball but dropped it. Bill Russell followed with an RBI single and the Dodgers clinched their second straight pennant.

This time, Larry Eichel of the *Inquirer*, penned the obituary. "Their death was sudden, and their death was cruel," he wrote, echoing Bill Conlin's description of the Phils' playoff loss a year earlier. "And, saddest of all, their death was self-inflicted."[139] In the visitors' clubhouse, Maddox, refusing to alibi for his error, demonstrated the courage and character to face the sportswriters. "The ball was right in my glove," said Garry. "It wasn't a tough play, just a routine line drive. I missed the ball and cost us a chance to be world champions. It's something I'll never forget for the rest of my life."[140] Schmidt wouldn't allow his teammate to shoulder the blame, though. "The Phillies didn't lose this game because of Garry," he insisted. "We lost because we put ourselves in a vulnerable position from the outset."[141]

The Phillies had run out of excuses. Despite having talent that was equal to or superior to the teams that had defeated them, they lost three straight playoffs. Fans and sportswriters alike accused them of "choking" and a "lack of mental toughness."[142] Ruly Carpenter wondered how much longer he should keep the team together, or whether to break it up and rebuild.[143] Even some of the players questioned whether the team could win it all. "You go so long and you don't win, you begin to wonder," said Larry Bowa, recalling the disappointment years later. "Then you fall short in the playoffs three years in a row. You go from saying, 'We're just glad to be here,' to saying, 'This group can't win.' The more you read about it in the newspapers, you start thinking maybe we can't win, or aren't good enough to win."[144]

If the Phillies of the late-1970s were a failed dynasty, no one felt it more than Steve Carlton and Mike Schmidt. Three times Carlton pitched the team into the postseason, only to lose. In four playoff starts, he was 1-2 with a 5.79 ERA, his regular season brilliance failing him when it mattered most. Three times Schmidt's bat carried the Phillies to a playoff berth, only to lose each time. In 44 post-season at bats, one of the majors' most feared power hitters failed to collect a single home run with just 8 hits for a mediocre .182 batting average.[145]

Some people began to question whether Lefty and Michael Jack had what it took to lead the Phillies to a world championship.

CHAPTER 7

CHARLIE HUSTLE
COMES TO TOWN

FOR THREE STRAIGHT YEARS the Phillies clinched the National League's Eastern Division only to lose in the playoffs. The young team that Paul Owens cultivated was getting older, their chemistry, less dynamic. The window of opportunity to reach the World Series was closing and Owens knew it. Something drastic had to be done, something ownership chafed at. That "something" was to enter a bidding war for the services of free agent Pete Rose, the one player who many believed could deliver a world championship to Philadelphia.

Only baseball could have created Rose. Consistent with the origins of the game, he was a working-class player from a working-class town. Born and raised in Cincinnati, Ohio, Rose was a throwback to an earlier era when players were reckless and carefree, sharp-witted and shamefully self-indulgent. He didn't have much natural ability, but he took advantage of the exceptional hand-eye coordination he did possess to turn himself into one of the finest hitters in the game. And like the old-timers, Rose would go on to set records and standards that became touchstones for future players to be measured against.[1]

Peter Edward Rose signed with the Cincinnati Reds as a second baseman and immediately won over the hometown fans being named Rookie of the Year in 1963. The brash youngster played the game with a competitiveness that burned white hot, season after season. A switch hitter, he slashed line drives to all fields. He ran the bases instinctively and with reckless abandon, antagonizing opponents and inspiring more laid-back teammates. He revived the headfirst slide and popularized running to first base on a walk, idiosyncrasies that earned him the nickname "Charlie Hustle."[2] "I didn't get to the majors on God-given ability," he admitted. "I got there on hustle, and I have had to hustle to stay."[3] Rose's passion for the game was, like his personal ambition, endless. In fact, he once said that he'd "walk through hell in a gasoline suit to keep playing baseball."[4]

By 1975 Rose had won three batting titles (1968, '69, '73) and a Most Valuable Player Award (1973). That year the Reds star, who had moved to third base, was the sparkplug that vaulted Cincinnati's "Big Red Machine" to a world championship. He was named the MVP of the Fall Classic for his .370 average, a refreshing change from the power pitchers and power hitters who usually won the award.[5] The following year, the Reds swept the New York Yankees in the World Series, earning a rightful place as one of the best teams in the history of the game.[6]

Rose's playing achievements were only part of his success, though. His was one of baseball's most colorful personalities. Adored by the media, Rose enjoyed an insightful ability to reduce the complexities of the game in a way that was understandable. "I don't think any player gets tired when he's hitting good," he explained in a 1978 interview, when asked how he was able to continue a hitting streak for 44 games. "The ball looks bigger than usual and the fielders seem spaced way out. When you're not hitting, the ball looks smaller and it seems like even the umpires have gloves and you can't find a hole."[7] He was quick with a witty one-liner that made for good copy. Asked to compare his speed to the game's top base stealers, Rose quipped: "I'm not bad. I ain't no Joe Morgan [the Reds' black second baseman], but I'm pretty good for a white guy."[8] More impressive was Rose's ability to disarm critics. When he was taken to task for endorsing Japanese baseball products, he told reporters, "If there was ever a war, I'd fight for the United States."[9] On another occasion, when a sportswriter questioned his intelligence, Rose, by then a multimillionaire, remarked, "I wish there was some way I could have gotten a college education. I'm thinking about buying a college, though."[10]

But if Rose embodied the best qualities of the game, he also reflected some of the worst. A chronic philanderer, he seemed to have a girlfriend in every National League city. He tended toward the youngest and prettiest women, whom he referred to as "hard bodies" because of their trim figures. At least one of the party girls filed a paternity suit against him. Rose's spouse, Karolyn, like many baseball wives, chose to look the other way. Her only request was that he not embarrass her or their children by having an affair in Cincinnati. But Rose couldn't even keep that promise, believing that his extramarital affairs were a fringe benefit of being a ballplayer.[11]

There was also a dark side to the aggressive way he played. It was a killer instinct that occasionally surfaced from his blue-collar competitiveness. Rose's father, Harry, cultivated the "win-at-all-costs" attitude in his son.[12] He was a rugged, handsome man who worked as a bank teller. But his real passion was sports. "My dad played semi-pro football until he was forty-four years old," Rose boasted when he spoke of his father. "One day when he was in his forties, he kicked off and somebody hit him with a helluva block. He fractured his hip on the play, but he kept crawling, broken hip and all, and made the tackle. That's the kind of guy my father was, tough and aggressive."[13] Harry Rose also dreamed of becoming a professional baseball player, but didn't have the talent to make it. As a result, he "deposited his own boyhood dreams onto the shoulders of his son."[14]

Pete Rose did his father proud. Not only did he reach the majors, but his insatiable desire to win made him one of the game's biggest stars and one of the most controversial, as well. During the 1970 All-Star Game, for example, Rose, scored the winning run on a bone-shattering collision at home plate. With the score tied 4-4 in the twelfth inning, Rose, on second base, broke for home on a sharp single to center. Amos Otis, the American League's center fielder, wielded and threw home. Catcher Ray Fosse snared the ball three feet up the third base foul line. Instead of sliding, Rose bowled over Fosse, permanently damaging the catcher's left shoulder. The National League won, 5-4. Fosse, a promising slugger, was never again able to hit with his former power. People began to ask why the cocky young Reds star would play so viciously in an exhibition contest like the All-Star Game, which was primarily a showcase for the best players in baseball.[15] Again, during the 1973 National League playoffs against the New York Mets, Rose's play raised questions about his ability to control his intensity. With the Mets leading the Reds, 9-2, in the third game of the series, Rose transformed a routine double play into a wild bench-clearing brawl when he took out shortstop Bud Harrelson on a hard slide at second base. Rose, who enjoyed a fifty-pound advantage over Harrelson, wrestled the Mets infielder to the ground, adding to the spectacle, which was viewed on national television.[16] Why would Rose slide so hard in a lopsided game?

To be sure, Pete Rose played to win. It was a quality that made him both appealing and detested. He put winning above everything else, even in a contest in which winning and losing was of no real consequence. As a result, he was endlessly compared to the surly Hall of Famer Ty Cobb, whose career hits record he pursued with the passion of a camp revival preacher. Rose, like Cobb, played with an arrogance that exceeded the limits of aggressive play. Predictably, the Reds star was hated and jeered by opposing fans. In Philadelphia, a city infamous for its own blue-collar sports culture, Rose was envied as much as hated. Phillies fans begrudgingly admired his "take-no-prisoners" mentality, wishing that he played for them. Their wish would eventually come true.

During the 1978 season, Rose was locked in a contract dispute with Reds general manager Dick Wagner. The All-Star third baseman was demanding a significant raise from the $365,000 a year deal that expired at the end of the year. Rose, a shameless egotist, believed he deserved to be the highest paid player in the game. He had compiled more than 3,000 hits, helped the Reds win four pennants and two World Series, and had recently mounted a serious challenge to Joe DiMaggio's record 56-game hitting streak by hitting safely in 44 straight games. Those achievements were so outstanding that the *Sporting News* named Rose "Player of the Decade for the 1970s."[17]

Wagner refused the demand and, after the season ended, took out an advertisement in the *Cincinnati Enquirer*, pleading his case before the fans in order to prepare them for the star's departure. Infuriated by the action, Rose directed his agent, Reuven Katz, to explore the free agent market. While Rose went on a baseball tour of Japan, Katz mailed letters to the eight teams in which his client expressed an interest: the Boston Red Sox, California Angels, Kansas City Royals, Los Angeles Dodgers, New York Yankees, Philadelphia Phillies, San Diego Padres, and Texas Rangers. By the time Rose returned from Japan, the search had narrowed to five teams, three of which weren't even on his list—the Phillies, Royals, Atlanta Braves, Pittsburgh Pirates, and St. Louis Cardinals. Katz chartered a Lear jet and the two men set off on a tour to explore the offers.[18]

The suitors were impressive. Braves owner Ted Turner offered one million dollars a year for three seasons and $100,000 per-year pension. Ewing Kauffman, owner of the Royals, presented a four-year contract with an additional option season that equaled Turner's offer. As an incentive, Kauffman also offered Rose a share of his considerable oil investments. Gussie Busch of the Cardinals, who made a fortune selling Budweiser beer, offered a lesser salary, but added one of his distributorships. John Galbreath, a multimillionaire horseman who owned the Pirates, did not enjoy the financial advantages of the others, but offered Rose $400,000 a year and two of his finest brood mares as well as the stud services of his top stallions.[19] While Rose was intrigued by the offers, he was hoping that the Phillies would win the bidding for his services and made them the final stop on his tour.

It was no secret that Rose wanted to play for the Phillies. Two years earlier when the Reds met them in the playoffs, he called Philadelphia the "second best organization in baseball" and stated that if he were traded he "wouldn't mind going to the Phillies" because he knew he "could help them."[20] Rose also relished the idea of playing with Mike Schmidt, whom he considered to be "the best player in baseball three days a week."[21] He believed that the Phillies were similar to the Reds of the late 1960s and early '70s—a talented, young club that contended but had yet to win the pennant. Rose believed that he could provide the veteran leadership and post-season experience necessary to bring a world championship to the City of Brotherly Love. But the initial discussion was not fruitful.

Rose and Katz flew into Philadelphia on a private jet, compliments of Phillies president Ruly Carpenter, and then drove to his Montchanin, Delaware, estate, along with Bill Giles, a longtime friend of Rose's. When Carpenter asked about the other offers, Katz reported that some "ran to seven figures a year."

"My God," said Carpenter in disbelief. "That's a million dollars. We can't make an offer like that." The duPont heir might have been wealthy, but he certainly wasn't going to be foolhardy with his family's fortune.

"Money isn't everything," replied Katz, suggesting that his client would settle for some special incentives.

But Carpenter would only offer $700,000 a season for three years and refused to add any incentives or long-term security. Rose couldn't accept the offer and Carpenter knew it. "I'm afraid there won't be a signing," sighed the Phillies president, stating the obvious. "I've got all the press assembled at Veterans Stadium, and there won't be a signing."[22]

Rose, sorely disappointed, somehow managed to muster some humor. "Can we still take the private jet back to Cincinnati?" he asked.

Carpenter wasn't amused. "You can if you pay for it," he replied.

"I felt sick," Rose admitted later. "I really wanted to play for the Phillies. But their package was worth millions less than Atlanta's or Kansas City's. I'd play for less, but not *that* much less."[23]

On the return trip to the airport, Bill Giles salvaged the negotiations. Pulling out a National League record book, he pointed out that Rose was third or fourth in almost every all-time hitting category. "If you decide to play for an American League club, like Kansas City, you'll never break these records," said Giles. "Your kids and grandchildren will never see your name at the top of these records." Rose was moved by the argument.

Before boarding the private plane for Cincinnati, Katz pulled Giles aside. "Why don't you see if Ruly will go to $800,000," he whispered to the Phils vice president. "I think I can talk Pete into signing because I believe he really wants to stay in the National League and play for Philadelphia."

Realizing that Carpenter would not increase his offer, Giles concocted his own plan. "I knew that if we signed Pete, more people would be watching our games on television," he recalled in a recent interview. "So, WPHL-TV, the station that carried the Phillies, should be willing to kick in some more money. I went to the station's owners and asked if they'd guarantee us an additional $600,000 over four years if we signed Rose to a four-year deal. It took them a couple of days, but they got back to me and agreed to increase their rights fee. The rest is history."[24]

On December 5, 1978, at baseball's winter meetings in Orlando, Florida, the Phillies announced that the thirty-seven-year-old Rose "signed a four-year contract for $810,000 a year" and was now the "highest paid player in the game."[25] Rose, his thick brown hair newly trimmed in a Prince Valiant style and smiling from ear to ear, stepped to the band of microphones and quipped: "You can stack all that money up and a show dog can't jump over it!"

After the laughter subsided, he became more serious. "Philadelphia is the place I always wanted to play," he admitted. "That was my first priority. I said all along that I might take less money if I could go to a team where I'd be happy. All of the offers were very similar, but it came down to a decision of where I was going to be the happiest."[26] In the end, Rose, who signed for $3.2 million over four years, accepted the lowest of all bids to play for the Phillies. Giles had saved the day by tapping into the club's television revenue. It was the kind of creative deal that a family-owned franchise would have to concoct in order to remain competitive in the new era of free agency.

Baseball had always been a business disguised as a boys' game. But in the 1970s, the innocence of the game was destroyed by the ongoing battle between players and owners over the reserve clause. Although Curt Flood had lost his battle to overturn the system in 1972, his legal action hastened the onset of free agency and million-dollar contracts for players. A year later, Marvin Miller, the negotiator for the Players Association, maneuvered the owners into accepting the impartial arbitration of salary disputes. Owners would no longer enjoy the final say in setting player salaries. Instead, the arbitrator would select either the player's final demand or the owner's last best offer. Now the balance of wealth and power would shift to the players.

In 1974, Jim "Catfish" Hunter, a star pitcher for the Oakland Athletics, used arbitration to win his release from the A's and owner Charlie Finley, who had reneged on his contract. Once Hunter was declared a free agent, twenty-two teams bid for his services. The New York Yankees prevailed with a record offer of $3.75 million over three years. Hunter had shown other star players the lucrative possibilities that existed if the reserve clause was eliminated.[27]

Realizing that he couldn't rely on the courts, Miller turned to the new arbitration board to challenge the reserve system. He found a loophole in the standard player's contract in a section that read, "If the Player and the Club have not agreed upon terms of such contract . . . the Club shall have the right to renew the contract for the period of one year on the same terms." Traditionally, the clause had been interpreted to mean that the team could renew the player's contract year after year, in perpetuity. But Miller argued that the clause only bound a player to his team for one year, after which time he was free to sell his services to the highest bidder.

To test his premise, Miller, in 1975, persuaded star pitchers Andy Messersmith of the Los Angeles Dodgers and Dave McNally of the Montreal Expos to play a year without a contract, declare themselves free agents, and, when their teams objected, file a grievance to force arbitration. When their respective teams filed grievances, the two cases were brought before the new three-man arbitration board, which consisted of Marvin Miller, the players' representative; John Gaherin, the owners' representative; and Peter Seitz, a seventy-year-old lawyer and professional arbitrator.

After three days of hearings, the board, on December 23, 1975, ruled in favor of the players by a vote of two to one. Seitz, the swing vote, was immediately fired by the owners, who took their grievance to the courts, claiming that the decision would "bankrupt baseball." But they lost their appeal in a federal district court, and again, in the court of appeals. The arbitration committee's decision was binding and the reserve clause was officially dead. Messersmith signed a three-year deal with the Atlanta Braves for $1 million, a $400,000 signing bonus, and a no-trade clause.[28]

During the next year, the owners and players agreed on what should be done about free agency. Miller offered the owners what appeared to be a compromise. To address their concern that top players would sell themselves each year to the top bidder, guaranteeing a championship for the owner with the biggest payroll, Miller proposed that the players would agree to remain ineligible for free agency until they had played six years in the majors. The owners agreed, believing that they could control the players for six successive seasons. To preserve a competitive balance among the teams, a reentry draft would be held every November to determine which teams could negotiate with a free agent. A maximum of 13 teams could draft one player. Finally, the owners and the Players Association agreed that following a championship season, any player with five years service in the major leagues could demand a trade. If he wasn't traded by the following spring, he could become a free agent. By agreeing to these terms, the owners inadvertently escalated player salaries. "As it turned out, the owners didn't make a wise decision," said Bob Boone, the Phillies player representative. "If every player had become a free agent every year, the value of each one would have been greatly reduced. But by limiting the number of free agents each year, Marvin assured that the bidding would go higher, and it did. I guarantee you that the first day he began negotiating with [owners' representative] [John] Gaherin, Marvin knew exactly where he wanted to end up and all the steps he needed to take to achieve his objective."[29]

Indeed, players' salaries escalated. The average salary would rise 41 percent from $52,300 in 1976 to $74,000 in 1977, with some twenty players earning over the $300,000 level. Baseball's total payroll would increase from $31.3 million to $48.1 million. By the time of the first reentry draft, 24 free agents remained unsigned and the owners had divided into two groups: those who were willing to spend lavish sums, like George Steinbrenner of the Yankees, and those who sat by and watched horrified by how the economics of the game had spiraled out of control, like Ruly Carpenter.[30] While Steinbrenner bought the New York Yankees back-to-back world championships in 1977 and 1978 by purchasing Reggie Jackson, Don Gullett, and Rich "Goose" Gossage, Carpenter's only foray into the free agent market produced Richie Hebner, who signed for a modest $600,000 over three years in 1977. Had Giles not negotiated the television deal, Carpenter would have passed on the opportunity to sign Pete Rose, whose $810,000 quickly became eclipsed by Dave Parker of the Pittsburgh Pirates, the first $900,000-a-year player and, shortly after, Nolan Ryan, who signed with the Houston Astros for $1 million a year.[31]

Giles realized that television had become a powerful force in baseball during the 1970s and that the marriage between TV and baseball could be a profitable one. By 1979, shared television revenue for nationally televised games resulted in a windfall of $1.8 million for each major league team. More handsome profits could be secured from local television contracts, especially for an organization like the Phillies, which enjoyed a lucrative media market. Cable television added to the revenue stream by allowing the team to televise even more games during prime time. As a result, the Phillies would be able to secure even more money by selling subscription baseball to the thousands of homes in their viewing area that paid for cable television.[32] "Sure, Pete Rose made a lot of money for himself, but we also made a lot of money on him," admitted Giles. "The Phillies picked up the extra $600,000 from TV and our ratings increased by 20 percent, which I attribute entirely to Pete. The additional television exposure resulted in greater gate receipts as well. We sold an extra 5,000 season tickets, which translated to about $2 million a year. So, while we paid Rose $810,000, we increased our revenues by at least $2.6 million."[33] The Phillies would become prime-time entertainment in Philadelphia and Rose, the team's biggest celebrity (Figure 17).

"I want to bring the world championship to a town that hasn't won it in half a century," said the thirty-seven-year-old Rose. "If I can get the Phillies to win the World Series, I can do anything." The Phillies new first baseman was only half joking. Just as important was his own desire to return to the Fall Classic, something he hadn't achieved since 1976 when the Reds won their last championship. "You have to lose a World Series before you realize how much you really wanted it," he confessed. "I keep telling the younger guys not to be satisfied with just being in the Series. I had to lose two in '70 and '72 before I found that out. Then we won two in '75 and '76 with Cincinnati." It wasn't that Rose didn't appreciate the personal successes—the batting titles, All-Star appearances, and hitting streaks—but that those things paled in comparison to winning the Series. "The statistics are just something that pile up over the years," he admitted. "You use those records as a way to motivate yourself day-to-day. But the only satisfaction that really stays with you is winning it all. After you've won the World Series, nothing else is enough. Frankly, it's all been disappointment since '76.[34] Apparently, some of the Phillies did not share Rose's enthusiasm.

"It might be hard to believe," said Danny Ozark in 2005, "but not everyone on the team was happy to get Pete. A lot of the players really liked Richie Hebner. He played regardless of injury. He hustled all the time, always had a dirty uniform. He was real good in the clubhouse. Everyone liked him. I think losing him wasn't too popular with some of the players."[35] To be sure, the Phillies needed

FIGURE 17. Free agent Pete Rose signed a four-year Phillies contract worth more than $3.2 million, but still less than what he was offered by four other clubs. Courtesy of the *Philadelphia Daily News*.

to find a position for Rose, who had, at various times, played third base, second base, and the outfield for the Reds. Mike Schmidt, who had become the team's franchise player, was firmly entrenched at third. Owens had recently acquired Manny Trillo, one of the best second basemen in the game, from the Cubs. The outfield of Luzinski, Maddox, and McBride provided an exceptional combination of speed, defense, and offense. Under the circumstances, the only position left for Rose was first base, which made Hebner expendable. Owens sent him to the Mets for pitcher Nino Espinosa.[36] "I hated to leave Philadelphia," Hebner admitted in a recent interview. "I thought I had two good years. We won the division both years. One year I platooned with Jose Cardenal, the next with Davey Johnson. Each of those years the platoon drove in over 100 runs, which wasn't too bad. When Rose came in I was out of a job. It was just that simple. There was nowhere for me to play."[37] If there was any unhappiness over Rose's acquisition among the players, however, it had more to do with how the new first baseman would fit into the Phillies clubhouse.

Much has been made of Rose's invaluable role in leading the Phillies to their first and only world championship.[38] Rose himself insists that he was "exactly what [the team] needed." Pointing to the homegrown nucleus of Schmidt, Bowa, Luzinski, and Boone, the former Reds star claimed that his leadership tempered the jealousy that existed among them. "Those guys were always arguing among themselves," Rose recalled. "They were a little jealous of each other and they were all around the same age, so no one would let the other guy become the team's leader. They'd always compare stats. Bowa was afraid Boonie would get more hits than him. Schmitty didn't want Bull to get more homers than him. Bull didn't want Schmitty to get more ink than him. There was a lot of that. So, when I got there, I said, 'Hey, take a look at my stats and shut up.'"[39]

While Rose did exercise a significant influence on the team, it wasn't immediate. He was careful not to upset the chemistry that already existed in a clubhouse where many of the players were born-again Christian athletes. Of the 25 players on the roster, 15 to 20 attended Baseball Chapel and took part in Bible study and fellowship on a weekly basis.[40] Instead, Rose adopted a "wait-and-see" attitude, quite different from the cocky, cheerleading demeanor he displayed with the Reds. It was an interesting marriage.

Born-again Christianity had its detractors among the players as well as the media. It was not uncommon, for example, for teammates to charge that the commitment to Christ lessened the intensity a born-again carried onto the playing field with him, or to question whether he was trivializing religion by attributing his on-field performance to it, the assumption being that a born-again Christian asked God for victory. The media proved to be most skeptical of the evangelical movement, tending to cast Baseball Chapel—the weekly service held in the clubhouse—as a misguided use of religion by a cadre of athletic groupies who call themselves "ministers." Team chaplains were portrayed as little more than good-luck charms who misused religion when in fact they worshipped sport and the players as much as Jesus. According to the skeptics, their call for religion was superficial, because their real focus was on winning and had little to do with faith at all.[41]

"At the time, Christianity was taboo in baseball," recalled Bob Boone, who established the weekly chapel services for the Phillies. "To be a Christian was considered a sign of weakness by other players because you put your relationship to Christ before the game. It also meant that you tried to lead a more devout life than many ballplayers do. We were called 'Bible-toters' and occasionally made the object of locker room humor. You had to be pretty tough to stand up to that. But if you believe that the Lord wants you to give everything you have to your personal and professional lives, I don't see that as a sign of weakness. It's a sign of strength. Baseball Chapel allowed those of us on the team who were Christians to find strength and fellowship with each other."[42]

Founded in 1973 by Watson Spoelstra, a former alcoholic and sportswriter, Baseball Chapel was a nondenominational Christian organization that arranged pregame Sunday services for both home and away teams in clubhouses across the nation. Initially, the service was established to address the practical dilemma of how to provide ballplayers with the opportunity for religious fellowship on Sunday with the game's hectic schedule. Since Sunday games began at 1:00 P.M., most players arrived at the park by 10:00 A.M. in order to dress, stretch, and take infield and batting practice. That left little time for church attendance.

Speakers were enlisted from a church or organizations such as Fellowship of Christian Athletes or the Moody Bible Institute. Each speaker was allotted 20 minutes and often addressed personal conversion experiences or brief explanations of scriptural passages. Most often a very simple theology was emphasized, consisting of four points: (1) that Jesus is the Son of God; (2) that God and man are separated by sin; (3) accepting Jesus as the intermediary; and (4) whether or not the individual will make the decision to do so.[43] "We had some great speakers," said Boone. "Pat Williams, then general manager of the Sixers basketball team, was a very dynamic and engaging speaker. Wendell Kempton, president of the Association of Baptists for World Evangelism, was probably the most intellectually inspiring. A lot of people came to the Lord because of him. It's not as if the speakers were saying anything earth shattering. But they were fascinating people and interest among the players spread because of that."[44]

When Baseball Chapel began in 1973, only seven teams held a regular chapel service, but five years later Baseball Chapel had programs on all 26 major league teams, drawing more than 10,000 players, coaches, and clubhouse personnel. Teams were not only scheduling Sunday services, but had also begun to arrange Bible study groups as well.[45] The dramatic growth of Baseball Chapel can be attributed to the increasing pressures of a changing sport and the players' need to find more stability in their lives.

Free agency introduced a narcissistic era in which many players defined themselves by how much they made rather than how they performed on the field. They challenged the authority of the manager, who earned only a fraction of their salary. Those players with incentive clauses were not shy about demanding more playing time so they could secure the bonus that came with so many more at bats or innings pitched. Owners were also less willing to part with a highly paid player just because he bad-mouthed the manager or abused alcohol or drugs.

Just as the quest for money and power intensified, so did the players' pursuit of a fast-paced lifestyle. It was "macho," for example, to be sexually active. During the season, players are on the road for two, sometimes three weeks at a time. Being constantly pursued by fawning women and lonely for female companionship, the temptation for infidelity is great. While there was nothing new about promiscuity in the major leagues, it became so prevalent during the 1970s that many wives resigned themselves to it or simply blocked it out.

Under such constant temptation and great stress to perform, many players began turning to Christianity in the 1970s. Some realized that they had everything a person could desire at a young age—money, fame, women—and yet still felt a sense of emptiness, or perhaps they saw faith as a solution to dealing with their fame and the extraordinary highs and lows of a very public occupation. The feeling of being unfulfilled led them to ask questions of a born-again teammate: "How can I balance faith, family, and career?" "How can I not only survive in an intensely competitive career, but also prosper?" "How can I give back to the community?" Gradually these players overcame their doubts and, in a quiet moment knelt and asked Christ to enter their life. Known as "born-again Christians," these ballplayers accepted the full authority of the Bible and made a personal spiritual commitment to Jesus Christ, including the responsibility to witness their Christian faith to others.[46]

Mike Schmidt attributed his conversion to Christianity to many of these same concerns. "My original desire for a spiritual relationship with the Lord was more selfish than anything else," admitted Schmidt. "The idea that God actually wanted to take the pressure off of my life was extremely appealing to me. That included everything, ranging from a dilemma in my personal life to going to bat with the bases loaded in the bottom of the ninth. So I looked at Baseball Chapel as an opportunity to take all the pressures out of my life and put them on the shoulders of Jesus Christ, allowing the outcome to be what he wanted it to be. After attending on that first occasion, I found myself reading scripture more and more and reflecting on my faith. It was the beginning of my spiritual journey."[47] Initially, Schmidt relied on Baseball Chapel to give him the emotional strength to cope with a batting slump or the criticism of the fans. He also found fellowship with other Christian athletes on the team, including Boone, Jim Kaat, and Garry Maddox. They spoke with him about how accepting Christ into one's life "doesn't guarantee clear sailing all the time" and that as a baseball player he had "put the worship of God above 'success.'" Of greater importance was "having a personal relationship with Christ." If Mike truly believed that "Jesus Christ was living inside of him" and that he was "doing everything for Him and through Him, then the burden of life in general will be lifted" from his shoulders.[48]

Intellectually, Schmidt understood what they were saying and was ready to commit his life to Christ. But he had yet to encounter the kind of adversity that would validate such a spiritual commitment. Wendell Kempton, president of the Association of Baptists for World Evangelism, began meeting with Mike and his wife, Donna, on a regular basis for Bible study. The sessions proved to be fruitful and, on January 9, 1978, Mike dedicated his life to Christ.[49] In February, he left for the Phillies' spring training camp in Clearwater, Florida, a new man. Schmidt was convinced that 1978 would be a banner year for him. Manager Danny Ozark reinforced his optimism by naming him team captain that spring. Then, when the Phillies broke camp and came north, Schmidt's fortunes began to change.

He suffered a severe pull to a rib cage muscle during the first week of the regular season. The injury put him on the disabled list for three weeks. After he came off, he wasn't able to play without pain for another two weeks. By June, Schmidt was pressing, trying to make up for lost time. He was showered with boos on a regular basis and the more he pressed, the worse he seemed to perform. Despite all the negativism of the Phillies' fans, the third baseman never made excuses for his performance. He played through nagging injuries that season and never let up. He also tried to put the fans' criticism into a proper perspective. After one particularly frustrating series against the Mets in late August, he admitted that he "deserved to be booed." He even confessed that "If I had a 'boo' sign in my back pocket, I would pull it out and join them!"[50]

The '78 campaign was a trial for Schmidt. Because he had accepted Christ into his life, he believed that personal and professional success was assured. However, he discovered that there was much more to faith than the initial commitment. Bible study sessions with Kempton became more frequent. "What's this all about?" Schmidt demanded to know. "I become a Christian and this is what happens?" Kempton reminded him that faith is a journey, not a destination. That if he genuinely and willingly gave himself to God that God will always be there to support him, win or lose. "Mike, when you go to bat, tell the Lord outright that you're going to give Him one hundred percent," suggested the Baptist minister. "If you strike out, you'll strike out doing your best. If you get a hit, that'll be doing your best, too. Put the outcome in His hands."[51]

Kempton was emphasizing the importance of the "Try Ethic," a philosophy based on First Corinthians 9: 24–27 and adopted by the Fellowship of Christian

Athletes. Years later, Schmidt would explain it as "the idea of being a winner whether you win or lose as long as you give everything you have." Kempton's advice to place the outcome in Christ's hands allowed Schmidt to let go of the pressure he felt of having to control each at bat or, in a larger sense, the outcome of the game itself. He gradually came to accept that he could only control certain things, like his "fear of failure, metabolism, and mind-set by placing all the pressure on Jesus Christ." Other things, such as whether or not he got a hit, were beyond his control.[52]

Other players dedicated themselves to Christianity because of a severe crisis in their lives. Garry Maddox's conversion, for example, came as the result of his experience as a soldier in Vietnam.[53] A deeply religious and intensely private man, Maddox preferred not to discuss that experience, but insisted that "God is the key to me" and has been "a big help in my life." Like Boone, Kaat, and Schmidt, Maddox readily admitted that he is "not perfect by any means," but that his spiritual journey is "progressing" as long as he understands that whatever success he has experienced in life "comes from God."[54]

Still others, took a more natural path to conversion. Boone, for example, had been raised in a religious family and discovered a natural attraction to the fellowship provided by born-again teammates as well as a meaningful way of dealing with adversity in his career. "I was religious before I began attending Baseball Chapel," said Boone, who graduated from Stanford with a degree in psychology. "I'd say that I was a good guy and that I tried to lead a moral life. But I really didn't know what was meant by 'giving up the reigns of my life to Jesus Christ' until I started studying the Bible. The intellectual and the spiritual came together for me through Baseball Chapel."[55]

There were also those Phillies who simply followed the crowd, not really committing themselves to faith but attending Baseball Chapel in the hope that it would give them some better luck. Those were the players who were vulnerable to charges of hypocrisy by their teammates. "I remember one of our better players who proclaimed himself to be a born-again Christian," recalled Tug McGraw. "Everyone knew that was a crock of shit because he always had the finest women on the road. Once, when we were playing in Houston, this 'born-again' imported one of his [playmates] from the Chicago Playboy Club. He was in the clubhouse when another guy started to needle him, 'Born-again Christian, my ass!' he said. Then he asked the 'born-again,' 'Who's the beef you brought up from Chicago?'

"They went at each other's throats. It took four guys to separate the two of them. That's how volatile our clubhouse was. Before his religious declaration, nobody ever criticized him for his running around. Nobody cared about it. But after he went around calling himself a 'born-again Christian,' it was a different story."[56]

Despite clubhouse differences, the Phillies looked unbeatable through the spring of '79. The prognosticators were choosing the Phils to "run away with their division" and "perhaps, finally clinch that elusive pennant." On May 7, the Phils, behind Steve Carlton, pounded the Padres in San Diego, 11-6. Interestingly, Tim McCarver was not behind the plate for the first time in three years. Ozark, critical of the veteran catcher's pitch selection and his inability to throw out base runners, benched him. The Phils' manager felt that McCarver was calling for too many breaking pitches, many of which were leading to costly walks for Carlton. His .167 batting average didn't help the offense either, when Lefty, who hadn't won a game in his three previous starts, wasn't getting much run support. As a result, Ozark called on Boone, who would become Carlton's regular catcher from that point on. "I realized a long time ago not to worry about things I have no control over," Boone said, when asked about Carlton's refusal to pitch to him three years earlier. "I tried not to let the situation get to me. I just accepted it. Besides, I've got a bigger ego when it comes to catching than anybody else."[57]

In fact, Boone admitted years later that, initially, he *did* take Carlton's snub personally. His father, Ray, a former major leaguer himself, offered the best advice on how to cope with it. "My dad knew I was feeling sorry for myself," said the Phillies catcher in a recent interview. "He sat me down and said, 'Well, I'll be damned if I'd let anybody else ever turn me out of a job.' He taught me to take a more positive approach. When I did get the chance to catch, I'd show Lefty just how good I was at calling a game." To his credit, Boone never complained about Carlton's preference to pitch to McCarver, a fact that earned him the respect of both teammates. "Why complain?" said Boone. "If I had challenged Timmy's role, maybe all three of us would have been traded. Besides, my job as a catcher was to get the best out of a pitcher every game. Earlier in my career, I wasn't doing that for Lefty, whether it was my fault or his, it didn't matter. The fact is that he pitched better to Timmy and I knew my time would come. Lefty got to watch me catch the other pitchers and saw how good I was and by 1979 I was back behind the plate whenever he took the mound."[58]

On May 17 the Phillies won a 23-22 slugfest against the Cubs at Wrigley Field on a tenth inning homer by Schmidt. The victory gave the Phils a 24-10 record and a four-game lead in the division.[59] Then their fortunes changed dramatically. They lost 16 of the next 21 games, falling to fifth place, 7½ games out. Injuries decimated the team. Trillo missed 46 games, having suffered a broken arm after being hit by a pitch. Luzinski missed 26 games with assorted leg problems. Boone was out for 23 games, first with a broken finger and then an injured knee. Bowa missed 16 games with a thumb injury. [60] Rose, the only regular who wasn't sidelined, was enjoying a stellar season. Shortly before a game against the New York Mets at Shea Stadium, he was served with divorce papers from his wife's lawyer. Instead of allowing the unpleasantness to affect his performance, Rose went on a batting spree, collecting 20 hits in his next 28 plate appearances. When Luzinski asked him how he could hit so well when he was under such stress, Rose replied: "Stress is facing a divorce when you don't want one. I'm finally free from the distractions of a bad relationship."[61]

Despite Rose's hot hitting, the Phillies continued to descend in the standings. Some of the players blamed their new first baseman, who was contending for the batting title. "There was a lot of resentment towards Rose on that team," recalled Bill Conlin of the *Philadelphia Daily News*. "Many of the veterans bad-mouthed him behind his back for being such a hot dog. Some even thought he was a selfish player and not the 'team leader' he was supposed to be. Others resented the fact that he had completely taken over the clubhouse and became the media darling. It got so bad at one point that there was a near fistfight between Rose and reliever Ron Reed after an exhibition game at Oklahoma City against the Phils' Triple-A club."[62]

Ozark struggled to break his team out of the slump. He held numerous clubhouse meetings, some were encouraging and others were more heated. He had his players take extra hitting and infield practice. He even shook up the team by fielding an unusual lineup on a nationally televised Saturday afternoon game in Cincinnati. McCarver went behind the plate to catch Randy Lerch. Boone moved to third base, his collegiate position. Schmidt moved to shortstop, his high school position. And Bud Harrelson, a substitute shortstop, played second. None of it helped. George Foster hit a home run in the sixth inning to lead the Reds to yet another victory. "I don't mind breaking out my old high school position in front of a small crowd," Schmidt complained after the game, "but the whole country was watching."[63] Other players began to question their manager's authority, too.

On June 30, the Phillies were playing the Cardinals in St. Louis and Carlton, struggling with his control, surrendered a base hit to pitcher John Fulgham allowing the Cards to go ahead. When Ozark went to the mound to relieve him, the team's ace threw the ball at his feet and stomped off to the dugout in disgust. Carlton had never been a supporter of Ozark's, but the action was grossly insubordinate. When the Phils' skipper fined him $500, Lefty marched to the front office and demanded that the fine be rescinded.[64]

The Phillies played .500 baseball through most of July, but by the beginning of August they were out of contention. Between August 3 and 5, the Phillies suffered a five-game sweep by the Pirates and were now six full games behind first-place Pittsburgh.[66] They were performing so poorly that they were being blown out of games by the third or fourth inning. On August 7, Phils president Ruly Carpenter, for the very first time, gathered the manager, coaches, and highly paid players in the clubhouse, closed the doors and blasted them. Carpenter criticized the team for their dismal performance and the lackadaisical atmosphere that existed in the clubhouse. Afterward, the Phillies played one of their best games of the year, defeating the Montreal Expos 4-2, to start what would become a three-game sweep.[65] But a few days later the team returned to its losing ways.

During home stands Owens, Bill Giles, Dallas Green, Howie Bedell, and Hughie Alexander would meet in Ruly Carpenter's office at the Vet to have dinner and commiserate over the team's pathetic performance. The situation reached a nadir on August 29. The Phillies, 11½ games out, were playing the Reds at the Vet. Early in the game, the fans began to cheer Cincinnati and boo the Phils. Homemade signs demanding Ozark's firing adorned the outfield, and a group of Boo Birds hung the Phillies skipper in effigy. The braintrust, assembled in Carpenter's office minus Green who was away on a scouting assignment, watched the horrific scene unfold as their team blew a 6-2 lead to lose to the Reds, 7-6.[67] The Phillies had won just one of the last nine games and even the fans had turned against them, considering the players lazy, overpaid, and undermotivated.

"We're going to have to do something," said Giles, breaking the silence.

Bedell seized the moment. "Let's send Dallas down there," he blurted out. "I think he'll clean up the clubhouse and get us going in the right direction. He knows the players and he's got enough moxie to be successful."[68]

The silence in the room was deafening. Bedell knew he shouldn't have made the suggestion. But he had always spoken his mind and had been encouraged to do so by his superiors. He was a "team player," a man who spoke and acted with the best interests of the organization in mind. Nor was he afraid to accept the consequences.[69]

"You're sure of what you're saying, aren't you?" erupted Owens, incredulously. "You're not afraid of me are you?" he screamed, this time pointing his index finger in Bedell's face. The general manager had had a few too many cocktails. The thought that anyone but himself was fit to assume the role of interim manager was a personal insult. He had done it before seven years earlier and, in his mind, he could certainly do it again.

Bedell, stone-cold sober, knew that Owens was looking for a fistfight, whether he wanted it or not. That particular group of baseball executives was known to resolve internal problems that way. In fact, it was preferred. "Paul," said Bedell, calmly, "those are my feelings."[70]

There was silence. Bedell's resolve seemed to disarm Owens, probably because no one came to his defense. Perhaps he was hurt that Carpenter, his star pupil, had not given him a vote of confidence earlier. None would be forthcoming, either. "I just felt that Paul had already made the move from the front office to the field once and had done a commendable job," said Ruly in a recent interview. "It wouldn't have been fair for me to ask him to do it again. He was getting along in years and his wife wasn't in very good health. It would have been asking too much of him. Besides, I had a lot of trust and confidence in Dallas, who was a younger version of Pope. He was an 'in-your-face' kind of guy and if we wanted to win, I knew he was the man for the job."[71]

After the meeting, Bedell phoned Green and told him what had transpired.

The forty-five-year-old farm director was surprised that Owens had not been selected, but felt comfortable with assuming the managerial duties on an interim basis.[72] The following day, Green met with Carpenter and Owens. They agreed Dallas was the best man to replace Ozark since he knew all the players and Owens's thought process as well as the vision of the organization. They also agreed that the season was "too far gone" to make any "significant changes in player personnel." Instead, Green would go down for the last 30 days of the season on an evaluative basis, to "get the information that Pope needed to make decisions about the future of the team."[73]

On August 31, Danny Ozark was fired and replaced by Green. Owens made the announcement at a 5:45 P.M. press conference in a vacant locker room at Atlanta's Fulton County Stadium, where the Phillies would play the Braves later that evening. "The decision was a very painful one, but it had to be made," he insisted. "We were disappointed in the way the club has performed and felt that something had to be done."[74] Carpenter echoed his general manager. "This is the most difficult decision I have ever made," he admitted. "We had to do a lot of soul searching. There aren't too many managers around who have won three straight division championships, but Danny did that for us. I don't want people to think we are placing the total blame for what happened on him. That is not the case. We just felt we had to make a change. The only thing I can say is I want to thank Danny Ozark for the contributions he has made to this organization."[75] Years later, Carpenter would still speak fondly of Ozark. While he strongly defended his decision to hire Ozark back in 1972 and applauded the manner in which he cultivated a young group of Phillies, the Phils' president admitted "that if Danny had a fault it's that he was too damned nice." "He was extremely loyal to the players when there were times he should have been a lot tougher on them."[76]

Carpenter's assessment was accurate. Ozark's contributions had been considerable. In the seven seasons he spent in Philadelphia, the manager with the sad, hound-dog expression, compiled 594 victories, which placed him fourth on the all-time list of Phillies managers. More impressive, Ozark lifted the Phils from perennial losers to three straight division titles. While the press chided him for his malapropisms and criticized him as a "simpleton, who wasn't smart enough to manage a big league team," Ozark's record spoke for itself. Perhaps his greatest accomplishment was to survive seven seasons in the City of Brotherly Love, one of the most demanding cities in all of professional sports.[77] Regardless of his personal circumstances, Ozark's achievements came second to a fierce allegiance to the players, whom he considered to be "like family."[78] He was always accessible, whether his players wanted to discuss their status on the team or a personal problem. He preferred to criticize them to their faces and behind close doors, rather than on the sports pages. His wife, Ginny, was just as supportive. The couple spent hours punching ballots during the annual All-Star

Game voting so his players would be elected to the National League squad. In the end, he "felt worse saying goodbye to them, than for being fired."[79] The feelings were mutual.

According to Larry Bowa, "there were a lot of tears in the clubhouse" when Ozark said his farewell. "He was a players' manager," said the Phillies shortstop.[80] Greg Luzinski was especially hurt by Ozark's firing. The former pilot was like a surrogate father to him, teaching him the game, how to handle the daily pressures of the big leagues, and being a patient listener when Bull needed one. "I don't think Danny got enough credit for what he did," insisted Luzinski. "He brought a lot of good, fundamental baseball to this organization and took us to the playoffs three straight years. But what people don't see is all the hard work he put into it, especially getting to know the players."[81] Bob Boone, who also attributes much of his early success to Ozark, was even more emphatic about the "raw deal" his first manager received. "While the press portrayed Danny as a dummy," he said, "the fact is that we won the division three straight seasons and over 100 games two of those years. I'd laugh when I'd read the press accounts. If Danny was so dumb, how did he become so successful? Truth is, he knew his personnel. He knew which players would quit on him if he gave them a day off. He knew when to hand the responsibility to the players, and when to shoulder it himself. Danny knew what his teams were all about, and, if you ask me, that takes some brilliance."[82]

If Ozark was "too damned nice," as Carpenter insisted, his replacement was just the opposite. Dallas Green was a self-confessed "screamer, yeller, and cusser." He was outspoken to a fault and harsh in his public criticism of the players. But Green was also ambitious. He conducted long workouts, stressed the fundamentals, and had very little tolerance for what he perceived to be "lackadaisical play."[83] He believed that Ozark's "low-key attitude" left most of the veteran players ill prepared for the criticism that followed when the Phillies failed to win. Instead, the team "became divided into the eight regulars, the bench, the bullpen, and the starters" and there was a distinct feeling among the players that "no one should step over those lines." "It wasn't a team," said Dallas, "and that had to change."[84]

Green didn't endear himself to many players when he conducted his first clubhouse meeting on September 1. But he did set a different tone that made personal accountability and teamwork the top priorities of his tenure. "Each and every one of you has to accept some of the responsibility for my being here," he began. "Each and every one of you has to accept some responsibility for getting Danny Ozark fired. You are professional baseball players and you are good players, but for some reason you haven't been playing like it. Because Danny wasn't able to solve the problem, he was fired."

Green had quickly captured their attention. The players were very familiar with his reputation as a "no-nonsense" baseball man. Some had played for him in the minor leagues. Others had crossed his path during previous seasons in spring training or during practice sessions at the Vet. All of them knew he meant business.

"I expect each and every one of you to take a look in the mirror and ask if you've played up to your capabilities," Green continued. I expect each and every one of you to grind it out for the next thirty days to see if we can't accomplish something with pride and dignity. At the end of those thirty days, I will report to Paul Owens and tell him who can and who can't help the Phillies. We will make every effort to see that those who can't will no longer be in a Phillies uniform."[85]

Few players were pleased with the speech, but they understood Green's expectations. When asked, a few days later, about the change in managers, Mike Schmidt replied diplomatically. "I don't know if Dallas's screaming is all that important," he reported. "What is significant is that we're working harder and we're getting more accomplished. We'll execute better. We won't give as many games away. If he screams at me, more than likely, I'll deserve it. Besides, it doesn't hurt to get kicked in the rear end once in a while. It might just make me a better ball player!"[86]

Under Dallas Green, the Phillies completed the '79 campaign winning 19 of their last 30 games. Despite the their fourth place finish, there were some bright spots. Schmidt rebounded from a dismal '78 season to set a club record with 45 home runs, also good enough to finish second in the league in that category while also collecting 114 RBI. Steve Carlton won 18 games, and Nino Espinosa, acquired from the Mets for Richie Hebner, added another 14 victories. Pete Rose was simply sensational. He played in all 163 games at first base (a brand new position for him), batted .331 (second best in the National League), collected over 200 hits for a record 10th time, stole a career high 20 bases, and hit safely in 23 straight games. He also passed Honus Wagner as the National League's all-time singles hitter with 2,490.[87] But Rose also continued to be his own worst enemy.

In September, Rose did an eleven-page interview with *Playboy* magazine, which was especially damaging to his image as a hero of the baseball world. Calling himself the "number one" player in the game, the Phillies first baseman clarified his statement by pointing to his on-field performance as well as his ability to "sell the game" and "make the most money." He also admitted to taking amphetamines as a way to lose weight and gain more energy. "There might be a night when you play a double header," he explained, "and you go to the ballpark the next day for a Sunday afternoon game. You just want to take a diet pill to mentally think you are 'up.'" While Rose confirmed that he only took "prescribed pills," the revelation raised concerns about drug abuse in the major leagues. Just as damaging was his response to a question about an alleged paternity suit filed against him. Insisting that the issue was "private," Rose, who was in the midst of a divorce, declared the interview over. "I don't want to talk to fuckin' reporters any more," he fumed. "I ain't gonna talk about that shit."[88]

Afterward, Rose admitted that he had "made a mistake" by "losing [his] cool" with *Playboy*. But he also insisted that there was "some good baseball stuff" in the interview and that the "best thing about the magazine is the pictures."[89] It was classic Rose, employing a witty, one-liner to artfully disarm his critics. Still, he could not completely hide the pressures of his personal life, a fact that became apparent on the final day of the season. Standing in front of his locker at the Vet, a reporter suggested that his off-field problems might have distracted the team during the season. Rose played dumb. But when asked to explain the difference between first and fourth place, the Phillies star replied: "Uh . . . 'bout three, asshole!"[90]

Despite three straight divisional titles and the addition of Pete Rose, the Phillies were still the underachievers of major league baseball. They had tremendous potential with their mix of youth and seasoned veterans, speed, power, depth, and pitching, but not a single world championship to show for it. Ownership had become just as impatient as the fans and the media. If the team could not deliver a pennant—if not a world championship—within the next year, they would be dismantled, another one of the many missed opportunities in Phillies history.

CHAPTER 8

"WE, NOT I"

WHEN DALLAS GREEN BECAME the Phillies' field manager in 1979, he scrutinized all the players' performances, criticized the smug attitudes he saw, and made everyone accountable to his rules and policies. Near the end of the season, Tug McGraw expressed his frustration to Stan Hochman of the *Philadelphia Daily News.* "The one area there should be peace and tranquility is in the clubhouse," he told the scribe. "But the players seem to hate the fans, they seem to hate the press, and when they come into the clubhouse they act like they hate the manager and each other."[1] But it was exactly Green's controversial style that the Phillies needed and the front office knew it. Although he was only supposed to manage the team for the remainder of the '79 season in order to determine "who really wanted to play baseball for the Phillies," Green was asked by owner Ruly Carpenter and general manager Paul Owens to stay on for the following season.[2]

"A lot of guys on that team weren't going to go out and have dinner with Dallas, but if you wanted to win, he was the man for the job," explained Carpenter in a recent interview. Dallas was like "a younger Pope . . . , an 'in-your-face' kind of guy," and that 1980 team needed someone like that because they weren't getting enough out of their talent.[3]

Had Green refused, Carpenter and Owens would have hired Whitey Herzog, who had won three straight division titles in Kansas City but had failed in the playoffs against the New York Yankees each time. Herzog had been fired by the Royals and would have gladly taken the Phillies job if it had been offered.[4] But Green quickly became convinced that he had a better understanding of the organization, its players, and how to motivate them than anyone else and agreed to stay on for the '80 season. "I figured I'd take a shot," explained Green. "I knew

Pope's and Ruly's thinking. I had a good feel for the players after I had spent the last part of the '79 season with them. I knew the farm system inside out. Just as important, I wasn't worried about getting fired, so I didn't have any secret agenda. I wanted to do the same thing that everybody else said they wanted and that was to win."[5]

There never was a honeymoon period. Green met with resistance from the very beginning of spring training. When the players arrived at Clearwater, they were greeted by huge white signs with foot-high lettering that read, "We, Not I!" The phrase would be Green's mantra throughout the season. When Bowa strutted into the clubhouse and saw the signs, he rolled his eyes and sneered: "Christ! What time do the fucking pom-pom girls come in to lead the cheers?"[6] The wisecracking shortstop proved to be one of Green's most difficult converts.

Bowa never really trusted Green. In 1972, when Dallas became minor-league director, he had a middle infielder in his system by the name of Craig Robinson. By that time Bowa was in his third season as the Phillies' regular shortstop, but Green insisted that Robinson could play the position better. Bowa went out and proved him wrong. Seven years later, in '79 when Green became Phillies manager, he told the players that he didn't want to "get into any shouting matches through the newspapers," and then proceeded to do just the opposite. Bowa struggled to control his temper, but believed that Dallas's tenure was short-term and held his tongue.[7] The following spring when Green returned, their relationship quickly deteriorated.

Bowa arrived at Clearwater, Florida, for spring training embroiled in a salary dispute. He had two seasons left on a five-year contract that paid him $300,000 a year, which ranked in the middle of the pay scale for National League shortstops. But when Bowa learned that Garry Templeton, the St. Louis Cardinals shortstop, had recently signed for $500,000 a year, he wanted to renegotiate his contract.[8] "I'm not saying that I'm worth $600,000," he complained to the press, "but some of these guys making more than me . . . it's a fucking joke."[9]

Centerfielder Garry Maddox was another problem. He was not only resistant to Green's hard-line approach, but he was also involved in a salary dispute with the Phillies. Maddox was in the final year of a five-year, $375,000 contract. He had won five Gold Gloves and posted a .293 average during the previous five seasons in Philadelphia. His agent, Jerry Kapstein, believed that those achievements warranted a four-year deal worth $3.6 million. But Green, taking the company line, criticized the request. "He's a singles [and] doubles hitter," fumed the Phillies manager. "You can't do much with him offensively because he doesn't execute. I can't bunt with him. I can't give him a take sign. What am I supposed to do?"[10]

Underscoring these tensions was the grim reality that the Phillies were running out of time. Green realized that 1980 might be the last chance to reach the playoffs for an aging team that was built to win in the mid- to late 1970s. In fact,

Sports Illustrated had already written the Phillies' obituary, picking them to finish fourth behind Pittsburgh, Montreal, and St. Louis.[11] Now he faced the unenviable task of taking twenty-five individuals with personalities as diverse as their talents and molding them into a winning team.

During his first clubhouse meeting that spring, Green was brutally honest with the players. He told them that they "didn't have enough desire, character or heart to carry through a 162-game schedule." He insisted that in the past, they "were able to win on raw talent alone," but that now "the abilities of the other National League teams had caught up with them" and they would "have to rely on character and a new approach to the game in order to win." That "new approach" revolved around the "team concept of baseball—to play hit-and-run, to bunt, to squeeze, to beat the other team by using all twenty-five players on the roster by executing the fundamentals." Just as important, Green's "new approach" emphasized a style of play that demonstrated "more emotion, aggressiveness, and enthusiasm." No longer would the Phillies be able to "act cool," to "sit back and wait for a home run to pull out a game." There was one other message that Green delivered: "If the veterans couldn't do it, they would sit and he'd bring up younger players from the minors who could play just as well."[12]

At 6'5" and 230 pounds, the Phillies manager cut an imposing figure. It was clear to anyone who heard his deep, booming voice that he meant business. Predictably, Green followed up his speech with immediate action. He refused to tolerate the smug attitudes of players like Rawly Eastwick, Doug Bird, Mike Anderson, and Bud Harrelson, individuals who acted as if their place on a major league roster was a birthright. Green replaced them with younger prospects like Keith Moreland, Lonnie Smith, George Vukovich, Bob Walk, Marty Bystrom, and Dickie Noles.[13] "We had to create competition," said Green. "Veterans no longer had the right to play just because they were veterans. I have to give a lot of credit to Ruly Carpenter, who supported that policy all the way. He had to eat a million dollars' worth of dead-weight salary to do it. But if we didn't have those kids, I felt in my heart that we would have been back in the same old 'Mr. Cool' situation."[14] Throughout the upcoming season, Green would exploit the enthusiasm and work ethic of these youngsters to deliver the message that the team was more important than any single individual (Figure 18).

Next he broke up the cliques that existed among the veterans, the rookies, the starters, and the relievers. Mike Schmidt's locker was purposely relocated next to Lonnie Smith's, a rookie outfielder. Steve Carlton lockered next to rookie pitcher Marty Bystrom. That way they had to talk with each other, the veterans being forced to share their knowledge with the younger players. The camaraderie carried onto the practice field as well. There were no separate workouts for infielders, outfielders, starting pitchers, and relief pitchers; all the players were on the field together. If Green had to split the squad, he made sure that the youngsters went with the established stars, and the bench players with the regulars. He also made the players stay at the ballpark longer. As a result, they were too tired to play golf or go to the dog track, common diversions during the Ozark regime. Together with his coaches—Bobby Wine, Ruben Amaro, Billy DeMars, Lee Elia, Herm Starrette, and Mike Ryan—Green enforced his program, with little concern for trampling on the egos of a highly talented, but complacent veteran team.[15]

At the same time, Green knew when to ease up on the "team" concept. He was openly criticized, for example, when he excused Steve Carlton from running wind sprints with the other pitchers. But after going through the same conditioning program that trainer Gus Hoefling created for Carlton, Green believed that his ace was in better condition than anyone else on the team. "His program is as much mental as it is physical," the Phillies pilot told the press. "It requires total concentration and a total commitment. His mental preparation for each game is a direct result of this program. On the physical side, Steve Carlton is one of the strongest men in baseball. Besides, he's a Cy Young Award winner, so why mess with his success?"[16] Green also knew how desperately Carlton wanted to win a World Series. Lefty had been frustrated under Ozark's leadership, believing that he didn't pay much attention to the pitchers. But Green was once a hurler himself and took the time to learn about Carlton's idiosyncratic training regimen. He respected that. As a result, the two men developed a mutual respect

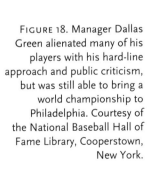

FIGURE 18. Manager Dallas Green alienated many of his players with his hard-line approach and public criticism, but was still able to bring a world championship to Philadelphia. Courtesy of the National Baseball Hall of Fame Library, Cooperstown, New York.

for each other that carried through the regular season. "Steve had a great mental attitude," said Green. "And part of that was his acceptance of me as the manager. It's no secret he had little love for Danny Ozark and I'm not sure he loves me, but I know he's happier. I allowed him to conduct his own conditioning without constant questions as to whether he was working. I never had to worry about him."[17]

As spring training unfolded, some of the problems dissipated. Maddox and Bowa came to terms with the Phillies on new, more lucrative contracts. Veterans like Carlton, Rose, and Schmidt began to promote the team concept among the other players. Green himself revealed a more zany side that none of the players could have predicted. One day, as he walked off the practice field with several pitchers, the Phils' skipper spotted a huge mud puddle left by the previous night's rain. Taking a running start, he flung himself, headfirst, into the muddy water. McGraw, the consummate flake, followed his manager's lead and soon other, younger hurlers were flinging themselves into the puddle as well.[18] Green had sealed an important and necessary bond with his closer, and he had won over the allegiance of other pitchers as well. Unfortunately, spring training would be cut short because of labor issues taking place off the field.

The collective bargaining agreement had expired in 1980 and had to be renegotiated. Free agency was the focal point of those negotiations. The average player salary had ballooned to $113,558, a figure that had more than doubled during the previous four years. The owners insisted that "free agency and skyrocketing salaries were killing the competitive balance in baseball" and that the "only way to remedy the situation was to compensate those clubs who lost a free agent." It was a smokescreen to hide their true intention, which was to end free agency. In fact, the growing free agent market had benefited baseball. By 1980 attendance and gate receipts were up and television and radio revenues increased as did the value of each major league franchise.[19] Marvin Miller was wise to the owners. "Competitive balance is a phony issue," he insisted. "If the real profit figures were revealed the owners' true intentions—ending free agency, restoring the reserve clause, and reducing player salaries—would come to light."[20]

On April 1, the Players Association voted to cancel the final week of spring training, return to play on opening day, and consider the possibility of a strike beginning on May 23, Memorial Day weekend. The strategy was designed to inflict a greater financial loss on the owners since the early weeks of the season often drew poor attendance. Miller suggested that the subject of free agent compensation be submitted to a one-year study group. Ray Grebey, the negotiator for the owners, agreed. Shortly after, a study group was established, composed of American League player representative Sal Bando of the Milwaukee Brewers, Phillies catcher Bob Boone, who represented the National League players, and club officials Frank Cashen of the Baltimore Orioles and Harry Dalton of the

California Angels.[21] If nothing else, the creation of the study group averted a player strike for another year since its work would take place over the remainder of the season.

When news of the Players Association's decision to cancel the remaining exhibition games reached the Phillies, they were en route by bus from a game against the Texas Rangers in Pompano Beach, Florida, to another game against the Houston Astros in Cocoa. Owens phoned Dallas Green and ordered him to continue onto Cocoa, where the team would stay overnight and then return to Clearwater the next morning. The decision was a stroke of genius. While players from other teams packed up and left their camps, the Phillies agreed to remain at Clearwater for the final week of spring training so they could work out at their own expense and prepare for the season when it opened.[22] As a result, they were probably more prepared to play than most teams when the regular season began.

Besides, the veterans were getting off easy. Green had subjected them to a more grueling camp than they had experienced in years under Ozark. Now they were free to do as they pleased. "We were like kids when school lets out," admitted Schmidt. "Tug McGraw, Steve Carlton and I chartered a forty-five-foot sport fishing boat that we called home for a week. We docked at the Clearwater Marina, where we partied for the final week of spring training. Sure, we worked out each morning at a local field—throwing, running and hitting. But the remainder of the day was spent on the water."[23] The party was short-lived. It was back to business on opening day, April 11.

When the Phillies reported to the Vet for the first day of the regular season, Green resumed his hard-line approach. He directed clubhouse manager Pete Cera to distribute the following list of rules to each player:

1. There will be no jeans, unless they're designer jeans, when the team is on the road.
2. No drinking on team flights without the manager's permission
3. Curfew will be 1:00 A.M. after day games and 2:00 A.M. after night games.
4. Players are not permitted to leave the clubhouse until the game is over.
5. Card games are banned once the pitchers' batting practice begins.
6. Any player acting unprofessionally or embarrassing the club will be fined at the manager's discretion.[24]

Predictably, the new policies were extremely unpopular with the veterans. At first, Bowa dismissed them as "high school stuff." Carlton refused even to read the list, tossing it into a nearby trash can. Most of the other veterans simply shook their heads in disgust.[25] If the rules had an immediate impact on the players' performance, it was a negative one.

After defeating the Montreal Expos on opening day, 6-3, the Phillies' pitching folded. The team went 6-9 in the month of April. Randy Lerch, a promising prospect a few years earlier, lost his first six decisions. Dick Ruthven was 5-5 after his first ten starts. Larry Christenson, plagued by a sore elbow since spring training, was placed on the disabled list at the end of May to undergo surgery.[26] "The big question mark coming out of camp was our starting pitching," admitted Mike Schmidt. "We knew we were going to score some runs. We knew we could catch the ball with anyone. We had pretty good team speed. But heading north, we didn't know what was going to happen to the rotation beyond Lefty and Ruthven."[27] In fact, the Phillies' mediocre performance was due to more than just poor pitching.

Rose was barely hitting .300 through May. Boone, Luzinski, and Maddox were under .250.[28] "Some of us were still upset about Danny Ozark being let go," explained Boone years later. "We felt that he had gotten a raw deal. Some of the players also felt guilty because we knew Danny was fired because we just didn't get the job done in '79."[29] Although he would never admit it, Boone was also under tremendous pressure because of his role as the National League players' representative. Insisting that it was "simple to separate baseball from the labor issues," he continued to meet throughout the season with the study group on free agency and report back to the players' union. In addition, Boone and Luzinski were hobbled by bad knees, making it difficult for them to drive the ball for distance at the plate. Boone, in particular, was never really able to heal from his off-season surgery because he had to get down into a crouch and catch, even when the pain was excruciating. Yet, he never complained, saying that he was "blessed with a high threshold for pain."[30] The anomalies were Rose and Maddox. Rose, a consistent .300 hitter throughout his career, usually hit much higher in the spring. Questions about his age were beginning to surface. Maddox, having signed a new contract, might have been pressing too hard to prove himself worthy of his multimillion-dollar contract. But his resentment for Green's bullying tactics must have also played a role in his failure to produce offensively.

Carlton's pitching carried the team through the spring. Lefty returned to his Cy Young Award-winning form in 1980. He was responsible for four of the Phillies' six victories in April and compiled another six in May, when he was named the National League's "Pitcher of the Month."[31] On April 26 he set a modern National League record when he recorded his sixth one-hitter in a 7-0 rout of the St. Louis Cardinals.[32] On May 5, Carlton took a no-hit bid against Atlanta into the eighth inning when Braves catcher Bill Nahorodny singled to break it up. The Phillies ace regrouped and completed the game with a three-hit, 7-1 victory.[33] Even when he lost, Carlton was able to shake it off much easier than he had in the past. When Green pulled Carlton for a pinch hitter in the seventh inning of a 2-0 losing effort against the New York Mets that spring, Lefty told his manager that he "did the right thing." A year before, Carlton would have torn apart the clubhouse.[34]

"Steve was a much happier person with Dallas," observed shortstop Larry Bowa. "I don't really think Lefty had anything personal against Danny Ozark. I think he just felt that Danny was an incompetent manager. He respected Dallas more because Dallas actually learned the ropes as a big league pitcher. Danny had a tendency to go with the hot hand. If Tug McGraw was hot, Danny went with him. Dallas knew how to use his pitchers and Steve appreciated that."[35]

Through June 22, Carlton had a 13-2 record and a 1.83 ERA and was ahead of his pace in 1972 when he captured his first Cy Young Award with a 27-10 record. "We had the comfort in knowing that Lefty was going out there every fourth or fifth day," said Tim McCarver. "We knew we could put a win in our pockets every time he took the mound. That slider of his made him remarkably successful. Willie Stargell of the Pirates used to say that trying to hit Lefty's slider was like trying to drink coffee with a fork. You just can't do it."[36]

Pete Rose, who watched Carton's brilliance from first base, was amazed at the number of hitters who worked a base on balls against the Phillies ace on a 3-2 count. After they trotted down to first, they'd ask, "How can Lefty throw me a slider on 3-2?" Rose just gave them a smirk and said, "'cause he's going to beat you with his best stuff."[37] Carlton was so confident in his ability to throw the slider for a strike that he insisted his fielders play straightaway, instead of moving a few steps to the right or left on a particular hitter. "If fielders overshifted behind Lefty, they took his breaking ball away," explained McCarver. "Batters were more inclined to pull his breaking ball than his fastball. If a right-handed batter put his slider into play, it invariably was a ground ball to third. When he was pitching, the two most important people on the field were his third baseman and the first base umpire. The third baseman had to handle a lot of ground balls, and the first base umpire was important because, with Lefty's slider, you'd have one check swing after another."[38]

Of course, McCarver, as a catcher, was much more analytical than Carlton. He could identify the pitcher's mistakes as well as his successes by watching his delivery, the rotation of the ball, and the release point. Lefty, on the other hand, kept it simple. "To me, pitching is like an elevated game of catch," he once told a teammate. "If I get the ball to the hitter that isn't success. But if I get the ball to the catcher, that is success."[39] Nor could he explain how to throw a slider. Once, when fellow hurler Dick Ruthven asked him how to throw the pitch, hoping to add it to his repertoire, Carlton picked up a ball, gripped the seams, and said, "I hold it like this and throw the shit out of it."[40]

Whether consciously or not, Carlton didn't share his thoughts on pitching with many individuals. He was a tremendous competitor who preferred to isolate himself on days he was scheduled to pitch. "You just didn't want to mess with him on those days," said Ruly Carpenter. "It was like he was in a trance. He'd lock everything out. Just sat near his locker reading books on metaphysics and Eastern philosophy. He wanted to be left alone. The writers never really understood that. But I did. We were paying him to pitch. That was his job and if it took isolating himself from everyone else to do it, then I for one wasn't going to question it."[41] In fact, the Phillies catered to Carlton's eccentricity by building him a "mood room" just off the clubhouse where he could seclude himself. The small room had blue carpeting, blue walls, a large, easy chair, and a tape deck. Reclining on the cushioned chair in the dimly lit room, Carlton would close his eyes and listen to the lull of crashing waves emitting from the sound system. When he emerged, the tall southpaw was a picture of tranquillity, ready to do battle against the best teams in the National League.[42] But some teammates insisted that Carlton could be rather friendly, even to the press.

"It's not true that Lefty won't talk to the writers," insisted Rose. "He won't talk to the writers about *baseball*. But he loves wine. Ask him about the French red wine crop of 1978, he'll talk to you till *you* want to get away from him!"[43] In fact, Carlton refused to grant a single interview in 1980. Not until the following winter, in the wake of the good feelings generated by the world championship, did he make an exception. When sportswriter Hal Bodley asked him if he'd reconsider his "no talking" policy for a book he was writing about the Phillies championship season, Lefty agreed. "There are a lot of reasons I feel the way I do about the press," he explained. "One thing that comes to mind is an incident that happened three years ago. All the Philadelphia writers were around my locker after a game. I talked for thirty minutes about various things. The next day in the papers they ripped the hell out of me. None of the questions I answered were in their stories. They just ripped me. So, I felt that if that's the way it was, I had better things to do after games than spend it with them. As far as I'm concerned, the press is one of the biggest enemies you have in Philadelphia. You have to first worry about the opposition, then all the things that are written in the paper. I just have to cut all those distractions off."[44] Carlton insisted that his refusal to grant interviews was also part of his "obligation to the fans and the Philadelphia Phillies." In no other way could he "give the best" of his mental and physical capabilities to win.[45] It was simply a convenient excuse.

Carlton didn't want to be bothered by the fans. He regularly refused requests for his autograph and made a conscious effort to avoid promotional events like camera night. "Lefty would drive me up a wall on camera night," recalled Bill Giles, then Phillies executive vice president. "Every year he'd hide on me in a closet or a concession stand and I'd have to go looking for him."[46] Carlton dismissed his responsibility with the rhetorical question: "If you're an introvert, why would you want to stand out on the field and have your picture taken with thousands of people?"[47] He refused to acknowledge the fact that those "thousands of people" were paying his salary and that they wanted to feel connected to him, to feel like they shared in his winning. Instead, Carlton deprived the fans of knowing much about him or about his views on the team, sports, or life in general. While he might have rationalized his dismissive attitude as an "introverted disposition" or an "obligation to the fans and the Phillies to win," Carlton's aloofness was purposeful and based on an inflated view of himself and his pitching talent. If anything, he lacked the emotional maturity to have a relationship with the fans and yet he depended on their approval to remain in the major leagues. As special as Carlton was as a pitcher, his refusal to make himself accessible to the fans was the epitome of ingratitude. And yet, his teammates saw another, more attractive side.

The Phillies ace was "always very open and happy to spend any amount of time with the younger pitchers," according to rookie pitcher Bob Walk, "especially if we were out of the public eye. He wasn't the kind of guy who'd walk around handing out advice. But if you asked him for it, he'd certainly oblige. We'd sit in back of the weight room and talk about pitching all day. In fact, Lefty was a *much* different person than the aloof prima donna that the media portrayed. He was fun to be around, at least for the pitchers."[48]

Carlton also possessed a humorous, if not wacky, streak that is said to be common among left-handers. If a major league clubhouse can be compared to a college fraternity, Steve Carlton was the president of the Phillies' frat house. He loved quoting from movies like *Animal House, Caddyshack,* and *Blazing Saddles.* He also loved food fights and didn't think twice about using the postgame spread for his ammunition. Head-butting was another favorite pastime, though some teammates scurried to avoid him because he could "crack your head open."[49] Nor did Carlton limit his antics to the Phillies clubhouse, often taking his show on the road. Once, while being feted at a fine restaurant in Los Gatos, California, outside San Francisco, Lefty reverted to his adolescent behavior. After a large vanilla-frosted cake was delivered to his table, Carlton tore up the cake and began a huge food fight. Still not content, he started head-butting anyone in sight, including the mayor's wife, who left the event with an enormous knot on her forehead.[50] On another occasion, Carlton decided to practice his golf swing in the hallway of a four-star hotel where the team was staying. Greg Luzinski, hearing the constant banging, ducked his head outside the door of his room and asked the eccentric pitcher what he was doing. Carlton, standing at one end of the hallway with a three-wood and a bucket of golf balls, explained that he was trying to chip the ball to the door at the opposite end without hitting the walls or the ceiling. Satisfied with the explanation, Luzinski shut the door and went back to bed. The next day, Eddie Ferenz, the Phils' traveling secretary, called a brief team meeting to announce that the "green fees on the sixteenth floor came to $1,600."[51] While the behavior did not please manager Dallas Green, it was tolerated because of Carlton's enormous talent and probably because of the tremendous pressure he experienced.

Whether he liked it or not, Carlton faced the constant pressure of living in a fishbowl. There was the pressure of maintaining his physical condition over a demanding, 162-game season, the pressure of performing at a consistently high level, and the strain of having his private life scrutinized, even though he avoided the press. These were the "distractions" he struggled to eliminate in order to perform at his best. "You can't let yourself get on that emotional roller coaster over wins and losses," he told Hal Bodley. "That's why you have to try to keep an even level of intensity. It becomes harder rather than easier with the years."[52]

Carlton's adolescent behavior in the clubhouse and at restaurants and hotels on the road reflected his ability—or inability—to deal with constant pressure. At the same time, Lefty's quiet cockiness as well as a sense of entitlement—the notion that he could do whatever he wanted without much regard for others or their property as long as he won—allowed him to become one of the finest pitchers in the history of Major League Baseball. He was the Phillies' ace . . . as well as their greatest enigma.

CHAPTER 9

SAME OL' SCHMIDT

S TEVE CARLTON, THOUGH ENIGMATIC, was the Phillies' unquestionable ace
    and arguably the best left-hander in baseball during the early 1980s. He
    set a high standard for the club's other pitchers by contending for the
major league title in victories, strikeouts, and earned run average on an annual
basis. While Carlton led the pitching ranks, Mike Schmidt was team's franchise
player.

"Consistency" is the hallmark of a truly great ballplayer and by the summer
of 1980, Mike Schmidt was, if anything, "consistent." He had captured three
National League home run titles and four Gold Glove Awards and played in four
All-Star Games since he had become the Phillies' regular third baseman in 1973.
With the exceptions of his rookie year and a subpar '78 season, Schmidt averaged 40 home runs and 100 RBI a year. Yet, he hadn't come close to fulfilling
his extraordinary potential.

Schmidt was a natural, which is not always a blessing. He was born with certain abilities that allowed him to excel in the major leagues: a strong arm with a
quick, accurate release; excellent reflexes; a fearlessness that enabled him to take
screaming line drives and blistering one-hoppers off his body; and an exceptional
intelligence. When he knew he had no play at first, for example, Schmidt was
known to fake a throw, whirl, and catch the lead runner between second and
third. He was just as talented as a power hitter.

Hitting home runs is a science that depends on much more than brute
strength. It takes exceptional hand-eye coordination, quick wrists, and timing.
Schmidt was blessed with all of these qualities. With one swing of his bat, he could
determine the outcome of a game—or as he did in 1980—a season. A generation of fans was beginning to adopt the Phillies third baseman as a hero because

of his home run prowess. Phillies broadcaster Harry Kalas endeared him to those young fans with his silky-smooth signature call, "Outta here! Home run, Michael Jack Schmidt!"

Watching Michael Jack play was captivating not because of *what* he did as much as *how* he did it. He played with such natural grace and intelligence that there was a sense of magic to his performance. Yet, he was dogged by personal insecurity because of his own high expectations as well as those of the fans.

The Phillies power hitter struggled with a deep-seated fear that he wasn't as good as he should be. His unyielding perfectionism was cultivated by a father who was a quiet but demanding individual. Rarely, if ever, did Jack Schmidt compliment his son, regardless of his achievements. Instead, he instilled a fierce intolerance for losing or even finishing second. "My dad was proud of me and what I accomplished as a young kid, but he always made it clear that I could be better than I was," recalled the Phillies third baseman. "He was on me all the time in everything I did. It was really never good enough for him and because of that I owe a great deal to him. I probably wouldn't be a major league baseball player if it wasn't for him." As a result, Schmidt was haunted and inspired by an almost pathologic fear of failure that stayed with him from little league through the majors.[1] An ambivalent relationship with Phillies fans made the situation worse.

Schmidt was not easily embraced at first by the hometown faithful. Fans couldn't relate to a naturally gifted athlete who sported an impressive physique. Although the young slugger worked hard to improve his performance, the physical aspect of the game came more easily to him than for others. His broad shoulders and muscular build allowed him to excel at the physical aspects of the game and stand out in a sport that had never been distinguished by handsome, sculpted bodies. In fact, Pete Rose jokingly coveted Schmidt's physique so much that he offered to trade his own body as well as his wife's and throw in some cash besides to acquire it.[2] Predictably, Michael Jack was labeled a "natural" in terms of his God-given talent and appearance, and that didn't play well in Philadelphia.

Phillies fans are "blue collar." They admire gritty players who get their uniforms dirty and show their emotion, warts and all. They embrace those who, like themselves, live in the black-and-white world of heroes and bums. Schmidt didn't fit that mold. He was scorned as baseball's "Mr. Cool" because he gave the impression that he wasn't putting forth his best effort. Philly fans don't want "cool." They wanted Schmidt to emote when things didn't go his way, to throw his batting helmet after a strikeout, to get tossed out of the game when he disagreed with the umpire's decision. Instead, Schmidt, after striking out, would simply return to the dugout thinking about the at bat. He realized that his inability to show emotion on the field annoyed the fans, admitting that he "often wished [he] didn't have the 'Mr. Cool' label." But he found it necessary to "remain as calm as possible under all circumstances" in order to "succeed at his game."[3]

At times, it appeared as if the local press conspired with the fans to make Schmidt's life miserable. Sportswriters from the *Philadelphia Bulletin, Daily News,* and *Inquirer* took turns criticizing the third baseman for "striking out too much," "choking in the clutch," "having a chip on his shoulder," and "not caring."[4] All the criticism weighed heavily on Schmidt, who was a highly sensitive and introverted person by nature. "Believe me," said Phillies owner Ruly Carpenter, "Mike Schmidt had great natural talent, but he also worked hard and cared very deeply about his performance when he stepped between the white lines. Unfortunately, when he first came up, the writers labeled him as 'lackadaisical' because he didn't wear his emotions on his sleeve. Once the fans started reading stuff like that, Mike was never really able to shake that label."[5] Thanks to Pete Rose, Schmidt was able to establish some necessary distance from the press.

Rose deflected the media attention away from his younger teammate. The Phillies first baseman had a special knack for handling the press. His sharp wit and personal insight into the game gave the media the kind of colorful copy they desired. Rose gloried in the spotlight and became a wonderful salesman for the team almost from the very beginning of his tenure in Philadelphia. He also understood the necessity for catering to the writers. "Pete believed that the media put people in the seats," explained Larry Shenk, the Phillies' director of public relations. "And if you put people in the seats, you get paid more. He did anything we asked. He'd go on the winter press caravan to places like Wilkes-Barre, Scranton, Lancaster—anywhere we had fans—just to talk baseball. When he took on that responsibility, he took a lot of pressure off Schmitty."[6]

Rose also took Schmidt to a higher level as a player (Figure 19). To be sure, when the former Red came to Philadelphia in 1979, Schmidt was a bona fide star, but one who had not yet realized his full potential. Nor would his reserved personality and sensitive disposition allow him to enjoy the game. Rose convinced him of his exceptional abilities, giving the young power hitter the confidence he needed to become the greatest third baseman ever to play the game. Pete's presence on the team and the press coverage he attracted took some of the attention and pressure off Schmidt, who became more relaxed and actually began to enjoy his successes. Rose had a special way of making the game fun for Schmidt. He nicknamed his younger teammate "Herbie Lee" after a boyhood friend. He boosted his spirits, getting him to laugh at himself on occasion, showing him that he didn't have to take the game so seriously all the time and yet he could still be consumed by a love for it.

"There's no doubt about it," admitted Schmidt, "Pete Rose had a tremendous influence on my career. He made a major difference for me and for the Phillies. You have to remember that from 1976 to 1978 our team captured the National League East title each season, but nothing seemed to go right for us in the playoffs. I'm not sure we knew how to win in that 5-game, postseason series and it didn't matter if you won 100 games during the regular season—if you couldn't win in the playoffs, you were labeled a 'loser.' The Phillies lived with that label until Pete Rose showed up. In 1980, Pete provided the kind of dynamic leadership that took the pressure off the other players. He was the finest team player I had ever seen. He always had something to say to pump you up, to play harder every game. At the same time, he was the kind of athlete who was boastful and could go out on the field and back it up. That allowed the rest of us to raise our level of play and, ultimately go on to win the World Series."[7]

Michael Jack, with Rose's support, improved his performance. Although he had been a successful power hitter with his previous, slightly closed stance, Schmidt tended to pull the ball to left field. Throughout the '79 season he experimented with different positions in the batter's box, finally settling on one patterned after two of the game's greatest hitters. "I wanted a stance that gave me a strike zone like Pete Rose's and production like Roberto Clemente, who stood off the plate because he liked the ball out and away, on the outside corner," Schmidt explained. "Clemente had to force his upper body to go out after the ball. The same is true for Rose. I thought that kind of stance would suit me best as a hitter too. So I backed up about eight inches off the plate and moved a bit deeper in the box. From that position, I could stride into the plate instead of striding toward the pitcher. That forced me to take my left shoulder into the ball, rather than to open

FIGURE 19. Mike Schmidt was the offensive leader of the 1980 Phillies. His .286 batting average, 48 home runs, and 121 RBI earned him the first of three National League Most Valuable Player Awards. Courtesy of the National Baseball Hall of Fame Library, Cooperstown, New York.

up, allowing me to hit the ball more to center and to the right and left-centerfield gaps than down the left side."[8]

The adjustment enabled Michael Jack to become more of a pure hitter, spraying the ball to all fields. At the same time he didn't lose any of his power, hitting home runs to right and center as well as to left field. By moving off the plate, he also became less vulnerable to the inside pitch, allowing him more decision-making time. It was the kind of change that would make a significant difference in his career, enabling him to stay at the top of his game while so many other sluggers tended to become one-dimensional hitters.

Rose also helped Schmidt defensively by encouraging him to think about the other facets of the game and not just his hitting. "Mike is human," said Rose during the '79 season. "He slumps like anybody else. One time he was slumping pretty bad and I thought he was carrying that onto the field, not giving 100 percent at third base. I offered him a little advice: 'When you're not hitting, that's the time to work extra hard on fielding. You're doing nothing with the bat, but you can still contribute with the glove.'"[9]

When the 1980 season began, Schmidt was a much better hitter, able to have just as great an impact on the game by moving the runner or by rapping a line-drive single as he was by hitting the home run. The power-hitting third baseman carried the team through the spring. His most outstanding game that spring came on April 22 when he became the first player to drive in six runs at Veterans Stadium en route to a 14-8 victory over the New York Mets. By the end of May he had slugged 16 home runs to lead the National League and was named the circuit's "Player of the Month." A few months later, Schmitty would go on to hit his 260th home run to break the Phillies club record held by Del Ennis. At the same time, he had transformed himself into a better hitter, reducing the number of strikeouts he suffered in previous years and was hitting at a .290 clip through the early summer.[10]

Rose had predicted that he would elevate his younger teammate's performance. "When I arrived in Philadelphia last year, Mike Schmidt was the best player in baseball three days a week," he boasted during the summer of 1980. "Now, after watching me, he's the best player in baseball seven days a week. I helped change his attitude. I stayed on his case until he believed that he was as good as he really was. Sure, there are players who run faster, or hit for higher averages, or steal more bases, but he does everything. He's the best player in the game."[11] Rose's impact on Schmidt was evident to others as well. "Pete pumped up Schmitty," recalled utility outfielder Del Unser. "All he wanted to do was win, no matter what it took, and that rubbed off on Mike."[12]

Schmidt realized that he did not possess the kind of leadership that Rose could offer the club and happily resigned as captain. "Pete was the central figure at a time when the team needed someone other than me to be the leader," he admitted years later. "I did not have the foundation or the confidence for it. Instead, Pete fired me up to be me."[13] When Green asked Schmidt why he resigned as team captain, the power-hitting third baseman replied: "You've got Pete Rose who exemplifies what a captain ought to be. Me, I'm a lot less outgoing."[14] Green accepted Schmidt's resignation and decided not to fill the vacancy. "We don't have a captain because we don't need one," insisted the Phillies manager. "With my open door policy, I don't need a go-between. A player has every right to come in at any time and say, 'Skip, can I have a few minutes?' Besides, I don't see the need for a captain on a veteran ball club, other than Pete Rose and Pete doesn't want the responsibility."[15]

Whether or not he accepted the title, Rose was the leader of the Phillies in 1980, and still the team had difficulty regaining their winning form. Carlton carried the pitching staff through the first half of the season, while the other starters struggled. After fifty-one games, the starting rotation turned in just seven complete games, five from Lefty. The bullpen also had a shaky start, but was stabilized in June by the additions of Kevin Saucier, Dickie Noles, and free agent, Lerrin LaGrow. Noles was the most impressive. Having been converted from a starter, the Phillies farmhand was scored on just four times in his first eighteen appearances and collected four saves. Tug McGraw, at age thirty-five, was still the closer, though he was showing signs of vulnerability. During the spring McGraw suffered from tendonitis in his throwing arm and was placed on the disabled list in early July. Ron Reed, usually a middle reliever, stepped into the closing role and did well. During the month of June he saved three games, won two, and posted an earned run average of 1.13.[16]

At the All-Star break in mid-July, the Phils managed to climb into second place in the National League's Eastern Division with a 41-35 record. Montreal was in first by a game and the defending world champion Pittsburgh Pirates were in third place, a game and a half out. Once again, Carlton, Rose, and Schmidt were selected as All-Stars for their impressive performances over the first part of the season. The Phillies' second-place standing, however, was primarily due to the failures of Pittsburgh and Montreal to take charge of the division while the Phils were mired in an off-field controversy that detracted from their on-field performance.

On July 8, a story appeared in the *Trenton Times* reporting that Pennsylvania authorities wanted to question "at least eight members of the Phillies about allegedly acquiring amphetamine pills illegally" from a Reading, Pennsylvania, physician, Dr. Patrick Mazza. Mazza was a fifty-six-year-old family practitioner, who worked as a team doctor for the Phillies Double-A ball club. Schmidt, Rose, Bowa, and Luzinski were among the players identified in the story.[17] Schmidt and Rose immediately denied the allegations, calling them "totally ridiculous," but they were still asked to testify in court. Mazza was more indignant about the

charges. "I'm angry and puzzled," he told the press. "It's not good medical practice to prescribe drugs without a physical examination and I've never done it. In
the case of amphetamines or barbiturates, it is also not allowed to issue refills
without a physical."[18]

There was nothing new about drug abuse in baseball. Scores of players took
amphetamines in the 1960s and 1970s in order to stay focused and combat the
fatigue of a grueling 162-game schedule. Nicknamed "greenies" because they
originally came in green capsules, amphetamines provided a quick energy boost,
especially for a player who had a day game less than twelve hours after the previous night's game had ended. Despite revelations that amphetamines were potentially addictive, many players defied the warnings and continued to abuse the
drug as well as painkillers and muscle relaxants. More educated trainers stopped
dispensing the pills in the clubhouse and gave vitamin B12 shots instead. Nevertheless, amphetamine use was not illegal if the drug was obtained with a prescription.[19] Not until the late 1970s did ballplayers begin using more lethal drugs
like heroin and cocaine. Since the Players Association consistently opposed drug
testing, it was extremely difficult to address the problem. When, in 1980, Ken
Moffett, director of the Players Association, admitted that as many as 40 percent
of major league players might be drug abusers, federal authorities launched a
wholesale crackdown without drawing any distinctions between the types of stim-
ulants that were being abused.[20] The Phillies' investigation was a result of that
crackdown.

Initially, the front office minimized the investigation. General manager Paul
Owens denied any knowledge of it until July 8 when the story broke in the *Trenton Times*. In fact, Owens knew about the investigation as early as June 26 when
Pennsylvania narcotics agents Phoebe Teichert and William Johnson met with
him. Vice president Bill Giles went further. After the story broke, Giles confronted
J. Stryker Meyer, the investigative reporter who broke the story, in the Vet's press
room. Charging him with "irresponsible journalism," Giles only made matters
worse by piquing the curiosity of the other local newspapers.[21] Finally, on July
12, Phillies president Ruly Carpenter diffused the situation by calling a press
conference and insisting that none of his players had "broken any laws" and that
the allegations were "all speculative." Carpenter added that the Phillies had "con-
tinually cautioned their players against the use of drugs" and that the team's
trainers did "not dispense drugs without a doctor's prescription."

When Berks County district attorney George Yatron was questioned about the
report, he admitted that an investigation had been under way for nearly a month
prior to the newspaper story but that it "did not involve Schmidt or Bowa." He
also mentioned that there was "no indication that any specific individual violated the law."[22] By the end of July most of the negative publicity had subsided,
but the accused players were still bitter toward the media. Bowa refused to talk

to the press. Schmidt found himself in a "limbo situation," trying to decide whether he "owed anything to the media" after it had "taken the liberty of tarnishing" his name."[23] Years later, however, when baseball was investigating the use of performance enhancing steroids by players, Schmidt admitted that the Phillies weren't "squeaky clean" when it came to "performance-enhancement chemicals." "In my day, amphetamines, basically diet pills, were widely available in major league clubhouses," he explained. "They were obtainable with a prescription, but the name on the bottle did not always coincide with the name of the player taking them before game time."[24] In other words, some of the Phillies were taking diet pills—containing five milligrams of amphetamines—that had been prescribed to their wives.[25]

Although the investigation focused on Mazza—and not the Phillies—Bill Conlin of the *Daily News* believes that the players were not totally innocent. "The relationship between Mazza and Schmidt, Bowa, and Luzinski had been forged as each one of those players went through Double-A ball at Reading," he explained. "Since everybody in those days was taking amphetamines, what better way to get the really good stuff than to have the team physician get it for you, or in this case, for your wife. Mazza was the *unpaid* team physician. He liked doing it because he loved baseball and loved being around the players. One of those players turned out to be the biggest Judas of all. Not only did he refuse the subpoena to testify in court, but [he] turned his back on Mazza who had voluntarily done all the legwork for a golf tournament he sponsored."[26]

Rose also continued to dodge the issue. He had long been suspected of taking amphetamines and had admitted as much in a 1979 *Playboy* interview.[27] When questioned under oath by Mazza's lawyer as to whether he had ever taken any form of amphetamine, Rose replied: "Why would I need them? I'm a natural." Shortly after, Mazza took the stand and admitted that he had prescribed pills for Rose "basically because there was a lot of strain on his thirty-eight-year-old body." Mazza was eventually acquitted because the players' testimony was not believable. Rose, in particular, was singled out as a "world class liar" by Mazza's attorney after the trial.[28] The drug scandal wasn't the only difficulty facing the Phillie first baseman in 1980, either.

Rose was experiencing a bitter divorce that dragged out over the course of the season. Karolyn Rose had accepted the fact that her husband, like many ballplayers, cheated on her when he was on the road. But when Rose was slapped with a paternity suit in 1979 and took up with a young Cincinnati woman, Carol Woliung, she filed for divorce.[29] Karolyn, an unemployed mother of two children, was asking the court to award her 60 percent of Rose's net worth, which amounted to the house in Cincinnati, a lump sum payment, alimony payments for eleven years, child support approximating $600 a month, and all educational costs. What's more, she took her case to the national press, humiliating her husband as "cold to the point of cruelty" in interviews with *Sports Illustrated*, the *Cincinnati Post*, and the *Philadelphia Inquirer*.[30]

Despite his personal difficulties, Rose managed to distance himself from the problems and produce on the playing field. "The night Karolyn Rose filed for divorce, Pete went five-for-five," recalled Bill Conlin. "I asked him how he could do that given the stress of a divorce. He said, 'I never let my personal life interfere with what I do between the white lines.'"[31] It was classic Rose—the consummate ballplayer. No matter what was going on in his life, baseball came first. He drew his strength from the game as well as his eternal optimism. As long as he could go to the ballpark each day, put on a uniform, engage in the banter of the clubhouse, and compete on the playing field, Pete Rose had a sanctuary from the unattractive realities of life itself.

The drug scandal and the negative media attention generated by the Rose divorce plagued the Phillies during the summer of 1980. On the field, the team was inconsistent. They would win one game and drop two, win one and lose the next three. In late July, the team suffered a six-game losing streak that dropped them to third place, four games behind the first-place Pirates. Returning to Philadelphia on July 23 after a miserable, 3-7 road trip, Green revealed his frustration to the press. "All I can do is scream and yell and kick and holler," he said, diverting the blame for his team's poor performance away from his coaching staff. "You still go back to character; that's what makes a ball club. But we've told 'em that a thousand times."[32]

Outfielder Greg Luzinski, on the disabled list with a knee injury, had heard enough. The Bull was never a big Dallas Green fan, but all the ranting and raving about the team's lack of character caused him to explode. Before a home game against the Cincinnati Reds, Luzinski nodded in the direction of the manager's office and told the local press: "I think he's hurting us. He's trying to be a fucking Gestapo. I read his quotes in the newspaper, and it really pisses me off." Then, realizing how negative he sounded, the left fielder backtracked. "Don't get me wrong," he told the sportswriters gathered around his locker. "I like playing for the guy; it's just some of the things he says about character affect some of the guys. They're sensitive guys who are getting singled out for one bad pitch or one bad play." Pointing to the large sign hanging above the clubhouse door, Luzinski stressed the contradictory nature of his manager's pronouncements. "That sign says, 'We, Not I,'" he continued. "It should go both ways. But he says 'we' when we win, and he says 'they' when we lose. The thing is—and Dallas has said this himself—he's got some shortcomings and one of them is his mouth."[33]

Relations between Green and his players deteriorated further in August as the Phillies skipper, with the full support of general manager Paul Owens, continued to criticize his players in the press. Larry Bowa feuded with Green in the local press and on his WWDB radio show. Bob Boone and Garry Maddox were

riding the bench and neither player was speaking to the manager. Larry Christenson was puzzled by Green's refusal to pitch him. Although Christenson suffered from a bad back, he had pitched through the problem before, but Green
put him on the disabled list without even discussing the action with him. "I
wasn't one to cause trouble," said the tall right-hander years later, "but Dallas
came in with his own agenda. He knew I had a lot of physical problems, but that
I could still pitch with them. It didn't matter. He'd find someone to replace me.
As a result, I only went 5-1 that season when I could have started many more
games." Green's controversial treatment wasn't limited to the veterans either.
Pitcher Randy Lerch was a frequent recipient of Green's tirades. By the end of the
season, Lerch was so intimidated by his manager that he purposely avoided him.[34]

"Every day you would walk into the clubhouse and wonder what was waiting
for you," recalled Mike Schmidt. "Who said who was a gutless jerk? Who said
who was lazy? Or who was selfish? It was like a soap opera. There was a feeling
among the players that this wasn't the way to do things. If you were going to
preach togetherness, then you'd better practice it. If you had a problem with a
player, call him in and read him the riot act behind closed doors. Don't take
every dispute public."[35]

Ruly Carpenter couldn't have cared less about Green's unpopularity among the
players. If a ballplayer came to him to complain, he'd send them right back to the
manager. "What's the old saying?" asked the Phillies' owner. "A third of the players are going to like the manager. Another third aren't going to like him, and the
job of the owner is to keep the third that is undecided from joining the mutiny.
I couldn't have cared less what the players thought. If they had a difference with
Dallas, they'd have to straighten it out with him. It wasn't my responsibility."[36]

Among the third who understood Green was reliever Sparky Lyle, who was
acquired from the Texas Rangers when Tug McGraw went on the disabled list.
Lyle had played for several different managers during his career, including Billy
Martin, Ralph Houk, Bob Lemon, and Bill Virdon in New York and Dick Williams
in Boston. He compared Green to Williams in that they both had a "gruff style
in motivating players and didn't beat around the bush but got straight to the
point." Lyle liked Dallas because he knew where he stood. Nor was he bothered
by Green's venting. "I felt that if you didn't do your job, you left yourself open
for ridicule," said the reliever. "That's all there is to it, and Dallas played by those
rules."[37]

Utility infielder John Vukovich was another Green loyalist. Vukovich had played
in the Phillies farm system with Bowa, Luzinski, Boone, and Schmidt. But he
had also played with Milwaukee and Cincinnati, so he had a basis for comparison, unlike many of his Phillies teammates. While Vukovich did not have great
offensive production, he was an outstanding third baseman with a hard-nosed
attitude about the game and how to play it. Like the old-time players, he firmly

believed that playing the game "right" was more important than playing it "good." In other words, being a team player who respected yourself, your teammates, and your manager as well as the game was more important than individual statistics or accolades.[38] "Vuke was a spearhead to that team," recalled Green. "He didn't play much, but he wasn't afraid to get up and scream and yell. He would tell the Bull, Schmitty, Bowa or any of the other guys when they needed to get off their butts."[39]

The rookies were probably Green's greatest supporters, though. Some, like Lonnie Smith, were grateful to him for giving them a chance to crack the lineup. "I had spent four full seasons at Triple-A," recalled Smith. "Danny Ozark was in no hurry to bring up the younger players. He was more comfortable with the veterans. Dallas gave me the opportunity and I tried to make the best of it. I'm grateful to him for that."[40] Others had grown accustomed to Green's temper and his penchant for accountability in the minors. They accepted his authority without question. "Many of us the rookies had come up in the farm system together," said Bob Walk. We had been dealing with Dallas for a long time. We'd already gotten called into his office to get yelled at. He'd been telling us what to do for three or four years by the time we had gotten to Philadelphia. It was nothing new for us. Sure, we gave him a lot of respect, but we weren't intimidated by him. It was the older guys—the future Hall of Famers and veteran players—who had to get used to him."[41]

Still, the factions that had formed around Green's leadership were tearing the team apart. On August 6, the St. Louis Cardinals shut out the Phillies, 14-0, in the most lopsided victory in Veterans Stadium's history. The team then traveled to Pittsburgh for a four-game weekend series. Somehow they were still just four games behind the Pirates and could have made a run for the division title. Instead, the Phils continued their losing ways, dropping the first two games of the series, 6-5 and 4-1.[42] Lerch lost the first game of the Sunday doubleheader 7-1. It was his thirteenth defeat in sixteen decisions.[43] Between games, Green corralled his team into the visitors' clubhouse at Three Rivers Stadium and locked the steel doors behind him. Thanks to the manager's booming voice and Bill Conlin's shorthand, the manager's speech was preserved for history:

> This game isn't easy. It's fucking tough, and we're fucking hurting with injuries. But you fucking guys got your fucking heads down. You got to stop being so fucking cool. If you don't get that through your fucking heads, your gonna be so fucking buried it ain't gonna be fucking funny. Get the fuck up off your butts and go beat somebody. You're a fucking good baseball team. But you're not now. You can't look in the fucking mirror. You keep telling me you can do it, but you fucking give up. If you don't want to play, get the fuck in that office and tell me, "I don't fucking want to play anymore!" Because if you feel that way, I don't want to play you![44]

Of course, the passage of time has a way of eliminating some of the more colorful details of that speech. When Green was asked to recount the talk twenty-five years later, he said: "It really wasn't that long. I just told them I was sick of their 'Mr. Cool' approach and that if they didn't want to play to turn in their uniforms."[45] Tug McGraw told a different version. "As a player I've been in lots of meetings and most of them were bullshit," said the Phils closer. "This one was real. Dallas called everyone out, challenging our character. It was a slap in the face. What he said went right to the core."[46] Even Luzinski, who was at odds with Green's approach, was hard-pressed to disagree. "I think Dallas exploded to get us over the hump," said the burly outfielder. "Sometimes you have to take those explosions with a grain of salt. But on that occasion, Dallas forced us to look in the mirror and it produced some results."[47] The "results" were not immediate, however, as the Phillies emerged from the clubhouse tirade to lose the second game of the doubleheader, 4-1. During the game, Green almost came to blows with pitcher Ron Reed in the dugout, before the two men were separated by teammates and coaches. The four-game sweep dropped the Phillies to third place, six games out of first.[48]

"After we lost those four straight games in Pittsburgh, everybody wrote us off," recalled Reed. "But when we landed in Chicago the players got together and said, 'Hey, we're better than a fourth-place club. Let's forget all the other stuff and play for ourselves. The hell with Dallas and the coaches. Let's win for us.' And we turned it around. There was no rah-rah stuff, no cheerleading. But we came together as a team by pulling for each other. Individual performances went out the window."[49]

In the end, Green's public criticism of the players, clubhouse tirades, and dugout tantrums accomplished more than his "We, Not I" signs. He created so much controversy that he united the team against himself. Regardless of the approach, the Phillies manager achieved his goal—to win as a team. The Phillies responded by winning six games against Chicago and New York, cutting the first-place Expos' lead to just one game.[50] Again they slumped.

In late August the Phils lost back-to-back games against the San Diego Padres. Owens was in the stands to see the second contest, a disastrous Sunday afternoon implosion, in which Garry Maddox made two errors. Early in the game, Maddox chased down a high fly ball in right center but had difficulty locating the ball because of the bright sun. Maddox, sunglasses tucked inside his back pocket, raised his right hand to shield his eyes. Although he managed to get his glove on the ball, he couldn't hold onto it. A few innings later, another ball was hit to the same spot and again Maddox dropped it. Owens went ballistic. "Jesus Christ!" he roared. "He still isn't wearing sunglasses!"

No sooner had Owens calmed down than Larry Bowa, playing deep at short, hesitated on an Ozzie Smith grounder. Instead of charging, Bowa backed up and hurried his throw. Smith beat it out and was safe on first. "God dammit!" Owens exploded, livid at the sight. "It looks like he's more worried about messing up some damned defensive record."[51]

When the dust settled, the Phillies were handed another defeat, this one by a score of 10-3. Later that evening, when the team's plane touched down in San Francisco, Owens told Green that he wanted to meet with them the following day. On September 1, after the Phillies took batting practice and infield at Candlestick Park, they entered the visitors' clubhouse to find their general manager waiting for them. "Pope, you're still pissed, aren't you?" Green asked.

"God damned right I'm still pissed!" snapped Owens.

"What about the kids?" said Green, referring to the four Triple-A players who had just joined the club. "You want them in here?"

Owens was oblivious to the fact that he had chosen the very same day for his tirade that the roster was expanded for the minor league call-up. "Do they have a 'P' on their fucking uniforms?" he shot back. "They're Phillies, too, and they're going to hear what I have to say!"[52]

The team's losing had become a personal insult to Owens, who had scouted, signed, and cultivated many of the players. His patience had run out. He knew that they were capable of much more than they were showing. "His" team, the team he struggled so hard to build, had suffered the worst fate of all in baseball— they had become complacent. They weren't hungry. The desire to win no longer existed. Instead, they had become a collection of talented individuals, who cared more about personal statistics than team success. That attitude contradicted everything Owens, the consummate "company man," valued and it infuriated him.

Now, with the veterans seated in front of their lockers, heads bowed, and the rookies nervously huddling together in the back of the room, Pope would put an end to the selfishness. According to several of the players who were present, Owens pulled no punches:

> You guys have been playing for yourselves, fighting among yourselves, and complaining for five months. It's going to stop. Dallas has been trying to tell you to straighten out. Now I'm telling you—and Ruly agrees with me 1,000 percent— stop your God damned pouting and crying.
>
> You don't give a shit about winning this thing for yourselves. You don't give a shit about winning it for Dallas. Well, then, win it for me and Ruly because we're the ones that put this team together. You've got talent, but you don't use it. You worry too damn much about your own little problems. Dallas screamed at you in Pittsburgh, and now you're back doing the same God damned sloppy things.
>
> Well, let me tell you something. I stuck my neck out after '79. I kept you together for one more run at it. I wanted to give you guys another chance! Now it's my turn. The last month belongs to me and you had better deliver![53]

The message was loud and clear—the Phillies had run out of "next years." There would be no future for the team if they didn't deliver a pennant.

Bake McBride had never seen the Pope so angry and was taken aback by his rant. "Normally, the Pope was nice and easygoing," recalled the Phillies veteran outfielder. "We all expected Dallas's blowup. But when Pope lost it with us I knew we had a problem. Everyone in that room sat up and paid attention."[54]

Owens was so agitated that his face and bald forehead were flush. His hands were trembling and his right leg tapped, unconsciously, on the clubhouse floor. "When Pope started out, he was pretty calm," recalled infielder John Vukovich. "But as he got into it, he got so mad that his leg was bouncing. I'm sitting there saying to myself, 'Slow down, Pope, or your going to have a heart attack.'"[55] But Owens's sermon was just beginning.

Turning to Larry Bowa, Pope continued his tirade: "I've been watching you play since you were a little shit in Sacramento. You're one of the best fielding short-stops ever. But lately you've been letting the ball play you. If I see you one more time short-arm a ball or not take that extra step because you're going after some god damned record, I'm going to pinch your little head off like a god damned grape."

Next, Owens directed his wrath at Garry Maddox, berating him for sulking: "Anybody can forget their sunglasses and lose a ball in the sun. But when you do it twice, I've got to wonder what the hell's going on with you. I'm god damned sick of your moods and your pouting. All you guys can pout someplace else. I don't want it in this clubhouse anymore."

In case they didn't get his message, Owens ended by challenging anyone to fight him. "You don't like what I'm saying?" he asked sarcastically. "Come knock on my door. I'm in Room 413. I'm also fifty-six years old and you might knock me down, but I'll get back up. And I'll keep coming back until you sons of bitches understand that you're a good ball club."[56]

Green's tirade wasn't unexpected. Nor did it register the impact of Owens's explosion. The team had already united against Dallas and decided to win to spite him. But the Phillies general manager was loved by the players. "Pope's more like a father to this team," said Pete Rose. "He developed Boone, Bowa, Christenson, Luzinski and Schmidt. He traded for some of the other key guys. He signed me. He means more to this ball club than Al Rosen means to the Yankees, or Dick Wagner means to the Reds. When he speaks, ballplayers know he didn't go to Harvard or Yale. He speaks a ballplayer's language."[57] The impact of Owens's speech went beyond loyalty, though. He knew how to motivate players, both pos-itively and negatively. On this occasion, Owens chose to use guilt. "No one was going to fight him when he got in our faces," admitted outfielder Del Unser. "We not only knew he was right, but we were embarrassed. And if you play this game long enough you don't want to be embarrassed, especially by the individuals who were responsible for getting you to that level."[58]

Owens's sermon accomplished its desired effect. The players understood that they couldn't force Green's firing because he enjoyed the full support of the general manager and the owner. Owens had challenged each one of the players to take a good hard look in the mirror in order to resolve their own shortcomings as individuals and put aside their petty grievances for the good of the team.

The Phillies defeated San Francisco that night, 6-4, and went on to sweep the series. But the true test of character would be played out over the month of September.

CHAPTER 10

TUGGING AT THE HEART

OR TUG MCGRAW, 1980 WAS THE HIGHLIGHT of an impressive fifteen-year career that began in the glitzy fishbowl of New York and climaxed with the final pitch of the World Series that October. If Paul Owens and Dallas Green had it their way, though, McGraw would not have thrown that pitch. The '79 campaign had been a nightmare for him. Although he managed to save 16 games, the comic reliever surrendered four grand slam home runs and watched his ERA balloon to 5.14. What's more, he would become a free agent after the '80 season. With little trade value, the Tugger, at the age of thirty-five, appeared to be finished as a player.

During the off-season, Owens and Green tried to deal McGraw along with right fielder Bake McBride to the Texas Rangers for reliever Sparky Lyle. Owens, in particular, had coveted the left-handed closer ever since 1977 when he won the Cy Young Award with the New York Yankees. But Ruly Carpenter nixed the trade at the last minute. Carpenter believed that McGraw and McBride could still contribute to the Phillies' fortunes. Nor did he want to offer Lyle the same incentive the Rangers had offered in his contract—a guaranteed broadcasting job with the club at $50,000 a season for ten years after he retired as a player.[1] In the end, the Phillies gained more than what they had anticipated.

McGraw was retained by the team for the 1980 season and, though he landed on the disabled list with tendonitis in early July, he returned at the end of the month and proceeded to pitch the Phils to a pennant (Figure 20).[2] Owens was also able to pry Lyle away from the Rangers on September 13 for a player to be named later. While the left-handed reliever was not eligible for the post-season, he was able to take a lot of pressure off McGraw down the stretch. What's more, the acquisition of Lyle reunited the two relievers who did a lot of moonlighting together during their seasons in New York. "It was refreshing for me to come to Philadelphia," admitted Lyle. "We weren't winning in Texas and I wasn't pitching much. I also valued pitching on the same team with Tug. The fans absolutely loved him in Philadelphia and he felt the same way about them."[3]

In many ways, McGraw was the spirit of the 1980 Phillies. On the field, he wore his heart on his sleeve and competed with an intensity that was second to none. After baling the Phillies out of a bases-loaded jam, he'd bounce off the mound thumping his chest with his hand or pumping his glove off his knee. In fact, there were times that the Tugger worked himself into such a frenzy that he'd "actually shit his pants." But when he reached the mound, "he was totally focused, ready to do battle."[4] His unusual behavior was consistent for southpaws. Left-handed pitchers have a reputation as being "slightly different," but left-handed relievers tend to be flaky. Once, when asked what it takes to be a good relief pitcher, McGraw replied: "A sound mind is something you don't need to be a reliever, especially if you're a left-hander."[5] The response did have a certain degree of truth to it.

The mental and physical preparation for a game are very different for relievers and starters. Since a starting pitcher is part of a rotation, he only pitches once

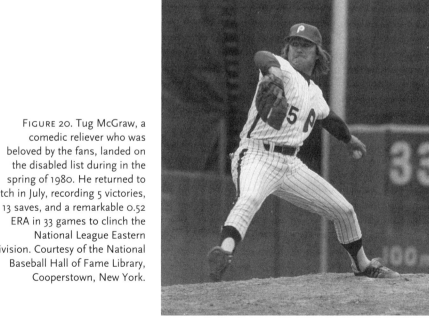

FIGURE 20. Tug McGraw, a comedic reliever who was beloved by the fans, landed on the disabled list during in the spring of 1980. He returned to pitch in July, recording 5 victories, 13 saves, and a remarkable 0.52 ERA in 33 games to clinch the National League Eastern division. Courtesy of the National Baseball Hall of Fame Library, Cooperstown, New York.

every four or five days and is expected to throw for at least six innings. As a result, everything he does—his diet, sleeping patterns, workouts—is gauged toward that one day he takes the mound. A reliever, on the other hand, must be ready to pitch every day, though he may only pitch for a single inning, or sometimes to a single hitter. That means he must be able to ready himself, both mentally and physically, within minutes of the phone call to the bullpen. McGraw prepared himself by "sitting in the dugout for six or seven innings" in order to "feel the pace or tempo of the game." It was easier for him to "feel part of the game that way."[6] For Tug, who tended to pitch on emotion as well as physical ability, the tempo of the game was often controlled by the excitement of the fans and he thrived on their energy.

Off the field, McGraw provided the kind of comic relief that's invaluable during the pressure of a pennant race. He kept his teammates loose with his quick wit and clubhouse pranks, remaining aloof from the turmoil that often surfaced between the players and their manager. In a clubhouse divided by cliques he was the one player who felt comfortable to circulate among all his teammates. "Tug was the most supportive veteran in terms of embracing the rookies on the team," recalled Marty Bystrom in a recent interview. "In spring training he seemed to prefer hanging out with the younger guys off the field."[7] Bob Walk remembers Tug spending many a night at a hotel bar with a younger pitcher who experienced a tough loss. "He was the kind of guy who felt for us, I guess because he had been through it all before," said Walk. "But he was also comfortable breaking through the different cliques on the team. It didn't matter if you were a pitcher, catcher, infielder, or outfielder, rookie or veteran, Tug would strike up a conversation with anyone."[8]

Like Pete Rose, McGraw also understood the importance of good relations with the press and the fans as well as the reciprocal relationship that existed between those two groups. As a result, Tug never hid from the writers after he blew a save. His explanations often elicited a laugh, especially when he identified the pitch he threw for a crucial out or a walk-off home run. In fact, McGraw had a humorous name for every pitch in his repertoire. The "John Jameson" was a fastball thrown "straight, the way I like my whiskey." The "Frank Sinatra" was any pitch thrown for a home run, also known as "Fly Me to the Moon." Of course, there were more suggestive references as well. The "Peggy Lee," for example, was code for "Is that all there is?" and the "Bo Derek" had a "nice little tail on it."[9] Sportswriters relished the interviews because of the colorful copy they gleaned from them. "Tug had such an infectious, off-the-wall personality," said Bill Conlin of the *Philadelphia Daily News*, "that anytime he walked into the clubhouse the whole place would light up. I think he was the beginning of the love affair between the fans and the team, even though there were so many pain-in-the-ass players on it."[10] Naturally, the fans worshipped the comedic reliever.

To be sure, McGraw's humor and personality were "infectious." He always had fun and he made sure that those around him did too. He also made time for the fans, often at the expense of his own family.[11] Truth is, Tug wanted—and needed—to be loved. "I think the fans understood my feelings for them," he admitted near the end of his life. "There's no question that I drew my motivation from performing in front of them. I loved the fans."[12] The fact that McGraw came from a broken home left him with that deep-seated need.

Raised in California's Napa Valley, Frank Edwin "Tug" McGraw, whose nickname refers to the enthusiastic way he responded to his mother's breast-feeding as an infant, was the middle son in a dysfunctional family. His mother was institutionalized for mental illness when he was in elementary school and his father became the sole parent for Tug and his two brothers. Frank McGraw Sr. floated from job to job—truck driver, fireman, salesman—but was "always working" when Tug was young. When his wife was hospitalized, he became "overwhelmed with the responsibilities of holding the family together." But he quickly adjusted taking a job "working the graveyard shift at the Water Department" so he could care for his sons. While they were sleeping, Frank, Sr., was at work. He'd come home, catch a few hours of sleep, and then "get involved in [his sons'] school activities." He drove the team sports bus, chaperoned dances, and always made sure to attend his sons' football, basketball, and baseball games. Frank McGraw did his best to discipline his three sons, though he relied primarily on the local Catholic school to take care of that responsibility. As an adult, Tug remembered his father mostly as a "pal" and home was "more like a fraternity house" than a stable environment.[13]

Most likely, McGraw's need for fan acceptance came from a lifelong struggle he waged against depression. "One of the greatest misperceptions about me," he once admitted, "is that everyone views me as a happy-go-lucky person. But there have been long stretches where my life was a roller coaster heading downhill, being mired in a series of personal crises."[14] In fact, Tug's upbeat persona was a conscious effort to battle depression. One can only admire the man for just how successful he was, personally and professionally, in that battle. His personal circumstances made him more sensitive to others who struggled with a mental or physical disability. As a result, he tended to be a champion of the underdog and took rejection more personally than most players, whether it was real or perceived.

"When I first joined the Phillies in 1975, I felt like an outsider," McGraw once admitted. "I really didn't feel like I was part of the team. Most of the players were homegrown, having come up through the Phillies' farm system. I didn't. It was also clear that the Phillies had a different approach to the game than I had been used to in New York. There, you enjoyed the entertainment part of being a professional athlete and sharing that with the press and the fans. I always had a great relationship with the sportswriters and the fans. But when I came to Philly with that attitude, I felt as if it wasn't appreciated by the players. It took a long time for them to get used to me and for me to get used to them."[15]

But the trauma of experiencing the playoff losses of 1976, '77, and '78 allowed McGraw and his teammates to bond together. When he found himself on the disabled list with tendonitis in early July 1980, his teammates stood by him, making every effort to cheer him up. "The first half of the '80 season Tug was injured a lot and didn't pitch much," recalled fellow reliever Ron Reed. "I used to kid him and say, 'You ought to be strong in the second half because you did nothing in the first half.'"[16] Greg Luzinski was another close friend and cheerleader. "I'd tell him, enjoy the rest because you're going to be in the hot seat day in and day out down the stretch. When Tug would tell me that he was scared, I'd laugh because if there was anybody I'd want as a closer with the game on the line it was him. We knew we could win when he took the mound."[17] Luzinski's words were prophetic.

After Paul Owens's clubhouse explosion in San Francisco on September 1, the Phillies went on a tear, winning 17 of their last 25 games and McGraw was at the heart of their success. Since coming off the disabled list on July 17, the entertaining reliever, in 33 appearances, compiled a 5-1 record with 13 saves. He allowed just 3 earned runs in the $52^{1/3}$ innings he pitched for an amazingly low ERA of 0.52.[18] "Tug's been outstanding down the stretch," said Dallas Green. "He's been in every game I've asked him to work and he's shut the doors totally. He's been the one consistent guy I can go to."[19]

On September 17, McGraw and the Phillies eliminated the defending world champion Pirates from the race when they took two of three games in Pittsburgh. Five days later, on September 22, Carlton defeated the Cardinals to eliminate St. Louis from the race. The victory set the stage for a three-game showdown at Veterans Stadium between Montreal and the Phillies, who clung to first place by a half a game. Bake McBride won the first game for the Phils, 2-1, with a ninth inning home run, but the Expos came back to beat Carlton the next day. The two teams entered the Sunday afternoon finale with the series tied at one game apiece. In a cruel twist of fate, the Phillies lost the game when center fielder Garry Maddox, blinded by the sun once again, misplayed a line drive off the bat of Montreal shortstop Chris Speier. The hit went for a game-breaking triple and Montreal held a half game lead entering the final week of the season.[20]

When the Chicago Cubs arrived in Philadelphia for a four-game series the following day, Green benched Maddox as well as Boone and Luzinski, both of whom were mired in hitting slumps. Before the game, Maddox confronted Jayson Stark, the beat writer for the *Philadelphia Inquirer*, and accused him of blaming him for the Phillies' loss the previous day.[21] While Maddox continued to sulk, Bowa fumed, blasting Green for his decision on his WWDB radio program. "Dallas said he's going to let the veterans go to the hilt," Bowa began. "To me, benching Maddox, Boone, and Luzinski is not letting the veterans go to the hilt. He can't sit those guys for four days and then expect them to play against Montreal in the final weekend of the season. In order for them to find their batting stroke, they have to play every day. Dallas is trying to shake things up, which is understandable, but he's also talking out of both sides of his mouth by saying he wants to stay with the veterans."[22] Bowa should have ended his criticism there, but he couldn't resist taking a verbal swipe at the press and fans as well. The temperamental shortstop took issue with recent newspaper accounts comparing the team to the '64 Phillies because of their inability to take charge of the National League's Eastern Division. "Whenever things got hairy we'd read about '64," recalled Larry Bowa. "The writers wouldn't let anyone forget about the collapse of that team. No matter how well we played, that's the mind-set of the fans and the press— something bad is going to happen."[23] He would continue to excoriate the fans later that evening after the Phillies' come-from-behind victory against the Cubs.

Larry Christenson started the opening game for the Phillies. Clinging to a 2-1 lead after six innings, L.C. surrendered two runs in the top of the seventh. Although the Phillies tied the score at 3-3 in the bottom of that frame and took the game into extra innings, they stranded base runners in the eleventh, twelfth, and fourteenth. Each time the fans reminded them of their failure with a cascade of boos. In the top of the fifteenth inning, the Cubs scored two runs on a walk, a throwing error by rookie reliever Dickie Noles, a sacrifice fly and a double against Kevin Saucier. Again, the Phils were showered with boos from the crowd.

With the Cubs leading 5-3 in the bottom of the inning, rookie Lonnie Smith and Pete Rose walked and moved into scoring position when reliever Doug Capilla unleashed a wild pitch. McBride grounded in one run and advanced Rose to third. Next, Garry Maddox, who replaced starting center fielder Del Unser in the twelfth, stepped to the plate and stroked a game-tying single. The Phils won, 6-5, when Manny Trillo singled Maddox home to cap the three-run rally.[24]

As the Phils ran out of the dugout to congratulate their teammates, the fans went wild giving them a standing ovation. Bowa, still incensed by their fickleness, called them "front runners, the worst fans in baseball." His quote received ample attention on the next day's sports pages and he was soundly booed for the remainder of the Cubs series. "You can punch a writer in this city and rate a standing ovation and second-guess a manager with impunity," wrote Bill Conlin of the *Philadelphia Daily News* of Bowa's boorish behavior. "But tell a Philadelphia fan he's a 'front runner' and you'd have less chance of getting clawed milking a panther. I mean how can you 'front run' in a town which claims two National League pennants in a century which is four-fifths shot?"[25] Conlin points out, however, that the rest of the team didn't necessarily share their shortstop's negative opinion of the fans. "I don't think that Bowa was speaking for the majority of the players when he ripped the fans," he said in a recent interview. "Sure the 1980 Phillies were a pain in the ass to deal with, but most of them were smart enough to know that you don't crap where you eat."[26]

On a more positive note, Mike Schmidt identified the game as a turning point for the team, giving them the confidence they needed to win the Eastern Division. "That was the first of many 'must-win' situations we faced," recalled Schmidt. "That was the first time we really felt like things had come together for us as a team." Having failed to deliver the winning run on two occasions in that game, Schmidt was especially grateful for the Phillies' newfound sense of teamwork. "In the past, it seemed that my teammates couldn't pick me up and the burden of failure would be even greater on me than anyone else in the same situation. But this time, Garry Maddox came off the bench to tie the game, and later, Manny Trillo won it."[27] Maddox and Trillo had removed the pressure from Schmidt, allowing him to regroup. As a result, the Phillies slugger was able to hit two game-winning homers later in the series.

The Phils won 14-2 the following day behind a brilliant effort by rookie Marty Bystrom. It was the rookie pitcher's fifth victory in as many starts. Radio broadcaster Rich Ashburn was astonished by the rookie's poise in the heat of the pennant race. "The best thing this young pitcher had going for him," Ashburn explained with his wry sense of humor, "is that he simply doesn't realize the gravity of the situation he's in." Years later Bystrom would agree with the assessment. "Maybe Whitey was right," he said in a recent interview. "I remember being called up at the beginning of September and the very first hitter I faced was Ron Cey of the Dodgers. I threw him a fastball that ran in on his hands and he hit a ground ball to third for a routine out. At that moment I said to myself, 'Hey, I'm here to stay.' My next outing was a start against the New York Mets and I threw a five-hit, shutout. I even went the full nine innings. So, at that point I was having a lot of success and it gave me all the confidence I needed to pitch in a pennant race. Having Boonie behind the plate calling the pitches and the defense I had behind me, I couldn't lose. Besides, there wasn't any real pressure on me because I hadn't gone through the earlier playoff losses of 1976 to 1978 like the veterans on that team. It was a 'win-win' situation for me."[28]

On October 1, Carlton defeated Chicago, 5-0, for his 24th victory of the season. Boone and Luzinski also returned to the lineup and contributed some timely hits.[29] The Phils swept the series on October 2 with a 4-2 victory behind the pitching of another rookie, Bob Walk. "I was very nervous before that game," admitted Walk in a recent interview. "We were a half game behind Montreal and they had the day off. If we lose that game we go to Montreal one full game down and we have to sweep them instead of taking two out of three. Sweeping the Expos in their own ballpark would have been hard."[30]

McGraw, who notched his 19th save of the season in the final victory over the

Cubs, was pitching the best baseball of his entire career and, again, he credited the hometown fans for his success. "I really don't remember my statistics," he admitted years later recounting the stretch drive. "What I do remember was this intense energy coming from the crowd every time I took the mound. The Vet was charged. The fans were electric. They made it easy to pitch. All I had to do was agree on the sign with the catcher. Then, I just put in my mind what I wanted to do and let my body cash the checks."[31] Manager Dallas Green went even further, attributing McGraw's success to the reliever's ability to remain above all the tension that existed between the players and their manager. "With his screwball personality, Tug was oblivious to all the clubhouse tension swirling around," said Green. "In many ways, he was our saving grace."[32]

The Chicago series was significant for several reasons. First, as Schmidt pointed out, the Phillies' four-game sweep of the Cubs gave the team the confidence they needed to defeat Montreal for the division title in the final series of the season. Both the hitting and the pitching, which had been inconsistent, were coming together at the same time. There was an air of confidence among the players who adopted as their theme song the uplifting disco hit "Ain't No Stoppin' Us Now," by Gene McFadden and John Whitehead.[33] Second, Boone and Luzinski restored Green's faith in them by producing offensively in the final two games of the series. Those performances allowed them to return to their starting roles in Montreal, which, in turn, prepared them for the playoffs.

Third, the rookies proved their mettle and became instrumental in the Phillies' drive toward the postseason. Lonnie Smith was a dangerous leadoff hitter, contributing five hits, scoring four runs, and stealing two bases in the two games he played. He also provided Luzinski with some stiff competition in left field. Similarly, rookie catcher Keith Moreland prodded veteran Bob Boone behind the plate. Moreland had four hits and batted in three runs in the three games he caught against the Cubs, in addition to doing a fine job handling both rookie and veteran pitchers. Marty Bystrom was just as impressive. He notched his fifth win in the second game of the series, surrendering just four hits in the 14-2 victory. When named the National League "Pitcher of the Month" for September, the humble right-hander downplayed the achievement. "I was just concentrating on doing my job," he said. "It was primarily a veteran ball club and, as Ron Reed told me, 'Rookies are to be seen and not heard.'"[34] Without the contributions of the youngsters, though, it is doubtful that the Phillies would have clinched the division flag. Green had banked the fortunes of his team on the rookies from the start of the season. He was taking a big risk by benching his veterans and playing the youngsters, especially in such critical roles as catcher, left fielder, and starting pitcher. But their performances down the stretch reinforced his confidence in them. "Lonnie Smith and Keith Moreland made an immediate impact," observed Green. "They both hit .300 and brought a youthful exuberance to an otherwise 'Mr. Cool' clubhouse. Other young players like Bob Walk and Marty Bystrom stepped up and got the job done. The bullpen was filled with young-sters like Dickie Noles, Warren Brusstar, and Kevin Saucier. Had they failed to perform, it would have been hard to sell the program. I guess it just goes to show that you don't have to be old to have character."[35]

Finally, the benching of Garry Maddox allowed utility outfielder Del Unser to gain the playing time he needed to sharpen his batting eye and get his timing back. Unser would compile a .400 batting average during the playoffs and col-lect several key hits that kept the Phillies' quest for a pennant alive.

After the Phillies swept the Cubs, they headed for Montreal. With the two teams in a dead tie for first place, the three-game series was nothing less than a season-ending showdown. "We went into that series with Montreal with such an air of confidence that nothing could go wrong," recalled John Vukovich.[36] Pete Rose was in rare form. Throughout September he had paraded around the club-house egging on his teammates: "Just get me to the playoffs, boys. I'll take care of it from there."[37] Now, in Montreal for the finale, he ratcheted his enthusiasm up another notch. Before the first game, Rose went out onto the field as the Expos were taking batting practice and with a his trademark devilish smirk went from player to player telling them that there was "no way they were going to win."[38] But beating the Expos wouldn't be easy.

Montreal was an expansion club, coming into the National League in 1969. The organization had a short but hard-luck history. Until they finished second to Pittsburgh in the National League East in 1979, the Expos were largely a team of no-names. But now, under the leadership of a successful, experienced manager, Dick Williams, and such stars as Gary Carter, Steve Rogers, Warren Cromartie, Ellis Valentine, and Andre Dawson, Montreal was a formidable competitor in the division. "We were just coming into our own in the late 1970s," said Carter. "We had some unbelievable talent on that team and some pretty good pitching as well. But there were also some strong teams in the league and the Phillies were right up there. Every time we played Philadelphia we knew it was going to be a battle. That was certainly the case in 1980."[39] Of the 18 games the Phils and Expos played that season, Philadelphia won 9 and Montreal, 9. Ten of those con-tests were decided by one run. So the Phillies had their work cut out for them when they arrived at Olympic Stadium on October 3.

Dick Ruthven started the opening game against the Expos' Scott Sanderson. The Phillies scored first when Pete Rose led off the game with a single to center. Bake McBride doubled Rose to third and Schmidt hit a sacrifice fly to right to score him for a 1-0 Philadelphia lead. Michael Jack struck again in the top of the sixth when he crushed a Sanderson fastball into the lower deck for his 47th home run of the season, increasing the Phillies' lead to 2-0. Meanwhile, Ruthven held the Expos to two hits through 5 innings until surrendering Montreal's only run in the sixth. McGraw entered the game in the eighth to seal the 2-1 victory. He faced six batters and struck out four of them, including Andre Dawson and Gary Carter.[40] It was not only his fifty-sixth appearance of the season, but his most impressive performance. The Phillies' magic number was down to one game.

Interestingly, McGraw, who was known for his emotional displays, simply walked off the field after recording the final out. As he entered the clubhouse, he kept telling himself to "key down." When Dick Ruthven asked him why he was so calm, the Tugger reminded him, "There's one more win, then we'll go nuts."[41]

The clincher came on Saturday, October 4. Despite the flu, Mike Schmidt was penciled into the lineup for the afternoon game, which was delayed for over three hours by a steady rain. When the contest finally began, it was a sloppy affair. Larry Christenson started for the Phillies against Montreal's ace Steve Rogers. The Expos took a 2-0 lead in the third when Jerry White homered. But the Phils narrowed their lead to one run in the fifth on a walk to Bowa and successive singles by Christenson, Rose, and McBride. The 2-1 Montreal lead stood until the top of the seventh when Rose began a rally with a one-out single to right. McBride and Schmidt followed with singles loading the bases for Greg Luzinski. The Bull singled to center field, knocking in 2 runs for a 3-2 Philadelphia lead. But Luzinski got caught in a weird inning-ending double play. On the hit, Montreal's center fielder Andre Dawson recovered the ball and caught Schmidt in a rundown between second and third. Shortstop Chris Speier tagged Schmidt for the second out and flipped the ball to third baseman Larry Parrish who was covering second to catch Luzinski. By the time the Bull was tagged out to end the inning, the Expos had turned an extraordinary double play that began with the center fielder and included the shortstop, third baseman, and catcher. It was just one of four base-running blunders the Phillies committed that game. "I don't know what Bull and Schmitty were doing," Rose deadpanned after the game. "It looked like a relay race. Imagine that—Schmitty giving the baton to Bull. That's a hell of a relay race, ain't it?"[42]

The Expos took a 4-3 lead in the bottom of the inning on two Philadelphia errors. The first miscue came with one out when the usually sure-handed Manny Trillo dropped a routine fly off the bat of Expos shortstop Chris Speier. Ron Reed, who had just entered the game in relief of Christenson, could see Green emerging from the dugout to take him out. "Dallas, Manny dropped the ball!" Reed fumed in disbelief. "Take him out, not me!" But Green took the ball and went to Sparky Lyle.

Lyle surrendered two runs, one of them unearned. The score remained at 4-3 in Montreal's favor until the top of the ninth when pinch hitter Bob Boone, in the midst of a 2 for 25 slump, tied the game for the Phils with a run-scoring single to center field. Once again, Green called on McGraw, who came in to pitch scoreless baseball for the next three innings.[43]

With the score tied at 4-4, the Phillies came to bat in the climactic eleventh inning to face Montreal reliever Stan Bahnsen. Rose singled to lead off for his third hit of the game. McBride came to bat next and fouled out to catcher Gary Carter, setting the stage for Mike Schmidt. Rose had advanced to second base so first was open, and Don McCormack, a rookie catcher who had never batted in the majors, was on deck. Green had run out of experienced hitters on the bench. Logic would dictate that Schmidt be given an intentional walk and that Bahnsen take his chances with the inexperienced McCormack. But for whatever reason, Expos manager Dick Williams elected to pitch to Schmidt. "I don't know why Williams did that," said Carter, who kept looking for a signal from his manager to walk the Phillies third baseman. "But he never said a thing, not even to pitch around him. So, I called for three breaking balls and Bahnsen shook me off each time. He wanted to go fastball which was a mistake against a fastball hitter like Schmidt."[44] After taking Bahnsen's first two pitches for balls, Schmidt hammered a fastball into the left field bleachers for a 6-4 Philadelphia lead. As the slugger rounded the bases, the Phillies poured out of the third base dugout to greet him. He was met with a wild reception at home plate and, in a rare show of emotion, Schmidt found himself jumping, hollering and hand-slapping along with his teammates. McGraw shut down the Expos in the bottom of the eleventh, striking out Larry Parrish to end the game and clinch the division for the Phils.[45]

"Schmidt wins the game with McCormack coming up on deck," said a stunned Larry Bowa after the game. "I was sitting on the bench saying, 'There's no way they can pitch to Schmitty. We're out of players. I'll be damned if I'm going to let Schmidt beat me when there's a kid coming up next.' Then, the next thing I know, 'POW! Home run.' I said, 'Williams is going to get ripped in the papers tomorrow.'" Interestingly, the Montreal sportswriters never exposed the manager's mistake in the following day's newspapers. Bowa, shocked by the conspicuous omission and still reeling from the negative treatment of Philadelphia's sportswriters, continued his assault on the hometown press. "Next day I'm looking all over in the paper," he said. "Nothing's there except, 'Wait 'til next season.' I'll guarantee you, if we pitched to an established hitter in that spot, the Philly sportswriters would have picked us apart."[46]

Schmidt, on the other hand, was just grateful for the opportunity. "Hitting that home run to clinch the division in 1980 was the defining moment of my career," he recalled on the twenty-fifth anniversary of that championship season. "I needed that series. Philly fans were split on whether I was a money player. It hurt me to know they doubted me, but personally I doubted myself."[47]

Schmidt's home run, his 48th of the season, set a new record for homers by a third baseman in a single season. It also capped a brilliant performance by the 31-year old power hitter. In 1980, he captured his first MVP award, leading the National League in home runs, RBI (121), and slugging average (.624). His new batting style also allowed him to become a more complete hitter, as he raised his average to .286, the highest of his career to that date. Other players also enjoyed career years, including Bake McBride (.309), Manny Trillo (.292), and rookie Lonnie Smith, who hit .339 and stole 33 bases in the 100 games he played that season. Although Rose dropped to .282, his lowest average since 1964 when he hit .269, he led the league with 42 doubles and played in all 162 games for the seventh time in his career. Even the pitching, which had been so disappointing in the early going, was impressive during the final months of the season. Carlton's 24-9 record, 286 strikeouts, and 2.34 ERA earned him a third Cy Young Award. McGraw was among the National League's top relievers with 20 saves and a major reason for the Phillies' success down the stretch. Two rookie pitchers were also instrumental in the team's fortunes. Bob Walk won 11 games, and Marty Bystrom, called up on September 1, won all five decisions, surrendering just six runs in the 36 innings he worked that month.[48]

The Phillies' impressive pitching and explosive offense gave them an advantage heading into the National League Championship Series against the Houston Astros, who clinched the league's Western Division with a 7-1 victory over the Los Angeles Dodgers in an intradivisional elimination game. "Logic tells you that we'd rather take on the Astros," Tug McGraw told the *New York Times* on the eve of the playoffs. "We've already out hit them at the Vet, and nobody except Mike Schmidt hits as many long ones in the Astrodome. Besides, it's time to finish the job we didn't finish in our three previous playoff losses in 1976, '77, and '78."[49]

Houston was making its first appearance in postseason play in the franchise's 19-year history. The team was managed by Bill Virdon, who had enjoyed previous success with the Pittsburgh Pirates and New York Yankees. Outfielders Jose Cruz (.302, 11 HR, 91 RBI), Cesar Cedeno (.309), and Terry Puhl (.282) along with first baseman Art Howe (.283) led the offense. But veteran second baseman Joe Morgan (.243, 11 HR, 49 RBI), who had been acquired from the Cincinnati Reds, was the only player with any significant postseason experience. The Astros pitching staff was more formidable.

Joe Niekro (20-12, 3.55 ERA) was the ace of the staff, but Nolan Ryan (11-10, 200 SO, 3.35 ERA) was a more formidable pitcher because of a 100-mph fastball and several no-hitters. Ken Forsch (12-13, 3.20 ERA) and Vern Ruhle (12-4, 2.38 ERA) rounded out the starting rotation, and Joe Sambito was the closer with 17 saves and a 2.20 ERA. If J. R. Richard (10-4, 1.89 ERA) had not suffered a near-fatal stroke in July, the Astros would have enjoyed even stronger pitching heading into the best-of-five-game series.[50] Still, the 1980 National League Championship Series proved to be the most eventful, if not most exciting, series since the divisional playoffs began in 1969.

The series opened in Philadelphia, where 65,277 fans packed Veterans Stadium to see Steve Carlton face the Astros' Ken Forsch. Carlton had not lost a game to the Astros in nearly two years, compiling a 6-0 record. Still, he took nothing for granted. In addition to his usual pregame preparation, which included martial arts and transcendental meditation, Lefty decided to adopt what would become yet another personal idiosyncrasy. Carlton, insisting that "loud noises distorted [his] vision," plugged his ears with cotton before taking the mound; something that would allow him to be "more mentally acute during the game."[51] He was successful in shutting down the Astros' lineup until the third inning when Gary Woods put Houston ahead with a two-out, run-scoring single. It was the only run Carlton surrendered in the seven innings he pitched.

Forsch held the Phillies to four hits through five innings. But Pete Rose started a two-run rally in the sixth when he led off the inning with a single to left field. Forsch struck out McBride and got Schmidt on a fly ball to center before Luzinski stepped to the plate. The Bull was the team's most successful hitter in the postseason, having hit safely in all eleven previous Phillies playoff games. He was the ideal hitter for the situation. Luzinski worked a full count and then smashed a towering drive into the left-field bleachers for a two-run homer. "I really get charged up for the playoffs," admitted the Bull after the game, dismissing any notion that he harbored ill feelings about the regular season. "I wasn't worried about my season. We're in the playoffs and the season's past."[52]

The following inning the Phillies added an insurance run when Maddox singled to center, advanced to second on a sacrifice bunt, stole third, and scored on Greg Gross's pinch-hit single to left. Carlton was lifted for McGraw in the eighth and the comic reliever proceeded to shut down the Astros for the next 2 innings for the 3-1 win.[53] The victory was the Phillies' first in a postseason home game since Grover Cleveland Alexander defeated the Boston Red Sox in the first game of the 1915 World Series.[54]

Houston tied the series the following day when Nolan Ryan went to the mound. Dick Ruthven pitched for the Phillies and surrendered the first run of the game in the third on a walk to shortstop Craig Reynolds, a sacrifice bunt, and a two-out RBI single to Terry Puhl. The Phils took the lead in the fourth, 2-1, when Schmidt and Luzinski tagged Ryan for back-to-back doubles and Maddox singled home another run.

Houston would not be denied, though, and tied the game at 2-2 in the seventh when Puhl doubled home Ryan. Philadelphia blew a golden opportunity to regain the lead in the bottom half of the inning. With only one out and runners on second and third, Houston manager lifted Ryan and went to reliever Joe Sambito. Sambito intentionally walked Rose to load the bases, setting up the possibility for a double play. He struck out Bake McBride and was then lifted for right-hander Dave Smith, who kept the game knotted at 2-2 by striking out Mike Schmidt.

McGraw came in to pitch the eighth. Joe Morgan led off with a double and scored when Jose Cruz singled to center. It was the first earned run scored off McGraw since September 2. Houston clung to a 3-2 lead heading into the bottom of the eighth, but the Phils came back to tie on base hits by Luzinski and Maddox. Reed replaced McGraw in the ninth and retired the side in order.

The Phillies almost won the game in their half of the inning. With one out, McBride and Schmidt singled to put runners on first and second. Lonnie Smith stepped to the plate and sliced a single to right. Houston outfielder Terry Puhl decoyed a catch and then fired home, but third base coach Lee Elia held up McBride. "It appeared to me that Bake didn't break like he should have," Elia admitted after the game. "Or maybe I was just being a little cautious. So, I put my hands up out of instinct. When Puhl threw that strike to home plate, I knew in my heart, that Bake wouldn't have scored."[55] Either way, McBride never did cross home plate. Astro reliever Frank LaCorte then struck out Trillo and retired Maddox on a pop-up, sending the game into extra innings.

Houston prevailed in the tenth when Jose Cruz singled in one run and pinch hitter Dave Bergman tripled in two more in a four-run outburst, giving the Astros a 7-4 victory.[56] Neither side appeared too concerned about the outcome, however, as the two teams prepared to leave for Houston. "Getting out of there with a split is what we were hoping for," admitted Nolan Ryan. "Now the Phillies have their work cut out for them. We play pretty good at home."[57] But Dallas Green brushed aside any thought that the Astrodome would intimidate his team. "Hey, we had to win two out of three last week in Montreal to get here," he reminded the sports-writers. "We're not scared of playing in the Dome or anywhere else on the road."[58]

The series resumed at Houston's Astrodome on Friday, October 10. Despite arm trouble, Larry Christenson took the mound for the Phils, facing knuckle-baller Joe Niekro. It proved to be a classic pitcher's duel going eleven innings before the deciding run was scored. Christenson hurled three-hit shutout ball for six innings. Three times Houston put two men on base in an inning and twice L.C. got out of the jam by throwing a double-play ball. "I always pitched well in Houston," recalled the tall right-hander in a recent interview. "Although I strug-gled a little bit in that game, I wasn't about to tell Dallas because he'd just pull me. Truth is, my arm was dead. I couldn't even throw between starts by the end of the season. Those double-play balls saved me."[59]

Unfortunately, the Phillies didn't give Christenson much offensive support, stranding base runners in eight of the eleven innings. McGraw was tagged for the winning run in the eleventh. Houston's Joe Morgan led off the inning with a triple over Bake McBride's head in right center. Rafael Landestoy entered the game as a pinch runner for Morgan and Green ordered a pair of intentional walks to Cruz and Howe. Denny Walling stepped to the plate and hit a lazy fly ball to left field. Luzinski circled the ball giving himself momentum toward the plate,

made the catch, and threw home. Schmidt cut off the throw and made a hope-
less, off-balance relay as Landestoy crossed the plate with the winning run. The
Astrodome erupted as 44,000 cheering fans waved Texas flags and Astro pennants. Houston's 1-0 victory gave the Astros a two-games-to-one lead in the best-
of-five-game series. "Sometimes you wonder if you're ever supposed to get into
a World Series," mused Bowa in the clubhouse, echoing the feelings of all Phillies
fans.[60]

The Phillies' saving grace was that their ace Steve Carlton would take the
mound for Game 4 the next night. While Carlton wasn't at his very best, he still
limited Houston's offense to just two runs through 5⅓ innings. Lefty breezed
through the first three innings before surrendering a run in the fourth and another in the fifth for a 2-0 Houston lead. By that time, the game had already
become controversial.

With two Phillies on base and no outs in the fourth, Maddox hit a soft come-
backer to the mound. Houston's starting pitcher Vern Ruhle fielded the ball and
threw it to first baseman Art Howe for an apparent double play. Home plate
umpire Doug Harvey claimed that the Astros' pitcher had trapped the ball, but
the first and third base umpires insisted that Ruhle caught the ball on the fly. As
a result, the putout at first base stood as a double play. In the midst of the confusion, Howe ran to second base to complete an apparent triple play. Paul Owens,
sitting with Ruly Carpenter and Bill Giles behind the third base dugout, exploded
at the call. "I figured what else can happen to prevent us from winning it," he
later admitted.[61] Carpenter tried to restrain Owens, preventing him from going
onto the field. But he couldn't stop Giles, who had already taken off for the seats
behind the first base dugout where National League president Chub Feeney was
seated. "God dammit, Chub! It's wrong!" he cried as he tore threw the crowd.
"You've got to overrule that call!"[62]

After Dallas Green protested the ruling, Harvey consulted with the rest of the
umpiring crew and then with Feeney. When all was said and done, the umpires
concluded that there was no triple play, only a double play as time had been called
when Howe attempted to make the third out. Following the ruling, both teams
protested the game. Another controversy followed in the sixth inning. With a 2-0
lead and only one out, Houston loaded the bases. Astros catcher Luis Pujols flied
to right. The runner at third, Woods, tagged at third and sprinted home. The
Phillies dugout erupted again, protesting that Woods left too soon. On the appeal,
umpire Bob Engel called Woods out. It was a critical ruling, giving the Phils the
momentum they needed.

On the verge of another defeat, the Phillies rallied in the eighth inning. Pinch
hitter Greg Gross led off with a single. Ruhle was lifted for Dave Smith who
promptly surrendered back-to-back base hits to Greg Gross and Lonnie Smith.
Rose followed with a single to right scoring Gross for the Phillies' first run. When

right fielder Jeff Leonard tried to get Smith going to third, Rose took second base. Schmidt stepped to the plate and hit a scorching grounder up the middle. Houston second baseman Joe Morgan stabbed the ball behind the bag, looked at Rose hustling to third and threw late to first base. McBride struck out. Trillo hit a liner to Leonard in right field. Schmidt, on first, decided that the Houston outfielder trapped the ball and took off for second. But right field umpire Bruce Froemming signaled a catch. Rose, ever alert, remained at third, tagged, and scampered home with the go-ahead run before the Astros doubled Schmidt at first.[63]

Trailing 3-2 in the bottom of the ninth, Houston came back to tie the game when Terry Puhl singled to right to score Landestoy, setting the stage for the climactic tenth inning. Once again, the Phillies' fate was in the hands of Pete Rose, and he embraced the challenge as fervently as he had done so many times over the course of his eighteen-year career. With one out, the Phillies first baseman singled to center off reliever Joe Sambito. Schmidt flied to left for the second out. Then Green sent Luzinski to the plate to pinch-hit for McBride. The Bull smacked Sambito's second pitch for a double off the base of the wall in left. The ball ricocheted off the fence so hard that it got to left fielder Jose Cruz quickly. It seemed that Rose didn't have a chance to score from first, but he found a way. Third base coach Lee Elia took one look at him chugging toward the bag and knew he was determined to score. "No way was I going to stop him," recalled Elia. "Only Pete Rose can score on that play. If he wants to go from first to home, he's going to do it."[64]

Cruz threw the ball to the cutoff, Landestoy, on one hop. The Houston shortstop wielded and fired home. Although the ball arrived ahead of Rose, catcher Bruce Bochy had to handle it on a difficult short hop. Rose stepped on the plate with his right foot and slammed into the Astro catcher with his left forearm sending him to the ground (Figure 21). Bochy never had control of the ball. Rose was safe and the Phillies led, 4-3. Trillo added a big insurance run with a double to left center that scored Luzinski.

"I can still see Pete coming in to home," said John Vukovich in a recent interview. "We all knew he was going to score. I guess Bochy will always remember that forearm shiver."[65] When asked about the controversial play after the game, Rose shrugged off any suggestion of foul play: "What I saw when I came around third was the catcher fighting with the throw. The throw wasn't a good one. It would have been hard for anybody to handle it. So I went in any way I could." "Besides," he added, "the object of the game is to win. You have to do whatever you can and they made two bad relays there. The whole key was that the catcher didn't have the ball or he would have planted me."[66]

McGraw came in to seal the win in the bottom of the tenth, retiring the Astros in order and bringing some normalcy to what had been a crazy game. The Phillies come-from-behind 5-3 victory was the longest game ever in playoff history at three hours and fifty-five minutes. "There's never been a game I've seen that has been more exciting, controversial, or interesting than this one," said McGraw afterward. "It was like a motorcycle ride through an art museum. You see the pictures, but later you don't remember what you saw." Larry Bowa agreed. "It was the weirdest game I ever played." "There's no advantage now," he added. "It's down to one game. Whoever wins becomes the National League champ."[67]

The following morning Manny Trillo and his wife Maria were eating Sunday brunch together at Houston's Shamrock Hilton when the Phillies second baseman made a brash prediction. "I think I'm going to win the Most Valuable Player of the series," he said, sipping his coffee. "I really feel it." Maria Trillo was shocked since her husband was usually not that outspoken. "Are you sure?" she asked. "Don't those awards usually go to the big home run hitters?" Manny quickly dismissed the notion. "Why not a second baseman?" he shot back. "Frank White, the Royals' second baseman was named the MVP of the American League playoffs

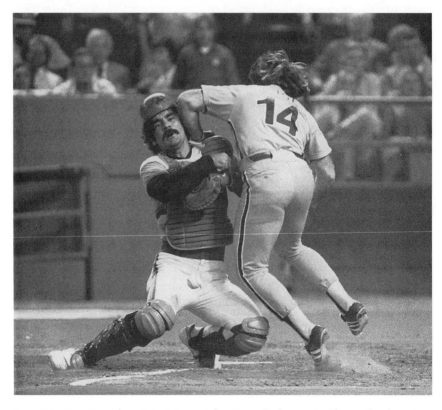

FIGURE 21. Pete Rose slams into Astros catcher Bruce Bochy, scoring the go-ahead run in the 10th inning of Game Four of the National League Championship Series. Courtesy of the *Philadelphia Daily News*.

against the Yankees a few days ago. Why not me?"[68] Trillo would find out that his prediction would come true later that night.

Despite the previous night's heady victory, the Phillies were facing some tough odds going into Game 5, since no National League team had ever won a fifth playoff game on the road. Additionally, Green bypassed Dick Ruthven, who was originally scheduled to start the game and went with rookie Marty Bystrom against Houston's Nolan Ryan. "I hadn't pitched in ten days going into that game," admitted Bystrom recently. "After Game 4, Dallas came up to me in the clubhouse and said, 'You got the ball tomorrow, kid.' I thought, 'Great, I'm ready!' But I was really very nervous when I got to the Astrodome the next day. I just told myself to keep the team close until we can get down to the late innings."[69] Bystrom's starting assignment was the kind of controversial decision Green had been making all season long. Instead of going with a veteran in a key spot, he chose a rookie and Rufus, who was told that he was being saved to start the first game of the World Series, was relegated to the bullpen.

The scoring started early. Houston took a 1-0 lead in the first on a single by Terry Puhl, who stole second and scored on Jose Cruz's double. The Phillies took the lead in the second when Boone singled to center to score Trillo and Maddox. The Astros tied the game in the sixth when Denny Walling's liner to left center was misplayed by Luzinski and resulted in a two-base error. Alan Ashby's single drove home Walling with the tying run.[70]

Green went to his relievers in the bottom of the seventh. Ron Reed, who had been throwing since the bottom of the sixth when Bystrom surrendered the tying run, believed he was being called in and started to run in from the bullpen. But Green held him up and motioned for Christenson, who had just pitched two days earlier. Although he had been told to warm up, L.C. didn't think he'd be called on and had only thrown eight warm-up pitches when the call came. "Oh shit! I'm not ready," he mumbled to himself, as he left the bullpen.[71] Ruthven was fuming. He'd already been passed over for the start and now he was being ignored again. "I got mad when they brought Larry in with only one day's rest," he admitted. "I'm saying to myself, 'What the hell am I, a sacrificial lamb? I've got more rest. Why don't you use me?'"[72]

It was a disastrous outing for Christenson, who surrendered three earned runs. When he was finally lifted for Reed, the Phillies were trailing 5-2. "I felt like a goat," he recalled. "I took a seat on the bench close to the bat rack. When the inning ended, Pete Rose comes in and he's looking right into me with those piercing eyes. It was as if he was saying, 'You motherfucker! You just screwed up everything. You blew our chances.' I was being sworn at, scolded, and ripped apart with one look of disgust that lasted maybe two seconds. I'll remember that look he gave me 'til the day I die."[73]

Nolan Ryan, on the other hand was firmly in control after the third inning.

Even Pete Rose's needling didn't seem to affect him. Before the game began, Rose approached the Houston pitcher and threw down a challenge. "You're not going to win today, Nollie," he chirped. "This is our ball game." Later, in the sixth inning when Ryan threw him a slow curveball, the Phillies first baseman lined it back into the pitcher's box for an easy out. "If you're so fuckin' proud of that curveball," Rose shouted as he returned to the dugout, "why don't you throw it to me the next time up and we'll see if you catch that one!"[74]

Ryan's luck finally ran out in the eighth. "We were down against Ryan, who never lost a lead in the late innings, especially at home," recalled Larry Bowa. "Pete Rose came up to me in the dugout and said, 'If you get on, we're going to win this damn game.'"[75] Inspired, Bowa led off with a single to center field. Boone followed with a hard chopper back to the mound. If Ryan had fielded the ball cleanly, it would have been a double play. Instead he tried to backhand the ball and it bounced off his glove for an infield hit. Now there were two runners on base with nobody out. Greg Gross came up next and laid a perfect bunt down the third base line to load the bases. Rose came to bat next. Having already needled Ryan about his curveball after his previous at bat, Rose had set the stage for himself. He was betting that the remark would earn him a steady diet of those slow curveballs, instead of the 100-mph fastballs Ryan favored. He was right. Ryan walked him on seven pitches, four of them curveballs. Rose had achieved his purpose. The walk had forced in another Philadelphia run and Ryan was sent to the showers.[76]

Joe Sambito entered the game to face pinch hitter Keith Moreland, who bounced a grounder to second, forcing in another run. The Phillies had cut the Astros' lead to one run, 5–4. With Schmidt coming to the plate, Astros manager Bill Virdon lifted Sambito and brought in Ken Forsch who had had success against the Phillies' power-hitting third baseman earlier in the series. It was a key moment: Schmidt could make or break the Phillies in that single plate appearance.

In a strange way, Schmidt's career had come down to that moment. The Phillies third baseman was so close to the championship that he could taste it. "It was my big moment, my chance to erase all doubts back in Philly that I'm a money player," recalled Schmidt, years later. "All I had to do was hit a grounder to short and we would've won the game and the pennant. Instead, I strike out and go in search of the nearest hole to crawl into. In that moment, walking from home to the dugout, I see my entire career flash before me. How can I live down this latest failure? No matter what good I did in the past I've failed in the moment of my team's greatest need."[77]

Redemption came off the bat of Del Unser, who hit a pinch single to right to tie the game. Trillo followed with a bases-clearing triple into the left field corner, giving the Phillies a 7–5 lead. After the Phillies second baseman reached third base, coach Lee Elia grabbed him and screamed, "I love you." Unable to control himself, Elia bit Trillo on the arm. "Gave him a pretty good bite, too," admitted Elia later. "But I didn't want to embarrass him with a kiss."[78] Houston wasn't finished, though.

The Astros tied the game in the home eighth off Tug McGraw, who surrendered two runs on four singles. "I was scared going into that game," McGraw admitted years later. "I could tell I was a little off and the hitters were on. The Astrodome was rocking, too. The noise was just phenomenal. It was so loud you could hardly hear yourself think. I threw a pitch to Jose Cruz that I thought was the best stuff I had and he hit a line drive single to center for the tying run. That was it. Dallas lifted me. To tell you the truth, I was relieved he took me out."[79]

Green called on Ruthven to pitch the ninth inning. "I was emotionally spent by the time I finally got out there," recalled Rufus years later. I was pissed off that I hadn't started the game and then even more pissed that I wasn't the first one out of the pen. But I guess it turned out all right because I could focus on

FIGURE 22. Garry Maddox, who had suffered earlier playoff losses in 1976, '77, and '78, is carried off the field by Manager Dallas Green and teammates after catching the final out of the National League Championship Series against Houston. Courtesy of the *Philadelphia Daily News*.

getting the job done instead of giving in to all the emotional stuff."[80] Ruthven retired the side in order to preserve the 7-7 tie. Now the momentum was with the Phillies. With one out in the tenth, Unser doubled to right. After Trillo flied out to center, Maddox stroked a double, scoring Unser with the go-ahead run. It was the biggest hit of his career.

Ruthven came out to pitch the bottom of the tenth with an 8-7 lead. "I knew we were going to win when I went out there," he said. "I'd never had that feeling in my career before. But I went out there knowing that there was no way I could lose that game."[81] Rufus was good to his word. He retired pinch hitter Danny Heep on a pop-up to Bowa at short for the first out. Next he got Terry Puhl to fly out to center, and he retired the side when Enos Cabell lifted a soft fly to Maddox, who squeezed it for the final out. The gangly center fielder rushed in to the infield where teammates converged on him from every direction (Figure 22).

Raising Maddox to their shoulders, the Phillies carried him off the field in celebration of their first pennant in 30 years.[82] "I'm elated," said Maddox after the game, trying to control his emotions. "All the disappointment, all the frustrations I felt in years gone by are washed away. I can't tell you how much it meant to have those guys pick me up and carry me off the field. I had never been carried off a field before. It was something you see happen as a kid growing up, but it's unreal when it happens to you. I felt like I was in a dream."[83]

Manny Trillo, who batted .381 with 8 hits and 4 RBI, was named the MVP of the National League Championship Series, fulfilling the prediction he made earlier in the day. But the victory was truly a team effort, a point that Phils owner Ruly Carpenter reinforced during the clubhouse celebration that followed. "I'm tremendously pleased," he said in a characteristically understated manner. "What's especially nice is that I've never seen a series where so many people contributed to the victory. The fact that Garry Maddox got the game winner is the most satisfying of all because I know in the back of his mind and the fans' minds was the ball he dropped in the playoffs two years ago in Los Angeles."[84]

Schmidt agreed: "The playoffs showed we had become the kind of team that finds a way to win. Of course, we really had so much at stake in that series as well. After our previous playoff losses, we had to get over this hurdle and we did, overcoming everything from the umpiring to left-on-base records to win as a team. To be honest, I don't think we could have survived another playoff loss as a team. We were on the edge individually and as a team. The organization would have taken another direction had we lost. But we got over the hurdle. All the negatives of the years before were wiped out by winning."[85]

CHAPTER 11

WE WIN!

W HEN THE PHILLIES WENT TO THE WORLD SERIES in October 1980 it
was a special experience not only for most of the players who had
never been there before, but also for the fans. A generation had passed
since 1950 when the Phils had played in their last Fall Classic. Many fans believed
they would never see their hometown heroes compete for the world championship, especially after the playoff losses in 1976, '77, and '78. Charles Smith of
Columbia, Pennsylvania, was one of those diehards who began following the
Phillies as a youngster and "took his lumps" throughout the 1960s and '70s.
"When they posted the sign—'Philadelphia Phillies World Champions'—on the
scoreboard," he recalled, "I started to cry. I went upstairs to my then-seven-year-
old son's bedroom and woke him up for the celebration. I wanted to share that
fabulous feeling with him because it was something he might never see again."[1]

Keri Evan of South Philadelphia had a similar experience. Her father was a
loading-dock worker at Seventh and Packer Streets and a huge Phillies fan. He
had to work the night the Phillies clinched the championship and she felt bad
that he couldn't see it.

When she returned home from celebrating downtown that evening, Keri found
her father sitting on the couch and grinning from ear to ear. "Did you see the
game?" she asked.

"Yeah, guess where?" he replied.

As it turned out, her father finished work early that night, walked over to the
Vet, and purchased a ticket for $60. He sat in center field and watched his boy-
hood team fulfill his own lifelong dream. That night taught Keri a valuable lesson—"work hard, be responsible, but stop to smell the roses when they bloom."[2]

For other fans, the 1980 World Series provided a cherished memory of a shared experience with a loved one before they passed away. In 1980, Carl Markau of Hamilton Square, New Jersey, followed each and every game of the National League playoffs and the World Series with his mother, who was confined to a wheelchair. "She couldn't speak, but we communicated with our eyes," he recalled. "Despite the incomprehensible ordeal she was going through, she was able to feel the excitement and happiness as the Phillies continued to win. She passed away shortly after the World Series, but I always believed that she would have died weeks sooner had the Phillies not advanced to the postseason. Because of that, I think she died a little happier."[3] Phil McCarriston wasn't as fortunate as Markau. His mother, another big Phillies fan who adored Tug McGraw, passed away shortly before Game 6. Struggling with mixed emotions, he returned from the viewing that night to watch the game with his family. "We all kept saying, 'Win it for Mom!'" he recalled, on the twentieth anniversary of the championship. "We went to Mom's burial the next morning with a happy heart, knowing she went out a winner."[4]

For all Phillies fans, though, the 1980 World Series and the extraordinary parade that followed it were indeed times to "stop and smell the roses."

In the World Series, the Phillies faced the Kansas City Royals a team whose fortunes had paralleled their own. Like the Phils, the Royals had clinched their division in 1976, '77, and '78 only to lose in the American League playoffs to the New York Yankees. In 1980, they finally dethroned the Bronx Bombers sweeping them in three straight games to capture the pennant. Also like the Phillies, Kansas City was loaded with talent. George Brett (.390, 24 HR, 118 RBI) was the American League's best hitter. First baseman Willie Aikens (.278, 20 HR, 98 RBI) also contributed some impressive firepower, while outfielder Willie Wilson (.326, 3 HR, 49 RBI) and designated hitter Hal McRae (.297, 14 HR, 83 RBI) were among the most consistent hitters in the league. Although second baseman Frank White and outfielder Amos Otis only hit .264 and .251 respectively during the regular season, their bats sparked the Royals to victory in the playoffs. White racked up a .545 average and batted in three runs and Otis hit .333 and scored 2 critical runs. The pitching was every bit as impressive. Dennis Leonard (20-11, 155 K, 3.79 ERA) was the ace of the staff. Larry Gura contributed 18 wins, Paul Splittorff, 14 and Rich Gale, another 13. Dan Quisenberry was the American League's top fireman with 33 saves and a 12-7 record as well as a 3.09 ERA.[5]

The World Series opened on Tuesday night, October 14, in Philadelphia before a crowd of 65,791. Since the Phillies had depleted their pitching staff in the grind-it-out five-game series against Houston, Green was compelled to start twenty-three-year-old rookie Bob Walk, the only starter who hadn't pitched in the playoffs. Known by his teammates as "Whirly-bird" because of his absent-mindedness, Walk was the first rookie to start an opening game of the World Series since Joe Black of the Brooklyn Dodgers faced the New York Yankees in

1952. A year earlier, the Phillies rookie was back home in Newhall, California, pumping gas. Now he was facing Dennis Leonard, the Royals' three-time 20-game winner. Kansas City pounded Walk early on a pair of two-run homers by Amos Otis in the second and Willie Aikens in the third for a 4-0 lead. "I was pretty shaky at the start and they were on my fastball," recalled Walk. "I put our team in the hole early. But I never doubted that we were going to come back."[6]

Just as they had done in the playoffs, the Phillies rallied in the bottom of the third when Larry Bowa jump-started the offense by singling with one out and then stealing second base. "Nobody thought I'd run," said Bowa. "First pitch, I'm gone. I'm on my own. Dallas had given me a hold sign because we were down 4-0. I thought, 'Forget that. I can get a jump on Leonard.' If I was out, I might as well have kept running. But I was safe. When I looked into the dugout I knew Dallas was ticked. But it was that kind of aggressiveness that turned the game around."[7] Bowa scored on Boone's double to left field. Lonnie Smith followed with a single but was caught in a rundown as Boone scampered home with the second Philadelphia run. Rose kept the inning alive by getting hit on the right leg by a pitch and Schmidt followed with a walk. McBride then cleared the bases with a three-run homer over the right field wall, giving the Phils a 5-4 lead. "I just wanted to make contact," the Phillies right fielder said of his home run. "The first time up Leonard threw me a sinker away and I hit a line drive to left field. I went back to the dugout and told Bowa, 'The next time up I'm going to hit a home run.' I knew he was going to throw me the same pitch and he did, only this time he got it a bit inside. As soon as I hit it, I dropped my bat and watched. I could tell it was going."[8]

The Phillies increased their lead to 6-4 the next inning when Manny Trillo beat out an infield hit, moved to second on a wild pitch, and scored when Boone doubled to right. The Phils added a seventh run in the fifth when Schmidt walked, advanced to second on a single by McBride, moved to third when Luzinski was hit by a pitch, and scored on a sacrifice fly by Maddox. But the 7-4 advantage was barely enough. Brett doubled to lead off the eighth and Willie Aikens hit another homer off Walk to cut the Philadelphia lead to one. McGraw came in from the bullpen to retire the side and pitched a perfect ninth for the save as the Phillies hung on for the 7-6 victory.[9]

When asked after the game if he relied on mental toughness for his pitching success, McGraw quipped: "If that were true, I'd be in the trainer's room right now soaking my head."[10] It was up to Pete Rose to provide the sportswriters with a more critical analysis of the Phils' first World Series victory since 1915. "When guys like Bowa and Boone get on, it just creates so much more pressure on the other team," Rose explained. "We're extra strong with the designated hitter now and when our 7, 8, and 9 hitters are going well, that makes it even tougher. I think we proved that we don't have to rely on Schmidt and the Bull to win ball games."[11]

In Ardmore, Pennsylvania, Maryellen and Bridget McCarthy were euphoric. The two sisters, ages thirteen and eleven respectively, "lived and breathed the Phillies." "That team meant everything to us," recalled Maryellen. "We memorized batting averages and ERAs. We checked the standings and box scores every day. We watched every pre-game show, game and post-game show. If the game wasn't on TV, we listened on the radio. We tried so hard to stay awake when the team played on the West Coast. Lying in our bunk-beds, eventually sleep would get the best of us and we'd wake up at 2:00 a.m. to the familiar background typewriter chatter of KYW News Radio—bummed because we missed the end of the game."

During the World Series the two sisters took turns pitching to each other on the front lawn of their suburban home, imitating the styles of their favorite players. Larry Bowa was Maryellen's hero and Mike Schmidt was Bridget's. "To this day, I can remember Bridget wiggling her butt when she was batting, just the way Michael Jack did. They were *our* Phillies. When they slumped, we defended them. When they won, we were proud. When they won the division and then the pennant, we won with them. And our worlds came to a grinding halt for the World Series."[12]

Game 2 was played the following evening and pitted Steve Carlton against Kansas City's Larry Gura. It was a scoreless, pitcher's duel through the first four innings. Then, in the fifth, Keith Moreland ignited a Phillies rally with an infield base hit. Maddox followed with a double down the left field line. Trillo sacrificed Moreland home, and Bowa's base hit to left gave the Phils a momentary, 2-0 lead.

The Royals scored their first run in the sixth and took a 4-2 lead in the seventh but lost the game in the eighth when the Phillies blasted reliever Dan Quisenberry for 4 hits and 4 big runs to clinch the game. After Boone walked, pinch hitter Del Unser doubled home the Phils' third run of the game. McBride tied the score with a base hit to right field. Schmidt came to the plate next, determined to deliver in the clutch. He jumped on Quisenberry's first offering for a double to right that put the Phillies ahead by a run.[13] "I didn't want to get behind him," Schmidt explained after the game." "Quisenberry is a one-pitch pitcher. He's got 33 saves and the best sinker in the American League. I guarantee you he's going to throw me a good hard first pitch. That was what I was looking for and I got it."[14] Schmidt later scored on Moreland's single to center field for the 6-4 victory and the Phillies went up by two games in the World Series.

The victory reinforced the value of the Phillies bench. "This team used to be eight regulars, four starting pitchers and a reliever," observed Larry Bowa, who once criticized Green for going with rookies when a game was on the line. "But Dallas has utilized twenty-five players. When the late innings come along, we have guys who know they'll contribute."[15]

Ed Rose, a native Philadelphian who lived in Baltimore, was at the game. "I had never experienced anything like it," he remembered. "The excitement was incredible, and to be there in person was a dream come true. Since I lived in Baltimore at the time, I usually had to sit in my car at night listening to the games on 1210, a clear channel station. But now I was living the dream. When Schmidt hit that double to lead the comeback win, the Vet went nuts and I drove home thinking, 'This could really happen. We could actually win a world championship.'"[16]

The Series moved to Kansas City for Game 3. George Brett, who was sidelined with a celebrated case of hemorrhoids in the previous game, returned to the Royals lineup, musing, "It's all behind me now!"[17] He went on to celebrate with a first-inning solo homer off Phillies starter Dick Ruthven. The Phils tied the game in the second when, with bases loaded and one out, Lonnie Smith smacked a grounder back to the box and Royals pitcher Rich Gale, confused, threw to first instead of home for an easy force out on Manny Trillo.

Willie Aikens put the Royals in front in the fourth when he tripled and later scored on Hal McRae's single to center. The following inning, Schmidt hit his first homer ever in postseason play into the Phillies' bullpen in left field. Two more hits were followed by an inning-ending double play. Although Philadelphia had collected eight hits in five innings, they had stranded eight base runners.[18]

Ruthven pitched effective baseball, holding the Royals to just four hits until the seventh when Otis homered to give Kansas City a 3-2 lead. The Phillies clawed their way back again the following inning. Bowa slashed a roller to the left side of the pitcher's mound and beat Rene Martin's throw to first base. He stole second one out later. Smith walked, and Rose followed with a single over the head of second baseman Frank White to tie the game at 3-3. The Phils were heading for their fifth extra inning contest in eight postseason games. They almost won in the tenth when they put runners on first and second with one out. Schmidt then hit a sharp liner to Frank White's right, but the Royals' second baseman speared the ball for an inning-ending double play.

Once again, McGraw was called in to pitch. It was his seventh appearance in the last eight games. But this time, he couldn't hold the Royals in check. U. L. Washington led off with a single. Wilson, trying to sacrifice, walked on four straight pitches. White struck out, but Wilson stole second base. Brett was intentionally walked to load the bases. Aikens followed with a single to left center to score Washington, giving the Royals a 4-3 victory. Afterward, sportswriters wisecracked that the "proctologists had come through in the end!"[19]

Patricia Kelley, who taught in the Archdiocese of Philadelphia, was saddened by the loss but continued to rally her students around the team. Throughout the postseason she encouraged her sixth graders to root for the Phillies in some unusual ways. "Everyone knew how excited I was during the playoffs and the World Series," she recalled. "I had the children's parents sign their homework in red pen. We would write baseball comments back and forth to each other. It gave students an incentive to do their homework. I also made the Phillies 'P' logo for the collars of my students and they would wear only red and white clothing when the Phils won. I'll never forget how everyone at the school cheered when the Phillies finally won the World Series, especially the sisters of St. Joseph."[20]

Larry Christenson started Game 4 for the Phillies, though he probably shouldn't have pitched. "My father had suffered a stroke during the playoffs in Houston and was placed on life support," he explained in a recent interview. "I was quietly fighting with what to do. Should I stay with the team or go to see my father?" Christenson didn't mention anything to the team, deciding to stay and pitch.[21] He never made it past the first inning, surrendering four runs on five hits while recording just one out.

The Phillies scored an unearned run in the second on a throwing error by shortstop U. L. Washington. Manny Trillo, who reached base on the miscue, later scored on a single to left by Bowa. But the Royals matched the run in the bottom of the inning when Aikens hit a towering shot into the Kansas City bullpen off reliever Dickie Noles, making the score 5-1 and putting the game out of reach for the Phillies.

Aikens's two home runs made him the only player in World Series history to enjoy two multiple home run games in a single series. It was also the only run Noles surrendered in his 4^2/$_3$ innings of work. It was an impressive outing for the rookie, who recorded six strikeouts in that span and changed the momentum of the Series back in the Phillies favor.[22] "After Aikens hit that homer off me, he stood there at home plate watching it leave the park," recalled Noles. "That pissed me off. I looked at him and said, 'If you don't get your fuckin' ass down the baseline you're going to be wearin' a baseball!' He still didn't move. So I swore to myself that if I was still in the game the next time he came up I would drill him."[23] Noles got his opportunity in the fourth inning.

Aikens was scheduled to hit second in that inning, following George Brett. After getting two quick strikes on Brett, the Royals slugger stepped out of the batter's box and looked down the third base line at Mike Schmidt. The two exchanged some words, apparently kidding each other about something. But Noles didn't appreciate it. He glared at Schmidt as if to say, "Hey, I'm out here pitching my butt off, don't talk to the hitter!" Then the rookie hurler turned to face Brett, who was still standing outside of the batter's box.

"Hey," shouted Noles, "Get back in the box or I'll drill your ass!"

Brett glared back at him, daring the young pitcher to deliver on his threat. Noles responded by throwing a fastball up and in, flipping the Royals slugger on his back (Figure 23).[24] There was a momentary silence and then the stadium erupted in a deafening "boo."

Royals manager Jim Frey came charging out of the dugout screaming at Noles and the home plate umpire. "You better stop it right now!" he demanded, running toward the mound. "He's throwing at him! He's going at his head. . . . No more of this! Stop it right now!"

Rose converged from first base, cutting off the infuriated manager. "Hey, Jim," he shouted. "Don't come out here. You have a heavyweight championship crowd on this field and you're going to get knocked on your ass!"[25]

"But he's throwing at him," protested Frey, pointing at Noles.

"He wasn't throwing at him," Rose shot back.

"How do you know?" asked Frey.

"Because if he was, he'd have hit 'im!"

The Royals dugout had been excoriating the young Phillies reliever with profanities and threats, but Rose's quip kept them at bay. "Pete turned and looked at their dugout," recalled Noles. "Walking to the mound he says to me, 'Pitch your own ball game.' It was loud enough for them to hear. Then, as he's walking back to first, Pete, still looking in their dugout, shouts: 'And if you want to knock anybody else down, go ahead.' That was Pete. He knew how to seize an opportunity. He wasn't worried about me being intimidated. He was concerned

FIGURE 23. Dickie Noles's brushback of the Royals' George Brett in Game Four has been credited with intimidating Kansas City, which batted .200 as a team in the remaining two games of the 1980 World Series. Courtesy of the *Philadelphia Daily News*.

about me taking it to another level and possibly starting a brawl. Pete figured, 'Lets take this and use it for what it was worth.'"[26]

To be sure, Noles was not the kind of pitcher who would back down from a fight. He had a tremendous amount of pride and a hair-trigger temper to go with it. As it turned out, the knockdown pitch to Brett proved to be more than a warning; it gave the Phillies the momentum they needed to defeat Kansas City in the Series. "Dickie was a gunslinger, the kind of guy you avoided making eye contact with in a bar," said Mike Schmidt. "When George Brett eased into his first pitch with his front foot so close to the plate, Dickie saw that as an insult. That was *his* plate, not Brett's. Noles rocketed the next pitch over his right ear, putting him on his back. That brushback pitch put an end to the Royals' hitting party. After that, Kansas City batted .200 the rest of the way and we went on to win it all."[27] Schmidt was correct. The Royals had been intimidated. Although Kansas City won the game, 5-3, it would be their last victory in the Series.

Back in Northeast Philadelphia, Stan Pawloski, who played with the Cleveland Indians in the 1950s, was impressed by Noles's brushback pitch. He told his twin sons that the Phillies reliever was a "throwback, the kind of ballplayer we had in baseball thirty years ago." "That Phillies team was special to me," Pawloski recalled. "They wanted to win. The game was more than a paycheck to them. Pitching inside has always been a fundamental part of the game. It's 'old school.' So is respect. I'm not taking anything away from George Brett, who was a fine player. But Noles had to restore some respect."[28]

Manager Dallas Green selected twenty-two-year-old rookie Marty Bystrom to pitch Game 5 against Larry Gura. For three innings both hurlers held each other's teams in check, Then, the Phillies erupted for two runs in the fourth when Bake McBride's one-out bunt was misplayed by Aikens at first and Schmidt followed with his second home run of the Series. Kansas City finally scored in the fifth when U. L. Washington singled, advanced on a base hit and sacrifice bunt, then scored as George Brett grounded to Trillo at second. Amos Otis tied the score at 2-2 with a leadoff home run in the sixth. When the Royals put runners on first and third on base hits by Clint Hurdle and Darrell Porter. Bystrom was lifted for Ron Reed. Reed surrendered a sacrifice fly to Washington that put the Royals in the lead, 3-2. But further damage was eliminated when Wilson doubled to right and Porter, trying to score from first, was gunned down at the plate on a brilliant relay from McBride, to Trillo to Boone. "I didn't have my best stuff, but I was just trying to keep us in the game," recalled Bystrom in a recent interview. "I knew Dallas was keeping me on a short leash. If I could hold 'em close and give our guys a chance to score, that was the job he wanted me to do. I just stuck to my game plan and tried to make good pitches when I needed to."[29]

McGraw came in to relieve Reed in the seventh and shut down Kansas City's offense for the remainder of the game. For the Royals, Quisenberry relieved Gura in the seventh, holding the Phils scoreless until the ninth. Schmidt, who led off that inning, ripped a bullet off of third baseman George Brett's glove. Brett's decision to cheat in a few steps because of Schmidt's bunt attempts in the first two games of the Series backfired. "I had no intention of bunting in that situation," said a surprised Schmidt after the game. "As a leadoff batter, I was just trying to drive the ball someplace. I did notice that Brett was playing me in, though. And maybe that helped me get on base. If he was playing me even with or just behind the bag, he might have had the time to make the play."[30]

Schmidt scored when pinch hitter Del Unser doubled to right field. It was Unser's third pinch hit and second RBI in the Series, making him 5-for-11 with three runs batted in and an impressive .454 average in the postseason. "Del's spoiling us," said Larry Bowa. "He's setting some very high standards. If he makes an out we'll get on him."[31] Moreland's sacrifice fly and Trillo's RBI single put the Phillies ahead 4-3. McGraw survived a shaky ninth in which he walked the bases loaded, but still managed to seal the victory. Tug is a very hyper and nervous type guy," observed Bob Boone after the game. "I was just trying to keep him under control as best I could in the ninth. We just don't seem to be doing anything easily."[32] Perhaps not, but the Phillies had regained momentum with their 4-3 victory in Game 5, sending the Series back to Philadelphia. There, they would send their ace Steve Carlton to the mound for Game 6. All they needed was one win in the remaining two games of the Series to clinch their very first world championship, and both would be played in the friendly confines of Veterans Stadium.

In the East Falls neighborhood of Philadelphia, John Grace, a history teacher at LaSalle College High School, was glued to the television set each evening watching the Series from his apartment. Afterwards, he'd call home to review the contest, play-by-play, first with his father and then with his brother. "We were a *huge* baseball family," said Grace. "The game was always on, either on the TV or the radio, and it was always followed by the 'Grace Brothers post-game analysis.' It didn't matter if we were all living under the same roof, or if I was down the shore for the summer at Ocean City. Of course, down there, I'd always celebrate a victory with a few cold ones at Twist's Bar."[33] Grace would have a lot to celebrate two nights later when the Phils returned to the Vet for Game 6.

To ensure that the contest would be played without incident, Phillies vice president Bill Giles contacted Wilson Goode, the City of Philadelphia's managing director, a few days before the game. "We have a chance for a riot here if we win this thing," Giles told Goode. "Can you beef up the stadium security with your mounted police?"

"I'll not only do that," replied Goode, "I'll bring the dogs, too."

Giles shuddered at the thought, considering the negative publicity such a scene might generate. "I really don't want the dogs," he protested. "I think it'll be a black eye for the city to have attack dogs out on the field. It would be like a police state."

But Goode wouldn't hear of it. "I'm bringing them both," he insisted. "The city owns the stadium and I don't want people destroying it."[34]

Plans were made to upgrade security at the stadium by Pat Cassidy, the Vet's operations director, in conjunction with George Solomon, the Philadelphia police commissioner. The police department canceled all vacations and provided 1,000 officers, including 10 mounted patrolmen, and 30 special riot control officers with attack dogs, while Cassidy added another 100 men to his already considerable security force.[35] By Tuesday morning, October 21, the Veterans Stadium grounds crew, security staff, and the City of Philadelphia were ready to go. Now the fate of the organization was left in the hands of the manager, coaches, and players themselves.

That afternoon, Tug McGraw hitched a ride to the Vet with his neighbor Mike Schmidt. Both players lived in suburban Media, a forty-minute drive from South Philadelphia down Interstate 95. Carpooling had become something of a superstition for them that season, just like the black-and-white milkshakes they'd buy and consume en route. "Schmitty and I were joking around, and he told me he felt tonight was the night," recalled McGraw. "He predicted that he'd drive in the winning run and make some great defensive play and that I'd come in, pitch the last inning, and get the big strikeout to end it. 'When that happens,' he said, 'I'm going to run over and dive on top of you so I can get my picture on the front page of the newspaper, maybe on the cover of *Sports Illustrated.*'"[36] Schmidt's words would prove to be prophetic.

At game time that evening, the Vet was packed with 65,838 fans, the largest ever in the ten-year history of the stadium. Security guards and policemen were positioned at each of the stadium's tunnels, ramps, and exits to prevent fans from the upper decks from leaving their seats and invading the box seat area.[37]

Steve Carlton faced Rich Gale in Game 6, which would prove to be the final game of the Series. Lefty was simply brilliant. In the first inning he struck out Willie Wilson and U. L. Washington and retired George Brett on a grounder to second. In the second Carlton walked two with one out but got John Wathan to ground into a double play. It was the first and last time the Royals would get more than a single base runner in the seven innings Carlton worked.

The Phillies began the scoring in the third inning. Boone led off with a walk. Lonnie Smith beat out a grounder, and Pete Rose bunted to load the bases. Schmidt followed with a single to left field, driving in two runs. "I couldn't have gotten a bigger hit than that," he admitted years later. "I got the game-winning hit in the final game of the World Series. I was so excited that I even made a gesture—hoisting my fist into the air—when I reached first base. It was one of the few times that I found myself showing emotion on the field."[38]

The Phillies increased their lead in the fifth. Lonnie Smith doubled and took third on Rose's fly to center. Schmidt walked and Paul Splittorff was called in to pitch to Bake McBride. The Phillies right fielder bounced a roller to the left of the mound, but Splittorff couldn't handle it. Shortstop U. L. Washington charged and barely got McBride at first. Smith scored the Phils third run on the play. The next inning the Phils padded their lead when Bowa, with two outs, doubled past Wilson in left field and Boone singled up the middle to score him.

In the seventh inning McGraw got up in the bullpen to warm up, but couldn't find his glove. When he finally located the mitt there was a police dog lying on top of it. As he reached for the glove, the K-9 began to growl at him. "Hey," McGraw shouted to the police officer standing nearby, "I need my glove and your dog has fallen in love with it."[39] Shortly after the Tugger retrieved his mitt, the inning ended and the ten mounted police officers stationed down the right field line next to the Phillies bullpen paraded in single file across the outfield warning track to the visitors' bullpen in left field. It was an effective deterrent to any fan planning to rush onto the playing field (Figure 24).[40]

FIGURE 24. Mounted police enter the outfield during Game Six. The Phillies and the City of Philadelphia took the action to ensure public order and were harshly criticized by the national media. Courtesy of the *Philadelphia Daily News*.

Carlton entered the eighth with a 4-0 lead. But when Lefty walked Wathan and Jose Cardenal singled, Green lifted him for McGraw. "It was a little scary to relieve Carlton," Tug admitted years later. "When I first came to the Phillies, I'd come in and say, 'I got this one for you, Lefty, don't worry about it.' And he'd look at me like he was about to tear my head off. He was intense and never wanted to leave the game. But by 1980 things had changed. I remember going in to the final game of the Series and we just made eye contact. We understood each other and I think he had the confidence to know I'd save the game for him. Besides, Lefty was great to relieve because no hitter could adjust from his slider to my screwball."[41] Unfortunately, that would not be the case on this evening.

After White fouled out to Rose for the first out of the inning, McGraw walked Wilson to load the bases. Washington stepped to the plate next and lofted a sacrifice fly to center scoring Wathan and cutting the Phillies' lead to 4-1. Brett followed with an infield hit loading the bases for Hal McRae. McRae fouled off two pitches and then hit a harmless grounder to second for the final out of the inning. The Phillies were retired in order by Quisenberry in the bottom of the eighth, setting the stage for the climactic ninth inning.

FIGURE 25. Phillies Catcher Bob Boone and Pete Rose converge on a pop-up near the first base dugout during Game Six. The ball has just glanced off of Boone's mitt, and Rose is about to catch it to record the second out of the ninth inning. Courtesy of the *Philadelphia Daily News.*

Always the showman, McGraw provided more drama. After retiring Amos Otis on five pitches, he walked Aikens and gave up singles to Wathan and Cardenal to load the bases. Frank White followed and popped a foul down the first base side near the Phillies' dugout. Boone sprang out of his crouch, shed his mask, and extended his arm to make the put-out. But the ball bounced out of his glove. Rose, ever alert, was there to grab the ball before it hit the ground to record the second out of the inning (Figure 25).

"At that point my dad popped a nitro to prevent cardiac arrest," recalled Phillies fan Donna Coppock.[42] Other fans breathed a huge sigh of relief before exploding into cheers. "Rose's catch was just awesome!" chirped Nick Halladay of West Chester, who was seated in the 700-level. "When that happened I just knew we were going to win. So did Pete because he ran back out onto the infield and spiked the ball in a show of confidence. The place just rocked. Everyone was pumped!"[43] That is, everyone with the possible exception of Bob Boone.

"Catchers are responsible for a pop-up in the area directly in front of them, the area behind them and the areas to their immediate left and right," explained Boone. "Everything else is for the first baseman on the right side or the third baseman on the left side. It's a much easier play for them coming to the ball. So on pop-ups to the left and to the right the catcher doesn't say anything—he just follows the pop-up, and listens for the first baseman or the third baseman to call him off.

"On this particular play, it wasn't my ball. I got to the end of the dugout and I'm listening for Pete to call me off, but I don't hear him. I can see the ball coming down, plus I'm real close to the edge of the dugout. I'm still listening for Pete and I don't hear anything. 'Where is he?' I'm asking myself, 'Where the hell is he?' As the ball is getting closer and closer I'm thinking, 'I know he's going to crash into me, but I just can't let the ball drop because he's not saying anything.'

"Normally, I'd just let the ball fall to me, but I figured I was going to have to out-rebound Pete for this ball, so I went up to grab it. It was like trying to catch a ball with a wooden board, the ball just sprang up on me. When the ball popped out of the glove, I remember thinking. 'Oh my God! I've never dropped one of these in my life!' But I dropped it because I was trying to catch it differently in order to avoid getting hit.

"At first, I was mad at Pete. I wanted to kill him. It was his ball. Then, all of a sudden, this glove appears and he catches the ball, so then I wanted to kiss him!"[44]

Rose told a slightly different story. "Not many people know it, but Boonie and I practiced that play!" he quipped. "Truth is, that it was my ball and his ball too. But with 65,000 people screaming, sometimes you don't always get it straight. Besides, I think it would have been a better play if I could have doubled off the runner on third base. It would have been a double play and nobody would have known the game was over!"[45]

Now there were two outs. The bases were still loaded and Willie Wilson, the Royals' dangerous leadoff hitter, was coming to the plate. The horses, attack dogs, and riot control police moved into position along the first and third base warning tracks. Just to avoid any confusion, the umpires, before the inning began, gave the most bizarre ground rule in the game's history: "Animals are in play."[46]

Boone, trying to regroup from the last heart-stopping play, approached McGraw on the mound. "Isn't this exciting, Tuggles?" he said, trying to reassure McGraw.

Tug was so exhausted that his fingers were numb. He told Boone that he couldn't throw any more screwballs, but the catcher didn't want to hear it. "You have to throw one more," said the Phils backstop. "We have to set up Wilson with the screwball to get him thinking about the outside corner. Then we should stay in on him after that."

Having agreed on strategy, Boone returned behind the plate and Wilson stepped into the batter's box. The catcher flashed three signs, none of which was the screwball. The mind game with Wilson had begun.

McGraw threw the scroogie for a strike. Next he threw a slider, down and in, for strike two. With the count at 0-2, the crowd was on its feet, cheering every pitch. McGraw, ever so close to living every young boy's dream, realized that he had to waste a pitch. The Tugger tried to throw a "Cutty Sark" fastball, up and inside. But he missed with it and the ball sailed high and right down the middle of the plate. Had Wilson chased the pitch, he might have nailed it for extra bases. Instead, he took it for ball one.

"Anyone watching that game who knew anything about pitching realized I had Wilson perfectly set up for a 1-2 screwball," recalled McGraw years later. "In fact there were 65,000 'pitching coaches' in the stands yelling, 'Screwball, Tug, screwball!' I swear, I even heard my dad who was sitting behind the Phillies dugout yell, 'Screw 'em, Tugger!' With all that help coming from the stands, surely Willie got the idea. He was looking for a screwball, too."[47]

McGraw and Boone were the only ones thinking differently. Boone called for another fastball, this one inside. If Wilson was looking for a screwball outside, there would be no way he could get around on a pitch like that. Tug toed the rubber, reared back, and threw the fastball. "I knew we were champions as soon as I released it," he admitted. "I saw Wilson start to lean towards the outside corner because he had mistakenly guessed screwball outside. We had fooled him. He swung and missed."[48]

McGraw leaped skyward as his teammates and coaches converged on the mound from the field and the dugout (Figure 26). Schmidt, smiling from ear to ear, purposely hesitated. McGraw was looking directly at him, waiting for the third baseman to deliver on the prediction he made earlier that day when the two men rode together to the Vet. Just as Phillies players were about to swarm around the reliever, Michael Jack, in a rare display of emotion, dove into McGraw's arms and was immediately engulfed by a mob of teammates and coaches.[49] Cameras recorded the scene for posterity and, like Schmidt predicted, the photograph graced the front page of the *Philadelphia Bulletin* the following day.

The celebration continued inside the Phillies clubhouse. Amidst the congratulatory hugs, the popping of corks, and the splashing of champagne, a hoarse Larry Bowa could still be heard stirring up the madness. "All the experts were wrong," he croaked. "D-E-A-D wrong! They picked Pittsburgh and St. Louis and Montreal. Well, adios to them. And then the experts picked Houston in the play-offs. Adios! And then they picked the Royals in the Series. Adios! We are the champions and no one can take that away. From now on until the next World Series, we are the best in the U.S. of A."[50]

When the commissioner Bowie Kuhn presented the World Series trophy to Ruly Carpenter, the Phils owner thanked Dallas Green and Paul Owens for their instrumental roles in "the greatest thing that ever happened to [him] in his life." Owens, overcome with emotion, had one arm wrapped around Green and the other around McGraw. Echoing Carpenter's feelings, the Phils' general manager

FIGURE 26. Tug McGraw jumps for joy after striking out the Royals' Willie Wilson to clinch the Phillies first world championship. Courtesy of the *Philadelphia Daily News*.

planted a kiss on McGraw's forehead, thanking him for his remarkable pitching in the playoffs and Series.

Accepting the trophy for the Phillies organization, Green thanked the ownership, Owens, his mentor, and all the players and coaches for "putting a lot of ghosts to rest." "I'm proud of all these guys, every one of them," he told Bryant Gumbel, who was covering the postgame celebration for NBC Sports. "You talk about courage, you talk about character, this team showed more guts the last month of the season than any team ever. Just look at all the games we won by one run, all the 'must' games we won."[51] Green was a different man than the one who had criticized his players, personally and publicly, throughout the season. He would later embrace Bowa and Maddox—two of his greatest critics—in bear hugs, thanking them for the season. Winning the Series had a special way of mending fences. Green could also appreciate the championship more than they could. He had sacrificed more, stopping at every level in the organization—player, coach, minor league manager, farm director. It was his time to shine in the national spotlight.

Three figures were conspicuously absent from the clubhouse mayhem: Steve Carlton, Greg Luzinski, and Mike Schmidt. Carlton had retreated to the trainer's room, just as he did after every game he pitched. There he sat quietly on the table sipping champagne as his fellow pitchers entered, one by one. Each one seemed to respect Lefty's privacy, staying long enough to give him a congratulatory hug and then return to the party outside.[52] Carlton appeared to be in a wonderful daze. For as wild and wacky as he could be with his teammates on road trips and in the clubhouse during the season, he didn't quite know how to handle the greatest achievement of his career: starting and earning the victory in the Series clincher. "You'll never know how much winning the championship meant to him," said his wife, Beverly, later. "After the season ended, he would sit up in bed in the middle of the night and almost shout, 'We're world champions!'"[53] Lefty would have a few more good seasons for the Phillies and make it back to the Fall Classic one more time. Luzinski, on the other hand, knew his days were numbered.

The Bull was a somber figure sitting quietly in front of his locker while getting dressed in his street clothes. Used sparingly during the Series, Luzinski was sidelined by an intestinal virus for three games and went hitless in nine at bats in the other three. Hampered by knee problems and fighting a losing battle with weight, the Bull, at age twenty-nine, could no longer play the outfield on a daily basis. Before the start of the next season, he would be sent to the American League to finish out his career as a designated hitter for the Chicago White Sox.[54]

Mike Schmidt, named the Most Valuable Player of the Series for hitting .381 with 2 home runs and 7 RBI, had been hustled into a separate room for a press conference. But there was a mix-up and he didn't return to the clubhouse until after the trophy presentation.[55] A few weeks later, he would be named the Most

Valuable Player of the National League, the first of three such awards he garnered in his career.[56] Michael Jack would go on to play for another eight and a half seasons, all with the Phillies. During that period he would lead the team to another World Series and compile the statistical totals to earn wide consideration as the "greatest third baseman in the history of the game."[57] But never again would he enjoy the kind of remarkable season he experienced in 1980 when, by his own admission, "my teammates carried me, when I needed it most."[58]

While the Phillies celebrated at the Vet, the fans basked in the glory of their first world championship in front of their television sets or at the corner bar. Parties broke out spontaneously across the city. People were dancing on Broad Street. McFadden and Whitehead's "Ain't No Stoppin Us Now" was the song of choice.[59] Mary Leimkuhler of the Fox Chase section of Northeast Philadelphia and her friends took the Broad Street subway from the Vet to Fern Rock Station and hopped into her car. "We were heading back to our own neighborhood, getting more revved-up as the night wore on into the early morning," she said. "We drove from Fern Rock to Five Points in Fox Chase, a distance of about five miles, with me on the hood of the car! It was something else. More than three thousand people had found their way to Five Points like us, all to pay homage to the home team and party on."[60]

Six-year-old Alex Carver of Wayne, Pennsylvania, was running around his neighborhood screaming with joy. "When Schmitty jumped on top of that pile of Phillies to begin the celebration, I went wild," he recalled. "I was screaming, 'THE PHILLIES ARE WORLD CHAMPIONS!' to anyone who'd listen. It was a great introduction to baseball for me and it began a lifelong love affair with the game and with the Phillies."[61]

Ray Angely, a native Philadelphian stationed at Elmendorf Air Force Base in Alaska, held his own little party. "When Tugger struck out Wilson, I spilled beer all over myself and let out a howl that rang through the entire barracks," he said. "Who cared! All those years of following every win and loss was worth it for one moment. I grabbed two of my friends and we painted downtown Anchorage red and sang the praises of the Philadelphia Phillies from bar to bar the whole night. Didn't matter that those two guys hadn't heard of the team, they were Phillies fans for at least that one memorable night."[62]

The following day the city closed. Businesses took a day off and absenteeism in schools was over 50 percent as more than one million Philadelphians turned out to cheer their Phillies. Preparations for a victory parade down Broad Street began early. Red and white streamers began floating from the windows of office buildings at 9:00 A.M. An hour later there were horns blowing, fireworks exploding, and kids hanging off lampposts cheering their heroes, as more than 500,000 fans lined the city's main thoroughfare (Figure 27). Signs could be seen proclaiming "Schmidt for President" and "Tugadelphia." The parade ended in

South Philadelphia at John F. Kennedy Stadium, where 85,000 gathered to hear speeches. It was a lovefest between the team and its fans.

Owens and Green told the Phillies faithful that they were "beautiful." Pete Rose reminded everyone that he had been in the World Series "five times," and there was "no doubt in [his] mind that you people are the greatest." Bowa, in a generous mood, dismissed his earlier criticism of Phillies fans as "the worst in baseball" and celebrated them as "the greatest fans in the world." Schmidt agreed. "I never saw so many sincere faces in my life as I did in that parade," he said. "Take this world championship and savor it because you all deserve it." Of course, McGraw, the closer, got the last word. Gripping that day's *Philadelphia Daily News* headline, "We Win!" the Tugger whipped the crowd into a wild frenzy when he thrust the newspaper skyward and proclaimed: "All through baseball history, Philadelphia has taken a back seat to New York City. Well, New York City can take this world championship and stick it!"[63]

Philadelphia would never again witness the outpouring of affection the city displayed for the Phillies that day. Not in 1983 when the Sixers won the city's next—and last—championship. Not in 2000 when Tug McGraw sponsored a

FIGURE 27. More than 500,000 fans lined Broad Street for the Phillies victory parade on October 22, 1980. Courtesy of the *Philadelphia Daily News*.

gala twentieth-anniversary celebration and replicated the parade down Broad Street. Even if the Phillies capture a second world championship in the future, the public celebration will pale in comparison to 1980 because of the deep emotion that world championship generated between the team and the city.

The 1980 Phillies and their fans had been working toward a world championship for five years. The playoff losses of 1976, '77, and '78 made 1980 so much more rewarding because the team had finally vindicated itself. Not that the 1980 Phillies were a better team than the earlier ones; they weren't. The '77 squad had a more explosive offense, greater speed, deeper pitching, and stronger defense. But the '80 Phillies were essentially the same team that had experienced all the frustration and disappointment of those earlier seasons.

Fans had grown up with the 1980 Phillies. We suffered in their losses and gloried in their victories. We took them personally. Like the team, we had become tired and frustrated with losing. Our standards for the players were higher, our expectations for a world championship, greater. Lesser athletes would buckle under the weight of those expectations in other cities. But not this collection of players. These Phillies delivered, in spite—or maybe because—of those great expectations and all the criticism that went with them. Call them what you will, but no one will ever call them "quitters." Ultimately, rooting for the 1980 Phillies was like rooting for ourselves.

CHAPTER 12

DYNASTY DENIED

T HE EUPHORIA GENERATED BY THE PHILLIES' first world championship was short-lived. Almost immediately after the World Series ended, the national press launched an attack on the Phils, blaming the team for problems that could be found on any baseball club during the era of free agency. New York's sportswriters began the assault in retaliation for McGraw's quip that their sports obsessed city could "take the [Phillies'] world championship and stick it." "The Phillies are miserable millionaires," wrote Mike Marley in the *New York Post.* "Their motto is meanness, rudeness and ignorance." Mike Lupica, who covered the warring Yankee teams of the late 1970s, was more sarcastic. "The Phillies are as much fun as a subway crime," he wrote in the *New York Daily News.* "They have made the New York Yankees seem like the Fellowship of Christian Athletes."[1]

The media bashing went national when Dick Young, writing for the *Sporting News,* used Carlton to launch an attack on Marvin Miller and the Players Association. Belittling the Phillies ace for "hiding out in the trainer's room" and "refusing to speak to the press" after Game 6, Young insisted that he wasn't "mad at Carlton as much as the ball clubs and the players' union that permit the Carltons of the world to hide from the press." He ended the article by calling on the union negotiator, Marvin Miller, to "do what he can to tear down the Berlin walls in the clubhouse for the benefit of the fans."[2] Another article by Joe Falls suggested that Phillies fans were as bad as their team. Falls reasoned that the mounted police and attack dogs that guarded the playing field during the final inning of Game 6 were necessary because the fans are "the toughest in the country." "Some of these people act up because it's the only way they can draw attention to themselves," he added. "These are people who are never noticed in life. If they suddenly disappeared from the earth not many would even care."[3]

No writer, however, was as scathing as *Newsweek*'s Pete Axthelm, who wrote two columns excoriating the Phillies. "For the Phillies, the Series had been a rite of redemption," wrote Axthelm in the October 27, 1980, issue of *Newsweek*. "In recent years they had earned a solid reputation as pampered and overpaid losers, talented masters of the near miss who had somehow contrived to stay out of the Series ever since 1950. It took some towering rages by square-jawed manager Dallas Green to prod them into this confrontation. Even then, the Phillies pursued their glories in a remarkably churlish and thin-skinned mood." Writing that the attack dogs "were pointed in the wrong direction," Axthelm went on to single out such "malevolent Phillies" as Larry Bowa, who "sneered that the boos of the fans inspired him"; Lonnie Smith, who "led a few teammates in obscene chants directed at the press"; Steve Carlton, who "withdrew in sullen splendor to the off-limits trainer's room while reporters maintained their demeaning vigil outside the door of the sanctuary"; and even Dallas Green, who answers the press "with a belligerent sneer." The only players who escaped criticism were Pete Rose and Tug McGraw, "both refugees from more easygoing clubhouses."[4] Axthelm must have been on a tight deadline, though. A week later, he directed his attack on McGraw for "belatedly joining the bullying and abrasive mood of his teammates" with his "'stick it' wisecrack." "Perfect," he concluded, "one of the last holdouts was in the fold."[5]

McGraw would put all the negative press into perspective years later. "The writers outside of Philadelphia didn't want us to enjoy the championship," he explained. "If anyone was a 'poor sport,' it was the New York sportswriters. They were jealous that Philadelphia had finally won a championship; something that they enjoyed for so many years. Even with the success the team had, the success the organization had coordinating security with the City of Philadelphia, those writers couldn't see clearly enough to realize that we established one of the most important precedents in American sports. Instead, they were bogged down by a handful of our players who didn't have very good relations with the press. At the time it bothered me, but in retrospect it was more embarrassing for them than it was for us."[6]

What was embarrassing for the city and the team was the way some of the *Philadelphia Daily News* sportswriters portrayed the Phillies. Despite one of the most exciting postseasons in baseball history and the club's first world championship, Tom Cushman advised readers that "winning the World Series will not cause the rest of the nation to forget the boorish behavior of the several athletes involved."[7] Bill Conlin went further, referring to the Phils as "hell's team" because of their "unattractive personalities."[8] Perhaps, but was it really necessary to turn on the hometown team in the wake of its greatest achievement? The Philadelphia press—and the *Daily News*, in particular—should have seized the moment to mend fences with the organization, or at least to allow the good

feelings that existed to linger into the next season before returning to their vit-
riolic ways.

The Phillies organization was experiencing internal problems as well. Howie
Bedell, who had been promoted to director of minor leagues after Green became
the Phillies manager in 1979, was under fire for the way he was running the farm
system. Ruben Amaro was the first to complain. Amaro, who had devoted himself to scouting top Latin American talent, was infuriated by Bedell's refusal to
act on his recommendations, specifically with two prospects who later became
major league stars.

"We lost George Bell in the Rule 5 draft because Howie didn't protect him on
the forty-man roster," insisted Amaro. "Bell hurt his leg in Double-A ball and
Howie didn't want to take a chance on him. I pleaded with Howie to protect him
on the roster. I told him that Bell had healed completely and that he was killing
the pitching in the Dominican winter league. But Howie went with another kid
instead. Of course, Bell went unprotected and he was picked up by the Toronto
Blue Jays, where he became a star."[9] Amaro also blamed Bedell for not acting on
his recommendation to sign Mexican pitcher Fernando Valenzuela. Amaro had
already arranged a deal with the owner of the Pueblo Club to exchange Valenzuela
for two players in the Phillies organization: pitcher Jesus Hernaiz, a veteran minor
leaguer; and a catching prospect by the name of Ramon Lura. Bedell wouldn't
make the deal, believing that Lura had a good future in the organization.[10]

According to Mark Winegardner, who wrote *Prophet of the Sandlots*, Bedell also
distanced himself from Tony Lucadello, one of the Phillies' most respected scouts.
Lucadello accused the Phillies farm director of "playing favorites" and "bad-
mouthing, then releasing" the kids he signed. Lucadello became so frustrated
with Bedell that he gave general manager Paul Owens an ultimatum: "get rid of
Bedell or get rid of me." When Bob Carpenter, Jr., learned of Lucadello's unhappiness, he was furious. "Bedell goes," he allegedly told his son Ruly. "Nobody fires
Tony. He's too good a man for us to lose." The next day, Dallas Green fired the
farm director.[11]

However, Bedell refutes both Amaro and Winegardner. "The decision to leave
George Bell unprotected on the forty-man roster was made by my successor, Jim
Baumer," he insists. "If I was still farm director, Bell would have been protected.
In fact, the day after I was dismissed by the Phillies I made sure to meet with Paul
Owens and told him that the two players he must protect were Bell and Ryne
Sandberg."[12]

Bedell's account appears to be the correct one. Jim Baumer was appointed
director of the minor leagues and scouting on November 6, 1980, just sixteen
days after the end of the World Series on October 21.[13] Bedell was dismissed either
on that day, or the day before. According to Julian McCracken, then general manager of the Double-A Reading Phillies, the 40-man roster was "not due for another

two weeks on November 20." Thus, it is highly doubtful that Bedell was responsible for the decision to leave Bell unprotected. Instead that responsibility would
have fallen to Baumer and his superior, Paul Owens.[14]

In addition, McCracken recalls that Bedell "sent Bell home to the Dominican
Republic in June 1980 so he could rest his injury." "Howie realized that it was
only going to frustrate Bell to sit on the bench in Reading," he said. "Bedell had
also given instructions to the Phillies' personnel covering Latin America to keep
an eye on Bell and to monitor his situation because he didn't want to lose a
player with the physical talent and potential of a Jorge Bell." Apparently, Bell decided to play in a few games in the Dominican Republic and that is when the
Blue Jays scouted him. After reading a favorable scouting report, Toronto felt it
would be worth the $50,000 price tag to take a chance on Bell in the Rule 5 draft
at the winter meetings that December in Dallas, Texas.[15] Of course, the "Phillies
personnel covering Latin America" would have been Ruben Amaro, who should
have monitored the situation and made sure that Baumer protected Bell on the
forty-man roster.

Interestingly, McCracken also insists that the Phillies "only had five openings
on the forty-man roster that they took to spring training in 1981" and that "those
five spots went to Wil Culmer, Julio Franco, Len Matuszek, Alejandro Sanchez,
and Ryne Sandberg, with Jorge Bell being omitted from the list."[16] Evaluations
for each player were included in the *Phillies 1981 Media Guide* and indicated the
following information:

WIL CULMER, 22, OF, came off a season at Peninsula (Carolina League, High
Class A) where he was named to the All-Star team, won the league batting championship (.369), led the league in runs scored and hits; had 28 doubles, 5 triples,
18 homers, 93 RBI and 26 SB; had been a professional for three seasons.

JULIO FRANCO, 22, SS, another player who was at Peninsula where he was named
the MVP of the league (made the All-Star team as well) while leading the league
in games played, at bats and RBI (99); hit .321 with 105 runs scored, 25 doubles,
6 triples, 11 homers and 44 SB; had been a professional for three seasons.

LEN MATUSZEK, 26, 1B/3B, a five-year minor league veteran . . . played in only 67
games at Triple-A Oklahoma City due to injury . . . was being protected on the
40-man roster for the first in his career by the Phillies . . . hit .305 with 16 doubles, 5 triples, 7 homers and 35 RBI in the aforementioned 67 games.

ALEJANDRO SANCHEZ, 21, OF, played the entire season at Spartanburg (South
Atlantic League, Low Class A) . . . led the team in most offensive categories but
did not lead the league in any category . . . hit .286, scored 84 runs, had 26 doubles, 8 triples, 15 homers, 76 RBI and 25 SB in 127 games; named to the league's
All-Star team; had been a professional for three seasons.

RYNE SANDBERG, 21, SS, played the entire season at Reading (Eastern League, Class AA) where he was named to the All-Star team . . . was the only player in the league to post double digit numbers in doubles (21), triples (12), homers (11) and SB (32) . . . had a .310 batting average, scored 95 runs, had 152 hits and 79 RBI; had been a professional for three seasons.[17]

Of the five players, the questionable one would have been Len Matuszek. Matuszek was an older player who had been in the organization for five years, but only played in half his team's games during the 1980 season and had never been previously protected by the Phillies. The real question here is why Matuszek—and not Bell—was protected. But the only people who can answer that question are Jim Baumer and Paul Owens, both of whom are deceased.

What's more, Baumer would have had a roster opening for Bell if Dallas Green had not called up pitcher Mark Davis from Reading in September of 1980.[18] Davis, the Most Valuable Player of the Eastern League that season, had only been with the organization for two years. There was no need to protect him on the roster. But once he had been called up to the Phillies, Davis took up one of the roster spots that could have gone to Bell. To make matters worse, Green, against Bedell's advice, allowed Davis to pitch for Amaro's Venezuelan team that winter after he had already thrown close to 200 innings during the regular season. Davis hurt his arm and it took him nearly seven years to pitch effectively again.[19]

When asked about the opportunity to sign Fernando Valenzuela, Bedell said that he "didn't recall that possibility." "But if Ruben [Amaro] had the chance to sign Valenzuela, it wouldn't surprise me because he really worked his tail off for the organization and came up with some excellent prospects," he said. "But that decision wouldn't rest with me. I would have had some input, but Dallas would have made the ultimate decision if it was a strictly minor league acquisition and Paul Owens would have been involved, too. So if the Phillies failed to sign Fernando Valenzuela, Dallas and Paul must have seen or heard something that Ruben didn't know."[20]

Bedell also disputes Winegardner's account of his relationship with Tony Lucadello. "As far as Tony Lucadello is concerned, I thought we had a wonderful relationship," he said. "I certainly treated all of Tony's players with the same respect I gave to all of our players in the farm system. They were promoted or released based on their abilities, nothing more, nothing less."[21]

Since Lucadello is deceased, Winegardner's account is the only source of the alleged conflict between the late Phillies scout and Bedell. But it is a skewed account. Winegardner cites the conflict with Bedell as a major reason for Lucadello's depression, which resulted in suicide in 1989. Bedell had been dismissed as farm director after the 1980 season and Jim Baumer, his successor, had held the position for eight years by that time. Many of the minor league players cited by Winegardener as being "bad-mouthed" and "released by" Bedell weren't even in the Phillies organization at the time he was farm director. But they do correspond with Baumer's tenure.

The question still remains: Why was Bedell dismissed, in November 1980, as director of minor leagues by the Phillies? "The reason for my dismissal was "the friction that was taking place between myself and Dallas Green," he said in a recent interview. "In fact, Ruly Carpenter didn't want me to leave, but rather to work things out with Dallas. Dallas was taking a lot of heat from the press, which accused him of running the entire organization—the parent club, the farm system, the front office—everything, and it just wasn't true. He began to question a lot of people's loyalty, wondering who was spreading these rumors to the press. It's funny. I came under fire because I held the company line. I always believed that each and every one of us was doing our own part to make the organization successful. That's what we had been taught. That's what Paul Owens and Ruly Carpenter preached to us. While Dallas was an important part of the organization, he was *not* the sum total of it. But there were those scouts who interpreted my loyalty to the organization as 'disloyalty to Dallas.' Some of them told Dallas that I couldn't be trusted."[22]

Whatever the case might have been, Bedell was dismissed by Green on or a day before November 6, 1980, just about two weeks after the Phillies clinched the world championship. It was a cruel twist of fate. Green, who owed his job as field manager to Bedell, more than anybody else in the organization, had turned on him. After all, Bedell was the one who dared to stand up to general manager Paul Owens and recommend Green as field manager. Although he was "sorry about leaving the organization because he considered the Phillies like a family," Bedell harbored no ill feelings toward Green, whom he still considers a "close friend." He went on to work for the Kansas City Royals, who won the World Series in 1985, and then for the Cincinnati Reds, who won a world championship in 1990.[23] That kind of track record suggests that Howie Bedell knew what he was doing when he worked with the Phillies. Bedell's firing was only the beginning of the organization's decline.

Many sportswriters quickly dismissed the Phillies, considering their world championship of the previous year a fluke. "The Phillies won against all odds last year," wrote Steve Wulf in *Sports Illustrated*, who predicted a second-place finish behind the Montreal Expos. Wulf believed that the '81 team was "headed for a breakdown." He pointed out that key players like Larry Bowa and Tug McGraw were past their prime, though "the Phillies will probably need another year to convince themselves of that." Even Schmidt and Carlton, he wrote, would be "hard pressed to match their exceptional 1980 performances." Finally, Wulf predicted "internal division between the players and their outspoken manager will also take its toll."[24] But even before the Phillies could prove the naysayers wrong, the organization was dealt a harsh blow.

During spring training, Ruly Carpenter announced that he intended to sell the team. He had had his fill of dealing with labor conflict, player agents, the escalating salaries created by free agency, and the pressure for revenue sharing created by lucrative television deals. The final straw came when Atlanta Braves owner Ted Turner signed Claudell Washington to a five-year deal worth $750,000 a year. "When Atlanta did that, I knew it was time to get out," Carpenter said recently. "That was a lot of money to pay a player at that time and Washington was certainly not a superstar. He was an average major league player whose strongest asset was base stealing. I knew at that point that common sense was not going to prevail and that it was time to sell."[25] It was the right decision.

Skyrocketing players' salaries and an unfavorable stadium contract with the City of Philadelphia made the sale inevitable. Although the Carpenter family resources were estimated by *Fortune* magazine at about $330,000,000, most of that money was tied up in DuPont company stock. Carpenter would have to dip into his inheritance to keep the club afloat with no assurance of a profit. In fact, the Phillies would need to draw 2,700,000 in home attendance each year just to break even. Clearly, the tax structure for baseball franchises no longer supported family ownership. The game was coming under the control of syndicates.[26]

News of Carpenter's decision quickly spread throughout the Phillies' Clearwater spring training camp. "I'll never forget that day," said Mark Carfagno, a member of the grounds crew. "We all knew something was going on that morning since Ruly called a meeting of all the players. I was working on field number 3 when John Vukovich came out. 'Hey Vuk!' I shouted. 'What's the meeting all about?' He said, 'Ruly's selling the team,' and just kept walking. It was like someone hit me in the stomach. From that day on, everyone was sitting on pins and needles, wondering what was going to happen to their jobs."[27] The players were in shock as well.

"You knew things just weren't going to be the same," recalled Larry Bowa. "Ruly did everything with a handshake. You could trust his word. Guys who came here from other clubs couldn't believe the closeness he had with us. He helped us in so many ways that you'd never hear about."[28] Greg Luzinski echoed his teammate's feelings. "Ruly cared much more than most of the owners," he said. "He could have easily broken up our team after 1978 when we failed to win [the National League pennant] for the third straight year, but he didn't because he had faith in us. That's why it was important for us to produce for him. We didn't want to let him down."[29] Ironically, the Bull was the first player to go in the gradual exodus of players from the world championship team.

Having acquired outfielder Gary Matthews from Atlanta on March 25, 1981, Luzinski was expendable and he knew it.[30] Convinced that they couldn't get a quality player for the Bull, who struggled with his weight and surgically repaired knees, the Phillies sold him to the Chicago White Sox for the bargain basement price of $150,000.[31] "Luzinski makes a big salary and he's eligible to become a free agent," said Dallas Green, explaining the transaction to the press. "He's looking for a four- or five-year deal for more money than he's making now. Put yourself in the shoes of another owner. Would you be eager to give up a player for Greg Luzinski, considering nothing more than the economics?"[32] The Bull's sale was especially sad because he had been part of the nucleus of homegrown players the Phillies had kept together for more than a decade in the hopes of securing a world championship. He had been a key part of a powerful offense and, in his earlier years, a leader whom Ruly Carpenter relied on in the clubhouse.

Perhaps Bill Conlin of the *Philadelphia Daily News* provided the most poignant epitaph to Luzinski's career when he wrote: "What appears to be the cold, heartless dumping of a man who helped build a franchise to greatness is really no more than a business decision made with heavy hearts." But even the surly sportswriter had to admit that the sale of the Bull "hurt me because I chronicled his deeds for over nine years" and because "he is a decent man whose career has been cut short for a paradoxical reason: God made him too damn big and strong."[33] Luzinski would still have four more productive years as a designated hitter in the American League, leading the White Sox to a division title in 1983.

If Luzinski's departure appeared to be a "cold, heartless business decision," Carpenter's decision to renegotiate Steve Carlton's contract at the end of spring training was a "moral obligation" based on Lefty's considerable contributions to the team. Carlton had been signed through the 1983 season at $400,000 a year, but Carpenter felt obliged to raise his ace pitcher's salary to $700,000 a year through the '84 campaign. At the time, Lefty was baseball's all-time left-handed strikeout leader and had won 181 games for the Phillies since he arrived in Philadelphia in 1972. The new deal could earn Carlton as much as $3 million with incentives for winning a Cy Young Award and leading the league in strikeouts and earned run average. Although the new contract made Lefty the second highest paid Phillie behind Pete Rose, who was making $800,000 a year, it still didn't make him the highest paid pitcher in the league. That distinction belonged to Nolan Ryan of the Houston Astros who was earning $1 million a year.[34] Carpenter had mixed emotions about the new deal. "It was something done in light of the inequities that have been created by some of the free agent signings," he admitted. "I didn't create the inequities, but I'm paying for them. We've renegotiated with a couple of players. It's always been a case of having a player signed and everybody being happy at the time. Then some owner pays a tremendous amount of money to a free agent. In Lefty's case, some tremendous amounts of money were given to pitchers who don't come close to his record." Carpenter was referring to Houston pitchers: Don Sutton ($850,000 per year); J. R. Richard ($800,000); and Joe

Niekro ($750,000).[35] While the Phillies owner had been forced to escalate player salaries as a matter of principle, free agency contradicted his own ethics and was driving him out of the game he loved. Baseball had always been more about success on the playing field, scouting, and player development to Ruly Carpenter and, secondarily, about profits. But the other owners felt differently.

To be sure, free agency had generated significant revenue, not only for the players but also for ownership. By 1981 attendance and gate receipts were up, and television and radio revenues increased as did the value of each major league franchise.[36] Still, the owners insisted that free agency was "destroying the competitive balance" in the game and were determined to eliminate it. That fact was made clear on January 1, 1981, when the study group appointed to examine free agency presented its report. Harry Dalton and Frank Cashen, the owners' representatives, demanded compensation for those clubs who lost a "quality" free agent (that is, one selected by eight or more teams in a reentry draft, which would thereafter be conducted in private). They also insisted that a club be allowed to protect fifteen players on its forty-man roster, leaving one of the remaining twenty-five available as compensation. Under these conditions, a club signing a free agent could possibly lose an established player who was more valuable than the free agent or lose a prospect with All-Star potential. Since the proposal was clearly unacceptable to the players, represented by Bob Boone and Sal Bando, the two sides had thirty days to try to forge an agreement. When that failed, the owners, on February 19, imposed their own compensation plan paving the way for baseball's second longest strike.[37]

Convinced that they held a strong position, the owners, led by diehards Gussie Busch of the St. Louis Cardinals, Gene Autry of the California Angels, and Calvin Griffith of the Minnesota Twins, were prepared for such an action. They believed that the players would not risk their already high salaries by alienating the fans with their demands for free agency. In addition to $15 million they had squirreled away in a strike fund, the owners paid Lloyd's of London $2 million for $50 million worth of strike insurance. The policy would eventually pay $100,000 for each lost game over a six-week period in the event of a strike.

The owners held a great advantage over the players, whose vote to strike on May 29, prevented them from obtaining any insurance. Instead, the majority of players stood to lose a considerable portion of their salaries. But they were determined to hold the line realizing that they would lose their future bargaining power if free agency was eliminated or if the Players' Union was weakened in any way.[38]

Commissioner Bowie Kuhn failed to help matters. As the strike date drew near, he became increasingly antagonistic toward the players' union. His bitterness was understandable. Kuhn's tenure was characterized by the decline of the commissioner's influence over labor relations. Over that time period the players won collective bargaining, salary arbitration, free agency, and safeguards against collusion. Kuhn viewed the strike as a personal insult and lambasted Marvin Miller, the players' negotiator, holding him directly responsible for all the labor problems and calling him a "prisoner of his own ego."[39]

Miller had heard enough. Tired of the owners' patronizing attitude, he filed a charge with the National Labor Relations Board against them for their refusal to negotiate. It was a clever ploy. Under the existing laws, an employer claiming an inability to pay in collective bargaining must document his income. Failure to provide the relevant data was interpreted as a refusal to bargain in good faith, which is an unfair labor practice. The owners' disclosure of their profits would show just how much they had profited from free agency. The NLRB ruled in favor of the Players Association and moved for an injunction in federal court to prevent the owners from implementing their own compensation plan until the board finally adjudicated the players' complaint. The ruling postponed the strike date until a ruling was made. If the courts granted the injunction, there would be no strike. If not, the owners' compensation proposal would become part of the new Basic Agreement and the strike would be a certainty.[40]

Judge Henry Werker, a conservative Republican, conducted the injunction hearing. On June 10, Werker ruled that free agent compensation was *not* an *economic* issue and ordered the players to "play ball."[41] Forty-eight hours later, the players went out on strike. For fifty days the major leagues shut down and all games—a total of 715—were canceled.[42] Tempers raged at the various negotiating sessions. The proceedings were so acrimonious that federal mediator Ken Moffett struggled to find any common ground between Ray Grebey, the owners' negotiator, and Miller, the players' agent. At one point, it appeared as if Miller had lost the support of the union. "Marvin was a master at never telling anybody what to do," recalled Boone, who provided a voice of reason during the contentious talks. "But he was also a master at leading you down the road he wanted by asking the 'right' questions. Sooner or later you would agree with his position because he made it so obvious. I think that began to rub some of the players the wrong way."[43]

Boone was a little more cautious in his approach to the negotiations. As a result, he quickly earned the respect of Grebey, who preferred to address the Phillies catcher directly during the sessions and even outside the boardroom. "I'm sorry you and I have to be on opposite sides of the negotiations," Grebey once told him. "I think you're the only reasonable one on their side."[44] While Boone might have appeared to be conciliatory, he was strongly behind the players' union. "Ray Grebey was a union breaker," Boone said in a recent interview. "He was a tough guy. That's why the owners hired him. He sold them on breaking the union. Their attorneys told the owners, 'Don't worry about the reserve clause, we'll win this thing.' That was the stupidest advice in the history of baseball. In 1975 Andy Messersmith didn't want to leave the Dodgers, but the owners were stupid enough to risk that clause to make him leave because he refused to be traded. It was a very unwise thing to do. I thank God the owners did it, though, because we wouldn't have enjoyed the benefits we, as players, have today without free agency."[45]

On July 28, the forty-eighth day of the strike, Miller, along with Boone and Doug DeCinces, an American League player representative on the negotiating team, met with the player representatives from the twenty-six clubs at Chicago's O'Hare Hilton. The session lasted five and a half hours. He explained the history of the negotiations, how the owners' plan for compensation was designed to punish those clubs who signed free agents, and his own plan for "pooled compensation," which addressed the owners' desire for "competitive balance" without destroying free agency. The players gave their negotiating team their unconditional support to stop the bargaining, even if it meant ending the season. Unable to break the player ranks, the more moderate owners forced Grebey to compromise.[46] The moderates were concerned about the real possibility of losing the entire season as well as the damage it would do to the game's image. To exploit their fears, Miller raised the possibility of players starting their own league in 1982. The owners finally agreed to settle on July 31 as the Lloyd's policy was about to expire and barely enough time remained for a credible resumption of play. By that time, the owners had sustained a total loss of about $72 million and the players, an estimated $4 million a week in salaries.

The new basic agreement stipulated that, beginning with the 1981 reentry draft, clubs that lost quality free agents were to receive a major leaguer or top minor leaguer in return. It was a limited victory for the owners, though, because all clubs would have to participate in a compensation pool. Each club was able to exclude their best twenty-four players and clubs not participating in the draft were allowed to protect twenty-six. This so-called "pooled compensation plan" alleviated player fears that lucrative free agent bidding might stop if the clubs were forced to surrender players directly. After the compensation issue was resolved, the two sides easily reached their fifth basic agreement, which ran through the 1984 season.[47]

The strike destroyed the momentum the Phillies had enjoyed at the beginning of the season.[48] The team was in first place with a 34-21 record when the strike began on June 12. Mike Schmidt was an offensive juggernaut, leading the majors in home runs (14) and RBI (41). In the game before the strike, against Nolan Ryan and the Houston Astros, Pete Rose tied Stan Musial's National League record for hits. The Phillies went on to win that game, 5-4, on a three-run homer by Garry Maddox to insure a one-and-a-half-game lead over the second-place St. Louis Cardinals.[49] "We were playing some of our best baseball," said Schmidt. "We had the 1980 world championship under our belts, and believed we could repeat. But then the strike stopped us."[50]

"We were firing on all cylinders before the strike," recalled Del Unser. "I felt we were better than the '80 team, more confident, and we had a better work ethic. But after the strike we didn't have the same spark."[51] Play resumed on August 9 with the All-Star Game, which was played at Cleveland's Municipal Stadium. Schmidt won the game for the National League, 5-4, with an eighth inning home run off Rollie Fingers.[52] But something was missing. The Phillies lacked the desire they had before the strike. When the games resumed, their play was mediocre at best for the first few weeks. On August 12, they were routed by the St. Louis Cardinals, 11-3. The Cards cranked out 14 hits, including 3 home runs, 4 doubles, and a triple. Dickie Noles surrendered five runs in the ninth inning alone.

After the game, Jayson Stark of the *Philadelphia Inquirer* approached Dallas Green and asked if he thought that the long strike had affected the performance of his pitchers more than the hitters. "Fuck you, Jayson!" Green exploded in a profanity-laced tirade. "You write what the fuck you want. I don't give a fuck. I'm fucking tired of that cynical shit. Ask a fucking question right. No, we're not trying to lose the fucking game. You cocksuckers think we don't have a nickel's worth of pride. The fuck we don't!"

Then, just as suddenly, Green calmed himself. "It ain't your fault, either," he admitted in a much lower voice. "All right, let's get to some serious talking. What do you guys want to know."[53]

Green, frustrated by the strike and the lethargy of his team, was trying to find a way to get his team motivated again. The playoff format didn't help matters, either. The Phillies had already won the first half of the strike-shortened season. They realized that the first-half winners would have to go on and play the second half winners in a divisional playoff anyway. If they won the second half as well they'd still have to play a wild card winner, the team with the second best record in either division. There was little incentive to win the second half. As a result, poor pitching, slumping hitters, and mental errors characterized the Phillies' second half. "If we didn't have the split season, we would've repeated," insisted Larry Bowa. "We dominated the first half. Then they told us, 'If you win the second half it doesn't matter, you're still going to have to play the second place team.' That's when everyone said, 'What are we playing for?'"[54] There were a few exceptions, though.

Mike Schmidt came close to winning the coveted Triple Crown with a .316 batting average and league-leading totals in home runs (31) and RBI (91) in the 102-game season. Gary Matthews had a remarkable September and finished with a .301 average and 67 runs batted in. And, of course, Pete Rose wound up with a .325 average and provided Phillies fans with a night to remember on August 10 when the regular season resumed.[55]On that evening, Rose connected for his 3,631st base hit to break Stan Musial's National League hits record. The milestone single came in the eighth inning off Mark Littell of the St. Louis Cardinals at Veterans Stadium. "Littell started me off with a slider for a strike," Rose said.

"It was the only breaking ball I saw all night. And then he came back with a fast-ball inside, and I knew it was going through when I hit it." When Rose reached first base, he took his usual aggressive turn, then clapped his hands as he returned to the bag. First base coach Ruben Amaro gave him a congratulatory hug as bat boy, Pete Rose Jr. led the charge from the dugout. "Nice going, Pop!" he said as his father flipped him the baseball.[56]

After the game, Rose attended a press conference where he was congratulated by Paul Owens, Ruly Carpenter, and Cardinal legend Stan Musial. "Me and Stan Musial, we've led the league in hits seven times," Rose boasted, displaying his knowledge of the game's history. "Nobody's ever done it eight. That kind of stuff keeps me going." When the reporters asked him about breaking Ty Cobb's all-time record of 4,191 hits, Rose replied: "I've only got three things on my mind now. A world championship. Leading the league in hits. Winning the batting title. You might think I'm an egomaniac, but I've got things that keep me pushing. If you're a good player and you've got pride, it's inside you to play good."[57] No sooner had he completed the remark than Rose was handed a red phone and told that President Reagan was on the other end of the line. Over the receiver he heard a voice say, "One moment, please."

Rose, always ready with a quip, said, "I've waited nearly twenty years for this hit. I can wait a little longer." But the wait lasted nearly a minute. As he stood there listening for the president's voice, Rose filled the awkward silence with one-liners. "Maybe the operators have gone on strike!" he joked.

"Mr. Rose?" asked the White House operator.

"Yes."

"Hold on, please, for the President of the United States."

Nothing. Then just the sound of the dial tone. Inexplicably, the Phillies first baseman had been disconnected. Rose hung up.

Seconds later the phone rang. It was the White House again. And again, Rose was cut off. "Good thing there ain't a missile on the way!" he cracked to break the tension in the room.

When Reagan finally got through, he said: "I'll tell you, I've had so much trouble getting this line. I think I had to wait longer than you did to break the record."

Without missing a beat, Rose replied: "We were going to give you five more minutes and then that was it."

There were muffled giggles in the audience. Some of the writers were shocked that Rose had the courage to make the wisecrack to the president. But Reagan seemed to take the remark in stride. "I just wanted to call and congratulate you," said the president. "I know how you must feel and I think it's great."

"Well, thank you very much," Rose said. "I know you're a big baseball fan and we appreciate your taking time out to call us here in Philadelphia. I know all the fans appreciate it and Pete Rose and Pete Rose the second appreciate it, too."

Reagan, never at a loss for words himself, continued. "I can tell you that you are right about being a fan," he said in a folksy manner. "As a matter of fact, I was a sports announcer, broadcasting major league baseball, before I ever had any kind of job like I have now. But this is really a thrill and I know how everyone must feel about it after the long dry spell waiting for the season to get under way and you've really brought it back in style."

"Well, thank you very much," Rose replied, before saying good-bye.

When some reporters questioned the wisdom of making a wisecrack to the president of the United States, Rose dismissed the criticism. "I learned a long time ago to be yourself," he said. "I was respectful, but I was just myself." "Look," he added, "I appreciate the president taking time out to call. I know how busy he is. How tough his job is."[58] Once again, Rose had disarmed the critics.

After the press conference ended, Larry Shenk, the Phillies publicity director, escorted Rose into the clubhouse where a South Jersey seafood restaurateur made a special presentation to the National League's new all-time hits leader. "The guy had read that Stan Musial had been in town all week dining at Bookbinder's every night on lobster," recalled Shenk in a recent interview. "He contacted me and said he had an eighteen-pound lobster and he'd like to give it to Pete after he broke the record." Shenk thought it was a nice gesture, so he agreed.

Rose took one look at the huge lobster, turned to Shenk and asked: "That thing ain't going to shit in my Rolls Royce, is it, Larry?"[59]

No one can argue that Pete Rose didn't enjoy every moment of his illustrious career, especially those years he spent with the Phillies. It seemed as if he broke some kind of record, no matter how insignificant, every time he took the field. He reveled in the clubhouse banter and the bench jockeying and shined in the national spotlight like no one else of his generation. "The older you get, you realize that the days are coming to an end," Rose, age 40, explained when asked how all the years of baseball had affected his performance. "So you want to enjoy them. You can't bear to give one away."[60]

His teammates continued to be amazed by him. "It wasn't just the way he played," said Manny Trillo. "He also knew the game. He could tell us what to expect from certain pitchers. He knew how to play certain hitters. Just watching the guy hit was an education."[61] To be sure, Rose was a walking encyclopedia when it came to knowing a pitcher's or hitter's idiosyncrasies, but his real genius lay in the intensity he brought to the game.

"Pete's intensity was unbelievable," said Larry Bowa. "He had a way of putting everything out of his mind whenever he stepped onto the field. He concentrated on every pitch better than any human being I've ever seen."[62] Ruly Carpenter recalled several occasions when Rose would recite, pitch for pitch, what he was thrown in an at bat that had taken place years before. "We'd be going up against a pitcher who'd been around for some time," said the Phillies owner, "and Pete would remember the first time he faced him, the sequence of pitches he threw, and how he fared as a hitter. I think he knew about 80 percent of the time what the pitcher was going to throw if he had faced him before, even if it was five or ten years ago."

Concentration and recall were just part of Rose's intensity, though. He got the most out of his limited abilities and rarely, if ever, made the same mistake twice. "There were many other players who were gifted with greater natural ability," said Carpenter. "Pete didn't have outstanding speed, power or an arm. He was only adequate defensively. But I never saw him make a mistake on a ball field. If I had to identify his most outstanding talent, it would be that Pete Rose simply knew how to win and that was a direct result of his intensity. He was the most intense athlete I've ever been around and he made his teammates 'play up' to his standards. Everyone on that 1980 team respected him. He had such a great reputation by that point in his career that no one was going to challenge him."[63] The fact that no one dared to make Pete Rose accountable would ultimately lead to his downfall. Few realize, however, that Rose had already embarked on a collision course with the commissioner's office during his years in Philadelphia. By 1981, his life off the field was beginning to spiral out of control due to a serious gambling addiction.

According to Mike Schmidt, Rose would often discuss point spreads with his teammates in the clubhouse and they "knew he bet on football and basketball games." But no one "had any idea that he had a gambling problem."[64] Dallas Green was more candid: "We knew Pete gambled like hell, but, to a man, we didn't have an inkling he bet on baseball. He got into that mess when he stopped playing.[65] To be sure, Rose, in a 2004 autobiography, admitted that he bet on baseball in 1987 when he managed the Cincinnati Reds, though he fervently denied betting on the game as a player.[66] Former commissioner Fay Vincent believes otherwise. In 1990, Vincent was approached by *USA Today* sportswriter Hal Bodley, who told him that he was with Rose in 1981 when he bet on baseball. Bodley, then a sportswriter for the Wilmington, Delaware, *News Journal* and a close friend of Rose's, described the incident in detail to the then-baseball commissioner:

> We were in a hotel dining room and Pete kept running out of the room to talk to someone on the phone and it was clear he was talking to bookies. I said to him, "Pete, are you betting on baseball?"
> He said, "Oh, sure. I've been doing that for a long time."
> I said, "If you don't stop that and they catch you, you'll be finished."
> Rose said, "They'll never bother with me. I'm too big."[67]

Bodley told Vincent that he "could never write" about the incident because "Rose and [he] were friends at the time." But after Rose reneged on a promise to collaborate with the sportswriter on his autobiography, Bodley had few reservations about exposing his former friend.[68] Vincent never pursued the issue because, by

1990, Rose had already been banned from baseball and his betting as a player was a moot point.[69]

Regardless, Rose's arrogance, the very same quality that made him such a great ballplayer, eventually resulted in his downfall. What's interesting is how he avoided being caught for as long as he did. Rose hid his gambling activities by befriending others and persuading them to place his bets for him. After he came to Philadelphia, for example, Rose exploited his "friendship" with Tommy Gioiosa, a drug trafficker who shared a condominium with him and assumed the role of a "gofer." Prior to being sentenced to five years in prison on cocaine trafficking and tax evasion in 1990, Gioiosa was among the first people to reveal that the former Phillie had indeed bet on baseball.[70] But Gioiosa was only one of many "friends" Rose used to shield his gambling activities over the course of his major league career. Others included members of the local media, who ingratiated themselves with him.[71] In 1989, Rose's gambling addiction caught up with him and resulted in his banishment from baseball, but the evidence suggests that the problem existed during his years in Philadelphia.

The split-season playoff proved to be a sorrowful ending for the '81 Phillies. Because they led the National League East when the strike occurred, the Phils, according to the split season plan, would play the Montreal Expos, the winners of the second half, to determine the winners of the division. While the plan might have been a creative solution to a difficult situation, it made the regular season meaningless for the Phils. That was not the case for Montreal. "We realized that we had a good team, said Gary Carter, the Expos All-Star catcher. "After the Phillies won the first half we just told ourselves we could win the second. We had so much talent on that team with Ellis Valentine, Andre Dawson, Warren Cromartie and Larry Parrish. Our pitching was pretty impressive too, with Steve Rogers, Charlie Lee, Scott Sanderson, and Bill Gullickson. We just knew we could win the divisional playoff."[72] The Expos seemed to be more excited about the series than either the Phillies or their fans.

An average attendance of 40,000 came to the Vet to watch the Phillies do battle with the Expos during the last three games of the divisional playoff. For fans who had sold out the stadium for postseason play just a year earlier, the showing was pathetic. Some of the indifference might have been due to the fact that a Wilmington newspaper leaked the story that Dallas Green was headed to Chicago after the season to become general manager of the Cubs, a position he had hoped to land with the Phillies. Whatever the case, Steve Rogers defeated Carlton, 3-1, in the series opener at Montreal on Wednesday, October 7. Bill Gullickson beat Dick Ruthven the following night by the same score on a Carter home run, and the Phillies were down two games to none in the best-of-five playoff.[73]

The series shifted to Philadelphia on Friday, October 9. Larry Christenson gave the Phils six strong innings surrendering just one run on four hits. Sparky Lyle and Ron Reed combined to limit Montreal to one other run as the Phils defeated the Expos, 6-2.[74] Dickie Noles started Game 4 on Saturday night and surrendered two runs on four hits in the five innings he pitched. But home runs by Mike Schmidt and Gary Matthews kept the Phillies in the game. McGraw entered the contest in the eighth inning with the score tied at 5-5 and proceeded to shut down the Expos offense for the next three innings, giving up just one hit. In the bottom of the tenth, reserve outfielder George Vukovich slammed a home run into the left field bullpen to keep the Phillies hopes of another division championship alive.[75]

The momentum now appeared to be in the Phillies' favor. Steve Carlton was on the mound for the decisive Game 5, which would also be played at the Vet. "We knew we had our backs to the wall," admitted Gary Carter. "Lefty was the best overall southpaw I ever faced, a true professional. He never gave anything away. With home field advantage and Lefty on the mound, the Phillies had everything in their favor."[76] But the Expos had their ace Steve Rogers going for them. Rogers had already defeated Carlton in Game 1 and provided the heroics in this contest as well. Not only did he blank the Phillies, scattering six hits over nine innings, but he got the key hit—a two-run single—in the 3-0 victory.[77] Montreal had made it into the postseason for the first time in the franchise's twelve-year history. They would lose in the National League Championship Series to the Los Angeles Dodgers, who went on to beat the New York Yankees in the 1981 World Series.

For the Phillies, there would be no return trip to the Fall Classic, no back-to-back world championships, no dynasty. The split season had broken their momentum and initiated the dismantling of the championship team. On October 29, 1981, Carpenter sold the Phillies to a group of investors headed by executive vice president Bill Giles.[78] For Giles, ownership of the Phillies was a dream come true. He had longed to become a general manager and soon realized that the only way that would be possible would be to buy the club.

When Carpenter announced that he would be selling the team in March '81, Giles put together a group of investors and purchased the organization for $30 million. His personal investment amounted to $50,000.[79] There were five other principal partners. Taft Broadcasting Company, a Cincinnati-based radio-TV corporation that owned Channel 29 in Philadelphia, was instrumental in the purchase. Taft agreed to front up to $30 million because of its longtime association with Giles's father, Warren, who had been president of the Reds in the late 1940s and later president of the National League. In return, Taft was granted rights to Phillies games for 10 years beginning in 1982. A second investor was J. D. B. Associates, a partnership consisting of John Drew Betz and Robert D. Hedberg. Hedberg was a financial consultant and Betz was chairman emeritus of Betz Laboratories Inc., which specialized in industrial water treatment. The third group of investors was Tri-Play Associates, a partnership of three brothers: Alexander K. Buck, J. Mahlon Buck, Jr., and William C. Buck. The Buck brothers were the chief executive officers of TDH Inc. and TDH Capital Corporation, private venture capital investment companies. The other two investors were Fitz Eugene Dixon, Jr., former owner of the NBA's Philadelphia 76ers, and Rochelle Levy, a prominent Philadelphia artist whose husband, Robert, made his fortune as chief executive officer of a small corporation engaged in bulk liquids and leisure-recreational activities.[80]

"I guess we could have stayed on as owners and made more money on the appreciation of the franchise," said Ruly Carpenter in a recent interview. "At the time we sold to the Giles group, the $30 million they paid was the highest ever paid. It was about three times the amount George Steinbrenner paid for the Yankees in the early 1970s. But all the labor conflict, the player agents, and especially free agency created so much aggravation, it just wasn't worth it anymore."[81] Now, Giles would have to confront those problems with his own baseball people. While he did not assume the title of general manager, the new Phillies president would have a major role in all player transactions. Tony Siegle, the new executive vice president would handle contracts. Jim Baumer was in charge of the minor league operations. The scouting department was splintered by the independent status of both Hughie Alexander and Ray Shore. Paul Owens was the odd man out. Although he would be given an administrative voice, his status was nebulous at best.[82] Giles insisted on "complete control of the baseball operation."[83]

The other owners agreed to let him run the day-to-day operations of the club. "I had complete authority with only two caveats," he recently admitted. "First, the owners didn't care if they made any money, but they certainly didn't want to borrow or lose any. The other, related caveat was that I was limited as to the amount of money I could spend on any given player or any large TV or concession deal without asking for their permission."[84] With that understanding, Giles, heading an amorphous chain of command, intended to make the Phillies the "team of the 1980s."[85] Ironically, he began by trading or selling some of the team's finest talent.

The first player to go was outfielder Lonnie Smith, who was traded on November 20 to the Cleveland Indians along with pitcher Scott Munninghoff for catcher Bo Diaz.[86] It was the first of many poor decisions by the new ownership and one that was roundly criticized by the fans. Smith, who had hit .324 in the strike-shortened season, was a good hitting outfielder with speed on the bases. He would go on to become a regular in the postseason, playing instrumental roles for the world champion Cardinals in 1982 and Royals in 1985. He also helped the Atlanta Braves to two pennants in 1991 and 1992.[87] Bake McBride followed Smith to Cleveland, being traded for pitcher Sid Monge. McBride's knees were gone and he was beginning to have problems seeing the ball as well.[88] As a result, his trade was more understandable than Smith's.

With the acquisition of Bo Diaz, catcher Bob Boone became expendable and was sold to the California Angels on December 6. Boone, who had been the National League player representative during the strike, was an easy target for the front office. Like Tim McCarver and Jim Bunning, the player representatives who preceded him, Boone was viewed as a source of labor agitation. In addition, he was criticized for being unable to throw out runners. "The Phillies thought I was through as a catcher," he said. "In fact my knee wasn't healed completely and it affected my throwing. I also think the fans soured on me because for them I was the face of a seven-week strike."[89] Boone's sale was another poor decision by Giles. He would go on to the American League, where he played another 9 seasons with the Angels and Kansas City Royals. During that time Boone won four more Gold Gloves (1982, '86, '87, and '88), was selected to another All-Star team, and established a career record for games caught with 2,225.[90]

Two days after Boone was sold, catcher Keith Moreland and pitchers Dan Larson and Dickie Noles were traded to the Chicago Cubs for starting pitcher Mike Krukow. Moreland had been Boone's backup, but the front office already had two other more promising young catchers in Darren Daulton and John Russell. Larson was still an unproven pitcher. Noles was fighting a losing battle with alcohol and drugs, which culminated in a hotel-bar brawl with Paul Owens during the '81 season.[91] It was the first of many trades the Phillies would make with new Cubs general manager Dallas Green, who was in a rebuilding process in Chicago. "My agenda in Chicago was to change the approach from a losing one to a winning one," Green explained years later. "I'd trade with any club. It didn't have to be the Phillies. It just so happened that Paul Owens and Hugh Alexander wanted to talk trade and I knew the kids the Phillies had. As a result it was easy to make deals with them."[92]

Green would make one of the biggest steals in baseball history on January 27, 1982, when he traded shortstop Ivan DeJesus to the Phillies for Larry Bowa and Ryne Sandberg. At the time, the deal seemed to make sense for both teams. Bowa was an aging shortstop whose best days were behind him. He was also locked in a salary dispute with Bill Giles, who didn't want to guarantee the infielder a three-year contract. Ivan DeJesus was a steady defensive shortstop who was younger than Bowa and could meet the Phillies' needs. Sandberg was a "throw in" in the deal. He had only played 13 games for the Phillies in 1981 and hit an unimpressive .167. Nor did he fit into the team's immediate plans. "The Phillies knew they weren't going to win another championship without a proven shortstop and that shortstop wasn't going to be Larry Bowa because of his bitching with Bill Giles," said Green, downplaying the notion that he fleeced his former employers. "Ivan DeJesus was a proven—and marketable—shortstop. At first the Phillies tried to keep Ryne Sandberg from us. But I insisted on him if I was going to make the deal. I think the Phillies knew that Ryne was a good athlete.

They just had no place to play him for two or three years. They were going for a pennant and there was some skepticism that he could play shortstop in the majors. Schmidt was at third. I always thought Ryne could play center field, but Maddox was there. The Phillies never really thought of him as a second baseman and besides, Trillo was already there. So, did the end justify the means for the Phillies? Hell yeah! DeJesus helped them to the World Series in 1983. You gotta go for the brass ring when you have a chance, and that's what the Phillies did when they traded Ryne Sandburg to the Cubs."[93] Of course, Sandberg went on to become a Hall of Fame second baseman with the Cubs, winning a National League MVP award and nine Gold Gloves (Figure 28). He also made ten All-Star teams and hit 282 home runs. But Bowa was also instrumental in Sandberg's success.

"Bowa really helped Ryno become a second baseman," Green admitted in a recent interview. "I had envisioned him as a third baseman and the Cubs played him there in 1982. But the following year we got Ron Cey from the Dodgers and moved Ryo to second base. With Bowa's help and his own tremendous work ethic, Ryno made himself into a great second baseman."[94] Dickie Noles, who had joined Green in Chicago, was astonished at Sandberg's transformation. "Ryne and Bowa were inseparable," he remembered. "They were at the ballpark before anyone else working their tails off, taking ground balls, hitting, working the double play. I think Bowa also loosened him up a bit. Ryne was a real quiet guy. But Bowa got

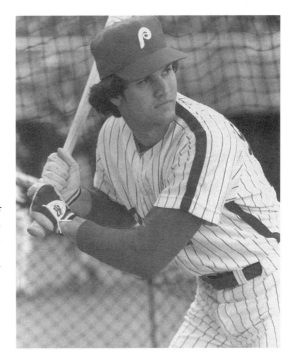

FIGURE 28. The trading of future Hall of Famer Ryne Sandberg to the Chicago Cubs was one of the worst deals made by the Phillies after 1980. Courtesy of the National Baseball Hall of Fame Library, Cooperstown, New York.

him to come out of his shell, to talk a little trash. He gave him a little cockiness, but in a good way. By 1984, Sandberg was the best second baseman in baseball and he was a power hitter with some speed on the base paths as well."[95]

Bowa probably viewed his mentoring of Sandberg as vindication for being traded.He was deeply hurt when he left Philadelphia and voiced his displeasure through the press. "When Ruly Carpenter owned the club the Phillies were like a family," he told Bill Conlin of the *Philadelphia Daily News*. "We did everything on trust and a handshake. But all that changed when Giles took over. It's all corporate now, no more family." Bowa insisted that Carpenter, before he sold the team, promised to sign him to a three-year contract and that if he didn't the shortstop could ask to be traded. Since Bowa had already been in the majors for ten years and had five straight years of service on the same team, he could veto any trade if he didn't like it. Giles reneged on the deal when he purchased the team, in spite of Carpenter's intercession. Infuriated, Bowa feuded in the newspapers with the new Phillies president, calling him a "liar" and insisting that the team would have to trade him "or there is going to be a problem here." After he learned of his trade to Chicago and that the Phillies "threw in" another player, the fiery shortstop asked who the "throw in" was. When he discovered that Ryne Sandberg was the player, Bowa remarked: "Well then, I was the guy they threw in because Sandberg is going to be a great player. That has got to be one of the all-time trades."[96]

Bowa's trade, like many of those to follow, was a ploy to avoid free agency. Giles, like most owners, traded those players who would soon become free agents rather than lose them for nothing. These were ballplayers with ten years of service in the majors and five straight years with one club, so-called "ten-and-five" players.[97] At the same time, the Phillies attempted to manipulate the contracts of their better younger players to prevent them from becoming free agents once they reached their sixth year of service. Again, Giles was following the lead of other owners, some of whom responded to the dilemma by agreeing to long-term contracts. Typically, this would occur sometime after the player's fourth year of service, before he became eligible for free agency. If the contract was for, say, a five-year period, the owner would, in effect, buy out three years' worth of the player's free agency rights, retaining his services without having to pay the escalating rate for a premier player in the future.[98] Mike Schmidt came under this category.

Schmidt was the Phillies franchise player. One of Giles's first priorities was to sign him to a new, long-term contract. The third baseman was in the final year of a six-year, $700,000 contract in 1981. He had recently purchased a new home in suburban Media and hoped to "retire as a Phillie."[99] Nevertheless, it would cost the Phillies a multiyear contract worth about $1.5 million a year to retain him. That was the going rate at the time for players of his caliber. Schmidt had emerged as the premier third baseman during an era that featured many stellar performers at the hot corner, including George Brett of the Royals, Graig Nettles of the Yankees, Ron Cey of the Dodgers, Bill Madlock of the Pirates, and Bob Horner of the Braves.

In the strike-shortened season of 1981, Schmidt led the National League in home runs (31), RBI (91) walks (73), runs scored (78) slugging average (.644) and on-base percentage (.435). He also compiled a career high .316 batting average, earned his sixth Gold Glove, and won the All-Star game for the National League with a 2-run homer off American League reliever Rollie Fingers. Not surprisingly, he received 21 of 24 first-place votes from the Baseball Writers, who named him the National League MVP for the second straight year. With the distinction, Schmidt became just the eighth player in baseball history and the third in the National League to capture consecutive MVP awards.[100] Together with his power hitting, which by 1982 resulted in 314 career home runs, Schmidt had established himself as a future Hall of Famer at the position. The Phillies realized that and knew they would have to meet his financial demands if they were to keep him in their red pinstripes. Only a long-term contract would allow him to complete his career in Philadelphia.

Schmidt was well aware of the politics surrounding salary negotiations. He hired Arthur Rosenberg, an accountant and senior vice president with the brokerage firm of Dean Witter Reynolds, to be his agent. Rosenberg and Paul Shapiro, the attorney he hired to assist him, had no previous experience negotiating player salaries. But he did his homework carefully, comparing Schmidt's statistical totals to the other high-salaried players in the game, calculating his worth in the current free agent market. He then approached Giles with a salary request "in the area of $1.7 million a year for six to eight years" with "the inclusion of a cost-of-living escalator clause," insisting that his client wanted a contract that would "let him retire as a Phillie."[101]

On December 21, 1981, Schmidt and Giles agreed to a new, six-year deal worth $10 million, making the Phillies third baseman the highest paid player in National League history at the time.[102] Giles did secure a clause that would allow the Phillies to trade their star third baseman after three years, if his knees would no longer allow him to play. "While Mike took a physical for purposes of insuring the contract, we wanted some way to get out of it after three years in case certain conditions arose," explained the Phillies president. "It's a very complicated thing, but the machinery exists for a trade should he become a guy who, for instance, can still swing the bat but can't play third base for some reason."[103]

The Phillies were one of only a few clubs that could afford to make such a deal to retain their star player. The television revenue they would receive over the next decade made the transaction possible. But Giles had no illusions about having tighter control of his club's finances in negotiating subsequent player contracts because of it. "Schmidt is a special commodity," he admitted. "My philosophy is you have to take care of the key guys like Rose, Schmitty and Carlton. While you have to treat everybody fairly, we can't afford to lose one of those three players. Unfortunately, we're going to have to have tougher negotiations with some of the other players down the road or we just can't make it financially."[104]

Conspicuously absent from Giles's list of "key guys" was Tug McGraw, who was earning less than $250,000 a year when his contract expired at the end of the '80 season. He became a free agent and entered the November reentry draft, but not a single team selected him. They believed that McGraw would probably re-sign with the Phillies anyway and they didn't want to waste a draft pick by selecting him. Nor did they believe that at age thirty-six McGraw was worth the $2 million, four-year contract he wanted.[105] But Tug "wasn't ready to retire" from something that he loved, and he also wanted to "stay in Philadelphia."[106] Giles realized that McGraw was the team's most popular player and any decision about his future would also affect the organization's marketing and public relations. As a result, the Phillies president re-signed the reliever to a two-year deal worth the same salary he had been making.

Giles had made public his modus operandi. The new regime would try to remain competitive with a nucleus of superstars while looking for ways to cut salary with impending free agents, aging veterans, and emerging young stars. That philosophy would allow the organization to eke out one more pennant.

CHAPTER 13

WHEEZE KIDS

THE PHILLIES ARRIVED AT CLEARWATER, Florida, in the spring of 1982 not knowing what to expect. Dallas Green's two-and-a-half-season tenure as manager had been a stormy one, punctuated by two post-season berths and the only world championship in the club's ninety-nine-year history. Few would miss Green. His volcanic temper, public criticism of the players, and "my-way-or-the-highway" approach had made many of the veterans uneasy. Managers of his ilk were usually hired for the short term. Their mission was to motivate a talented but complacent team to realize its full potential. Once that goal was achieved, he was gone just as quickly as he came. Negative motivation can only carry a team so far. There is no long-term future for managers like Dallas Green. He realized that fact, too, and jumped at the Cubs' offer to become their general manager.

The new Phillies skipper would have to embark on the delicate process of rebuilding with a mix of aging superstars, role players, and young prospects. Bill Giles believed he found the right man for the job in Pat Corrales, a 41-year-old journeyman catcher of Mexican-Indian descent. Corrales had managed the Texas Rangers between 1978 and 1980, compiling 160 wins and 164 losses. His team's highest finish was second place, but his players respected him for his low-key and fair-minded approach.

As the veterans and rookies began to stream into the Carpenter Complex clubhouse, Corrales flashed his Pepsodent smile and welcomed each one to the new season. When everyone was assembled, he began his maiden speech. "Be on time and give 100 percent on the field and no one will bother you," he said. Expecting the usual litany of rules and regulations that had characterized Green's clubhouse, the players waited to hear more.

"I don't have a lot of rules," added Corrales. "Managers did when I played and I broke all of them. I've been called a 'tough guy' and a 'disciplinarian,' but those aren't my labels. I don't think the players I've managed would say that about me either. But I can be tough. If I have to chew anybody out, I'll call him into my office and do it behind close doors. I don't like to make family matters public. That's pretty much it."[1]

Stunned by the brevity, the Phillies quickly embraced their new manager, a soft-spoken contrast to the human thunderstorm they had known as Dallas Green. Pat Corrales had begun with much promise what would become one of the shortest tenures in Phillies history.

The fans were less than happy, though. Still reeling from the trades that sent Larry Bowa to the Cubs for shortstop Ivan DeJesus and the three-cornered deal that sent Lonnie Smith to the St. Louis Cardinals for Cleveland Indians catcher Bo Diaz, the Boo Birds took their frustrations out on DeJesus and Diaz when the team got off to a poor start. DeJesus flirted with a .200 batting average through April, and Diaz, who suffered from a reputation as a malingerer, didn't hit much better.[2] Carlton was also suffering through the worst start of his seventeen-year career. He lost his first four decisions, and his earned run average had ballooned to 6.75. The critics said he was "washed up," that the more than 4,200 innings he had pitched over his illustrious career had "finally caught up to him."[3] When he heard about the negative press, Lefty fired back. "As far as I'm concerned, the press is one of the biggest enemies you have in Philadelphia," he snapped in a rare interview with Hal Bodley of *Sporting News*. "First, you have to worry about the opposition, then all the things that are written in the paper. I have to just cut all those distractions off, which is what I intend to do."[4]

Ironically, the biggest disappointment was the team's franchise player, Mike Schmidt. The Phillies third baseman had believed he was in the best physical condition of his career when he left for spring training and was ready for another MVP year. But only five games into the regular season he was sidelined with a severe injury. It happened on April 13, a raw, windy opening day at New York's Shea Stadium. During the top of the second inning, Schmidt lined a Randy Jones fastball into right field, a sure double. As he took off for first base, he felt a sharp stab in his back. It was so excruciating he doubled over in pain, holding his side. He had fractured a lower left rib with the force of his swing and, in the process, had torn the muscle away from his rib cage.[5] Schmidt would be sidelined for weeks. It was two months before he could play without any pain.

When he returned to the lineup in early May the Phils were barely playing .500 baseball and stuck in fifth place. Schmidt tried to make up for lost time, pressing to hit the long ball.[6] The more he pressed, the worse he performed. The Phillies third baseman entered the month of June with three homers and 13 RBI. A month later his power hitting totals modestly increased by four home runs and 11 RBI, but he was hitting .300. "Maybe I ought to bat him lead-off," joked Corrales. "Mike is a perfectionist. He wants to hit 40 homers, 120 RBIs, and finish with a .300 average. That's the perfect baseball player. Now there's nothing wrong with that kind of thinking, but it does take its toll on a player, even of his caliber."[7] By mid-July, Corrales saw signs that the slugger was finally coming out of his funk. Schmidt was driving the ball harder, but he had not completely healed from the injury, making it impossible for him to hit with the kind of power he had been accustomed to in previous seasons. The perfectionist in him refused to accept that fact. Amazingly, he still collected 33 homers and 80 RBIs by September and was hitting .300 on the mark.

On September 13, in the opener of a critical three-game series against the division-leading Cardinals, Schmidt hit a run-scoring double. The Phillies won the game, 2-0, behind the three-hit pitching of Steve Carlton and moved into first place by a full game. Having rebounded from a poor spring, Lefty was 20-9 with an ERA of 3.34. He had won 16 of his last 20 decisions, including 14 complete games.[8] But the other starters struggled to reach the .500 mark. Marty Bystrom, plagued by shoulder and elbow problems, struggled to keep his ERA under 5.00. Larry Christenson continued to pitch with pain and somehow managed to eke out a 9-10 record with a 3.47 ERA. Dick Ruthven, who had posted a 12-7 record the previous year and made the All-Star team, slumped to 11-11. He lost his spot in the starting rotation in August after throwing his glove into the stands when Corrales lifted him from a game. Ruthven would be traded to the Cubs for reliever Willie Hernandez the following season.[9] "I never like Corrales," admitted Ruthven in a recent interview. "He was nothing but a 'yes man' for Bill Giles. Giles wanted me out of Philadelphia. I was on the verge of becoming a 'ten-and-five' player, ten years in the majors with five years service on the same team. That meant I'd be able to veto any trade he tried to make. Giles wasn't going to be handcuffed. He told Corrales to make it miserable for me, and Pat thoroughly loved doing it. When I threw my glove into the stands, Giles labeled me a 'malcontent' and traded me. He probably saved a lot of money in the deal, too."[10]

Mike Krukow lost the second game of the Cardinals series the following night when Darrell Porter drove in two runs and Schmidt grounded into a bases-loaded double play. St. Louis took the final game of the series, defeating recently acquired pitcher John Denny to regain first place by a one-game margin. A week later, when the two teams met again, Schmidt was mired in a 1-for-25 slump. Anticipating the Phillies' ultimate collapse, the media were unmerciful, blaming the third baseman for his team's misfortunes.[11]

Rose came to his teammate's defense. "I don't think it's fair to put the load on his shoulders," he insisted. "When we've got guys not swinging the bat, he feels he has to get three hits and hit two out of the ballpark, and that puts too much strain on him." Rose reminded the press that the Phillies' swoon was a "team effort" and that Schmidt can't be blamed "if the rest of the team [was] slumping."[12]

The Cardinals went on to win the division with four games remaining in the season while the Phillies finished second, three games out with an 89-73 record. Still, there were many bright spots. Carlton won his fourth and final Cy Young Award with a league-leading 23 victories, 19 complete games, 286 strikeouts, and an impressive 3.10 ERA. Despite his offensive woes, Schmidt finished the season with a .280 average, 87 RBI, and 35 home runs. Bo Diaz also rebounded from a slow start with 18 homers, 85 RBI and a .288 batting average, and right fielder Gary Matthews turned in another fine performance hitting .281 with 19 home runs and 83 RBI.[13] Changes were on the horizon, though.

After the season the Phillies made one of the biggest and most controversial trades in club history. Second baseman Manny Trillo was packaged to the Cleveland Indians along with outfielder George Vukovich, shortstop Julio Franco, pitcher Jay Ballard, and catcher Jerry Willard for Von Hayes, a much heralded outfield prospect. The "five-for-one" deal was initially hailed as a good one. Hayes, a young left-handed power hitter, was being compared to both Ted Williams and Stan Musial by the baseball experts. The Phillies brass projected him as Garry Maddox's successor in center field.[14] Trillo, who was on the eve of free agency, wanted a long-term, multimillion-dollar contract; something that went against Giles's philosophy. While Vukovich had served the Phillies well as a reserve, he was viewed as a utility player. Of the three Phillies prospects who were dealt, Franco was the most promising. Signed by Dominican scout Quique Acevedo in 1976 for a bonus of $4,500, Franco, in five minor league seasons, impressed his coaches with 6'2" speed. He hit with power and consistency, but some coaches thought that his fielding was too erratic. With DeJesus at shortstop and plenty of middle infielders in the farm system, Franco was considered "expendable."[15]

Shortly after the Hayes acquisition, pitcher Mike Krukow and Mark Davis were traded to San Francisco for second baseman Joe Morgan and reliever Al Holland. Holland was the key to the deal. The Phillies needed a closer to replace McGraw who, at age 37, was in the twilight of his career. Krukow, who posted a 13-11 record with a 3.12 ERA, had the trade value to get Holland, who had been a setup man for Greg Minton in San Francisco. Davis was a twenty-two-year-old prospect who had led the Eastern League with 19 wins and 185 strikeouts in 1980. But he contracted tendonitis in '81 and finished his short rookie season at 1-4 with a 7.74 ERA. He would go on to win the Cy Young Award as a reliever with the San Diego Padres in 1989, but in 1982 he was still at least three to four years away from contributing at the big league level.[16] The Phillies needed to win now and they were willing to deal some of their promising youngsters to do it. The acquisition of Morgan, age 39 and past his prime, also made sense considering the club's "win now" philosophy.

Having traded Trillo, the Phillies needed an experienced second baseman that could mentor their young prospect, Juan Samuel. Signed by the Phillies in 1980 for a bonus of $3,000, Samuel was also discovered by Dominican scout Quique Acevedo. Like Julio Franco, Samuel possessed speed and power. But he had difficulty playing second base. Morgan, who helped to make the Astros and Giants contenders after leaving Cincinnati, was a perfect solution to the dilemma. He would serve to fill the void left between Trillo and Samuel.[17]

Giles, always eager to capitalize on marketing possibilities, saw a golden opportunity to reunite three key members of the "Big Red Machine" when power-hitting first baseman Tony "Mad Dog" Perez was released from the Boston Red Sox in November 1982. Realizing that the Phillies needed a right-handed pinch hitter with some clout and a player who could spell Rose at first base, Giles had Owens sign the former Red to a one-year contract. Perez, who helped to make a contender out of the Montreal Expos after leaving Cincinnati, fit nicely into the Phils' plans.[18]

Along with Rose and Morgan, Perez gave the Phillies the kind of experience necessary to make another run at the pennant. Cumulatively, they had played in a total of 7,925 games, collecting 8,711 hits, scoring 4,729 runs, and sported seven World Series championship rings.[19] The acquisition of the three former Reds also gave the Phillies a rather elderly complexion, as 22 of the players on the 40-man roster were over 30 years of age. Among the "most seasoned" veterans were Rose (42), Perez and pitcher Ron Reed (41), Morgan and outfielder Bill Robinson (40), and pitchers Steve Carlton and Tug McGraw (38). Collectively, the 1983 Phillies were more affectionately known as the "Wheeze Kids," an appropriate moniker considering that the 1950 pennant winners were called the "Whiz Kids" and that 1983 marked the centennial anniversary of the Phillies organization.[20]

Player transactions were not the only changes taking place in the Phillies organization. The minor league and scouting operation was also in flux. Many of the scouts were confused by the division of authority between farm director Jim Baumer, on one hand, and scouting director Jack Pastore, on the other. Top scouts Hughie Alexander and Ray Shore seemed to be working independently. Some members of the front office believed that the two scouts were funneling talent to Dallas Green in Chicago. To be sure, Green's departure triggered a chain reaction of resignations among his friends in the Phillies scouting system. The former Phillies skipper had badmouthed the organization after he resigned to become the Cubs' general manager, saying that the scouting and farm systems hadn't been working right since *he'd* quit directing them and that Baumer and Pastore should be fired.[21] Baumer anticipated the defections, though. Shortly after Green departed, he suspended the issuing of 1982 contracts to all scouts in order "to see who was going to Chicago and who wanted to stay with us."[22] Among those who eventually left to join Green were Hugh Alexander, Ruben Amaro, Brandy Davis,

Gordon Goldsberry, Lou Kahn, and Gary Nickels.[23] Baumer was less concerned about the defections than Giles's decision not to replace them.[24] He had learned about the politics and economics of scouting early in his scouting career.

After a mediocre seventeen-year playing career in the United States and Japan, Baumer joined the Houston Astros as a scout. Once a hungry expansion franchise ready to outhustle any other group of scouts, Houston, after the establishment of the amateur draft, placed a lower priority on player development. Instead, the Astros tried to attract fans through special promotions and trades aimed at short-term improvement. Disgusted by the new policy, Baumer left the Astros in 1972 to join the Milwaukee Brewers as a special assignment scout. Promoted to scouting director the following year, Baumer made the signing of his career when he snatched future Hall of Famer Robin Yount, then a high school shortstop from Danville, Illinois, in the first round of the June 1973 draft. Two years later, in 1975, Baumer became the Brewers' general manager. Although he engineered two significant trades that brought Cecil Cooper from Boston and Mike Caldwell from Cincinnati, Milwaukee remained a second division team. After a second last-place finish in 1977, Baumer was fired and forced to start over again as a special assignment scout with Philadelphia.[25]

When Baumer became farm director after the 1980 season, Ruly Carpenter still owned the Phillies and he had more money to play with than was the case in Milwaukee. In fact, the Phils led all major league organizations in spending on player development. In 1981, the final year of Carpenter's ownership, the club invested about $3.7 million in scouting and farm systems. That figure did *not* include administrative salaries and expenses.[26] Carpenter genuinely believed that scouting and player development were the keys to building a successful franchise. That was not the case with the new president Bill Giles, whose baseball values were shaped at Houston when he was the Astros' publicity director. Giles remained more interested in marketing the team than in developing it. Patching together the 1983 Wheeze Kids for one more run at the pennant confirmed that approach. So did Giles's decision not to replace the exodus of Phillies scouts to Chicago after they had been lured away by Dallas Green.

The organization's reduced scouting capabilities and some unwise decisions resulted in several years of bad drafts beginning in June 1981. That year the Phillies selected Johnny Ray Abrego, a sore-armed, high school pitcher from Mission San Jose, California. Signed by scout Eddie Bockman for a bonus of $70,000, Abrego sat out the entire 1982 season after reconstructive elbow surgery. The Cubs claimed him for $25,000 in the minor league draft in December 1983. He appeared in a total of six games, in September 1985, with Chicago, posting a 1-1 record with a 6.38 ERA. His only victory came against the Phillies. After laboring through four more minor league seasons and a shoulder operation, Abrego, at age twenty-five, was released in 1988.[27] What's worse, the Phillies' second through sixth picks in the '81 draft never made it to the major leagues. Their best selection was college pitcher Charles Hudson, a twelfth-round pick, who was signed by scout Doug Gassaway for a $5,000 bonus. In four seasons with the Phillies (1983-86), Hudson was 32-42 with a 3.98 ERA.[28]

The Phils continued to make poor draft picks throughout the decade of the 1980s, including the list of first-round selections shown in the table.[29]

PHILLIES' FIRST-ROUND DRAFT PICKS, 1982–89

Draft year	Player	Position(s)	Highest level/ years	Career record
1982	John Russell	Catcher/outfielder	Majors/10 years	.225 avg.
1983	Ricky Jordan	First baseman	Major /8 years	.281 avg.
1984	Pete Smith	Right-handed pitcher	Majors/11 years	47-71 / 4.55 ERA
1985	Trey McCall	Catcher	Double-A	
1986	Brad Brink	Right-handed pitcher	Majors/3 years	0-4 / 3.56 ERA
1987	No pick			
1988	Pat Combs	Left-handed pitcher	Majors/4 years	17-17 / 4.22 ERA
1989	Jeff Jackson	Outfielder	Double-A	

More telling are the prospects the Phillies bypassed in the first round during the 1980s. In 1985, the Phils could have signed outfielder Brian McRae (Royals), pitcher Joe Magrane (Cardinals), or Rafael Palmiero (Cubs), instead of Trey McCall, who never even made it to the majors. In 1989, the Phils could have selected power-hitting first basemen Frank Thomas (White Sox) or Mo Vaughn (Red Sox), but they chose Jeff Jackson instead.[30] The Phillies were so bad at judging prospective talent during the Giles regime that *Daily News* beat writer Bill Conlin offered the following composite description of the club's early round picks: "Billy Bob Crewcut from Cradle of Liberty Junior College in True Grit, Oklahoma—somebody who will go out and hit .212 at Batavia, .190 in the Florida Instructional League, .235 at Spartanburg, and be quietly released."[31]

As if the poor draft choices weren't bad enough, Giles, ever conscious of his budget, also abandoned the Phillies' Latin American scouting operation. Shortly after he became president, Giles approached Ruben Amaro, director of the team's Latin American operation, and asked him to continue in that capacity, which included both scouting and heading the Phillies' winter baseball program in Venezuela. Amaro insisted that his key personnel be paid more money. When Giles balked at the request, Amaro became infuriated. He considered going to Chicago. Green had already offered him a coaching position along with John Vukovich and Lee Elia. But Amaro wanted to remain with the Phillies. "I still thought I had a future with the club," he said in a recent interview. "After they hired Pat Corrales, I told them that I wanted to remain as a coach. I thought I could help in the adjustment because I knew all the players and had a good rapport with them. I could also continue in Venezuela in the winter time."[32]

Giles left the decision to Owens. Whether the Pope had questions about Amaro's loyalties to Green or he simply deferred to Corrales's wish to name his own coaching staff is unclear. But Amaro was refused the coaching position and offered a two-year contract to continue as director of the Latin American program. Insulted, Amaro left Philadelphia and joined Green in Chicago.[33]

Years later Giles admitted that he had deferred to farm director Jim Baumer on the decision to discontinue the Latin American program. "Baumer wasn't high on Hispanic players," said Giles. "Jim didn't think investing in the program was worth the money. Nor did he have any interest in pursuing that kind of initiative." When it was suggested that the Phillies failed to capitalize on the most talented pool of players that emerged in the 1980s and 1990s, Giles admitted that Baumer had given him "bad advice."[34] Still, it is difficult to escape the conclusion that Giles's decision was based primarily on finances. His background was marketing and promotions, not player development. Profit margins and savings were more important to him. Ultimately, the decision to abandon the Latin American program was a poor one that would have serious long-term consequences.

For now, the Phillies were the "Team of the Eighties," and Rose, Morgan, and Perez aimed to reinforce Giles's self-proclaimed title. "I did not come here for a reunion," snapped Morgan, downplaying the notion that he and Perez were acquired simply to draw more fans. "The Phillies got me to help them win another world championship."[35] To be sure, the Phillies' "Big Red Machine" still had enough gas left in the tank to inspire their younger teammates. Throughout spring training, Rose, Morgan, and Perez kept things loose, constantly badgering each other.

"You used to caddy for Yastrzemski, Doggie," Rose said to Perez, referring to his part-time role as a defensive replacement for Boston's aging superstar. "Now you're going to find out how it feels to caddy for a *real* ballplayer!"

"Hey, old man," Morgan chirped in. "I'm here to kick you in the rear end and Doggie's here to give you a rest once in awhile so you can raise that .271 average of yours."

"I'll rest plenty when I'm dead," Rose shot back, not missing a beat.

The three veterans continued the bantering on the practice diamond. During infield drills, they kept replaying the '75 World Series against the Boston Red Sox. Perez insisted that the trio wouldn't be wearing their diamond-studded championship rings if he hadn't hit two home runs in Cincinnati's Game 5 victory. Morgan, refusing to be outdone, said they wouldn't have their rings if he hadn't stroked the winning hit in Game 7. And Rose told them both that they owed their rings to him for hitting .370 in that Fall Classic.

"We're going to have a lot of fun this season," said Perez.

"Yeah, this could turn out to be the most enjoyable year of my career," added

Morgan. "It was great the first time around, but I didn't appreciate it as much as I should have. This time I'll be able to stop and smell the roses."[36]

Corrales appreciated the enthusiasm as well as the experience of his superstars. "The younger players see them on the field, and it makes it easier for them to develop good working habits," he said.[37] The Phillies had a lot of young players who could stand to learn from such a prominent group of veteran stars. Rose took outfielder Jeff Stone under his wing, remembering how difficult his own rookie year was. "When I came up to the Reds, nobody would associate with me," he said. "I was taking a popular veteran's job. I remember what it was like. That's why I like talking to the young players. It doesn't take nothing to be nice to people."[38] Juan Samuel, the Phillies' young second base prospect, was mentored by both Perez and Morgan. "It was like I was dreaming when I walked into that clubhouse," he recalled. "Here I am, a kid from a small Dominican neighborhood, and I'm playing with some of the greatest names in baseball. Not only that, but they're actually talking to me, helping me out.[39]

According to John Russell, who was a catching prospect, the mentoring had to be earned, it wasn't offered freely. "Rookies were treated a bit different back then," he said. "It was 'old school.' If you didn't do your job, you'd be alienated. And Pete Rose would be quick to put you in your place, though he did it in a funny way. But if you worked hard, kept your mouth shut, and did your job, guys like Lefty, Tug and Schmitty would take you under their wing."[40]

Schmidt, in particular, had a soft spot for the rookies. For all the criticism he took for being "aloof," Michael Jack made it a point to embrace the younger players. Samuel remembers Schmitty wrapping his muscular arm around him and saying, "C'mere, let's talk some baseball," whenever he made a mistake in practice.[41] Michael Jack was even more understanding with Von Hayes. "Don't forget that Schmidt, in his early years with the Phillies, was ridiculed by a lot of hard-bitten veterans, and it was done in the most personal terms," said Peter Pascarelli, the *Philadelphia Inquirer*'s beat writer. "To steel himself, he fashioned an insular existence and let his on-field performance do the leading. He was one of the few veterans who tried to help Von Hayes during his awful first season with the Phils in 1983. While others, like Pete Rose and Joe Morgan, took to derisively calling Hayes 'Five-for-One,' Schmidt refused to join in the chorus. Such class is worth an awful lot, especially in the 'take-no-prisoners' world of the major league clubhouse."[42]

While the 1983 Phillies might have been loaded with experience and talent, they were not favored to capture the National League's Eastern Division. The Montreal Expos were the favorites with the St. Louis Cardinals a close second. In fact, sheer good luck played a significant role in the Phillies' quest for the pennant. The division was an embarrassment that season. No team took command through the first half, and yet the Phils found themselves in second place

at the All-Star break, 1½ games behind Montreal. Several key Phillies were struggling. Rose was laboring at the plate and in the field and, as a result, was being
platooned with rookie Len Matuszek. Matthews, who had 17 game-winning RBI
the previous season, had only three. And Morgan was hitting an anemic .201,
splitting second base duties with rookie Juan Samuel. But Schmidt suffered the
worst slump.

In early May, the Phillies slugger was hitting .352 with 7 homers and 23 RBI.
But over the next month his average slipping to .245. The nadir of his 19-game
slump came on May 27 in a game against the Montreal Expos. Schmidt went
0-for-4, fouling out his first time up, then striking out in his next three at bats.
The following night he struck out on three pitches in each of his first four plate
appearances. Finally, in his fifth at bat, he hit the first pitch for a game-winning
home run.[43]

While Carlton continued to pitch every fourth day and led the league in
innings, he was replaced as the staff ace by John Denny, who was on pace to win
20 games. The pitching of Carlton, Denny and Al Holland, who assumed the
closer's role, kept the Phillies in 3rd place at the end of June, but Giles wanted
Corrales fired. Owens talked him out of it, explaining how difficult it was for a
journeyman major leaguer to manage a team with four or five potential Hall of
Famers.

One early July morning, Corrales sat at the bar at Cincinnati's Terrace Hilton
Hotel drowning his sorrows in a schooner of beer. Bill Conlin of the *Philadelphia
Daily News* pulled up a stool and began firing away questions. After three or four
half-hearted responses, Corrales finally snapped.

"You guys in the press don't know a lot of things that go on in the clubhouse,"
he barked. "You keep writing about how I've been able to keep my cool through
all this, but I don't always keep it. Tonight I thought Joe Morgan laid down on a
play and I told him about it in front of the whole team. After the game I told
Mike Schmidt that he stinks, right in front of his parents."

Conlin, knowing when he had a scoop, kept quiet, allowing Corrales to continue the rant.

"You know what I've been telling 'em, all these big stars?" asked the Phillies
skipper. "I've been telling 'em, I'm not gonna let you motherfuckers get me fired.
I'll sit your asses down and play the guys I think are gonna win, the guys who
hit. I'm not gonna sit back and let you guys cost me my job."[44]

Predictably, Giles fired Corrales a week later, on July 18. He was the first
manager in Phillies' history to be axed in midseason with his team in first place.
"Pat had to go," insisted Giles. "Every time I met with him he talked about how
much he hated the players and how much the players hated him. It just wasn't
working."[45]

With Corrales gone, Giles turned to Owens, the most logical candidate to assume the field post. Once before, in 1972, the Pope went down to evaluate a losing team composed of mediocre veterans and young prospects. At the time, he had recently become the team's general manager and felt it was the best way for him to determine which players to retain and which to trade. But now, eleven years later, the Phillies were a winning team with star players, some of whom were future Hall of Famers. And the Pope was also older, raising questions about his stamina. "After he fired Corrales, Bill asked me to take over," recalled Owens. "He said an interim manager wouldn't have any impact."

Owens struggled with the decision. He really didn't want to go back down to the field, but he played the good soldier and, once again, assumed the duties of manager. "So many times in my career, I've asked guys to do something for the good of the club. You can't turn people down. All the guys said, 'Pope, if anybody can handle 'em, you can.'"[46]

But Bill Conlin, a close friend of Owens, said that there was more to the decision than loyalty. "Pope was set up by Giles and Jim Baumer, the farm director," he insisted in a recent interview. "They wanted him to fail. Failing would make it easier for Giles to limit his role in the organization. Pope was fifty-nine years old at the time. He didn't want to go back down. Why do you think they sent Dallas Green down in 1979 instead of Owens? He was too old for that kind of pressure. But Hughie Alexander told Pope, 'You might as well take the job because Giles wants to be the general manager anyway. He might let you keep the title, but you'll be a figurehead. He'll be the one making all the moves.'"[47]

There does appear to be some validity in Conlin's explanation. After Giles took over the club, Owens's status was unclear. The new Phillies president insisted on being involved in player transactions and began to assert himself more. By '83, Giles had become more independent in that area, relying less on Owens's experience than his own intuition. Pope was pushed into the background, though he was still included as an adviser in all trade discussions.[48] In fact, Giles still boasts about the acquisitions of Joe Morgan, Tony Perez, and Al Holland as "*my* big signings"; transactions that Owens "had nothing to do with."[49] At the same time, however, Giles flatly denies any conspiracy against the Pope.

"I hired Paul for the job because he was the man to do it," insisted Giles recently. "That wasn't the way I had planned it, though." When Giles became president of the club in 1981 he hoped to retain Green as the manager. "I drew up a five-year contract for Dallas that had him continuing as manager for two years and then becoming general manager," he explained. "Paul knew about the arrangement and he was fine with it since he planned to retire in two or three years." When Green left, Giles hired Corrales to manage the team and when that didn't work out, he felt he had to stay inside the organization to find a replacement. "We were in first place with an established team," said Giles. "Why go outside the organization when we already had someone inside who built the team? If those players were going to listen to anybody, they'd listen to him. I just felt more comfortable putting Paul down there and he wanted to do it."[50]

If Giles wanted to be a general manager though, Owens's transition to the field was an auspicious, if not convenient, way to achieve the goal. The Phillies president had said, from his first days with the organization back in 1970, that "trading players was really my goal."[51] Now that Owens was the manager there were no obstacles in his way. Whether Giles had consciously planned it that way or not is debatable. What is clear, however, is that the Phillies responded to Owens's appointment by winning 9 of their next 16 games. "When Pope came down the team really jelled," recalled Al Holland. "We knew that he had put the team together and we wanted to win it for him. It would have been a real vindication, too, because all season we'd been hearing how a bunch of old guys couldn't win it all. Well, if we did win it all, it'd make him look like a genius."[52]

But when August rolled around, the Phillies bats went silent again. Owens constantly juggled the lineup, looking for the right offensive combination. He even began a platoon system in the outfield, alternating between Gary Matthews and Greg Gross in left, and Joe Lefebvre and Von Hayes in right. Through it all, the press ignored the poor hitting of Rose, Diaz, Matthews, Morgan, and Hayes and focused their criticism on Schmidt, who was struggling to hit .240. Peter Pascarelli of the *Philadelphia Inquirer* seemed to take special pleasure in criticizing him for "leaving more runners on base than anyone else in the line-up" and complaining that Schmidt's power production "comes in small stretches around long droughts." Pascarelli also projected that Schmidt's "strikeout total will be 150 for the year" and suggested that if Mike didn't "put together four explosive weeks" down the stretch, it would be his fault that the Phillies underachieved.[53]

After one especially vicious personal attack, Schmidt felt as if he had "just hit a brick wall with the media in terms of trust and respect." He considered joining Steve Carlton in taking an unconditional vow of silence, but decided against it, realizing that such criticism was the price he had to pay for being a successful professional athlete. Instead, he continued to be one of the most cooperative and approachable professional athletes in the city. "When you're up at the top, there are so many people who want to take shots at you," he explained. "Being a professional athlete though, means you're in the public eye and you get paid well. You have to realize that success breeds jealousy. Besides, nobody boos or gives bad press to a mediocre player, only the best ones get it."[54] All the criticism and lineup juggling had taken their toll on him, though.

On September 9, Schmidt lashed out against the Phillies' management. "We have no sense of direction," he complained. "Nobody is sure who is the manager around here. As a veteran player, I'm disappointed in the way the front office has handled this season. We have a team full of guys who are capable of turning on a switch, but two weeks later, you wouldn't know it was the same club if you looked at the lineup. What we've got is an organization full of soap opera problems."[55] It was an uncharacteristic outburst from a player who usually went about his business avoiding distractions and controversies. Owens was quick to reply. "Schmidt's problem is that he thinks too much," said the Phillies skipper. "He should just go out and play the game, using the ability God gave him."[56] But Schmidt's teammates appreciated his words, believing that only he, as the franchise player, could register their dissatisfaction with management.

When all the controversy died down, the Phillies were still in first place. The Expos, who had been favored to win the division, had self-destructed down the stretch. St. Louis, also considered a better team than the Phillies by the experts, choked in midseason and never regrouped. Once again, the Phils' pitching allowed them to take advantage of their rivals' misfortunes. When Ruthven was traded to the Cubs and Christenson went down with elbow problems, the starting rotation was bolstered by youngsters Kevin Gross, who posted four critical victories, and Charles Hudson, who added another eight. Tony Ghelfi and Steve Comer also contributed victories as spot starters when the team needed help with doubleheaders. Just as important was the success of the bullpen.[57]

While Owens could count on his starters for at least six good innings, he had confidence that the bullpen could hold the opposition. Closer Al Holland was on pace to save 25 games. Had he not suffered early season shoulder problems that limited his activity until late May, he could have posted more than 30 saves. "I loved the opportunity to become a closer when I came to Philadelphia," he said. "It wasn't a difficult transition either since I was a setup man in San Francisco. I just had to take a different mental approach. The only thing that was difficult was replacing Tug McGraw. We bumped heads a few times when I first came, but things got ironed out. In fact, we became pretty good friends and I learned a lot from him."[58]

Although it might have been difficult replacing McGraw, one of the most beloved players in the team's history, Holland, also a left-hander, forged his own colorful persona and was quickly accepted by the fans as well as the press. The two gold chains he sported around his neck and his muttonchop sideburns earned him the nickname "Mr. T," after one of the actors on the popular television show *The A-Team*.[59] While Holland anchored the bullpen, he wasn't the sum total of it.

Willie Hernandez, acquired from the Cubs in the Ruthven deal, was the setup man. While he kept the opposing offense in check for the eighth inning, he also picked up eight victories and seven saves that season. Together with right-handers Ron Reed and Larry Andersen, Hernandez buttressed the bullpen, making Holland's job easier. "I loved Willie," said Holland. "He probably could have closed a lot of those games himself. He was one of the most talented and unselfish teammates I ever had. And he made my role much easier."[60] So did the Phillies' offense, which became opportunistic, if not fearsome, down the stretch.

Rose, who had been demoted to the bench, came alive in September. He went 8-for-21 as a pinch hitter for a .380 average and led the team in sacrifice flies with 7. The left field platoon of Gary Matthews and Greg Gross yielded 21 of the season total 79 runs batted in in September. Diaz, who flirted with the .220 mark all season ended up with 64 RBI. Schmidt also struggled with a .255 batting average, but he still led the majors in home runs (40) and finished third in RBI (109). Morgan, who had been hitting .200, also found his stride. On September 19, he celebrated his 40th birthday by hitting two home runs, a single, and a double and batting in 4 runs as the Phils beat the Cubs, 7-6. The following day Morgan went 4-for-5 with a double and 3 runs batted in in the Phils' 8-5 victory over Chicago. "I don't think I've ever had a bad September," he chortled.[61]

On September 23, Carlton defeated the Cardinals, 6-2, in St. Louis for his 300th career win. He became only the sixteenth pitcher in major league history to achieve that feat. The victory, the Phillies' eighth straight in a streak that would reach 11 by that Monday, 9/26, eliminated the defending world champion Cardinals from the pennant race. Prior to the game, Carlton had agreed to give a televised interview with Phillies broadcaster Harry Kalas that would be simulcast on WTAF-TV and WCAU Radio in Philadelphia. But he reneged after reading Bill Brown of the *Delaware County Times*, who wrote: "Silent Steve is finally going to talk, but it will be like a Soviet news agency briefing because the questions are going to be screened."[62] Lefty phoned publicity director Larry Shenk and told him, "Milestones are nice, but honestly, they are secondary to winning" and that he didn't want to make the issue of his speaking "bigger than the pennant race." Although Carlton did do a brief, on-field interview after the victory with his former catcher Tim McCarver, by then a national broadcaster, he continued his no-talking policy until the day he was released from the Phillies in 1986.[63]

The Phillies clinched the division the following week with a 13-6 rout of the Chicago Cubs at Wrigley Field. Bo Diaz led the 19-hit attack with two home runs and three singles. Joe Morgan continued his hot September contributing four hits and three RBI. Manager Paul Owens, champagne dripping onto his shoulders, was the object of affection in the Phillies clubhouse as his players stopped to give him a hug. "We finally came together and the players realized that they were as good as I thought they were," Owens told Bill Conlin of the *Philadelphia Daily News*. "They're professionals who played good ball down the stretch, and will do it again before the year's through."[64]

The Phillies would have to prove themselves in the playoffs against the Los Angeles Dodgers, who had lost only once in their twelve regular season games with Philadelphia. But the Phillies had gotten hot at the right time, gaining momentum down the stretch, while Los Angeles struggled through September with a 14-14 record. Starting pitchers Fernando Valenzuela (15-10, 3.75 ERA) and Rick Honeycutt (16-11, 3.03) had been shelled in their most recent outings. Jerry

Reuss (12-11, 2.94) and Bob Welch (15-12, 2.65 ERA) also struggled down the stretch, though not as badly as the others. Steve Howe (4-7, 18 SV, 1.44 ERA), the Dodgers' best left-handed reliever, had been suspended for the third and final time that season for alleged drug abuse, leaving right-hander Tom Niedenfuer (8-3, 11 SV, 1.90 ERA) to close out the remaining games.[65] The team's offense was, at .250, not as potent as the earlier Dodger teams the Phillies faced in the late 1970s. Gone were the powerful bats of Steve Garvey and Reggie Smith, replaced by those of Greg Brock (.224, 20 HR, 66 RBI) and an aging Dusty Baker (.260, 15 HR, 73 RBI). Aside from power-hitting third baseman Pedro Guerrero (.298, 32 HR, 103 RBI), the offensive clout was more evenly distributed between second baseman Steve Sax, who hit for a .281 average, and outfielders Mike Marshall (.284, 17 HR, 65 RBI) and Ken Landreaux (.281, 17 HR, 66 RBI).[66] The Dodgers, with an average age of 28, were a younger, less experienced team than the Phillies. In fact, pitcher Jerry Reuss thought the team was so young he jokingly said he "half expected the training room to have a sandbox and swings."[67]

The Phillies, on the other hand, could count on their experience, a multifaceted offense, and strong pitching. "That's why I like our chances," boasted Rose. "We go into the playoffs with only a couple of guys having really good years, but a lot of guys who produced down the stretch. That kind of team is tougher to beat than one that has just one or two guys carrying it."[68] The fact that the Phillies also carried 9 players on their roster who had already been to the post-season (Marty Bystrom, Joe Lefebvre, Ron Reed, Steve Carlton, Gary Matthews, Garry Maddox, Tony Perez, Greg Gross, Mike Schmidt, Pete Rose, and Joe Morgan) also gave them an advantage.

The playoffs opened in Los Angeles on October 4 with Steve Carlton facing hard-luck pitcher Jerry Reuss, loser of five of his previous six postseason appearances. The game was decided in the first inning when Schmidt slammed a low fastball into the center field bleachers. Lefty pitched seven and a half masterful innings. The Dodgers launched their biggest threat in the eighth when singles by Steve Sax and Dusty Baker and a walk to Pedro Guerrero loaded the bases with two outs. Owens went to Holland, who promptly retired Mike Marshall on a fly ball to right. Mr. T retired the Dodgers in the ninth to preserve the 1-0 victory.[69] The Dodgers evened the series the following day, thanks, in part, to the Phillies' sloppy defense. Los Angeles scored a first-inning run off John Denny on an error by Ivan DeJesus, but the Phils came back to tie it on a solo homer by Matthews in the second. The score was deadlocked until the bottom of the fifth. Pitcher Fernando Valenzuela led off with a line drive to the warning track in deep right-center. Maddox got to the ball but dropped it for a three-base error. After walking Dusty Baker, Denny surrendered a two-run triple to Guerrero, making the score 3-1 in favor of the Dodgers. Los Angeles added another run in the eighth off reliever Ron Reed to even the series.[70]

The playoffs resumed in Philadelphia on Friday night, October 7. Rookie Charles Hudson faced Bob Welch of the Dodgers and pitched a complete game victory, 7-2. Though Dodger outfielder Mike Marshall hit a two-run homer in the fourth, Hudson allowed just three other hits and struck out nine. While many of his teammates maintained that the rookie pitcher "didn't have his best stuff," pitching coach Claude Osteen disagreed. "The thing about Charlie is that at some point in most of his games he becomes defensive," said Osteen. "When that happens his arm action stops and his stuff suffers. That's what happened on the two-run homer to Marshall. But I'm proud of Charlie because he regrouped. He's won so many pressure games for us this season and today's was the biggest."[71]

Gary Matthews proved to be a one-man wrecking crew, clubbing a solo homer in the fourth, a two-run single in the fifth, and another run-scoring base hit in the seventh. For Matthews, who had been demoted to a platoon player, it was redemption. His regular season totals—.258 average, 10 homers and 50 RBI—were pathetic by the standards he set in 1982, when Pete Rose dubbed him "Sarge" for his offensive leadership. "Sitting on the bench was certainly one of the low points of my career," he admitted after the game. "But I kept myself ready and have been feeling good at the plate lately. Today, I just made myself a pledge that everything I swung at would be low and that I would lay off the high pitches that have been getting me into trouble. It ended up being a day I'll always remember."[72]

Carlton returned to the mound for the pennant clincher the following day against Jerry Reuss. Matthews gave him all the offense he needed to win in the first inning when he clubbed a three-run homer into the seats in left. He was later named the Most Valuable Player of the series with a .429 average, 3 homers, and record-tying 8 RBI.

The Phillies sent Reuss to the showers in the fifth after Rose singled and Schmidt doubled him home. They added another two runs the following inning on a Sixto Lezcano home run, but by that time Carlton had retreated to the clubhouse with a sore back. Reed pitched the seventh inning and Holland entered the game in the eighth to retire five of the six batters he faced.[73] After he retired the final batter, Mr. T turned in the direction of third base, looking for Schmidt to begin the celebration. When the Phillies clinched the division in Chicago, Holland had jumped into the arms of Joe Morgan, the nearest teammate. Schmitty took exception, shouting, "Hey man! You're supposed to be jumping into my arms!" Holland promised that if "things worked out against the Dodgers, you'll be the first one I look for." Now on this warm October night, Mr. T kept his word. After striking out Dodger shortstop Bill Russell to end the game, he found Schmitty running in his direction and hurled his 210-pound frame into the third baseman's arms as the newspaper photographers captured the scene for posterity.[74]

The Phillies now found themselves in their second World Series in four years. Interestingly, their fans didn't show as much enthusiasm the second time around.

Perhaps the lethargy was due to the mediocre play of the team for most of the summer in a league that was just as bad. Nor did the four-game victory over the Dodgers in playoffs offer the same excitement as the 1980 League Championship Series, which went down to the wire. Whatever the reason, the Phillies entered the Fall Classic without the same spirited support they enjoyed three years earlier, but they still carried the determination to bring the city another world championship.

The Baltimore Orioles were the Phillies' opponents, having captured the American League East by six games and then quickly dispatching the Chicago White Sox in the league championship series, three games to one. Dubbed the "I-95 Series" by local pundits—a reference to the interstate highway that connected the two cities—the contest pitted two more established Eastern clubs, both with storied histories. The Orioles were managed by first-year skipper Joe Altobelli, who had replaced the highly successful Earl Weaver. Baltimore enjoyed an outstanding pitching staff, featuring left-handers Scott McGregor (18-7), Mike Flanagan (12-4), rookie right-handers Mike Boddicker (16-8) and Storm Davis (13-7), and closer Tippy Martinez (9-3, 21 SV). The Birds had a potent offense that centered around Cal Ripken, a 23-year-old shortstop who was also the league MVP (.318, 27 HR, 102 RBI), and veteran first baseman Eddie Murray (.306, 33 HR, 111 RBI). The Orioles also boasted an excellent defensive catcher in Rick Dempsey and an effective outfield platoon of six players who could all hit well.[75]

Game 1 was played October 11, a rainy Tuesday evening in Baltimore. Phillies ace John Denny, the National League Cy Young Award winner, faced the Orioles' Scott McGregor. President Ronald Reagan was in the stands to watch the classic pitchers' duel, with each team managing just five hits. After Joe Morgan reached base on an error to lead off the first inning, McGregor retired the next 8 batters. Denny surrendered a solo homer to Orioles right fielder Jim Dwyer in the bottom half of the inning and a two-out single to first baseman Eddie Murray. But after that the Cy Young Award winner retired 17 of the next 18 hitters. Denny was lifted in the eighth after serving Al Bumbry a two-out double. Al Holland came on to get the save.[76] "When Denny took the ball we knew we could win as long as we gave him a couple of runs," Holland recalled years later. "He was one of the most competitive athletes I've known and he prided himself in going deep into the ball game. I shudder to think what the clubhouse would have looked life if we lost. John would have torn the whole place apart. He took losing *very* personally."[77]

The Phillies scored their first run in the top of the sixth. Before the inning began, Joe Morgan told Pete Rose, "If McGregor throws the curveball to me again, I'm going to hit it out." True to his word, Little Joe smacked a 1-2 curveball over the right field wall to tie the game at 1-1. Garry Maddox hit a solo homer in the eighth, which gave the Phils a 2-1 win. "McGregor was throwing me fastballs all night," he said afterward, reflecting on his game-winning hit. "In the eighth, I just made up my mind to look for a fastball and hit it hard."[78] It was one of the few special moments for Maddox in a frustrating season in which he languished on the bench for long periods. Father time was catching up with him quickly and he knew his days as a Phillie were numbered. "When I look back on this season, I'll remember that home run," he said. "I know I'm definitely one of the guys who could be gone, and its something I think about. I guess that when your career winds down you start getting sentimental."[79]

The next day Baltimore rode a dazzling three-hitter by Mike Boddicker for a 4-1 win, evening the Series. The Phillies only serious threat came in the fourth inning when Joe Morgan singled, stole second, advanced to third on an error, and scored on a deep fly ball to center by Joe Lefebvre. The Orioles, on the other hand, got all the runs they needed in the fifth off Phillies starter Charles Hudson. Left fielder John Lowenstein led off the inning with a home run to center. Second baseman Rich Dauer followed with a single, third baseman Todd Cruz reached base on a bunt, and catcher Rick Dempsey doubled home Dauer. Boddicker then lined out to left field, scoring Cruz from third base.[80] Interestingly, the bats of both clubs' premier power hitters fell silent through the first two games. Eddie Murray of the Orioles suffered through a 1-for-8 performance while Schmidt found himself in an 0-for-8 slump. When Murray was asked about the coincidence and whether it bothered him, he replied: "I've been going through it all my life. I think Mike Schmidt is going through the same thing. The media keeps bringing it up. So it's difficult to ignore." As Murray spoke, he became more agitated by the question. "What do you expect?" he finally snapped. "We're out there doing the best we can and if we don't deliver, you jump in our faces. How would you like it?"[81]

The two teams traveled to Philadelphia for Game 3 on October 14. It was another pitcher's duel, this one between two southpaws, Steve Carlton and Mike Flanagan. But the game is probably best remembered for Owens's controversial decision to bench Pete Rose in favor of Tony Perez at first base. "I've got to do something to get more offense," the Phillies manager explained. "We've gotten only eight hits in two days. Besides, I've got a good feeling about Tony."[82] While Rose was only 1-for-8 in the first two games of the Series, he hit .283 against left-handers during the regular season, whereas Perez hit only .205. Benching a player with Rose's postseason experience was a panic move at a time when, with the Series tied at one game apiece, there was no reason to panic. "It's just not the way baseball is played," Rose told broadcaster Howard Cosell in a postgame interview. "Here we are, the third game of the World Series, and probably the two most surprised guys in this ballpark were myself and Tony Perez. It's just embarrassing."[83]

On the field, the Phillies jumped out to a 1-0 lead in the second inning on a Gary Matthews homer. The next inning Morgan increased the lead to 2-0 on a right field home run. Although the Phils put men on base for each of the next three innings, they failed to come up with a timely hit to break the game open. Carlton pitched masterfully through the first five innings surrendering just two hits. In the sixth he was tagged for a solo home run by right fielder Dan Ford. He was lifted in the seventh when Dempsey hit a two-out double to left center, went to third on a wild pitch, and scored on pinch hitter Benny Ayala's single to left. With the score tied at 2-2, Holland came in and promptly surrendered a single to John Shelby. The O's now had men on first and second. Ford stepped to the plate and smashed a hard grounder to short. The ball bounced off DeJesus's glove for an error as Ayala crossed the plate with what would prove to be the winning run. "I didn't catch it," said DeJesus after the game, refusing to hide from the horde of sportswriters. "When the ball hit the ground, it just kept going. It hit a wet spot and skidded. I tried to knock it down, but it hit off my glove. I should have had it." The Phils were on the losing end once again, 3-2, and down one game in the Series.[84]

John Denny faced Storm Davis in Game 4. It was a scoreless pitchers' duel until the fourth inning when Baltimore loaded the bases on consecutive singles by Jim Dwyer, Cal Ripken, and Eddie Murray. After fanning John Lowenstein, Denny surrendered a two-run single to Rich Dauer. The Phillies came back in the bottom of the inning. Rose singled and Schmidt, riding an 0-for-12 slump, followed with a broken-bat pop fly that fell into short left center. It would be his only hit of the Series. Joe Lefebvre doubled, cutting the score to 2-1. Philadelphia took the lead in the fifth on doubles by Bo Diaz and Pete Rose and a single by Denny, but the O's regained the lead in the sixth, 4-3, and added a fifth run in the seventh.

Schmidt had another opportunity to redeem himself in the eighth. Down by two runs with Rose on first base the Phillies were hoping that their slugger had finally broken out of his funk. Orioles reliever Sammy Stewart threw him a cut fastball out over the plate and Schmidt, trying to tie the game up with one swing, hit a pop foul down the third base line.[85] The Boo Birds let loose on him as he returned to the dugout. "That was the first time they booed me in the Series," he noted afterward. "They put up with me making outs as much as they could and I can understand that. I'm just as disappointed as they are. They're not making it tough on me. I guess I'm making it tough for myself to hit."[86] The Phils fell short by a run in the ninth and they lost a heartbreaker, 5-4.

Baltimore clinched the championship the following night with a 5-0 romp of the Phils. Scott McGregor yielded just five base hits and Eddie Murray broke out of his slump with two homers. Baltimore was simply a better team. The Phillies could only manage nine runs and a .195 team batting average over the five-game series and embarrassed themselves losing four straight games, including three at home. Schmidt wasn't the only Phillie who failed to hit, just the most conspicuous one. "I just couldn't get comfortable at the plate," he explained his 1-for-20 performance afterward. "I was constantly trying to adjust and it almost seemed like they knew what I was thinking. I tried as hard as I could, but it just didn't work out. I apologize for my performance, but not for my effort."[87]

The largest crowd in Philadelphia baseball history—67,064—attended the final contest. Most of the fans were there to witness Pete Rose's last game in red pinstripes. It was no secret that the Phillies intended to release the forty-two-year-old first baseman as well as his close friends and teammates Joe Morgan and Tony Perez before the next season.[88] Giles wanted to avoid the kind of collapse the Cincinnati Reds experienced in the late 1970s after their big names moved on. He realized that the 1983 World Series was the last hurrah for an aging team of veteran stars that had been built to win in the late 1970s and early '80s. What Giles refused to admit, however, was that the dynasty that "should have been" was over. His earlier statement that the Phillies would be the "Team of the Eighties" would return to haunt him, time and again, throughout the decade. It was time to rebuild.

The departures of Morgan and Perez were understandable and necessary. Both were at the end of their careers and their statistics reflected that fact. Morgan hit just .230 with 16 home runs and 59 RBI. Perez posted a .241 batting average 6 homers and 43 RBI as a reserve player. Rose's release was more difficult to accept for many of his teammates and the fans. But the first baseman's .245 average and the prospect of paying another $1 million for an athlete who would become a part-time player convinced Bill Giles to sever the relationship. There might have been more to Rose's release than his obvious decline in production, though.

According to Michael Sokolove in his book, *Hustle: The Myth, Life, and Lies of Pete Rose*, Giles knew Rose well enough before he came to the Phillies to realize that he had a gambling problem. Giles even admitted that, during his years in Philadelphia, Rose was "using friends to call bookies for him," but he "didn't think it was a big deal because Pete was betting on other sports, not baseball." Interestingly, when Giles became president of the Phillies in 1981 he said that there was "another player" on the team "who was believed to be betting through bookmakers" and "placing calls from a pay phone near the clubhouse." Giles not only had the pay phone removed, but reported the player—whom he refused to name—to the commissioner's office. When asked why he didn't do the same in Rose's case, Giles admitted that "it was probably because I loved and respected him so much that I didn't really think it was my place." "Baseball has a very large security operation," he added. "And you know, Pete was our bread and butter."[89]

By 1983, Henry Fitzgibbon, the FBI agent who was conducting the investigation of Rose, had been hot on the first baseman's trail for three years.[90] Was Giles feeling the heat? To be sure, the Phillies president was just as sensitive to public relations as he was to baseball's policies against gambling. In fact, he was a member of Major League Baseball's rules committee as well as the National League's executive committee.[91] Under the circumstances, cutting Rose loose might have been the safest, though not the most lucrative, thing to do. Whatever the reason, Giles gave Rose his outright release on October 19.

While Rose accepted the decision with his characteristic homespun philosophy, he made it clear that he intended to play elsewhere on an everyday basis. "If it's the best thing for me, then I'll hit the road," said the baseball legend. "I don't like to play part-time. I've been an everyday player for so many years it's hard for me to play three days a week. I'm sure there are some teams out there who want me."[92] Rose, just 201 hits shy of breaking Ty Cobb's all-time hits record of 4,191, could not shatter the record as a part-time player. He needed to be in the lineup everyday to have any consistency at the plate. As a result, the Phillies were no longer an option, but the Montreal Expos quickly signed Rose, agreeing to make him a regular.

Perhaps the most fitting epitaph to the Rose era in Philadelphia came from Mike Schmidt, who said, "The Phillies had gone a long, long time without being in a World Series, until Pete Rose arrived. Pete's been in two of them here. He's also been a great friend of mine. I've accomplished a lot during his time here and I think a great deal of that success has to do with him." While the third baseman hated to see his best friend go, he realized that "time marches on. So do careers as well as life itself and you can't ignore that. I'll be in the same boat some day. God willing, it will be four or five years down the road, but I'll be in the same boat, too."[93]

Now the weight of leadership rested squarely on Schmidt's shoulders, whether he wanted it or not.

CHAPTER 14

ORGANIZATION ADRIFT

ETWEEN 1984 AND 1989 the Phillies' fortunes changed dramatically. The front office, operating through an amorphous chain of command, made poor decisions and bad trades that would have serious implications for the long-term future. Paul Owens, whose experience and vision were most responsible for building a world championship baseball organization, was eased out of the decision-making process as the Giles regime struggled to rebuild its "Team of the Eighties."

Shortly after the completion of the '83 season, Owens announced that he was relinquishing the general manager's position to remain as field manager in 1984.[1] While he would retain coaches Dave Bristol, Claude Osteen, Deron Johnson, and Mike Ryan, Bobby Wine would be replaced as bench coach by John Felske, who had managed at Triple-A Portland the year before.

Felske's promotion was recommended by farm director Jim Baumer. The two men had been good friends since the late 1970s when they were both in the Milwaukee Brewers organization. When the Phillies had a managerial opening at Reading in 1982, Baumer jumped at the chance to bring his friend into the Phillies organization. In 1983, Felske was promoted to Portland where he led the Beavers to the Pacific Coast League Championship and a berth in the Triple-A World Series.[2] Giles, who "thought highly" of Baumer, accepted his farm director's advice.[3] Felske was made bench coach and given the opportunity to acquaint himself with the National League.[4] He was being groomed as the next manager. Owens was reduced to a figurehead in the dugout. Most of the playing decisions would be made by Felske and the other coaches.[5]

The 1984 Phillies, who had been picked to repeat as National League champions, were supposed to be an even better club than the '83 pennant winners thanks to the additions of outfielder Glenn Wilson and promising rookies Jeff Stone and Juan Samuel. Wilson was only in his third season in the majors when he came to the Phillies in '84, but he had demonstrated great promise with the Detroit Tigers. In 1982 he hit .292 with 12 homers in just 84 games and displayed a rifle arm in the outfield, occasionally throwing out runners at first base. The following season Wilson was made a regular in the outfield and hit second in the Tigers' lineup. The youngster responded with a .268 average, 11 home runs, and 65 RBI. He was traded to the Phillies on March 24, 1984, along with catcher John Wockenfuss for pitcher Willie Hernandez and infielder Dave Bergman.[6] To make room in the outfield, the Phillies dealt Gary Matthews to the Chicago Cubs along with Bob Dernier for reliever Bill Campbell and outfielder-first baseman Mike Diaz.[7] Wilson would become the Phillies new left fielder.

Initially, the trades were harshly criticized because Hernandez went on to become the closer for the Tigers and played an instrumental role in their 1984 world championship. Matthews played a similar role, leading the Cubs to the division title the same season. Wilson, on the other hand, had a disappointing first season in Philadelphia, hitting just .240 with 6 home runs and 32 RBI. But the following year, he rebounded to hit .275 with 14 homers and 102 RBI and was shifted to right field where he led the league's outfielders in assists for the next three years. The congenial Texan also became a fan favorite because of his dry wit and exciting style of play. He was voted the Phillies' Most Valuable Player in 1985, the same year he made the All-Star Team.[8]

Jeff Stone never realized his seemingly limitless potential. When the Phillies called him up in 1984 he looked to be a speedy outfielder with a solid bat. Named the Eastern League's Player of the Year in 1983 when he played for Double-A Reading, Stone, in four and a half minor league seasons, compiled a .294 batting average and stole 372 bases.[9] He gave some indication that his abilities carried over to the big league level in '84 when he hit .362 and stole 27 bases in just 51 games with the Phils. During the next three seasons, though, Stone struggled, shifting between Triple-A Portland and Philadelphia.[10] His difficulty was due, in part, to his naïveté. Stone was a Missouri farm boy who never did much traveling before he reached the pros. As a result, he was very limited in his understanding of urban life as well as foreign culture. One winter, while playing ball in Venezuela, he asked a teammate if the moon he saw at night in the Caribbean was the same one they had in Missouri. After the season was over, he left his portable television set in Venezuela. When asked why he made the decision, Stone replied, "I'd have no use for it in the States 'cause they only speak Spanish on it." Often the object of clubhouse humor, he was an easy target. Once, when asked if he'd like a shrimp cocktail, Stone declined saying, "No thanks, I don't drink."[11] By 1988, the Phillies had given up on Stone and shipped him to Baltimore.

Juan Samuel was the Phillies' brightest star during the mid-to-late 1980s and Ruben Amaro's legacy to the club's Latin American experiment (Figure 29). Amaro's scouts discovered the young Dominican working in a clothing factory and playing fast-pitch softball in the town of San Pedro de Macoris, the same town that produced Joaquin Andujar of the Cardinals, and Pedro Guerrero of the Dodgers, among other big league stars.[12] Samuel hesitated to sign with the Phillies because he was responsible for supporting his family after the death of his father. But his mother gave him her blessing and he signed with the Phils as a second baseman in 1980.[13]

Samuel's first stop was Bend, Oregon, where he hit .282 with 17 homers, 44 RBI, and 26 stolen bases. The following year Samuel moved on to Single-A Spartanburg where he hit .248 and collected 11 home runs and 74 RBI as well as 53 stolen bases. He spent the '82 season at Peninsula, where he boosted his numbers, hitting .320 with 28 home runs, 94 RBI, and 64 stolen bases. The performance caught the attention of the front office, which moved him more rapidly through the system. As a result Samuel began the '83 season at Double-A Reading but was quickly promoted to Triple-A Portland and then to Philadelphia where he hit .277 in 18 games.[14] "I just wanted to be able to contribute in any way I could in 1983," he recalled in a recent interview. "I knew it wasn't my time yet. I was a rookie. My job was to learn and do anything I could to help out.

FIGURE 29. Second baseman Juan Samuel was the most talented Hispanic player signed by the Phillies before they abandoned their Latin American program in the mid-1980s. Courtesy of the National Baseball Hall of Fame Library, Cooperstown, New York.

Pete Rose, Joe Morgan, and Tony Perez were the guys who got the Phillies to the post-season that year. But I also knew they'd all be gone after the season was over and the Phillies would bring up a lot of young kids. I was part of their future."[15]

Amaro knew that Samuel had a bright future with the Phillies if he could readjust his throwing, which was submarine style. As a result, the ball would rise as he threw it to first base, often resulting in wild throws. "[Roving infield instructor] Larry Rojas worked with Sammy for four years in the minors on his throwing," said Amaro. "He taught him how to throw the ball overhand. Then, the next thing you know, Sammy's promoted to the Phillies in 1983 and the first thing that [shortstop] Ivan DeJesus tells him is to go back to his old way of throwing. I was furious when I found out. It set him back quit a bit."[16] Predictably, Samuel committed 9 errors in the 18 games he played in 1983 and 33 the next year when he became the Phillies' regular second baseman. Still, 1984 was his breakout year. He hit .272 with 15 home runs and 69 RBI and set a major league record for rookies with 72 stolen bases.[17]

Felipe Alou, who coached Samuel on the Escogido ball club that winter, said that the Phillies second baseman was the "most popular player in the Dominican Republic." "Juan plays all out," said Alou, who later managed the Montreal Expos and San Francisco Giants. "He takes the extra base, makes the head-first slide, and does it down here in front of the local fans. He's not down here to take it easy, which many Dominican players do after they play all summer in the States. The fans here appreciate that and idolize him for it."[18]

Through 1987, Samuel's star continued to rise. Although he struggled with his defense, his offensive production was remarkable. Between 1984 and 1987, Samuel averaged 102 runs scored, 175 hits, 35 doubles, 15 triples, 19 home runs, 80 RBI, and 51 stolen bases a season as a leadoff hitter. He was the first player in major league history to reach double figures in doubles, triples, home runs, and stolen bases in each of his first four seasons in the majors and he accomplished that extraordinary feat before the age of 28.[19] Samuel looked to be on his way to the Hall of Fame. But the Phillies didn't have the pitching to reach the playoffs. The 1984 season reflected that frustrating reality.

From late May to late August, the Phillies contended for first place. Al Holland's relief pitching and Schmidt's bat kept them in the race. By early September, Holland was exhausted. Although he posted 29 saves for the season, he tailed off dramatically down the stretch, blowing 11 leads or ties in the final six weeks. With Hernandez gone, the Phillies had to rely on the less capable relief pitching of Bill Campbell, Larry Andersen, and Kevin Gross. The starting pitching had also faded. Carlton, who posted a 13-7 record, had his last effective year. John Denny, the '83 Cy Young Award winner, was injured most of the season and slumped to 7-7. Jerry Koosman, obtained from the Chicago White Sox early in the season, proved to be the club's most winning pitcher with a 14-15 record. After losing twelve of their last fourteen games, the Phils finished a disappointing fourth.[20] "We had a lot of young guys who tried to do too much," said Holland. "While a veteran team can deal with the adversity that comes with a 162-game season, younger guys panic. They're not as confident when they're losing. Things started to fall apart in September when the race was tighter. The pitching didn't do as well as we expected. We didn't execute the plays as sharply as we had the previous year with veterans like Rose and Morgan in the lineup. Every phase of our game dropped because of the lack of experience."[21]

At the end of the season, Giles waged a personal battle between his conscience and his budget. His conscience told him that he owed Owens another shot at managing after he had captured a pennant for the organization in '83. But his budget indicated that the team had lost favor with the fans. Home attendance had dropped and he needed to draw two million to break even in 1985. Eventually, Giles yielded to financial considerations and eased the Pope out as field manager by offering him a lucrative five-year contract as his "assistant."[22] Felske would become the Phillies' new manager, the third in as many years in Giles's brief tenure as president.[23]

Now the decision-making fell to a small group of front-office personnel called the "Gang of Six," composed of Giles, Owens, farm director Jim Baumer, and special assistants Hugh Alexander and Ray Shore. The "sixth" member of the group was supposedly a bottle of Jack Daniels, the group's preferred beverage and one, apparently, that often swayed their better judgment when making transactions.[24] Over the next four years, the "Gang" presided over the decline of what was once a first-rate baseball organization. Though Owens was still a highly visible member of the front office, he was muted by the other members and Giles exercised veto power over all acquisitions. Despite the considerable years of baseball experience among the group's members, it was almost comical to watch them operate at the winter meetings. "Some teams make trades only as a last resort while others are more willing but try to hide their intentions," explained beat writer Peter Pascarelli of the *Philadelphia Inquirer*. "Then there are the Phillies who unleash their front office point men like so many sharks in a feeding frenzy. They make no effort to hide whom they're talking to and what they're looking for, talking loudly about their intentions with an almost hyperactive openness and flair."[25]

The Gang's foremost intention between 1985 and 1989 was to find pitching at a cost-effective price. Al Holland wasn't in their plans since he was on the verge of being a "ten-and-five" player. Predictably, he was looking for a long-term contract with a substantial raise. When he approached Giles with the request at the end of the '84 season, the Phillies president told him, "Sorry, that's not the way things are being done these days."[26] Shortly after, Holland was traded to the

Pirates for pitcher Kent Tekulve, who was in a similar contractual dispute with Pittsburgh.[27] Later that season, the Gang of Six would trade catcher Bo Diaz to the Reds for pitcher Fred Toliver. John Denny, whose best days were behind him was also dealt to Cincinnati for outfielder Gary Redus and pitcher Tom Hume.[28] While Tekulve gave the Phillies some stability in the bullpen for two years, Toliver (1-7, 4.67 ERA, 1 SV, in 26 games over three seasons) and Hume (5-5, 3.98 ERA, 4 SV, in 86 games over two seasons) became part of a long list of forgettable acquisitions the Gang of Six made in the mid-to-late 1980s.[29] More frustrating was the club's inability to develop the pitchers in its own farm system.

The Phillies minor leagues had not yielded an All-Star caliber pitcher since Chris Short in 1966 or a bona fide ace since Robin Roberts in 1948. Although the failure dates to the Carpenters' ownership of the club, the Gang of Six not only failed to recognize the potential of those young pitchers in their system, they also traded away some remarkable talent. Mike Jackson, for example, compiled a 3-10 record with one save and a 4.11 ERA in the 64 appearances he made during his two-year career with the Phillies. He was traded along with Glenn Wilson in December 1987 for outfielder Phil Bradley, another forgettable player. Jackson would go on to become a closer for several pennant-contenders, including the 1997 American League champion Cleveland Indians.[30] Similarly, Dave Stewart appeared in only 12 games for the Phillies in 1985-86 with a 0-0 record and a 6.48 ERA. Released by the Phils after the '86 season, he would go on to become the ace of the Oakland A's, perennial contenders who captured a world championship in 1989. He would join the Toronto Blue Jays in 1993 and help that club to another world championship.[31]

Not surprisingly, the Gang of Six, in general, and Giles, in particular, were excoriated in the local press for many of their trades. Perhaps the harshest critic was Bill Conlin of the *Philadelphia Daily News*, who considers Giles an "elitist at heart," someone who "never understood what drove Phillies fans." "The fans in this city have an insane loyalty to the team," explained the sportswriter. "But that loyalty is mitigated by a sense of frustrated entitlement. They've waited and waited for years to have a world champion and only once, in 1980, did the Phillies come through for them. As a result, Phillies fans feel entitled to boo, to be critical of management on sports-talk radio. And Giles never understood that because he surrounds himself with other country clubbers who tell him what a great job he's doing. The fact is, Giles can't take criticism. When I began attacking his farm system, he told the *Daily News* that I was full of shit and that his farm system was ranked as one of the best in baseball. So the *Daily News* assigned four other writers to investigate the Phillies' minor leagues and they found out that I hadn't been critical enough."[32]

Giles, however, insists that he's always been sensitive to the local fan base. "I'm probably too much of a fan myself," he said in a recent interview. "People

know that I'm passionate and that I live and die with the team just as any dedicated fan does. I also think the fans liked me when I was president of the club.
True, some of the local sportswriters and sports-talk radio criticized the things I
did, but that's part of the game. Besides, I really believe those people are a small
minority of our fan base."[33]

To be sure, Bill Giles was not part of the blue-collar culture of his team's fan
base. As president and part-owner of the Phillies, Giles's income bracket distanced him from the majority of fans, making it impossible for him to relate to
them. Conlin's assertion that Giles "surrounded himself with other country clubbers who told him what a great job he was doing" has much validity. The Phillies
have always been an "old buddy" organization with a fierce loyalty among the
members of the front office. It began with the Carpenters, heirs of the DuPont
fortune, who cultivated strong ties to the powerbrokers of both Philadelphia and
Wilmington, Delaware. Members of the front office attended and later sent their
sons to private schools like Tower Hill, Penn Charter, and the Episcopal Acad-
emy before matriculating to the Ivy League, usually the University of Pennsylvania. There they learned the financial realities of running a corporation, and
later eagerly applied the lessons to their boyhood passion of baseball. They also
brought with them a fraternity-like culture and a network that included some of
the city's most influential politicians, successful bankers, and prominent busi-
nessmen. The front office operated on certain rules: never allow the press to
control the team's decision-making; build a winning team, but not at a significant financial loss; never admit a mistake in public; and, above all, cover for the
other members when mistakes are made.

While such a fraternity-like culture is patronizing, if not arrogant, Ruly Carpenter had the remarkable ability to make it tolerable, even attractive, to the players and fans. He was approachable, mixing with the team's employees whether
they were groundskeepers or the treasurer. He made them feel like they mattered, like they were an indispensable part of the organization, like "family."
Giles, on the other hand, was an "outsider" when he joined the Phillies in 1970.
He worked hard to promote and market the team and was instrumental in turning the organization into one of the major league's most lucrative franchises. He
also ingratiated himself with the Carpenter family and was eventually made an
"insider," the preferred successor to their regime.

By 1982, after he had purchased the team along with other well-heeled investors, Giles was at the head of the fraternity. He didn't have to answer to anyone
because the contractual agreement between him and the other owners stipulated
that he had complete authority for the day-to-day operation of the club and, hence,
its success on the playing field. The only difference between Giles's regime and
Carpenter's was that few members of the front office were made accountable for
their actions, or more accurately, their inaction. As a result, the Latin American

market was abandoned, scouts were not replaced when they left the organization, poor decisions were routinely made in the acquisition of players and in the June amateur draft, and the farm system, once the crown jewel of the organization, was routinely ranked near the bottom by publications like *Baseball America*.[34]

With a majority of absentee owners, the front office became complacent, resting on the laurels of the Carpenter regime. Certain individuals, like Hugh Alexander and Ray Shore, were allowed to operate with great independence, often to the detriment of the club. Others, like Paul Owens, who had experienced success and had a clear vision for the future, were stifled. The complacency filtered down to the players and, as a result, the organization languished. "Complacency" in any business is a death knell and in baseball the consequences cannot be hidden as easily from the public. The Phillies no longer "expected" to win when they took the field, they "hoped" they could win with as little effort as possible. In the process, the team and its owners held Philadelphia's die-hard baseball fans "hostage" to their mediocrity.

As the 1980s unfolded, the fans became increasingly bitter, feeling as if they no longer mattered. Yet, they still flocked to the Vet, driven by an insane loyalty to the team. "Philly fans were great," insisted John Russell, who played for the club during its tailspin into mediocrity. "I didn't understand them at first, but I learned pretty quickly that they were die-hard. For example, it was okay for them to boo you, but let a Mets fan try it and they'd be all over him. I'll be the first to say that it gets irritating when you're being screamed at. But I came to realize that it wasn't personal. You'd go out to eat at a restaurant and the same fan that booed you was the same one who'd buy you dinner. Besides, they pay their money to go to the game. They deserve to boo you if you strike out with the bases loaded."[35]

Whatever his shortcomings with the faithful, Bill Giles always demonstrated a strong sensitivity for their heroes. Tug McGraw's retirement, in 1984, serves as a fine example. McGraw was perhaps the most popular Phillie during the team's glory years and one of the pioneers of relief pitching.[36] He established a permanent residence for his family in suburban Media and had several business interests in the city, including a high visibility commercial endorsement for First Pennsylvania Bank. When Giles was encouraged by his advisers to give Tug his release in 1983, he refused to do so. The following spring McGraw pitched well enough to make the team, but he missed several weeks at the end of the season with shoulder problems. When the aging reliever approached Giles about a new contract for the '85 season, the Phillies president delayed his decision, hoping that McGraw would be picked up by another team in the reentry draft. But the only club to express any interest was Oakland. Again, Giles was torn. He knew that McGraw's pitching days were over, but he had a soft spot for the comedic reliever and wanted to keep him in the organization in some capacity.

On January 17, 1985, Giles met with McGraw and explained his dilemma. "I've sort of known that since last fall," said Tug. "But I just can't make that decision yet. I still think I can pitch."

It was a difficult conversation for the Phillies president, who was known to get teary-eyed on such occasions. "Don't apologize," said Giles, struggling to contain his emotions. "I understand. That's the way baseball is. You have to move ahead with things. But if I can keep you in the organization in some other way, please let me know."

McGraw thanked Giles, promising that if he couldn't "hook on with another club," they would "talk about some specific possibilities."[37]

On Valentine's Day, 1985, Tug held a press conference at Veterans Stadium to announce his retirement from baseball. There were no tears or regrets. "The Phillies are in a rebuilding movement, and it's time for me to move ahead with my life," said the veteran reliever. "They have some pretty young pitchers coming up and I'm already in my early forties. Besides, the hitters are telling me it's time to retire," he quipped, adding some humor to a somber occasion.

When asked for clarification, Tug explained the challenges he faced during the 1984 season: "I couldn't recover as quickly as I used to. If I pitched two or three innings one night and I was asked to pitch again the next night, I might have been able to give them an inning but no more than that. Afterwards I'd need a couple days off for my body to recover. I looked at the alternatives and those were pitching earlier in the game or being a mop up man and I didn't want to do either of those things. So I don't see any point in continuing."

At the same time, McGraw admitted that he "really didn't want to leave Philadelphia." "I'll never forget my years here. Obviously being part of the first championship club will always be something special and the parade was awesome. I won't forget the headache I had following our celebration, either." After thanking the Phillies organization, in general, and Bill Giles, in particular, McGraw took his leave. He would take his 96 victories, 180 saves, and career ERA of 3.14 with him, going down in history as one of the greatest relief pitchers in the game.[38]

Tug, over the next twenty years, would serve as a spokesperson for a variety of local businesses and community organizations, a features reporter for WPVI-TV in Philadelphia, the vice president of Major League Baseball's Alumni Association, a pitching instructor at the Phillies spring training camp.

Giles could also spend heavily on the free agent market when he believed a particular player could put the Phillies in the postseason. In 1987, he paid $1.6 million to bring All-Star catcher Lance Parrish to Philadelphia at the expense of alienating himself from the other owners.[39] It was a bold move at the time because the owners adamantly refused to sign free agents and would eventually be found guilty of collusion.[40] But Giles believed that Parrish was the missing piece in his team's quest to make it into the postseason. Parrish, who played for the 1984 world champion Detroit Tigers, was one of the best power-hitting catchers in baseball between 1982 and 1985. During that four-year span, he hit .266 and averaged 30 home runs and 100 RBI a season. He was also a four-time All-Star and three-time Gold Glove Award recipient who boasted a .992 fielding percentage. While Parrish's numbers declined in 1986 due to back problems, he was still able to hit .257 with 22 home runs and 62 RBI in the 91 games he played that season.[41] With Darren Daulton, the Phils' young prospect still a year or two away from taking over as the team's regular catcher, the Parrish acquisition looked like the perfect fit. After passing a medical exam, the Phillies acquired the Detroit slugger and made him their cleanup hitter in a lineup that featured Mike Schmidt, Von Hayes, Juan Samuel, Glenn Wilson, and Mike Easler.

Finally, the Giles regime has donated more money and time to the larger Philadelphia community than any other owner in the club's history. Recognizing the important relationship between the Phillies and the community, the Phillies president, in 1982, established a Community Relations Department in order to reach out to the many charities in the tristate area. The new department ushered in a variety of programs to support such concerns as cystic fibrosis, ALS, or Lou Gehrig's disease, Children's Hospital, Handicapped Boy Scouts, Gaudenzia Drug and Alcohol Rehabilitation House, the Philadelphia Child Guidance Clinic, and the No Greater Love organization, which benefits the children of American soldiers killed while serving their country. In the first year of operation, the Phillies raised over $50,000.[42] That amount grew to more than $250,000 in 1985 and continued to increase through the 1989 season.[43] Thus, while poor decision-making might have haunted Giles and the Gang of Six, the Phillies president did demonstrate a well-intentioned commitment to the fans and the Delaware Valley region. Still, Giles's teams struggled to capture another pennant throughout the 1980s.

During John Felske's three-year tenure as manager, 1985 to 1987, the Phillies finished fifth, a distant second, and fourth. Felske had lost touch with the players and was accused of being insensitive to the club's black players. The Phillies' on-field performance reflected their laid-back manager's approach. Lacking in the fundamentals, the team relied on their power hitters to secure a lead and then hoped the bullpen could protect it for the balance of the game, but the strategy didn't work. With the Phils buried in fifth place in June of 1987, Felske was replaced by Lee Elia.[44]

Elia, a native Philadelphian, had been a player and long-time coach with the Phillies before going to Chicago with Dallas Green in 1982. There, he coached and briefly managed the Cubs. When he returned to the Phillies as manager, Elia brought enthusiasm and an emphasis on fundamental baseball—tight defense, sharp execution, consistent run production, and aggressive base running—all the things that had constituted the so-called "Phillies Way" that had been taught in the organization's minor leagues during the 1970s.[45] But he, too, finished a discouraging sixth, 35½ games behind the division-clinching New York Mets in 1988 and was dismissed at the end of the season.[46]

Amid the plethora of changes, bad decisions, and mismanagement that were taking place in the Phillies organization, there was a desperate need for leadership among the players, especially after Pete Rose departed. It would have been natural for the younger players to look for leadership among the members of the 1980 world champions. But as the decade unfolded, those veterans were traded, released, or retired. Among the last to go were Garry Maddox, Steve Carlton, and Mike Schmidt. While none of the three veterans could provide the kind of assertive, vocal leadership of Rose, they all enjoyed reputations as mentors who provided leadership by example. But Maddox retired in the spring of 1986. Constant pounding on the artificial turf had taken its toll on his back and legs. He tried to return from back surgery after the '84 season. Appearing in 105 games during the '85 campaign, the Secretary of Defense hit just .239 with 4 home runs and 23 RBI. When his back continued to plague him the following season, Maddox retired.[47] Carlton also left the Phillies in 1986, though it was not his decision.

Lefty posted a 1-8 record in 1985, a season in which most of his time was spent on the disabled list with a rotator cuff injury. In '86 he lost two of his first four starts and failed to last beyond the fifth inning in any of his next four assignments. His control was gone and his slider had lost its bite. Giles, struggling with his own sense of loyalty, tried to convince his one-time ace to go back on the disabled list, but he refused. By mid-June, the future Hall of Famer was struggling with a 5.88 ERA and had surrendered over 96 hits. When Giles, on June 21, suggested that he retire, Carlton insisted that he could "still pitch" and "still win," and requested that he be given "until the All-Star break to straighten things out." Instead, Giles gave him one more start.[48] That night he lost a 4-0 lead against the Cardinals, surrendering 6 runs on 6 hits and 6 walks in just 5 innings. The Phillies president knew it was time to release Lefty, but it took him three full days to muster the courage to do it.[49]

On June 25, Giles called a press conference to announce that "Steve Carlton, the greatest left-handed pitcher in Phillies history and one of the greatest pitchers of all-time, will no longer be pitching in a Phillies' uniform." "Watching him pitch on Saturday night I just couldn't take any more," Giles admitted, his voice breaking repeatedly. "He pitched so many great games for the Phillies, it hurt me too much to watch him."[50]

The following night, before the Phils played the St. Louis Cardinals at the Vet, highlights of Carlton's remarkable fourteen-year career in red pinstripes beamed across the large scoreboard in right center field. Giles, watching from his 400-level executive suite, wept convulsively for ten minutes.[51]

"It was tougher on Bill than it was on me," said Carlton of his release from the Phillies after he finally retired in 1989. "He took it pretty hard. To me, it was just a matter of moving on. I still wanted to pitch. It was just a matter of finding someone that wanted me."[52] Carlton said that his decision to continue pitching was also based on a desire to break Warren Spahn's record of most career victories by a left-hander. As a result, Lefty struggled to hang on in the big leagues over the next two years with several teams, including the San Francisco Giants, Chicago White Sox, Cleveland Indians, and Minnesota Twins.[53] Predictably, "quitting" was not a part of Carlton's mentality. He had spent most of his professional career tuning out the negative, focusing on the positive, and willing himself to win. He had come back from adversity in the past, he *knew* he could do it again, even at the age of forty-one. Sadly, he was wrong.[54]

Essentially, the mantle of leadership fell to Mike Schmidt, who, by 1987, was nearing the end of his Hall of Fame career. He had already secured a reputation as the best third baseman in the history of the game and had the statistics to prove it. Schmidt was a three-time Most Valuable Player (1980, '81, and '86) and the MVP of the 1980 World Series. He had led the National League in home runs eight times, and in RBI four times. He was a ten-time Gold Glove Award winner and had been elected to ten All-Star squads. Nor had those achievements come easily. Over the years, Schmidt developed an impressive work ethic. Early in his career, he disciplined himself to hit the breaking ball and to cut down on his strikeouts. Later, in his early thirties, he reworked his batting style so he could hit for average as well as power. His experience would benefit the Phillies' other young power hitters he mentored during the twilight of his career.

Perhaps Schmidt's greatest achievement, however, was winning over the fans, who voted him the "Greatest Phillies Player of All-Time" in 1983. He was one of baseball's most admired role models. An active fund-raiser for the United Way, the Philadelphia Child Guidance Clinic, and the Christian Children's Fund, the Phillies slugger took his responsibility to youngsters very seriously, setting a refreshing example for other athletes during an era when many superstars reveled in the role of "antihero."[55] But where Schmidt succeeded with the fans was by learning how to deal with their fickle treatment and by showing more emotion on the playing field. Schmidt's headfirst leap onto a pile of teammates after the final out of the 1980 World Series, for example, is indelibly etched in the minds of many Philadelphians and is still one of the most treasured images in the city's sports history. After hitting his 500th career home run on April 18, 1987, against the Pirates at Pittsburgh's Three Rivers Stadium, Schmidt, once again, let down his guard. As the ball cleared the fence, Michael Jack broke out a huge smile, clapped his hands together, and, imitating a railroad engine, chugged his way to first base.[56] Other, less dramatic moments occurred as well. In one game, Schmidt, in pursuit of a foul pop-up down the left-field line, reached into a box seat to make a catch. Not only did he snag the ball, but also a fan's hat in the process.

The Phillies third baseman ceremoniously carried his glove—with the ball and the fan's hat—over to the umpire who proceeded to call the batter out.[57]

Schmidt also learned to appreciate the humorous side of all the criticism. On one occasion, when he was struggling through an especially bad slump, a Boo Bird regular jeered him relentlessly. Every time the Phillies slugger stepped up to the plate, the irascible fan would holler, "Hey, Schmidt, you better earn that million dollars!" Instead of dwelling on the negative, Schmidt admitted that he was actually "tempted to step out of the batter's box, walk over to the fence, and say to him, very softly, 'That's two million.'"[58]

What's more, Schmidt learned to laugh at himself once in a while. Perhaps the most memorable incident came in 1985 when he briefly switched positions to first base. Known as the "wig and sunglasses prank," it began when Schmidt gave an interview to Peter Hadekel of the *Montreal Gazette* in mid-April. Frustrated by a particularly abusive reception from the fans a few nights before, Schmidt described the hometown faithful as "beyond help" and "a mob scene." "Whatever I've got in my career now, I would have had a great deal more if I'd played in Los Angeles or Chicago," he said. "You name a town—a place where the fans were just grateful to have me around."[59]

As usual, the Phillies third baseman was direct. His words were tinged with frustration, disappointment, and bitterness. It was also a mistake to voice them in a public arena. Schmidt only served to alienate himself from the fans and the press, which was more than willing to capitalize on his mistake.

Two months later, on June 29, the interview was published in the *Gazette*. The next day, Schmidt's remarks made headlines in Philadelphia. After confirming that he did, in fact, give the interview, the Phillies star admitted that he "regretted saying what I said" and clarified his position. He pointed out that the interview had been done much earlier in the season, when the Phillies were "suffering through a miserable stretch" and the fans "were not sure which way to go." He then softened many of his criticisms. "I know that I'm a little too sensitive," he admitted. "But I do get disappointed with the behavior of Phillies fans when my performance is subpar. How soon they forget some of the good things that have happened. It's easy to play when you're in first place and it's easy to be a fan when your team is winning every day. But every team and every player is going to have their peaks and valleys. Philadelphia is the toughest town I've been around when you're in a valley." Offering a truce, Schmidt added that he "hoped the fans don't feel that I'm proud of my .237 batting average. I feel worse about my performance this season than any of the fans. But I can't quit. I've got to keep going out there every day to get out of the slump."[60]

Despite his controversial remarks, Schmidt dismissed the suggestion that he sounded as if he wanted to be traded. "I never want to be traded," he insisted. "I love my home, my kids are in school and they love the Philadelphia area. I also have friends in town as well as business interests. Our roots are here."[61]

When the Phillies returned home from Montreal on July 1, Schmidt braced himself for the ultimate Boo Bird reception. During the introductions preceding the Phils' game with the Cubs, the fans prepared to give him a greeting he would never forget. The hostility against the Phillies superstar was so thick you could feel it in the air. Then, suddenly, a bewigged figure wearing a pair of dark sunglasses trotted out onto the field to take his position at first base. The physique belonged to Mike Schmidt, so did the uniform number. But nobody could make out the face, which was hidden under a mass of dark brown dreadlocks. For a split second, the fans didn't know what to do. Was it actually Schmidt incognito? Had "Mr. Cool" lost his mind, or had he finally learned not to take himself so seriously?

Regardless of fan opinion, Schmidt was delivering a psychological masterstroke. He had defused a potentially embarrassing situation by borrowing the props from clubhouse clown and teammate Larry Andersen. His self-deprecating sense of humor had saved the day. After a few seconds of uncertainty, the fans took to their feet, responding with a boisterous round of applause.[62] No self-respecting Boo Bird, even in his wildest of dreams, could have predicted that Schmidt would get himself a standing ovation that day. More important, the incident marked the beginning of a new, more appreciative relationship between the Phillies slugger and the fans. Of course, they would continue to boo him in the future, but they did it with a certain degree of respect.

At the same time, Schmidt's feats were so legendary and his demeanor so private that it was difficult for many teammates to approach him. He was a devout family man and a self-proclaimed Christian athlete whose introspective nature gave the impression that he considered himself "better" than others, which wasn't the case. "Mike is hard to get to know because he's such a private person," said teammate Shane Rawley. "He likes being 'one of the guys,' but it's difficult for him to really let loose because of who he is. That may sound funny, but he can be very serious at times, maybe too serious. Then again, that seriousness is what makes him stand above the other players."[63] Manager John Felske was more direct. "The Phillies will never have a true leader until Mike Schmidt retires," he said shortly after being fired. "The young players are intimidated by him and they try too hard to emulate him."[64] After the '87 season, when the slugger signed a new, two-year contract worth $4.5 million, Phillies president Bill Giles insisted that Schmidt was "intelligent enough to be a leader if he wasn't so moody."[65] Instead of taking exception to all the criticism, Michael Jack agreed with it. "Moody's probably not that far off in terms of describing me," he admitted. "However, I think we all have that label at times. There's not a player around who has the ideal mood. Although I'm totally satisfied with myself in terms of my behind-the-scenes leadership, my approach to the game, my leading by example, I guess

I have to pat a few more butts and do a little more screaming in the clubhouse. I know that most of the young players on the team are a little scared of me. I've done my best to try to ease the pressure of that situation. I've been out to dinner with every kid on the team. Still, it's human nature. I mean, ten years ago, if I were playing with Hank Aaron, I'd be thinking, 'I've got to watch what I do, what I say,' So, maybe the best thing for me to do is let leadership happen more naturally."[66]

To be sure, Schmidt's aloofness was one of the major obstacles preventing him from becoming a more effective team leader than he might have been in his final years with the Phillies; the other was his unchecked candor with the press. "My overriding goal is to do whatever it takes to get the Phillies organization back on top," he told Stan Hochman of the *Philadelphia Daily News* in the spring of 1987. "We're not polished anymore. The minor league system is depleted. The front office has little to be desired in terms of positions that are held. And the jobs they're doing . . . the fields are the worst in the league. The dugouts are filthy. The clubhouse is dirty. The pride factor is not what it used to be. We used to have the best field, now it's the worst. We used to have the cleanest dugouts, now they're the dirtiest. We used to have the best minor league system, now it's one of the worst."[67] Tactfulness was never one of Schmidt's strengths. When he arrived in the clubhouse the following night, he found green ferns hanging from his locker and candles surrounding his folding chair. Workers were scrubbing the runway from the clubhouse to the dugout in a mock effort to eliminate the smell of "cat piss" that Schmidt had identified.[68]

"Mike wasn't a jerk," insisted Hochman in an effort to explain the enigmatic Phillies star. "He was just unsophisticated, unworldly, and he sure didn't understand the newspaper business. He didn't understand that he could say something to the writers here in Philadelphia or in Montreal and it would appear in papers across the country the next morning."[69] But Peter Pascarelli, who covered Schmidt's career for the *Philadelphia Inquirer*, believes that Schmidt's candor with and accessibility to the press was one of his greatest gifts. "Few players could more intelligently analyze the game than Schmidt," he said. "And even when he did it condescendingly, he was as accessible as any superstar. That's why I always thought the fans' preoccupation with his inability to lead was so much nonsense. Schmidt's performance and technical baseball experience did the leading."[70]

Whether or not he was the acknowledged leader, Schmidt was the most highly visible player on a team that was in sharp decline. His best seasons were behind him, as was the case, it seemed, for the Phillies. In '87 Schmidt enjoyed his last productive year, hitting .293 with 35 home runs and 113 RBI, but the team finished in fourth place. Von Hayes (.277, 21 HR, 84 RBI), Glenn Wilson (.264, 14 HR, 54 RBI), and Lance Parrish (.245, 17 HR, 67 RBI) did not produce the numbers or power hitting they were expected to deliver. Nor was the pitching very solid. Aside from reliever Steve Bedrosian (5-3, 2.83 ERA, 40 SV), who won the

Cy Young Award, the most consistent hurler was Shane Rawley (17-11, 123 K, 4.38 ERA). Bruce Ruffin (11-14, 93 K, 4.35 ERA), who took Steve Carlton's place in the rotation the previous season, put up some respectable numbers, but would never again win more than six games in a season with the Phils and was traded four years later.[71]

In 1988 the Phillies dropped to sixth place. The team played poorly from the start of the season and Schmidt's performance was partly to blame. He was hitting only .214 by the beginning of June with just 5 homers and 23 RBI. His play at third was just as dismal, having committed ten errors.[72] Predictably, the press began its Schmidt bashing. "If art is something that continuously gives you back more than you bring to it, then Mike Schmidt is no masterpiece," wrote Bruce Buschel of *Philly Sports*. "He demands too much. He is enervating. If baseball is where you go for simplicity, for good and bad, Schmidt dishes out ambiguity. He can win and lose at the same time. He can have the confidence to be Mike Schmidt and still be uncertain of his gifts. Somehow, this immortal player never fails to remind us of our own mortality. Athletes are not supposed to be wracked with the same doubts and fears as the rest of us; most need to block them out to perform. Schmidt seems to need them. He emanates neuroses. He blames the fans; he thanks the fans. They helped him; they hurt him. Sometimes, he appears so conflicted that he's paralyzed by crossed emotions. Or he looks bored. Bored!"[73]

In the midst of all the criticism came the announcement that Bill Giles hired Lee Thomas, director of player development for the St. Louis Cardinals, as the Phillies new general manager; a position Schmidt hoped to secure after his retirement. Giles's decision was a tacit admission that he and the Gang of Six had failed to build their own dynasty, the so-called "Team of the Eighties." Thomas made immediate changes. Before the end of the '88 season, he fired Lee Elia and named Cardinal coach Nick Leyva manager. Farm director Jim Baumer was also gone, replaced by Lance Nichols, who had served in a similar capacity in St. Louis. Thomas also traded unproductive veterans like Lance Parrish for younger prospects and began revamping the minor league and scouting systems.[74]

"The team was being rebuilt with people from the Cardinals organization," recalls veteran reserve catcher John Russell, who knew his days as a Phillie were numbered. "When they brought in Tom Nieto, who had been a backup in St. Louis, I saw the writing on the wall. I felt it was time to move on and asked to be traded. Don't get me wrong, I would love to have stayed with the Phillies, but at that point it wouldn't have been a good fit."[75] Russell was traded to the Atlanta Braves where he continued his career as a backup catcher.

No one was safe, not even the established stars like Juan Samuel, who was asked to change positions from second base to center field to make room for another former Cardinal, Tommy Herr. "I thought I had a choice in the matter," said Samuel in a recent interview. "But I really didn't. Thomas wanted to attract more fans with Herr, who was a local guy, and he could only play second base. I was told that I could make an easy adjustment to the outfield because of my speed. But I was already one of a handful of good second basemen in the National League, whereas I would be one of many outfielders in the Phillies organization. After I agreed to make the move I became expendable. I really didn't want to leave Philly. I was involved in the community and I had just bought a house in Cherry Hill, New Jersey. But the Phillies had other plans that didn't include me."[76] Samuel, one of the most popular Phillies at the time, was traded to the New York Mets on June 15, 1989, for reserve outfielder Lenny Dykstra and reliever Roger McDowell. He played another decade with the Mets, Dodgers, Reds, Tigers, Royals and Blue Jays before retiring in 1998.[77]

Changes were made throughout the organization. "All of a sudden good people who had been with the organization for years were let go or retired," said Mark Carfagno, who worked on the grounds crew. "Everyone was looking over their shoulder, just waiting to be replaced by someone from the Cardinals organization. There was no more 'Phillies family,' and anyone who tried to portray it that way was full of bullshit."[78]

In a series of cost-cutting measures, Giles and Thomas dropped their Latin American scouts and limited the expense money of their North American scouts. In some cases, they eliminated part-timers altogether. Tony Lucadello, one of the organization's most successful and devoted scouts, took the measures personally. He relied heavily on two part-timers to cover his extensive territory, which included Ohio, Indiana, Illinois, and Michigan. When he was ordered by Thomas to let them go, he contemplated retirement and eventually became so depressed that he committed suicide.[79] By 1989, the Philadelphia Phillies had the lowest rated farm system in major league baseball thanks to Giles and the Gang of Six.[80]

If the Giles regime had kept many of the young players they drafted and/or traded for but later released, the 1989 team would have featured two Hall of Famers, three Cy Young Award winners, four Most Valuable Players, and an All-Star at every position:

POSITION PLAYERS

C – Darren Daulton, National League All-Star with Phillies, 1992-93, '95
1B – John Kruk, National League All-Star with Phillies, 1991-93
2B – Ryne Sandberg, 1984 National League MVP with Chicago Cubs (Hall of Famer)
SS – Julio Franco, American League All-Star with Texas Rangers, 1989-91
3B – Mike Schmidt, 1980, '81, and '86 National League MVP with Phillies (Hall of Famer)
RF – Von Hayes, National League All-Star with Phillies, 1989
CF – Juan Samuel, National League All-Star with Phillies, 1984, '87, '91
LF – George Bell, 1987 American League MVP with Toronto Blue Jays

PITCHERS

Mark Davis, 1989 National League Cy Young Award winner with San Diego
   Padres

Willie Hernandez, 1984 American League Cy Young Award winner and MVP
   with Detroit Tigers

Steve Bedrosian, 1987 National League Cy Young Award winner with Phillies

Dave Stewart, 1987 American League Cy Young Award candidate, 1989 All-
   Star with Oakland A's

Mike Jackson, 1998 American League MVP candidate with Cleveland Indians

Instead, the 1989 Phillies were among the most undistinguished teams in the club's inglorious history. Players came and went with such regularity that it was almost impossible for manager Nick Leyva to keep track of them. Thomas was constantly trading and selling players or recalling them from the minor leagues in a desperate effort to find a lineup that could do something besides lose.[81] Looming on the horizon was what to do about Mike Schmidt, the team's 39-year-old third baseman and the lone survivor of the 1980 World Championship club.

Schmidt missed the last six weeks of the 1988 season with a torn rotator cuff, finishing with a .249 average and only 12 home runs and 62 runs batted in. He would have to undergo an arthroscopic operation to repair the injury in the off-season. When the Phillies did not pick up the option on his contract—which would have paid him $2.25 million—Schmidt filed for free agency.[82] Several teams expressed an interest in him, including the New York Yankees, the Cincinnati Reds, and the Los Angeles Dodgers.[83] But the veteran third baseman wanted to finish his career in Philadelphia and so he continued to negotiate with Giles and Thomas. On December 7, Schmidt and the Phillies came to an agreement on a one-year contract that would guarantee him $500,000, with incentives that could add up to a potential package of $2.05 million.[84]

When Schmidt returned for the '89 season, manager Nick Leyva found himself in an unenviable position. He was a first-year manager trying to put a competitive club on the field. The logical position for a thirty-nine-year-old veteran would be first base, but the Phils had already made a commitment to Ricky Jordan, a prospect whose .308 average, 11 home runs and 43 RBI in just 69 games the previous year made him a good candidate to be the team's cleanup hitter of the future. Jordan's one weakness was his throwing arm and that meant he could play nowhere but first base.[85] Leyva also had three younger players, Chris James, Von Hayes, and Steve Jeltz, who could step in to play third base. Predictably, Thomas and Leyva scrutinized Schmidt's performance throughout spring training, and it wasn't an impressive one. He struggled both in the field and at the plate. Despite the fact that he had gone 1-for-18 and hadn't hit a single home run through the first half of the Grapefruit League schedule, management gave him the nod at third base.

"If this were a situation of two kids going for the same job, Chris James would have beat him out," admitted Thomas. "But that isn't the situation. A veteran player cannot be judged on spring training. From the beginning, I've operated on the assumption that if Mike couldn't do the job, he'd know that and come to us. Since he hasn't come to us, he obviously thinks he can still do it. If we go into the season and he shows us that he can't do the job, then we'll have some decisions to make."[86] Leyva echoed Thomas's sentiments. "Of course I had my doubts about Mike coming into the spring," he admitted. "But he's busted his tail and is determined to get himself back together again. He's going to hit fourth in our lineup and, offensively, if he can still do the job like I think he can, he's going to drive in a lot of runs to help our club."[87] Schmidt, who had grown tired of being scrutinized by the press and the brain trust, was comfortable with the strategy, promising that he'd "retire" if he couldn't achieve the "high standards" he'd always set for himself.[88] Schmidt kept his word.

After a solid April, in which he hit five home runs and batted in 18 runs, the veteran third baseman went into a month-long tailspin. His fielding had deteriorated. There was very little consistency in his performance at the plate. The team was languishing in last place. At the end of May, Schmidt was hitting just .203 with only one homer for the month. Finally, on Sunday, May 28, Michael Jack reached the decision to retire after the Phils' 8-5 loss to San Francisco, where his own error preceded a game winning grand slam by Giants first baseman Will Clark. It was the team's fifth straight loss—and their ninth in eleven games—on what proved to be a dismal trip to the West Coast.[89]

During a hastily arranged news conference the following day before the Phillies' game against the San Diego Padres, Schmidt made the announcement (Figure 30). Stating that he had always set high standards for himself as a player and that he believed he could "no longer perform up to those standards," he admitted, "I feel like I could ask the Phillies to make me a part-time player in order to hang around for a couple of years and add to my statistical totals. However, my respect for the game, my teammates, and the fans won't allow me to do that."

Schmidt paused to compose himself, then continued: "The Phillies are a first-class organization and have always supported me with loyalty and security that few players, if any, will ever know. For that, I will be forever thankful to the Philadelphia Phillies." Fighting back tears, he said, "You probably won't believe this by the way I look right now, but this is a joyous time for me. I've had a great career. My family and friends and I are very content and excited about my decision. It's the beginning of a new life focus."

Schmidt tried to collect himself again. "Some eighteen years ago, I left Dayton, Ohio, with two very bad knees and a dream to become a major league baseball player," he concluded, as he began to cry. "I thank God that the dream came true."[90]

Unable to compose himself any longer, Schmidt broke down, sobbing uncontrollably. Phillies president Bill Giles took over the microphone. "Thank you from the bottom of my heart, and for all the Phillies fans who have seen you play for over 16 years," he continued. "In my opinion, you're the greatest third baseman of all time. It's been a real honor and pleasure to have seen you play."

Giles was somber, but dignified in his remarks.

"I think all of us who have followed your career will be grateful not only for what you did on the field, but for the way you lived your life off the field," he added. "And I think that is just as important."[91]

During the next few years, Bill Giles showered Schmidt with praise, retired his uniform number 20, and sent him and his family on an all-expenses-paid trip around the world, among other lavish gifts. In fact, the Phillies president seemed to give the future Hall of Famer everything except the one thing he wanted most—a job with the organization. Although Schmidt repeatedly expressed an interest in managing the Phillies or taking a position in the front office, Giles never gave him the opportunity, insisting that "very few great players have been good management people" and that "Mike isn't always a good communicator and communication is a big part of this business."[92]

FIGURE 30. Mike Schmidt brushes away tears after announcing his retirement on May 29, 1989. Courtesy of the *Philadelphia Daily News*.

Instead, Schmidt moved his family to Jupiter, Florida, and began a new, less scrutinized life. "There's just no place for me in the Phillies organization," he said before leaving Philadelphia. "I understand that. I'll always feel I could have helped people in baseball after I finished playing. But if it didn't happen immediately after my retirement, it wasn't going to happen."[93]

Sadly, the Phillies, who became perennial losers, had distanced themselves from the greatest player in their history, and with him went the integrity of an organization that was once the best in all of baseball.

CONCLUSION

Between 1976 and 1983, the Philadelphia Phillies captured five division titles, two pennants, and a world championship. Even in 1981 and 1982, when they didn't win the National League's Eastern Division, the Phils were in the chase down the stretch. That success was due to Ruly Carpenter and Paul Owens's vision, more than any other factor. Their goal was to keep the homegrown nucleus of Schmidt, Bowa, Boone, and Luzinski together at all costs because they genuinely believed that those players had the talent to win a world championship.

Carpenter and Owens emphasized player development and scouting as the two biggest keys to success. Owens took the feedback of his most trusted scouts and worked the amateur draft with a talent that left his competitors awestruck. He also paid careful attention to major league players on opposing teams. As general manager he traveled with the team on the road, making mental notes of those opposing players who might contribute to his team's chemistry and, when the circumstances dictated it, trading for them. Owens was successful in both areas because he could read a player's soul as easily as he could identify his skills. He looked for those athletes who "expected" to win because they had the desire, drive, hunger, and passion for it. In so doing, he surrounded the homegrown nucleus with the kind of talent and clubhouse chemistry they would need to compete at the highest levels.

Just as important to the success of the organization were the lieutenants hired by Owens, specifically Dallas Green and Howie Bedell. Ultimately, they were responsible for carrying out the vision articulated by the Pope and teaching the "Phillies Way," which emphasized hustle, hard work, aggressive play, and the pride in performance that came with playing the game the "right" way. They were men who understood the chain of command, believed in the team concept—both in the front office and on the playing field—and made their scouts and coaches accountable for their actions.

Green was a younger clone of the Pope. He was an intense worker with a special skill for identifying future stars in the amateur draft. Hard-drinking, tough-minded, and ambitious to a fault, Green was also a taskmaster who watched his scouts with an eagle eye. He maintained the same approach as field manager between 1979 and 1981, making his players accountable to the team concept, regardless of whether they were a rookie or a future Hall of Famer. He did it by benching seasoned veterans and playing rookies, criticizing his complacent stars in the press, and daring to fight anyone who challenged him. It wasn't a happy marriage for many of the players who had been with the team during the hard-luck playoff losses of 1976, '77, and '78, but they soon realized it was their last chance for a world championship, and it worked.

Bedell, who directed the minor league field operations and later became farm director, was a more low-key member of the brain trust. Unlike Green and many of his minor league coaches who hoped to advance through the system, Bedell's ambitions were intimately bound with the success of the Phillies organization. He was a master teacher-coach and a progressive thinker, who was responsible for introducing such innovations as continuous motion training, pitching coaches at every level of the minor leagues, and a formula for identifying the best middle relievers and starters; all of which were adopted by other major league organizations. Bedell was fair-minded, but he could also be tough when he needed to be.

Nor did Bedell or Green escape the scrutiny of Owens, who had his own most experienced scouts like Hughie Alexander and Lou Kahn keep a watchful eye on their progress and regularly report to him. But there was more than player development, scouting, and the accountability that went into building the 1980 Phillies.

Carpenter ran the organization like a family. There was an innate sense of trust between ownership and the players. Contract negotiations were never set in stone. Often one agreement would be torn up on the spot and another renegotiated. On other occasions, promises were made and kept on little more than a handshake. Owens and Carpenter made the time to listen to everyone's concerns. From star players to groundskeepers, employees felt as if they mattered. As a result, most of the players who came through the Phillies system tended to be very loyal, giving that extra effort that defines all winning organizations.

After Bill Giles and his partners purchased the Phillies in 1981, the front office operated like an inept business corporation where cost-effectiveness and profit margins mattered more than winning. Player development and the scouting system, as well as the accountability that made those areas so successful, quickly dissipated. With a majority of absentee owners, the front office became complacent, resting on the laurels of the recent past. Few members were made accountable for their actions. Certain individuals, like Hugh Alexander and Ray Shore, were allowed to operate with great independence, often to the detriment of the club. Others, like Paul Owens, who had experienced success and had a clear vision for the future, were marginalized in the club's decision-making process. As a result, the Latin American market was abandoned, scouts were not replaced when they left the organization, poor decisions were routinely made in the acquisition of players and in the amateur draft, and the farm system, once the crown jewel of the organization, went into sharp decline. The complacency filtered down from the brain trust to the players. As a result, the Phillies no longer "expected" to win when they took the field, they "hoped" they could win with as little effort as possible.

But poor leadership was not entirely to blame for the team's collapse. Free agency altered dramatically the manner in which baseball operated. While free agency rectified the financial exploitation players experienced under the reserve clause, it also destroyed the team concept and accountability that were the cornerstones of the Phillies' success during the club's glory years.

No longer could the Phillies produce a homegrown team by sending out their scouts to identify and sign the most talented players and cultivate them in their farm system. Now they were forced to compete with other bidders on the free agent market for the very best players, the highest bidder almost always prevailing. Giles, ever conscious of a limited budget, rarely dipped into the free agent market for a high-priced star, and when he did in 1987 with the signing of Lance Parrish, it was a crapshoot.

Free agency also created constant labor conflict. Lawyers and agents were every bit as important in the running of the club as the ever-changing stream of managers and coaches who served the organization during Giles's tenure. Profit sharing also became a critical consideration in determining the team's budget for player signings and transactions. During the Giles regime, player salaries escalated so quickly that the club struggled to balance its budget in order to re-sign their stars, or those who they felt were stars. As a result, the fans were held hostage, being forced to pay more money for tickets and concessions. Most of the time, the product—the Phillies teams between 1984 and 1989—was painfully disappointing.

Today, Philadelphia is once again excited about the Phillies. History seems to be repeating itself. In 2004, the team abandoned the cavernous sterile confines of Veterans Stadium and moved into Citizens Bank Ballpark, a cozy, state-of-the art facility reminiscent of the old, turn-of-the-century ballparks. The park appeals to fans of all ages. Youngsters test their pitching and base-running skills at games located on the concourse. Adults enjoy a variety of eateries, including the popular Bull's BBQ, operated by Greg Luzinski. And seniors reminisce about the "good old days" of Phillies baseball while visiting the Hall of Fame Club or taking a walk along Ashburn Alley with its historic timeline and Phillies Wall of Fame. Much as they did in the 1970s, the Phils are promoting baseball as a "family affair."

Just as important, the Phillies are once again fielding another homegrown nucleus that, if kept together, has the potential to clinch another world championship. First baseman Ryan Howard, the 2005 Rookie of the Year, slugged 58 homers in his sophomore MVP season, breaking Mike Schmidt's single-season record of 48 round trippers. Like Michael Jack, Howard promises to be one of the most feared power hitters in baseball for years to come. Chase Utley, a gritty second baseman along the lines of Pete Rose, has proven to be a clutch performer at the plate. Shortstop Jimmy Rollins, a three-time All-Star, is the indispensable leader of the team. Mentored by Larry Bowa earlier in his career, Rollins, at age twenty-eight, is the most experienced member of the young nucleus. Cole Hamels, a twenty-three-year-old left-hander who throws 94 mph, has the potential to be the "Steve Carlton" of the future. In 2007, this talented nucleus of players led the Phillies to their first National League Eastern Division title in fourteen years.

These are the Phillies who belong to my son Peter's generation. With a little luck, they, too, will experience the same heady exhilaration of a world championship, or perhaps even a dynasty. While I wish them the best, it'll never be the same for me. That, too, is only fitting.

The 1980 season was much more than the Phillies' first world championship. It was redemption for a miserable, century-old legacy of losing as well as the highlight of my love affair with baseball. I don't believe anything will ever match the emotion or pride I felt for my hometown team that year. Perhaps it's better that they didn't repeat as world champions in '81 or '83. It wouldn't have been as special.

Occasionally, Peter will walk into my study and stare at a framed print of Mike Schmidt taking Cincinnati Reds pitcher Fred Norman deep to left field as shortstop Dave Concepcion watches the trajectory of the ball. It's a scene that recalls an April 26, 1976, game at the Vet. In the background is Philadelphia Phil with bat in hand ready to clout the Liberty Bell and set off the green-colored dancing waters that once formed the "home run spectacular." "Happy Birthday" is written across the outfield wall in honor of the nation's bicentennial.

When Peter asks me why I like the print so much, I say that it reminds me of my boyhood, my hero, and a place I called my "baseball home" for more than thirty years. He doesn't quite understand how difficult it is for me to let go of the past and come to terms with the self-evident truth that "nothing lasts forever."

Maybe so, but in my mind, I'll see Schmitty's home run swing and the ball clearing that left field fence for the rest of my life.

APPENDIXES

Appendix A. Individual Statistics for 1980 Phillies

PITCHER	W-L	G	GS	CG	IP	H	BB	K	SHO	SV	ERA
REGULAR SEASON											
Brusstar, Warren	2-2	26	0	0	38	42	13	21	0	0	3.69
Bystrom, Marty	5-0	6	5	1	36	26	9	21	1	0	1.50
Carlton, Steve	*24-9*	38	*38*	13	*304*	243	90	*286*	3	0	2.34
Christenson, Larry	5-1	14	14	0	73	62	27	49	0	0	4.01
Davis, Mark	0-0	2	1	0	7	4	5	5	0	0	2.57
Espinosa, Nino	3-5	12	12	1	76	73	19	13	0	0	3.79
LaGrow, Lerrin	0-2	25	0	0	39	42	17	21	0	3	4.15
Larson, Dan	0-5	12	7	0	45	46	24	17	0	0	3.13
Lerch, Randy	4-14	30	22	2	150	178	55	57	0	0	5.16
Lyle, Sparky	0-0	10	0	0	14	11	6	6	0	2	1.93
McGraw, Tug	5-4	57	0	0	92	62	23	75	0	20	1.47
Munninghoff, Scott	0-0	4	0	0	6	8	5	2	0	0	4.50
Noles, Dickie	1-4	48	3	0	81	80	42	57	0	6	3.89
Reed, Ron	7-5	55	0	0	91	88	30	54	0	9	4.05
Ruthven, Dick	17-10	33	33	6	223	241	74	86	1	0	3.55
Saucier, Kevin	7-3	40	0	0	50	50	20	25	0	0	3.42
Walk, Bob	11-7	27	27	2	151	163	71	94	0	0	4.56
Totals:	**91-71**	**162**	**162**	**25**	**1,447**	**1,419**	**530**	**889**	**5**	**40**	**3.39**

KEY:
W-L: Win-Loss record
G: Games
GS: Games started

CG: Complete games
IP: Innings pitched
H: Hits

R: Runs
ER: Earned runs
BB: Base on Balls

K: Strikeouts
SHO: Shutouts
SV: Saves
ERA: Earned run average

*NOTE: Bold/italicized numbers indicate National League leader

Source: Rich Westcott and Frank Bilovsky, *The Phillies Encyclopedia*, 3rd ed. (Philadelphia: Temple University Press, 2004), 93.

NATIONAL LEAGUE CHAMPIONSHIP SERIES

	W-L	G	GS	CG	IP	H	R	ER	BB	K	SHO	SV	ERA
Brusstar, Warren	1-0	2	0	0	2.2	1	1	1	1	0	0	0	3.00
Bystrom, Marty	0-0	1	1	0	5.1	7	2	1	2	1	0	0	1.80
Carlton, Steve	1-0	2	2	0	12.1	11	3	3	8	6	0	0	2.25
Christenson, Larry	0-0	2	1	0	6.2	5	3	3	5	2	0	2	3.86
McGraw, Tug	0-1	5	0	0	8	8	4	4	4	5	0	0	4.50
Noles, Dickie	0-0	2	0	0	2.2	1	0	0	3	0	0	0	0.00
Reed, Ron	0-1	3	0	0	2	3	4	4	1	1	0	0	18.00
Ruthven, Dick	1-0	2	1	0	9	3	2	2	5	4	0	0	2.00
Saucier, Kevin	0-0	2	0	0	2	1	0	0	2	0	0	0	0.00
Totals:	3-2	5	5	0	48.8	40	19	18	31	19	0	2	3.18

WORLD SERIES

	W-L	G	GS	CG	IP	H	R	ER	BB	K	SHO	SV	ERA
Brusstar, Warren	0-0	1	0	0	2.1	0	0	0	1	0	0	0	0.00
Bystrom, Marty	0-0	1	1	0	5.0	10	3	3	1	4	0	0	5.40
Carlton, Steve	2-0	2	2	0	15.0	14	5	4	9	17	0	0	2.40
Chrstenson, Larry	0-1	1	1	0	.1	5	4	4	0	0	0	0	18.00
McGraw, Tug	1-1	4	0	0	7.2	7	1	1	8	10	0	2	1.17
Noles, Dickie	0-0	1	0	0	4.2	5	1	1	2	6	0	0	1.93
Reed, Ron	0-0	2	0	0	2.0	2	0	0	0	2	0	1	0.00
Ruthven, Dick	0-0	1	1	0	9.0	9	3	3	0	7	0	0	3.00
Saucier, Kevin	0-0	1	0	0	.2	0	0	0	2	0	0	0	0.00
Walk, Bob	1-0	1	1	0	7.0	8	6	6	3	3	0	0	7.71
Totals:	4-2	6	6	0	51.8	60	23	22	26	49	0	3	3.68

KEY: W-L: Win -Loss record
       G: Games
       GS: Games started

CG: Complete games
IP: Innings pitched
H: Hits

R: Runs
ER: Earned runs
BB: Base on Balls

K: Strikeouts
SHO: Shutouts
SV: Saves
ERA: Earned run average

*NOTE: Bold/italicized numbers indicate National League leader

Source: Larry Shenk, ed., *The World Champion Phillies and the Road to Victory* (Philadelphia: Phillies, 1980), 39.

REGULAR SEASON

HITTER	G	AB	R	H	2B	3B	HR	RBI	SB	AVG
Aguayo, Luis	20	47	7	13	1	2	1	8	1	.277
Aviles, Ramon	51	101	12	28	6	0	2	9	0	.277
Boone, Bob	141	480	34	110	23	1	9	55	3	.229
Bowa, Larry	147	540	57	144	16	4	2	39	21	.269
Dernier, Bob	10	7	5	4	0	0	0	1	3	.571
Gross, Greg	127	154	19	37	7	2	0	12	1	.240
Isales, Orlando	3	5	1	2	0	1	0	3	0	.400
Loviglio, Jay	16	5	7	0	0	0	0	0	1	.000
Luzinski, Greg	106	368	44	84	19	1	19	56	3	.228
Maddox, Garry	143	549	59	142	31	3	11	73	25	.259
McBride, Bake	137	554	68	171	33	10	9	87	13	.309
McCarver, Tim	6	5	2	1	1	0	0	2	0	.200
McCormick, Don	2	1	0	1	0	0	0	0	0	1.000
Moreland, Keith	62	159	13	50	8	0	4	29	3	.314
Rose, Pete	162	655	95	185	*42*	1	1	64	12	.282
Schmidt, Mike	150	548	104	157	25	8	*48*	*121*	12	.286
Smith, Lonnie	100	298	69	101	14	4	3	20	33	.339
Trillo, Manny	141	531	68	155	25	9	7	43	8	.292
Unser, Del	96	110	15	29	6	4	0	10	0	.264
Virgil, Ozzie	1	5	1	1	1	0	0	0	0	.200
Vukovich, George	78	58	6	13	1	1	0	8	0	.224
Vukovich, John	49	62	4	10	1	1	0	5	0	.161
Totals:	162	5,625	728	1,517	272	54	117	674	140	.270

KEY:
G: Games
AB: At-bats
R: Runs scored

H: Hits
2B: Doubles
3B: Triples

HR: Home runs
RBI: Runs batted in
SB: Stolen bases

AVG: Batting average

*NOTE: Bold/italicized numbers indicate National League leader

Source: Westcott and Bilovsky, *Phillies Encyclopedia*, 93.

HITTER	G	AB	R	H	2B	3B	HR	RBI	SB	AVG
NATIONAL LEAGUE CHAMPIONSHIP SERIES										
Aviles, Ramon	1	0	1	0	0	0	0	0	0	.000
Boone, Bob	5	18	1	4	0	0	0	2	0	.222
Bowa, Larry	5	19	2	6	0	0	0	0	1	.316
Gross, Greg	4	4	2	3	0	0	0	1	0	.750
Luzinski, Greg	5	17	3	5	2	0	1	4	0	.294
Maddox, Garry	5	20	2	6	2	0	0	3	2	.300
McBride, Bake	5	21	0	5	0	0	0	0	2	.238
Moreland, Keith	2	1	0	0	0	0	0	1	0	.000
Rose, Pete	5	20	3	8	0	0	0	2	0	.400
Schmidt, Mike	5	24	1	5	1	0	0	1	1	.208
Smith, Lonnie	3	5	2	3	0	0	0	0	1	.600
Trillo, Manny	5	21	1	8	2	1	0	4	0	.381
Unser, Del	5	5	2	2	1	0	0	1	0	.400
Vukovich, George	3	3	0	0	0	0	0	0	0	.000
Pitchers (cumulative)		12	0	0	0	0	0	0	0	.000
Totals:	**5**	**190**	**20**	**55**	**8**	**1**	**1**	**19**	**7**	**.290**

Source: Shenk, *World Champion Phillies*, 39.

HITTER	G	AB	R	H	2B	3B	HR	RBI	SB	AVG
WORLD SERIES										
Boone, Bob	6	17	3	7	2	0	0	4	0	.412
Bowa, Larry	6	24	3	9	1	0	0	2	3	.375
Gross, Greg	4	2	0	0	0	0	0	0	0	.000
Luzinski, Greg	3	9	0	0	0	0	0	0	0	.000
Maddox, Garry	6	22	1	5	2	0	0	1	0	.227
McBride, Bake	6	23	3	7	1	0	1	5	0	.304
Moreland, Keith	3	12	1	4	0	0	0	1	0	.333
Rose, Pete	6	23	2	6	1	0	0	1	0	.261
Schmidt, Mike	6	21	6	8	1	0	2	7	0	.381
Smith, Lonnie	6	19	2	5	1	0	0	1	0	.263
Trillo, Manny	6	23	4	5	2	0	0	2	0	.217
Unser, Del	3	6	2	3	2	0	0	2	0	.500
Designated Hitters	—	23	1	4	0	0	0	1	0	.174
Pinch Hitters	—	3	2	2	2	0	0	2	0	.667
Others	—	0	0	0	0	0	0	0	0	.000
Totals:	6	201	27	59	13	0	3	26	3	.294

KEY: G: Games   H: Hits   HR: Home runs   AVG: Batting average
        AB: At-bats   2B: Doubles   RBI: Runs batted in
        R: Runs scored   3B: Triples   SB: Stolen bases

*NOTE: Bold/italicized numbers indicate National League leader

Source: Shenk, *World Champion Phillies*, 39.

Appendix B. 1980 National League Championship Series Box Scores

GAME 1:
TUESDAY, OCTOBER 7, AT PHILADELPHIA

HOUSTON	AB	R	H	RBI	PHILLIES	AB	R	H	RBI
Landestoy, 2b	5	0	0	0	Rose, 1b	4	1	2	0
Cabell, 3b	4	0	1	0	McBride, rf	4	0	1	0
Cruz, lf	3	1	1	0	Schmidt, 3b	3	0	0	0
Cedeno, cf	3	0	1	0	Luzinski, lf	4	1	1	2
Howe, 1b	4	0	0	0	Unser, lf	0	0	0	0
Woods, rf	4	0	2	1	Trillo, 2b	4	0	0	0
Pujols, c	3	0	0	0	Maddox, cf	3	1	1	0
Bergman, pr	0	0	0	0	Bowa, ss	2	0	1	0
Reynolds, ss	2	0	0	0	Boone, c	3	0	1	0
Puhl, ph	1	0	0	0	Carlton, p	2	0	0	0
Forsch, p	2	0	2	0	Gross, ph	1	0	1	1
Leonard, ph	1	0	0	0	McGraw, p	0	0	0	0
Totals	**32**	**1**	**7**	**1**	**Totals**	**30**	**3**	**8**	**3**

Houston	001	000	000	- 1
Phillies	000	002	10x	- 3

Game-winning RBI: Luzinski. Error: Bowa. Double play: Phillies 1. Left on base:
Houston 9, Phillies 5. Home run: Luzinski. Stolen bases: McBride, Maddox.
Sacrifices: Forsch, Bowa.

HOUSTON	IP	H	R	ER	BB	SO
Forsch	8	8	3	3	1	5

PHILLIES	IP	H	R	ER	BB	SO
Carlton (W)	7	7	1	1	3	3
McGraw (S)	2	0	0	0	1	1

Umpires: Engel, Tata, Froemming, Harvey, Vargo, and Crawford. Time, 2:35.
Attendance, 65,277.

Source: Shenk, *World Champion Phillies*, 19–25.

GAME 2:
WEDNESDAY, OCTOBER 8, AT PHILADELPHIA

HOUSTON	AB	R	H	RBI	PHILLIES	AB	R	H	RBI
Puhl, rf	5	1	3	2	Rose, 1b	4	0	2	0
Cabell, 3b	4	0	0	0	McBride, rf	5	0	1	0
Morgan, 2b	2	1	1	0	Schmidt, 3b	6	1	2	0
Landestoy, pr, 2b	0	1	0	0	Luzinski, lf	4	1	2	1
Cruz, lf	4	1	2	2	L. Smith, pr, lf	1	1	1	0
Cedeno, cf	5	1	1	1	Trillo, 2b	3	0	1	0
Howe, 1b	4	0	0	0	Maddox, cf	5	0	2	2
Bergman, 1b	1	0	1	2	Bowa, ss	4	1	2	0
Ashby, c	5	0	0	0	Boone, c	4	0	1	0
Reynolds, ss	3	1	0	0	Ruthven, p	2	0	0	0
Ryan, p	1	1	0	0	Gross, ph	0	0	0	0
Sambito, p	0	0	0	0	McGraw, p	0	0	0	0
D. Smith, p	0	0	0	0	Unser, ph	1	0	0	0
Leonard, ph	1	0	0	0	Reed, p	0	0	0	0
LaCorte, p	1	0	0	0	Saucier, p	0	0	0	0
Andujar, p	0	0	0	0	G. Vukovich, ph	1	0	0	0
Totals					**Totals**				

```
Houston     001  000  110  4-7
Phillies    000  200  010  1-4
```

Game-winning RBI: Cruz. Error: Schmidt, McBride, Reynolds. Double play: Phillies
1. Left on base: Houston 8, Phillies 14. Two base hits: Puhl, Morgan, Schmidt,
Luzinski. Three base hit: Bergman. sacrifices: Ryan, Trillo 2, Gross, Cabell.

HOUSTON	IP	H	R	ER	BB	SO
Ryan	6.1	8	2	2	1	6
Sambito	.1	0	0	0	1	1
D. Smith	1.1	2	1	1	1	2
LaCorte (W)	1	4	1	0	1	1
Andujar (S)	1	0	0	0	1	0

PHILLIES	IP	H	R	ER	BB	SO
Ruthven	7	3	2	2	5	4
McGraw	1	2	1	1	0	0
Reed (L)	1.1	2	4	4	1	1
Saucier	.2	1	0	0	1	0

Umpires: Tata, Froemming, Harvey, Vargo, Crawford and Engel. Time, 3:34.
Attendance, 65,476

GAME 3:
FRIDAY, OCTOBER 10, AT HOUSTON

PHILLIES	AB	R	H	RBI	HOUSTON	AB	R	H	RBI
Rose, 1b	5	0	1	0	Puhl, rf, cf	4	0	2	0
McBride, rf	5	0	1	0	Cabell, 3b	4	0	2	0
Schmidt, 3b	5	0	1	0	Morgan, 2b	4	0	1	0
Luzinski, lf	5	0	0	0	Landestoy, pr	0	1	0	0
Trillo, 2b	5	0	2	0	Cruz, lf	2	0	1	0
Maddox, cf	4	0	2	0	Cedeno, cf	3	0	0	0
Bowa, ss	3	0	0	0	Bergman, 1b	1	0	0	0
Boone, c	4	0	0	0	Howe, ph	0	0	0	0
Unser, ph	1	0	0	0	Walling, 1b, rf	3	0	0	1
Moreland, c	0	0	0	0	Pujols, c	3	0	0	0
Christenson, p	2	0	0	0	Reynolds, ss	3	0	0	0
G. Vukovich, ph	1	0	0	0	Niekro, p	3	0	0	0
Noles, p	0	0	0	0	Woods, ph	1	0	0	0
McGraw, p	1	0	0	0	Smith, p	0	0	0	0
Totals	**41**	**0**	**7**	**0**	**Totals**	**31**	**1**	**6**	**1**

Phillies   000 000 000 00 -0
Houston   000 000 000 01 -1

One out when winning run scored. Game-winning RBI: Walling. Errors: Christenson, Bergman. Double plays: Phillies 2. Left on base: Philles 11, Houston 10. Two-base hits: Puhl, Maddox, Trillo. Three-base Hits: Cruz, Morgan. Stolen bases: Schmidt, Maddox. Sacrifices: Reynolds, Cabell. Sacrifice fly: Walling.

PHILLIES	IP	H	R	ER	BB	SO
Christenson	6	3	0	0	4	2
Noles	1.1	1	0	0	1	0
McGraw (L)	3	2	1	1	3	1

HOUSTON	IP	H	R	ER	BB	SO
Niekro	10	6	0	0	1	2
Smith (W)	1	1	0	0	1	2

Hit by pitch: by Niekro (Maddox). Passed ball: Pujols Umpires: Froemming, Vargo, Harvey, Crawford, Engel, and Tata. Time, 3:22. Attendance, 44,443.

GAME 4:
SATURDAY, OCTOBER 11, AT HOUSTON

PHILLIES	AB	R	H	RBI
L. Smith, lf	4	1	2	0
Unser, lf, rf	1	0	0	0
Rose, 1b	4	2	2	1
Schmidt, 3b	5	1	2	1
McBride, rf	4	0	2	0
Luzinski, ph	1	1	1	1
G. Vukovich, lf	0	0	0	0
Trillo, 2b	4	0	2	2
Maddox, cf	4	0	0	0
Bowa, ss	5	0	1	0
Boone, c	4	0	0	0
Carlton, p	2	0	0	0
Noles, p	0	0	0	0
Saucier, p	0	0	0	0
Reed, p	0	0	0	0
Gross, ph	1	1	1	0
Brusstar, p	1	0	0	0
McGraw, p	0	0	0	0
Totals	**40**	**5**	**13**	**5**

HOUSTON	AB	R	H	RBI
Puhl, rf, cf	3	0	1	1
Cabell, 3b	4	1	1	0
Morgan, 2b	3	0	0	0
Woods, rf	2	0	0	0
Walling, ph	1	0	0	0
Leonard, rf	1	0	0	0
Howe, 1b	3	0	1	1
Cruz, lf	3	0	0	0
Pujols, c	3	1	1	0
Bochy, c	1	0	0	0
Landestoy, ss	3	1	1	1
Ruhle, p	3	0	0	0
D. Smith, p	0	0	0	0
Sambito, p	0	0	0	0
Totals	**30**	**3**	**5**	**3**

Phillies   000 000 003 02 -5
Houston   000 110 000 10 -3

Game-winning RBI: Luzinski. Error: Landestoy. Double Plays: Phillies 3, Houston 2. Left on base: Phillies 8, Houston 8. Two-base hits: Howe, Cabell, Luzinski, Trillo. Three-base hit: Pujols. Stolen bases: McBride, L. Smith, Landestoy, Woods, Puhl, Bowa. Sacrifice: Sambito. Sacrifice flies: Howe, Trillo.

PHILLIES	IP	H	R	ER	BB	SO
Carlton	5.1	4	2	2	5	3
Noles	1.1	0	0	0	2	0
Saucier	0*	0	0	0	1	0
Reed	.1	0	0	0	0	0
Brusstar (W)	2	1	1	1	1	0
McGraw (S)	1	0	0	0	0	1

HOUSTON	IP	H	R	ER	BB	SO
Ruhl	7x	8	3	3	1	3
D. Smith	0xx	1	0	0	0	0
Sambito (L)	3	4	2	2	1	5

* Pitched to one batter in 7th
x Pitched to three batters in 8th
xx Pitched to one batter in 8th

Umpires: Harvey, Vargo, Crawford, Engel, Tata, and Froemming. Time, 3:55. Attendance, 44,952

GAME 5:
SUNDAY, OCTOBER 12, AT HOUSTON

PHILLIES	AB	R	H	RBI	HOUSTON	AB	R	H	RBI
Rose, 1b	3	0	1	1	Puhl, cf	6	3	4	0
McBride, rf	3	0	0	0	Cabell, 3b	5	1	1	0
Moreland, ph	1	0	0	1	Morgan, 2b	4	0	0	0
Aviles, pr	0	1	0	0	Landestoy, 2b	1	0	1	1
McGraw, p	0	0	0	0	Cruz, lf	3	0	2	2
G. Vukovich, ph	1	0	0	0	Walling, rf	5	2	1	1
Ruthven, p	0	0	0	0	LaCorte, p	0	0	0	0
Schmidt, 3b	5	0	0	0	Howe, 1b	4	0	2	1
Luzinski, lf	3	0	1	0	Bergman, pr, 1b	1	0	0	0
Smith, pr	0	0	0	0	Pujols, c	1	0	0	0
Christenson, p	0	0	0	0	Ashby, ph, c	3	0	1	1
Reed, p	0	0	0	0	Reynolds, ss	5	1	2	0
Unser, ph, rf	2	2	2	1	Ryan, p	3	0	0	0
Trillo, 2b	5	1	3	2	Sambito, p	0	0	0	0
Maddox, cf	4	1	1	1	Forsch, p	0	0	0	0
Bowa, ss	5	1	2	0	Woods, ph, rf	1	0	0	0
Boone, c	3	1	2	2	Heep, ph	1	0	0	0
Bystrom, p	2	0	0	0	**Totals**	**43**	**7**	**14**	**6**
Brusstar, p	0	0	0	0					
Gross, lf	2	1	1	0					
Totals	**39**	**8**	**13**	**8**					

Phillies	020	000	005	1	-8
Houston	100	001	320	0	-5

Game-winning RBI: Maddox. Errors: Trillo, Luzinski. Double Plays: Houston 2. Left on base: Phillies 5, Houston 10. Two-base Hits: Cruz, Reynolds, Unser, Maddox. Three-base hits: Howe, Trillo. Stolen base: Puhl. Sacrifices: Cabell, Boone

PHILLIES	IP	H	R	ER	BB	SO	HOUSTON	IP	H	R	ER	BB	SO
Bystrom	5.1	7	2	1	2	1	Ryan	7	8	6	6	2	8
Brusstar	.2	0	0	0	0	0	Sambito	.1	0	0	0	0	0
Christenson	.2	2	3	3	1	0	Forsch	.2	2	1	1	0	1
Reed	.1	1	0	0	0	0	LaCorte (L)	2	3	1	1	1	1
McGraw	1	4	2	2	0	2							
Ruthven (W)	2	0	0	0	0	0							

Wild pitch: Christenson. Umpires: Vargo, Crawford, Engel, Tata, Froemming, Harvey. Time, 3:38. Attendance, 44,802.

Appendix C. 1980 World Series Box Scores

TUESDAY, OCTOBER 14, AT PHILADELPHIA

KANSAS CITY	AB	R	H	RBI	PHILLIES	AB	R	H	RBI
Wilson, lf	5	0	0	0	Smith, lf	4	0	2	0
McRae, dh	3	1	1	0	Gross, lf	1	0	0	0
G. Brett, 3b	4	1	1	0	Rose, 1b	3	1	0	0
Aikens, 1b	4	2	2	4	Schmidt, 3b	2	2	1	0
Porter, c	2	1	0	0	McBride, rf	4	1	3	3
Otis, cf	4	1	3	2	Luzinski, dh	3	0	0	0
Hurdle, rf	3	0	1	0	Maddox, cf	3	0	0	1
a-Wathan, rf	1	0	0	0	Trillo, 2b	4	1	1	0
White, 2b	4	0	1	0	Bowa, ss	4	1	1	0
Washington, ss	4	0	0	0	Boone, c	4	1	3	2
Leonard, p	0	0	0	0	Walk, p	0	0	0	0
Martin, p	0	0	0	0	McGraw, p	0	0	0	0
Quisenberry, p	0	0	0	0	**Totals**	32	7	11	6
Totals	34	6	9	6					

```
Kansas City    022  000  020 - 6
Phillies       005  110  00x - 7
```

a-Grounded into double play for Hurdle in 8th

Error: Leonard. Two-base hits: Boone 2, G. Brett. Home Runs: Otis, Aikens 2, McBride. Stolen bases: Bowa, White Caught stealing: Smith. Sacrifice fly: Maddox. Hit by pitch by Leonard (Rose), by Martin (Luzinski). Wild pitch: Walk. Double play: Phillies 1. Left on base: Kansas City 4, Phillies 6. Umpires: Wendelstedt, Kunkel, Pryor, Denkinger, Rennert, and Bremigan. Time, 3:01. Attendance, 65,791.

KANSAS CITY	IP	H	R	ER	BB	SO
Leonard (L)	3.2	6	6	6	1	3
Martin	4	5	1	1	1	1
Quisenberry	.1	0	0	0	0	0

PHILLIES	IP	H	R	ER	BB	SO
Walk (W)	7*	8	6	6	3	3
McGraw (S)	2	1	0	0	0	2

*Pitched to two batters in 8th

Source: Shenk, *World Champion Phillies*, 26–33.

GAME 2:
WEDNESDAY, OCTOBER 15, AT PHILADELPHIA

KANSAS CITY	AB	R	H	RBI	PHILLIES	AB	R	H	RBI
Wilson, lf	4	1	1	0	Smith, lf	3	0	0	0
Washington, ss	4	0	1	0	b-Unser, cf	1	1	1	1
G. Brett, 3b	2	0	2	0	Rose, 1b	4	0	0	0
Chalk, 3b	0	1	0	0	McBride, rf	3	1	1	1
a-Porter	1	0	0	0	Schmidt, 3b	4	1	2	1
McRae, dh	4	1	3	0	Moreland, dh	4	1	2	1
Otis, cf	5	1	2	2	Maddox, cf	3	1	1	0
Wathan, c	3	0	0	1	c-Gross, lf	1	0	0	0
Aikens, 1b	3	0	1	0	Trillo, 2b	2	0	0	1
LaCock, 1b	0	0	0	0	Bowa, ss	3	0	1	1
Cardenal, rf	4	0	0	0	Boone, c	1	1	0	0
White, 2b	4	0	1	0	Carlton, p	0	0	0	0
Gura, p	0	0	0	0	Reed, p	0	0	0	0
Quisenberry, p	0	0	0	0	**Totals**	29	6	8	6
Totals	34	4	11	3					

Kansas City	000	001	300	-4
Phillies	000	020	04x	-6

b-Doubled in one run for Smith in 8th.
c-Grounded into double play for Maddox in 8th.
a-Called out on strikes for Chalk in 9th.

Error: Trillo. Two-base hits: Maddox, Otis, Unser, Schmidt. Stolen bases: Wilson,
Chalk. Sacrifice: Washington. Sacrifice flies: Trillo, Wathan. Wild Pitch: Carlton.
Double plays: Phillies 4, Kansas City 2. Left ob base: Kansas City 11, Phillies 3.
Umpires: Kunkel, Pryor, Denkinger, Rennert, Bremigan and Wendelstedt.
Time, 3:01. Attendance, 65,775

KANSAS CITY	IP	H	R	ER	BB	SO
Gura	6	4	2	2	2	2
Quisenberry (L)	2	4	4	4	1	0

PHILLIES	IP	H	R	ER	BB	SO
Carlton (W)	8	10	4	3	6	10
Reed (S)	1	1	0	0	0	2

GAME 3:
FRIDAY, OCTOBER 17, AT KANSAS CITY

PHILLIES	AB	R	H	RBI
Smith, lf	4	0	2	1
a-Gross, lf	0	0	0	0
Rose, 1b	4	0	1	1
Schmidt, 3b	5	1	1	1
McBride, rf	5	0	2	0
Moreland, dh	5	0	1	0
Maddox, cf	4	0	1	0
Trillo, 2b	5	1	2	0
Bowa, ss	5	1	3	0
Boone, c	4	0	1	0
Ruthven, p	0	0	0	0
McGraw, p	0	0	0	0
Totals	**41**	**3**	**14**	**3**

KANSAS CITY	AB	R	H	RBI
Wilson, lf	4	1	0	0
White, 2b	5	0	0	0
G. Brett, 3b	4	1	2	1
Aikens, 1b	5	1	2	1
McRae, dh	4	0	2	1
Otis, cf	4	1	2	1
Hurdle, rf	4	0	2	0
b-Concepcion	0	0	0	0
Cardenal, rf	0	0	0	0
Porter, c	4	0	0	0
Washington, ss	4	0	1	0
Gale, p	0	0	0	0
Martin, p	0	0	0	0
Quisenberry, p	0	0	0	0
Totals	**38**	**4**	**11**	**4**

Phillies	010	010	010	0	3
Kansas City	100	100	100	1	4

b-Ran for Hurdle in 9th.
a-Sacrificed for Smith in 10th.

Two out when winning run scored

Two-base hits: Trillo, G. Brett. Three-base hit: Aikens. Home runs: G. Brett, Schmidt, Otis. Stolen bases: Hurdle, Bowa, Wilson. Caught stealing: Washington. Sacrific: Gross. Double Plays: Kansas City 2, Phillies 1. Left on base: Phillies 15, Kansas City 7. Umpires: Pryor, Denkinger, Rennert, Bremigan, Wendelstedt, and Kunkel. Time, 3:19. Attendance, 42,380.

PHILLIES	IP	H	R	ER	BB	SO
Ruthven	9	9	3	3	0	7
McGraw (L)	.2	2	1	1	2	1

KANSAS CITY	IP	H	R	ER	BB	SO
Gale	4.1	7	2	2	3	3
Martin	3.1	5	1	1	1	1
Quisenberry (W)	2.1	2	0	0	2	0

GAME 4:
SATURDAY, OCTOBER 18, AT KANSAS CITY

PHILLIES	AB	R	H	RBI	KANSAS CITY	AB	R	H	RBI
Smith, dh	4	0	0	0	Wilson, lf	4	1	1	0
Rose, 1b	4	1	2	0	White, 2b	5	0	0	0
McBride, rf	3	0	1	0	G. Brett, 3b	5	1	1	1
Schmidt, 3b	3	0	1	1	Aikens, 1b	3	2	2	3
Unser, lf	4	0	1	0	McRae, dh	4	1	2	0
Maddox, cf	4	0	1	0	Otis, cf	4	0	2	1
Trillo, 2b	4	2	1	0	Hurdle, rf	2	0	1	0
Bowa, ss	4	0	2	1	Porter, c	3	0	0	0
Boone, c	3	0	1	1	Washington, ss	4	0	1	0
Christenson, p	0	0	0	0	Leonard, p	0	0	0	0
Noles, p	0	0	0	0	Quisenberry, p	0	0	0	0
Saucier, p	0	0	0	0	**Totals**	**34**	**4**	**10**	**5**
Brusstar, p	0	0	0	0					
Totals	**33**	**3**	**10**	**3**					

Phillies	010 000 110	3
Kansas City	410 000 00x	5

Errors: White, Christenson, Washington. Two-base hits: McRae 2, Otis, Hurdle. McBride, Trillo, Rose. Three-base hit: G. Brett. Home runs: Aikens 2. Stolen base: Bowa. Caught stealing: McBride. Sacrifice flies: Boone, Schmidt. Wild pitches: Leonard, Saucier. Doubleplay: Kansas City 1. Left on base: Phillies 6, Kansas City 10. Umpires: Denkinger, Rennert, Bremigan, Wendelstedt, Kunkel, and Pryor. Time, 2:37. Attendance: 42,363.

PHILLIES	IP	H	R	ER	BB	SO
Christenson (L)	.1	5	4	4	0	0
Noles	4.2	5	1	1	2	6
Saucier	. 2	0	0	0	2	0
Brusstar	2.1	0	0	0	1	0

KANSAS CITY	IP	H	R	ER	BB	SO
Leonard (W)	7*	9	3	2	1	2
Quisenberry (S)	2	1	0	0	0	0

*Pitched to one batter in 8th.

GAME 5:
SUNDAY, OCTOBER 19, AT KANSAS CITY

PHILLIES	AB	R	H	RBI
Rose, 1b	4	0	0	0
McBride, rf	4	1	0	0
Schmidt, 3b	4	2	2	2
Luzinski, lf	2	0	0	0
a-Smith, lf	0	0	0	0
b-Unser, lf	1	1	1	1
Moreland, dh	3	0	1	0
Maddox, cf	4	0	0	0
Trillo, 2b	4	0	1	1
Bowa, ss	4	0	1	0
Boone, c	3	0	1	0
Bystrom, p	0	0	0	0
Reed, p	0	0	0	0
McGraw, p	0	0	0	0
Totals	**33**	**4**	**7**	**4**

KANSAS CITY	AB	R	H	RBI
Wilson, lf	5	0	2	0
White, 2b	3	0	0	0
G. Brett, 3b	5	0	1	1
Aikens, 1b	3	0	1	0
c-Concepcion	0	0	0	0
McRae, dh	5	0	1	0
Otis, cf	3	1	2	1
Hurdle, rf	3	1	1	0
d-Cardenal, rf	2	0	0	0
Porter, c	4	0	2	0
Washington, ss	3	1	2	1
Gura, p	0	0	0	0
Quisenberry, p	0	0	0	0
Totals	**36**	**3**	**12**	**3**

Phillies	000	200	002	4
Kansas City	000	012	000	3

a-Ran for Luzinski in 7th.
d-Flied out for Hurdle in 7th.
b-Doubled in one run for Smith in 9th.
d-Ran for Aikens in 9th.

Errors: Aikens, G. Brett. Two-base hits: Wilson, McRae, Unser. Home runs: Schmidt, Otis. Stolen base: G. Brett. Sacrifices: White Moreland. Sacrifice fly: Washington. Double plays: Kansas City 2. Left on base: Phillies 4, Kansas City 13. Umpires: Rennert, Bremigan, Wendelstedt, Kunkel, Pryor and Denkinger. Time, 2:51. Atten. 42,369.

PHILLIES	IP	H	R	ER	BB	SO
Bystrom	5*	10	3	3	1	4
Reed	1	1	0	0	0	0
McGraw (W)	3	1	0	0	4	5

KANSAS CITY	IP	H	R	ER	BB	SO
Gura	6.1	4	2	1	1	2
Quisenberry (L)	2.2	3	2	2	0	0

*Pitched to three batters in 6th.

GAME 6:
TUESDAY, OCTOBER 21, AT PHILADELPHIA

KANSAS CITY	AB	R	H	RBI
Wilson, lf	4	0	0	0
Washington, ss	3	0	1	1
G. Brett, 3b	4	0	2	0
McRae, dh	4	0	0	0
Otis, cf	3	0	0	0
Aikens, 1b	2	0	0	0
a-Concepcion	0	0	0	0
Wathan, c	3	1	2	0
Cardenal, rf	4	0	2	0
White, 2b	4	0	0	0
Gale, p	0	0	0	0
Martin, p	0	0	0	0
Splittorff, p	0	0	0	0
Pattin, p	0	0	0	0
Quisenberry, p	0	0	0	0
Totals	**31**	**1**	**7**	**1**

PHILLIES	AB	R	H	RBI
Smith, lf	4	2	1	0
Gross, lf	0	0	0	0
Rose, 1b	4	0	3	0
Schmidt, 3b	3	0	1	2
McBride, rf	4	0	0	1
Luzinski, dh	4	0	0	0
Maddox, cf	4	0	2	0
Trillo, 2b	4	0	0	0
Bowa, ss	4	1	1	0
Boone, c	2	1	1	1
Carlton, p	0	0	0	0
McGraw, p	0	0	0	0
Totals	**33**	**4**	**9**	**4**

```
Kansas City    000  000  010   1
Phillies       002  011  00x   4
```

a-Ran for Aikens in 9th.

Errors: White, Aikens. Two-base hits: Maddox, Smith, Bowa. Caught stealing: Rose. Sacrifice fly: Washington. Double plays: Phillies 2, Kansas City 1. Left on base: Kansas City 9, Phillies 7. Umpires: Bremigan, Wendelstedt, Kunkel, Pryor, Denkinger, and Rennert. Time, 3:00. Attendance, 65,838.

KANSAS CITY	IP	H	R	ER	BB	SO
Gale (L)	2	4	2	1	1	1
Martin	2.1	1	1	1	1	0
Splittorff	1.2*	4	1	1	0	0
Pattin	1	0	0	0	0	2
Quisenberry	1	0	0	0	0	0

PHILLIES	IP	H	R	ER	BB	SO
Carlton (W)	7**	4	1	1	3	7
McGraw (S)	2	3	0	0	2	2

*Pitched to one batter in 7th.
**Pitched to two batters in 8th.

Appendix D. Phillies Team Standings, 1971-1989

YEAR	RECORD	FINISH IN NL EAST	GAMES BEHIND	MANAGER
1971	67-95	Sixth	30	Frank Lucchesi
1972	59-97	Sixth	37 $\frac{1}{2}$	Frank Lucchesi / Paul Owens
1973	71-91	Sixth	11 $\frac{1}{2}$	Danny Ozark
1974	80-82	Third	8	Danny Ozark
1975	86-76	Second	6 $\frac{1}{2}$	Danny Ozark
1976	101-61	First	—	Danny Ozark
1977	101-61	First	—	Danny Ozark
1978	90-72	First	—	Danny Ozark
1979	84-78	Fourth	14	Danny Ozark / Dallas Green
1980	91-71	First	—	Dallas Green
1981	59-48	First (1st half) / Third (2nd half)	4 $\frac{1}{2}$ (2nd half)	Dallas Green
1982	89-73	Second	3	Pat Corrales
1983	90-72	First	—	Pat Corrales / Paul Owens
1984	81-81	Fourth	15 $\frac{1}{2}$	Paul Owens
1985	75-87	Fifth	26	John Felske
1986	86-75	Second	21 $\frac{1}{2}$	John Felske
1987	80-82	Fourth	15	John Felske / Lee Elia
1988	65-96	Sixth	35 $\frac{1}{2}$	Lee Elia / John Vukovich
1989	67-95	Sixth	26	Nick Leyva

Source: Westcott and Bilovsky, *Phillies Encyclopedia*, 85–101.

NOTES

INTRODUCTION

1. "Phantastic," *Philadelphia Bulletin*, October 22, 1980; see also "Phils Win Series; City Goes Wild," and "We Win!" in the same issue.

2. Tug McGraw with William C. Kashatus, *Was It as Good for You? Tug McGraw and Friends Recall the 1980 World Series* (Media, Pa.: McGraw and Co., 2000), 70–71.

3. Larry Bowa, quoted in Frank Fitzpatrick, *You Can't Lose 'Em All: The Year the Phillies Finally Won the World Series* (Dallas: Taylor, 2001), 9.

4. Tug McGraw, Interview by author, West Chester, Pennsylvania, May 3, 2000. See also Tug McGraw with Don Yaeger, *Ya Gotta Believe! My Roller-Coaster Life as a Screwball Pitcher and Part-Time Father, and My Hope-Filled Fight Against Brain Cancer* (New York: New American Library, 2004), 149.

5. McGraw interview; and McGraw, *Ya Gotta Believe!*, 151.

6. McGraw, *Was It as Good for You?*, 73.

7. McGraw, quoted by Bob Ibach and Tim Panaccio, *The Comeback Kids* (Philadelphia: Bel Air, 1980), 1.

8. Gil Spencer, "Celebrate! Celebrate!" *Philadelphia Daily News*, October 22, 1980.

9. See Rich Westcott and Frank Bilovsky, *The Phillies Encyclopedia* (Philadelphia: Temple University Press, 2002), 93–94.

10. Rob Neyer and Eddie Epstein, *Baseball Dynasties: The Greatest Teams of All Time* (New York: W.W. Norton, 2000). For more on the 1910–14 Philadelphia Athletics, see William C. Kashatus, *Money Pitcher: Chief Bender and the Tragedy of Indian Assimilation* (University Park: Pennsylvania State University Press, 2006). For more on the 1929–31 Philadelphia Athletics, see William C. Kashatus, *Connie Mack's '29 Triumph: The Rise and Fall of the Philadelphia Athletics Dynasty* (Jefferson, N.C.: McFarland, 1999).

11. Westcott and Bilovsky, *Phillies Encyclopedia*, 93.

12. Geoffrey C. Ward, *Baseball: An Illustrated History* (New York: Knopf, 1994), 421.

13. Westcott and Bilovsky, *Phillies Encyclopedia*, 220.

14. McGraw, *Ya Gotta Believe!*, 140.

15. McGraw, quoted in Paul Dickson, *Baseball's Greatest Quotations* (New York: Edward Burlingame, 1991), 286.

16. Westcott and Bilovsky, *Phillies Encyclopedia*, 146–48.

17. William C. Kashatus, *Mike Schmidt: Philadelphia's Hall of Fame Third Baseman* (Jefferson, N.C.: McFarland, 2000).

18. Westcott and Bilovsky, *Phillies Encyclopedia*, 244–45.

19. Only two books have been written about the 1980 Phillies and they tend toward interpretive extremes. Hal Bodley's *The Team That Wouldn't Die: The Philadelphia Phillies, World Champions, 1980* (Wilmington, Del.: Serendipity Press, 1981) is a celebratory treatment. Bodley, a columnist for *USA Today's Sports Weekly* who began his career with the *Wilmington News Journal*, wrote the book in the wake of enthusiasm over the Phils' only world championship. Consequently, the book reads more like a laudatory anthology of newspaper columns and player interviews. It lacks the kind of objectivity that only time and distance from the subject can give it. Nor does it place the Phillies' achievement in the broader context of baseball history, which is necessary for a critical study of the team. The other book, Frank Fitzpatrick's *You Can't Lose 'Em All*, is a much more cynical treatment. Fitzpatrick, a sportswriter for the *Philadelphia Inquirer*, depicts a team of prima donnas, innocents, and malcontents bullied into the post-season by Dallas Green, their outspoken and physically intimidating manager. Fitzpatrick's focus on legal calamities and communications problems tend to overwhelm the shining moments of that unique season as well as the significant economic and social patterns that influenced the game at the time.

Chapter 1. Legacy of Losing

1. James A. Michener, "Life and Death Through the Years with the Phillies," *New York Times*, November 19, 1978.

2. James A. Michener, *Sports in America* (New York: Random House, 1976), 412.

3. See Sheldon Stewart, "Chicago Cubs," in *The Ballplayers: Baseball's Ultimate Biographical Reference*, ed. Mike Shatzkin (New York: William Morrow, 1990), 183-85. The Cubs won the World Series in 1907 and 1908 and captured National League pennants in 1876, '80–82, '85–86, '06–08, '10, '18, '29, '32, '35, '38, and '45.

4. Dan Shaughnessy, *The Curse of the Bambino* (New York: Penguin, 2000), 1–4. According to the "Curse," Harry Frazee, the Red Sox owner, sold the team's star player, Babe Ruth, to the New York Yankees in 1919 in order to finance his Broadway shows. Ruth, nicknamed the "Bambino," had been responsible for helping Boston to three of its six world championships between 1903 and 1918. When he was sold, Ruth "cursed" the Red Sox by going on to lead the Yankees to 7 pennants and 4 World Series titles. The Red Sox, on the other hand, failed to win another fall classic until 2004.

5. Shaughnessy, *Curse of the Bambino*, 18.

6. Rich Westcott and Frank Bilovsky, *The Phillies Encyclopedia* (Philadelphia: Temple University Press, 2002), 595–97; Jeré Longman, "Milestone Marks What Phillies Fans Already Knew," *New York Times*, June 12, 2007.

7. See William C. Kashatus, *September Swoon: Richie Allen, the '64 Phillies, and Racial Integration* (University Park: Pennsylvania State University Press, 2004).

8. Westcott and Bilovsky, *Phillies Encyclopedia*, 467–72.

9. Robin Roberts and C. Paul Rogers, III, *The Whiz Kids and the 1950 Pennant* (Philadelphia: Temple University Press, 1996), 339–45.

10. David M. Jordan, *Occasional Glory: A History of the Philadelphia Phillies* (Jefferson, N.C.: McFarland, 2002), 195–207.

11. Rich Westcott, *Phillies '93: An Incredible Season* (Philadelphia: Temple University Press, 1994), 122-27; see also Philadelphia Inquirer, *Worst to First: The Story of the 1993 Phillies* (Philadelphia: Philadelphia Inquirer, 1993), 178–80; John Kruk with Paul Hagen, *"I Ain't an Athlete, Lady . . ."* (New York: Simon & Schuster, 1994), 28–30; and Robert Gordon and Tom Burgoyne, *Beards, Bellies, and Biceps: The Story of the 1993 Phillies* (New York: Sports Publishing, 2002), 231–33.

12. Allen Lewis, *The Philadelphia Phillies: A Pictorial History* (Virginia Beach: JCP Corporation, 1981), 17.

13. Rich Westcott, *Philadelphia's Old Ballparks* (Philadelphia: Temple University Press, 1996), 9–12.

14. Jordan, *Occasional Glory*, 8–11.

15. Westcott, *Philadelphia's Old Ballparks*, 27–30.

16. Lewis, *Phillies*, 18–19.

17. See Jerrold Casway, *Ed Delahanty in the Emerald Age of Baseball* (Notre Dame, Ind.: University of Notre Dame Press, 2004).

18. Lewis, *Phillies*, 18–19.

19. Nathaniel Burt and Wallace E. Davies, "The Iron Age, 1876-1905," in *Philadelphia: A 300-Year History*, ed. Russell F. Weigley (New York: W.W. Norton, 1982), 519.

20. Harold Seymour, *Baseball: The Early Years* (New York: Oxford University Press, 1989), 75–85.

21. Donald Honig, *The Philadelphia Phillies: An Illustrated History* (New York: Simon & Schuster, 1992), 21.

22. Lewis, *Phillies*, 19.

23. Rick Wolff, ed., *The Baseball Encyclopedia*, 8th ed. (New York: Macmillan, 1990), 109.

24. Seymour, *Early Years*, 135–71.

25. Westcott and Bilovsky, *Phillies Encyclopedia*, 14–22.

26. Wolff, *Baseball Encyclopedia*, 838.

27. Wolff, *Baseball Encyclopedia*, 1121.

28. John M. Rosenburg, *The Story of Baseball* (New York: Random House, 1970), 39–40.

29. David M. Jordan, *The Athletics of Philadelphia: Connie Mack's White Elephants, 1901-1954* (Jefferson, N.C.: McFarland, 1999), 15–16. Shibe purchased original investor Charles Somers's stock in the A's. Mack owned another 25 percent and two Philadelphia newspapermen, Frank Hough and Sam Jones, shared the remaining 25 percent.

30. Wilfred Sheed, "Manager: Mr. Mack and the Main Chance," in *The Ultimate Baseball Book*, ed. Daniel Okrent and Harris Lewine (Boston: Houghton Mifflin, 1981), 106.

31. Robert Warrington, "The Story of the 1902 American League Champion Athletics," *Along the Elephant Trail* 6, 1 (Winter 2002): 4; and J. M. Murphy, "Napoleon Lajoie: Modern Baseball's First Superstar," *National Pastime* (Spring 1988): 14–15. Mack continued to snare players from the Phillies just before the opening of the '02 season when he lured right fielder and future Hall of Famer Elmer Flick, pitcher Bill Duggleby, and shortstop Monte Cross to his A's. Nor was Mack the only American League manager to raid the Phillies' roster. The St. Louis Browns stole pitcher Red Donahue, who posted a 21-13 record in 1901, and Washington snared power hitter Ed Delahanty, a future Hall of Famer, third baseman Harry Wolverton, and pitchers Jack Townsend and Al Orth, a 21-game winner in '01.

32. Warrington, "Story of the 1902 American League Champion Athletics," 4.

33. *Philadelphia Ball Club, Limited, v. Lajoie,* 202 Pa. 210, 217, 219, 221 (1902). Although Cross, Flick, and Duggleby were not named in the litigation, the ruling also applied to them.

34. John McGraw, quoted in Sheed, "Manager," 108.

35. Jordan, *Athletics of Philadelphia,* 23–24; and Warrington, "Story of 1902 American League Champion Athletics," 4. Fraser willingly returned to the National League.

36. Connie Mack, quoted in *Philadelphia Public Ledger,* April 22, 1902.

37. See William C. Kashatus, *Money Pitcher: Chief Bender and the Tragedy of Indian Assimilation* (University Park: Pennsylvania State University Press, 2006). Bender was a star pitcher of Mack's first championship dynasty. His story is told in the context of the 1903–14 Philadelphia Athletics teams.

38. Lewis, *Phillies,* 25.

39. Seymour, *Baseball's Early Years,* 145–48; and G. Edward White, *Creating the National Pastime: Baseball Transforms Itself, 1903–1953* (Princeton, N.J.: Princeton University Press, 1996), 60–63.

40. Westcott and Bilovsky, *Phillies Encyclopedia,* 24–29.

41. Westcott and Bilovsky, *Phillies Encyclopedia,* 30.

42. Westcott and Bilovsky, *Phillies Encyclopedia,* 32–33.

43. Westcott and Bilovsky, *Phillies Encyclopedia,* 469–71, 542.

44. Lewis, *Phillies,* 40.

45. Westcott and Bilovsky, *Phillies Encyclopedia,* 549.

46. Eloit Asinof, *Eight Men Out: The Black Sox and the 1919 World Series* (New York: Henry Holt, 1963); Daniel E. Ginsburg, *The Fix Is In: A History of Baseball Gambling and Game Fixing Scandals* (Jefferson, N.C.: McFarland, 1995), 100–182.

47. Wolff, *Baseball Encyclopedia,* 1104.

48. William C. Kashatus, *Connie Mack's '29 Triumph: The Rise and Fall of the Philadelphia Athletics Dynasty* (Jefferson, N.C.: McFarland, 1999). In addition to the Athletics, Philadelphians could enjoy the flashy, fast-paced style of the city's Negro League teams, created in the wake of the owners' "gentlemen's agreement" barring African Americans from the major leagues. By the 1920s, both black and white fans were flocking to the old wooden-frame ballparks where the Hilldales and, later the Stars, played. There they could revel in the exploits of such remarkable players as William "Judy" Johnson, Oscar Charleston, and Gene Benson. See Neil Lanctot, *Fair Dealing and Clean Playing: The Hilldale Club and the Development of Black Professional Baseball, 1910–1932* (Jefferson, N.C.: McFarland, 1994).

49. Westcott and Bilovsky, *Phillies Encyclopedia,* 553.

50. Lawrence S. Ritter, *Lost Ballparks: A Celebration of Baseball's Legendary Fields* (New York: Viking, 1992), 12.

51. Westcott, *Philadelphia's Old Ballparks,* 91–98.

52. Bill Dooly, "Phillies Lose Finale at Baker Bowl," *Philadelphia Record,* July 1, 1938.

53. Lewis, *Phillies,* 50–60.

54. Westcott and Bilovsky, *Phillies Encyclopedia,* 374–75.

55. Westcott and Bilovsky, *Phillies Encyclopedia,* 377.

56. Jackie Robinson, *I Never Had It Made* (New York: G.P. Putnam's Sons, 1972), 71–76; Jules Tygiel, *Baseball's Great Experiment: Jackie Robinson and His Legacy,* expanded ed. (New York: Oxford University Press, 1997), 182–87; David Falkner, *Great Time Coming: The Life of Jackie Robinson from Baseball to Birmingham* (New York: Simon

& Schuster, 1995), 163–64; and William Ecenbarger, "First Among Equals," *Philadelphia Inquirer Magazine*, February 19, 1995, 14.

57. Tom McGrath, "Color Me Badd," *The Fan* 11 (September 1996): 39; and Michael Sokolove, "Nice Is Not Enough," *Philadelphia Inquirer Magazine*, March 30, 1997, 21.

58. Roberts and Rogers, *Whiz Kids and the 1950 Pennant*.

59. Jordan, *Athletics of Philadelphia*, 172–86.

60. Eddie Sawyer quoted in Honig, *Philadelphia Phillies History*, 167.

61. Norman Macht, "Gene Mauch," in *Ballplayers*, ed. Shatzkin, 686.

62. Westcott and Bilovsky, *Phillies Encyclopedia*, 452–54.

63. "Can the Phils Keep Losing Forever?" *New York Herald Tribune*, August 17, 1961.

64. Ray Kelly, "Phils Win . . . Finally," *Philadelphia Bulletin*, August 21, 1961.

65. Westcott and Bilovsky, *Phillies Encyclopedia*, 77–78.

66. Kashatus, *September Swoon*.

67. Bob Uecker, quoted in Westcott and Bilovsky, *Phillies Encyclopedia*, 542.

68. Joe Queenan, *True Believers: The Tragic Inner Life of Sports Fans* (New York: Picador/Holt, 2003), 11.

CHAPTER 2. DOWN ON THE FARM

Earlier versions of portions of this chapter appeared in William C. Kashatus, *Mike Schmidt: Philadelphia's Hall of Fame Third Baseman* (Jefferson, N.C.: McFarland, 2000). Reprinted by permission.

1. Ruly Carpenter, interview by author, Wilmington, Delaware, June 2, 2005.

2. Carpenter interview.

3. Carpenter interview.

4. Frank Dolson, *Beating the Bushes: Life in the Minor Leagues* (South Bend, Ind.: Icarus Press, 1982), 207.

5. Hal Bodley, "The Pope and His Pupil," *Phillies 1978 Yearbook* (Philadelphia: Phillies, 1978), 45.

6. Carpenter interview.

7. Bodley, "Pope and His Pupil," 46.

8. Bodley, "Pope and His Pupil," 46.

9. Jack Carney, "Paul Owens: Success at Every Level," *Phillies 1984 Yearbook* (Philadelphia: Phillies, 1984), 3.

10. Carney, "Paul Owens," 4

11. Paul Owens, quoted in Carney, "Paul Owens," 5.

12. Paul Owens, quoted in Bodley, "Pope and His Pupil," 47.

13. Carney, "Paul Owens," 5; Bodley, "Pope and His Pupil," 46.

14. Carpenter interview.

15. Paul Owens quoted in Carney, "Paul Owens," 5; and Bodley, "Pope and Pupil," 47.

16. Carpenter interview.

17. George Gmelch, *Inside Pitch: Life in Professional Baseball* (Washington, D.C.: Smithsonian Institution Press, 2001), 6–17.

18. Mark Winegardner, *Prophet of the Sandlots: Journeys with a Major League Scout* (New York: Atlantic Monthly Press, 1990), 1–6.

19. Carpenter interview.

20. Carpenter interview.

21. Paul Owens, quoted in Frank Fitzpatrick, *You Can't Lose 'Em All: The Year the Phillies Finally Won the World Series* (Dallas: Taylor, 2001), 97.

22. Carpenter interview.

23. Carney, "Paul Owens," 5.

24. Eddie Bockman, quoted in Larry Bowa with Barry Bloom, *Bleep! Larry Bowa Manages* (Chicago: Bonus Books, 1988), 89.

25. Eddie Bockman, quoted in Bowa and Bloom, *Bleep!*, 95.

26. Eddie Bockman, quoted on Larry Bowa, October 2, 1965, in "Exclusive Scouting Reports," *Phillies 1978 Yearbook*, 50.

27. Allen Lewis, "Larry Bowa," *Phillies 1971 Yearbook* (Philadelphia: Phillies, 1971), 5–6.

28. Paul Bowa, quoted in Bowa, *Bleep!*, 87.

29. Larry Bowa, interview by author, Radnor, Pennsylvania, August 15, 1992; Bowa, *Bleep!*, 90.

30. Bill Conlin, quoted in Bowa, *Bleep!*, 260.

31. Gene Mauch, quoted in Bowa, *Bleep!*, 260.

32. Larry Bowa, interview by author, Ardmore, Pennsylvania, November 12, 2005.

33. Dolson, *Beating the Bushes*, 144.

34. Dolson, *Beating the Bushes*, 144.

35. Bowa, *Bleep!*, 260.

36. Dolson, *Beating the Bushes*, 143.

37. Frank Piet, quoted on Greg Luzinski, April 6, 1968, in "Exclusive Scouting Reports," *Phillies 1978 Yearbook*, 48.

38. Bill Conlin, *"Batting Cleanup, Bill Conlin"*, ed. Kevin Kerrane (Philadelphia: Temple University Press, 1997), 115. *Philadelphia Daily News* sportswriter Bill Conlin shortened Luzinski's nickname to "Bull."

39. Paul Owens, quoted in Fitzpatrick, *You Can't Lose 'Em All*, 72.

40. Manny Trillo, interview by author, Scranton, Pennsylvania, June 27, 2005.

41. Greg Luzinski, interview by author, Philadelphia, August 3, 2005; Dolson, *Beating the Bushes*, 135.

42. Luzinski interview.

43. Dolson, *Beating the Bushes*, 136–37.

44. Paul Owens, quoted in Chris Wheeler, "Paul Owens: I've Got a Feeling," *Phillies 1976 Yearbook* (Philadelphia: Phillies, 1976), 9.

45. Luzinski interview.

46. Dolson, *Beating the Bushes*, 135.

47. Bob Boone, quoted in Dolson, *Beating the Bushes*, 134.

48. Dolson, *Beating the Bushes*, 134.

49. Howie Bedell, interview by author, Pottstown, Pennsylvania, September 20, 2005.

50. Bedell interview.

51. Bob Boone, interview by author, Atlantic City, New Jersey, October 15, 2005.

52. Eddie Bockman, quoted on Bob Boone, April 2 and May 17, 1969 in "Exclusive Scouting Reports," *Phillies 1978 Yearbook*, 49.

53. Boone interview.

54. Boone interview.

55. Boone interview.

56. Boone interview.

57. Rich Westcott and Frank Bilovsky, *The Phillies Encyclopedia* (Philadelphia: Temple University Press, 2002), 136.

58. Tony Lucadello, quoted in Winegardner, *Prophet of the Sandlots*, 61.

59. Lucadello, quoted in Jay Searcy, "Few Saw the Potential," *Philadelphia Inquirer*, June 1, 1989.

60. Stan Hochman, *Mike Schmidt: Baseball's King of Swing* (New York: Random House, 1983), 15–16.

61. Palsgrove and Galvin, quoted in Paul Meyer, "Prep Honorable Mention to Series MVP," *Dayton Journal Herald*, October 23, 1980; Hochman, *Mike Schmidt*, 18.

62. Mike Schmidt, in William C. Kashatus, "Pride of the Philadelphia Phillies: An Interview with Mike Schmidt," *Pennsylvania Heritage* (Fall 1995): 14–15. See also Mike Schmidt with Barbara Walder, *Always on the Offense* (New York: Atheneum, 1982), 22–23.

63. Mike Schmidt, interview with author, Jupiter, Florida, October 8, 1998.

64. Schmidt, *Always on the Offense*, 24.

65. Wren, quoted in Ritter Collett, "Schmidt, Pride of Dayton," *Dayton Journal Herald*, October 20, 1980.

66. Hochman, *Mike Schmidt*, 23–24.

67. Lucadello, quoted in Winegardner, *Prophet of the Sandlots*, 61.

68. Hochman, *Mike Schmidt*, 25; Dolson, *Beating the Bushes*, 125.

69. Mike Schmidt with Glen Waggoner, *Clearing the Bases: Juiced Players, Monster Salaries, Sham Records and a Hall of Famer's Search for the Soul of Baseball* (New York: HarperCollins, 2006), 6–8.

70. Ken Tuckey, "Phillies Win, 4-3, on Draftee's Home Run," *Reading Times*, June 18, 1971.

71. Dolson, *Beating the Bushes*, 125

72. Westcott and Bilovsky, *Phillies Encyclopedia*, 251–52.

73. Lucadello quoted in Winegardner, *Prophet of the Sandlots*, 61.

74. Schmidt interview, October 8, 1998.

75. Schmidt interview, October 8, 1998; Schmidt, *Clearing the Bases*, 13–14.

76. Schmidt, quoted in Dolson, *Beating the Bushes*, 128–29.

77. John Vukovich, interview by author, Scranton, Pennsylvania, May 11, 2006.

78. *Sporting News*, August 19, 1972.

79. Schmidt, *Clearing the Bases*, 14–16.

80. Mike Schmidt, "Who's on Third . . . And Why He's There," *Temple University Alumni Magazine* (December 1995): 10.

81. Hochman, *Mike Schmidt*, 34; Rich Westcott, *Baseball Legends: Mike Schmidt* (Philadelphia: Chelsea House, 1995), 27.

82. Schmidt, quoted in Dolson, *Beating the Bushes*, 127.

83. Bowa interview, August 15, 1992; Boone interview; Luzinski interview; Schmidt interview,; Vukovich interview; Howie Bedell, interview by author, Pottstown, Pennsylvania, August 14, 2006.

CHAPTER 3. THE VET

Portions of this chapter appeared in an earlier form in William C. Kashatus, *September Swoon: Richie Allen, the '64 Phillies, and Racial Integration* (University Park: Pennsylvania State University Press, 2004), reprinted by permission.

1. Rich Westcott, *Philadelphia's Old Ballparks* (Philadelphia: Temple University Press, 1996), 106, 113; and Lawrence Ritter, *Lost Ballparks: A Celebration of Baseball's Legendary Fields* (New York: Penguin, 1992), 178.

2. Westcott, *Philadelphia's Old Ballparks*, 167.

3. Interview of Larry Shenk, Philadelphia, October 28, 2005.

4. Allen Lewis, interview by author, Clearwater, Florida, December 29, 2001.

5. Linda Belsky Zamost, "The Year That Almost Was," *Philly Sport* (June 1989): 17–20.

6. Ritter, *Lost Ballparks*, 185.

7. Bobby Wine, quoted in Johnny Callison with John Sletten, *The Johnny Callison Story* (New York: Vantage, 1991), 127.

8. Bruce Kuklick, *To Every Thing a Season: Shibe Park and Urban Philadelphia, 1909–1976* (Princeton, N.J.: Princeton University Press, 1991), 148–49; Phillies Hall of Fame artist Dick Perez, interview by author, Wayne, Pennsylvania, April 16, 2001.

9. Kuklick, *To Every Thing a Season*, 165–66.

10. Kulick, *To Every Thing a Season*, 155.

11. Kulick, *To Every Thing a Season*, 155; for statistics on Phillies attendance, see B. G. Kelley, "And There Used to Be a Ballpark Right Here," *Philly Sport* 2 (June 1989): 49.

12. Rich Westcott, *Veterans Stadium: Field of Memories* (Philadelphia: Temple University Press, 2005), 2–3.

13. Ruly Carpenter, quoted in Westcott, *Veterans Stadium*, 4.

14. Westcott, *Veterans Stadium*, 4–5. The bond had increased from the original estimate of $22.7 million in 1962 to $25 million in 1964.

15. For a complete treatment of Dick Allen's early career in Philadelphia, see William C. Kashatus, *September Swoon: Richie Allen, the '64 Phillies, and Racial Integration* (University Park: Pennsylvania State University Press, 2004).

16. "Phils Trade Allen to St. Louis, Phila. Gets Hoerner and Browne—Flood Plans to Retire as Player," *New York Times*, October 9, 1969.

17. Curt Flood to baseball commissioner Bowie Kuhn, December 24, 1969, quoted in Geoffrey Ward and Ken Burns, *Baseball: An Illustrated History* (New York: Knopf, 1994), 411.

18. See *Flood v. Kuhn*, U.S. District Court of New York (1970); Curt Flood, "Why I Challenged Baseball," *Sport* 32 (March 1970): 10–13; Edmund P. Edmonds and William H. Manz, eds., *Baseball and Antitrust: The Legislative History of the Curt Flood Act of 1998, Public Law No. 105-297, 112 Stat. 2824* (Buffalo, N.Y.: William S. Hein, 2001); and William Gildes, "Curt Flood: Baseball's Angry Rebel," *Baseball Digest* 12 (February 1971): 55–61. Brad Snyder's *A Well-Paid Slave: Curt Flood's Fight for Free Agency in Professional Sports* (New York: Viking, 2006) is the best secondary source on the subject.

19. Rick Wise, interview by author, Camden, New Jersey, September 5, 2001.

20. Frank Lucchesi, interview by author, Colleyville, Texas, January 6, 2002.

21. Rich Westcott and Frank Bilovsky, *The Phillies Encyclopedia* (Philadelphia: Temple University Press, 2002), 352.

22. Lucchesi interview.

23. Lucchesi interview.

24. Billy DeMars, quoted in Larry Bowa with Barry Bloom, *Bleep! Larry Bowa Manages* (Chicago: Bonus Books, 1988), 259, 262.

25. Lucchesi interview.

26. Tim McCarver with Ray Robinson, *Oh, Baby, I Love It!* (New York: Dell, 1988), 123.

27. Westcott and Bilovsky, *Phillies Encyclopedia*, 84–85.

28. William Y. Giles, interview by author, Philadelphia, July 15, 2005.

29. Westcott, *Philadelphia's Old Ballparks*, 192; and Frank Dolson, "Nostalgia Evening Ends in Nightmare," *Philadelphia Inquirer*, October 2, 1970.

30. Kulick, *To Every Thing a Season*, 180

31. Art Wolfe, quoted in Westcott, *Philadelphia's Old Ballparks*, 193.

32. Wolfe, , 194.

33. Kulick, *To Every Thing a Season*, 180.

34. "Saying Goodbye to Connie Mack," *Philadelphia Daily News*, October 2, 1970. Connie Mack Stadium was badly damaged by fire in 1971 and totally demolished in 1976. Today, the block on which it stood is occupied by the Deliverance Evangelistic Church.

35. "How an Empty Lot in South Philadelphia Became One of the Finest Stadiums in the World," *Phillies 1971 Yearbook* (Philadelphia: Phillies, 1971), 15.

36. Westcott, *Veterans Stadium*, 13.

37. "How an Empty Lot Became a Stadium," 14.

38. Westcott, *Veterans Stadium*, 16–18; and "The Stadium," *Phillies 1971 Yearbook*, 6–7.

39. Westcott, *Veterans Stadium*, 16–18; "The Stadium,"6–7.

40. Bill Giles, quoted in "The Stadium," 6–7.

41. Westcott and Bilovsky, *Phillies Encyclopedia*, 379.

42. Giles interview.

43. Giles interview.

44. Giles interview.

45. Westcott and Bilovsky, *Phillies Encyclopedia*, 379.

46. Giles interview.

47. Giles interview.

48. Shenk interview.

49. Giles interview.

50. Giles interview.

51. Robert Gordon, *Legends of the Philadelphia Phillies* (Champaign, Ill.: Sports Publishing, 2005), 83.

52. Westcott, *Veterans Stadium*, 20–22.

53. Gene Mauch, quoted in "D-Day in South Philadelphia," *Phillies 1972 Yearbook* (Philadelphia: Phillies, 1972), 4.

54. Bowie Kuhn, quoted in "D-Day in South Philadelphia," 5.

55. Westcott, *Veterans Stadium*, 22–23.

56. Westcott and Bilovsky, *Phillies Encyclopedia*, 85–86.

57. Ray Ripplemeyer, quoted in Bill Conlin, "Now Rick's Immortal, Too," *Philadelphia Daily News*, June 24, 1971.

58. Rick Wise, quoted in Conlin, "Now Rick's Immortal, Too."

59. Westcott and Bilovsky, *Phillies Encyclopedia*, 453.

60. Tim McCarver, quoted in Conlin, "Now Rick's Immortal."

61. Westcott and Bilovsky, *Phillies Encyclopedia*, 452–53.

62. Westcott and Bilovsky,, *Phillies Encyclopedia*, 226.

63. Rick Wolff, *The Baseball Encyclopedia* (New York: Macmillan, 1989), 701.

64. Larry Bowa, interview by author, Radnor, Pennsylvania, August 15, 1992.

65. Bowa interview.

66. Chris Wheeler, "Gone But Not Forgotten: Greg Luzinski," *Phillies 1985 Yearbook* (Philadelphia: Phillies, 1985), 56.

67. Westcott and Bilovsky, *Phillies Encyclopedia*, 86.

68. Westcott and Bilovsky, *Phillies Encyclopedia*, 85.

CHAPTER 4. LEFTY

1. Tim McCarver with Ray Robinson, *Oh, Baby, I Love It!* (New York: Dell, 1988), 51.

2. McCarver, *Oh, Baby, I Love It!*, 50.

3. Bob Broeg, "Even Bubble-Gum Cards Can't Keep Up with Carlton," *Sporting News*, March 23, 1968.

4. Carlton, quoted in Neal Russo, "Cards Foes Slipping on Steve's Slider," *Sporting News*, August 30, 1969.

5. Carlton, quoted in Russo, "Cards Foes Slipping on Steve's Slider,"

6. John Thorn and Pete Palmer, eds., *Total Baseball* (New York: Warner, 1989), 1630.

7. Dick Young, "Allen and Carlton Draw More Fire from Gussie," *New York Daily News*, March 13, 1970. Carlton wasn't the only Cardinal holdout. Richie Allen, recently acquired from the Phillies, refused to report to spring training until he was offered a $90,000 salary by Busch. "If Allen doesn't take our offer," said the St. Louis owner, "he won't ever play for the Cardinals." Hours later, Allen showed up at spring training.

8. Bob Broeg, "Birds Toss Book at Richie and Steve," *Sporting News*, March 21, 1970. The New York Yankees invoked the renewal clause a few years earlier when pitcher Jim Bouton refused to report to spring training, threatening him with a $100-a-day fine.

9. Gussie Busch, quoted in Young, "Allen and Carlton Draw More Fire."

10. "Carlton Accepts Two-Year Contract," *New York Times*, March 18, 1970.

11. Thorn and Palmer, *Total Baseball*, 1630.

12. Joseph Durso, "Cards Trade Carlton to Phillies for Wise in Pitcher Exchange," *New York Times*, February 26, 1972.

13. John Helyar, *Lords of the Realm: The Real History of Baseball* (New York: Villard, 1994), 36–37, 79.

14. Helyar, *Lords of the Realm*, 37–38.

15. Helyar, *Lords of the Realm*, 110.

16. Helyar, *Lords of the Realm*, 110.

17. Helyar, *Lords of the Realm*, 111.

18. Durso, "Cards Trade Carlton to Phillies for Wise."

19. Rick Wise, quoted in Durso, "Cards Trade Carlton to Phillies for Wise."

20. Rick Wise, interview by author, Camden, New Jersey, September 5, 2001.

21. Steve Carlton, quoted in Frank Dolson, "Steve Carlton," *Annual Baseball Hall of Fame Program* (Cooperstown, N.Y.: National Baseball Hall of Fame/Sporting News, 1994), 4.

22. Bing Devine, quoted in Larry Fox, "Carlton-Wise Trade: Strictly Business," *New York Daily News*, February 26, 1972.

23. Steve Carlton, quoted in Fox, "Carlton-Wise Trade: Strictly Business."

24. Carlton, quoted in Fox, "Carlton-Wise Trade: Strictly Business." The Phillies had been after Carlton for two years and had all but given up on him. In fact, Quinn, during the winter of 1971–72, had been pursuing a trade with the Mets for Nolan Ryan using catcher Tim McCarver as the bait.

25. Gussie Busch, quoted in Helyar, *Lords of the Realm*, 113.

26. "No April Fools—Players Go on Strike," *Sporting News*, April 3, 1972.

27. Helyar, *Lords of the Realm*, 120–22.

28. Helyar, *Lords of the Realm*, 127; see also Alex Belth, *Stepping Up: The Story of Curt Flood and His Fight for Baseball Players' Rights* (New York: Persea, 2006). Belth's carefully

researched book on Flood's challenge to the reserve clause argues that the Cardinal center fielder knew he wouldn't win his Supreme Court case against Major League Baseball, but was still willing to sacrifice his career and whatever income he might have made on principle.

29. Geoffrey C. Ward and Ken Burns, *Baseball: An Illustrated History* (New York: Knopf, 1994), 423.

30. Senator Samuel Ervin, quoted in Ward and Burns, *Baseball*, 423–24.

31. Ervin, quoted in Ward and Burns, *Baseball*, 424.

32. Allen Lewis, "Carlton Retrieves Discarded Slider and Zooms," *Sporting News*, May 20, 1972.

33. Steve Carlton, quoted in Bill Conlin, *Batting Cleanup* (Philadelphia: Temple University Press, 1997), 83–84.

34. Ray Ripplemeyer, quoted in Conlin, *Batting Cleanup*, 84.

35. Lewis, "Carlton Retrieves Discarded Slider."

36. Tim McCarver, quoted in Lewis, "Carlton Retrieves Discarded Slider."

37. Steve Carlton, quoted in Lewis, "Carlton Retrieves Discarded Slider."

38. McCarver, *Oh, Baby, I Love It!*, 155.

39. Chris Wheeler, "Paul Owens: I've Got a Feeling," *Phillies 1976 Yearbook* (Philadelphia: Phillies, 1976), 8.

40. Rich Westcott and Frank Bilovsky, *The Phillies Encyclopedia* (Philadelphia: Temple University Press, 2004), 352.

41. Frank Lucchesi, interview by author, Collegeville, Texas, January 6, 2002.

42. Larry Bowa, interview by author, Ardmore, Pennsylvania, November 12, 2005

43. Ruly Carpenter, interview by author, Wilmington, Delaware, June 2, 2005.

44. Paul Owens, quoted in Wheeler, "Paul Owens," 8.

45. Owens, quoted in Wheeler, "Paul Owens," 9.

46. "Countryside: A Look at the Farm System," *Phillies 1973 Yearbook* (Philadelphia: Phillies, 1973), 65.

47. Owens, quoted in Wheeler, "Paul Owens," 9. See also author's interviews with Bill Conlin, Turnersville, New Jersey, June 16, 2005; Dallas Green, West Grove, Pennsylvania, July 5, 2005; Howie Bedell, Pottstown, Pennsylvania, September 20, 2005.

48. Westcott, *Veterans Stadium*, 86–87.

49. Bill Conlin, "Just Super Steve!" *Philadelphia Daily News*, August 17, 1972.

50. Tommy Hutton, interview by author, Palm Beach Gardens, Florida, August 12, 2005.

51. Bowa interview.

52. Steve Carlton, quoted in Allen Lewis, "Think Positive! That's Carlton's Credo," *Sporting News*, September 2, 1972.

53. Westcott and Bilovsky, *Phillies Encyclopedia*, 86.

54. Bob Carpenter, quoted in Hal Bodley, "The Pope and His Pupil," *Phillies 1978 Yearbook* (Philadelphia: Phillies, 1978), 47.

55. Ruly Carpenter interview.

56. Bill Giles, quoted in Bill Conlin, "Direction '73," *Phillies 1973 Yearbook* (Philadelphia: Phillies, 1973), 5.

57. Frank Dolson, *The Philadelphia Story: A City of Winners* (South Bend, Ind.: Icarus Press, 1981), 182–83.

58. Dolson, *The Philadelphia Story*, 183–84.

59. Bill Giles, interview by author, Philadelphia, July 15, 2005.

60. Giles interview.

61. Danny Ozark, interview by author, Vero Beach, Florida, August 8, 2005.

62. Ruly Carpenter interview.

63. Danny Ozark, quoted in Bill Conlin, "Ozark, the Fundamentalist," *Philadelphia Daily News*, March 16, 1973.

64. Westcott and Bilovsky, *Phillies Encyclopedia*, 86.

65. Westcott and Bilovsky, *Phillies Encyclopedia*, 86.

66. Ozark, quoted in Conlin, "Direction '73," 4.

67. Westcott and Bilovsky, *Phillies Encyclopedia*, 87; Stan Hochman, *Mike Schmidt: Baseball's King of Swing* (New York: Random House, 1983), 43.

68. Ozark, quoted in Ray Didinger, "He Remained in Schmidt's "Hot corner," *Philadelphia Daily News* (Special Feature), July 26, 1995.

69. Ray Kelly, "Schmidt's 'Strikes' Putting Crimp in Ozark Schedule," *Sporting News*, August 18, 1973; Hochman, *Mike Schmidt*, 49.

70. Mike Schmidt, interview, "Michael Jack City," *The Fan* (May 1995): 27; see also Kelly, "Schmidt's 'Strikes' Putting Crimp in Ozark Schedule"; Schmidt, quoted in Westcott, *Mike Schmidt*, 30.

71. Hochman, *Mike Schmidt*, 39.

72. See Schmidt, "Michael Jack City," 29; and Larry Bowa with Barry Bloom, *Bleep! Larry Bowa Manages* (Chicago: Bonus Books, 1988), 161–63.

73. Schmidt, quoted in George Vass, "Talent Explosion at the Hot Corner," *Baseball Digest* (May 1975): 20.

74. Hochman, *Mike Schmidt*, 40.

75. Larry Christenson, interview by author, Malvern, Pennsylvania, August 12, 1005.

76. Frank Fitzpatrick, *You Can't Lose 'Em All: The Year the Phillies Finally Won the World Series* (Dallas: Taylor, 2001), 80–81.

77. McCarver, *Oh, Baby, I Love It!*, 56.

78. Ozark interview.

79. Jim Lonborg, interview by author, Scituate, Massachusetts, August 9, 2005.

80. Conlin interview.

81. Bill Conlin, "It Wasn't My Fault He Wouldn't Speak," *Philadelphia Daily News* supplement, August 1, 1994.

82. McCarver, *Oh, Baby, I Love It!*, 83.

83. Dolson, *The Philadelphia Story*, 186.

84. Dolson, *The Philadelphia Story*, 215.

85. Christenson interview.

86. Dolson, *The Philadelphia Story*, 188.

87. Christenson interview.

88. Westcott and Bilovsky, *Phillies Encyclopedia*, 86–87, 354.

CHAPTER 5. "YES WE CAN"

1. Dallas Green, interview by author, West Chester, Pennsylvania, October 13, 1999.

2. Paul Owens, quoted in Frank Fitzpatrick, *You Can't Lose 'Em All: The Year the Phillies Finally Won the World Series* (Dallas, Taylor, 2001), 72

3. Dallas Green, interview by author, West Grove, Pennsylvania, July 5, 2005.

4. Hal Bodley, *The Team That Wouldn't Die: The Philadelphia Phillies, World Champions, 1980*, 97; and Tom Jozwik, "Dallas Green," in Mike Shotzkin, ed. The *Ballplayers:*

Baseball's Ultimate Biographical Reference Book (New York: Arbor House/William Morrow, 1995), 409.

5. Green interview, July 5, 2005.

6. Howie Bedell, interview by author, Pottstown, Pennsylvania, September 20, 2005.

7. Bedell interview; Ruben Amaro, interview, Weston, Florida, May 16, 2006.

8. Amaro interview; Bedell interview; Green interview, July 5, 2005.

9. Amaro interview; Bedell interview; Green interview, July 5, 2005.

10. Tug McGraw, interview, West Chester, Pennsylvania, May 3, 2000.

11. Bedell interview.

12. Bedell interview; Green interview, July 5, 2005.

13. Bedell interview.

14. Bedell interview.

15. Bedell interview.

16. Amaro interview.

17. Amaro interview.

18. Peter C. Bjarkman, *Baseball with a Latin Beat: A History of the Latin American Game* (Jefferson, N.C.: McFarland, 1994); Bruce Markusen, *The Team That Changed Baseball: Roberto Clemente and the 1971 Pittsburgh Pirates* (Yardley, Pa.: Westholme, 2006).

19. Amaro interview.

20. Bedell interview.

21. Amaro interview. Shortstop Jorge Lebron at fourteen was the youngest player ever signed to a professional contract. He played for two years at the Phillies Single-A club at Auburn, New York, where he was joined by another Amaro signee, Orlando Isalis, a fifteen-year-old catcher-third baseman. Isales played in 3 games with the Phillies; Lebron never made it past Double-A ball.

22. Mark Carfagno, interview, South Philadelphia, June 24, 1006.

23. John Vukovich, interview, Scranton, Pennsylvania, May 4, 2006; see also interviews with Ruly Carpenter, Wilmington, Delaware, June 2, 2005; Greg Luzinski, South Philadelphia: August 3, 2005; of Tug McGraw, West Chester, Pennsylvania, May 8, 1999.

24. Paul Owens, quoted in Chris Wheeler, "Paul Owens: I've Got a Feeling," *Phillies 1976 Yearbook* (Philadelphia: Phillies, 1976), 8–9.

25. "Phillies Send Brett to Bucs for Dave Cash," *Philadelphia Daily News*, October 18, 1973.

26. Paul Owens quoted in Ron Reid, "Oops, Here Comes Philly Again," *Sports Illustrated* (June 10, 1974): 24–25.

27. Dave Cash, interview, Scranton, Pennsylvania, July 26, 2005; Reid, "Oops, Here Comes Philly Again"; Mark Heisler, "Dave Cash: Key Man in Phillies' Upsurge," *Baseball Digest* (October 1974): 40–42.

28. "Schmidt Powers Phils Past Mets," *Philadelphia Inquirer*, April 4, 1974.

29. Dave Anderson, "The 'Home Run' That Raised the Roof," *New York Times*, July 2, 1974; Ray Kelly, "Schmidt's Blast—Longest Single Ever?" *Sporting News*, June 29, 1974.

30. Cedeno, quoted in "Schmidt's Mighty Blast," *Philadelphia Bulletin*, June 12, 1974.

31. Schmidt, quoted in "Schmidt's Mighty Blast."

32. Reid, "Oops, Here Comes Philly Again."

33. Dave Cash, quoted in Reid, "Oops, Here Comes Philly Again."

34. Larry Bowa, quoted in Reid, "Oops, Here Comes Philly Again."

35. Cash interview, July 26, 2005.

36. Larry Bowa and Dave Cash, "Ting-a-ling, Double Play" (Philadelphia: Molly Records, 1974).

37. Cash interview, July 26, 2005; Cash, quoted in Larry Platt, "The Unloved: Mike Schmidt," *Philadelphia Magazine* (July 1995): 82.

38. Anderson, "'Home Run' That Raised the Roof"; Stan Hochman, *Mike Schmidt: Baseball's King of Swing* (New York: Random House, 1983), 53.

39. Rich Westcott and Frank Bilovsky, *The Phillies Encyclopedia* (Philadelphia: Temple University Press, 2002), 87–88.

40. Schmidt, quoted in Ray Kelly, "New-Style Schmidt Fires Phils' Frenzy," *Sporting News*, June 8, 1974; Ed Rumill, "Schmidt Finds His Other Batting Eye," *Christian Science Monitor*, June 11, 1974.

41. Schmidt quoted in "Michael Jack City," *The Fan* (May 1995): 29; Hochman, *Mike Schmidt*, 55–56; Schmidt, quoted in Platt, "The Unloved," 81; and Frank Dolson, *Beating the Bushes: Life in the Minor Leagues* (South Bend, Ind.: Icarus, 1982), 128.

42. Luzinski interview.

43. Bob Boone, interview, Atlantic City, New Jersey, October 15, 2005.

44. Westcott and Bilovsky, *Phillies' Encyclopedia*, 226; for Montaniz's statistics see Rick Wolff, ed., *The Baseball Encyclopedia*, 8th ed. (New York: Macmillan, 1990), 1248.

45. See Frank Dolson, "The Majors' Next Home Run King?" *Baseball Digest* (June 1974): 18–20; Pat Calabria, "Greg Luzinski: The Maturing of a Major League Slugger," *Baseball Digest* (November 1975): 45–48; for Luzinski's statistics see Wolff, *Baseball Encyclopedia*, 1162.

46. Luzinski interview.

47. Larry Bowa with Barry Bloom, *Bleep! Larry Bowa Manages* (Chicago: Bonus Books, 1988), 163.

48. Mike Schmidt, interview, Jupiter, Florida, October 8, 1998.

49. Bowa, *Bleep!*, 164.

50. Schmidt interview, October 8, 1998.

51. Bowa, *Bleep!*, 165.

52. "Phils Get Tug McGraw from Mets," *Philadelphia Daily News*, December 3, 1974.

53. Red Foley, "Mets Believe! Give Tug 90G," *New York Daily News*, February 15, 1974.

54. Tug McGraw with Don Yaeger, *Ya Gotta Believe! My Roller Coaster Life as a Screwball Pitcher and Part-Time Father, and My Hope-Filled Fight Against Brain Cancer* (New York: New American Library, 2004), 136.

55. Jack Lang, "Mets Hang Stiff Price Tag on Tug," *New York Daily News*, November 30, 1974.

56. McGraw, *Ya Gotta Believe!*, 134.

57. Dallas Green, quoted in Fitzpatrick, *You Can't Lose 'Em All!*, 217.

58. Paul Owens, quoted in Bill Conlin, "A Baseball Man Unlike Any Other," *Philadelphia Daily News*, December 29, 2003.

59. McGraw, *Ya Gotta Believe!*, 136.

60. See "Sports Editor's Mailbox: Tug at the Heart and Soul," *New York Times*, December 15, 1974.

61. See Tug McGraw and Joe Durso, *Screwball* (Boston: Houghton Mifflin, 1974). McGraw's slogan was inspired by M. Donald Grant, the Mets chairman of the board. Grant, in an attempt to rally the last-place Mets in June 1973, met with the players in the clubhouse. During his pep talk he repeatedly said, "You have to believe that you can

still win the division." McGraw made the saying a rally cry, screaming to his teammates, "Ya gotta believe!" See Dave Nightingale, "You Gotta Believe . . . And Relieve," *Chicago Daily News*, October 2, 1973.

62. See Zalon, Jennings, and Glitelman, quoted in "Sports Editor's Mailbox: Tug at the Heart and Soul," *New York Times*, December 15, 1974.

63. McGraw, *Ya Gotta Believe!*, 134–35.

64. Dick Young, "Tug Faces Arm Surgery, Cancer Test," *New York Daily News*, March 17, 1975.

65. Young, "Tug Faces Arm Surgery, Cancer Test."

66. Ray Kelly, "Tug Taken Aback by Surgery, But Arm's Okay," *Sporting News*, April 5, 1975.

67. McGraw interview, May 3, 2000.

68. Kelly, "Tug Taken Aback."

69. Tug McGraw, interview, West Chester, Pennsylvania, July 3, 2000.

70. Ray Kelly, "'Yes We Can!' Phillies Boast, With Eyes on N.L. East Title," *Philadelphia Bulletin*, March 8, 1975; Kelly, "The Bull and Bullpen Raise Phillies Flag Stock," *Philadelphia Bulletin*, April 12, 1975; Westcott and Bilovsky, *Phillies Encyclopedia*, 86–88.

71. Bill Conlin, "Tug No Boone to Tiger Trade," *Philadelphia Daily News*, December 4, 1974.

72. "Philadelphia Negotiating for Allen," *Philadelphia Inquirer*, February 17, 1975.

73. Dick Allen and Tim Whitaker, *Crash: The Life and Times of Dick Allen* (New York: Ticknor and Fields, 1989), 153.

74. Allen and Whitaker, *Crash*.

75. Ozark, quoted in Frank Dolson, *The Philadelphia Story: A City of Winners* (South Bend, Ind.: Icarus, 1981), 194

76. Ray Kelly, "Phils Kick Up Their Heels After Steve Stubs His Toe," *Sporting News*, April 26, 1975.

77. Allen Lewis, "Montañez Traded to Giants for Maddox," *Philadelphia Inquirer*, May 5, 1975.

78. Chris Wheeler, "Garry Maddox . . . No One Did It Better," *Phillies' 1987 Yearbook* (Philadelphia: Phillies, 1987), 65; Westcott and Bilovsky, *Phillies Encyclopedia*, 213.

79. Bill Conlin, "Can Allen Answer Trade Riddle?" *Philadelphia Daily News*, May 5, 1975; see also Conlin, "A Baseball Man Unlike Any Other," *Philadelphia Daily News*, December 29, 2003.

80. "Phils Sign Allen, Give Up Essian," *Philadelphia Daily News*, May 7, 1975; and interview of Dick Allen, West Chester, Pennsylvania, April 21, 2001.

81. Stan Hochman, "Dick Allen: 'I'm No Messiah,'" *Philadelphia Daily News*, May 8, 1975.

82. For Allen's statistics see Wolff, *Baseball Encyclopedia*, 625; Barry Rosenberg, "Two for the See-Saw," *Philadelphia Magazine* (September 1975): 130–44.

83. Allen interview.

84. "Danny Ozark's Five Simple Rules for Dick Allen," *Philadelphia Daily News*, May 8, 1975.

85. Ozark, quoted in Dolson, *Philadelphia Story*, 194.

86. Carfagno interview.

87. Carfagno interview.

88. Rosenberg, "Two for the See-Saw," 138.

89. Rosenberg, "Two for the See-Saw," 131–32.

90. Carpenter, quoted in Rosenberg, "Two for the See-Saw," 135.

91. Westcott and Bilovsky, *Phillies Encyclopedia*, 246–47.

92. Dick Ruthven, interview, Alpharetta, Georgia, August 9, 2005.

93. Ruthven interview

94. Dolson, *Beating the Bushes*, 65–66.

95. Dolson, *Philadelphia Story*, 271.

96. Ray Kelly, "Return of McCarver Revives Phils Ace Carlton," *Sporting News*, August 2, 1975.

97. Boone interview.

98. Larry Eldridge, "Mike Schmidt Would Rather Be Consistent," *Baseball Digest* (September 1976): 68–71.

99. Ozark quoted in Rosenberg, "Two for the See-Saw," 142.

100. Hochman, *Mike Schmidt*, 58.

101. Ray Kelly, "Schmidt Star Still Is Rising, Phillies Assert," *Sporting News*, February 22, 1975.

102. Schmidt, quoted in Hochman, *Mike Schmidt*, 67; Schmidt, quoted in Allen and Whitaker, *Crash*, 189.

103. Allen and Whitaker, *Crash*, 161.

104. "Ozark feeling pressure," *Philadelphia Inquirer*, September 24, 1975.

105. Westcott and Bilovsky, *Phillies Encyclopedia*, 88.

106. Ray Kelly, "Carlton, Lonborg and Allen at Seat of Phillies' Failure," *Sporting News*, November 8, 1975.

107. Westcott and Bilovsky, *Phillies Encyclopedia*, 150.

108. Allen Lewis, "Jay Johnstone's Long Journey to Success," *Baseball Digest* (December 1976): 56–61.

109. Thomas Boswell, "Cast Offs, Stars—They Do It for the Phillies," *Washington Post*, July 15, 1976.

CHAPTER 6. CONTENDERS

1. Rich Ashburn, "Schmidt Needs Change in Batting Order," *Philadelphia Bulletin*, April 14, 1976.

2. Ashburn, "Schmidt Needs Change in Batting Order."

3. Allen, quoted in Stan Hochman, *Mike Schmidt: Baseball's King of Swing* (New York: Random House, 1988), 62.

4. Allen, quoted in Hochman, *Mike Schmidt*, 62

5. Allen Lewis, "Schmidt Hits 4 HRs as Cubs Bow, 18-16," *Philadelphia Inquirer*, April 18, 1976.

6. McGraw, quoted in Lewis, "Schmidt Hits 4 HRs."

7. Schmidt, quoted in Hochman, *Mike Schmidt*, 66.

8. Schmidt, quoted in Larry Keith, "It's Either a Clout or an Out," *Sports Illustrated* (May 3, 1976): 22.

9. Larry Shenk, "The Summer of '76 . . . A Memorable Season," *Phillies' 1986 Yearbook* (Philadelphia: Phillies, 1986), 64.

10. Shenk, "The Summer of '76."

11. Shenk, "The Summer of '76."

12. Tim McCarver, interview, Gladwyne, Pennsylvania, December 21, 1999.

13. Ray Kelly, "McCarver's Helping Hand Bringing Out Best in Carlton," *Sporting News*, June 12. 1976.

14. Bill Conlin, "It Wasn't My Fault He Wouldn't Speak," *Philadelphia Daily News* supplement, August 1, 1994.

15. "Phillies Fever" (Philadelphia: Grand Prix Records, 1976).

16. Rich Westcott, *Veterans Stadium: Field of Memories* (Philadelphia: Temple University Press, 2005), 89.

17. Rich Westcott and Frank Bilovsky, *The Phillies Encyclopedia* (Philadelphia: Temple University Press, 2002), 89.

18. "Vet History," *Phillies 1981 Yearbook* (Philadelphia: Phillies, 1981), 48.

19. Thomas Boswell, "Cast Offs, Stars—They Do It for the Phillies," *Washington Post*, July 15, 1976.

20. Shenk, "Summer of '76," 65.

21. Westcott and Bilovsky, *Phillies Encyclopedia*, 89.

22. Bill Conlin, "Anatomy of a Slump," *Philadelphia Daily News*, September 13, 1976.

23. Danny Ozark, interview, Vero Beach, Florida, August 8, 2005.

24. See Stan Hochman, "Is Anxiety Key to Phils' Slump?" *Philadelphia Daily News*, September 7, 1976; see also Ozark, quoted in Bill Conlin, *Batting Cleanup*, ed. Kevin Derrane (Philadelphia: Temple University Press, 1997), 89; Ozark, quoted in Rich Westcott, *Tales from the Phillies Dugout* (Champaign, Ill.: Sports Publishing, 2003), 123.

25. See Bill Conlin, "Not the Time to Panic," *Philadelphia Daily News*, September 8, 1976; see also Ray Kelly, "Sudden Skid Surprises and Bewilders Phillies," *Sporting News*, September 25, 1976; Frank Dolson, *The Philadelphia Story: A City of Winners* (South Bend, Ind.: Icarus Press, 1981), 198.

26. Schmidt, quoted in Red Smith, "The Unmaking of a Reds' Fan," *New York Times*, October 9, 1976.

27. Dolson, *Philadelphia Story*, 198.

28. Tug McGraw, quoted in Red Foley, "New Experience for Tug—He's Feeling Pressure," *New York Daily News*, October 8, 1976.

29. Allen Lewis, "Phils Win, Take Division Title," *Philadelphia Inquirer*, September 27, 1976.

30. Jim Lonborg ,quoted in Bill Conlin, "Lonborg Revels in Another Clinching," *Philadelphia Daily News*, September 27, 1976.

31. Tug McGraw interview, September 15, 1999.

32. Dick Allen and Tim Whitaker, *Crash: The Life and Times of Dick Allen* (New York, Tickner and Fields, 1989), 166.

33. See Bill Conlin, "Phils Do Their Flying Without Dick Allen," *Philadelphia Daily News*, September 27, 1976; Conlin, "Dissension Brewing on Phillies?" *Philadelphia Daily News*, September 29, 1976; Conlin, "Phils Feuding over Allen's Flight?" *Philadelphia Daily News*, September 30, 1976.

34. Dave Cash, interview, Scranton, Pennsylvania, August 11, 1999.

35. Garry Maddox, quoted in Conlin, "Phils Feuding over Allen's Flight?"

36. McGraw interview; see also McGraw, quoted in Chuck Slater, "Phils Weigh Dropping Allen for Playoffs, World Series," *New York Daily News*, October 1, 1976.

37. Garry Maddox, quoted in Slater, "Phils Weigh Dropping Allen."

38. McGraw, quoted in Slater, "Phils Weigh Dropping Allen."

39. See Conlin, "Phils Feuding over Allen's Flight?"

40. Ozark, quoted in Conlin, "Phils Feuding over Allen's Flight?"; Ozark interview.

41. Allen and Whitaker, *Crash*, 164.

42. Allen and Whitaker, *Crash*, 165

43. Ozark, quoted in Slater, "Phils Weigh Dropping Allen."

44. Ozark, interview.

45. Tony Taylor, interview, Philadelphia, July 27, 1999.

46. For Reds 1976 statistics, see Rick Wolff, ed., *The Baseball Encyclopedia*, 8th ed. (New York: Macmillan, 1990), 457; see also Robert H. Walker, *Cincinnati and the Big Red Machine* (Bloomington: Indiana University Press, 1988).

47. For Phillies 1976 statistics, see Wolff, *Baseball Encyclopedia*, 458.

48. Lonborg interview.

49. Bruce Keidan, "Ninth-Inning Rally by Phils Falls Short as Reds Win, 6-3," *Philadelphia Inquirer*, October 10, 1976.

50. Lonborg interview.

51. Bruce Keidan, "Phils' Backs to Big Red Wall," *Philadelphia Inquirer*, October 11, 1976.

52. Dave Cash interview, Scranton, Pennsylvania, July 26, 2005.

53. Bruce Keidan, "Two Homers in 9th Lead to 7-6 Reds Win and NL Pennant," *Philadelphia Inquirer*, October 13, 1976.

54. Dick Allen, interview, West Chester, Pennsylvania, April 21, 2001; for Allen's statistics, see Westcott and Bilovsky, *Phillies Encyclopedia*, 125–26.

55. Cash interview.

56. John Helyar, *Lords of the Realm: The Real History of Baseball* (New York: Villard, 1994), 206.

57. Cash interview.

58. Westcott and Bilovsky, *Phillies Encyclopedia*, 89, 354; Chris Wheeler, "Garry Maddox . . . No One Did It Better," *Phillies 1987 Yearbook* (Philadelphia: Phillies, 1987), 65.

59. Dolson, *Philadelphia Story*, 194–96.

60. Ozark, interview.

61. Peter Binzen, ed., *Nearly Everybody Read It: Snapshots of the Philadelphia Bulletin* (Philadelphia: Camino Books, 1997).

62. Russell F. Weigley, ed., *Philadelphia: A 300-Year History* (New York: W.W. Norton, 1982), 690–91.

63. Allen Lewis, interview, Clearwater, Florida, December 29, 2001.

64. See "Stories from the Press Box," History Channel documentary, aired May 10, 2001; Conlin, *Batting Cleanup*, xi–xii. Sportswriters Dick Young of the *New York Post* and Stan Isaacs of *Newsday* set the precedent for the new breed of sportswriter in the 1960s. Young once observed that a chipmunk "had to tell people they're full of shit and then go out and face them the next day." Isaacs is widely credited with popularizing the intrusive questioning. After New York Yankees pitcher Ralph Terry defeated the San Francisco Giants in Game 5 of the 1962 World Series, Terry excused himself from a group of sportswriters to take a telephone call from his wife. When he returned, Terry mentioned that his wife was feeding their baby. From the back of the group, Isaacs asked, "Breast or bottle?" It was the kind of intrusive personal question that became a trademark of the chipmunks.

65. Bill Conlin interview, Turnersville, New Jersey, June 16, 2005.

66. Conlin interview

67. Carpenter interview.

68. Ozark interview.

69. McGraw interview, West Chester, Pennsylvania, May 8, 1999.

70. Schmidt, quoted by Conlin, *Batting Cleanup*, xii.

71. Conlin interview.

72. Taylor interview.

73. Schmidt, quoted by Hochman, *Mike Schmidt*, 61.

74. Ibid., 59.

75. Lonborg interview.

76. Frank Dolson interview, Merion, Pennsylvania, December 28, 2001.

77. Rich Marazzi, "Ted Sizemore," in *The Ballplayers: Baseball's Ultimate Biographical Reference*, ed. Mike Shatzkin (New York: William Morrow, 1990), 1006.

78. Merritt Clifton, "Richie Hebner," in Shatzkin, *Ballplayers*, 456; Richie Hebner interview, Scranton, Pennsylvania, June 27, 2006.

79. Larry Shenk, "The Offensive Juggernaut of '77," *Phillies 1987 Yearbook* (Philadelphia: Phillies, 1987), 66.

80. Hebner interview.

81. Jay Johnstone and Rick Talley, *Over the Edge: Uncensored Exploits of Baseball's Craziest Player* (New York: Bantam, 1987).

82. Johnstone and Talley, *Over the Edge*, 166.

83. Ray Ripplemeyer, quoted in Bob Pacitti, "McGraw's Antics Still Vivid for Coach," Scripps News Service, January 7, 2004.

84. McGraw interview, West Chester, Pennsylvania, September 15, 1999.

85. McGraw interview, June 3, 2000.

86. McGraw interview, June 3, 2000; Christenson interview.

87. See Ray Kelly, "A Cast of Characters," in *1977 National League Championship Series Program* (Philadelphia: Phillies, 1977), 52–55; see also Tug McGraw and Mike Witte, *Scroogie* (New York: New American Library, 1974); Tug McGraw and Mike Witte, *Scroogie #2* (New York: New American Library, 1976).

88. "McGraw's Boost for Bicycling," *Sporting News*, April 1, 1978.

89. McGraw interview, June 3, 2000; John T. Nicholson interview, West Chester, Pennsylvania, July 10, 2004.

90. Nicholson interview.

91. Ozark, quoted in Ray Kelly, "Schmidt Upset at Ozark," *Philadelphia Bulletin*, April 27, 1977.

92. Schmidt, quoted in Kelly, "Schmidt Upset at Ozark."

93. Westcott and Bilovsky, *Phillies Encyclopedia*, 217–18.

94. Schmidt, quoted in Frank Bilovsky, "Morganna Generous on Dad's Day," *Philadelphia Bulletin*, June 20, 1977.

95. Bowa, quoted in Conlin, *Batting Cleanup*, 89–90.

96. Westcott, *Veterans Stadium*, 86–90.

97. Shenk, "Offensive Juggernaut of '77," 66.

98. Stargell, quoted in Paul Dickson, *Baseball's Greatest Quotations* (New York: HarperCollins, 1991), 409.

99. Shenk, "Offensive Juggernaut of '77," 66.

100. Carlton, quoted in Ray Didinger, "Carlton: Profile," *Philadelphia Daily News* supplement, August 1, 1994.

101. McCarver interview. See also Tim McCarver with Ray Robinson, *Oh, Baby, I Love It!* (New York: Dell, 1988), 90. Carlton was a protégé of St. Louis Cardinals pitcher

Bob Gibson, who taught him to divide the plate into three lanes and focus on throwing to the 2½ inches that represented the inside and outside lanes.

102. Tim McCarver, *Oh, Baby, I Love It!*, 53.

103. Conlin interview; Conlin, "Silent Steve."

104. McCarver interview; see also, McCarver, *Oh Baby, I Love It!*, 54; Stan Hochman, "Carlton Wins his 200th," *Philadelphia Daily News*, July 24, 1978.

105. Carlton, quoted in Ray Didinger, "Carlton: Profile."

106. Westcott and Bilovsky, *Phillies Encyclopedia*, 90; see also Allen Lewis, *The Philadelphia Phillies: A Pictorial History* (Virginia Beach, Va.: JCP Corp., 1981), 207–9; Donald Honig, *The Philadelphia Phillies: An Illustrated History.* (New York: Simon & Schuster, 1992), 203–7.

107. Phillies, *1977 National League Championship Series Program*, 463.

108. Bruce Keidan, "Phils Win Wild One in West," *Philadelphia Inquirer*, October 5, 1977; Bill Conlin, "Phils Get the 1st One," *Philadelphia Daily News*, October 5, 1977.

109. Schmidt, quoted in Conlin, "Phils Get the 1st One."

110. Luzinski, quoted in Conlin, "Phils Get the 1st One."

111. Bruce Keidan, "Sutton Cools off Phils, 7-1," *Philadelphia Inquirer*, October 6, 1977; and Bill Conlin, "Don Sutton Revives Dodgers," *Philadelphia Daily News*, October 6, 1977.

112. Bruce Keidan, "It Was Give Away Day at the Vet; Dodgers Score 3 in 9th for 6-5 Win," *Philadelphia Inquirer*, October 8, 1977.

113. Stan Hochman, "Bad Bounces Tell the Tale," *Philadelphia Daily News*, October 10, 1977.

114. Keidan, "It Was Give Away Day at Vet."

115. Bowa, quoted in Barry M. Bloom, *Larry Bowa: "I Still Hate to Lose"* (Champaign, Ill.: Sports Publishing, 2004), 31.

116. Keidan, "It Was Give Away Day at the Vet."

117. Hebner interview.

118. Ozark, quoted in Bill Conlin, "Phillies Can't Dodge Disaster," *Philadelphia Daily News*, October 8, 1977; Dolson, *Philadelphia Story*, 207. Years later, Ozark would stay with the same reasoning, that he "wanted to keep Luzinski's bat in the line-up if we fell behind"; see Ozark interview, August 8, 2005.

119. Keidan, "It Was Give Away Day at the Vet."

120. Dolson, *Philadelphia Story*, 207.

121. Ozark, quoted in Dolson, *Philadelphia Story*.

122. Ozark, quoted in Conlin, "Phillies Can't Dodge Disaster"; Frank Fitzpatrick, *You Can't Lose 'Em All: The Year the Phillies Finally Won the World Series* (Dallas: Taylor, 2001), 52.

123. Hebner interview.

124. Bill Conlin, "Phils Couldn't Win Big One—Again," *Philadelphia Daily News*, October 10, 1977.

125. Lasorda, quoted in Bruce Keidan, "There Is No Joy in Mudville; John Drowns Phillies Hopes," *Philadelphia Inquirer*, October 9, 1997.

126. Conlin, "Phils Couldn't Win Big One—Again"; "Phillies Can't Dodge Disaster."

127. Bill Lyon, "Phillies Powerhouse a Tribute to Builder Owens," *Philadelphia Inquirer*, October 8, 1977.

128. Tracy Ringolsby, "Top Paid Club? Phils at $140,000 Average," *Sporting News*, January 28, 1978. The Cincinnati Reds were a distant third with a total payroll of

$2,759,800. Figures are based on each team's 25-man roster as of August 31, 1977, with bonuses, signing bonuses, and deferred payments pro-rated over the term of a player's contract.

129. Ozark, quoted in Ray Kelly, "Phillies Loaded—And They Know It," *Philadelphia Bulletin*, March 4, 1978.

130. Westcott, *Veterans Stadium*, 99–104; Larry Shenk, "A Star Is Born," *Phillies 1986 Yearbook* (Philadelphia: Phillies, 1986), 44–45.

131. Westcott and Bilovsky, *Phillies' Encyclopedia*, 90–91; Larry Shenk, "Can They Repeat?" *Phillies 1988 Yearbook* (Philadelphia: Phillies, 1988), 62–63.

132. Bill Conlin, "Game 1: Phils' Play Off," *Philadelphia Daily News*, October 5, 1978; Larry Eichel, "Garvey's 2 Homers Lead the Way," *Philadelphia Inquirer*, October 5, 1978.

133. Stan Hochman, "Raindrops Fall on Schmidt," *Philadelphia Daily News*, October 5, 1978.

134. Ozark, quoted in Dolson, *Philadelphia Story*, 210.

135. Bill Conlin, "Will the Sun Rise in West for Phils?" *Philadelphia Daily News*, October 6, 1978.

136. Jim Murray, "The Phillies Were Made for Philly," *Los Angeles Times*, October 4, 1978.

137. Bill Conlin, "Lefty Gives Phils a Lift," *Philadelphia Daily News*, October 7, 1978.

138. Garvey, quoted in Larry Eichel, "Phils Bounce Back Smartly, 9-4," *Philadelphia Inquirer*, October 7, 1978.

139. Larry Eichel, "Dodgers Take Phils, 4-3, in 10th," *Philadelphia Inquirer*, October 8, 1978.

140. Maddox quoted in Frank Dolson, "Maddox to be Remembered for What He Can't Forget," *Philadelphia Inquirer*, October 8, 1978.

141. Schmidt, quoted in Dolson, "Maddox to be Remembered."

142. Larry Mcmullen, "Fans Disappointed Once Again," *Philadelphia Daily News*, October 9, 1978.

143. Carpenter interview.

144. Larry Bowa interview, Ardmore, Pennsylvania, November 12, 2005.

145. For Carlton's and Schmidt's post-season statistics for 1976–78, see Wolff, *Baseball Encyclopedia*, 1426, 1729.

Chapter 7. Charlie Hustle Comes to Town

1. Pete Rose holds the major league record for all-time hits with 4, 256. He also holds major league records for most games, lifetime (3,562); most singles, lifetime (3,215); most seasons and most consecutive seasons, 100 or more games (23); most seasons, 200 or more hits (10); most seasons, 150 or more games (17); most at bats, lifetime (14,053); most plate appearances, lifetime (15,861); most consecutive seasons, 600 or more at bats (13); most seasons, 600 or more at bats (17); most plate appearances, season (771), 1974; most doubles by a switch hitter, season (51), 1978. Rose shares major league records for most consecutive seasons leading major leagues in runs scored (3); fewest sacrifice flies, season, most at bats (0 and 680), 1973; most games, first baseman, season (162), 1980 and 1982; most stolen bases, inning (3), May 11, 1980, seventh inning. Rose holds National League records for most years and most consecutive years played (24); most runs, lifetime (2,165); most seasons leading league in hits (7); most doubles, lifetime (746); most singles by a switch-hitter, season (181), 1973; fewest

stolen bases, season, most at bats (0 and 662), 1975; most times five or more hits in one game, lifetime (10). Rose shares National League records for most consecutive games, one or more hits, season (44), 1978; most seasons leading league in at bats (4). He also holds the modern National League record for most 20-game hitting streaks, lifetime (7); and shares modern National League records for most seasons leading league in fielding percentage by outfielder, 100 or more games (3); and most consecutive years leading league in fielding percentage by outfielder, 100 or more games (2). See Craig Carter, ed., *Daguerreotypes: The Complete Major and Minor League Records of Baseball's Greats* (St. Louis: Sporting News, 1990), 249.

2. Pete Rose and Roger Kahn, *Pete Rose: My Story* (New York: Macmillan, 1989), 9. Rose is credited with reviving the headfirst slide after seeing Enos Slaughter do it. But he popularized running to first base on a walk. Yankee pitcher Whitey Ford is credited with giving Rose the nickname "Charlie Hustle." During a spring training game between the Reds and the New York Yankees in the mid-1960s, Ford, who was known for his casual approach to the game, saw Rose run down to first base after a walk and shouted: "Hey! "Look at Charlie hustle."

3. Rose, quoted in Rich Westcott and Frank Bilovsky, *The Phillies Encyclopedia* (Philadelphia: Temple University Press, 2002), 244.

4. Rose, quoted in Paul Dickson, *Baseball's Greatest Quotations* (New York: HarperCollins, 1991), 370.

5. Stewart Wolpin, "Pete Rose," in *The Ballplayers*, ed. Mike Shatzkin (New York: William Morrow, 1990), 938.

6. Rob Neyer and Eddie Epstein, *Baseball Dynasties* (New York: W.W. Norton, 2000), 303–18.

7. Rose, quoted in Dickson, *Baseball's Greatest Quotations*, 369

8. Rose, quoted in Dickson, *Baseball's Greatest Quotations*, 370.

9. Rose, quoted in Dickson, *Baseball's Greatest Quotations*, 370.

10. Rose, quoted in Dickson, *Baseball's Greatest Quotations*, 370.

11. Michael Y. Sokolove, *Hustle: The Myth, Life, and Lies of Pete Rose* (New York: Simon and Schuster, 1990), 183–87.

12. Rose and Kahn, *My Story*, 68.

13. Rose, quoted Rose and Kahn, *My Story*,, 43.

14. Rose and Kahn, *My Story*, 94.

15. Sokolove, *Hustle*, 83–85; Rose and Kahn, *My Story*, 133–34.

16. Sokolove, *Hustle*, 93; Rose and Kahn, *My Story*, 156–57.

17. Wolpin, "Pete Rose," 937.

18. Rose and Kahn, *My Story*, 189–202.

19. Ibid., 202–4.

20. Rose, quoted in Bruce Keidan, "Rose in Phillies Future?" *Philadelphia Inquirer*, October 12, 1976.

21. Pete Rose with Rick Hill, *My Prison Without Bars* (Emmaus, Pa.: Rodale, 2004), 109.

22. Ruly Carpenter interview, Wilmington, Delaware, June 2, 2005; Rose and Kahn, *My Story*, 205.

23. Rose, quoted in Rose and Kahn, *My Story*, 205.

24. Bill Giles interview, Philadelphia, July 15, 2005; see also Giles, quoted in Rose and Kahn, *Pete Rose: My Story*, 205–6.

25. Joseph Durso, "Rose Signs with Phillies," *New York Times*, December 6, 1978.

26. Rose quoted in Durso, "Rose Signs with Phillies."

27. John Helyar, *Lords of the Realm: The Real History of Baseball* (New York: Villard, 1994), 132–53.

28. Ibid., 153–70. Messersmith was a legitimate star. In 1974, he led the Dodgers to the pennant with a 20-6 record and a 2.56 ERA. The following season he played without a contract and was almost as effective, posting 19 wins and a 2.29 ERA. McNally's case was a bit different. As a key pitcher of the Orioles dynasty in the late 1960s, he won at least 20 games in four straight years, 1968 through 1971. Although he won 16 games for the Orioles in 1974, Baltimore traded him to the Montreal Expos. Because the trade was without his consent, McNally refused it and initially intended to sit out the '75 season. After Miller persuaded him to challenge the reserve clause, he played for the Expos without a contract, but retired in midseason with a 3-6 record and a chronically sore shoulder. His grievance still remained active, though.

29. Bob Boone interview, Atlantic City, New Jersey, October 15, 2005.

30. Helyar, *Lords of the Realm*, 214.

31. Randy Rieland, *The New Professionals: Baseball in the 1970s* (Alexandria, Va.: Redefinition, 1989), 59–60.

32. David Q. Voigt, *American Baseball: From Postwar Expansion to the Electronic Age* (University Park: Pennsylvania State University Press, 1983), 314–17.

33. Giles interview; see also Giles, quoted in Rose and Kahn, *My Story*, 206–7.

34. See Mark Whicker, "Rose Is Forever Young," *Philadelphia Bulletin*, October 14, 1980; Rose, quoted in Thomas Boswell, "For Rose, Nearly 40, Series Could be the Last Hurrah," *Washington Post*, October 19, 1980; Stan Hochman, *Mike Schmidt: Baseball's King of Swing* (New York: Random House, 1983), 13, 80–82.

35. Danny Ozark interview, Vero Beach, Florida, August 8, 2005.

36. Rich Westcott and Frank Bilovsky, *The Phillies Encyclopedia* (Philadelphia: Temple University Press, 2002), 91. Owens traded Ted Sizemore, Jerry Martin, Barry Foote, and two minor leaguers to the Cubs for Manny Trillo, Greg Gross, and Dave Rader.

37. Richie Hebner interview, Scranton, Pennsylvania, June 27, 2006.

38. Westcott and Bilovsky, *Phillies Encyclopedia*, 244–45; Hal Bodley, *The Team That Wouldn't Die: The Philadelphia Phillies, World Champions, 1980* (Wilmington, Del.: Serendipity Press, 1981); 111; Frank Dolson, *Philadelphia Story: A City of Winners* (South Bend, Ind.: Icarus Press, 1981), 287; Donald Honig, The *Philadelphia Phillies: An Illustrated History* (New York: Simon & Schuster, 1992), 212.

39. Rose, quoted in Frank Fitzpatrick, *You Can't Lose 'Em All: The Year the Philies Finally Won the World Series* (Dallas: Taylor, 2001); 55–56; Rose, quoted in *Glory Days: The Story of the 1980 World Champion Phillies*, VHS video, written and produced by Dan Stephenson (Philadelphia: Phillies, 2000).

40. Major league teams that had a strong Christian influence during the 1970s and 1980s included the California Angels, Los Angeles Dodgers, Montreal Expos, New York Mets, Philadelphia Phillies, Pittsburgh Pirates, San Francisco Giants, and Texas Rangers.

41. Chris Smith, "God Is an .800 Hitter," *New York Times Magazine*, July 27, 1997, 27–28; George Vecsey, "Religion Becomes an Important Part of the Baseball Scene," *New York Times*, May 10, 1981; Rieland, *The New Professionals*, 43; Steve Hubbard, *Faith in Sports: Athletes and Their Religion on and off the Field* (New York: Doubleday, 1998), 41. In the most critical series of articles, appearing in *Sports Illustrated* in 1976, Frank Deford wrote: "In the final analysis, sport has had a greater impact upon religion than the other way around. While athletics does not appear to have been improved by the

religious blitzkrieg, the religious people who work that side of the street seem to have been colored by some of the worst attitudes found in sport. The temper of the athletic religion is competitive, full of coaches and cheerleaders, with an overriding sense of wins and losses, stars and recruiting, game plans, and dugout chatter." See Deford, "Religion in Sports," *Sports Illustrated*, April 19, 26, May 3, 1976.

42. Bob Boone, interview, Villa Park, California, January 3, 2006.

43. Watson Spoelstra, interview, Largo, Florida, April 8, 1998; see also Phil Elderkin, "Religion and Baseball," *Christian Science Monitor*, August 2, 1977; Watson Spoelstra, "How 'Real Hell-Raiser' Found God," *National Tattler* (Chicago), December 8, 1974. Spoelstra, admittedly, was a "heavy drinker and "hell-raiser" in his sportswriting days. Once president of the Baseball Writers Association of America, he was a popular figure among sports celebrities. He became born again in 1957 as part of a bargain he made with God to care for his eighteen-year-old daughter who had suffered a brain hemorrhage. When she recovered, Spoestra quit drinking. Later, when he retired from sportswriting, he founded Baseball Chapel, gaining the official sanction of commissioner Bowie Kuhn.

44. Boone interview, January 3, 2006.

45. For growth of evangelical Christianity in Major League Baseball, see *Christian Science Monitor*, August 2, 1977; Watson Spoelstra, "Baseball Chapel: Church at the Ballpark," *1978 Cleveland Indians Scorebook*, 42; Joe Falls, "God and the Gladiators," *Parade Magazine*, April 23, 1978, 1; Peter Becker, "At Play in the Fields of the Lord," *M Inc.* (August 1991): 74; and William C. Kashatus, "The Origins of Baseball Chapel and the Era of the Christian Athlete, 1973–1990," *NINE: A Journal of Baseball History and Social Policy Perspectives* 7, 2 (Spring 1999): 75–90.

46. For the narcissistic trends in baseball during the 1970s, see Rieland, *The New Professionals*, 124–25; Steve Mann, "The Business of Baseball," in *Total Baseball*, ed. John Thorn and Pete Palmer (New York: Warner, 1989), 628–41. For accounts on why athletes became born again Christians, see Hubbard, *Faith in Sports*; "Baseball Chapel Offers Alternatives to Players," *San Francisco Chronicle*, August 14, 1990; Dave Branon and Joe Pellegrino, *Safe at Home: Winning Players Talk About Baseball and Their Faith* (Chicago: Moody Press, 1992).

47. Mike Schmidt interview, Jupiter, Florida, October 8, 1998.

48. Schmidt, quoted in Skip Myslenski, "Mike Schmidt: It's Just a Question of Mind over Batter," *Boston Globe*, July 10, 1977.

49. Schmidt interview, October 8, 1998; see also Mike Schmidt, "Something More," *Guideposts* (July 1987): 4; Mike Schmidt with Glen Waggoner, *Clearing the Bases: Juiced Players, Monster Salaries, Sham Records, and a Hall of Famer's Search for the Soul of Baseball* (New York: HarperCollins, 2006), 45–46.

50. Mike Schmidt interview, Jupiter, Florida September 28, 1994; see also Schmidt, quoted in Rich Ashburn, "Schmidt: Boobirds Are on target," *Philadelphia Bulletin*, August 20, 1978.

51. Kempton, quoted in Schmidt, "Something More," 5.

52. Schmidt interview, October 8, 1998.

53. Ray Didinger, "Garry Maddox: The Man with the Golden Glove," *Baseball Digest* (September 1978): 50–54; and Phil Elderkin, "Garry Maddox: The Phils' Premier Ball Hawk," *Baseball Digest* (August 1979): 68–70.

54. Garry Maddox, quoted in Stan Hochman, "God Is Key to Maddox's Life," *Philadelphia Daily News*, October 4, 1978.

55. Boone interview, January 3, 2006.

56. Tug McGraw interview, West Chester, Pennsylvania, September 15, 1999.

57. Hal Bodley, "Boone Shatters Carlton-McCarver Battery," *Sporting News*, May 26, 1979.

58. Boone interview, October 15, 2005; Tim McCarver with Ray Robinson, *Oh, Baby, I Love It!* (New York: Dell, 1998), 56.

59. Bill Conlin, "Phils Do Number on Cubs," *Philadelphia Daily News*, May 17, 1979.

60. Allen Lewis, *The Philadelphia Phillies: A Pictorial History* (Virginia Beach, Va.: JBC Corp., 1980), 147; Honig, *Phillies*, 213–14.

61. Sokolove, *Hustle*, 97; Rose, *My Prison Without Bars*, 109.

62. Bill Conlin interview, Turnersville, New Jersey, June 16, 2005.

63. Dolson, *Philadelphia Story*, 212.

64. Hal Bodley, "Angry Boss Tells Wealthy Phils They're Not so Hot," *Sporting News*, August 25, 1979.

65. Bodley, "Angry Boss,"

66. Bodley, "Angry Boss."

67. Hal Bodley, "Ozark Pays the Price for Phils' Sad Season," *Sporting News*, September 15, 1979.

68. Howie Bedell interview, Pottstown, Pennsylvania, September 20, 2005; Giles interview.

69. Bedell had been fired by the Phillies in 1973 when he refused to complete the season as manager of Single-A Auburn. His refusal was based on the mismanagement of funds by the minor league club's front office, which had promised to make improvements to the ballpark but diverted the revenue elsewhere. Bedell also shouldered the blame for firing Jim Bunning as the Phillies' Triple-A manager in 1976 because he felt Bunning's personal interests in securing a major league managerial post did not complement the developmental needs of that particular club. Although Bedell offered Bunning a position as a roving pitching instructor, the former Phillies ace rejected the offer. Bedell was harshly criticized by sportswriter Frank Dolson, a good friend of Bunning's in two subsequent books. See Frank Dolson, *Beating the Bushes: Life in the Minor Leagues* (South Bend, Ind.: Icarus, 1982), 77–80; Frank Dolson, *Jim Bunning: Baseball and Beyond* (Philadelphia: Temple University Press, 1998), 180–86.

70. Bedell interview.

71. Carpenter interview.

72. Bedell interview.

73. Dallas Green interview, West Grove, Pennsylvania, July 5, 2005; Carpenter interview.

74. Owens, quoted in Jayson Stark, "Danny Ozark Fired by Phillies," *Philadelphia Inquirer*, September 1, 1979.

75. Carpenter, quoted in Bodley, "Ozark Pays the Price."

76. Carpenter interview.

77. Dolson, *Philadelphia Story*, 181–82.

78. Ozark interview.

79. Ozark interview. Ozark returned to his former position as third base coach for the Los Angeles Dodgers in 1980. Two years later, he joined the San Francisco Giants, where he coached for Frank Robinson. When Robinson was fired in 1984, Ozark replaced him. After that season, he retired from baseball.

80. Bowa, quoted in Bodley, "Ozark Pays the Price."

81. Greg Luzinski interview, Philadelphia, August 3, 2005.

82. Boone interview, October 15, 2005.

83. Westcott and Bilovsky, *Phillies Encyclopedia,* 459–60; Tom Jozwik, "Dallas Green," in Shatzkin, *Ballplayers,* 409; Lewis, *Phillies: A Pictorial History,* 147.

84. Dallas Green interview, West Chester, Pennsylvania, October 13, 1999.

85. Green interview, October 13, 1999.

86. Schmidt, quoted in Hochman, *Mike Schmidt,* 85.

87. Westcott and Bilovsky, *Phillies' Encyclopedia,* 92–92, 244.

88. Pete Rose, quoted in Maury Levy and Samantha Stevenson, "Pete Rose Slams Fans, Management, Media, Plugs Self," *Playboy Magazine* (September 1979): 77–79, 102–7.

89. Pete Rose, quoted in Rose and Kahn, *My Story,* 210.

90. Rose, *My Prison Without Bars,* 109.

CHAPTER 8. "WE, NOT I"

1. Tug McGraw quoted in Frank Dolson, *The Philadelphia Story: A City of Winners* (South Bend, Ind.: Icarus, 1981), 269.

2. Jayson Stark, "Phillies Make It Official: Dallas Green Is Manager," *Philadelphia Inquirer,* October 19, 1979; Dallas Green, interview, West Chester, Pennsylvania, October 13, 1999.

3. Ruly Carpenter, interview, Wilmington, Delaware, June 2, 2005.

4. Dolson, *Philadelphia Story,* 263.

5. Dallas Green interview, West Grove, Pennsylvania, July 5, 2005.

6. Bowa, quoted in Bill Conlin, *Batting Cleanup* (Philadelphia: Temple University Press, 1997), 100.

7. Hal Bodley, *The Team That Wouldn't Die: The Philadelphia Phillies, World Champions, 1980* (Wilmington, Del.: Serendipity Press, 1981), 194–95.

8. Frank Fitzpatrick, *You Can't Lose 'Em All: The Year the Phillies Finally Won the World Series* (Dallas: Taylor, 2001), 79.

9. Bowa quoted in Fitzpatrick, *You Can't Lose 'Em All,* 96.

10. Fitzpatrick, *You Can't Lose 'Em All,* 95–96.

11. *Sports Illustrated,* April 10, 1980.

12. Green interview, October 13, 1999.

13. Fitzpatrick, *You Can't Lose 'Em All,* 99.

14. Green interview, October 13, 1999.

15. Green interview, October 13, 1999.

16. Green, quoted in Hal Bodley, "Super Steve: Silent Ace," *Sporting News,* June 21, 1980.

17. Green, quoted in Bodley, *The Team That Wouldn't Die,* 245.

18. Fitzpatrick, *You Can't Lose 'Em All,* 92.

19. Marvin Miller, *A Whole Different Ball Game: The Inside Story of the Baseball Revolution* (Chicago: Ivan R. Dee, 1991), 286–88; John Helyar, *Lords of the Realm: The Real History of Baseball* (New York: Villard, 1994), 223–30.

20. Miller, *A Whole Different Ball Game,* 288.

21. Miller, *A Whole Different Ball Game,* 291–92.

22. Bodley, *The Team That Wouldn't Die,* 7.

23. Mike Schmidt with Glen Waggoner, *Clearing the Bases: Juiced Players, Monster*

Salaries, Sham Records, and a Hall of Famer's Search for the Soul of Baseball (New York: HarperCollins, 2006), 48.

24. Green interview, July 5, 2005.

25. Fitzpatrick, *You Can't Lose 'Em All*, 110–11.

26. Rich Westcott and Frank Bilovsky, *The Phillies Encyclopedia* (Philadelphia: Temple University Press, 2002), 92.

27. Mike Schmidt, interview, Jupiter Florida, October 8, 1998.

28. Westcott and Bilovsky, *Phillies Encyclopedia*, 92.

29. Bob Boone, interview, Atlantic City, New Jersey, October 15, 2005.

30. Boone, interview; Dolson, *Philadelphia Story*, 270–71.

31. *Philadelphia Inquirer*, May 6, 1980.

32. *Philadelphia Daily News*, April 27, 1980. Cardinals catcher Ted Simmons's lead-off single in the second inning was the only hit off Carlton in the game.

33. *Philadelphia Inquirer*, May 6, 1980.

34. Bodley, *Team That Wouldn't Die*, 245.

35. Larry Bowa. quoted in Bodley, *Team That Wouldn't Die*, 245.

36. Tim McCarver, interview, Gladwyne, Pennsylvania, December 21, 1999.

37. Pete Rose, quoted in *Lefty: The Life and Times of Steve Carlton*, VHS video written and produced by Dan Stephenson (Philadelphia: Phillies, 1994).

38. Tim McCarver, quoted in Dave Anderson, "Finally, Limitations for Lefty," *New York Times*, June 29, 1986.

39. Steve Carlton, quoted in Anderson, "Finally, Limitations for Lefty."

40. Dick Ruthven, interview, Alpharetta, Georgia, August 9, 2005.

41. Carpenter interview.

42. Tug McGraw, interview, West Chester, Pennsylvania, August 11, 1999.

43. Pete Rose and Roger Kahn, *Pete Rose: My Story* (New York: Macmillan, 1989), 227.

44. Steve Carlton, quoted in Bodley, *The Team That Wouldn't Die*, 246.

45. Steve Carlton, quoted in Westcott and Bilovsky, *Phillies Encyclopedia*, 146. Carlton wasn't the only player who refused to talk to the press. Among others were Dave Kingman of the Chicago Cubs, George Hendrick of the St. Louis Cardinals, Vida Blue of the San Francisco Giants, and Mike Marshall of the Minnesota Twins. See Furman Bisher, "Carlton Big Windbag Next to Some," *Sporting News*, June 14, 1980.

46. Bill Giles, quoted in *Lefty*.

47. Carlton quoted in *Lefty*.

48. Bob Walk, interview, Fairless Hills, Pennsylvania, July 8, 2006.

49. Don Carmen and Larry Anderson, in *Lefty*.

50. Darren Daulton in *Lefty*.

51. Greg Luzinski in *Lefty*.

52. Carlton, quoted in Bodley, *The Team That Wouldn't Die*, 246.

CHAPTER 9. SAME OL' SCHMIDT

1. Mike Schmidt, interview, Jupiter, Florida, May 28, 2006; Schmidt, quoted in Dick Wimmer, *Baseball Fathers, Baseball Sons* (New York: William Morrow, 1988), 56–57.

2. Rose, cited in Bill Fleischman, "The Weight of Philly on His Shoulders," *Inside Sports* (June 1984): 24.

3. Schmidt, quoted in Stan Hochman, *Mike Schmidt: King of Swing* (New York: Random House, 1983), 112; Schmidt, *Always on the Offense*, 29.

4. For especially negative press of Schmidt, see "Schmidt Makes 'All-Cool' Team," *Philadelphia Bulletin*, August 11, 1975; Barry Rosenberg, "Two for the See-Saw: Mike Schmidt and Dick Allen," *Philadelphia Magazine* (September 1975): 130–44; Ray Kelly, "Schmidt Upset at Ozark," *Philadelphia Bulletin*, April 27, 1977; Peter Pascarelli, "Phillies Need a Mr. September," *Philadelphia Inquirer*, August 21, 1983; Bruce Buschel, "Even Superstars Get the Blues," *Philly Sport* (June/July 1988): 4–8.

5. Ruly Carpenter, interview, Wilmington, Delaware, June 2, 2005.

6. Larry Shenk, interview, Philadelphia, October 28, 2005.

7. Mike Schmidt interview, Jupiter, Florida, October 15, 1994.

8. Schmidt, *Always on the Offense*, 55–57.

9. Rose, quoted in Michael V. Sokolove, *Hustle: The Myth, Life and Lies of Pete Rose* (New York: Simon and Schuster, 1990), 227.

10. William C. Kashatus, *Mike Schmidt: Philadelphia's Hall of Fame Third Baseman* (Jefferson, N.C.: McFarland, 2000), 52–58.

11. Pete Rose, quoted in Hochman, *Mike Schmidt*, 92; Pete Rose, *My Prison Without Bars* (Emmaus, Pa.: Rodale, 2001), 109.

12. Del Unser, interview, Fairless Hills, Pennsylvania, July 17, 2005.

13. Mike Schmidt, quoted in *Glory Days: Story of the 1980 World Champion Phillies*, written and produced by Dan Stephenson (VHS video).

14. Schmidt, quoted in Frank Fitzpatrick, *You Can't Lose 'Em All: The Year the Phillies Finally Won the World Series* (Dallas: Taylor, 2001), 102.

15. Dallas Green, quoted in Hochman, *Mike Schmidt*, 184.

16. Hal Bodley, "Bullpen a Real Life-Saver to Phils," *Sporting News*, June 28, 1980.

17. J. Stryker Meyer, "Penna. Authorities Investigate Phillies Players," *Trenton Times*, July 8, 1980.

18. Dr. Patrick Mazza, quoted in Associated Press, "No Evidence Found Involving Phillies," *New York Daily News*, July 10, 1980.

19. David Q. Voigt, *American Baseball: From Postwar Expansion to the Electronic Age* (University Park: Pennsylvania State University Press, 1983), 260–61; Will Carroll, *The Juice: The Real Story of Baseball's Drug Problems* (New York: Viking, 2005); Tug McGraw with Dan Yaeger, *Ya Gotta Believe! My Roller-Coaster Life as a Screwball Pitcher, and Part-Time Father, and My Hope-Filled Fight Against Brain Cancer* (New York: New American Library, 2004), 67–69, 141.

20. David Q. Voigt, "The History of Major League Baseball," in *Total Baseball*, ed. John Thorn and Pete Palmer (New York: Warner, 1989), 47; Sokolove, *Hustle*, 80. In 1983, three Kansas City Royals were sentenced to jail terms as convicted users and a Dodger pitcher was suspended. In 1985, a San Diego Padres player was traded because of drug abuse. Most damaging, however, were revelations coming from two Pittsburgh court cases of seventeen players who abused drugs. Baseball commissioner Peter Ueberroth's attempt to force all players to submit to periodic drug testing was blocked by the Players Association, which insisted that the issue be addressed through collective bargaining.

Undaunted, Ueberroth suspended the accused players from the game and required each one to donate up to 10 percent of his salary to charity and to participate in antidrug campaigns as a prerequisite for reinstatement. Not until 2006, however, did Major League Baseball establish a strict policy for drug testing, spurred on by the abuse of performance-enhancing steroids.

21. Frank Dolson, *Philadelphia Story: A City of Winners* (South Bend, Ind.: Icarus, 1981), 266; Larry Kramer, "Editorial from the Trenton Times," *Sporting News*, August 16, 1980. Kramer, editor of the *Trenton Times*, took issue with the Phillies' charges of "irresponsible journalism" as well as similar allegations made by *Philadelphia Daily News* sportswriter Bill Conlin. Kramer defended his investigative reporter, J. Stryker Meyer, calling him "one of the best, most experienced, law enforcement reporters around."

22. Carpenter and Yatron, quoted in Hal Bodley, "Angry Phils Deny Drug Report," *Sporting News*, July 26, 1980; Bodley, "Phils 'Scandal' Fizzles Out," *Sporting News*, August 16, 1980.

23. Schmidt quoted in Bodley, "Angry Phils Deny Drug Report," *Sporting News*, July 26, 1980.

24. Mike Schmidt with Glen Waggoner, *Clearing the Bases: Juiced Players, Monster Salaries, Sham Records, and a Hall of Famer's Search for the Soul of Baseball* (New York: HarperCollins, 2006), 90.

25. McGraw, *Ya Gotta Believe!*, 141–42.

26. Bill Conlin, interview, Turnersville, New Jersey, June 16, 2005.

27. Pete Rose interview by Samantha Stevenson, "Pete Rose Slams Fans, Management, Media, Plugs Self," *Playboy Magazine* (September 1979): 102–3; Jim Salisbury and Todd Zolecki, "Baseball's Problem with Pills," *Philadelphia Inquirer*, March 8, 2006. In 2003, Milt Pappas, who pitched in the majors between 1957 and 1973, told ESPN that Rose "took hand fulls" of greenies in order to enhance his on-field performance.

28. Sokolove, *Hustle*, 79-81.

29. Sokolove, *Hustle* 147, 183–87.

30. Sokolove, *Hustle*, 184–85. When Pete and Karolyn Rose were finally divorced on December 29, 1980, she secured the award she asked for, while Pete kept another house and the Rolls Royce he received from the Reds for being the National League MVP in 1978. Ten years later, Rose would admit to his biographer Roger Kahn that the divorce was "one hundred percent my fault" and that he still believed that Karolyn was "a terrific woman." See Rose and Kahn, *Pete Rose: My Story* (New York: Macmillan, 1989), 210–13.

31. Conlin interview. Mike Schmidt and Greg Luzinski were also amazed by Rose's exceptional performance and asked him how he could play so well when he was under such stress. Rose replied: "Stress is facing a divorce when you don't want one. I'm finally free from the distractions of a bad relationship." Rose, quoted in Sokolove, *Hustle*, 109.

32. Dallas Green, quoted in Hal Bodley, "Green Talks a Blue Streak over Colorless Phillies," *Sporting News*, August 9, 1980.

33. Luzinski, quoted in Bodley, "Green Talks a Blue Streak"; Dolson, *Philadelphia Story*, 267.

34. Fitzpatrick, *You Can't Lose 'Em All*, 79, 147–48; Bob Boone and Garry Maddox quoted in *Glory Days: The Story of the 1980 World Champion Phillies*; Larry Christenson, interview, Malvern, Pennsylvania, August 12, 2005.

35. Mike Schmidt, quoted in Fitzpatrick, *You Can't Lose 'Em All*, 147.

36. Carpenter interview.

37. Sparky Lyle, interview, Vorhees, New Jersey, August 10, 2005.

38. John Vukovich, interview, Scranton, Pennsylvania, May 4, 2006.

39. Dallas Green, quoted in Hal Bodley, "Green Yelled; Finally, Phils Heard," *Sporting News*, November 8, 1980.

40. Lonnie Smith, Lonnie, Fairless Hills, Pennsylvania, July 8, 2006.

41. Bob Walk, interview, Fairless Hills, Pennsylvania, July 8, 2006.

42. *Philadelphia Daily News,* August 11, 1980.

43. Dolson, *Philadelphia Story,* 268.

44. Bill Conlin, *Philadelphia Daily News,* August 9, 1980

45. Dallas Green, interview, West Grove, Pennsylvania, July 5, 2005; Green, quoted in Sam Carchidi, "The Mouth That Roared: Green's Tirade Was Shot Heard Round The World," *Philadelphia Inquirer,* July 10, 2005.

46. Tug McGraw interview, West Chester, Pennsylvania, August 11, 2000.

47. Greg Luzinski interview, Philadelphia, August 3, 2005.

48. Hal Bodley, "25 Years Ago, the Phillies Win the World Series," *Phillies 2005 Yearbook* (Philadelphia: Phillies, 2005), 10.

49. Ron Reed, quoted in Dolson, *Philadelphia Story,* 268.

50. Donald Honig, *The Phillies: An Illustrated History* (New York: Simon & Schuster, 1992), 215; Allen Lewis, *The Philadelphia Phillies: A Pictorial History* (Virginia Beach, va.: JCP Corp., 1981), 149–50.

51. *Philadelphia Daily News,* August 31, 1980; Dolson, *Philadelphia Story,* 65–66.

52. Dolson, *Philadelphia Story,* 67–68; McGraw interview, August 11, 2000.

53. Owens, quoted in Dolson, *Philadelphia Story,* 67–68; Bob Boone interview, Atlantic City, New Jersey, October 15, 2005; Vukovich interview; McGraw interview, August 11, 2000; Unser interview; Christenson interview; Rich Westcott and Frank Bilovsky, *The Phillies Encyclopedia* (Philadelphia; Temple University Press, 2002), 92.

54. Bake McBride, interview, Fairless Hills, Pennsylvania, July 8, 2006.

55. Vukovich interview.

56. Dolson, *Philadelphia Story,* 67–68; Boone interview; Vukovich interview; McGraw interview, August 11, 2000.

57. Rose, quoted in Dolson, *Philadelphia Story,* 70.

58. Unser interview.

CHAPTER 10. TUGGING AT THE HEART

1. Hal Bodley, *The Team That Wouldn't Die: Philadelphia Phillies, 1980 World Champions* (Wilmington, Del.: Serendipity Press, 1981), 9–10; interviews of Ruly Carpenter, Wilmington, Delaware, June 2, 2005; Tug McGraw, West Chester, Pennsylvania, August 11, 2000; Bake McBride, Fairless Hills, Pennsylvania, July 8, 2006.

2. Carrie Seidman, "Phillies' McGraw: He's Still a Believer," *New York Times,* September 30, 1980.

3. Sparky Lyle, interview, Vorhees, New Jersey, August 10, 2005.

4. Larry Christenson, interview, Malvern, Pennsylvania, August 12, 2005; Tug McGraw with Dan Yaeger, *Ya Gotta Believe! My Roller Coaster Life as a Screwball Pitcher and Part-Time Father, and My Hope-Filled Fight Against Brain Cancer* (New York: New American Library, 2004), 192.

5. McGraw interview, August 11, 2000.

6. McGraw interview: August 11, 2000

7. Marty Bystrom, interview, Geigertown, Pennsylvania, July 6, 2006.

8. Interview of Bob Walk, interview, Fairless Hills, Pennsylvania, July 8, 2006.

9. Tug McGraw quoted in Ron Fimrite, "One Heartstopper After Another," *Sports Illustrated* (October 27, 1980): 26–27.

10. Interview of Bill Conlin, Turnersville, New Jersey, June 16, 2005.

11. McGraw, *Ya Gotta Believe!*, 91.

12. McGraw, *Ya Gotta Believe!*, 191.

13. McGraw, *Ya Gotta Believe!*, 29–33; McGraw, interview, West Chester, Pennslyvania, May 5, 2000.

14. McGraw, *Ya Gotta Believe!*, 14–15, 85–86.

15. McGraw interview, May 5, 2000.

16. Ron Reed, quoted in Sam Carchidi, "McGraw: Heart of a Champ," *Philadelphia Inquirer*, July 11, 2005.

17. Greg Luzinski, interview, Philadelphia, August 3, 2005.

18. Carchidi, "McGraw: Heart of a Champ."

19. Dallas Green, quoted in Seidman, "Phillies' McGraw: He's Still a Believer."

20. Frank Dolson, *The Philadelphia Story: A City of Winners* (South Bend, Ind.: Icarus, 1981), 272.

21. See Jayson Stark, "Phils Lose on Maddox Error," *Philadelphia Inquirer*, September 29, 1980; Dolson, *Philadelphia Story*, 272.

22. Larry Bowa, quoted in Frank Dolson, "Torment Stokes Fire Within Bowa," *Philadelphia Inquirer*, October 2, 1980; Dolson, *Philadelphia Story*, 273.

23. Bowa, quoted in Barry M. Bloom, *Larry Bowa: "I Still Hate to Lose"* (Champaign, Ill. Sports Publishing, 2004), 28.

24. *Philadelphia Inquirer*, September 30, 1980.

25. Bill Conlin, "Bowa Does It Again," *Philadelphia Daily News*, September 30, 1980.

26. Conlin interview.

27. Schmidt, *Always on the Offense*, 178–79.

28. Bystrom interview.

29. Jayson Stark, "Phils Down Cubs on Carlton's 2-Hitter," *Philadelphia Inquirer*, October 2, 1980.

30. Walk interview.

31. McGraw interview, August 11, 2000.

32. Dallas Green, interview, West Chester, Pennsylvania, October 13, 1999.

33. See Rob Watson, "Gene McFadden, R & B Songwriter, Dies," *Philadelphia Inquirer*, January 28, 2006.

34. Bystrom interview.

35. Dallas Green, interview, West Grove, Pennsylvania, July 5, 2005.

36. John Vukovich, interview, Scranton, Pennsylvania, May 4, 2006.

37. Pete Rose, quoted in in *Glory Days: Story of the 1980 World Champion Phillies*, VHS video, written and produced by Dan Stephenson (Philadelphia: Phillies, 2000).

38. Mike Schmidt, quoted in *Glory Days*.

39. Gary Carter, interview, West Palm Beach, Florida, July 20, 2005.

40. *Philadelphia Inquirer*, October 4, 1980.

41. Tug McGraw quoted in Dolson, *Philadelphia Story*, 275.

42. Pete Rose, quoted in *Glory Days*.

43. Allen Lewis, *The Philadelphia Phillies: A Pictorial History* (Virginia Beach, Va.: JCP Corp., 1981), 150–52.

44. Carter interview.

45. Steve Wulf, "Dilly of a Win for Philly," *Sports Illustrated*, October 13, 1980.

46. Larry Bowa, quoted in Dolson, *Philadelphia Story*, 276.

47. MikeSchmidt with Glen Waggoner, *Clearing the Bases* (New York: Harper-Collins, 2006), 50.

48. For Phillies 1980 statistics, see Appendix A..

49. Tug McGraw, quoted in Joseph Durso, "Phillies Prefer Opposing the Astros," *New York Times*, October 7, 1980.

50. For Houston Astros 1980 statistics, see Rick Wolff, ed., *The Baseball Encyclopedia*, 8th ed. (New York: Macmillan, 1990), 481.

51. Steve Carlton, quoted in Frank Dolson, "Steve Carlton," in *Basefall Hall of Fame Annual Program* (Cooperstown, N.Y.: National Baseball Hall of Fame and Sporting News, 1994): 5.

52. Greg Luzinski, quoted in Larry Shenk, ed., *The World Champion Phillies and the Road to Victory* (Philadelphia: Phillies, 1980), 19.

53. *Philadelphia Inquirer*, October 8, 1980.

54. Ron Fimrite, "Wow, What a Playoff," *Sports Illustrated*, October 20, 1980.

55. Lee Elia, quoted in *Glory Days*.

56. *Philadelphia Inquirer*, October 9, 1980; Fimrite, "Wow."

57. Nolan Ryan quoted in Shenk, *World Champion Phillies*, 20.

58. Dallas Green, quoted in Shenk, *World Champion Phillies*, 20

59. Christenson interview.

60. *Philadelphia Inquirer*, October 11, 1980; Fimrite, "Wow."

61. Owens, quoted in *Glory Days*.

62. Bill Giles, interview, Philadelphia, July 15, 2005.

63. *Philadelphia Inquirer*, October 12, 1980.

64. *Philadelphia Inquirer*, October 12, 1980; Lee Elia, quoted in Dolson, *Philadelphia Story*, 286.

65. Vukovich interview.

66. Rose, quoted in *Philadelphia Bulletin*, October 12, 1980.

67. *Philadelphia Bulletin*, October 12, 1980; Fimrite, "Wow."

68. Manny Trillo interview, Scranton, Pennsylvania, June 27, 2005.

69. Bystrom interview.

70. Jayson Stark, "Phillies Rule National League! Astros Are Beaten in 10th, 8–7," *Philadelphia Inquirer*, October 13, 1980.

71. Christenson interview.

72. Dick Ruthven interview, Alpharetta, Georgia, August 9, 2005..

73. Christenson interview; Christenson quoted in Michael Y. Sokolove, *Hustle: The Myths, Life, and Lies of Pete Rose* (New York: Simon & Schuster, 1990), 92.

74. Rose, quoted in Thomas Boswell, *How Life Imitates the World Series* (New York: Penguin, 1983), 275.

75. Bowa, quoted in Bloom, *Larry Bowa: "I Still Hate to Lose"*, 35.

76. Boswell, *How Life Imitates the World Series*, 275.

77. Schmidt, *Clearing the Bases*, 51–52; Schmidt, quoted in Bob Ibach and Tim Panaccio, *The Comeback Kids: 1980 World Series Flashback* (Bel Air, Calif.: Bel Air Printing, 1980), 10; Schmidt, quoted in *Philadelphia Daily News*, October 16, 1980.

78. Lee Elia, quoted in Rich Westcott, *Tales from the Phillies Dugout* (Champaign, Ill.: Sports Publishing, 2003), 144.

79. McGraw interview, August 11, 2000.

80. Ruthven interview.

81. Ruthven interview.

82. Stark, "Phillies Rule National League!"; Fimrite, "Wow."

83. Garry Maddox, quoted in Ray Didinger, "Maddox Takes Ride of His Life," *Philadelphia Daily News*, October 13, 1980.

84. Ruly Carpenter, quoted in Larry Eichel, "The Happy End to a Long Ordeal," *Philadelphia Inquirer*, October 13, 1980.

85. Mike Schmidt with Barbara Walder, *Always on the Offense* (New York: Atheneum, 1982), 179–80.

CHAPTER 11. WE WIN!

1. Charles Smith, quoted in Tug McGraw with William C. Kashatus, *Was It as Good for You? Tug McGraw and Friends Recall the 1980 World Series* (Media, Pa.: McGraw and Co., 2000), 5.

2. Keri Evan, quoted in McGraw, *Was It as Good for You?*, 18.

3. Carl Markau, quoted McGraw, *Was It as Good for You?*, 29.

4. Phil McCarriston, quoted in McGraw, *Was It as Good for You?*, 26–27.

5. Rick Wolff, ed., *The Baseball Encyclopedia* (New York: Macmillan, 1990), 484, 2728.

6. Bob Walk, interview, Fairless Hills, Pennsylvania, July 8, 2006.

7. Barry M. Bloom, *Larry Bowa: "I Still Hate to Lose"* (Champaign, Ill.: Sports Publishing, 2004), 36–37.

8. Bake McBride, interview, Fairless Hills, Pennsylvania, July 8, 2006; McBride, quoted in Bill Lyon, "Homer and Two Singles Help Ease McBride's Pain," *Philadelphia Inquirer*, October 15, 1980.

9. Jayson Stark, "Rally Beats Royals as McBride Homers, McGraw Saves Walk," *Philadelphia Inquirer*, October 15, 1980; Ron Fimrite, "One Heart Stopper After Another," *Sports Illustrated*, October 27, 1980.

10. Tug McGraw, quoted in Fimrite, "One Heart Stopper," 27.

11. Pete Rose, quoted in Larry Shenk, *The World Champion Phillies and the Road to Victory* (Philadelphia: Phillies, 1980), 26.

12. Maryellen McCarthy Rampata, quoted in McGraw, *Was It as Good for You?*, 23–24.

13. Jayson Stark, "Schmidt RBI Keys 6-4 win," *Philadelphia Inquirer*, October 16, 1980; Fimrite, "One Heart Stopper."

14. Schmidt, quoted in Bill Lyon, "Schmidt Ready to Join the Phils' Hit Parade," *Philadelphia Inquirer*, October 16, 1980.

15. Larry Bowa, quoted in Fimrite, "One Heart Stopper."

16. Ed Rose, quoted in McGraw, *Was It as Good for You?*, 8–10.

17. George Brett, quoted in Bob Ibach and Tim Pannacio, *The Comeback Kids: 1980 World Series Flashback* (Bel Air, Calif.: Bel Air Printing, 1980), 8.

18. Fimrite, "One Heart Stopper," 29.

19. Danny Robbins, "Leaving 8 on Base, Schmidt Can Only Welcome New Day," *Philadelphia Inquirer*, October 19, 1980.

20. Patricia M. Kelley, quoted in McGraw, *Was It as Good for You?*, 34.

21. Larry Christenson, interview, Malvern, Pennsylvania, August 12, 2005.

22. Jayson Stark, "Aikens Homers Twice in First Two Innings to Spark 5-3 Victory," *Philadelphia Inquirer*, October 19, 1980.

23. Dickie Noles, interview, Aston, Pennsylvania, August 26, 2005.

24. Frank Dolson, "Brett Sprawls, Manager Howls," *Philadelphia Inquirer*, October 19, 1980.

25. Pete Rose, quoted in *Glory Days: The Story of the World Champion Phillies*, VHS video written and produced by Dan Stephenson (Philadelphia: Phillies, 2000).

26. Noles interview.

27. Mike Schmidt with Glen Waggoner, *Clearing the Bases: Juiced Players, Monster Salaries, Sham Records, and a Hall of Famer's Search for the Soul of Baseball* (New York: HarperCollins, 2000), 52–53.

28. Stan Pawloski, quoted McGraw, *Was It as Good for You?*, 58.

29. Marty Bystrom, interview, Geigertown, Pennsylvania, July 6, 2006.

30. Schmidt, quoted in Jayson Stark, "Unser, Schmidt Key Win," *Philadelphia Inquirer*, October 20, 1980.

31. Larry Bowa, quoted in Danny Robbins, "All Good Things Come to Del Unser, Who Sits and Waits," *Philadelphia Inquirer*, October 20, 1980.

32. Bob Boone, quoted in Shenk, *World Champion Phillies*, 31.

33. John Grace, quoted in McGraw, *Was It as Good for You?*, 45–46.

34. Bill Giles, interview, Philadelphia, July 15, 2005.

35. Bill Conlin, "Philly Crowd Control a Model for All Clubs," *Sporting News*, November 8, 1980.

36. McGraw interview, West Chester, Pennsylvanis, May 8, 1999; McGraw as told to Diana V. Smartt, "We Were the Champions," *Philadelphia Magazine* (October 1991): 40.

37. Conlin, "Philly Crowd Control."

38. Schmidt, quoted in Ibach and Panaccio, *Comeback Kids*, 10.

39. Tug McGraw, interview, West Chester, Pennsylvania, August 11, 2000.

40. Conlin, "Philly Crowd Control."

41. McGraw interview, August 11, 2000.

42. Donna Coppock, quoted in McGraw, *Was It as Good for You?*, 71.

43. Nick Halladay quoted in McGraw, *Was It as Good for You?*, 71–72.

44. Bob Boone, interview, Atlantic City, New Jersey, October 15, 2005.

45. Pete Rose, quoted in McGraw, *Was It as Good for You?*, 72.

46. Thomas Boswell, *How Life Imitates the World Series* (New York: Penguin, 1982), 265.

47. McGraw interview, August 11, 2000.

48. McGraw interview, August 11, 2000

49. McGraw, "We Were the Champions," 41.

50. Larry Bowa, quoted in Bill Lyon, "And Then There Was Steve Carlton . . .," *Philadelphia Inquirer*, October 22, 1980.

51. Dallas Green, quoted in Dick Kaegel, "Phils Phinally Win the Series," *Sporting News*, November 8, 1980.

52. Lyon, "And Then There Was Steve Carlton."

53. Beverly Carlton, quoted in McGraw, *Was It as Good for You?*, 49.

54. Lyon, "And Then There Was Steve Carlton."

55. Schmidt, *Clearing the Bases*, 53.

56. Frank Dolson, "MVP Mike: Schmidt Flattered at Unanimous Vote by Writers," *Philadelphia Inquirer*, November 27, 1980.

57. Ted Silary, "When It Came to Chores, Mike Could Do It All," *Philadelphia Daily News* (Special Report: "Legends in Their Own Time"), July 26, 1995; William C. Kashatus,

Mike Schmidt: Philadelphia's Hall of Fame Third Baseman (Jefferson, N.C.: McFarland, 2000).

58. Schmidt, *Clearing the Bases*, 53.

59. Donald Kimelman, "Phils Win Series; City Goes Wild," *Philadelphia Inquirer*, October 22, 1980.

60. Mary Leimkuhler, quoted in McGraw, *Was It as Good for You?*, 91.

61. Alex Carver quoted in *Was It as Good for You?*, 87.

62. Ray Angely quoted in *Was It as Good for You?*, 90.

63. Hal Bodley, "Phillies and Fans: Mutual Admiration," *Sporting News*, November 8, 1980.

CHAPTER 12. DYNASTY DENIED

1. See Marley and Lupica, quoted in Frank Fitzpatrick, *You Can't Lose 'Em All: The Year the Phillies Finally Won the World Series* (Dallas: Taylor, 2001), 5.

2. Dick Young, "The Mute Ballplayers," *Sporting News*, November 22, 1980.

3. Joe Falls, "Show of Force at Philly—Was it Needed?" *Sporting News*, November 8, 1980.

4. Pete Axthelm, "Those Malevolent Phillies," *Newsweek*, October 27, 1980.

5. Pete Axthelm, "World Series Postscript," *Newsweek*, November 3, 1980.

6. Tug McGraw interview, West Chester, Pennsylvania, May 8, 2000.

7. Tom Cushman, quoted in Fitzpatrick, *You Can't Lose 'Em All*, 5.

8. Bill Conlin, *Batting Cleanup* (Philadelphia: Temple University Press, 1997), 100.

9. Ruben Amaro, interview, Weston, Florida, May 16, 2006. According to the Rule 5 draft, any player who has played for three seasons in the minor leagues must be elevated to the 40-man roster or another major league club would have the opportunity to draft any unprotected players, provided that the drafting team has room on its own 40-man roster.

10. Amaro interview.

11. Mark Winegardner, *Prophet of the Sandlots: Journeys with a Major League Scout* (New York: Atlantic Monthly Press, 1990), 219–21.

12. Howie Bedell, interview, Pottstown, Pennsylvania, July 3, 2006.

13. *Phillies: 1981 Media Guide* (Philadelphia: Phillies, 1981), 8.

14. Julian McCracken, interview, Phoenixville, Pennsylvania, July 3, 2006.

15. McCracken interview; see also Terry Pluto and Jeffrey Neuman, eds., *A Baseball Winter: The Off-Season Life of the Summer Game* (New York: Macmillan, 1986), 103.

16. McCracken interview

17. *Phillies: 1981 Media Guide*, 28–29, 36, 49.

18. *Phillies: 1981 Media Guide*, 28; Rich Westcott and Frank Bilovsky, *The Phillies Encyclopedia* (Philadelphia: Temple University Press, 2002), 93.

19. Howe Bedell interview, Pottstown, Pennsylvania, August 14, 2006; Julien McCracken interview, Phoenixville, Pennsylvania, August 14, 2006.

20. Bedell interview, August 14, 2006.

21. Howe Bedell interview, Pottstown, Pennslyvania, September 20, 2005.

22. Bedell interview, September 20, 2005. During the interview, Bedell produced a November 12, 1980, handwritten letter from Ruly Carpenter that corroborated his statement that the Phillies owner had hoped to retain him and that the Carpenter family

was "forever indebted" to him. Carpenter also volunteered to "do anything I can to help you in the transition period."

23. Bedell interview, September 20, 2005.

24. Steve Wulf, "National League East: Scouting Report," *Sports Illustrated*, April 13, 1981.

25. Ruly Carpenter interview, Wilmington, Delaware, June 2, 2005. According to one Phillies executive, Ruly Carpenter would have kept the team if the decision was solely his and not his father's. Ruly targeted his anger at owners like Atlanta's Ted Turner, who had signed Claudell Washington for the five-year, $3.5 million contract. "Some of the other owners," he said, "are just nouveaux riches as far as baseball in concerned. They have a hell of a lot of money, and it could be an ego trip for them. Or they just want to buy instant success—they don't want to do it through development in the minor leagues or scouting." See Kevin Kerrane, *Dollar Sign on the Muscle: The World of Baseball Scouting* (New York: Simon & Schuster, 1984), 78–79.

26. Kerrane, *Dollar Sign on the Muscle*, 78–79.

27. Mark Carfagno, interview, South Philadelphia, June 24, 2006.

28. Larry Bowa, interview, Radnor, Pennsylvania, August 15, 1992.

29. Greg Luzinski, interview, South Philadelphia, August 3, 2005.

30. Westcott and Bilovsky, *Phillies Encyclopedia*, 574. Matthews was acquired in a trade that sent Phillies pitcher Bob Walk to Atlanta.

31. Westcott and Bilovsky, *Phillies Encyclopedia*, 212, 583.

32. Green, quoted in Conlin, *Batting Cleanup*, 117.

33. Dallas Green, quoted in Conlin, *Batting Cleanup*, 117.

34. Hal Bodley, "Ruly Pays Carlton 'Moral' Debt," *Sporting News*, July 11, 1981. The highest paid Phillies entering the regular season in 1981 were Rose ($800,000); Carlton ($700,000); Maddox ($675,000); and Schmidt ($560,000). Schmidt would renegotiate his contract for a much more lucrative deal later that year.

35. Bodley, "Ruly Pays Carlton 'Moral' Debt."

36. Marvin Miller, *A Whole Different Ball Game: The Inside Story of the Baseball Revolution* (Chicago: Ivan R. Dee, 1991), 286–88; John Helyar, *Lords of the Realm: The Real History of Baseball* (New York: Villard, 1994), 223–30.

37. Miller, *Whole Different Game*, 292; Helyar, *Lords of the Realm*, 258–59.

38. Miller, *Whole Different Game*, 293–96; Helyar, *Lords of the Realm*, 261.

39. Bowie Kuhn, *Hardball: The Education of a Baseball Commissioner* (New York: Times Books, 1987), 346.

40. Miller, *Whole Different Game*, 288; Helyar, *Lords of Realm*, 262–63.

41. Steve Twomey, "Baseball Strike Looms as Judge Denies Injunction," *Philadelphia Inquirer*, June 11, 1981; Miller, *Whole Different Game*, 289; Helyar, *Lords of the Realm*, 263.

42. Geoffrey C. Ward and Ken Burns, *Baseball: An Illustrated History* (New York: Knopf, 1994), 447.

43. Bob Boone, interview, Atlantic City, New Jersey, October 15, 2006.

44. Ray Grebey, quoted in Helyar, *Lords of the Realm*, 266.

45. Boone interview.

46. Helyar, *Lords of the Realm*, 283.

47. Helyar, *Lords of the Realm*, 286.

48. Jayson Stark, "Baseball to Resume on Aug. 9," *Philadelphia Inquirer*, August 1, 1981.

49. Jayson Stark, "One for the Record," *Philadelphia Inquirer*, June 11, 1981.

50. Mike Schmidt with Glen Waggoner, *Clearing the Bases: Juiced Players, Monster Salaries, Sham Records, and a Hall of Famer's Search for the Soul of Baseball* (New York: HarperCollins, 2000), 33.

51. Jayson Stark, "Schmidt's Homer Wins It for NL," *Philadelphia Inquirer*, August 10, 1981.

52. Del Unser, interview, Fairless Hills, Pennsylvania, July 17, 2005.

53. Dallas Green, quoted in Conlin, *Batting Cleanup*, 117–18.

54. Larry Bowa, interview, Radnor, Pennsylvania, August 15, 1992.

55. Westcott and Bilovsky, *Phillies Encyclopedia*, 93; Jayson Stark, "Phillies Stay on a Surge, Pound Cubs," *Philadelphia Inquirer*, September 26, 1981.

56. Stan Hochman, "Rose Just Keeps on Ticking," *Philadelphia Daily News*, August 11, 1981.

57. Pete Rose, quoted in Jayson Stark, "Pete Rose: A Man for Any Season," *Philadelphia Inquirer*, August 11, 1981.

58. Larry Shenk, interview, Philadelphia, October 28, 1006; Stan Hochman, "New Hot Line: Reagan to Rose," *Philadelphia Daily News*, August 11, 1981.

59. Shenk interview.

60. Pete Rose, quoted in Thomas Boswell, *How Life Imitates the World Series* (New York: Penguin, 1983), 275.

61. Manny Trillo, interview, Scranton, Pennsylvania, June 27, 2005.

62. Barry M. Bloom, *Larry Bowa: "I Still Hate to Lose"* (Champaign, Ill.: Sports Publishing, 2004), 33.

63. Ruly Carpenter, interview, Wilmington, Delaware, June 2, 2005.

64. Schmidt, *Clearing the Bases*, 47–48.

65. Dallas Green quoted in Sam Carchidi, "'80 Phils Agree: Rose a Winning Influence," *Philadelphia Inquirer*, July 13, 2005; Green interview, West Grove, Pennsylvania, July 5, 2005.

66. Pete Rose with Rick Hill, *My Prison Without Bars* (New York: St. Martin's Press/ Rodale, 2004), 133–35.

67. Fay Vincent, *The Last Commissioner: A Baseball Valentine* (New York: Simon & Schuster, 2002), 127.

68. Michael Sokolove, *Hustle: The Myth, Life, and Lies of Pete Rose* (New York: Simon & Schuster, 1990), 143–44. Bodley vehemently denied that he ever told Vincent about Rose betting on baseball (Bodley, cited in Sokolove, *Hustle*; Carchidi, "'80 Phils Agree"). But he did admit that Rose is "not a very good human being" or a "very good friend" and that if he "said what was in his heart it wouldn't be very good for him" (see *Hustle*, 144).

69. Vincent, *Last Commissioner*, 127.

70. See depositions of Tommy Gioiosa and Pete Rose, in John M. Dowd et al., *Report to the Commissioner in the Matter of Peter Edward Rose, Manager, Cincinnati Reds Baseball Club* (New York, May 9, 1989), summary vol. 181: 123–27, National Baseball Hall of Fame Library.

71. Sokolove, *Hustle*, 141–43, 266–67; Bill Conlin, interview, Turnersville, New Jersey, June 16, 2005.

72. Gary Carter, interview, West Palm Beach, Florida, July 20, 2005.

73. Westcott and Bilovsky, *Phillies Encyclopedia*, 496–97.

74. Jayson Stark, "Phils Out-Hit Expos to Stay Alive," *Philadelphia Inquirer*, October 10, 1981.

75. Jayson Stark, "Phils Win on Vukovich's 10th Inning Homer," *Philadelphia Inquirer*, October 11, 1981.

76. Carter interview.

77. Jayson Stark, "Expos Win NL East Behind Rogers, 3-0," *Philadelphia Inquirer*, October 12, 1981.

78. Chuck Newman, "Bidding Ended Early for Some; Persistence Helped Giles Win the Battle," *Philadelphia Inquirer*, October 30, 1981.

79. Bill Giles, interview, Philadelphia, July 15, 2005.

80. See Larry Shenk, "President Bill Giles and the New Ownership," *Phillies 1982 Yearbook* (Philadelphia: Phillies, 1982), 2; Newman, "Bidding Ended Early for Some."

81. Carpenter interview.

82. Pluto and Neuman, *A Baseball Winter*, 174–75.

83. Bill Giles quoted in Shenk, "President Bill Giles and the New Ownership."

84. Giles interview.

85. Giles interview.

86. Westcott and Bilovsky, *Phillies Encyclopedia*, 574.

87. Westcott and Bilovsky, *Phillies Encyclopedia*, 260.

88. Bake McBride, interview, Fairless Hills, Pennsylvania, July 8, 2006.

89. Bob Boone, interview, Villa Park, California, January 3, 2006.

90. Westcott and Bilovsky, *Phillies Encyclopedia*, 136. Boone's major league record for most games caught was later broken by Carlton Fisk.

91. Westcott and Bilovsky, *Phillies Encyclopedia*, 574; Bill Conlin, "Noles' Expertise Will Help Spoiled Brett," *Philadelphia Daily News*, July 17, 2006; Dickie Noles, interview, Aston, Pennsylvania, August 26, 2005.

92. Green interview, July 5, 2005.

93. Green interview, July 5, 2005.

94. Green interview, July 5, 2005.

95. Noles interview.

96. Larry Bowa with Barry Bloom, *Bleep! Larry Bowa Manages* (Chicago: Bonus Books, 1988), 74–77. Years later when he was managing the Phillies, Bowa said he understood that Giles was "just representing the new ownership" and "had to be fiscally responsible." He also admitted that as a player "you don't look at the big picture." It was a "hard lesson to learn." See Bloom, *Larry Bowa: "I Still Hate to Lose"*, 50.

97. Schmidt, *Clearing the Bases*, 56.

98. Steve Mann, "The Business of Baseball," in *Total Baseball*, ed. Pete Palmer and John Thorn (New York: Warner, 1989), 636. A multiyear contract also had benefits for the player. No matter what might happen to him during the term of the contract, most, if not all, of the money would be guaranteed. Even if he was injured and his performance declined dramatically, his financial future was assured. Considering the wild rate of salary escalation during the 1980s, the only risk involved for the player in signing a long-term contract occurred if his performance improved dramatically. Then, he would be locked in to a specific salary when, in fact, his relative dollar value would be much higher.

99. Mike Schmidt, quoted in Gene Fraley, "2d MVP for Mike: Time to Talk Money," *Philadelphia Bulletin*, November 18, 1981.

100. Chuck Newman, "Phils' Third Baseman Wins His Second MVP," *Philadelphia Inquirer*, November 18, 1981. In winning his second straight MVP Award, Schmidt joined National Leaguers Ernie Banks of the Chicago Cubs (1958–59) and Joe Morgan of the Cincinnati Reds (1975–76), In the American League, those who won back-to-

back MVP Awards were Jimmie Foxx of the Philadelphia Athletics (1932–33), Hal New-houser of the Detroit Tigers (1944–45), and New York Yankees Yogi Berra (1954–55), Mickey Mantle (1956–57), and Roger Maris (1960–61).

101. Ben Yagoda, "What's the Big Deal?" *Philly Sport* (July 1989): 32–33.

102. Bill Conlin, "Most Valuable ($10 M) Player," *Philadelphia Daily News*, December 22, 1981. Only Dave Winfield of the New York Yankees who had a $21 million, ten-year contract made more money than Schmidt at the time.

103. Bill Giles quoted in Conlin, "Most Valuable ($10 M) Player."

104. Conlin, "Most Valuable ($10 M) Player."

105. Dave Anderson, "McGraw: Ignored World Series Hero," *New York Times*, November 16, 1980; Hall Bodley, "Free Spirit McGraw Enjoying Hero Status," *Sporting News*, November 29, 1980.

106. Tug McGraw with Dan Yaeger, *Ya Gotta Believe! My Roller-Coaster Life as a Screwball Pitcher, and Part-Time Father, and My Hope-Filled Fight Against Brain Cancer* (New York: New American Library, 2004), 152.

CHAPTER 13. WHEEZE KIDS

1. Larry Shenk, "Manager Pat Corrales," *Phillies 1982 Yearbook* (Philadelphia: Phillies, 1982), 5.

2. Rich Westcott and Frank Bilovsky, *The Phillies Encyclopedia* (Philadelphia: Temple University Press, 2004), 94.

3. Hal Bodley, "Carlton Stays Strong with Grueling Work," *Sporting News*, September 27, 1982.

4. Carlton quoted in ibid.

5. Mark Bowden, "The Short, Sad Spring of Michael Schmidt," *Philadelphia Inquirer Magazine*, May 16, 1982.

6. Frank Dolson, "Schmidt Fights to Stay on Top," *Philadelphia Inquirer*, June 3, 1982.

7. Pat Corrales, quoted in Jayson Stark, "Phils Wait for the Power in Schmidt's Bat to Resurface," *Philadelphia Inquirer*, July 4, 1982.

8. Bodley, "Carlton Stays Strong."

9. Westcott and Bilovsky, *Phillies Encyclopedia*, 94–95.

10. Dick Ruthven, interview, Alpharetta, Georgia, August 9, 2005.

11. Stan Hochman, *Mike Schmidt: Baseball's King of Swing* (New York: Random House, 1983), 123–24.

12. Pete Rose, quoted in Hochman, *Mike Schmidt*, 125.

13. Westcott and Bilovsky, *Phillies Encyclopedia*, 94–95.

14. Rich Westcott, *Tales from the Phillies Dugout* (Champaign, Ill.: Sports Publishing, 2003), 148; David M. Jordan, *Occasional Glory: A History of the Philadelphia Phillies* (Jefferson, N.C.: McFarland, 2002), 201.

15. Manny Trillo, interview, Scranton, Pennsylvania, June 27, 2005. See also Kevin Kerrane, *Dollar Sign on the Muscle*, 346.

16. Kerrane, *Dollar Sign on the Muscle: The World of Baseball Scouting* (New York: Simon & Schuster, 1984), 344–45.

17. Jordan, *Occasional Glory*, 201; Kerrane, *Dollar Sign on the Muscle*, 356.

18. Steve Wulf, "In Philadelphia, They're the Wheeze Kids," *Sports Illustrated* (March 14 1983): 26.

19. Steve Wulf, "Philly Is Streaking for Home," *Sports Illustrated* (October 3, 1983): 20–25.

20. Wulf, "In Philadelphia, They're the Wheeze Kids," 27–28.

21. Kerrane, *Dollar Sign on the Muscle*, 301, 319.

22. Baumer, quoted in Kerrane, *Dollar Sign on the Muscle*, 319.

23. Kerrane, *Dollar Sign on the Muscle*, 334. According to Brandy Davis, the result of the Phillies' scouting defections to Chicago was the creation of a nucleus of home-grown Cubs players who would go on to capture a division title for Chicago in 1984. Among the players were Mark Grace, Greg Maddux, Jamie Moyer, and Rafael Palmiero.

24. Kerrane, *Dollar Sign on the Muscle*, 310.

25. Kerrane, *Dollar Sign on the Muscle*, 301–4.

26. Kerrane, *Dollar Sign on the Muscle*, 310.

27. Kerrane, *Dollar Sign on the Muscle*, 187, 339.

28. Bill Conlin, interview, Turnersville, New Jersey, June 16, 2005; Kerrane, *Dollar Sign on the Muscle*, 349.

29. List of Philadelphia Phillies first round draft picks, ESPN.com and Baseball-almanac.com.

30. Phillies first round draft picks.

31. Bill Conlin, quoted in Kerrane, *Dollar Sign on the Muscle*, 335.

32. Amaro, interview, Weston, Florida, May 16, 2006.

33. Amaro interview.

34. Bill Giles, interview, Philadelphia, July 15, 2005.

35. Joe Morgan, quoted in Wulf, "In Philadelphia, They're the Wheeze Kids," 27.

36. Wulf, "In Philadelphia, They're the Wheeze Kids," 33.

37. Corrales, quoted in Wulf, "In Philadelphia, They're the Wheeze Kids."

38. Rose, quoted in Wulf, "In Philadelphia, They're the Wheeze Kids."

39. Juan Samuel, interview, Binghamton, New York, May 24, 2006.

40. John Russell, interview, Scranton, Pennsylvania, May 3, 2006.

41. Samuel interview

42. Peter Pascarelli, "Confessions of an Ex-Phillies' Beat Writer," *Philly Sport* (July 1989): 31–32.

43. Hal Bodley, "Phillies' Schmidt Should Stop Thinking About Slump," *USA Today*, June 6, 1983; Frank Dolson, "The Trials of '83 Could Not Keep Schmidt Down," *Philadelphia Inquirer*, October 4, 1983.

44. Bill Conlin, *Batting Cleanup* (Philadelphia: Temple University Press, 1997), 122–23.

45. Giles interview.

46. Paul Owens, quoted in Westcott and Bilovsky, "The Golden Decade," *Phillies Encyclopedia*, 531.

47. Conlin interview.

48. Terry Pluto and Jeffrey Neuman, eds., *A Baseball Winter: The Off-Season Life of the Summer Game* (New York: Macmillan, 1986), 4–5.

49. Giles interview.

50. Giles interview.

51. Giles interview.

52. Al Holland, interview, Roanoke, Virginia, August 12, 2005.

53. See Peter Pascarelli's daily columns in the *Philadelphia Inquirer* during the periods May 11 to June 6 and July 14 to August 30, 1983. Quote is taken from Pascarelli, "Phillies Need a Mr. September," *Philadelphia Inquirer*, October 4, 1983.

54. Schmidt, quoted in Dolson, "Trials of '83."

55. Schmidt, quoted in Ralph Bernstein, "Schmidt Lashes Out at Management," *New York Times*, September 9, 1983; Bill Fleischman, "The Weight of Philly on His Shoulders," *Inside Sports* (June 1984): 22.

56. Paul Owens, quoted in Bernstein, "Schmidt Lashes Out at Management."

57. Peter Pascarelli, "Pitching, Depth and Teamwork Got Phils to Top," *Philadelphia Inquirer*, October 4, 1983.

58. Holland interview.

59. Holland interview.

60. Holland interview.

61. Steve Wulf, "Philly Is Streaking for Home," *Sports Illustrated* (October 3, 1983): 23–24.

62. Bill Brown, "Silent Steve to Talk About 300th Win," *Delaware County Times*, September 28, 1983.

63. Wulf, "Philly Is Streaking for Home," 22–23; Larry Shenk, interview, Philadelphia, October 28, 2005.

64. Bill Conlin, "Phils Clinch Division, Crush Cubs, 13-6," *Philadelphia Daily News*, September 29, 1983.

65. Charles Leerhsen, "Pushing Toward the Pennant," *Newsweek* (October 10, 1983): 41.

66. Rick Wolff, ed., *The Baseball Encyclopedia*, 8th ed. (New York: Macmillan, 1990), 499.

67. Jerry Reuss, quoted in Leerhsen, "Pushing Toward the Pennant."

68. Pete Rose, quoted in Pascarelli, "Pitching, Depth and Teamwork Got Phils to Top."

69. Peter Pascarelli, "Carlton and Holland Blank L.A.," *Philadelphia Inquirer*, October 5, 1983.

70. Peter Pascarelli, "Errors Are Costly in Phils' 4-1 Loss," *Philadelphia Inquirer*, October 6, 1983.

71. Osteen, quoted in Peter Pascarelli, "Hudson, Matthews Are Key," *Philadelphia Inquirer*, October 8, 1983.

72. Gary Matthews quoted in Pascarelli, "Hudson, Matthews Are Key."

73. Ron Fimrite, "The Old and Relentless Beat the Young and Restless," *Sports Illustrated* (October 17, 1983): 18–20.

74. Holland interview.

75. See Wolff, *Baseball Encyclopedia*, , 501.

76. Bill Livingston, "Denny Takes Control of First Game," *Philadelphia Inquirer*, October 12, 1983.

77. Holland interview.

78. Maddox, quoted in Peter Pascarelli, "Maddox's Homer Beats Orioles," *Philadelphia Inquirer*: October 12, 1983.

79. Frank Dolson, "Cheers for a handful of Phils, Whose Future Is Right Now," *Philadelphia Inquirer*: October 12, 1983.

80. Peter Pascarelli, "O's Even Series on 4-1 Win," *Philadelphia Inquirer*, October 13, 1983.

81. Eddie Murray, quoted in Al Morganti, "When a Power Hitter Doesn't Hit," *Philadelphia Inquirer*, October 14, 1983.

82. Paul Owens, quoted in Peter Pascarelli, "Rose Is Benched in Surprise Move," *Philadelphia Inquirer*, October 5, 1983.

83. Pete Rose, quoted in Frank Dolson, "Unexpected Move Stuns and Embarrasses Rose," *Philadelphia Inquirer*, October 15, 1983.

84. Peter Pascarelli, "O's Take Lead in Series on 3-2 Win." *Philadelphia Inquirer*, October 15, 1983.

85. Peter Pascarelli, "Orioles Push Phils to the Brink," *Philadelphia Inquirer*, October 16, 1983.

86. Schmidt, quoted in Frank Dolson, "Schmidt Toughs Out Pressures of Slump," *Philadelphia Inquirer*, October 16, 1983.

87. Schmidt, quoted in Steve Wulf, "The Orioles All Pitched In," *Sports Illustrated* (October 24, 1983): 24–28; Tim Callahan, "A Series of Replacements," *Time*, October 24, 1983.

88. Jayson Stark, "For Rose, Retirement Is Out, But So Is Future with Phils," *Philadelphia Inquirer*, October 17, 1983; Peter Pascarelli, "The Early Line: Owens to Manage, Rose to Go," *Philadelphia Inquirer*, October 18, 1983.

89. Bill Giles, quoted in Michael Y. Sokolove, *Hustle: The Myth, Life and Lies of Pete Rose* (New York: Simon & Schuster, 1990), 213–16. Giles, in a July 15, 2005 interview, confirmed his statements that he had "no inkling that Rose bet on baseball" when he played for the Phillies and that he had the pay phone removed from the clubhouse because of suspicions that "another player" was placing bets. He also insisted that Rose's release from the Phillies "had nothing to do with gambling"; see Giles interview.

90. Sokolove, *Hustle*, 213. Fitzgibbon's investigation lasted 10 years and, in 1989, resulted in an agreement signed by Commissioner Bart Giamatti and Pete Rose, making Rose permanently ineligible from baseball. By that time Rose had returned to Cincinnati, first as a player-manager and later as manager.

91. Westcott and Bilovsky, *Phillies Encyclopedia*, 379.

92. Pete Rose, quoted in "Release 'the Best Thing' for Rose; Sure He'll Find Another Team," *Philadelphia Bulletin*, October 20, 1983.

93. Schmidt, quoted in Stark, "For Rose, Retirement Is Out, But So Is His Future with Phils."

Chapter 14. Organization Adrift

1. Rich Westcott and Frank Bilovsky, *The Phillies Encyclopedia* (Philadelphia: Temple University Press, 2002), 353.

2. Larry Shenk, "John Felske: Phillies 40th Manager," *Phillies 1985 Yearbook* (Philadelphia: Phillies, 1985), 3.

3. Bill Giles, interview, Philadelphia, July 15, 2005.

4. Larry Shenk, ed., *Phillies 1984 Yearbook* (Philadelphia: Phillies, 1984), 6.

5. Terry Pluto and Jeffrey Neuman, eds., *A Baseball Winter: The Off-Season Life of the Summer Game* (New York: Macmillan, 1986), 4–5.

6. Westcott and Bilovsky, *Phillies Encyclopedia*, 575; Rich Ashburn, "Glenn Wilson: Texas' Gift to the Phillies," in *Phillies 1986 Yearbook* (Philadelphia: Phillies, 1986), 67.

7. Westcott and Bilovsky, *Phillies Encyclopedia*, 575.

8. Westcott and Bilovsky, *Phillies Encyclopedia*, 279.

9. Shenk, *Phillies 1985 Yearbook*, 30, 52.

10. Larry Shenk, ed., *Phillies 1987 Yearbook* (Philadelphia: Phillies, 1987), 51.

11. Rich Westcott, *Tales from the Phillies Dugout* (Champaign, Ill.: Sports Publishing, 2003), 152.

12. Jim Barniak, "Young Samuel, Already a Star," *Phillies 1985 Yearbook*, 62.

13. Juan Samuel, interview, Binghamton, New York, May 24, 2006.

14. Shenk, *Phillies 1985 Yearbook*, 51.

15. Samuel interview.

16. Ruben Amaro, interview, Weston, Florida: May 16, 2006.

17. Wolff, *Baseball Encyclopedia*, 1414.

18. Felipe Alou, quoted in Barniak, "Young Samuel, Already a Star."

19. Westcott and Bilovsky, *Phillies Encyclopedia*, 247.

20. Westcott and Bilovsky, *Phillies Encyclopedia*, 96–97.

21. Al Holland, interview, Roanoke, Virginia: August 12, 2005.

22. Pluto and Neuman, *A Baseball Winter*, 5.

23. Shenk, "John Felske," 3.

24. Michael Y. Sokolove, *Hustle: The Myth, Life, and Lies of Pete Rose* (New York: Simon & Schuster, 1990), 213.

25. Peter Pascarelli, quoted in Pluto and Newman, *A Baseball Winter*, 15–16.

26. Holland interview.

27. Westcott and Bilovsky, *Phillies Encyclopedia*, 575.

28. Westcott and Bilovsky, *Phillies Encyclopedia*, 575

29. Westcott and Bilovsky, *Phillies Encyclopedia*, 301, 316.

30. Westcott and Bilovsky, *Phillies Encyclopedia*,, 301, 575.

31. Westcott and Bilovsky, *Phillies Encyclopedia*, 315.

32. Bill Conlin, interview, Turnersville, New Jersey: June 16, 2005.

33. Giles interview.

34. Giles interview; Kevin Kerrane, *Dollar Sign on the Muscle: The World of Baseball Scouting* (New York: Simon & Schuster, 1984), 334. In a 2005 interview, Bill Giles did admit that his organization had "overrated the farm system" and "we weren't getting the draft picks." As a result, the Phillies "didn't have many good young players in the late 1980s." But Giles was quick to add that the poor draft picks were due to the fact that "we were drafting way down the list" because the Phillies "had won so much during the period 1976 to 1983."

35. John Russell, interview, Scranton, Pennsylvania, May 3, 2006.

36. Tug McGraw was among the first pitchers to adopt and excel at relief pitching during the 1960s and 1970s as the complete game became less common. Among the others were Hoyt Wilhelm, Rollie Fingers, Lindy McDaniel, Elroy Face, Sparky Lyle, and Lee Smith. When McGraw retired at age forty in 1984, he ranked 15th on the all-time list for games pitched with 824. He had also recorded 180 career saves, ranking him 8th all-time, with a 96-92 career record and a 3.14 ERA. See Paul Votano, *Late and Close: A History of Relief Pitching* (Jefferson, N.C.: McFarland, 2002), 85, 152.

37. Tug McGraw, interview, West Chester, Pennsylvania, August 11, 2000.

38. Larry Shenk, "Gone But Not Forgotten: Tug McGraw," *Phillies 1985 Yearbook*, 57.

39. John Helyar, *Lords of the Realm: The Real History of Baseball* (New York: Villard, 1994), 353–54.

40. Helyar, *Lords of the Realm*, 353–54; Geoffrey C. Ward, *Baseball: An Illustrated History* (New York: Knopf, 1994), 451.

41. Rick Wolff, ed., *The Baseball Encyclopedia*, 8th ed. (New York: Macmillan, 1990), 1319.

42. Larry Shenk, "Community Relations," *Phillies 1985 Yearbook*, 70.

43. Shenk, "Community Relations," 58.

44. Westcott and Bilovsky, *Phillies Encyclopedia*, 357.

45. Westcott and Bilovsky, *Phillies Encyclopedia*, 357–58; Chris Wheeler, "A Dream Come True," *Phillies 1988 Yearbook*, 4–5.

46. Westcott and Bilovsky, *Phillies Encyclopedia*, 100.

47. Chris Wheeler, "Garry Maddox, No One Did It Better," *Phillies 1987 Yearbook*, 65.

48. Dave Anderson, "Finally, Limitations for Lefty," *New York Times*, June 29, 1986.

49. Frank Dolson, "Decision Was Long Overdue," *Philadelphia Inquirer*, June 26, 1986.

50. Bill Giles, quoted in Dolson, "Decision Was Long Overdue."

51. Helyar, *Lords of the Realm*, 353.

52. Steve Carlton. quoted in Paul Domowitch, "Carlton Proving He's Not the Retiring Type," *Philadelphia Daily News*, July 8, 1988.

53. Frank Dolson, "Steve Carlton," in *Baseball Hall of Fame Annual Program* (Cooperstown, N.Y.: National Baseball Hall of Fame and Sporting News, 1994), 5. Carlton never did break Spahn's record of 363 lifetime wins by a lefthander. When he finally retired in 1989, Lefty had 329 victories, 34 shy of Spahn's record.

54. Life wasn't easy for Steve Carlton after he retired in 1989. Most of the $10 million he earned over his twenty-four-year baseball career was lost on bad investments. Carlton was represented by agent David Landfield in the late 1970s and early 1980s. Although Mike Schmidt, once a client of Landfield's, had warned Carlton about the agent, the Phillies ace refused to heed his teammate's advice to fire him. Finally, in 1983, Carlton became suspicious and asked Landfield for a complete accounting of his money. When the agent refused to comply, Carlton fired him, and filed a lawsuit claiming that Landfield had written large, interest-free loans to himself with the pitcher's money, taken kickbacks from companies in exchange for bringing in Carlton as an investor, mixed the pitcher's funds with the money of other athletes he represented, rewrote several of Carlton's life insurance policies so he could collect the commission, and allowed his relatives to live, rent-free, in condominiums owned by the Phillies pitcher. The suit was settled out of court in 1985, but by that time it was too late; Carlton had lost millions of dollars (Domowitch, "Carlton Proving He's Not the Retiring Type"). Carlton, who was inducted into the Baseball Hall of Fame in 1994, leads a reclusive life in Durango, Colorado. On occasion, he emerges from his bunker-like house for paid appearances. See Tim Wendel, "Carlton's Philosophy Strikes Out," *USA Today Baseball Weekly*, July 27, 1994; Pat Jordan, "Carlton Still an Enigma," *Philadelphia Magazine* (July 1994): 32–35.

55. Jay Searcy, "The Transfiguration of Mike Schmidt," *Philadelphia Inquirer Magazine*, October 26, 1986, 13.

56. Jayson Stark, "Schmidt Slugs His 500th and Gives Phils a Victory," *Philadelphia Inquirer*, April 19, 1987.

57. Bill Fleischman, "The Weight of Philly on His Shoulders," *Inside Sports* (June 1984): 24.

58. Fleischman, "The Weight of Philly on His Shoulders."

59. Schmidt, quoted in Peter Hadekel, "Schmidt Calls Philly Fans a 'Mob Scene,'" *Montreal Gazette*, June 29, 1985.

60. Schmidt, quoted in Peter Pascarelli, "Schmidt Hits the Fans as Being 'Beyond Help,'" *Philadelphia Inquirer*, June 30, 1985.

61. Schmidt, quoted in Peter Pascarelli, "New Target: Schmidt Now Focuses His Ire on Media Instead of Phillies Fans," *Philadelphia Inquirer*, July 1, 1985.

62. Frank Dolson, "A Bewigged Schmidt Tries to Repair the Hurt," *Philadelphia Inquirer*, July 2, 1985; Mike Schmidt with Glen Waggoner, *Clearing the Bases: Juiced Players, Monster Salaries, Sham Records, and a Hall of Famer's Search for the Soul of Baseball* (New York: HarperCollins, 2000), 59–60.

63. Shane Rawley, "Michael Jack Schmidt," *Phillies 1987 Yearbook*, 12.

64. John Felske, quoted in Angelo Cataldi, "Phils Look for Their Leader and Find Only Their Star," *Philadelphia Inquirer*, May 29, 1988.

65. Bill Giles, quoted in Frank Dolson, "Old Pro May Try a New Attitude," *Philadelphia Inquirer*, November 11, 1987; Jayson Stark, "Phils Get Schmidt for 2 More," *Philadelphia Inquirer*, November 11, 1987.

66. Schmidt, quoted in Dolson, "Old Pro May Try New Attitude."

67. Schmidt, quoted in Stan Hochman, "Schmidt Critical of Phillies," *Philadelphia Daily News*, May 16, 1987.

68. Larry Bowa with Barry Bloom, *Bleep! Bowa Manages the Phillies* (Chicago: Bonus Books, 1988), 161–62.

69. Stan Hochman, quoted in Larry Platt, "The Unloved: Mike Schmidt," *Philadelphia Magazine* (July 1995): 82.

70. Peter Pascarelli, "Confessions of an Ex-Phillies Beat Writer," *Philly Sport* (July 1989): 32.

71. Westcott and Bilovsky, *Phillies Encyclopedia*, 99–100.

72. Jayson Stark, "Elia Considering Moving Schmidt to First Base," *Philadelphia Inquirer*, July 10, 1988.

73. Bruce Buschel, "Even Superstars Get the Blues," *Philly Sport* (June/July 1988): 22.

74. Westcott and Bilovsky, *Phillies Encyclopedia*, 157–58, 495–96.

75. Russell interview.

76. Samuel interview.

77. Westcott and Bilovsky, *Phillies Encyclopedia*, 247.

78. Mark Carfagno, interview, South Philadelphia, June 24, 2006.

79. Mark Winegardener, *Prophet of the Sandlots: Journeys with a Major League Scout* (New York: Atlantic Monthly Press, 1990), 264–72.

80. Winegardener, *Prophet of the Sandlots*, 279.

81. Westcott and Bilovsky, *Phillies Encyclopedia*, 101.

82. Diane Pucin, "Schmidt Is a Free Agent," *Philadelphia Inquirer*, October 22, 1988.

83. Bill Madden, "Yankees Plan to Make Bid for Schmidt," *New York Daily News*, October 25, 1988; Pascarelli, "For the Phillies, the Off-Season Is Where the Action Is," *Philadelphia Inquirer*, October 30, 1988; Frank Dolson, "Rose's Dream Was Only That," *Philadelphia Inquirer*, December 8, 1988.

84. Paul Hagen, "Schmidt Takes First Step," *Philadelphia Daily News*, December 8, 1988; Peter Pascarelli, "Phils Sign Schmidt to a 1-Year Pact," *Philadelphia Inquirer*, December 8, 1988; Schmidt, *Clearing the Bases*, 63–65.

85. Frank Dolson, "First Base Would Be Just Perfect for Schmidt but . . .," *Philadelphia Inquirer*: February 22, 1989.

86. Lee Thomas, quoted in Peter Pascarelli, "Schmidt to Start at 3rd Base, But with Question Marks," *Philadelphia Inquirer*, March 31, 1989.

87. Nick Leyva, quoted in Pascarelli, "Schmidt to Start at 3rd Base."

88. Schmidt, quoted in Jay Searcy, "Mike Schmidt Says the Season for Holding Back Is Past," *Philadelphia Inquirer*, April 2, 1989.

89. Peter Pascarelli, "Giants Deal Phils Fifth Loss in a Row," *Philadelphia Inquirer*, May 29, 1989; Schmidt, *Clearing the Bases*, 67.

90. Excerpts from Schmidt's statement appeared in the *Philadelphia Inquirer*, May 30, 1989.

91. Giles, quoted in Pascarelli, "Schmidt's Career Ends with Tears," *Philadelphia Inquirer*, May 30, 1989.

92. Bill Giles, quoted in Ray Didinger, "Schmidt Trying to Connect; Phils' Rebuffs Take Glow Out of Retirement," *Philadelphia Daily News*, May 29, 1991. Giles, in a 2005 interview, revealed that Schmidt believed that a "front office job with the Phillies was going to be automatic after he retired." But he repeatedly told Schmidt that he would "never be general manager as long as I'm president." Giles also stated that if Lee Thomas and Nick Leyva wanted Schmidt as the Phillies hitting coach he'd "have no problem with it."

93. Schmidt, quoted in Jayson Stark, "Time Cruel Foe for 2 Great Phils," *Philadelphia Inquirer*, February 10, 1991.

SELECTED BIBLIOGRAPHY

Allen, Dick and Tim Whitaker. *Crash: The Life and Times of Dick Allen*. New York: Ticknor & Fields, 1989.

Bloom, Barry M. *Larry Bowa: "I Still Hate to Lose"*. Champaign, Ill.: Sports Publishing, 2004.

Bodley, Hal. *The Team That Wouldn't Die: Philadelphia Phillies, 1980 World Champions*. Wilmington, Del.: Serendipity Press, 1981.

Carroll, Will. *The Juice: The Real Story of Baseball's Drug Problems*. New York: Viking, 2005.

Conlin, Bill. *Batting Cleanup*. Ed. Kevin Kerrane. Philadelphia: Temple University Press.

Dolson, Frank. *Beating the Bushes: Life in the Minor Leagues*. South Bend, Ind.: Icarus Press, 1982.

——. *The Philadelphia Story: A City of Winners*. South Bend, Ind.: Icarus, 1981.

Fitzpatrick, Frank. *You Can't Lose 'Em All! The Year the Phillies Finally Won the World Series*. Dallas: Taylor, 2001.

Giles, Bill with Doug Myers. *Pouring Six Beers at a Time and Other Stories from a Lifetime in Baseball*. Chicago: Triumph Books, 2007.

Helyar, John. *Lords of the Realm: The Real History of Baseball*. New York: Villard, 1994.

Hubbard, Steve. *Faith in Sports: Athletes and Their Religion on and off the Field*. New York: Doubleday, 1998.

Jordon, David. *Occasional Glory: A History of the Philadelphia Phillies*. Jefferson, N.C.: McFarland, 2002.

Kashatus, William C. *Connie Mack's '29 Triumph: The Rise and Fall of the Philadelphia Athletics Dynasty*. Jefferson, N.C.: McFarland, 1999.

——. *Mike Schmidt: Philadelphia's Hall of Fame Third Baseman*. Jefferson, N.C.: McFarland, 2000.

McCarver, Tim with Ray Robinson. *Oh Baby, I Love It! Baseball Summers, Hot Pennant Races, Grand Salamis, Jellylegs, El Swervos, Dingers, and Dunkers*. New York: Dell, 1988.

McGraw, Tug with William C. Kashatus. *Was It as Good for You? Tug McGraw and Friends Recall the 1980 World Series*. Media, Pa.: McGraw and Co., 2000.

McGraw, Tug with Don Yaeger. *Ya Gotta Believe! My Roller-Coaster Life as a Screwball Pitcher and Part-Time Father, and My Hope-Filled Fight Against Brain Cancer.* New York: New American Library, 2004.

Miller, Marvin. *A Whole Different Ball Game: The Inside Story of the Baseball Revolution.* Chicago: Ivan R. Dee, 2004.

Neyer, Rob and Eddie Epstein. *Baseball Dynasties: The Greatest Teams of All Time.* New York: W.W. Norton, 2002.

Rose, Pete with Rich Hill. *My Prison Without Bars.* New York: Rodale, 2004.

Rose, Pete and Roger Kahn. *Pete Rose: My Story.* New York: Macmillan, 1989.

Schmidt, Mike with Glen Waggoner. *Clearing the Bases: Juiced Players, Monster Salaries, Sham Records, and a Hall of Famer's Search for the Soul of Baseball.* New York: Harper-Collins, 2006.

Shenk, Larry, ed. *The World Champion Phillies and the Road to Victory.* Philadelphia: Phillies, 1980.

Sokolove, Michael Y. *Hustle: The Myth, Life, and Lies of Pete Rose.* New York: Simon & Schuster, 1990.

Teitelbaum, Stanley H. *Sports Heroes, Fallen Idols: How Star Athletes Pursue Self-Destructive Paths and Jeopardize Their Careers.* Lincoln: University of Nebraska Press, 2005.

Voigt, David Q. *American Baseball: From Postwar Expansion to the Electronic Age.* University Park: Pennsylvania State University Press, 1983.

Westcott, Rich. *Veterans Stadium: Field of Memories.* Philadelphia: Temple University Press, 2005.

Westcott, Rich and Frank Bilovsky. *The Phillies Encyclopedia.* 3rd ed. Philadelphia: Temple University Press, 2004.

Winegardner, Mark. *Prophet of the Sandlots: Journeys with a Major League Scout.* New York: Atlantic Monthly Press, 1990.

Wolff, Rick, ed. *The Baseball Encyclopedia.* 8th ed. New York: Macmillan, 1990.

INDEX

ACKNOWLEDGMENTS

This book is dedicated to two individuals who hold a very special place in my heart, Tug McGraw and Mike Schmidt. Tug and I planned to collaborate on a comprehensive treatment of the Phillies' 1980 championship season based on an earlier collector's edition we co-authored in 2000. Irreverently titled, *Was It as Good for You? Tug McGraw and Friends Recall the 1980 World Series*, the slender volume was a collection of player and fan memories celebrating the twentieth anniversary of the Phils' only world championship. We hoped that the book would remind readers of how the City of Philadelphia and the Phillies came together as winners during that very special season. Three years later, Tug died of brain cancer and I was on my own for the sequel.

For all his celebrity, Tug never considered himself a "star" and he was often at a loss when he was treated that way. He was my friend and a person who truly loved the game of baseball and its rich history. Tug tended to embrace others who felt the same way and agreed to several interviews in anticipation of this book. I will always be grateful to him for his friendship, wonderful sense of humor, and for teaching me that life is too short to be taken too seriously.

Mike Schmidt was my boyhood hero. As a kid growing up in Northeast Philadelphia, I was impressed by his 300-foot shot off the centerfield speaker on the ceiling of Houston's Astrodome and the four consecutive home runs he hit in a single game at Wrigley Field. But it was the way Michael Jack led his life that made him my hero. He has lived the very same way he played the game, with grace and dignity. Over the years since his retirement, he has become a friend whose example continues to encourage me both personally and professionally. I am extremely grateful to him for his willingness to be interviewed on several occasions as well as for his support and friendship.

Special thanks are also due to all the other individuals who agreed to be interviewed: Dick Allen, Ruben Amaro, Sr., Howie Bedell, Bob Boone, Larry Bowa, Marty Bystrom, Mark Carfagno, Ruly Carpenter, Gary Carter, Dave Cash, Larry Christenson, Bill Conlin, Frank Dolson, Bill Giles, Dallas Green, Richie Hebner, Al Holland, Tommy Hutton, Allen Lewis, Frank Lucchesi, Jim Lonborg, Greg Luzinski, Sparky Lyle, Bake McBride, Tim McCarver, Julian McCracken, Sam Milluzzo, John Nicholson, Dickie Noles, Danny Ozark, Dick Perez, John Russell, Dick Ruthven, Juan Samuel, Larry Shenk, Lonnie Smith, Watson Spoelstra, Tony Taylor, Manny Trillo, Del Unser, John Vukovich, Bob Walk, and Rick Wise.

Special thanks are due to several others as well. Michael Schefer, my editor at the *Philadelphia Daily News* and a good friend, was instrumental in securing the right of reproduction for photographs and reviewed an earlier draft of the book. Jayson Stark of ESPN, who covered the 1980 Phillies for the *Philadelphia Inquirer*, and Bob Boone were kind to write endorsements of the book. Andrew Newman, Assistant Photo Archivist, at the National Baseball Hall of Fame Library, was helpful in securing photographs and the right to reproduce them. The color photo that graces the front cover of this book could not have been located or secured for reproduction without the efforts of Dan Katzman at Corbis-Betteman. Mike Zuckerman, professor of history at the University of Pennsylvania and a dear friend, encouraged me to publish with Penn Press. Bob Lockhart and his staff at the Press were extremely helpful in guiding me through the editorial process and allowing this book to come to fruition. I am extremely appreciative to all these people for their efforts.

Finally, a special thanks is owed to my family. My parents, Balbina and Bill, encouraged my early love of baseball and gave me their unconditional support in my decision to become a writer. My sons, Tim, Peter and Ben, have tolerated those twin passions all their lives. Some day they will hopefully understand, like their mother, Jackie. Words cannot adequately describe, the love and respect I have for her.